BURT FRANKLIN: RESEARCH & SOURCE WORKS SERIES 541
Essays in Literature & Criticism 83

TRISTAN AND ISOLT

A Study of the Sources of the Romance

TRISTAN AND ISOLT

A Study of the Sources of the Romance

By

Gertrude Schoepperle Loomis

Second edition, expanded by a bibliography and critical essay on Tristan Scholarship since 1912.
by ROGER SHERMAN LOOMIS

VOLUME I

BURT FRANKLIN

The first edition of this work was published in Frankurt a. M. in 1913 as "New York University: Ottendorfer Series of Germanic Monographs No. 6 and 7."

Published by BURT FRANKLIN
235 East 44th St., New York, N.Y. 10017
Originally Published: 1913
Reprinted: 1970
Printed in the U.S.A.

S.B.N. 31610
Library of Congress Card Catalog No.: 71-131396
Burt Franklin: Research and Source Works Series 541
Essays in Literature and Criticism 83

IN REMEMBRANCE OF

CAROLA WOERISHOFFER

> How beautiful upon the mountains
> are the feet of him that bringeth good
> tidings!   Isaiah LII, 7.

PREFACE.

The present study of the origins of the Tristan story was undertaken in 1906, when I was a graduate student in Radcliffe College. Part of it was presented as a.thesis for the degree of doctor of philosophy in that institution in 1909. Professor W. H. Schofield, under whom I began the study of Arthurian romance, helped me greatly with advice and encouragement in the early stages of the work. To fellowships granted me by the Women's Educational Association of Boston and by the administrators of the Ottendorfer Memorial Fellowship of New York University in 1907, and to the Alice Freeman Palmer Fellowship of my Alma Mater, Wellesley College, which I received in 1909, I am indebted for the opportunity of continuing my research abroad. I cannot refrain from acknowledging here the many kindnesses extended to me by Professor McLouth, Secretary of the Ottendorfer Memorial Fellowship Committee, and by Mrs. Woerishoffer, the step-daughter of Mr. Ottendorfer. The design on the cover of the book is the work of my friend Miss Ella Mackinnon.

In connection with the chapter on the Celtic elements in the Tristan story I owe much to the lamented H. d'Arbois de Jubainville, who first turned my attention more particularly to that subject, and to Professor Kuno Meyer, Professor O. J. Bergin, and Mr. R. I. Best, who have assisted me in many ways.

To the learned and kindly librarian of the Sorbonne, M. Emile Chatelain, and to his courteous associates I owe lasting gratitude for the hospitality that made my four years in Paris a period of richest opportunity. To the Library of Columbia University I am likewise indebted for gracious hospitality. I am also under obligations to MM. Paul Meyer, Antoine Thomas, A. Jeanroy, J. Vendryes, and G. Glotz, and to Dr. E. Gierach, and Dr. H. G. Leach.

I owe much to the Tristan studies of M. Bédier. I owe even more to the interest with which he has followed mine. It is in the passages of my book in which my conclusions diverge most widely from his that his influence is most clearly to be read. When I brought the tentative results of my work to him it was these expressions of variant opinion that he received with most sympathetic attention, emphasizing their significance, even suggesting more effective ways of presenting my evidence.

There is hardly a page of my book that is not in some way an expression of the influence of M. Ferdinand Lot, as there was hardly a day, during my years in Paris, that a word of his did not serve to vitalize and clarify some problem of my investigation.

M. A. Smirnov and Mr. R. I. Best have read the study in manuscript and in proof. It is a pleasure to have this opportunity of acknowledging their invaluable suggestions and corrections.

For the mistakes and failings which the book exhibits I beg the reader's indulgence and rectifying hand.

New York University, March 1913.

GERTRUDE SCHOEPPERLE.

TABLE OF CONTENTS.
(VOLUME I.)

TABLE OF CONTENTS.

(VOLUME II.)

TRISTAN AND ISOLT.

A STUDY OF THE SOURCES OF THE ROMANCE.

I. INTRODUCTION.

In his admirable study of the sources of the Tristan story in the second volume of his edition of the poem of Thomas, M. Bédier points out the weakness of the evidence that had been adduced to establish the antiquity of the tradition. Of the portions that have been cited as 'mythological', 'pagan' or 'Celtic', he shows that there are only four which present any feature unfamiliar to the twelfth century French *trouvères*: the story of Mark of the horse's ears, Tristan's ability to imitate the songs of the birds, the *arc qui ne faut*, and the fairy castle of Tintagel[1]. From his own study of the tradition M. Bédier adds a few traits that seem to him sufficiently foreign to French romance to be regarded as survivals of a Celtic period of the tradition[2]. The stream flowing through Isolt's chamber, and the room in which the knights of Arthur sleep side by side with King Mark and his queen, are traits that would not have been invented by a poet

---

[1] J. Bédier, *Le roman de Tristan par Thomas, Société des anciens textes français*, Paris 1902, 1905, II, 130—55.

[2] *loc. cit.* II, 155—60. Celtic parallels to the first trait mentioned were noted by K. Meyer, *Zeitschrift für Rom. Philol.* XXVI, p. 716, XXVIII, p. 353.

familiar with the twelfth century French castle. The
third incident which M. Bédier takes to be genuine
Celtic tradition is that found in the Welsh triad:
Tristan, disguised as a swineherd, tends the royal
swine while the real keeper bears a message to
Isolt[1].

M. Bédier concludes: These are the only features
of the Tristan tradition that seem to be genuinely
Celtic. They are brutal tales of a husband duped
by a lover redoubtable for his physical strength and
master of primitive arts. It is not this 'barbaric De-
cameron' that we think of as the story of Tristan and
Isolt. The story of Tristan and Isolt is significant
only as it is tragic — the tale of two hapless mortals
bound to each other by a supernatural power, and
living in the midst of a society in which their love
violates a sacred and indissoluble tie.

M. Bédier cites a passage from the Welsh laws
to show that among the Celts the marriage tie was
neither sacred nor indissoluble. He infers from
this that we must attribute to the French the first
tragic treatment, and hence the real invention of
the story[2].

We shall find that M. Bédier is right in affirm-
ing that the extant versions reflect the personality of
the French redactors. We shall find that Gaston Paris

---

[1] There are several allusions to Tristan in Welsh documents.
cf. *Black Book of Carmarthen, Facsimile* 50 v., 51 r. — J. Loth,
Les Mabinogion, Paris 1889, Index *sub voce* Drystan, Essylt,
March On account of their vagueness or of the uncertain date
and authenticity of the texts in which they appear, we do not
utilize them as data in our study of the tradition. — cf. Bédier
II, 112—116; W. Golther, *Tristan und Isolde in den Dichtungen
des Mittelalters und der neuen Zeit*, Leipzig 1907, 237—42;
J. Loth, *Contributions à l'étude des Romans de la Table Ronde*,
Paris 1912, 112—23.

[2] II, 160—7.

was also right in his feeling that the tragic story of
Tristan was of Celtic origin. M. Bédier pointed out
with justice that the evidence by which Gaston Paris
supported his view was inconclusive. The few traits
which M. Bédier accepts as indicating Celtic influence
are unfortunately no less so. For example, the *arc qui
ne faut*, which he takes to be a weapon of Celtic
magic, is really a prosaic contrivance familiar to the
Anglo-Normans [1]. The incident of the Blades at the
Bed, which he regards as Celtic on account of the
primitive sleeping arrangements involved, is a popular
tale, universally current, which we find adopted, sleeping arrangements included, in late French romances [2].
There is, however, as will be seen, other evidence of
Celtic influence in the Tristan story.

M. Joseph Loth has pointed out that M. Bédier
was mistaken in concluding from the passage which
he cited from the Welsh laws, that a tragic story of
Tristan could not have existed among the Celts [3].
Our own study, already considerably advanced when
M. Loth's article appeared, shows not only that a
tragic treatment of unlawful love was possible among
the Celts, but that there were numerous tragic versions
of the theme in Old Irish literature. It shows further
that a considerably larger number of Celtic traits
survive in the extant redactions of Tristan than
M. Bédier recognized.

M. Bédier uses the following method to determine
what lies between the Celtic tradition and the extant
texts: He analyzes the narrative as it is preserved in
the five oldest versions, and points out two striking

---

[1] cf. infra, Ch. VI.
[2] cf. infra, Ch. V.
[3] *Rev. Celt.* XXX, 270—82; reprinted in *Contributions, op.
cit.* 1—14.

general characteristics: the logical progress of the action from one step to another, and the harmony of each step in the action with the characters of the persons involved. These two characteristics prove, according to M. Bédier, that the tragic story of Tristan was invented by a poet of great genius at one stroke in the form in which we find it in the extant versions.

M. Bédier then proceeds to an examination of the texts of Béroul[1], Eilhart[2], Thomas[3], the *Folie*[4], and the Prose Romance[5]. He arrives at the conclusion that they derive from a single twelfth century poem now lost. He identifies the author of this lost French poem with the single poet of great genius, the author of the first tragic treatment of the story.

This reasoning is open to serious objections. M. Bédier has taken the logical progress of the narrative and the subordination of incident to character to indicate the original unity of the story. But the progress of the narrative and the treatment of the characters vary strikingly in the different versions. M. Bédier would perhaps say that the lost common

---

[1] *Le roman de Tristan par Béroul*, ed. E. Muret, *Société des anciens textes français*, Paris 1903. M. Bédier, op. cit. II, p. 309 represents the continuation of Béroul as of unknown provenience, and as independent of the common source.

[2] *Eilhart von Oberge*, ed. F. Lichtenstein, *Quellen und Forschungen* XIX, Strassburg 1877.

[3] *Le roman de Tristan par Thomas*. ed. J. Bédier, *Soc. des anc. textes français*, Paris 1902. Only fragments of the latter part of the poem are extant. M. Bédier reconstructs the first part by a comparison of its derivatives, the Norse *Tristrams saga ok Isondar*, ed. with German translation by E. Kölbing, Heilbronn 1878; the English *Sir Tristrem*, ed. with German translation by E. Kölbing, Heilbronn 1882; and the German Gottfried von Strassburg *Tristan*, ed. K. Marold, Leipzig 1906.

[4] *Les deux poèmes de la Folie Tristan*, ed. Bédier, *Soc. des anc. textes français*, Paris 1907, p. 85 ff.

[5] *Le roman en prose de Tristan, analyse critique par* E. Löseth, *Bibliothèque de l'école des hautes études*, LXXXII. Paris 1891.

source possessed this logical progress of action and this subordination of action to character and that the inconsistencies of the extant versions are due to their imperfect reflection of their lost original. There is no evidence, however, that the lost poem was as perfect artistically as M. Bédier supposes. Even if there were, it would be unjustifiable to infer, merely from such evidence, that it was created at one stroke by a single poet. We may admire the symmetry of Canterbury Cathedral, but the aesthetic justification our admiration cannot make Canterbury Cathedral the work of one man or of one century.

M. Bédier's view as to the stage of development represented by the extant versions of the Tristan story, no less than his view as to the Celtic tradition at the basis of it, is sharply opposed to the views of his predecessors. According to them, the extant texts were compiled from episodic poems which were originally independent[1]. They represent various efforts to unite a body of tradition into a consistent narrative. According to M. Bédier, they are redactions of a single French poem the author of which owed but an insignificant debt to previous redactors[2].

The present study tends to support M. Bédier's conclusion that the extant texts are dependent on an earlier biographical poem. This poem contained, however, a more important body of tradition than M. Bédier recognized.

In our analysis of the tradition we have followed a different method from that of our predecessors, but our endeavor, like theirs, has been to throw light on the origin and development of the tradition. In under-

---

[1] Bédier II, 168—71.
[2] Bédier II, 160—1, 186—8.

taking our study we proceeded as follows: In connection with each incident we gathered from French literature more or less contemporary with the extant texts, and from popular tradition, parallels that may have been known to the redactor who introduced it into the narrative. We also compared the customs and ideas reflected in the Tristan stories with those appearing in other twelfth century French romances. At the same time we collected examples of similar elements in Celtic and Scandinavian literature.

We frequently found in the version of Eilhart von Oberge, features to which we found no analogues in French literature but which we frequently met in accounts of primitive belief and custom or in Celtic romance. In other versions of Tristan these were replaced by traits more familiar in twelfth century romance. In Scandinavian literature, except in the romances drawn from foreign sources, we seldom found anything that seemed connected with the Tristan tradition. Eilhart's version invariably corresponded to current folktales, whereas in the other redactions of the Tristan story, the incidents appeared with modifications characteristic of the redactor's personal conception of the story. We should not have attributed a trait to the initiative of the redactor from the mere fact of its deviation from the type. The individual bias of the poet was discernible in three other ways: first, in the ensemble of traits peculiar to his version; second, in the remarks made by him in the course of the story in his own person, especially those in which he criticized the narrative which he presented; third in the contradictions and ambiguities peculiar to his redaction and explicable by comparison with the other versions.

As a result of our comparison of the Tristan texts with the analogues which we had collected, we were thus led to attribute a higher value to the Béroul-Eilhart version than to that of Thomas or the Prose Romance as preserving an earlier version of the tradition. As for the *Folie Tristan* of the Berne manuscript, its allusions are frequently so vague as to make it useless for comparison. The specific traits which it presents, however, correspond closely to those of the Eilhart version. We decided therefore, in presenting our collection of analogues, to use as a basis what seemed to us the most primitive complete version of Tristan extant, the version of Eilhart von Oberge.

Up to this point in our study we had not referred to the reconstruction of the *poème primitif* made by M. Bédier. On consulting it now we found that M. Bédier had drawn up the outlines of the common source by adopting traits now from one, now from another of its derivatives. How was the disparity between our conception of the lost poem and that of our predecessor to be accounted for? On comparing the poem of Eilhart with the M. Bédier's reconstruction we found that, in all the important points, and in most of the minor points in which they differed, it was possible to demonstrate that the version of Eilhart better represented the lost original.

It was curious to observe, in following M. Bédier's study, that he had frequently included details from Eilhart in violation of the conditions of the method which he had set for himself in making the reconstruction. At other times he had disregarded both his method and the more primitive character of the Eilhart version to include an especially charming trait from Thomas. M. Bédier's reconstruction is not based entirely, as it purports to be, upon a mechanical comparison of the traits of the different versions and a preference for those which are supported by two or

more redactions. It is constructed in accordance with
the considerations of taste, sentiment, and logic which
appear in his discussions.

We are disposed to believe that the poem of
Eilhart von Oberge represents more accurately than
any reconstruction that has been made, and more
faithfully than any other version (except perhaps the
fragment of Béroul) the French poem to which the
Folie of the Berne manuscript alludes, and which
Thomas remodelled according to his personal taste.
We do not feel justified, however, in calling this poem,
as does M. Bédier, the *common source*, and in considering it as the archetype from which proceed all the
extant versions of the Tristan story, and all those that
ever existed [1]. It is certain that this poem is the source
of several versions — the Béroul-Eilhart version,
Thomas, and the *Folie Tristan* of the Berne manuscript. We should hesitate to call it the source of the
continuation of Béroul, or of the Prose Romance. To
prevent misunderstanding we shall therefore refer to
it as the *estoire*. We take the term from the passage
in which Béroul alludes to his source:

> Si conme l'estoire dit,
> La ou Berox le vit escrit [2].

We should prefer to allude to it as Eilhart's
buch [3], since we have no evidence that the source of
Béroul contained the continuation which we find in
Eilhart, Thomas, and the *Folie*. But this term, borrowed from the German text, fails to convey the idea
that the poem is French.

---

[1] Bédier II, 313.
[2] Béroul 1789—91.
[3] cf. Lichtenstein, *Int.*, CXV—VII.

The reader will observe that we distinguish the *poem of Béroul* from the *continuation of Béroul*. We do not attempt to decide whether or not the continuation is by the same author as the first part. The sources of the continuation of Béroul are unknown. We point out in the course of our study that the episodes which compose it seem to be variants of incidents found respectively in Thomas, Béroul, and the Prose Romance. None of them are in Eilhart, a fact which may indicate that the continuation is independent of the *estoire*, and, perhaps, founded on a version anterior to it.

We are not at all convinced that the story of Tristan in the Prose Romance is derived directly or exclusively from the *estoire*. M. Bédier bases his discussion of the Prose Romance on the version given in manuscript 103[1]. In this manuscript the story of the combat with the dragon and the final incidents of the romance are given in a form similar to that which we find in Eilhart. Prof. Röttiger has shown that these incidents have been interpolated from the poetic versions[2]. In all the other manuscripts of the Prose Romance we find an account of the birth and childhood of Tristan, of his quest of Isolt, of the return from the forest, and of the death of the lovers which differs from the story told in the poems. We have no reason to affirm that in these passages the poems offer an older tradition. In the late and hopelessly corrupt redaction in which it has come down to us, the Prose Romance has been strongly influenced by the poems. But it is hazardous to term it a *derivative* of the

---

[1] Bedier II, 321 n.
[2] W. Röttiger, *Der heutige Stand der Tristanforschung, Programm des Wilhelm-Gymnasiums zu Hamburg*, Hamburg 1897, p. 26.

estoire. It may even be that in the passages mentioned, the Prose Romance preserves traces of an earlier
version than the *estoire.*

We have devoted three chapters to an analysis
of the *estoire.* In the chapter on the *Date of the
Estoire* we have brought together the traits of the
poem which seem be the latest additions to the tradition, the passages composed under the influence of
French ideas of courtly love. In the chapter on the
Narrative Technique of the Estoire we have studied
those portions of the story that are too commonly
paralleled in popular tradition for us to hope to trace
their origin. By comparing them with numerous analogues we have been able to form an idea of the
methods and the artistic purpose of the author of the
estoire. In the chapter on the *Celtic Tradition in the
Estoire* we have discussed those passages in which it
seems possible to discern here and there the fossils of
an older story. We have not always attempted to
decide whether a passage represents Celtic tradition
modified in view of a French audience or the invention
of a French redactor.

II. AN OUTLINE OF THE *TRISTRANT*[1] OF EILHART VON OBERGE.

A. RIVALIN AND BLANCHEFLEUR. THE CHILD-HOOD OF TRISTAN.

It is a tale of joy and sorrow that I shall tell you. Hearken it well; there is none better of worldly tales, for deeds of prowess and for love.

Introduction. 1—54.

There was once a king called Mark, who ruled in Cornwall. He was at war with the king of Ireland, a monarch of overweening arrogance, who had many a time already harried King Mark with his fleet from across the sea.

Mark's struggle with Ireland. 54—71.

Tidings of this war reached a noble king called Rivalin in the land of Loonois, and he came with a goodly troop in right knightly fashion to king Mark at Tintagel. And Rivalin served the king as if he had been his own vassal, for King Mark had a fair sister and he hoped by his prowess to win her for his wife. In this he succeeded; for when the war was ended and Rivalin returned to his kingdom, Blanchefleur went with him.

Rivalin of Loonois comes to Mark's aid. 71—88.

He wins Blanchefleur. 88—95.

---

[1] In this outline I have given the names of the persons, when possible, in their French form.

But on the sea the pains of childbirth came upon her and in them she died. The man-child that was cut from her womb was brought safely to land. And there the women carried Blanchefleur to her grave with lamentations. Rivalin exceeding sorrowful gave his son the name Tristan.

When the child no longer needed the care of a nurse, the father confided him to a worthy tutor, Gorvenal, who taught him to run and leap, to wrestle, to throw the lance, to cast the stone, to ride, and to wield the sword. He trained him in honor and courtesy and in all the virtues and all the exercises that beseem a perfect knight.

When Tristan was of sufficient age, Gorvenal suggested that he might obtain his father's permission to travel, and learn the customs of other lands and see what honor he could command among men who were not his father's vassals. Rivalin was well content to hear this request, and a good ship was fitted out under the direction of Gorvenal, well laden with fine stuffs and gold and silver. Eight squires und two young noblemen were chosen to accompany them. They bade fare-

well to Rivalin and set sail for Cornwall. When they arrived, Tristan bade his companions not to reveal his identity. The little company was graciously received, and Tristan's offer of service was at once accepted. Mark recommended him to the special care of the Lord High Steward, Dynas of Lidan.

So Tristan remained at the court of Mark, and proved himself worthy of the courtesy men showed him there until the time approached when he should be made a knight.

B. THE MORHOLT.

Now the king of Ireland had given his sister in marriage to a redoubtable knight called the Morholt, who himself alone had the strength of four men and who subdued the kingdoms round about to Ireland's rule. The Morholt now determined to subdue Mark. He set sail in the direction of Cornwall, sending ahead messengers to tell the king that he must pay the tribute withheld these fifteen years or more. If he refuse, let him furnish a champion of equal birth and the Morholt will defend the right of Ireland in single combat. 'One other way still I offer him', said the Morholt, 'let him defend himself in battle'. The tribute the Morholt required was every third child born in the Cornish land within the fifteen years.

The tribute to the Morholt. 351—533.

Mark sent to all the corners of his kingdom, summoning his vassals, to announce to them the dire conditions. Now the young Tristan had secretly resolved to undertake the combat, and he confided his design to Gorvenal. The tutor hesitated on account of his pupil's youth, but at last yielded. He advised him first to ask the king to make him knight. Mark's efforts to persuade his nephew to delay were vain and Tristan was knighted together with sixty others in seven days of ceremony.

When the assembled vassals had learned from Mark the conditions laid down by the Morholt, they retired to take counsel among themselves. But no one dared undertake a combat which meant certain death. Tristan entered and offered to be their champion. He urged them to obtain the king's word that permission would not be withheld from anyone who wished to defend Cornwall. Only when they had obtained this

Tristan offers to defend Cornwall. 533—742.

promise were they to reveal to the king that the champion was Tristan.

The Irish declared that they would not accept the Cornish champion unless he was of lineage equal to theirs. Tristan then revealed his identity. Mark was torn between the joy of finding in his favorite his own nephew and the anguish of seeing his youth put to so sore a trial. He implored Tristan to desist from the combat, reminding him that Cornwall's shame was not his. But entreaty and command were alike vain. Tristan insisted on Mark's holding to his promise. Word was sent to the Morholt that the sister's son of Mark would offer him single combat on the third day on an island near his halting place.

The island combat. 742—1012. King Mark came thither with his men and encamped. He bade them bring out his favorite steel armor and he put it on Tristan with his own hands. He gave Tristan a trusty sword, a shield wrought with skill, a noble horse with fair trappings, a saddle of gold and a burnished bridle. Then he embraced him, committing him to God. The weeping multitude followed him with their prayers. He entered the boat with his horse and rowed to the island. The Morholt was already there and had moored his boat. Tristan, disembarking, pushed his off into the sea. 'Why have you not moored your boat?' inquired the Morholt. 'Why should I?' replied Tristan. 'The victor will have enough with one.' The Morholt, wondering at the youth and valor of his adversary, offered him his friendship and half his possessions if he would desist from the combat. Tristan refused to accept any terms except the delivery of Cornwall. They mounted for the struggle.

They spurred on their steeds and assailed each other fiercely. Both were wounded, Tristan with a poisoned wound. After a long struggle he succeeded in cutting off the Morholt's hand, and, when the Irish champion attempted to flee, he gave him a terrible blow with his sword. A fragment of the steel was broken off and remained in the Morholt's skull. Mortally wounded, the Irish champion fled to his boat, pursued by the taunts of Tristan.

Mark sent to the island then for the victor, and the companions of the Morholt took their champion on board, still alive, and sailed back to Ireland.

Messengers were sent from the ship to the princess Isolt, his niece; for she was renowned for her skill in healing and could surely save her uncle, if she found him still alive. When she came he was already dead. She extracted from his skull the broken fragment of Tristan's sword and preserved it. The Morholt was buried with wailing and lamentation. The Irish king commanded that all persons landing in Ireland from Cornish ships should be hanged without mercy.

C. THE VOYAGE FOR HEALING. PRO OF IEMSETIR.

But the Irish champion had not fought utterly in vain. Tristan too had received a wound. No leech-craft but that of Isolt of Ireland could heal the poison of the Morholt's weapon, and he would rather have died than heal the slayer of her uncle. Her beauty and graciousness and skill were honored throughout the kingdom of Ireland, where many a sick man had been healed by her of his ills.

But the leeches who tended the wounded Tristan could not help him. He took neither sleep nor food, and grew thin and feeble. Because the stench from

The seclusion of the invalid. 1012—1092.

his wound made it intolerable to be near him, he begged the king to have a little house built for him outside the town on the shore of the sea. Then he was borne thither, followed by the mourning people as one lost to them forever. Only the king, Dynas, and Gorvenal ventured near him. There he remained, awaiting his end.

The rudderless boat. 1092—1192. At length he begged Mark to allow him to be set adrift upon the sea. He preferred, if he must die, to die alone, rather than to remain among his people and be loathsome to all. The king resisted at first, but at length gave his consent. Tristan took with him only his sword and harp, and embarked amid general mourning. If he did not return, Gorvenal was to be the heir of his realm. The king watched him with tearful eyes as the boat was borne off without oars or rudder, driven hither and thither by the wind. He was long tossed about on the waves. At last to his horror he found himself driven upon the coast of Ireland.

The Irish king saw the little boat and came to examine its wretched burden. He bade his men carry the wounded man into a house. Tristan gave his name as Pro of Iemsetir. He explained that he was a minstrel and that he had been thus wounded by pirates who had attacked and pillaged the ship on which he had set out for purposes of trade. The The healing of Tristan by the messenger of Isolt. 1192—1337. king sent to his daughter for a remedy. At last the poison yielded to the herbs brought by her messenger. Tristan was thus healed by Isolt without once seeing her.

There was famine in Ireland at that time. It was Pro who gave the king counsel how to relieve the people. He was put in charge of a ship and sent to England for provisions. Having seen the cargo

safely on its way to Ireland, Pro himself embarked
for Cornwall. He was welcomed there with joy.

D. THE QUEST OF THE PRINCESS OF THE SWALLOWS' HAIR. TANTRIS.

The king was so glad to recover his nephew that
he resolved never to take a wife. He declared that
Tristan should be his heir. In spite of the efforts of
his barons to induce him to marry, he persisted in being of this mind. At last they presented themselves
before him, with Tristan in their midst, and insisted
that he delay no longer to choose a wife. He appointed
a day on which to give his decision.

When the day arrived he was in great anxiety,
While he waited for the entrance of the barons
he was still seeking a way to elude their demand.
Suddenly he noticed two swallows quarreling, and
saw a long beautiful hair fall from their beaks. The
sight suggested to him the ruse he had been seeking.
When Tristan and the barons entered, he told them
that he would comply with their wishes but declared
he would have no woman other than her to whom
the hair belonged which had fallen from the swallows'
beaks. The barons saw that he was mocking them,
and believed that the stratagem was of Tristan's invention. To clear himself of this suspicion, the latter
asked Mark to confide the hair to him and to allow
him to go in quest of the princess. *Mark is forced to yield to the barons and agrees to marry. 1337—1435.*

Having chosen a hundred knights to accompany
him, he set off in a richly equipped ship. He was
resolved to search all lands until he found the princess
whose hair the swallows had brought in their beaks.
At the end of a month, in spite of their efforts to
avoid the Irish coast, they were cast ashore at the *Tristan sets out at hazard in quest of the Princess of the Swallows' Hair. 1435—1598.*

Schœpperle, Tristan.   2

very town in Ireland in which Tristan had been
healed. Terrified, they sought a ruse to save themselves. Tristan offered a golden cup to the marshal
who was sent by the king to put them to death. He
gave his name as Tantris and pretended to be a
merchant who, having heard of the famine in Ireland, had set out from England with his companions
in twelve ships, richly freighted, in hope of profitable
trade. They had met boats fleeing from the Irish
shore, they said, and had learned that none were
allowed to land. Nevertheless, rather than lose their
cargo, they had cast lots. It had fallen to Tristan's
ship to venture upon the coast. If the king would
spare him and agree to accept his stores, he would
return to the other ships and bring the cargo. The
marshal departed ot communicate this explanation to
the king.

E. THE COMBAT WITH THE DRAGON.

Tristan under-
takes the com-
bat with the
dragon.
1598—1686.

As Tristan and his men lay in the harbor,
waiting to know their fate, they learned that a
dragon was devastating the country and that the king
of Ireland had promised his daughter and the half
of his kingdom to anyone who would kill the monster.
Tristan determined to destroy it in order to save
himself and his companions from the vengeance of
the Irish king. He armed himself next morning and
set out. He learned the whereabouts of the dragon
from a man whom he met fleeing from it. He rode
into a deep hollow and awaited the approach of the
monster.

His lance broke in the first attack and he and
his horse were burned by the dragon's flames. He
succeeded at last in dealing the dragon a mortal blow

with his sword and cut out its tongue as a trophy. Almost dead from his burns, he lay down in a brook near by.

The man whom Tristan had met fleeing was the king's seneschal. Having first made sure that the dragon was dead, this individual and his followers ventured to turn their faces in its direction. The seneschal concluded that the knight he had met had been swallowed by the dragon, and, returning to the court, told the king that he himself had performed the exploit. His men supported his statement and the king was at last convinced of its truth. He went to announce to Isolt that the country had been delivered and that it was the seneschal who had won her. His daughter was less credulous, and at her request he fixed a delay until the next morning. *The seneschal pretends to have slain the dragon. 1686—1766.*

At dawn Isolt commanded the horses to be saddled and set out accompanied by Perenis and Brangien, to investigate the scene of the combat. They found the print of horse's shoes such as were not used in Ireland, and, following these, they came to the place where the dragon lay dead. Beside it was a shield burned by the flames. Farther on they found Tristan's horse. A little later Brangien espied the gleam of a helmet in the brook where the hero lay unconscious. Isolt took off his armor and bound up his wounds. They carried him to the town and there she bathed and tended him. *The princess investigates the seneschal's claim and finds Tristan. 1766—1863.*

When Tristan opened his eyes at last and saw the woman before him, he smiled. He knew at once that his quest was accomplished — her hair was like that which had fallen from the swallows' beaks. Noticing his smile, Isolt asked herself what it was that amused him. She remembered that she had neglected to clean his sword. Hastening to fulfil this *The princess won is the Princess of the Swallows' Hair. 1863—1872.*

duty, she noticed that a fragment of the blade was missing. It occured to her that the form of the missing fragment was similar to that which she had taken from the head of the Morholt. She fetched the bit of steel she had preserved and convinced herself that the hero's sword was the same that had slain her uncle.

The deliverer is the slayer of the Morholt. 1872—2157.

She swore that the Morholt should be avenged. Tristan confessed his identity and attempted to reason with her: she should not wish to avenge the death of the Morholt upon him; he had slain her uncle because he must. And if harm should befall him while under her protection, she must avenge him. But his plea was fruitless. It was Brangien who obtained his pardon, for she reminded her mistress that if Tristan were slain she would be forced to become the wife of the hateful seneschal. Isolt had not thought of that. She went to her father then and announced that she had found the knight who had really slain the dragon. He would appear on the next day and confound the imposter. She required the king to promise pardon in advance for any harm the hero might have done him in the part.

The next day the followers of the king and the seneschal's men came to the assembly. Tristan sent word to his companions in the harbor to appear at the gathering sumptuously dressed. The Irish wondered at these silent strangers so richly attired, who rose deferentially at the entrance of Tristan. Isolt, having required her father to give the stranger the promised kiss of peace, revealed the fact that he was the champion who had slain the Morholt. She reminded her father that he had slain him for the sake of his country, and that he had now done a great service to the Irish by delivering them from the dragon.

The king was faithful to his promise to pardon Tristan.

The seneschal declared that it was he who had killed the dragon. Tristan offered to disprove the assertion by a wager of battle, and produced the tongue to show that he had performed the exploit. After taking counsel with his men, the impostor acknowledged that his claim was false, and left the court in disgrace.

The impostor is put to shame. 2157—2226.

Tristan then told the king that he wished to take Isolt to Cornwall to become the wife of **Mark,** saying that he himself was too young to marry. The king approved his plan, since Isolt might not be able to forget that Tristan had slain her kinsman.

Tristan receives Isolt for Mark. 2226—2264.

F. THE LOVE POTION. THE MARRIAGE OF ISOLT WITH MARK.

Before their departure the queen prepared a potion and confided it to Brangien. She charged her to guard it with the greatest care and to give it to Mark and Isolt on their wedding night. No one must touch it until then. It was a love potion, so tempered that those who drank of it could not be separated for four years. However they might long to free themselves from its spell, they must love each other with all their power throughout their lives. If they were separated for a day during the first four years they would fall ill; if they did not see each other for a week they would surely die.

The mother of Isolt prepares a love potion. 2264—2336.

When they had sailed for some distance, Isolt complained of the swiftness of the voyage. Tristan accordingly ordered the ship to be moored, and they disembarked and rested. He went to Isolt and asked her if she was ready to continue their course. While he was talking with her he became thirsty. A courteous maid offered them wine. Little did Tristan know, as he took it, what an ill starred drink it was. He offered it to Isolt and she too drank. It was as if they had lost their senses. On the instant they loved each other. Four days and nights they lay in torture. Isolt in her cabin reproached herself: 'Alas the great change that has been wrought in my heart by that dear foe! He has taken from me hunger and thirst and I grow so ill that I shall lose my life. What shall I do? Wretched that I am, I fear he has no kindness toward me. How can I then have kindness toward him? Kindness? Why do I say that? How could I cherish unkindness toward him? There is no better man nor more valiant between heaven and earth. He has proved his prowess many a time. I know him to be gracious and good, beautiful and single hearted, loyal and of gentle bearing. Alack, my heart and desire, when will you turn from him? We cannot, for love has taught us and we dare not disobey. I had thought love were sweet, but I find it bitter. O Cupid, whate'er I may have done against thee, thou hast thy vengeance now. Alas, Love, what have I done that I should be thus punished? What wilt thou of me? I submit myself to thee, I seek thy feet, O Love. It is a hard fate that has befallen me, to love the man who ne'er had thought of loving me. When my father would have given me to him to wife, he cared not at all to take me.'

Now she bade her heart hide its love, and again she thought to go to Tristan and beg pity. Thus she was tortured and Tristan too, for night and day he thought of naught else but her.

Brangien and Gorvenal saw the anguish which Tristan and Isolt sought to hide. They took counsel

Tristan and Isolt drink the potion.
2336—2398.

Love monologue of Isolt.
2398—2611.

The lovers are brought together.
2611—2798.

together. The maid bethought herself of the potion. She hastened to the place where she had put it and she found it gone. She told Gorvenal the terrible news. They knew then what the illness was and that their lord and lady must die unless they possess each other. They agreed then that they dared not make themselves answerable for their death.

The boat reached a haven. Gorvenal begged Tristan to go to Isolt's cabin and inquire how she felt. Tristan hesitated, fainting, at the door, and Isolt called to him to come to her. Brangien and Gorvenal withdrew, sure of their success. In the cabin remained only those two, Tristan and Isolt, and Love. Which told the other how it was with him, I know not, only that both, ere they departed, were healed of their pain. Until they neared the land of Mark they were together in great joy of their love.

Unless they deceived Mark on the wedding night, they were now surely lost. Isolt went to Brangien and begged her to lie with the king for a while on that first night. The maid yielded unwillingly, to save her mistress and herself.

Mark came to meet the vessel, and Isolt was led to Tristan in great honor. Tristan told the king that the bride begged him to observe her country's custom on the wedding night — to leave no light by the nuptial bed that none might see her until the dawn. The king gladly assented and asked Tristan to act as chamberlain. That night, when the lights had been quenched, Tristan brought Brangien silently to the king. That was the falsest deed that ever Tristan did, for in that same place he lay with Isolt. Yet it was not treachery; for he did it against his will. It was the cursed drink that brought him to

The Marriage of Isolt with Mark. 2798—2831.

Brangien substituted in the marriage bed. 2831—2863.

it. At midnight Brangien came to the queen and told her she might go now to her husband. Thus was Mark deceived. For a year Tristan was in the court; not even for a day could he depart. Truly, he said to Gorvenal, he knew that if he were two days without seeing the queen, he would surely die.

G. BRANGIEN AND THE MURDERERS.

Isolt gives Brangien over to be slain. 2863—3001.

Not long after, the queen determined to reward Brangien with death for the service she had done her. She feared that the maid would reveal her secret. She offered two poor knights sixty silver marks, and bade them go to a certain spring and take the life of the person who should come to draw water there, bringing back to her the liver as a sign. The queen then made as if ill and bade Brangien bring her water from the spring in the orchard.

When the assassins saw Brangien preparing to draw water in her golden jug, they fell upon her. She realized that it was the queen who had sent them. She thought of a plan to save herself. One of the knights should remain to guard her and the other return to the queen and tell her that her command had been fulfilled. 'Tell her', continued Brangien, 'that I know no cause for her to punish me thus. I have done naught to harm her. I left all to follow her to this land. When we set sail, her mother gave us two white shirts, but before we reached the shore, hers was not fit to be put on with honor before the king. Mine was fair and new, and she begged me to lend it to her for the bridal night. Surely I have never deserved death of her.'

Brangien is saved and Isolt rejoices. 3001—3081.

The knights considered that it would be indeed shame to them to kill this maid. A dog chanced to

run past, and one of them killed it and took its liver
to the queen. When Isolt heard that Brangien had
died without betraying her, she reproached herself
bitterly for her cruelty. 'Now may God destroy me',
she cried, 'and may neither man nor woman trust me
more, treacherous that I am'. So terrible was her
anguish that the knight revealed the truth, and offered
to bring Brangien to her. Isolt fell at the maid's
feet. 'It would be just, if God, who has saved thee
from this death, should strike me down myself', she
cried repentant. Brangien in turn begged forgiveness.
The two women lay for a long time prostrate with
grief.

Tristan was hunting with the king and knew
nothing of all this. When Gorvenal told him, he was
very angry, and bade the queen be doubly good to
Brangien thenceforth.

H. THE KISS AT THE QUEEN'S COUCH.

It was not long after this that Tristan was sorely
slandered by three wicked dukes and four counts at
the court, who envied him his exploits and his fame.
Thus indeed it is with the excellent. Him would
the envious ever fain destroy. Tristan's case is proof
of this: he had no other fault than to be ever first
where men strove in doughty deeds, and ever generous
as long as he lived. It was for this, and because the
king loved him more than they, that they hated him.
So the seven determined to destroy him. They had
a chief called Andret, the king's sister's son. They
told envious lies to the king of Tristan: 'May it
please your Majesty, we would tell you that your
nephew loves the queen and betrays you. It is a
shame for you to prefer him to us all.' 'Be silent',

Tristan's ene-
mies try to
rouse Mark's
suspicions.
3081—3250.

cried the king. 'I will not distrust Tristan, whatever you say. It was he who withstood the Morholt. Had he never done aught but that, he were worthy of far more favor than any of you. But he has proved his faithfulness in many another way'. They were angry then, and sought to discover Tristan alone with the queen. They made slanderous verses and recited them to the king. In vain. All the ill they said of Tristan, Mark reckoned as honor to his nephew.

But, when the king went to the royal couch, he found reason in their words, for Tristan was standing beside it, holding Isolt in his arms and pressing her lovingly to his breast. Mark was very angry then. 'This is evil love', he cried. 'How can my honor fail to suffer, when you do me such wrong with your false love. It is not permitted to have aught of joy or pain of another's wife. I would not believe though they told me often. It would have been better if I had. You are a faithless man. Be off from the court and thank God that you get away alive. It is such kissing as this that rouses envy.'

Mark finds Tristan at the queen's bed. 3250—3277.

I. THE TRYST UNDER THE TREE.

Never, I ween, did two hearts suffer as those two. Tristan went to his inn and stayed there. He could not go away. They would both die unless they saw each other. The queen sent Brangien to Tristan to tell him he must find a way. When he heard her message, he declared that no man's threats should keep him longer from Isolt. 'When she sees, on the stream that flows through her chamber, a branch followed by a piece of bark carved with a five pointed cross, she will find me under the linden by the bank.' The queen rejoiced when she heard the message. After

The whittlings on the stream. 3277—3382.

that the two met in the evenings under the linden,
and during the day they lay as though very ill.

The envious barons disputed among themselves
whether the lovers still saw each other. 'There is a
dwarf here', said Andret, 'who can read in the stars
all that is and will be. We shall give him a reward
for telling us'. The dwarf declared that Tristan indeed
had the queen's love. 'If the king will follow my
advice, he will see for himself; if he find I lie he
may cut off my head.' Mark accordingly made the
announcement that he was going hunting and that
he would be seven days absent. The dwarf followed
the king to the linden and bade him get up into it.
The devil must have helped the dwarf. How else
could he have climbed alone?

The moon was bright. They had not been there
long when Tristan came. He broke off a branch and
sent it down the stream, the piece of bark after it.
Then he saw in the water the shadow of two figures
in the tree. 'We are both lost', he groaned. 'If only
the queen knew!' But the branch and the bark flowed
down to Isolt's chamber where the two women were
watching for it, and Isolt hastened to her lover. 'God
protect me', thought the queen, as she saw Tristan
sitting motionless by the spring, 'what ails the youth
that he does not rise and come to meet me? I am not
used to this. What can be the cause of it?' Then she
saw that he motioned backward and she caught sight
of the spies in the tree. She gave no sign of seeing
them, but said to Tristan: 'Tristan, why was I to
come to you?' 'Lady', he replied, 'to help me gain
the king's permission to return to the court'. 'You
may be sure that I shall not do that', cried Isolt,
'for I have come into ill repute by your fault. I was
gracious to you for my lord's sake, because you are

*Tristan's ene-
mies determine
to convince
Mark of his
nephew's guilt.
3338—3472.*

*The meeting at
the fountain.
3472—3626.*

his nephew, and because you do him more service than the others, but now I am made common talk through you. I should be best pleased if my lord would put you to death.' 'Nay, my lady, I have undertaken great exploits for your sake, and it is only through your favor that I can regain the king's.' 'I shall not help you', declared the queen. 'Let him pardon you of his own accord.' 'Then I must leave the country', said Tristan, 'and little as my lord may regret it, he will never live down the shame if I go under his displeasure. My lord prefers to forget it, but in my own country I am as powerful a king as he. And if I went otherwhere I should be received with honor, and given mounted men to attend me. Persuade the king, then, to give me back my pledges, and I will at once leave the kingdom.' 'No, I will not', declared Isolt, and with that she departed. 'It is a crime against God', said Tristan, 'the wrong he does me', and with that he turned away to his lodging. The king drew his sword then and would have slain the dwarf, but he escaped, and Mark pondered on how he might persuade his nephew to remain in the kingdom.

Mark begs Isolt to persuade Tristan to return to the court. 3626—3772. Early in the morning he came to his wife and begged her to tell him what had passed between her and Tristan the night before. 'My lord', she replied, 'I have not seen him for twelve days'. 'You saw him last night', declared the king, 'for I was in the tree and heard what you said. Help me to persuade him to remain here; I will make the whole court obey him.' 'I shall not help you', said the queen, 'we parted last night in anger. I would rather he were gone, for if your cherished favorites slander us again I shall be shamed the more. Let Tristan go where ne will.' The king implored her to relent. 'I am not allowed to speak to him', she said. 'I give you permission to be

with him as much and as often as you will. When
he kissed you that time I was too angry. It will not
happen again. I know now that you are true to me.'
'As you will', said Isolt, 'but you must have Brangien
go to him. I fear, however, that she will be as loath
to do it as I.'

'Why did you drive him away, if you wish to
keep him?' said Brangien, when the king appealed
to her. 'It was because he was slandered to me.' 'Who
did the slandering?' 'A duke.' 'Then let the duke
bring him back again.' Brangien's resistance was no
less obstinate than that of Isolt, but she yielded when
the king promised to put Tristan's bed in the royal
chamber and to let him be with the queen early and
late, though his enemies should tear themselves to
pieces with spite. The king publicly declared Tristan's
innocence and the lovers were free for a time from
restraint and suspicion.

J. THE FOOTPRINT ON THE FLOOR.

One day Dynas, who had heard nothing of the
dwarf's part in this affair, was riding in the forest and
found the little man. Not knowing how the creature
had lost the king's favor, he brought him back to
court and obtained his pardon. *Dynas brings back the dwarf. 3772—3792.*

The dwarf swore to the enraged Andret that
it was Tristan's wit and not his innocence that had
saved him that night at the fountain. They prevailed upon the king to put his nephew again to the
test. Tristan was told that he must go next morning
to King Arthur on an errand that would require seven
days. 'To-night', said the dwarf, 'I shall spread flour
on the floor between the queen's bed and Tristan's. *The dwarf spreads flour on the floor. 3792—3891.*

Tristan will not be able to resist his desire. I myself shall be in hiding under the bed, and others will be at the door.' Tristan saw the trap, but the power of the potion was stronger than his prudence. He leaped over to Isolt's couch. With the effort his wound broke open and her bed was stained with blood. At the word of the dwarf Aquitan, the king and his guards hastened forward. Tristan endeavored to leap back to his place, but this time his foot touched the floor. He was taken and bound.

Tristan and the queen are sentenced to death. 3891—3991.

The king swore that the shame of this love should be remembered till the world's end. He commanded Andret to break Tristan on the wheel and to burn Isolt at the stake.

K. THE FLIGHT TO THE FOREST.

At daybreak preparations were made for the punishment of the lovers, and men were summoned from far and near to see. The people lamented in vain. The steward Dynas alone dared approach the king and implore mercy, but it was to no avail.

They came to a chapel beside the road, built on a cliff above the sea. The quick-thoughted Tristan begged them to let him enter to pray. 'Let the poor sinner find him pardon if he may; this chapel has but this one small door; it is not difficult to guard. Besides, the sea lies below on the other side in great waves.'

When Tristan went in, he bolted the door as a wise man should, and not a word of prayer did he say. But out of the tiny window he forced himself,

Tristan leaps from the cha- pel on the cliff. 3991—4140.

leaped down to the sea, and swam to land. He crept stealthily along the shore, watching lest some one follow.

Now Gorvenal, well nigh dead with grief for the loss of Tristan, was riding out of the city, bringing away his master's horse and sword. As he rode, he reflected sadly how easily the good Tristan might make his way to freedom, if he but had these idle tools. Suddenly he saw his lord before him. Right glad were those two to see each other.

'Now let us ride', cried the squire, 'for when the king hears of this, it were best that we be far off'. 'No, I shall die with the queen or save her. At worst I shall have vengeance on some of those who would destroy her.' *He is determined to save the queen. 4140—4221.*

With this Tristan hid himself in a bush from which he had a view of the place where the queen was to be executed.

In the meantime those who waited at the chapel door grew impatient. 'His prayer is too long', they said. One called: 'You must leave off your praying on your knees to-day; it is too much to ask us to stand here so long.'

No man answered. Then they broke down the door, for they were angry. But they found no Tristan.

Word was brought to Mark that Tristan had escaped. 'He that finds him shall never lack aught I have to give', cried the king. The knights sprang to their horses and were off. But they found him not, nor would they, I dare swear, had they sought him to this day. Many a one was glad, and some were sorry. *Mark learns of Tristan's escape. 4221—4243.*

When those who sought had sought in vain, the king resolved to cool his wrath upon the woman. He swore there should be no escape this time, and he bade her be brought and burned at the stake.

At that moment there came a leper running and calling to the king to grant him a boon. 'The queen', said he, 'is to die, and you would choose for her a *Mark gives Isolt to the lepers. 4243—4302.*

shameful death. I will tell you a worse one than
hanging or burning. Give her to me and let her
live with us. There will be more shame in dying by
our love.'

'Thou speakest truth', said the king, and gave
the queen to the leper. It was long that men in the
land spoke ill of him for that.

The lepers' route led past the place where Tristan
lay in the bush. It was a grief to Tristan to see his
lady touched by those foul hands. As they drew near
the place where he lay hid, he fell upon the lepers,
and only one of them lived to bring the news to
the king. Mark swore that he would give half his
possessions to anyone who would avenge him on Tristan

*Tristan saves
Isolt from the
lepers.
4302—4368.*

L. THE LIFE IN THE FOREST.

Now Tristan's dog Husdent began to howl loudly
for his master, and the king bade that he be hanged.
But the servant, who loved Tristan, spared the dog,
who followed his master's scent deep into the forest.
When Tristan heard him, he believed that he was
followed by the king's men. The fugitives were in
terror. Gorvenal, determined to save his master, advanced alone in the direction of the sound, and the
lovers, yielding to his entreaty, withdrew deeper into
the forest. But the dog was alone. Gorvenal now set
out to rejoin Tristan, but lost his way. It was well
he had the dog then to guide him.

*Husdent joins
the lovers.
4368—4512.*

The fugitives rode deeper into the forest and built
themselves a hut of wood and branches. Except for
the game and fish that Tristan caught, they had only
herbs to eat. It is said that Tristan was the first to
take fish by angling, and that he was the first to put

*Life in the fo-
rest.
4512—4617.*

hounds on the scent of game. It was a hard life they had there in the forest, he and the fair Isolt, but for them it was child's play, so much joy did they have from the great love they bore each other. It was only Gorvenal that suffered. The wonder was that he did not die.

Now it was a custom with Tristan and Isolt, when they had lain down and had had enough of talk with each other, that Tristan drew out his sword and laid it between them. It was a strange habit, to be sure, but it turned out luckily for him, for it happened that one of the king's huntsmen came to the hut one morning early while they were sleeping. When he saw the sword and recognized Sir Tristan, he hastened to the king and informed him. Mark bade him be silent and bring him to the place. The king finds the sword between the lovers. 4617—4688. What he had in mind I cannot tell you. When they came near he bade the man remain with the horses and went alone to where Tristan lay. He took the sword that lay beside him and put his own in its place. During all this the lovers did not awaken. He laid his glove upon the queen then and went away.

When the two awoke they saw the glove and the sword. 'We shall never escape from the place alive', cried Tristan. 'The king has been here; he is near. We owe our lives but to his courtesy; for, finding us sleeping, he would not kill us. As soon as we get up, we shall be slain.'

They fled from the place, wondering every instant that the king did not fall upon them. All the long day they rode deeper and deeper into the forest. At vesper time they came to a place hemmed in by trees and cliffs. There they remained, subsisting on such scanty herbs as they could find, and I may tell you

Life in the forest. 4688—4702.

that they were sensible enough to have chosen better fare if they had had a choice.

Near the place there was a holy hermit named Ogrin, who was wont to shrive the king. One day Tristan rode to the good man, but, unless he would promise to give up the queen, Ogrin would grant him no forgiveness. Tristan rode away unshriven, for shrift was not so dear to him as was the queen.

First visit to the hermit Ogrin. 2—4724.

M. THE RETURN FROM THE FOREST.

Thus he lived in the forest with Isolt, as love constrained him, until the power of the potion waned. That was, as those say who have read the book (and surely this is true) until four years after they had drunk the draught. It seemed to them then that they must leave the forest. They could not endure the misery of it another day. At dawn Tristan took Isolt to Ogrin and told him he was sorry he had not followed his counsel. The good hermit asked Tristan if he repented of his sin and if he would give Isolt back to the king. 'Yes', replied Tristan, and Ogrin rejoiced and showed them such kindness as he could.

The influence of the potion abates. 4724—4742.

Second visit o the hermit Ogrin. 4742—4771.

He wrote a letter and Tristan carried it that night to Tintagel to the king. When he reached the orchard he tied his horse to the linden under which he had known so much of joy and pain, and from whose branches Mark had watched his meeting with Isolt. Then he went and spoke to the king through the wall, and asked him if he slept.

Tristan takes a letter to the king. 4771—4863.

'I should, if you would let me', replied the monarch.

'I say for a sooth, you must be awake for a while', replied Tristan, and telling him that he brought a message from the hermit, he threw the letter into the window. He told the king to hang the answer on the cross at the fork of the roads.

The king recognized the voice. 'It is you, Tristan. Stay, I would speak with you.' But Tristan was off, and Mark's attempt to overtake him was vain. Impatiently the king waited for the dawn to have the letter read to him.

> 'My lord, Ogrin prays thee earnestly for the love of God, to take back his lady thy wife. Tristan will bring her to thee. Receive her graciously and take back Tristan. He will repay thee with his love as he should.'

When this had been read to the king, he told his counsellors how he had found the lovers lying in the forest, and he swore that there had never once been between Tristan and Isolt aught but pure love, though indeed Tristan was fond of her beyond reason. Then he had a letter written, saying he would take back his wife, since Tristan was willing, four days thereafter. As for Tristan himself, he had done him so much harm that at no man's counsel or command would he allow him to remain in his country. But he should be protected from high and low while he was bringing Queen Isolt, for this at least was right doing. *The king agrees to take back his wife. 4863—4904.*

Ogrin gave the lovers such poor clothes as he could spare to cover them, and in these Tristan brought back Isolt to Mark. He begged to be allowed to stay in the country, but Mark refused. He had suffered too much from Tristan, and he hated him too bitterly ever to forgive. He did not wish his service. Tristan departed angrily. 'Take the queen then. You will never live to see the day that I beg your favor again. And look to it that you take no vengeance upon Isolt. You will answer to me for any harm that comes to *Tristan brings Isolt to Mark and goes into exile. 4904—5016.*

her. It is for her sake that I take no vengeance upon
you.' 'Alas', he continued, 'it is hard for me to part
from my lady'. And with that he committed the queen
to Mark, who held her in kindness many a year after.
Tristan gave the queen his little dog, bidding her show
her love for him by her care of it.

Then he rode away and came one morning to the
realm of the king of Ganoie. There he was well received, and won glory in many exploits that would
be too long to tell here. But he resolved at last to
seek another country, and having said farewell to the
king, he set off with Gorvenal to the realm of Arthur
in Britain.

N. TRISTAN AT ARTHUR'S COURT.

Tristan is
welcomed at
Arthur's court.
5016—5059.

There he was joyously welcomed, and by none
more joyously than by Sir Gawain. With him Tristan
became fast friends and won great honor at the court.
Now once when he had been riding in disguise, as
was customary, he met another knight and they fell
to fighting. This was the fashion of men who sought
to gain honor at Arthur's court. The knight was one
of the most excellent of Arthur's following, but Tristan

Tristan over-
comes
a knight of
Arthur's court.
5059—5129.

struck him from his horse, so that he had to go home
on foot. Tristan gave the horse to a poor man that
he chanced to meet, and withdrew quickly. Gawain
and the king decided that it must have been Tristan
who had distinguished himself in this joust, and
Gawain determined to sift the matter. But Tristan
stoutly denied all knowledge of the occurrence. At
last Gawain put his request in Isolt's name. At that

---

1 I have taken Eilhart's *Delekors schevalier* (*OX* 5061) to
be a translation of a *chevalier de la cour* in his original.

Tristan yielded. If he were to die for it he would not refuse anything thus begged.

In this talk Gawain learned how Tristan longed to see his lady, and he promised to help him. To this end he arranged a hunting party. He contrived to have the hunt prolonged until night fall, when the party found themselves near Mark's castle and had to seek shelter there. Arthur was displeased, for he knew that Tristan was in disfavor at that court. He sent Kay ahead to announce the visit. Mark received the party hospitably, and gave his word to take no vengeance for old wrongs, but he warned them to make no new attempt against his honor. The guests were greeted by the queen with the customary kiss, but Gawain, out of loyalty, denied himself the favor that was denied to Tristan.

Gawain's plan to aid Tristan to see Isolt. 5129—5285.

O. ARTHUR'S KNIGHTS AT MARK'S COURT: THE BLADES AT THE BED.

I must explain to you that the kings of those times did not have such fine chambers as lords have to-day, and Mark had no place to lodge his guests but in the great room. There they lay all together. As was the custom, the king and his wife lay at one end, and according to their habit, each lay alone.

Now the angry host set sharpened blades on a block of wood, and placed it where Tristan must be cut if he came to the queen. Thus he guarded his wife. But when Tristan felt the wound, he bound his shirt around it and came to the queen in spite of it. It was not long before the blood soaked through the cloth; Tristan had to leave her before they had more than embraced. He returned to his bed, bleeding

Tristan is wounded on the trap set by Mark. 5285—5354.

like a wounded beast, and bemoaned his fate. Gawain heard him and grieved in sympathy. He confided Tristan's desperate strait to the other knights, and through the quick wit of Kay they found a way to protect Tristan from discovery. They all got up, and making a great commotion in the room, wounded themselves on the blades. Kay tried to escape but Arthur's knights wound themselves. 5354—5488. he was pushed on by the rest. 'Are there wolves in this hall that you must set traps here?' cried Kay. 'It is strange hospitality that we find'. Mark awoke and reproached Arthur for the brawling of his knights. 'They always behave thus', said Arthur.

They lay down then and Tristan could go to Isolt in safety. At daybreak he rose and bound up his wounds like the others. It was a shame to Mark to see his guests go limping. They went home then, but Tristan, in spite of the pleading of Gawain and the efforts of Arthur to retain him, set out for new adventures.

P. TRISTAN AT THE CASTLE OF HOWEL.

Tristan learns of King Howel's distress. 5488—5583. Tristan rode for seven nights and came at last to a land that had once been fair but now was waste and burned. Not a house was to be seen far and near. He rode for three days more and in all that time met not so much as a dog or a cock. At noon on the third day, however, he spied an old chapel on a height, and beside it a little house that looked as if it might be a hermit's cell. Such indeed it was. The hermit, who was called Michael, gave Tristan shelter for the night, and when they had eaten their meal, they sat down by the fire and the old man replied to Tristan's questions about the country. 'The

lord of it, King Howel, is a good lord', said he, 'and
it is but lately that the land is thus desolate'.
Tristan learned that Rivalin of Nantes, a powerful
duke, had asked for the daughter of Howel in
marriage, and the father had refused to give his
child to a vassal. Duke Rivalin had then determined
to take her by force; for he was no craven. 'Indeed', continued Michael, 'if it were not for this
wrong to his lord, he would be a worthy man enough'.
Michael related how the other lords had all joined
with Rivalin, and had broken down all King Howel's
castles. 'The king is in Carhaix now', concluded the
hermit, 'with a small following. His one son,
Kaherdin, is a dauntless warrior, who would not
shrink from an equal contest. But the foes are so
many that the besieged dare not venture out'.

Tristan learned that the castle was but two
miles distant, and next morning he took leave of
the hermit and set out to Carhaix. He found the
king standing on the battlements in front of the castle,
and told his name and offered his services. The king
was sorry to refuse them, but the besieged party, he
said, had no food but a few beans, and could not allow
Tristan to share their hardships. 'My lord', replied
Tristan, 'for two years I lived in the forest and knew
not the taste of bread. I can bear that'. Kaherdin,
the king's son, who had come forward to look at the
stranger, added his entreaties to Tristan's and prevailed upon the king to admit him.

'Come with me now', said Kaherdin, when he had
entered, 'and the ladies will welcome you. You must
see my sister, There was never a fairer woman. She
is fit to be a king's bride'.

'What is your sister's name?'
'Friend, she is called Isolt'.

He offers his
services.
5583—5678.

He meets the
second Isolt.
5678—5700.

Then it seemed to Tristan that she had chosen him. 'Isolt it is that I have lost. Isolt it is that I have found again'.

In that same hour he entered where she was, and saw her. He did not say that he knew a fairer woman. So much I may tell here.

As Tristan and Kaherdin went out, hand in hand, Tristan learned that no one in the castle dared accept Rivalin's challenge to single combat. Tristan prevail-

Tristan
overcomes the
rebellious
Rivalin.
5700—6106.

ed upon Kaherdin to help him to go out of the castle secretly next morning at dawn. He overcame Rivalin and forced the rebel duke to agree to obey his commands. Although Rivalin's men rushed to their master's aid, he did no treachery but was true to his promise. Of the alternatives offered by Tristan, to provision the town for a week or to be immured in the deepest dungeon of the castle, he chose the former. Although the duke's men threatened to destroy everyone in the castle unless their master was given up, Tristan retained his captive.

Meanwhile the king received word that two of his nephews were on their way to the city, bringing two hundred knights and twelve weeks' provisions. The king welcomed them and placed the new troops under Tristan's command. In the encounter many of Rivalin's men were killed and forty were taken prisoners. The numbers of the enemy enabled them to renew the attack again and again. As Kaherdin was returning to the castle to summon the king to his aid, he was assailed by King Bedenis, one of Rivalin's allies, and, had it not been for Tristan's assistance, would surely have been taken captive. The fight continued until the blood was so deep that the combatants must wade to the knee. Rivalin's men fled, but most of them were slain or taken captive. The rebel vassal

was forced to submit, and to agree to restore to Howel
all his land and to make good all his losses.

Q. THE MARRIAGE OF TRISTAN.
THE AUDACIOUS WATER. TRISTAN'S DEFENSE.

Then the swift Kaherdin began to fear that his
comrade Tristan might leave him, and he began to
cast about in his mind how he might so attach Tristan
to himself that he would remain at Carhaix. He said
to Tristan: 'My valued friend, my father is fond of
you, why do you not ask him to give you my sister?'

Tristan is offered Isolt of the White Hands. 6106—6138.

'I would ask him gladly', replied Tristan, 'if I
knew he were disposed to do it, but if I should be
so unfortunate as to displease him, I should lose my
service'.

'But what if it is pleasing to him? What if he
wishes to give her to you?'

'In truth I should take her right willingly.'

So the lady was given to Tristan. She was with
him more than a year, as I have heard for a truth,
and never did he make her his wife. This she
bore without resentment. Nor, indeed, did she ever
speak of it, until one day when the king and queen
and Tristan and his wife, and Kaherdin with them,
were riding on a low lying páth near the town.
Isolt's horse stepped into a pool of rain-water and it
splashed up along her knee under her shift.

The maiden marriage. 6138—6143.

'Water, thou art strange indeed. Ill luck to thee!
How darest thou spring under my clothes farther than
ever the hand of any knight has yet dared come or
ever came?'

The audacious water. 6143—6205.

Her brother Kaherdin heard her words and declared that they could not be true. Isolt was dis-

tressed that he had heard her, but she could not
deny what she had said. She had been a year with
Tristan and she was not yet his wife. Kaherdin, in
distress, placed the matter before his father and his
trusted friends. 'Tristan shall pay for this insult to
us', he declared, 'it is clear that his purpose is to
desert her.' The king swore that he would have
vengeance. Tristan should be taken secretly and slain.
Kaherdin objected to this plan: he would allow no
treachery to be practised on his comrade. He went
to Tristan therefore and spoke to him frankly.

Kaherdin
threatens
Tristan.
Tristan's boast
of the other
Isolt.
6205—6264.
'There can be friendship between us no longer.
You have cast shame upon my sister and upon us
all.' He told Tristan then that he had learned his
secret and that he knew his intention. Tristan swore
that he had no thought of leaving his wife. 'But
she has shown me slight affection. There is another
who for my sake treats my dog with greater love.'
He offered to bring Kaherdin where this other was,
and prove his boast. If it were false, he might take
what vengeance he would.

R. THE VOYAGE OF TRISTAN AND KAHERDIN TO CORNWALL.

They departed together for Cornwall. When they
had crossed the sea, they made their way to Lidan,
to Dynas, and Tristan begged the faithful seneschal
to go to the queen and tell her the straits that he
was in, and how his life hung in the balance. 'Let
The
hunting party.
The lover in
the thornbush.
6264—6423.
her arrange a two days hunting party at the Blanche
Lande', he said. 'On the road thither there is a
thornbush near a hunting lodge. In this I shall be
hidden. I will shoot a twig into her horse's mane.
Let her stop at this sign and caress the dog with so

much fervor that my companion must confess that my boast is justified. Let her bring with her many maidens, the fairest that she has, and ride in state.'

Dynas went to Tintagel, as Tristan bade him, and, joining in a game of chess with the royal pair, contrived to draw the queen's attention to the ring which she had given Tristan. She recognized at once that he was her lover's messenger, and, when she had learned his request, she lost no time in carrying out his plan.

Kaherdin and Tristan watched from the thorn-bush as the hunting party passed. First there were the cooks with their pots and pans and provisions, then the cup-bearers and those who dealt out the bread. The huntsmen followed with their hounds; then came those bearing the king's wardrobe, next the chaplain with the host. At length the king appeared with his hounds and falcons. When he had passed, the chamberlains of the queen came by, and the maids and youths that tended her, in pairs, at such intervals from each other that the first couple was out of hearing of the second. The ladies were adorned with gold and wore long rich mantles — each was fairer and more richly dressed than the one before. Kaherdin was struck with amazement by all this, and when there came one fairer and more nobly clad than all the rest, he cried out. 'See, the queen is coming.' 'No' declared Tristan, 'in dark clouds she would be in truth as the sunlight, but her radiance is naught compared to that of the queen.' To Kaherdin it seemed that there could be nothing so fair as this maid, whose name, I will tell you, was Camille of Montrelles. Then came the courteous wise Brangien. When Kaherdin saw her he cried out that she was still more beautiful than Camille. Then there passed

The procession of beautiful ladies. The dog carried in state. 6423—6512.

two richly decked palfreys, bearing a litter adorned
with gold. Kaherdin begged his companion to tell
him what lay in the litter.

'It is my dog', replied Tristan. 'The queen
carries it thus for my sake.'

'You yourself have not been so honored by my sister.'

Scarcely had he pronounced these words when he
saw such a light that it seemed to him there must
be two suns, and he cried out quickly to Tristan to
tell him what it might be. 'It is the queen that
comes now', said Tristan. Never would Kaherdin
have believed that a woman could so give radiance
to the day.

The coming of
Isolt.
6512—6542.
She rode alone. Andret had been her escort, but
she had sent him for something that he could not find.
Indeed, it matters little what he was doing. When
Kaherdin beheld the queen, he confessed that he had
never seen so fair a woman. 'Alas', he cried, 'my
sister cannot be compared with her.'

The signal o
the twig.
6542—6575.
Then Tristan let fly the twig into the horse's
mane. The queen halted and pretended to be suddenly taken ill. She sent word to the king, begging him
to bid the train halt for the night where they were,
and to take care that there be no barking of dogs
nor blowing of horns near the place where she was.
She dismounted then unaided — a thing that had
happened seldom to her before — and approached the
golden litter. She took out the little dog and began
to stroke him lovingly with her jeweled mantle. She
Isolt caresses
Tristan's dog.
6575—6595.
lifted him in her arms and caressed him so tenderly
that Kaherdin exclaimed: 'Comrade mine, thou art
quit of thine oath. Thou had'st never such treatment
from my sister.'

As Queen Isolt went back to her horse, she let
her mantle fall away from her, and when Kaherdin

beheld this, I ween he swore to Tristan that he had never seen so fair a woman.

Kaherdin acknowledges that Tristan's boast is justified. 6595—6610.

She spoke to the little birds singing there: 'You have much joy in varied song. I will give you twelve golden chains if you will fly with me to the forest of Blanche Lande and stay with me this night.'

Isolt gives the cue to her lover. The tryst at the Blanche Lande. 6610—6672.

It was to tell Tristan where to find her that she said this. Then she wrapped her mantle about her and the wretch Andret lifted her to her horse. The king came alone to inquire for his wife before he went to rest with his men, for she had begged him in her message to leave her to herself that night. Brangien told him that the queen was not well enough to see him until the next morning.

But when Tristan presented himself with Kaherdin, she received him after the old fashion, in all love. She sent Kaherdin to Camille of Montrelles. None knew the queen's secret save this Camille, Brangien, and Perenis.

Now Kaherdin began to seek favor with Camille, but she would have none of him. When he pressed her she retorted.

Kaherdin courts Camille. 6672—6708.

'Where is your wit, good sir? Do you not see that I am no country wench, that you think to win me with so brief a wooing? You must be a country lout, indeed. How else? I give you warning by my troth that you will do well to cease your clamoring. I will take no lover, neither to-day, nor ever. That I swear. And had you been five years in my service, obedient to my every command, you would be still a-begging for what you ask.' Then she considered within herself and added: 'You are a seemly fellow enough, and if you were my countryman and of my rank, and if it pleased my kinsmen to grant me to you, I think indeed that I might take you.'

Then I warrant Kaherdin wished he had not begun. But when the queen withdrew with Tristan, she said to him: 'For Tristan's sake I will give you one of my maids to bear you company. Choose Brangien or Camille as may please you, and I will bid her be with you to-night.' For a moment Kaherdin thought that she was mocking him but then he realized that she meant it well. He thanked her and asked for Camille.

The lady's maid given to the lover's companion. 6708—6745.

While he stretched himself on the bed to allow his shoes to be taken off, Camille went to the queen to inquire if it was indeed her wish, as Kaherdin had told her, that she should lose her honor.

'No', replied the queen. 'You shall take the pillow that I lay under my head when my longing for Tristan is so great that I cannot sleep. You know the power of the pillow. Lay it under his head and he will sleep soundly all the night. Thus you can lie beside him without fear.' The pillow was so made that whoever had it under his head, slept day and night as one dead. Camille took it softly and said to Kaherdin: 'Lift up your head. I will lay you on my arm as my lady bade me.' Thus was Kaherdin befooled.

Kaherdin is duped by the magic pillow. 6745—6805.

When Camille had dressed herself next morning she drew the pillow from the hero's head. He awakened then and felt with his hand. There was no one beside him and it was already morning. He would have liked to be twenty miles away. But he could not get off so easily. Before he escaped he must listen for a while to the taunts of the women.

'If I had but known that you could lie so decorously', said Camille as he dressed, 'I should not have refused when you asked me.'

Kaherdin was almost mad with vexation. If his
ears had been cut off, not a drop of blood would have
come out of them.

S. IN ISOLT'S NAME.
THE FALSE ACCUSATION. TRISTAN THE LEPER.
ISOLT'S REPENTANCE.

Tristan parted from Isolt in great love and
sorrow, and rode away with Kaherdin, innocent of
all knowledge of his companion's mortification. They
came to a difficult pass in the road and could not
cross on foot. Tristan accordingly sent word by Perenis *The delay in*
to Gorvenal and Kaherdin's squire to hasten to join *the journey.*
them with the horses. While the two squires were *6805—6828.*
seeking their masters, Breri, one of the king's courtiers,
and seven of his men pursued them. Breri thought that
one of the fugitives was Tristan, and having in vain
called upon him to turn for the sake of his own honor,
he conjured him to turn for the honor of Isolt if she
was dear to him. The fugitive did not turn. Breri
returned to the queen and told her that he had seen *Breri tells Isolt*
Tristan, that he had pursued him and won a horse of *. that Tristan .*
his. Although he had conjured him to turn for her *request made*
sake, Tristan had refused to do so. Isolt was very *in her name.*
angry. *6828—6885.*

'I would you had thrown him into the sea and
that I might never more hear his name. But you
should have torn out your eyes rather than pursue
him.' When Breri saw how angry she was, he with-
drew, for he was a courteous man. Isolt sent Perenis *Isolt sends Pe-*
to Tristan and bade him tell her lover that he had *renis to Tristan*
done ill not to turn when Breri called in her name. *her anger.*
Perenis delivered the message. *6885—6913.*

'I am innocent', declared Tristan, 'you can see for yourself that the horses have not yet come. No matter how dear it had cost me, although he who conjured me had a thousand knights, I should not have failed to turn. Let her believe this, for it is true.'

As he spoke Gorvenal came up, and Kaherdin's squire was with him bringing three horses. The fourth was lost.

Kaherdin's revenge.
6913—6947.

Now Kaherdin believed that Tristan had some hand in the trick that had been played on him the night before, and he resolved to take his vengeance now. 'You have found good pasture', he said to the squires, 'since we were chased this morning.'

'Why do you say that?' cried Tristan angrily.

'Because it is true. And if your eyes were to leap out of your head for it, I should have to speak as I have spoken.'

The two men disputed angrily. Tristan would have struck down Kaherdin for his lie, but he remembered in time that he had brought him thither and that he must therefore bear with him, whatever injustice he might do.

Tristan in vain protests his innocence.
6947—6998.

'Tell the queen that I am innocent', he said to Perenis. 'Let her be sure that I have never refused a request made in her name. You see yourself that the charge is unjust. I shall wait here until you return to tell me if she still believes me guilty.'

'Alas, you are bribed by him to deceive me', cried Isolt, when Perenis delivered his message. She would not listen to his explanation.

When Tristan heard that Isolt held him guilty, he resolved to seek her and clear himself. When he saw Tristan's distress, Kaherdin repented his spiteful talk, and promised to await with Gorvenal his friend's

return. Tristan sought the queen disguised as a
leper. She saw him, and bade him be sent away.
When he persisted, she ordered them to drive him
away with blows, and laughed to see her commands
obeyed. Then Tristan went on his way and rejoined
Gorvenal. When the squire heard what welcome his
master had received, he hated the queen. He swore
he would not serve Tristan another day unless he
promised neither to see or speak to her for a year.

Tristan forgot his quarrel with Kaherdin, and
Kaherdin's family forgot their anger against him, for,
in his displeasure against the queen, Tristan took the
other Isolt indeed to wife, and the two had much joy
together, and recked not of the other Isolt whether or
not she might repent. Tristan's joy was untroubled.

Now it was in May that Tristan was driven away
by the queen, and this great wretchedness lasted until
Michaelmas. Then Isolt began to lament bitterly that
she did not see Tristan.

'It is but just that you should suffer', declared
Perenis: 'You were wrong in punishing him when he
was innocent'.

She was more willing now to listen to Perenis'
defense of her lover. She decided at length to send
him a letter confessing that she had sinned and offering
to do penance.

'No, it is better not to risk a letter', she thought,
'I will send the clever young Pilois, who is quick
with words. He will plead my cause.'

She confided to him how she had lost her lover's
favor. She begged him to tell Tristan that she
repented truly for her fault and in penance wore
a hair-shirt next her skin night and day. She would
surely die unless he forgave her.

Tristan, disguised as a leper, seeks the favor of Isolt. 6998—7038

Isolt has Tristan driven away with blows. 7038—7070.

Tristan consummates his marriage with Isolt of Brittany. 7070—7081.

Isolt repents. 7081—7110.

She sends Pilois to Tristan. The hair-shirt. 7110—7191.

Pilois pleads
in vain with
Tristan to for-
give Isolt.
7191—7292.
Pilois left Cornwall, and, when he came so near
to Carhaix that he could see the castle, he espied
Tristan riding in the field by the road hawking. The
falcon had caught a bird and perched, with full crop,
joyous on his master's hand. When Tristan saw young
Pilois, he asked him of the queen, how she fared, for
he thought the messenger might be from her.

'She fares indeed like the poor woman she is',
Pilois replied.

'Why?'

'Because she is almost dead on your account.'

'And why?'

'She fears your wrath.'

'She does?'

'Yes, in truth.'

'She need not.'

They questioned each other for a while. Pilois
begged Tristan to forget the blows he had received.
'I can not', declared Tristan. 'They went too near my
heart.'

'But she has suffered for it.'

'Perhaps she did, for a while, but she is glad
that we are strangers now. She ordered me to be
beaten and driven away from her. She laughed to
see it.'

'She begs you to punish her for it now', said
Pilois. 'She truly repents her sin. Because she has
done ill to you she comes to you for mercy. She offers
you her service. She will obey you in everything, and,
as penance for her sin against you, she wears a hair-
shirt next her skin. Come soon to where she is and
heal her of her sorrow.'

'No, I shall never go to her again', declared
Tristan. 'It might happen to me again, as it happened before.'

Pilois continued to beseech him but Tristan refused
to relent. At last he begged him, in Isolt's name, Pilois begs in
Isolt's name.
and for the sake of her great suffering, to forget his Tristan relents.
wrongs. Tristan's anger was melted then. 'For Isolt's 7292—7370.
sake, for thine, Pilois, and God knows, most for my
own, I will forget my grief against her. But I may
not break my word to Gorvenal. I cannot go to her
until the spring.'

Tristan told Pilois to come to him at his inn, and
there, according to the custom of the country, he bade
a gift be given him. With those hundred shillings Tristan
rewards Pilois.
the youth bought himself many a fine fairing at the 7370—7392.
yearly market in Mont Saint Michel. Fast as his
heart would have taken him back to Tintagel, his
feet must perforce make slower speed. When he
reached there, the king asked him where he had
been that he came back with such riches. Then Isolt
feared so greatly lest he should speak unguardedly
that the sweat broke out all over her body. Pilois
saw well that she was anxious, and he answered
cleverly enough. He had won it all at Saint Michel. Pilois returns
to Cornwall.
They all misunderstood him, as he intended they 7392—7445.
should. Isolt alone knew what he meant and wept
for joy.

T. TRISTAN THE PILGRIM. THE GAMES.
IN ISOLT'S NAME.

As soon as May came, Tristan and Gorvenal Tristan and
Gorvenal set
out for Corn-
clothed themselves as pilgrims and departed for Cornwall. Not finding Dynas at home, they concealed wall.
7445—7513.
themselves in the thornbush in which Tristan had
hidden himself in his other visit. Many passed along
the road, but none whom Tristan could trust with his
message. At last, at daybreak, a dear friend of his

came by. So heavy were his eyes with sleep that he did not see Tristan, although he approached him and was about to speak. Tristan reflected that he had probably spent the night with his love, and so courteous was he that he refrained from awakening him. The horse took fright, however, and the rider, startled from his dream, was delighted to see Tristan before him. Tristan accepted his friend's offer to do him a service, and sent him with the ring as a token to the queen. He begged her to ride hunting again to the Blanche Lande, and told her that she would find Tristan again in the thornbush. At Isolt's request the king directed Andret to ride behind with her and her ladies.

The ring.
The hunting party.
7513—7560.

The queen had had a great misfortune. Brangien, her favorite, had died All had grieved for her, but none so bitterly as the queen. That is how it was that Camille rode with her now and was wholly in her confidence. When they reached the thornbush the queen sent ahead all the train, except Andret and Camille.

The death of
Brangien.
7560—7584.

Now how was the queen to speak to her lover in the thornbush without Andret's knowledge? She began to pluck flowers. As she was doing so the hounds came rushing past, and her frightened horse broke his strap and ran. Andret sprang on his horse and made after it. Then the queen could go and speak to her love. She dared not go into the thornbush, however, nor did he dare come out. How was she to arrange it? I wager that she contrived some means to tell him where to follow her.

The lover in the
thornbush;
Isolt gives the
cife.
7584—7690.

Just then a huntsman started the stag in the direction of this look-out, and the animal headed for the very thornbush in which Tristan was hiding. When he neared it, recognizing that someone was

there, he suddenly ran off another way. The king
was on the point of entering the bush to learn what
had frightened the deer, when Isolt saved her lover
by rushing after the animal and screaming. The king's
attention was thus diverted. The hunt took another
direction and Isolt was left with her lover for a little
while. But Andret soon found the horse and she was
compelled to ride on with him.

That night the lovers met at the trysting place
and were happy. Tristan forgot the blows he had
suffered and Isolt forgot her penance.

The tryst at the
Blanche Lande.
7690—7704.

The lover set out next morning to return to
Brittany. He had some difficulty in finding Gorvenal.
In seeking him, he stumbled upon the place where
the king and his followers had halted and were
engaged in sports. Some were casting the lance, some
leaping, some putting the stone. Tristan was making
his way through the crowd, rejoicing that no one had
recognized him, when a friend, hurrying after him,
called him by name, and begged him to go back with
him and outdo the others in feats of strength. Tristan
refused. It would be too dangerous. The friend
insisted, promising to get him safely away, but Tristan
was firm.

The delay in
the journey.
7704—7787.

At last the other put his request in the name of
Isolt. At this Tristan at once yielded. But when he
took the leap, the gray breeches split, and the spectators caught a glimpse of fine crimson stuff beneath.
When he put the stone, the gray pilgrim's coat broke
and the crimson showed through it. Tristan made off
then and none marked him. But when the king came
that evening and heard of the strong pilgrim, and of
how he had outdone all the others, and of the fine
scarlet underneath his gray cloak, he thought in his
heart that it must have been Tristan. He sent his

Tristan
is requested in
Isolt's name to
take part in the
games.
7787—7865.

men to seek him, but in vain. Tristan was already on his way to Brittany, where he was welcomed home.

U. KAHERDIN AND GARGEOLAIN. NEWS OF THE DEATH OF TRISTAN'S FATHER.

There was a powerful noble called Bedenis who had his seat near Carhaix. He was a great man for knightly deeds and hunting, and he had a handsome wife called Gargeolain, whom he kept so strictly guarded that it was an injury to his own honor.

The jealous Bedenis immures his wife. 7865—7945.

I wonder what the man is thinking of who guards his wife thus. If her heart is not with him willingly, he may use all his ingenuity to keep her, and she will love another, if she chooses, in spite of him. This is proved by what happened to Bedenis.

He' had built a high castle wall, with three moats around it, deep and wide. Though he had men enough to serve him, it was he himself who bore the keys. When he went out, there was no one so old or so young or so stupid that he would leave him there with his wife. She must stay alone, much as it irked her. Almost every day he went hunting, and left his wife thus, and when he returned she dared not look on anyone but him. This was the Bedenis who had so nearly taken Kaherdin prisoner.

Gargeolain's previous promise to Kaherdin. Their meeting. 7945—7964.

Now this lady had secretly promised that before she would receive her husband, she would receive Kaherdin, if he would come to her. But she had not been able to fulfil her vow; for Bedenis had heard it, and, as soon as he took her, he arranged this guard. Yet the lady still loved Kaherdin in her heart, nor did he forget her. He set all his thoughts on her love as you will see.

One day, when Bedenis was hunting, Kaherdin took his way alone to a place whence he could see his lady standing on the battlement. She bade him welcome.

'God reward thee', he cried earnestly, 'and curse him who so built this castle that I cannot see thee as I would. It would be some comfort to me, however, if these ladies would allow me a moment of private speech with thee.'

When the ladies had withdrawn, Kaherdin reminded her of what she had promised him to do before she took her husband, and told her that she was never out of his thoughts. Gargeolain renews her promise. 7964—8028.

'Gladly enough would I have done your will', she replied, 'if it had been possible, and would still, if it might be. But you see my case. My lord has locked me up and none can come to me. I will grant you what you wish, if you can but devise a way to reach me.'

Kaherdin withdrew joyfully then, and studied diligently to find a way to realize his desire. At Tristan's suggestion he obtained from Gargeolain wax impressions of the keys of the castle. Tristan himself sought out a smith, a Cornishman who had come with him from Tintagel, to make him keys. Tristan aids Kaherdin to form a plan. 8028—8135.

'Do you want to go a-thieving', the smith asked laughing.

While the keys were being made, Tristan received word that his father was dead and that war had broken out among the barons in his kingdom. He determined to reward Gorvenal for his faithful service by giving him the inheritance. Gorvenal refused, fearing that he might not be able to keep the vassals in subjection. He preferred that Tristan should come to News of the death of Tristan's father. 8135—8201.

Loonois and put the realm in order, and then leave it in his charge. Tristan could not bear to set out on the journey without first seeing Queen Isolt.

V. TRISTAN THE MINSTREL. HAUPT AND PLOT. TRISTAN WOUNDED IN A SIEGE.

He and Gorvenal set out for Cornwall disguised as minstrels, wearing little red caps and short cloaks of yellow stuff. Tristan sent word by Dynas as usual, and asked Isolt to meet him in the orchard by the linden tree. Next morning he joined Gorvenal and they departed. But Andret caught sight of them and gave chase. The fugitives found a little boat by the shore of a stream and saved themselves by leaping in and pushing off. Now Andret had no horse and could not wade across. He cast a spear after the fugitives. It broke, and Tristan, catching a part of it and using it as a paddle, guided the boat safely to the other shore.

When the king heard of this, he set guards on all the roads and adjured them as they loved the land and their own eyes, to stay there until Tristan was caught. Dynas were given the same directions, but when he chanced to come upon Tristan, he secreted him in his own house and bade his wife take care of him.

Now Queen Isolt was in great distress lest her lover be captured. One day, while she was pondering on a way to save him, two minstrels, Haupt and Plot, who had been brought to dire straits by gaming, came to the castle. The queen took them aside and asked them to do her a favor. She told them of Tristan's situation and promised to reward them richly if they would pretend to be the fugitives, and allow themselves

The tryst in the orchard. 8201—8268.

The pursuit by Andret. 8268—8363.

Isolt bribes Haupt and Plot. 8363—8476.

to be taken. It could bring them to no harm, and
it would deliver her lover. She gave them little red
caps such as Tristan and Gorvenal had worn, and told
them to make as if they were bent on getting out of
the country. When they were captured, they were to
say: 'Tristan, our lord, is in Carhaix. His father is
dead and he is about to set out with three hundred
men to take possession of his kingdom. We were pursued and fled to a stream where we found a boat and
pushed our way safely down the stream by using a
broken part of a spear hurled at us.' Isolt cautioned
them to hold to these statements in spite of threats
or bribes.

The strangers were indeed captured. They were
taken apart separately, questioned, and threatened, but
both held staunchly to the story.

'You shall be slain for this, and it is foolish, for
if you had told the truth, as your comrade has done,
you would have been spared.'

Haupt and Plot
pretend to be
the minstrels
pursued by An-
dret.
8476—8549.

'Does he say otherwise than I?'

'In truth, yes.'

'Let him take shame to himself then.'

'Why?'

'Because he lies.'

'How stubborn you are that you will not recant.'

'Well, do you want the truth?'

'Yes, indeed.'

'That you have already.'

So the ruse of Isolt succeeded. The two minstrels
were set free, and the king removed the guards. Tristan
returned in safety to Carhaix, mustered three hundred
knights, and set out to his own land. He remained
there among his vassals a little more than two years.
Then he left the realm to Gorvenal and returned to
Carhaix.

Tristan at Loo-
nois. Gorvenal
rewarded.
8549—8574.

He found King Howel and his wife dead, and
Kaherdin again besieged by Duke Rivalin. Isolt and
her brother rejoiced greatly at Tristan's return. With
his help the rebellion was soon put down. Tristan
then set to work to reduce the mutinous vassals to
complete subjection. While he was engaged in this
work, he was one day besieging a tower, and was
struck with a stone and carried from the fray for
dead. He recovered from his wound but slowly, and
when, after a year, he could ride and walk again,
no one could recognize in his changed looks the
Tristan of other days.

Tristan
is wounded
during a siege.
8574—8658

W. TRISTAN THE FOOL.

Now' one day he was riding with his sister's son,
a boy who had come with him from his own country,
and they came down to the sea. Tristan turned his
longing eyes toward Cornwall and murmured to
himself:

'Alas, dear Queen, can it be that I shall never
see thee more?'

The youth heard and asked him why he spoke
thus. Tristan told him then of the perilous ending
of the last visit.

The
lad's counsel
to Tristan.
8658—8725.

'But, uncle', said the lad, 'there would be no
danger now. You are not as you were then. Your
hair is shorn. Put on a jester's motley and act the
part, and they will believe you are a fool.'

'Now God bless thee, my child', cried Tristan
laughing, and kissed him for his counsel.

In motley then, and carrying a jester's club, Tristan
crept stealthily to the Cornish boats and found a merchant ship from Tintagel. The merchant thought him

indeed a fool, and resolved to bring him to his lady the queen. So merry did Tristan make them during the voyage that they all swore there never was a better fool. They gave him cheese to eat, but he did not forget his lady. He put the cheese in his pocket for her, and ate of other things.

Tristan disguised as a fool, is taken to King Mark at Tintagel. 8725—8768.

The king was on the shore, and Tristan was presented to him at once. Andret wished to play with the fool like the others, but Tristan fell upon him in a fury to avenge himself for all the harm that he had suffered from him. The king chid the fool for casting loving looks at the queen.

'I must and dare look so. She owes me fond looks too, for I am dear to her.'

The fool furnishes diversion for the court. 8768—8914.

'Be silent', cried the king, 'if you must speak thus, let it be of other women.'

'I have done much for her sake', said the fool. 'and suffered much — indeed it is she that has made of me a fool.'

So earnest was he that for an instant they felt some truth in the words.

'I will prove my love for her', he cried. 'See the treasure I have brought with me for her across the sea', and he offered the queen the cheese.

They laughed then, declaring that this was indeed the foolishest fool they had ever seen. When the king had departed, he again pressed the queen to eat the cheese which he had for seven days carried in his hood. When she refused, he put it into her mouth The queen struck him a slight blow then. 'Ah, my lady, if you but knew who I am, you would not strike me thus. If Tristan were dear to you, you would not.' He showed her the ring then, and Isolt knew that it was Tristan himself.

Tristan makes himself known to the queen. He is with her for three weeks 8914—8942.

During the three weeks that followed, the lovers
had much joy, but two of the guards of the chamber
learned the queen's secret and lay in wait for Tristan
one night at the door to kill him. But he knew their
plan and entered in spite of them. For no one's threats
would he refrain. She loved him as he loved her,
above all the world. The spies quailed before him
as he passed them to go to his lady. He kissed her
lovingly, saying sadly:

Tristan is dis-
covered and
must depart.
The ring shall
be a token.
8942—9033. 'Now we must part. We are discovered. I can
come no more, alas, to see you. Be true to me as I
shall ever be to you. If messenger of mine bring you
this ring, do secretly what I ask of you then. Mav
God destroy those who part us two so soon.'

The queen cursed them likewise, and wept
full sorely. And Tristan went out, holding high his
jester's club.

X. KAHERDIN AND GARGEOLAIN. THE WISPS
IN THE WALL.

You all know how it was with Kaherdin and
Bedenis' wife — their desire was still unfulfilled. One
fine day therefore, when the husband was hunting,
Kaherdin set out to see his lady, and Tristan accompanied him. The wind blew off his garland of flowers
Kaherdin and
Tristan at the
castle of Be-
denis.
9033—9076. as they passed the moat. He was in right joyous
mood, I promise you, as they opened the gates with
the keys and entered. The ladies received them
graciously. Gargeolain withdrew with Kaherdin into
an inner chamber, and Tristan was left sitting with
the others.

Now Tristan had more skill in shooting twigs
than any one else, and as he sat there he beguiled

the time thus. He shot one twig into the wall and Tristan shoots the wisps into the wall. 9076—9112.
another into the first, and a third into that, and
a fourth and a fifth, each into the other. The ladies
were astonished by his skill. So absorbed were they
all in the play that he shot the wall full of twigs
without realizing that they would be deadly tokens
against him when he had gone back to Carhaix.

The two friends rode away at last, taking care The friends depart. 9112—9136.
to lock the gates behind them. In the forest they
gave chase to a roe, and wearied and lamed their
horses without taking it. While they were thus
occupied, Bedenis returned home. As he entered the Bedenis finds the chaplet in the moat and the wisps in the wall. 9136—9161.
castle, he saw Kaherdin's garland lying in the moat,
and above in the chamber he saw in the wall the
twigs that Tristan had shot. He thought to himself:

'None but Tristan can have done this, and if he
has been here, Kaherdin has been with him.'

He drew his sword over his wife and threatened
to kill her unless she confessed.

'Has Kaherdin been with you?' Bedenis accuses his wife. 9161—9180.
'Yes.'
'What did he do to you?'
'He kissed me.'
'Did you give him your love?'
'No.'
'You lie.'
'My lord, I do. He forced me. I know not how
he entered the castle.'

Bedenis sprang on his horse and set out with seven
men in pursuit. Tristan and Kaherdin, with their He sets out in pursuit. Kaherdin is killed and Tristan wounded. 9180—9256.
lame horses, could not outrun them. In the struggle
that followed, Kaherdin was killed and Tristan was
wounded with a poisoned spear. Bedenis rode sadly
away. He was unharmed, and he had avenged his
shame, but he had lost his men, and he knew that

the allies of these two friends would not rest until
he had paid dearly for their death.

When the news was brought to Carhaix, Tristan's
wife was overcome with grief. She buried her brother
with great mourning and sent swiftly for skilled leeches
to heal Tristan. But it was of no avail. His wound
was such that none could heal him but King Mark's
wife Isolt.

Y. THE MESSENGER TO QUEEN ISOLT.

Tristan sends
for Isolt to
come and heal
him.
9256—9297. Tristan sent for his host from the town and asked
him to be his messenger. The man agreed gladly, for
he had come with him from Tintagel. Tristan told
him to remind the queen of all that he had done and
suffered for her sake, and of their last meeting, and to
beg her to come to him quickly. 'Unless she comes'.
continued Tristan, 'I must surely die.'

The daughter
of the messeng-
er is to watch
for his arrival.
9297—9309. He gave him the ring as a token. 'When you
return', he concluded, 'put up a white sail if you bring
my lady, and if she does not come, put up a black
one. Tell your daughter secretly to watch for you
every day by the shore, that she may tell me what
is the color of your sail. Let her be careful, and tell
no one why she looks out upon the sea.'

The host did not fail. He went home and told
the matter to his daughter, as Tristan had commanded
him, and he told her what to do when she saw him
coming. Solemnly he bade her to conceal it from
everyone.

Isolt departs
with the mes-
senger for Brit-
tany.
9309—9346. He set sail then and hastened to Queen Isolt and
told her secretly of Tristan's message. When she saw
the ring, she left her husband, her honor, and her
country, her royal robes and treasure, and all she

ever had, and fled with the merchant. Of all her possessions she took with her only the things that she needed for her leechcraft.

Every day all day long the child watched for her father's ship in order to bring Tristan word of the color of the sail. I do not know who told it to Tristan's wife. She commanded the girl, as soon as she should learn of her father's coming, to tell her at once the color of the sail, and to conceal it from Tristan till her father came. It might easily do him harm.

Tristan's wife commands the child to announce the arrival to her. 9346—9372.

When she returned to the shore, the girl saw on the sea a ship approaching, with a sail as white as snow. She did not disobey the lady; she dared not neglect her command. She returned to her and told her that the sail was white.

Z. THE DEATH OF TRISTAN AND ISOLT.

'I see the boat of your host approaching', said his wife then to Tristan.

She tells Tristan that the sail is not white. 9372—9385.

At this the sick man rejoiced. He raised himself in the bed and asked her if she could tell him the color of the sail. The lie that she told him then she afterward mourned bitterly; she did not know that it would break his heart. She told him that the sail was not white. Tristan laid his head down on the bed; his bones cracked; he stretched himself out and died.

Tristan dies. 9385—9391.

When his wife saw him thus, she well nigh died of grief, for it was she who had spoken the word that had killed him. Ah, how she screamed then! 'Alas and alas, that ever such evil should befall me', she cried. She saw that it was through her fault that he was dead.

Grief for
Tristan.
9391—9413.
Then mourning and lamentation was raised throughout the city. Tristan was borne into the great church and buried with mournful song.

The death
of Isolt.
9413—9446.
Isolt of Ireland heard the tolling of the bells as she stepped upon the shore, and she knew that Tristan was dead. She did not turn pale or red; she did not weep. But her heart was sore. Silently she went to the bier. His wife stood beside it weeping and lamenting. 'Lady', said Queen Isolt to her, 'you must take a place yonder and let me draw nearer. I mourn him with more cause than you. I loved him more.'

She uncovered the bier and silently she made a little place beside him. There she lay down then and died.

There was loud weeping in the place, and saddest of all was the wife of Tristan. Indeed it were a hard heart that had not been moved.

Eilhart's testimony.
9446—9464.
It was Master Eilhart of Oberg that put this story into verse and related it to us — the story of how Tristan was born and died. Another may perhaps say that it was otherwise. We all know that the story is told in different ways. But Eilhart has the true account.

The grief of
Mark.
9464—9510.
The wife of Tristan, tortured with grief, had the bodies laid in noble tombs. News came to King Mark that Tristan and the queen had been brought to death by their love and that it had been a potion that had bound them to each other thus against their will. He grieved to learn this too late. God knows he would have pardoned them and kept them with him, had they told him that it was the potion that had made them mad. He would have given them his kingdom and his lands for their own, if he could have brought them to life again.

He crossed the sea to Brittany and brought the bodies back to Cornwall with much mourning, and he buried them there with great state in one grave.

I know not if I should tell you, but I have heard it told that the king had a rose bush set over the woman and a vine over the man. They grew together so that they could in no wise be sundered. It was the potion, men told me, that did this thing. Now I have finished all that is written of Tristan. May Christ accept it [1].

The rosebush and the vine. 9510—9525.

---

[1] In making this outline we have followed the text edited by Lichtenstein, *Quellen und Forschungen* XIX. For the relation of this redaction to the lost original see Appendix I.

III. THE *ESTOIRE*.

A. M. BÉDIER'S STUDY OF THE RELATION OF THE EXTANT TEXTS.

THE TABLE OF CONCORDANCES AS A METHOD OF PROOF.

In his study of the relation of the poem of Thomas to the other early versions of the Tristan romance — the poem of Béroul, the poem of Eilhart von Oberge, the *Folie Tristan* of the Berne manuscript, and the French Prose Romance — M. Bédier employed the following method[1]. First he compared the five versions trait for trait. He examined each detail of the narrative in each of the versions and asked himself: Of the two or three or four variants which these redactions present, which is the oldest form? He decided the question for himself on the more or less archaic treatment of each detail and its more or less perfect and logical combination with the details in proximity to it.

This method did not seem to him entirely satisfactory; he hesitated to make the primitiveness of a

---

[1] *Le roman de Tristan par Thomas,* Paris 1902. 1905, II, 191—193, 309.

trait dependent on his own taste and his own syllogisms. But having examined the poems again and again from this point of view, he noticed, not without surprise, he says, that the traits which, for reasons of taste, of sentiment, or of logic, he had considered primitive, were attested by all three versions, or by two at least, when there were three available for comparison. Those which he had judged remodelled and posterior appeared, on the contrary, in a single version. The only exception was that Béroul and Eilhart in a few cases agreed in giving what seemed to him a less satisfactory account than the others. This he took to be an indication that the Béroul-Eilhart version, Thomas, the Prose Romance, and the *Folie Tristan* of the Berne manuscript, were independent derivatives of the same poem [1].

M. Bédier in consequence decided not to present his conclusions as to the outlines of the common source as the result of considerations of logic and taste. On the contrary he drew up a table of concordances and a table of variants. In the first table he placed all the traits that are found in at least two versions (counting Eilhart and Béroul together as one version y); in the second he placed all those that occur in one version only. The table of concordances represents, to M. Bédier's mind, the outlines of the common source.

M. Bédier declares that the making of this reconstruction was a purely mechanical process. 'In this task', he says, 'our preference has no part.' But it is clear from his own description of his procedure, which we have given above, that it was not until he had reached his conclusions, that the idea of presenting them in a table of concordances occurred to him.

---

[1] *op. cit.* II, 192.

His classification of the texts — *y* (Eilhart-Béroul), Thomas, the *Folie*, and the Prose Romance — as independent derivatives from a common source, is founded on considerations of taste, sentiment, and logic. On this classification the tables of concordances are entirely dependent. Moreover, it is on considerations of taste, sentiment, and logic, not at all on the mere correspondence of two or more versions, that he depends at every point in selecting the traits of his reconstruction.

This may be illustrated by a few examples. Let us take his procedure in the reconstruction of the Quest episode. It is first necessary to determine what was the version of Thomas, for the text of Thomas in this passage is not extant[1]. The situation in the different redactions is as follows: *Sir Tristrem* is too condensed to throw any light on Mark's attitude toward the demand of the barons that he should marry. The *Saga* represents him as acceding at once to their request, Gottfried as resisting until overborne by Tristan's threat to withdraw from the court unless he satisfies the barons. M. Bédier attributes to Thomas the motives and course of action represented by Gottfried, since these alone accord with his own idea of the necessities of narrative and character at this point. He then reconstructs the common source according to Eilhart and the Thomas version[2].

But this cannot be said to be using the method of a table of concordances. It is well known that Gottfried developed the characters and elaborated the narrative of Thomas independently, and by borrowings from Eilhart. We cannot safely attribute to Thomas traits in Gottfried's version coinciding with Eilhart

---

[1] *op. cit.* I, 105, n. 1.
[2] *op cit.* II, 214 ff.

and not supported by the *Saga* or *Sir Tristrem*. The mere coincidence of Gottfried and Eilhart on this point does not prove that their version was that of the source of Eilhart and Thomas[1]. It is on other grounds, on the literary grounds which M. Bédier has developed in his *Discussion*, that Eilhart's version is here to be accepted.

We cite another example of the fact that M. Bédier's reconstruction is not determined by the concordance of two or more versions: He represents the account of the return from the forest as follows[2]:

> On awakening, the lovers realize that the king has been there and that he has spared them (OBT). They are terrified at first, fearing that he has gone to bring help, but they soon understand his clemency and realize that it will be possible to arrange a reconciliation with him (OBT). Negotiations (OBT) ... Mark takes back Isolt, and Tristan remains exiled from the court (OBR) by the terms of an agreement with the king (OB).

As a matter of fact, neither Eilhart nor Béroul connect the lovers' appeal for reconciliation and the return from the forest in any way with the discovery scene in question. Nor do the lovers interpret as indications of the king's clemency the tokens which he leaves. On the contrary they are terrified and flee.

The various texts give the following various treatments of the return from the forest[3]. After the account of the episode of the separating sword, Béroul and Eilhart tell us that the lovers live in constant fear until the influence of the potion abates. At this moment they are suddenly stricken with repentance.

---

[1] Piquet, *L'originalité de Gottfried de Strasbourg*, Lille 1905, pp. 181—9.

[2] *op. cit.* II, 257—8.

[3] *Le roman de Tristan par Béroul*, ed. E. Muret, Paris 1903, 2131 ff.; Eilhart von Oberge, ed. F. Lichtenstein, Strassburg 1877, *Quellen und Forschungen* XIX, 4724 ff.

By the intercession of the hermit Ogrin they prevail upon the king to take back Isolt. Tristan brings her to the appointed place, gives her over to Mark, and goes into exile. The allusions in the *Folie* of the Berne manuscript are not detailed, but the mention of Ogrin and the *parlement* suggests the Béroul Eilhart version [1]. In the Prose Romance the king abducts Isolt [2]. In Thomas he recalls them both to the court because he is convinced of their innocence, having seen them sleeping with a sword between them [3]. The reconstruction of M. Bédier does not correspond to any version. It is determined by motives of taste, sentiment, and logic, and must be judged on that basis. It is a compromise due to his conviction that neither the garden scene, the device by which Thomas subsequently brings about the exile of Tristan [4], nor the expiration of the influence of the potion by which Eilhart and Béroul bring it about, represent the version of the *estoire*.

M. Bédier himself realizes how untrustworthy a table of concordances would be if used as a method of proof. He notes as probably fortuitous the correspondence of the Prose Romance and Thomas in the trait that Tristan, recovering from his swoon after killing the dragon, is recognized by Isolt [5]. He further recognizes that the correspondence between two versions may in some cases be due to secondary influence, or to independent borrowing of an incident in a widely popular tale. For example, in Thomas and in the

---

[1] *La Folie Tristan,* ed. Bédier, Paris 1907, 225 ff., 464 ff.

[2] *Le roman en prose de Tristan,* ed. Löseth, Paris 1890, § 53; Bédier II, 362—4.

[3] *Le roman de Tristan par Thomas,* ed. Bédier, I, ch. XXVIII.

[4] Bédier II, 262.

[5] Bédier II, 227—8.

Prose Romance, Tristan kills the dragon *by one blow piercing through the throat to the heart*[1].

The most important conclusion which M. Bédier drew from his comparison of the versions is that to which the studies of Lichtenstein[2], Muret[3], Röttiger and Golther[4] had long pointed, namely that the source of Thomas and that of the Béroul-Eilhart version was the same. But it is by the *Discussions*[5] and not by the table of concordances that M. Bédier has established it.

The table of concordances proves nothing[6]. It is merely a convenient index of some of the traits which occur in two or more versions and which M. Bédier takes to be primitive. It is only the problems that are treated in the *Discussions* that can be considered solved. Such questions as whether the Prose Romance is based on the *estoire* or merely influenced by it[7], or whether the *Folie Tristan* of the Berne manuscript is drawn from the *estoire* or from Béroul, are still matters of doubt[8].

---

[1] Bédier II, 219 d.

[2] *QF*. XIX, cxxxii—cl.

[3] *Romania* XVI, 288—363; XXVII, 611.

[4] W. Röttiger, *Der heutige Stand der Tristanforschung*, Hamburg 1897, p. 36; Golther, *Zeitschr. f. frz. Sp. u. Lit.* XXII, 23.

[5] Bédier II, 196—8 et seq.

[6] cf. Zenker, *Romanische Forschungen* XXIX, 328 ff.; J. Kelemina, *Untersuchungen zur Tristansage*, Leipzig 1910, *Teutonia* 16, VIII; Muret, *Zeitschr. f. frz. Sp.* XXXVII, 171 ff.

[7] M. Bédier uses MS. 103 as representative of the Prose Romance. But this version has been interpolated by a redactor acquainted with the poems. Cf. Röttiger, *Der heutige Stand der Tristanforschung*, op. cit. 26.

[8] Muret, *Zeitschr. f. frz. Sp. u. Lit.* XXXVII, 171, and *Béroul* LXXIII, considers that the *Folie* of the Berne manuscript is based on the Béroul version; cf. Bédier II, 263: *si on avait la preuve assurée que F, qui connaît ce personnage, est indépendant d'y.*

B. CRITICISM OF M. BÉDIER'S RECONSTRUCTION OF THE *ESTOIRE*.

1. IMPORTANT POINTS
IN WHICH THE VERSION OF EILHART IS CLOSER TO
THE *ESTOIRE* THAN M. BÉDIER'S RECONSTRUCTION.

a) The potion.

The most important point in which it seems to us that M. Bédier's reconstruction of the source of Eilhart and Thomas is mistaken is in regard to the duration of the influence of the potion. We have already discussed this question in an article in the *Romania* (XXXIX, 277—97) but we take this opportunity to present the evidence in what seems to us now a more convincing form.

In Béroul we have the statement that the influence of the potion was confined to three years[1]. In Eilhart von Oberge it is represented as lasting forever, but as suffering a certain diminution in its efficacy at the end of four years[2]. Thomas[3] and the Prose Romance[4] make no mention of this diminution.

b) The return from the forest.

The attributes of the potion must be considered in connection with the account of the lovers' return

---

[1]   2133—2141.

[2]   ed. Lichtenstein (cited as OX), 2279—2300; The Dresden manuscript and the Heidelberg manuscript, from which Lichtenstein made his critical edition, are cited respectively as OD and OH. Prose redaction ed. F. Pfaff, *Literarischer Verein in Stuttgart*, CLII (cited OP), p. 43—44; Bohemian translation ed. Knieschek, *Zeitschr. f. d. Alt.* (cited *OČ*) XXVIII, 86_{15}—87_{15}. On these redactions v. infra Appendix I.

[3]   Bédier I, 142.

[4]   Löseth § 38—9; Bédier II, 340—1.

from the forest, for in Béroul and in Eilhart the
return is a direct consequence of the abatement of
its influence. When the destined hour arrives, the
compulsion which has lain upon the lovers is lifted.
In Béroul[1] their sudden change of feeling is described
at length. For the first time they realize the privations
of their life in the forest, the misery of exile, and the
suffering they have caused each other. Their relief at
being freed from the curse of the potion, their remorse
for their sin, their regret for the injury they have
done Mark, and their aspirations toward a better life
are couched in all the the pious formulae of mediaeval
orthodoxy. Moved by the desire to obtain remission
of their sins and counsel for amendment, they again
seek the hermit Ogrin. To his greeting:

> 'Gent dechacie, a con grant paine
> Amors par force vos demeine!
> Conbien durra vostre folie?
> Trop avez mené ceste vie.
> Et, queles, quar vos repentez[2]!'

Tristan replies:

> 'Si longuement l'avon menee,
> Itel fu nostre destinee.
> .iii. anz a bien, si que n'i falle,
> Onques ne nos falli travalle[3].'

Released from the influence of the potion, the
lovers at once abandon their life in the forest.
Through the good offices of the hermit Ogrin, Mark
is prevailed upon to receive Isolt. Tristan brings her
back to him, and submits to exile.

---

[1] Béroul 2133—89.
[2] Béroul 2295—2300.
[3] Béroul 2301—5.

Since the return from the forest is represented in the same way in the *Folie Tristan* of the Berne manuscript, we may suppose that the treatment of the potion in its source was similar to that in Eilhart.

'En la forest fumes un terme,
O nos plorames mainte lerme.
Ne vit encore l'hermite Ugrin?
Dex mete s'ame a boene fin[1].'

and

Encor ai l'anel près de moi
Que me donestes au partir
Del parlemant que doi haïr.
Maldite soit ceste asanblee!
Mainte dolereuse jornee
En ai puis aüe et soferte[2].'

Béroul fixes the term of the influence of the potion as three years. He describes its abatement at the end of that period, and the lovers' abandonment of each other. But the continuator[3] of Béroul carries on the story of the lovers' passion as if there had been no mention of a term to the potion's influence. Eilhart states that during the first four years the lovers must be together daily; after that they can endure separation, but they must love each other with all their

---

[1] *Folie* (Berne MS.), ed. Bédier (*La Folie Tristan*, Paris 1907) 462—6.

[2] *op. cit.* 223—9.

[3] For a discussion of the continuation in Béroul, cf. Muret, *Béroul* p. II—XXV. He concludes XXIII—IV: 'Ainsi nous sommes amenés à reconnaître dans le manuscrit 2171 deux, et même trois groupes de récits, nettement distincts et parfois contradictoires ... On sait déjà que les récits de la première partie dérivent de la même source perdue que le poème allemand d'Eilhart d'Oberg. Dans le morceau de raccord, un récit de même provenance a sans doute été remanié pour accueillir les données de la dernière partie.' Similarly *Zeitschr. f. frz. Sp. u. Lit.* XXXVII, 171.

souls as long as they live[1]. The *Folie* gives the same
narrative, and we may suppose that it understands
similarly the abatement of the influence of the potion
and the lovers' return from the forest.

The expiration of the influence of the potion, the
repentance of the lovers, and their reconciliation with
Mark at the counsel of the hermit are entirely lacking
in the Thomas version. The question is therefore:
are the versions of Eilhart, Béroul, and the *Folie*
dependent on a secondary source which differs from
the source of Thomas in this point, or does Thomas,
here as in the narrative as a whole, revise his model
in accordance with more courtly tastes[2]?

c) *The hypothesis of a secondary source for Béroul and Eilhart.*

M. Bédier postulates a secondary source for Eilhart
and Béroul in order to support the first hypothesis[3].
M. Bédier states it somewhat as follows: In the
estoire the period of the potion's efficacy was not
limited. A redactor y, whose version is the source
of Béroul and Eilhart, observing that in the second
part of the romance the lovers see each other less
frequently, introduced the idea which we find in
Eilhart that the influence of the potion partially

---

[1] *OX* 2274—2300.

[2] M. Bédier and other critics who have discussed this
question have been influenced in the study by a feeling that
it was necessary to suppose the version of the *estoire* such as
would seem appropriate to a 'primitive' or 'original' version.
We are not here discussing the original conception of the potion,
nor even the most primitive French version; we are discussing
the particular French poem of which the versions in question are
redactions. This poem represents in our opinion a late development of the tradition. Cf. W. Foerster, *Cligès* [3] LXV.

[3] Bédier II, 238.

abated after four years. He did this in order to make
their passion appear more spontaneous, more voluntary,
more human. Béroul, who represents the influence of
the potion as expiring after three years, either neglects
to mention, or deliberately misinterprets, the clause in
his original which stated that after that time its
influence, although slightly less potent, should continue
throughout their lives.

It seems to us unjustifiable to attribute to the
redactor of the Béroul-Eilhart version the purpose of
rendering the love of Tristan and Isolt more spontaneous, more voluntary, and more human. But whether
or not the explanation appeals to us as plausible,
there is no evidence for it. Moreover it implies the
supposition, for which, as has been shown, there is no
evidence, that the return from the forest took place
in the *estoire* as it is represented in M. Bédier's reconstruction.

It seems to us unjustifiable to suppose that Thomas
has preserved the version of the *estoire* in the treatment of the potion, when we have evidence, as
M. Bédier has shown, that he has altered it in every
other important particular in which he differs from the
other redactors [1]. It seems especially improbable since
his departures from them in the treatment of the potion
are in accord with his habitual tendency to make the
lovers' conduct the mirror of his own ideal of love [2].

On the other hand the facts fit in perfectly with
the hypothesis that the *estoire* was the hybrid thing
which is preserved in Béroul, Eilhart, and the *Folie*,
and that it is Thomas who has modified it. In the
first place, this supposition is in accordance with the

---

[1] Bédier II, *Discussions* passim.
[2] Bédier I, p. 1, p. 416, l. 3125—45. cf. Bédier II, 279—280.

fact that the Thomas version, in other cases that have
been examined, is the revision of a model which Béroul
and Eilhart and the *Folie* preserve substantially un-
changed[1]. Further, the conception of the potion which
we have pointed out in this section of the Béroul-Eilhart
version, a conception which condemned the relation of
the lovers as criminal, is one with which Thomas would
certainly not have been in sympathy. It was almost
inevitable that he should alter such a version in accordance with his own attitude toward love, an attitude less naive, less ascetic, more impregnated with
the courtly ideals of his time[2]. In his version the
return from the forest is not due to the abatement of
the influence of the potion and the repentance of the
lovers. On the contrary the two lovers give up the
life together only when forced by Mark, who, having
chanced to come upon them sleeping and seen a sword
between them, is convinced of their innocence and
commands them to come back[3].

This termination is certainly more fitting in a
poem dedicated to the glorification of love than that
in which the first step in the return is due to the
lovers' regret for their sin and discomfort.

Mark's discovery of the lovers in the forest is
found also in Béroul and Eilhart, but is there without
influence upon the narrative. Mark finds them sleeping
in their leafy hut. He is about to destroy them
when he notices that Tristan's sword lies between
them. His resolution fails him. He takes the sword
and leaving his own in its place as a token of his

---

[1] Bédier II, 259—63. Golther accepts Bédier's conclusion,
op. cit. (1907), p. 152—3.

[2] cf. Brakelmann, *Les plus anciens chansonniers français*,
Paris 1870—1, Chrestien de Troyes II, 28—34. To efface the
love-potion entirely was, however, too bold a move for Thomas.

[3] Bédier I, Ch. XXVIII.

presence, departs unobserved. When Tristan and Isolt awake, they are terrified and flee from the place[1].

We might think perhaps that the Thomas redaction, in which the episode forms a turning point in the story, represents the version of the *estoire*. On the contrary it is certainly a modification of it. The recall of Tristan and Isolt together, as we have it in Thomas, fails to bring the lovers into the position which is the necessary point of departure for the remainder of the story, namely Tristan in exile making stolen visits to Isolt at the court of Mark. Thomas is forced to invent a new episode in order to bring them into this position.

His expedient is the following: Mark again finds the lovers asleep together, this time in a garden, no sword between them. He again withdraws, this time on the pretext of seeking witnesses. As he departs the lovers awake, terrified, and Tristan flees[2].

The scene is full of improbabilities. Would Mark, finding the lovers in each others arms, feel the necessity of departing to call witnesses? Would Tristan, awakening and seeing the king departing, be so cowardly as to flee, leaving Isolt to her fate? Knowing that Mark might return at any instant, would the lovers have leisure to bid each other a long farewell and to exchange rings? M. Bédier considers that these improbabilities betray the invention of Thomas, who was less concerned to maintain the dignity of the characters than to avoid those features of the Eilhart version which were displeasing to him on account of their brutality[3].

---

[1] Béroul 1774—2133; *OX* 4581—701.
[2] Bédier I, Ch. XXIX.
[3] Bédier II, 262.

It seems to us hazardous to assert that an incident did not belong to the *estoire* on the mere ground of its improbability. The episode of the discovery in the forest which undoubtedly belonged to the *estoire* is full of improbabilities. Even the mediaeval reader seems to have asked: would Tristan and Isolt, alone in the forest, sleep with a sword between them? And would Mark, finding them thus, depart without making an effort toward a reconciliation? The description of the long farewell is a convention of the *chansons de geste* and the romances. The poet would not be likely to stop to consider whether or not it was realistic. We may agree with M. Bédier that in the garden scene in Thomas the treatment of Tristan is not in accordance with the conception of his character which appears in other parts of the narrative. Yet we are not prepared to maintain that the version of the *estoire* would always correspond to our ideas of consistency. As we shall attempt to show in the final chapters of our study, the redactor was continually under the necessity of adapting to his purpose heterogeneous material already possessing the authority of tradition.

Our conclusion that the discovery in the garden is the invention of Thomas is due rather to the following considerations: the version in which the lovers' return from the forest is explained by the abatement of the influence of the potion is supported by Béroul, Eilhart, and the *Folie*, whereas the garden scene by which it is brought about in Thomas is peculiar to that version. This fact establishes a presupposition against the authenticity of the garden scene, since Thomas is known to have remodelled in many points the version given in the three other texts. We have shown that Thomas had good reasons for utilizing as

he did the discovery in the forest which he found in
his source. By doing so he was enabled to suppress
Tristan's appeal to Mark to take back Isolt. As a
consequence of the suppression of this passage he is
now in need of some means of introducing the following narrative, in which Tristan is in exile, making
stolen visits to the queen at the court of Mark. Recognizing the advisability of avoiding as far as possible
any innovation in the tradition, he introduces the sequel
by a variant of the discovery scene already familiar.
The similarities between the discovery in the forest
and the discovery in the garden are obvious. Besides
those noticeable in the summaries above, it may be
noted that the terror of the lovers in Béroul, on
awakening after the discovery in the forest, is similar
to that described in Thomas after the discovery in
the garden.

In Béroul:

'Par cest change poon parçoivre,
Mestre, que il nos veut deçoivre;
Qar il ert seus, si nos trova;
Poor li prist, si s'en torna.
Por gent s'en est alé arrire,
Dont il a trop et baude et fire:
Ses amerra, destruire veut
Et moi et la roïne Yseut;
Voiant le pueple, nos veut prendre,
Faire ardoir et venter la cendre.
Fuion; n'avon que demorer[1].'

In Thomas:

'Tristan se dreche et dit: A! las!
Amie Yseut, car esvelliez:

---
[1] Béroul 2111—22.

Par engien somes agaitiez.
Li rois a veu quanque avon fait,
Au palais a ses omes vait;
Fra nos, s'il puet, ensenble prendre,
Par jugement ardoir en cendre.

. . . .

Fuïr deport et querre eschil,
Guerpir joie, siouvre peril[1].'

It would thus seem that Thomas suppressed the
abatement of the influence of the potion because it
was out of harmony with his ideal of love. Explain-
ing the return of the lovers from the forest as due to
the command of Mark, he at one stroke secured a
justification for a charming episode which had before
only impeded the narrative, and avoided attributing
the abandonment of the forest life to the initiative of

---

[1] Bédier I, p. 249, l. 17—29. Similar also is the trait of
the ring given by Isolt to Tristan at their parting.

In Béroul, at the parting at the *parlement*:

'Ami Tristran, or m'escoutez.
Par cele foi que je vos doi,
Se cel anel de vostre doi
Ne m'envoiez, si que jel voie,
Rien qu'il deïst ge ne croiroie ...
Mais, des que reverrai l'anel,
Ne tor ne mur ne fort chastel
Ne me tendra ne face errant
Le mandement de mon amant,
Solonc m'enor et loiauté
Et je sace soit vostre gré.'

ed. Muret 2794—2805.

In Thomas at the parting in the garden:

'Nequedent cest anel prenez:
Por m'amor, amis, le gardés.'

The manuscript of Thomas breaking off here, M. Bédier reconstructs the version as follows from the *Saga*: 'qu'il vous tienne
lieu de bref, de sceau et de serment, qu'il vous console et vous re-
mémore notre amour et cette séparation.' Bédier I, p. 250. l. 51—3.

the lovers themselves[1]. It seems established therefore that the treatment of the potion and of the return from the forest in Béroul, Eilhart, and the *Folie* represents the *estoire*, and that the treatment of Thomas is a revision of that model[2].

In regard to the treatment of the potion and the return from the forest in the Prose Romance, three possibilities are open. It may be that it preserves a version independent of the *estoire*. We have no authority to assert that the *estoire* was the first French romance that dealt at length with the adventures of Tristan. Second, it may have been influenced by the version of Thomas in the conception of the potion. Third, the redactor may have effaced independently, with his characteristic freedom, the limitation of the influence of the potion, the repentance of the lovers, and the voluntary return from the forest — traits that were no doubt as shocking to him as they were to Thomas.

The influences that led to the development of the account of the potion which we find appropriated by the *estoire* will be discussed in a later chapter in connection with the sources of the tradition. This poet was fortunately or unfortunately under the necessity of accepting the treatment of the return from

---

[1] Professor Golther also considers the garden scene to be an invention on the part of Thomas. *Tristan und Isolde in den Dichtungen des Mittelalters und der neuen Zeit*, Leipzig 1907, pp. 51, 62, 153.

[2] I no longer find convincing the considerations advanced in the discussion of this incident in my article in the *Romania* XXXIX, 285 — 90, where I attempted by another method to prove the point that I have endeavored to prove here, namely, that Thomas found the Béroul-Eilhart version in his source and that his variants are his improvements on that account. The conclusion seems to me to be warranted by the arguments presented in the present study. Cf. M. Bédier's discussion of the two discovery scenes in Thomas. I, p. 242. II, 261.

the forest with the other traditional elements of the story. The necessity of including in the same version with it the various returns of the exiled Tristan to Isolt, satisfactorily accounts for the attributes of the potion which we find in Eilhart. In Béroul these attributes are noted[1], as they were perhaps noted in the *estoire*, at the moments when the variations of the influence of the potion occur. The absence, in the continuation of Béroul, of the important trait that the influence of the potion continues to dominate the lovers after the expiration of the three years, is sufficiently accounted for by the fact that the continuator of Béroul did not have access to the *estoire*.

Our rejection of M. Bédier's reconstruction in regard to the return from the forest involves the rejection of his classification of the versions.

His hypothesis of a sub-source, y, as the model of Eilhart and Béroul, is based entirely on their treatment of the return from the forest and their naïve provision for it in the definition of the potion. The genesis of y is as follows: M. Bédier considered it impossible that the *estoire* should contain anything false to the tradition. He felt that the Béroul-Eilhart treatment was false to the tradition. He accordingly saw in the Béroul-Eilhart account of the potion a later invention. He therefore felt it necessary to postulate a common secondary source, y, for those two poems[2]. Since we have proved that the Béroul-Eilhart account of the potion was also in the *estoire* (whether it is false to the original tradition is another question), all necessity and all justification for postulating this secondary source y disappears.

---

[1] Béroul 2133—47.
[2] Bédier II, 238.

The characteristics of y as determined by M. Bédier[1] will therefore coincide with those of the *estoire*. These are the following: Dynas' pleading with Mark for Tristan, Tristan's slaughter of the lepers, the visits of the lovers to the hermit Ogrin[2], and his intercession with Mark on their behalf.

d) The quest of the princess. The recognition of Tristan by Isolt on his second arrival in Ireland.

We shall now turn to another passage of the narrative in which it appears to us that M. Bédier has adopted in his reconstruction of the *estoire* a trait which was introduced by later redactors. The reader will recall that in Eilhart, Béroul, and Thomas, Tristan makes two visits to Ireland, the first in quest of healing, after his combat with the Morholt, the second in quest of a wife for Mark. On his second arrival he lands secretly and sets off in pursuit of a dragon which he learns is devastating the country. Having killed the monster, he is found by Isolt unconscious.

In Thomas she recognizes Tristan at this point as the hero she has healed a few months before. As a second authority for the recognition scene, M. Bédier cites the Prose Romance[3]. The agreement of the Prose Romance with Eilhart in this point is purely accidental. The recognition scene takes place in the Prose Romance under entirely

---

[1] Bédier II, 264.

[2] M. Bédier appears to have overlooked the fact that the first visit of the lovers to the hermit Ogrin is also found in Eilhart. Lichtenstein, *Eilhart von Oberge, op. cit.* 4702—30 (cited hereafter as *OX*).

[3] Bédier II, 221 i, cf. 227.

different circumstances: Tristan, whose wound is being tended by Isolt, goes out secretly from the castle to destroy the dragon and is disfigured beyond recognition by the swelling due to the monster's poison. Isolt, finding him thus, nevertheless recognizes him as the hero whom she is healing. The incident of the dragon combat appears in but one manuscript of the Prose Romance and has been shown to be an interpolation due to the influence of the poems [1]. M. Bédier is, however, forced to include the recognition scene in his table of concordances, in order to be consistent. He has represented Isolt as seeing Tristan during his previous visit [2]. If she has already seen him, it is inevitable that she should recognize him on his return

e) *The meeting of Tristan with Isolt on his first arrival in Ireland.*

According to Eilhart, Tristan does not see Isolt during his first visit in Ireland; he is healed by a plaster which she sends him in response to her father's message [3]. There is accordingly no scene of recognition between them [4].

In the meeting of Tristan and Isolt during the first visit as well as the scene of recognition in the

---

[1] Röttiger, *op. cit.* p. 26.
[2] Bédier II, 210 j.
[3] *OX* 1193—220; *OP* 19_{21}—20_3; *OČ* 39_{15}—40_{18}.
[4] cf. *OX* 1863—7. In the *Folie Tristan* of the Berne manuscript we find (401 ff.):

'Car de la plaie que je oi,
Que il me fist par mi l'espaule, ...
Me randistes et sauf et sain;
Autres de vos n'i mist la main.'

We should account for this agreement with Thomas as due to the same tendency as that by which Brangien is represented as having given the potion to the lovers with her own hand. Cf. infra, Ch. III.

second, M. Bédier's reconstruction of the *estoire* seems
to us mistaken. Our reasons for preferring the version
of Eilhart involve a rather complicated argument.
The episode, as given in Eilhart, presents almost
without modification, a folk tale which was common
in the fiction of the Middle Ages, as it still[1] is
in popular tradition: A king sees a hair on the
waters of a stream or in the beak of a bird. He decides that he must have to wife the woman to whom
the hair belongs. A young hero undertakes the quest
and succeeds in obtaining her for the king.

As will be observed on examining versions of the
folk tale of the Swallows' Hair, one of the essential
elements of the story is that the princess and her whereabouts are unknown. This requirement seems incompa-
tible with the story of the hero's healing at the hands
of that same princess a few months before. The difficulty is met in Eilhart by the slightest possible change
in the first narrative — we are told that Isolt does
not tend the wounded Tristan in person: she sends a
messenger to him with healing herbs and he departs
from Ireland without seeing her.

In Thomas the two incidents have undergone a
thorough remodelling, and are fused to the advantage
of the story. Tristan is healed by Isolt in person
during the first visit. The second voyage is not
introduced by a story of two swallows and a mysterious hair; the quest which Tristan undertakes is no
longer for a princess whose identity is unknown. On
the contrary, it is introduced by Tristan's praises, on
his return from his first visit to Ireland, of the princess
who has healed him there. It is decided that this
princess would be a suitable wife for Mark, and Tristan

---

[1] cf. infra, Ch. V.

undertakes to set out and win her [1]. When Isolt finds
him, after the slaying of the dragon, they of course
recognize each other. It is clear, however, from the
passages in Gottfried and *Sir Tristrem* which allude
to the Swallows' Hair and reject it as improbable [2],
that Thomas' model gave the Béroul-Eilhart version
and that Thomas has given it, on his own responsability,
the modified form which we have just read.

It is certain, therefore, that the *estoire* represented
Tristan as setting out in quest of a princess to whose
identity a hair was the only clue [3]. If that princess
is to be Isolt, the poet must arrange that Tristan
shall have had no sight of her up to that time. If he
wishes to do this, he cannot represent her as healing
Tristan in person previously. The scene where Tristan
is found by Isolt after 'the combat with the dragon
must be their first meeting. Any question of their
recognizing each other there is impossible. The opening for a scene of recognition between Tristan and
Isolt in the second episode is first created when Thomas
rejects the story of the Swallows' Hair and allows
Tristan to set out on the quest for a wife for Mark
with the definite purpose of bringing him the Isolt he
has met in Ireland. One may object, on artistic grounds,
to Eilhart's use of a messenger in the healing of Tristan.
But it is a mistake to consider this objection evidence
that in the *estoire* Tristan was healed by Isolt in person.

It is unanimously agreed that both the Voyage for
Healing and the Quest of the Princess of the Swallows'
Hair, belong to the *estoire* [4]. If the hero and heroine

---

[1] Bédier I, Ch. XII p. 103—113.
[2] Gottfried von Strassburg, *Tristan*, ed. Marold, 8605—32;
Sir Tristrem, ed. Kölbing, Heilbronn 1882, 1365—6.
[3] cf. Bédier II, 213—8; similarly Golther (1907), 43—4.
[4] Bédier II, 207—33; Golther (1907), 42—4.

of the one story are to be identified with the hero
and heroine of the other, some way must be found to
combine them. The hero must set out in search of a
princess whom he has never seen and of whose whereabouts he is entirely ignorant, although he has been
healed by that very person only a few months before [1].
The only combination of these two episodes which has
authority in the texts is that which we find in Eilhart.
Since Eilhart's is the only version which is faithful to
the *estoire* in preserving both episodes, it is only reason-
able to suppose that it represents the *estoire* in the
way it combines them.

f) Tantris in the quest for the princess.

If the reader concurs in the foregoing conclusion,
he will agree that Eilhart represents the *estoire* in
another point in which Bédier rejects his version [2].
It will be recalled that in Tristan's first visit to
Ireland he passed, according to Eilhart, under the
name Pro [3]; in the second, under the name Tantris [4].
In Thomas, Tristan uses the pseudonym Tantris on
his first visit and is recognized as Tantris on his
second arrival [5]. Unless we suppose the *estoire* to have
contained the recognition scene (which, as we have
seen, is impossible), it is not surprising that it should
have contained two pseudonyms. M. Bédier makes

---

[1] M. Bédier's reconstruction contains the trait of the healing
of the hero by the princess in person and the recognition scene
(II, 221 i., 227, cf. supra) from Thomas. But for his combination
of the story of the Swallows' Hair from Eilhart, and these traits,
which depend upon a rejection of the story of the Swallows' Hair,
from Thomas, he has no authority in the texts.

[2] Bédier II, 209 i and note.

[3] *OX* 1182.

[4] *OX* 1585.

[5] Bédier I, 93, 121.

Tristan give the name Tantris on his first arrival,
because he erroneously considers that the recognition
scene formed part of the *estoire*: He cites the Prose
Romance, Thomas, and the *Folie* as authority for this
trait[1]; but it really appears only in Thomas. The name
Tantris appears in only one manuscript of the Prose
Romance (MS. 103), and there not before the combat
with the dragon[2]. In the *Folie*, the occasion of the
use of the pseudonym is not specified[3]. It appears
therefore that Eilhart preserves the version of the
estoire in depicting Isolt as healing Tristan by a messenger, in depicting him as seeing her for the first
time after his combat with the dragon, and in depicting him, on his second arrival in Ireland, as giving a
different name from that by which he was known
during his first visit there.

2. POINTS IN WHICH M. BEDIER'S RECONSTRUCTION CONTAINS TRAITS WHICH HE HAS NEGLECTED TO NOTE AS OCCURRING IN EILHART.

Having made a list of the remaining traits[4] noted
in M. Bédier's table of concordances as drawn from
versions other than Eilhart, we remarked that some
of those given on the authority of Thomas, the Prose
Romance, or the *Folie*, actually occur in Eilhart also.
M. Bédier had overlooked their presence in the German
version.

---

[1] Bédier II, 209 h.

[2] MS. 103. Bédier II, 332; cf. Löseth p. 475, p. IV, note.

[3] *Folie* (MS. Berne). Of the occasion when Tristan came
to Isolt disguised as a fool the poet relates: *Change son non, fait
soi clamer Tantris*, 1. 126—7. On this occasion Tristan addresses
the king thus: *Rois, tu n'iés mie encor bien duit; Esgarde moi
en mi lo vis: Don ne sanble je bien Tantris?* 1. 183 ff.

[4] v. Appendix II.

a) Tristan is admired by all the court.

M. Bédier notes only Thomas and the Prose Romance as stating that the young Tristan, when almost of age to be dubbed knight, is *loved by all the court*[1]. This trait is found in Eilhart as well as in the versions mentioned.

b) . Tristan takes his harp in the rudderless boat.

In the Voyage for Healing M. Bédier adopts from Thomas and the Prose Romance the trait that Tristan, thrown on the coast of Ireland, plays his harp as the boat nears the land[2]. This detail is, indeed, not expressly mentioned in the extant redactions of Eilhart, but there are traces of it. In both the prose and the verse redaction, it is mentioned that Tristan took his harp in the rudderless boat:

> 'dô bat der hêre nicht mê
> mit im an daz schif tragin,
> wen sîne harfin, hôrte ich sagin,
> und sîn swert des he begerte[3].'

'Hiemit ward er getragen in das schiflin mit grosser klage, mitt im sein schwert unnd ein härpffen[4].'

Since the poet mentions that Tristan took his harp with him, he probably mentioned it with some purpose. At any rate the reasons for including the trait in a reconstruction of the lost common source, are as clear in Eilhart as in Thomas, which version M. Bédier cites in support of the trait.

---

[1] II, p. 196.
[2] II, 209 h.
[3] *OX* 1134.
[4] *OP* p. 18.

c) The Irish king offers the half of his kingdom.

The trait that the Irish king offers the half of his kingdom, in addition to his daughter, to the slayer of the dragon, is cited by M. Bédier from Thomas and the Prose Romance [1]. It is found also in the Bohemian translation of Eilhart [2].

d) The influence of the potion is for life.

M. Bédier cites from the Prose Romance the following words, describing the effect of the potion, *or sont entrez en la rote qui jamais ne leur fauldra jour de de leurs vies, car ils ont beu leur destruction et leur mort* [3]. The course of the story not only in Thomas, which M. Bédier cites, but also in Eilhart, testifies to the same theme.

e) The blood from Tristan's wound stains the bed of Isolt.

In the episode in which the dwarf spreads the floor with flour as a trap for the lovers, Tristan, it will be remembered, reaches Isolt's side by leaping. from his bed to hers. His wound breaks open and she is covered with blood. When Tristan, upon realizing himself discovered, leaps back to his own bed, he leaves a footprint on the floor. M. Bédier seems to have overlooked the line in Eilhart

'si wart von im recht als ein blût [4]',

for he says that in Eilhart the only evidence against the lovers is the footprint on the floor [5].

---

[1] II, 218 a.
[2] Knieschek, *ZfdA.* XXVIII (cited hereafter *OC*), p. 285; § 57, 1. 20; cf. Appendix I.
[3] II, 234 c.
[4] *OX* 3927.
[5] II, 249 c, note, 250—2.

f) The dwarf gives the signal for capture.

M. Bédier follows Béroul and Thomas in making the dwarf leave the room after spreading the flour on the floor [1]. In Eilhart he conceals himself under the bed of Isolt [2]. The significance of both movements is the same: it must be possible for the dwarf to give the signal for capture without being seen by Tristan. In Eilhart he does it from under the bed, in Béroul from outside the room [3]. The version of Thomas contains no signal from the dwarf. The king is absent for some time. When he returns, Tristan has already successfully regained his bed. The blood is the only evidence to confirm the king's suspicion [4].

g) Isolt gives Tristan a ring as a token.

No mention is made in Eilhart, at the time of the parting of the lovers after the return from the forest, of a ring given to Tristan by Isolt. M. Bédier takes this detail from Béroul, the *Folie*, and Thomas, where it occurs in a different setting [5]. This ring is, however, mentioned later in Eilhart, when Tristan sends his messenger to Isolt:

'Tristrant ir ein vingerlîn
zu wârzêchene sante
daz sie vor vil wol erkante
wen sie hâtiz im gegebin [6].'

---

[1] II, 249 b.
[2] OX 3846—8.
[3] Béroul 736.
[4] Bédier I, 204.
[5] II, 258 g.
[6] OX 6356—60.

h) Isolt knows of Tristan's marriage.·

M. Bédier includes in his reconstruction of the *estoire* the mention, which he cites from Thomas and the Prose Romance, that Queen Isolt learns of Tristan's marriage to Isolt of Brittany[1]. There is no account of this in Eilhart, but it seems from the following narrative that she is acquainted with the fact. When Tristan is under the necessity of justifying his failure to consummate his marriage, he tells Dynas, on his arrival in Cornwall, of his sore strait, and bids him tell the queen and ask her aid:

> 'Tristrant in dô bî sich nam
> und begunde ·im clagen sîne nôt.
> sîner vrauwin her entbôt,
> daz he komen wêre
> und sagete ir daz mêre:
> sîn lîp stunde ûf der wâge[2].'

The statement is of course not definite.

i) The second Isolt wilfully deceives Tristan about the color of the sail.

M. Bédier ascribes the motive of jealousy to the second Isolt, to account for her telling the dying Tristan that the sail of the ship which is seen approaching is black. He cites Thomas and the Prose Romance as supporting this detail[3]. The reader will recall the incident: Tristan is wounded with a poisoned spear and sends to Queen Isolt to come and heal him. The ship is to have a white sail if it brings her, a black

---

[1] II, 268 f.
[2] *OX* 6274—80.
[3] Bédier II, 300.

one if she does not come. The daughter of the messenger is to go daily to the shore to watch for the ship, and to tell Tristan as soon as it approaches.

According to the Eilhart version, the wife of Tristan learns of this plan[1]. The redactor says he does not know who told her. She commands the child to bring the word of the vessel's arrival, not to Tristan, but to her, for

'her mochte es lîchte nemen schaden[2].'

When the girl brings her word that the sail is white, she goes at once to Tristan and tells him that the ship of his messenger is approaching. He asks her what is the color of the sail:

'dô loug sie leider sêre
daz ez ir sît wart gar leit
âne aller slachte valscheit
sprach sie sô, tumlîchen,
und sagete im lugelîchen,
der segil wêre wîz nît.

Dô Tristrant tôd was,
vor leide kûme genas
sin wîb, die daz wort sprach,
dâ von im sîn herze brach.
eia! wie lûte sie do schrê
„owê, ach und owê
daz mir î sô obele geschach!"
selbe sie daz wol sach,
daz he von iren schulden starb[3].'

---

[1] *OX* 9346—8. Cf. Ch. II, Y.
[2] *OX* 9355.
[3] *OX* 9378—9399.

Lichtenstein[1], Hertz[2], Paris[3], M. Bédier[4], and all
the other critics, interpret the expressions *tumlichen*
and *âne aller slachte valscheit* as meaning that Isolt did
not tell the lie out of jealousy, but by mistake, by a
peculiar sort of distraction. They consider her answer
to be one of those foolish remarks which, according to
Hartmann von Aue, are characteristic of women:

> 'wir wîp bedurfen alle tage
> daz man uns tumbe rede vertrage,
> wande sî under wîlen ist
> herte und âne argen list
> gevarlich und doch âne haz,
> wan wirne kunnen leider baz[5].'

It is difficult to believe that a poet should have
conceived Isolt of the White Hands as taking the
precaution of going to the child and telling her
to bring the message not to Tristan but to her, and
then have attributed to thoughtlessness the lie so
carefully planned. The explanation of the lie as
not due to jealousy is surely a mistake. M. Bédier
accordingly adopts the version of Thomas and the
Prose Romance and relegates the version of Eilhart
to the variants[6].

---

[1] *OX* cxx—cxxi *aus törichtem Unverstand.*

[2] *Tristan und Isolde von Gottfried von Strassburg*, Stuttgart
and Berlin 1907, p. 567, *ohne falschheit.*

[3] *Revue de Paris*, avril 1894, p. 140, *par mépris.*

[4] *Le roman de Tristan par Thomas* II, 304. Chez Eilhart
d'Oberg, Iseut aux Blanches Mains ne ment point par jalousie
préméditée; si elle dit que la voile est noire, alors que la voile
est blanche, c'est sans mauvaise intention, par caprice de femme,
par une sorte de bizarre distraction.

[5] *Iwein* 7679—85, ed. E. Henrici, Halle a. S. 1891.

[6] II, 300 j. In saying that Isolt of the White Hands knows
nothing of Queen Isolt, M. Bédier seems to have forgotten for the
moment the lines *OX* 9346 — 8.

As we have pointed out in a short article in the *Zeitschrift für deutsche Philologie*[1], the passage in Eilhart has been misinterpreted, owing to a misunderstanding of the bearing of the words *tumlichen* and *âne aller slachte valscheit*. The idea that Eilhart represents Isolt as not jealous is erroneous. The passage reads: she lied grievously, in a way that she afterward sorely repented. She spoke without any evil intention, stupidly, saying falsely that the sail was not white. . . . When Tristan was dead, his wife was almost overcome, she who had spoken the word that broke his heart. Ah me! how loudly she cried then, 'alas, oh, and alas, that ever such evil should befall me!' She herself saw clearly that she had caused his death[2].

The expressions *tumlichen* and *âne aller slachte valscheit* are not intended, it seems to us, to account for Isolt's motive in telling the lie. They are the poet's comment on it in the light of its consequences. He wishes to assure us that she did not intend to cause Tristan's death. *tumlichen* and *âne aller slachte valscheit* are to be understood in connection with the lines following: *daz ez ir sît wart gar leit*, and *sîn wîb, die daz wort sprach, dâ von im sîn herze brach.* That is, it was stupid of Isolt to lie, but she did not know that Tristan would die in consequence of her words — she was without any such evil intention.

The treatment of the passage by the mediaeval redactors, as we have pointed out in the article referred to, supports this interpretation. The prose redaction distinctly qualifies the lie of Isolt as murder:

---

[1] *Isolde Weisshand am Sterbebette Tristan's*, Zeitschr. für deutsche Philol., vol. XLIII (1911), p. 453—5.
[2] *OX* 9377—9400. Cf. Ch. II, 2.

und fraget, ob sy icht weste, wie der segel gestalt were.
Ach waffen! des grossen mordes, den die fraw do unwissen-
lich mit unwarheit begieng, das ir doch hynach yemerlich
leid ward. Sy sprach also, der segel wer schwartz[1].

Ulrich von Türheim similarly refers to Isolt's lie
as murder. He does not add that she did not intend
as such:

'„vrowe, nû ruoch mich wizzen lân,
wie der segel sî getân.“
„der ist swarz als ein kol.“
diu wîzgehande tet niht wol,
daz si ime benam daz leben,
dô si sach ûf dem schiffe sweben
einen segel wîz als ein snê[2]

grôze sünde Îsôt erwarp
daz si in tôte âne nôt[3].

ir waren man und wîp gehaz
daz si Tristanden tôte[4].

mit leitlîcher vrâge
vrâgete Îsôt Îsôten:
„wes sitzet ir bî dem tôten,
den ir, vrouwe, ertoetet hât?
durch got, hin von der bâre gât!
ir habet getân ein michel mort“[5].'

Eilhart does not say, as do Thomas and the Prose
Romance, that Isolt of the White Hands was jealous.
He merely represents her as acting like a jealous

---

[1] *Tristrant und Isalde*, ed. E. Pfaff, *Lit. Verein in Stuttgart*
(cited hereafter *OP*), CLII, p. 197₁₇.
[2] ed. Massmann, 582₅ — ₁₁.
[3] *op. cit.* 582₁₆ — ₈.
[4] *op. cit.* 582₂₈ — ₈.
[5] *op. cit.* 582₃₆ — 583₂.

person. Her motive is self evident. In this absence
of psychological interpretation, Eilhart probably faithfully reproduces the *estoire*.

3. MINOR POINTS
IN WHICH THE VERSION OF EILHART IS CLOSER TO
THE *ESTOIRE* THAN M. BÉDIER'S RECONSTRUCTION.

In two cases in which M. Bédier has rejected the
version of Eilhart, there seems to be some ground
for believing that it may preserve the version of
the *estoire*.

M. Bédier represents Brangien as the person who
offers the potion to the lovers. The evidence of the
texts is as follows: In the *Saga* it is a servant[1]; in
Gottfried it is *der juncfröuwelin einez*[2]; in the *Folie*
of manuscript Douce, it is a valet[3]. In Béroul the
sentences are in the impersonal construction[4]. In
Eilhart it is a *juncfrauwelin*[5]. In *Sir Tristrem*[6] and
the *Folie* of manuscript Berne[7], it is Brangien; in
the Prose Romance it is Brangien and Gorvenal[8].
We should incline to believe that the fatal action
was attributed in the *estoire* to some such colorless
person as Eilhart's *juncfrauwelin*. The tendency in
successive redactions of a romance seems to us to be
to substitute a familiar character for an indefinite
one[9]. It is natural that Brangien should come to
assume the role, since, no matter who actually offered

---

[1] Cap. XLVI, p. 56, l. 29; p. 157.
[2] l. 11674.
[3] l. 649.
[4] l. 2260.
[5] l. 2343.
[6] l. 1666.
[7] l. 316.
[8] Löseth § 39; Bédier II, 341.
[9] cf. the substitution of Brangien for Camille, Ch. V infra.

the drink, she is the person really responsible for the error. The contrary supposition — that Brangien was first given the role and was ousted by an insignificant servant — seems to us improbable.

M. Bédier is inclined to follow MS. 103 of the Prose Romance in representing Isolt of the White Hands as learning the secret of the sails from the daughter of the messenger whom Tristan has sent to bring Queen Isolt to heal his wound. Here it is clearly stated that Tristan confides to the girl the significance of the sails and that it is the frequent interviews between her and Tristan that arouse the wife's suspicion . Thomas on the contrary represents the wife of Tristan as listening at the wall while Tristan charges the messenger with his errand[2].

In Eilhart, all that the messenger's daughter knows is that at the sight of her father's returning ship, she is to hasten to Tristan to announce the color of its sails. She is ignorant of the significance of the information she brings[3]. Eilhart represents Isolt of the White Hands as knowing the secret, but declares he does not know how she learned it.

> 'ich enweiz wer ez dô sagete
> Tristrandes wîbe[4].'

The accounts of how Tristan's wife learned the significance of the sails were perhaps provided by MS. 103 of the Prose Romance and by Thomas, each on his own account, to supplement the *estoire*, which probably corresponded with Eilhart in giving no explanation.

---

[1] II, 299.
[2] I, 396, l. 2608 — 22.
[3] 9300 — 9; 9341 — 8.
[4] 9346 — 8.

4. MINOR POINTS
AT WHICH M. BÉDIER'S RECONSTRUCTION, BASED ON THOMAS AND THE PROSE ROMANCE, FURNISHES DETAILS LACKING IN EILHART.

In the following cases, Thomas and the Prose Romance agree in giving details not in Eilhart. The presence of these details in Thomas and the Prose Romance may be interpreted in one of two ways: They may represent details of the *estoire* lost in Eilhart, or they may be due to secondary influence between Thomas and the Prose Romance.

The explanation that Tristan was thus named on account of the tragic circumstances of his birth[1] is not given in Eilhart. It is a natural omission, since German hearers could not be expected to appreciate the French etymology.

In the account of the tribute demanded by the Morholt, M. Bédier includes, from Thomas and the Prose Romance, the trait, lacking in Eilhart, that the tribute paid to Ireland by Cornwall was an ancient institution[2]. In Eilhart the Morholt claims the tribute from Mark on the ground that it has been paid for many years by Mark's neighbors[3]. The significant point is common to both, namely that up to this time Mark has refused it[4].

M. Bédier follows Thomas and the Prose Romance in representing Isolt's mother as assisting her in taking the steel from the head of the Morholt and in

---

[1] II, 195 c.
[2] II, 199.
[3] 362—372.
[4] It may be that the trait is due to secondary influence between Thomas and the Prose Romance, or it may be that each independently gave the tribute the authority of precedent. It is also possible that the *estoire* represented the tribute as paid both by Mark's ancestors as in the French versions and by his neighbors as in the German one.

seeking for the slayer of the dragon. It is with her
as well as with her daughter that Tristan makes
peace when he is discovered to be the Cornish
champion [1].

In M. Bédier's reconstruction, as in Thomas and
the Prose Romance, it is two serfs who conduct
Brangien into the forest [2]. In Eilhart the assassins hired are two poor knights who are directed to
attack the maid when she goes to the fountain in
the orchard [3]. In Thomas and the Prose Romance
they have her tied to a tree while they return to
inform Isolt; in Eilhart one remains to guard her.
M. Bédier remarks that the version of Eilhart is
less plausible, inasmuch as Brangien's cries from the
orchard might rouse the castle. This consideration
does not seem to us weighty. We have no reason
to believe that the most plausible version was that of
the *estoire*.

The harp and the rote.

The episode of the harp and the rote [4] appears in Thomas, and in a modified form in the Prose
Romance. It may have belonged to the *estoire* and
been omitted by Eilhart. It has no bearing on the
narrative.

Both Thomas and the Prose Romance give the
detail that while the dying Tristan awaits the arrival
of Isolt of Ireland, until he is too weak to be moved,
he is carried every day to the shore to scan the
horizon for ships [5].

---

[1] II, 204, 220, 223.
[2] II, 240—1.
[3] 2873—4.
[4] II, 244.
[5] II, 299.

5. MINOR POINTS
IN WHICH M. BÉDIER'S RECONSTRUCTION, BASED ON BÉROUL AND THE PROSE ROMANCE, FURNISHES DETAILS LACKING IN EILHART.

In the following four points, Béroul and the Prose Romance agree in giving details which are not in Eilhart. We see no way of determining with certainty whether or not these traits were contained in the *estoire*.

Returning to the castle after the tryst under the tree, the queen tells Brangien what has occurred, and congratulates herself on having escaped the danger that threatened her, and appeased the king[1]. The people of Cornwall raise loud lamentations when Tristan is condemned to death, after his guilt has been proved by the footprint on the floor. They remember what Tristan suffered to free Cornwall from the tribute to Ireland, and they deplore the ingratitude of Mark[2]. The rock upon which Tristan leaped, when he escaped from the chapel window, is known since that time as *Tristan's Leap*[3]. The name of the forest in which the lovers take refuge is *Morrois*[4].

In one of the remaining cases in which other versions agree in giving a trait not in Eilhart, it seems possible to prove that they preserve the version of the *estoire*. This is the mention, by the Prose Romance and *Erec*, of the name of the island on which the combat with the Morholt took place[5]. In Eilhart the Morholt is represented as having advanced with his army from Ireland in the direction of Cornwall to an unspecified point, where he halts and sends

---

[1] II, 247 f.
[2] II, 253 a.
[3] II, 253 b.
[4] II, 254 c.
[5] II, 201 j.

messengers to Mark to demand the tribute[1]. Mark
responds to the Morholt's demand by appointing a
time and place for a judicial combat — an island near
by, on the third day[2]. The combat is to take place
in the morning[3]. The messengers return to the Morholt
and deliver the message. The Morholt asks them at
once when and where the combat is to take place.
They reply that it is to be fought on the following
morning near by[4]. The Morholt prepares for the combat; Mark arrives with an army and encamps near
the place appointed.

These indications, if we interpret them correctly,
define the island where the Morholt waited, as a place
between Ireland and Cornwall. Mark replies to the
messengers appointing the combat for the third day.
The messenger, upon reaching the Morholt, tells him
that the fight is to take place the next day. At
the beginning of the description of the combat, it is
again specified as taking place on the third day[5].
The texts define the island of combat as close to the
Morholt's halting place. The Morholt's messenger, on
returning to his master, says that the champion will
meet him at a place near by.

Given the habitual looseness of the romances in
geographical details, the Scilly Islands between Ire-

---

[1] According to the redaction in German verse (*OX*): dô
vûr he obir des meres vlût.   Dô he quam obir sê, l. 402—3.
According to the Bohemian redaction (*OČ*): fuhr er über das meer,
dorthin von wo er, wie er meinte, ohne schaden widerkehren würde.
ZfdA. XXVIII, p. 266, § 12,15.

[2] daz her komen solde bî den sê ûf ein wert ... dar nâch
an dem dritten tage. *OX* 711—6; similarly *OP* 13,10—13; *OČ* 271,
24,2—7.

[3] zu rechter streytzeit *OP*; früh *OČ*.

[4] hîr gar nâ — daz sal geschên morgen vrû. *OX* 732—4.
Similarly *OP* 13,16—19, *OČ* 24,20—3.

[5] *OX* 742.

land and Cornwall, would correspond closely enough
to the indications of the halting place of the Morholt.
It is therefore possible that the allusion in *Erec* and
the statements of the Prose Romance, which place the
combat on the island St. Samson, here preserve a
localization which the Eilhart version, with its habitual avoidance of names, omitted. Eilhart preserves,
however, as we have seen, the indications for this
localization. In the Thomas versions, where the
Morholt appears in person at Tintagel to demand the
tribute and receive the challenge, this localization disappears entirely, and the combat takes place on an
island directly off the coast of Cornwall [1].

In his outline of the arguments used by Tristan to
appease Isolt when she discovers him to be the slayer
of her uncle, M. Bédier adds to the ones given by
Eilhart, an additional one on the authority of Thomas
and the *Folie*. He represents Tristan as appeasing
Isolt by telling her that he has come to seek her as
a bride for Mark [2]. This may have been in the *estoire*;
it may, on the contrary, be the invention of Thomas.
Considering his characteristic enthusiasm for the glory
of the United Kingdom of England and Cornwall [3], the
idea that Tristan could depend upon his mission as the
proxy of Mark to win grace from the Irish princess
would be natural enough. The conclusive consideration
for Isolt in Eilhart is that if she destroys Tristan there
will be no one to contest the claim of the steward
who pretends to have won her by killing the dragon [4].
In both Eilhart and Thomas the Irish kingdom is bitterly hostile to Cornwall on account of the slaying of the

---

[1] I, 83—5.
[2] II, 222 k.
[3] II, 40.
[4] 1944—68.

Morholt[1], and it is only by a ruse that Tristan's ship has been allowed to land.

In the *Folie*, the lines

'En po d'ore vos oi paiee
O la parole do chevol [2]'

are perhaps simply the loose form of statement characteristic of that version[3]. On the other hand it is possible that the argument was in the *estoire* and that Eilhart omitted it.

M. Bédier mentions the episode of the Ambiguous Oath in his reconstruction, but recognizes that the fact of its occurrence in Thomas and in the continuation of Béroul is not sufficient to establish its presence in the *estoire*. The model of the continuator of Béroul is unknown[4].

C. CRITICISM OF PROFESSOR GOLTHER'S RE- CONSTRUCTION OF THE *ESTOIRE*.

Thus far we have confined ourselves to establishing the authority of the version of Eilhart as representing the *estoire* in the points in which M. Bédier's reconstruction differs from it[5]. It remains to examine briefly the points in which the reconstruction of the

---

[1] II, 215 f.
[2] 421—3.
[3] cf. supra Ch. III.
[4] cf. Bédier II, 309.
[5] Further criticism of M. Bédier's reconstruction is found in J. Kelemina, *Untersuchungen zur Tristansage, Teutonia* 16; and R. Zenker, *Romanische Forschungen* XXIX, 322—69. For reviews of these see the *Romania* XL, 114—9, and *Literaturblatt für germ. u. rom. Philol.* XXXII, 362—3. Cf. also Zenker, *Zeitschr. f. rom. Philol.* XXXV, 715—31. Professer Zenker seems to have overlooked *OX* 9346—8. Also *Rom.* XL, 117, n. 1.

estoire proposed by Professor Golther differs from the version of Eilhart[1]. They are of secondary importance and might be passed over as unessential[2].

Professor Golther adopts the episode of Petit Crû for the following reason: Eilhart and Béroul mention a journey of Tristan to the realm of the king of Gavoie without giving any details as to what he did there. This seems to Professor Golther to be an indication that they are here omitting an episode which was in their source and he believes that this episode was the story, contained in Thomas, of Petitcrû[3]. It is of course possible that the absence in Eilhart of this and other episodes, is due to abridgement. We have, however, nothing that can be regarded as evidence on the point.

Professor Golther is inclined to believe that the incident of the Ambiguous Oath belonged to the *estoire*, because it appears in the continuation of Béroul as well as in Thomas[4]. But, as we have said above, there is no evidence that the continuation of Béroul is a derivative of the *estoire*. It seems to us rash, therefore, to regard material in the continuation of Béroul as evidence of what the *estoire* contained.

Professor Golther considers that the episodes of Haupt and Plot and of Tristan the Fool were not in the *estoire*, because they form an awkward interruption in the account of Kaherdin's *amour* with Gargeolain, and because the episode of Haupt and Plot repeats numerous details which have already appeared in Tristan's visits in disguise to Isolt[5]. This does not

---

[1] *Tristan und Isolde in den Dichtungen des Mittelalters und der neueren Zeit*, von Wolfgang Golther, Leipzig 1907, 40—59.
[2] Golther, *op. cit.* p. 39.
[3] 62—3.
[4] 59—62.
[5] 66, 77 ff.

seem to us satisfactory evidence. We have other instances of the embarassment of the redactor of the
estoire in combining the episodes which form the narrative, and of his repeated use of the same details[1].
The only data which we possess for determining the
artistic ability of this redactor is the reconstruction
which we are engaged in making. It is not permis-
sible to base the' reconstruction upon a preconceived
idea of that ability.

Professor Golther excludes from his reconstruction of the *estoire*: Camille, the successor of Brangien;
Pilois, the messenger who tells Tristan of Isolt's
penance of the hair shirt; and the *wirt* whom Tristan
sends to bring Isolt to Brittany. For his rejection of
Camille and Pilois he gives no reason[2]. He rejects
the *wirt* in favor of Gorvenal on the authority of a
version mentioned by Thomas[3]. Professor Golther
thinks it only fitting that this last service should be
attributed .to the faithful Gorvenal. The reader is
of course at liberty. to share this feeling. The solution given in the version of Eilhart seems to us
equally fitting: On the death of his father Tristan
has placed Gorvenal in charge of his paternal inheritance[4]. The authority of Eilhart[5] and the Prose
Romance MS. 103[6] seems to us more important than
Thomas' allusion to a version which, perhaps, never
existed[7]. Thomas' reference to it, like his reference

---

[1] cf. infra, Ch. V.
[2] 80.
[3] 67; cf. Bédier I, p. 377, l. 2124 ff.
[4] *OX* 8562—76.
[5] *OX* 9256—8.
[6] Bédier II, 385$_{5-6}$ *il avoit en la ville ung sien compere
marinel, qui avoit a nom Genes*; Löseth § 542 a.
[7] I, 377, l. 2124—37. *Ensurquetut de cest' ovraingne Plusurs de noz granter ne volent Ço que del nain dire ci solent,
Cui Kaherdin dut femme amer: Li naim redut Tristrant navrer
E entuscher par grant engin, Quant ot afolé Kaherdin; Pur ceste*

to Breri, seems to us a pleasant literary fraud. Thomas wished to anticipate objections against the more important innovations which he had made in this passage. The question of who took the message to Isolt was of no great consequence, but the fact that Kaherdin should do it was disconcerting to conservative readers, for, according to the *estoire*, Kaherdin had met his death at the hands of Bedenis.

It is to the tendency of the later redactors to substitute a definite and familiar minor character for an indefinite and unfamiliar one, that we attribute the substitution of Kaherdin for the anonymous messenger, and of Brangien for Camille and for the *juncvrouwelein* who gave the lovers the potion [1].

The suggestions of Professor Golther are traceable to the inclination to reconstruct a version in which detail and episode are rigorously subordinated to the main theme. We have no reason to believe that the *estoire* was such a composition.

D. CONCLUSION.

In the foregoing study we have sought to establish that the version of Eilhart is a faithful reproduction of its French original and that this original was the same poem as the source of Thomas. The effort of the German redactor seems to have been to reproduce conscientiously the narrative of his source [2]. This is

---

plaie e pur cest mal Enveiad Tristan Guvernal En Angleterre pur Ysolt. Thomas ico granter ne volt, E si volt par raisun mustrer Que iço ne put pas ester.

[1] cf. supra, Ch. III.
[2] cf. Lichtenstein, Introduction, *Quellen und Forschungen* XIX, cxixff.

precisely what we should have expected of the first poet
to introduce the courtly literature of France into North
Germany[1]. At numerous points in the narrative he
expresses surprise at what he finds in his source, but
he makes no attempt to modify it:

> 'daz mag ûch grôz wundir hân,
> wan ich ez ûch nicht sagen kan[2].

> daz hât mich wundir gar genûg.
> îdoch sô sagit uns daz bûch
> und ouch die lûte vor wâr[3].

> daz was ein vromder mannes sin[4].'

In treating the refinements of courtly love it
appears that he was himself as much impressed as
he expected his auditors to be by what he found in
it. When Tristan disguises himself as a leper and goes
to seek Isolt's pardon, the redactor exclaims:

> 'wâ hât ir î vornomen
> um einer vrauwen hulde
> dorch alsô cleine schulde
> sô vlîzlîchen werben?'[5]

In some passages the narrative is so condensed as
to be unintelligible[6]; in others it proceeds with much
detail. Tristan's successful exploits against the rebellious vassal of Howel are recounted at great length[7].
On the other hand the hero's failure to consummate

---

[1] Lichtenstein cxviii, Gierach, *Zur Sprache von Eilharts
Tristrant*, Prag 1908, § 107—8.
[2] 4615—7.
[3] 4575—8.
[4] 4592; cf. also 5054—9; 5285—99.
[5] 7020—4.
[6] eg. 86—92; 6138—42; 9330.
[7] 5700—6103.

his marriage is barely mentioned. It seems probable that the German poet in most cases condensed the portions of the narrative which involved elaborate psychological analysis.

It sometimes seems possible to discern an effort on the part of Eilhart to gather together details which in the *estoire* were scattered in different passages. In this effort Eilhart merely changes the position, not the character of the detail. He informs the reader at the beginning of his account[1], of the entire number of his hero's enemies, Béroul[2] first mentions each individual in the episode in which he becomes active. Similarly, Eilhart may be individually responsible for giving the complete account of the potion at the first mention of it in the narrative[3], whereas in Béroul, and perhaps in the *estoire*, the modifications in its influence are first noted as they make themselves felt[4].

Without considering the version of Eilhart authoritative in every detail, we are disposed to believe that most of the minor points of the narrative faithfully represent the *estoire*. We should expect to find in it as in Eilhart, for example, Tristan's birth upon the sea[5], his being cut from his dead mother's womb[6], the stream flowing through Isolt's chamber[7], and Mark's saying before the dwarf strews the flour on the floor, that Tristan must set off next morning to the court of Arthur[8].

---

[1] *OX* 3084—88, 3154—7.
[2] 581—3; cf. Muret, *Béroul* VI—VII.
[3] 2279—2300.
[4] 2133—2147.
[5] cf. Bédier II, 195 c, note; 196.
[6] cf. Bédier II, 196—7.
[7] cf. Bédier II, 157, 248.
[8] cf. Bédier II, 249 b.

Having established in detail the validity of the traits in the Eilhart version which M. Bédier and Professor Golther had considered it impossible to attribute to the *estoire*, we must conclude that the poem of Eilhart is the best representative of the lost poem accessible to us. The editor of Eilhart long ago pointed out that the German poet followed a French original with almost absolute fidelity [1]. The present study points to the conclusion that the French original was the same as that of which Béroul represents a part, the same original as that which the *Folie Tristan* of the Berne manuscripts envisages as reminiscence, the same original as that of which we have traces in the Prose Romance. It is to this same original, or one of its derivatives, that the redactor of manuscript 103 of the Prose Romance again referred, and from which he interpolated the dragon combat and the final incidents.

---

[1] Lichtenstein, *QF XIX*, cxx.

IV. COURTLY ELEMENTS IN THE *ESTOIRE:* ITS DATE.

A. THE DATE GIVEN BY M. BÉDIER.

1. M. BÉDIERS *TERMINUS AD QUEM.*

M. Bédier takes the year 1154 as a *terminus ad quem* for the *estoire*[1]. He is led to do this by an allusion to Tristan in a lyric of Bernart de Ventadour:

> 'Tan trac pena d'amor
> Qu'a Tristan l'amador
> non avenc tan de dolor
> Per Yzeut la blonda[2].'

The allusion is of such brevity as to make it certain that the poet supposed his hearers familiar with the fame of Tristan as a lover.

The lyric in question has been supposed to be addressed to Eleanor of Poitou[3]. According to the

---

[1] II, 154—5. Golther, like Bédier, considers the mention of Tristan by Bernart de Ventadour as giving a *terminus ad quem* for the date of the *estoire*. He takes the treatment of Arthur, Gawain and Kay in the episode of the Blades at the Bed as giving a *terminus a quo*. The *estoire*, according to Golther, must have been written between 1140 and 1150, after these characters had become familiar to French audiences in the dress given them by Geoffrey of Monmouth in his *Historia Regum Britanniae*. *Op. cit.*, 1907, p. 69—73.

[2] Bartsch, *Chrestomathie provençale*, p. 63.

[3] Diez, *Leben und Werke der Troubadours*, reedited by K. Bartsch, Leipzig 1882, p. 26 ff.

troubadour biographer, Bernart was at the court of
Eleanor after her marriage with Henry, Duke of Normandy[1]. In 1154, Henry became Henry II of England
and Eleanor left Normandy. The poem has therefore
been dated approximately 1154.

It is extremely hazardous, however, to accept the
date of Eleanor's departure from Normandy as the
date of the lyric in question. Crescini prints the
following readings for the stanza which has led to its
association with that date. In one manuscript:

'Lo cor ai pres d'amor,
que l'esperitz lai cor,
e lo cors estai alhor
pres de leis en Fransa[2].'

In another manuscript:

'Que·l cor ai en amor
pus de nulh amador
car l'esperitz en lay cor
lonh de mi en Franza[3].'

A group of three manuscripts gives:

'Mon cor ai en amor
e l'esperitz lai cor;
e si·m sui ieu sai aillor
loing de lieis, en Fransa[4].'

Another group of three manuscripts has:

---

[1] C. Appel, *Provenzalische Chrestomathie*, Leipzig 1902
p. 190.
[2] Crescini, *Atti del Reale Istituto Veneto* LXIX, dispensa I,
p. 78. This is the reading of *Ms. C*, preferred by Zingarelli,
Studi medievali III, fasc. 1, pp. 49—68.
[3] This is the reading of *Ms. R*. Crescini, *loc. cit.*
[4] *Mss. AIS*. Crescini, p. 78.

'Lo cor ai pres d'amor,
que l'esperitz lai cor,
e'l cors estai sai alhor,
lonh de leis, en Fransa?[1]'

Owing to these variants, it is impossible to determine where the poet was when he wrote the poem or where the lady was to whom he addressed it. There is no evidence that this lady was Eleanor of Poitou[2]. Even if these points were settled, the date of the lyric would still be uncertain, Bernart's movements between northern and southern France and England being unknown. His allusion to Tristan is therefore of slight value in determining a date at which the story was familiar in France[3].

It would be interesting to know at how early a period the love story of Tristan and Isolt was known on the continent. But even if the allusion of Bernart de Ventadour gave us a definite answer to this question, we have no assurance that the story familiar to his hearers was the version that Thomas, Béroul, and Eilhart had under their eyes[4]. The allusion of the

---

[1] *Mss. C M Va. C* has *Pres* for *lonh* in the last line. cf. Crescini, *op. cit.* 78.

[2] Crescini p. 79: Lo Zingarelli sentenzia: 'così Bernart era indubbiamente in Inghilterra, mentre pensava e scriveva all' amore lontano, in Francia . . .' No: tutto il contrario: Bernart era indubbiamente in Francia, e pensava e scriveva a chi non c'era. A chi? Non lo so. D'Eleonora nessun cenno preciso.

[3] M. Bédier also refers II, 154 to an allusion in Augier Novella. Cf. Sudre, *Rom.* XV, 544. According to Johannes Müller, *Zeitschr. f. rom. Philol.* XXIII, 48, Augier Novella lived between 1185 and 1235. The poem in which the allusion to Tristan occurs (Müller, *Zeitschr. f. rom. Philol.* XXIII, 72, No. 7) is assigned to the years following 1231 or, with less probability, to 1226 (*loc. cit.* p. 52).

[4] The allusions to the Tristan story scattered through French, Provençal, Italian, and German literature are seldom precise; in many cases they refer to scenes similarly treated in various extant redactions. They might accordingly have been based on any of

troubadour would not furnish a *terminus ad quem* for
the date of the *estoire*, any more than for the poem
of Béroul or of Thomas, or for the Prose Romance.
The poet of the *estoire*, like many redactors after him
and probably several redactors before him in France,
only retold the story.

The Tristan romance is not the creation of one
poet or of one day[1]. There may well have been
redactions of it in France previous to the *estoire*. It
appears from certain passages in Eilhart and Thomas
that there were. The similarity of these passages
suggests the possibility that they are based on a
similar passage in their source.

In Eilhart[2]:

> 'nû saget lîchte ein ander man
> ez sî andirs hîr umme komen:
> daz habe wir alle wol vornomen,
> daz man daz ungelîche saget:
> Eilhart des gûten zûg habet,
> daz ez recht alsus ergîng.'

---

the extant versions or on lost ones. Collections of allusions to
the Tristan story have been made by Sudre, *Rom.* XV, 534—7;
A. Graf: *Appunti per la storia del ciclo brettone in Italia*
(*Giornale storico della letteratura italiana*) V, 102 ff.; Bédier II,
Appendice II, cf. Bédier II, 57—60; Elvira Sommer-Tolomei,
La leggenda di Tristano in Italia, Roma 1910 (reprinted from
Rivista d'Italia).

[1] In a note M. Bédier himself suggests two stages in the
development of the tradition previous to the *estoire*. The first is
a Celtic stage, in which the tradition consisted of episodes more
or less loosely related to the hero; the second is a stage in which
these episodes had been united in a biography, a biography
which lacked, however, the feature which M. Bédier considers
a fundamental characteristic of the *estoire*, Tristan's offer,
when taken and bound, after the discovery of the footprint
on the floor, to prove his innocence by wager of battle. Bédier
II, 311, n. 1.

[2] *OX* 9452—8; Lichtenstein CXVII.

In Thomas [1]:

> 'Seignurs, cest cunte est mult divers,
> E pur ço l'uni par mes vers
> E di en tant cum est mester
> E le surplus voil relesser.
> Ne vol pas trop en uni dire:
> Ici diverse la matyre.
> Entre ceus qui solent cunter
> E del cunte Tristran parler
> Il en cuntent diversement:
> Oï en ai de plusur gent.
> Asez sai que chescun en dit
> E co qu'il unt mis en escrit,
> Mès sulun co que j'ai oï,
> Nel dient pas sulun Breri
> Ky solt les gestes les cuntes
> De tuz les reis, de tuz les cuntes
> Ki orent esté en Bretainge.'

We find Gottfried reproducing the passage from Thomas in the following form [2]:

> 'ich weiz wol, ir ist vil gewesen,
> die von Tristande hânt gelesen,
> und ist ir doch niht vil gewesen,
> die von im rehte haben gelesen;
>
> . . . .
>   si sprâchen wol
> und niwan ûz edelem muote
> mir unde der werlt ze guote
>
> . . . .
> aber als ich gesprochen hân,
> daz sî niht rehte haben gelesen,

---

[1] I, 377, ll. 2167—24.
[2] ed. Marold, ll. 131—55.

daz ist, als ich iu sage, gewesen:
sine sprâchen in der rihte niht,
als Thômas von Britanje giht,
der âventiure meister was
und an britûnschen buochen las
aller der lanthêrren leben
und ez uns ze künde hât gegeben.'

Just as Gottfried reproduced the passage from Thomas, so, we believe, Eilhart and Thomas reproduced it from the *estoire*. If this idea be correct, it would appear that the redactor of the *estoire*, in claiming authenticity for his account, alluded to other redactions known to his audience.

2. M. BÉDIER'S *TERMINUS A QUO*.

M. Bédier proceeds as follows to determine a *terminus a quo* for the *estoire*[1]: Between the Norman Conquest (1066) and the earliest extant romance of Crestien de Troyes, we have reason to believe that there was a considerable development of Arthurian tradition. The *estoire* would seem to belong to this period. It contains numerous primitive traits in which it resembles the *chansons de geste*.

M. Bédier analyzes with especial care the series of events in the Béroul-Eilhart version from the Flour on the Floor to the return of the lovers from the forest, and makes the following observations[2]:

The whole course of the narrative is founded on a specific moral and social principle, on a peculiar conception of justice; namely, the idea that the inno-

---

[1] II, 152—5; 183—7; 313—4.
[2] II, 185—6.

cence or guilt of the lovers is not to be determined
by the fact of their crime, but by the judgment which
God will pronounce upon them by means of an ordeal
or a judicial combat. The poet of the *estoire* regarded
the lovers as innocent. He believed that in the sight
of God, who knew the secret of the potion, they were
absolved. He believed that if Tristan were allowed
a judicial combat, heaven would pronounce on his
side. This is the idea that gives unity, significance,
and dignity to the romance. It had already lost its
significance when the story reached the hands of
Thomas. The series of events from the Flour on the
Floor to the Return from the Forest must therefore
have been invented at the precise moment when the
wager of battle was still recognized as a test of innocence, but people were beginning, almost unconsciously
still, to admit that ruse and force might sometimes
aid one of the combatants.

M. Bédier concludes that the *estoire* must have
been written in the early years of the twelfth century.

It seems to us a mistake to assign an early date
to the *estoire* because it contains traces of customs ante-
dating the latter half of the twelfth century. Such primitive traits as are preserved in it are fossils of earlier
tradition. The redactor of the *estoire* retained them
because they had a certain charm, or because it would
have involved serious modifications of the narrative
to alter them. Such traits are valuable in some cases[1]
as showing the antiquity of the tradition; but they lend
no aid in determining the date of a particular version. As
the Norman walls of Canterbury Cathedral are evidence

---

[1] The primitive sleeping arrangements in the scene of the
Blades at the Bed are no indication of antiquity; cf. Ch. V. For
the stream flowing through the house, cf. Ch. VI.

that the beginnings of the pile date from the time of
Lanfranc, so the primitive traits in the extant Tristan
versions show that the tradition antedates the redaction. Of the date of the particular redaction they
tell nothing.

M. Bédier's reasoning in regard to the peculiar
idea of justice underlying the *estoire* does not aid us
in determining its date. In the first place, the moment
when men began to waver in their confidence in the
wager of battle as the judgment of God cannot be
fixed as an historical date. There were probably men
who doubted the validity of the judicial duel in the
time of Charlemagne; there are probably men in our
own time who would trust it still. In the second place,
the series of events in which the paradox of the lovers'
technical guilt and real innocence is the center of the
poet's interest survives, like the other primitive traits,
from an earlier period. As we shall point out, the
estoire also contains a series of events which reflect
a social attitude peculiar to the latter part of the
twelfth century.

We shall not urge the fact that the appeals for
a judicial combat on which M. Bédier lays stress, are
peculiar to the version of Béroul[1]. The moral conception underlying them exists in the *estoire*, for the

---

[1] Béroul 779—827 (when Tristan is taken and bound, his
guilt having been proved by the blood drops on the floor)
esp. 809 ff.:

Ja, se Tristran ice seüst
Que escondire nel leüst,
Mex se laisast vif depecier
Que lui ne lié soufrist liër.
Mais en Deu tant fort se fiot
Que bien savoit e bien cuidoit,
S'a escondist peüst venir,
Nus n'en osast armes saisir
Encontre lui, lever ne prendre.
Bien se quidoit par chanp defendre.

lovers, being brought under the influence of the potion through no fault of their own, are regarded by the poet as innocent. Their sin may be proved, but an ordeal would acquit them.

B. COURTLY ELEMENTS IN THE *ESTOIRE*.

1. INTRODUCTION.

It is not to the *most* primitive traits in the *estoire* it is to the *least* primitive ones, that we would turn in our endeavor to determine its date. Let us proceed by this method.

The early portion of the poem implies the condemnation of adultery, whereas in the narrative that follows the return from the forest[1] the fundamental conception is courtly and unmoral[2]. It implies the cult of unlawful love characteristic of the latter half of the twelfth century.

If we examine carefully the incidents of the latter part of the *estoire*, we find that several of them present the favorite situations of the conventional courtly lyrics of that period. Others present problems of courtly love in the same manner. Others imply the currency of the notions of courtesy and the conceptions

---

[1] cf. Bédier II, 265—306.

[2] In the story of Brangien's fatal carelessness, of Tristan's broken faith to Mark, of the lovers' hopeless struggle against themselves, the long agony of desire, their reckless hazards, their hair breadth successes and their shameful defeats — in these there is something of the high seriousness of tragedy. Their appeal is to one age as to another. Kaherdin's *amours*, on the other hand, are the creation of the season. They are in the tone of *badinage* characteristic of the *pastourelles* and *chansons de mal mariée*. Produced under the same influences are the incidents in which Tristan is adjured *dorch Isalden willen*.

of Arthur and his knights which then first came into
vogue. These conventional situations appear in the
Tristan story in too developed a form for us to believe
that the narrative was composed before they were
universally familiar. Their relation to the biography
as a whole is too vital for us to look upon them as
the interpolations of this or that version. It is impossible to imagine that it is to the Tristan poet we
owe their introduction into French literature. The
appearance of these traits in the *estoire* can be accounted for in only one way: the series of incidents
from the return from the forest to the death of
Tristan must have been composed under the influence
of the courtly literature which came into vogue during
the time of Eleanor.

2. KAHERDIN AND CAMILLE: THE *PASTOURELLE*.

In order to measure justly the significance of the
traits which seem to associate the *estoire* with the
movement of which the lyric types of which we have
spoken are a part, it will be necessary to analyze in
some detail the incidents in which *motifs* familiar in
the lyrics occur.

On his first return to Cornwall from Brittany,
Tristan is accompanied by his wife's brother Kaherdin.
While Tristan is with Isolt, his companion courts her
maid Camille[1].

It is usual in the romances and the *chansons de
geste* for the lady to offer her maid to the companion
of her lover. In the numerous examples we have found
of this occurrence, the maid submits with all docility[2].

---

[1] *OX* 6255—6805.
[2] cf. infra, Ch. V.

In Tristan, Camille resists. The passage that follows
is strikingly similar to the type of courtly lyric known
as the *pastourelle*. These *pastourelles*, of which we
have numerous examples from the latter part of the
twelfth and the thirteenth centuries, relate the following incident[1]:

A knight, wandering musing through the fields
at sunrise, meets a pretty young shepherdess weaving
a garland of flowers. He descends from his horse and,
without much ceremony, demands her favor.

He is usually successful, by dint of persuasion or
force, in gaining his desire. In some cases the shepherdess pretends to yield to his importunities, but,
when he thinks he has only to enjoy his success, she
escapes him by some ruse, and, slipping from his hands,
taunts him with his defeat.

Kaherdin addresses Camille as the gallant of the
pastourelle addresses the shepherdess. With a person
of her station he is confident of his success and loses
no time in coming to the point[2]:

'do begunde der hêre Kehenîs
zu Gymêlen minne sûchen,
do enwolde sie es nicht rûchen.
îdoch en lîz her des nît,
ez wêre ir leit adir lîp,
vaste he ir ane lach.'

Camille is shocked at his precipitation. She reminds him that she is not a peasant girl that he
should ask her to yield to so short a siege[3]:

---

[1] K. Bartsch, *Romances et pastourelles françaises*, Leipzig
1870, Bks. II and III. — For studies of the *pastourelle* see
A. Jeanroy, *Les origines de la poésie lyrique en France*, Paris 1904,
p. 1—43; G. Paris, *Journal des Savants* 1891—2, p. 674—88,
729—42, 155—67, 407—29.
[2] *OX* 6672—8.
[3] *OX* 6679—86.

'wâ tût ir hen ûwirn sin?
jâ sêt ir wol daz ich nicht bin
eine gebûrinne
daz ir mich bittet umme minne
in sô gar korzir zît:
ich wêne ir ein gebûr sît.
wie mochte ez anders geschîn?'

She declares that if Kaherdin had been five years
in her service, obedient to all her commands, he would
not yet have received this favor[1]:

'hêtet ir ouch vunf jâr
zu allem mîme bote stân,
dennoch wêrez ungetân
des ir gewûgit wedir mich'.

Kaherdin is thus informed that Camille is no
pastoure. She is to be wooed as a lady is to be
wooed, with patience and prayers, with subtleties
and reserves, and won by slow and painful steps that
are recognized stages of initiation.

Camille, like the shepherdess, escapes Kaherdin by
a ruse[2] and in her raillery of him the next morning,
there is the light mischievous note characteristic of
the *pastourelle*[3].

'„wiste ich nechtin daz ir sô
togentlîchen kundet legin,
ich hête ûch nicht vorzegin
so getâner dinge:
daz ir mich bâtet umme minne,

---

[1] *OX* 6690—94.
[2] Isolt commands Camille to yield to Kaherdin, but gives
her a magic pillow. The moment this is put under his head he
falls asleep, and does not awaken until she withdraws it the next
morning. cf. Ch. II R; Ch. V, infra.
[3] *OX* 6794—6805.

> ich hête es ûch wol irloubit.
> des was vorleide nâ irtoubit"
> Kehenis dâ ûf der stete.
> swer sîne ôren ersnete,
> kein blûttropfe wêre komen ûz.
> he wêre gerne ze hûs!'

As the *pastourelle* expresses it[1]:

> 'Et il demeure com musart.
> l'ame de lui soit la honie
> quant la bele li eschapa.'

3. KAHERDIN AND GARGEOLAIN: THE *MAL MARIÉE*.

Kaherdin's *amour* with Gargeolain, in spite of
its tragic ending, is dealt with in the same light
tone as the adventure with Camille.

The elements of the situation are conventional
in the *chanson de mal mariée*: the lady has promised,
before her marriage, to give herself to her young
lover. The husband hears this promise and swears
to prevent its fulfilment. He locks up his wife and
keeps guard over her day and night The lady laments
her fate; she holds an interview from the parapet with
her lover below, and succeeds, in spite of her husband,
in fixing a rendezvous. The poet reflects on the wicked-
ness and folly of the husband[2].

In Tristan, Bedenis, the husband of Gargeolain,
is a noble lord distinguished in knightly exercises and
especially devoted to hunting[3]:

---

[1] Bartsch, *op. cit.*, p. 194, No. 68.
[2] cf. Jeanroy, *op. cit.* p. 84—102, *La chanson dramatique;*
cf. Bartsch, *op. cit.* p. 13, No. 9; p. 30, No. 35; p. 35, No. 38; p. 41,
No. 41; p. 48, No. 47; p. 50, No. 49; p. 52, No. 51; p. 57, No. 56 etc.
[3] *OX* 7872—8; cf. chapter II, U X.

'ein schônez wîp her habete,
die was Gariôle genant.
der hûte der wîgant
sô freislîchen sêre,
daz her sîn selbes êre
dâ mete hâte gekrenkit.'

Bedenis' anxiety is, however, not surprising[1]: his
wife, like the lady of the lyric, had promised that
before she would accept her husband she would
grant Kaherdin her love if he would come to her.
Bedenis had overheard this and had at once built
three moats and three walls around his castle. Keeping these locked and the keys always in his own
hands, he saw to it that no one had access to his
wife. One day when the husband is hunting, the lover
rides under the battlements and gets speech with his
lady. They curse the *jalous* who keeps them from each
other. Kaherdin reminds her of what she had promised
to grant him before she would take her husband.
She declares that she is still ready to give him her
favor; she has always loved him; she would gladly
have granted him his wish before, and she is of the
same mind still, if he can devise a way to approach
her. In spite of the difficulties, Kaherdin finds a way.

The ladies in the *chansons de mal mariée* are in
a similar situation. We quote but one example[2]:

'En un vergier lez une fontenele,
dont clere est l'onde et blanche la gravele,
siet fille a roi, sa main a sa maxele:
en sospirant son douz ami rapele.
    „ae cuens Guis amis!
    la vostre amors me tout solaz et ris.

---

[1] *OX* 7865—8135; 9033—9190.
[2] Bartsch, *op. cit.* p. 13, No. 9.

Cuens Guis amis, com male destinee!
mes pere m'a a un viellart donee,
qui en cest mes m'a mise et enserree:
n'en puis eissir a soir n'a matinee."
　　ae cuens Guis amis!
　　la vostre amors me tout solaz et ris.

Li mals mariz en oi la deplainte,
entre el vergier, sa corroie a desceinte:
tant la bati q'ele en fu perse et tainte.
entre ses piez por pou ne l'a estainte.
　　ae cuens Guis amis!
　　la vostre amors me tout solaz et ris.'

There is no attempt to regard the relation of
Kaherdin and Gargeolain from a moral point of view.
The poet considers the jealous husband justly served
when his wife betrays him and he comments thus on at-
tempting to constrain women to faithfulness by force[1]:

'mich wundert, wes he denkit
der sînes wîbes hûtet,
wen stât ir ir gemûte
nicht williglîchen dar,
sô mag he nimmer sie bewarn
mit allen sînen sinnen.
wen, wil sie einen minnen,
sie tût ez âne sînen dang.
es were korz adir lang.'

The poet's criticism in the *chanson de mal mariée*
si invariably the same[2]:

'damë qui a mal mari
s'el fet ami
n'en fet pas a blasmer.'

---

[1] *OX* 7878—87.
[2] Bartsch p. 51, No. 49; p. 81, No. 64.

The lady's attitude is unambiguous[1]:

> 'li jalous
> envious
> de cor rous
> morra,
> et li dous
> savourous
> amourous
> m'avra.'

The situation not infrequently becomes part of the courtly narrative poems from the middle of the twelfth century. In Marie de France's *Guigemar*, for example, there is a lady similar to Gargeolain[2]:

> 'Li sire, ki la mainteneit
> mult fu vielz huem et femme aveit,
> une dame de halt parage,
> franche, curteise, bele e sage.
> Gelus esteit a desmesure.'

The thirteenth century Provençal romance *Flamenca* sustains throughout more than eight thousand lines the mood of moral *insouciance* which we find in the lyric. Here the husband, like Bedenis, is represented as a handsome and amiable young knight, who after his marriage becomes the most intolerable *jalous*. He immures his wife in the castle, allows no one to go out or to come in, and carries the keys himself. Like Gargeolain, his wife betrays him without compunction[3].

It would be difficult to deny that in these adventures of Kaherdin, the Tristan poet may have

---

[1] Bartsch p. 52, No. 51.

[2] *Die Lais der Marie de Franee*, ed. K. Warnke, Halle 1900, No. 1, *Guigemar*, ll. 209—17.

[3] P. Meyer, *Le Roman de Flamenca*[2], Paris 1901.

appropriated his theme from popular poetry. If we affirm that he did not, however, we are forced to suppose that he introduced for the first time into the range of courtly literature, the themes of the *pastourelle* and the *mal mariée*. It is easier to suppose that the incidents in Tristan, with their conventional features and moral irresponsibility, are part of the same literary movement as the *pastourelles* and *chansons de mal mariée* of the latter part of the twelfth and thirteenth centuries. We are personally inclined to interpret them as due to the influence of an already developed courtly lyric.

4. ISOLT'S REPENTANCE: THE *CHANSON A PERSONNAGES*.

There is a third incident in the *estoire* that corresponds to a conventional type of thirteenth century lyric.

It is the account of Isolt's repentance for her cruelty to Tristan. Breri has told her that Tristan failed to turn his horse, although adjured in her name to do so. Tristan's denial of the charge has fallen on deaf ears. Isolt persists in believing the accusation. Her lover makes a desperate effort to regain her favor, seeking to approach her disguised as a leper, but she orders him driven away with blows, and laughs at his humiliation. Some months afterward she is stricken with remorse for this sin against her lover. As a penance she puts on a hair shirt and wears it next her skin night and day. She vows that she will not put it off until Tristan comes to her[1]:

---

[1] *OX 7181—4.*

'ich enkunne nicht genesin,
he wil mir denne gnêdig wesin;
ich bin sicherlîchen tôd,
he en helfe mir schîre ûz der nôd.'

She sends a messenger to Tristan, imploring him
to forgive her and come to her[1].

'daz wil sie nû immermêre
bûzen, swie dû gebûtest:
daz meiste teil der lûte
brichet unde bûzzet echt,
wen gnade ist bezzir denne recht.
sie sûchit dîne genâde,
ire trûwe saltû entphâhen
swaz sie dir hât zu leide getân,
des wil sie dir zu bûzze stân
nâch gnâdin und nach rechte,
sie enmag dir nicht vechtin,
sie enwil sîn nicht geruchen:
sie wil genâde sûchen,
wen daz recht ist ir zu swâr.
ab sie dir daz entbîten tar,
sie entbûtet dir iren dinist
und allez daz dir lîp ist,
daz sie daz alles gerne tû
und entbûtit dir dar zû,
daz sie dir zu êrin
treget ein hemede hêrîn
allir nêhist irem lîbe.
wiltu sie nû lenger mîden,
sô wert ir nimmir leides bûz.
hêre, ich sûche dînen fûz
daz du schîre kumest dâr sî sî:
sô wirt sie allir sorgin vrî.'

<hr>

[1] *OX* 7252—79.

Schœpperle, Tristan.

9

In the *chanson à personnages* the lady has discouraged the lover by her severity and he has at last left her to seek a new love[1]. She loves him now, and in her turn learns the anguish of unrequited affection. She implores him to forgive the wrong she has done him. She repents her cruelty. She is dying for love of him. She reminds him that the path to heaven is the forgiveness of injuries. She encourages herself by the reflection that a drop of water will finally wear away a stone.

The characteristic note is given in this refrain:

'Qu'en dirai?
   Forssenée
fui, plus que desvée
quant le refusai.
   G'en ferai
droit a son plesir
s'il m'en daigne oïr.

. . . .

Chançon, va sanz delaier
à celui qui tant m'agrée:
por Deu li pri et requier
viengne a moi sanz demorée:
en sa merci me metrai,
tost avrai
pès trovée
se il li agrée,
que je trop mal trai
   g'en ferai
[droit a son plesir,
s'il m'en daigne oïr.]'

The man covers her with reproaches and recom-

¹ Jeanroy p. 97—9; citation, *op. cit.*, 499—501.

mends her to seek another lover. In one version he is finally touched by her tenacity.

We have a narrative fragment representing a similar theme in the biography of the troubadour Guillem de Balaun[1].

Here it is the lover who, for a whim, is angry with his lady. She humiliates herself before him, coming to his inn to seek his pardon, and is driven away, as Tristan is driven away by Isolt, with blows. Later the knight repents of his cruelty and begs her forgiveness through an intermediary. He declares himself willing to perform any penance to prove his sincerity. Where Isolt puts on a hair shirt, this penitent cuts off his finger nail. The two lovers are at last reconciled and love each other thereafter the more. It is possible that this, like many passages in the troubadour biographies, is founded on lost lyrics of the poet in question.

The courtly poets of the twelfth and thirteenth centuries seem to have been interested in the question of how far the lover should suffer humiliation for love's sake. In Crestien's *Charrette*[2], Guinevere withdraws her favor from Lancelot because she has heard that he hesitated an instant to mount the ignominious cart which offered him a possible means to serve her. Lancelot does not know how he has offended, but he accepts his punishment with entire submission. It is enough for him that it is his lady who lays it upon him. She continues to put his unquestioning devotion to the test. According to her command he is by turns ignominiously cowardly and surpassingly courageous.

---

[1] Raynouard, *Choix des poésies originales des Troubadours*, Paris 1820, V, 180 ff.

[2] ed. Foerster, *Der Karrenritter* (Halle 1899), 3955 ff.

She rewards him when she has at last tested him to her satisfaction. At no point do we find either the lover or the poet permitting himself to question or criticize her conduct.

In the *estoire*, as we have seen, Tristan is represented as less submissive. Isolt's cruelty is not accepted by him without question. When she seeks his forgiveness, confessing her wrong and imploring mercy in all humility, he sternly refuses her. It is only after long supplication that he is moved[1].

In several late romances we find the poet thus taking revenge for his sex[2]. In one, the *Chevalier au Perroquet*, the hero has submitted to his lady's command to bear himself with cowardice at the tourney, but when she summons him that night to reward him, he covers her with insults and reproaches. He even goes so far as to beat her and drag her by the hair.

5. FOR ISOLT'S SAKE.

Not without significance for the date of the *estoire* are the numerous instances in the latter part of the romance in which the poet uses the phrases *dorch Isalden willen* and *dorch Tristrandes willen*.

Gawain adjures Tristan *for Isolt's sake* to confess if it was he who overthrew *Delakors schevalier (chevalier de la cour?)*. Tristan acknowledges the exploit. He declares that if he were to die for it, he would never refuse a request made in these terms[3].

---

[1] cf. Bédier II, 270 ff. and bibliography.
[2] *Hist. Litt.* XXX, 107.
[3] *OX* 5123—9.

'geselle, ich habez jâ getân:
swes man mich vrâgin î began
dorch willen mîner vrauwin,
daz lâze ich offinbêrlîch schauwin.
ich hele des dorch keine nôt
solde ich dar umme ligen tôt.'

Gawain responds that it is an honor to her that
he has done this for her sake[1].

'gnâde mûze sie des hân,
mîne vrauwe die koninginne,
daz dû dorch ire minne
mir dese ding hâst vorjên.'

Tristan boasts to Kaherdin that *for his sake*, Isolt
the Queen shows more favor to his dog than Isolt of
Brittany shows to him[2].

'jâ helt eine vrauwe baz
ein hundelîn dorch mînen willen
obir lût und stille
den mich ûwir swestir hât getân.'

Kaherdin sees the dog borne in state in the queen's
train. Tristan explains that it is for his sake[3].

'den vûret die koningîn
alsus dorch mînen willin.'

When Isolt gives her maid to Kaherdin the night
that he comes with Tristan to the Blanche Lande, she
says that it is for Tristan's sake[4].

'ich wil ûch zu nacht lîen
eine behegelîche amîen
dorch Tristrandes willen.'

---

[1] *OX* 5130—4.
[2] *OX* 6244—8.
[3] *OX* 6506—8.
[4] *OX* 6711—4.

When Breri sees the squires in the distance he calls to them, thinking one of them is Tristan, to turn for the sake of Isolt[1].

> 'Dô bat her in umme kêrin
> dorch der koninginne êre,
> ab sie im wêre lîp.'

Isolt is very angry when she hears that Tristan has failed to comply with a request made in these terms[2]:

> '„zu lest manete ich in dô
> daz he dorch ûch wolde kêren.“
>
> . . . .
>
> dô môgete die vrauwe [gar] sêre
> daz he nicht wolde wedir kêrin
> dorch iren willen[3].
>
> . . . .
>
> enbôt sie dem helde sân,
> her hête gar obele getân
> daz he nicht umme kârte
> dô Pleherîn rîf sô harte.
> und in dorch mich kêren bat[4].'

Tristan protests his innocence and reiterates his principle[5]:

> 'swer mich des dorch sie bête,
> und ab her tûsent ritter hête,
> ich kêrte im undir die ougen.'

When Perenis returns to tell him that Isolt is still convinced of his guilt, he repeats that he never

---

[1] *OX* 6841—4.
[2] *OX* 6862—4.
[3] *OX* 6885—8.
[4] *OX* 6889—94.
[5] *OX* 6903—6.

has refused and never will refuse a request made in
her name[1].

> 'des sî sie sicher und gewis,
> daz ich des nî nicht gelîz,
> swes man mich bat adir hîz
> dorch mîner vrauwin willen tûn.
> ez wệre ouch nû ze vrû,
> ab ich des nû nicht entête,
> swes man mich dorch sie bête.'

When Isolt repents her cruelty, she puts on a
hair shirt next her skin as penance for his sake[2].

> 'daz tûn ich dorch den willen sîn'.

Her messenger conjures Tristan to return to her
for her sake[3].

> 'hêre, dû salt dar komen
> dorch mîner vrauwin lîbe
>
> . . . .
>
> und dorch die grôze arebeit
> die mîn vrauwe nâch dir hât.'

Tristan has been insensible to every other plea,
he cannot resist this. He bids the messenger tell his
lady for his sake to take off the hair shirt[4].

> 'und sage der werdin vrauwen dîn
> daz sie dorch den willen mîn
> daz hêrîn hemede ûz tû.'

When Tristan, returning to Cornwall in his pilgrim
disguise, is recognized by a friend, and begged to take

---

[1] *OX* 6950—7.
[2] *OX* 7170.
[3] *OX* 7292—8.
[4] *OX* 7363—6.

part in the court games, he refuses. His friend knows
a way, however, to gain his consent. He asks him to
do it for the queen's sake [1].

> 'ich wil dich es betin alsô hô
> daz du ez âne zwîvel tûn mûst:
> ich bete dich daz dû es tûst
> dorch der koninginne willen.'

When Tristan sends the messenger to beg Isolt
to come to Brittany to heal him, he tells him to
remind her of all Tristan has done for her sake. At
sight of the ring which he sends as a token, Isolt for
Tristan's sake leaves all to follow his messenger [2].

> 'sie lîz dorch den willen sîn
> ir koninglîche êre
> und entrachtete ir nicht mêre [3].'

The poet takes for granted among his audience
a complete familiarity with the notion that the appeal
in the name of his lady is all powerful to influence
the lover [4]. This idea has an important influence on
the narrative. The presence of it in the *estoire* is
attested not only by the German poem, but by Thomas
and the *Folie* [5].

6. THE ARTHURIAN KNIGHTS.

The treatment of Arthur and his knights [6] in the
estoire implies an audience already acquainted with

---

[1] *OX* 7788—91.
[2] *OX* 9265—84.
[3] *OX* 9338—41. Cf. also 8830—2, 8835, 8910—2.
[4] cf. Bédier I, 342.
[5] Bédier II, 276—80; Schoepperle, *Rom.* XL, 86—8. *Sur un vers de la Folie Tristan de Berne (Je ai sailli et lanciez jons,* l. 184).
[6] *OX* 5016—5462.

Kay and Gawain in the stereotyped rôles in which we
find them in French Arthurian romance. Gawain is the
mirror of courtesy, the faithful friend, the most distinguished of Arthur's knights. His prowess is familiar
to the hearers, and his affection is the highest tribute
that can be given a hero. The humorous treatment
of Kay is a similar indication that this figure also
had become conventional.

It is hardly possible that in an episode of such
secondary importance, so loosely related to the main
story, the Tristan poet should have created two of
the most striking figures in Arthurian romance. We
must suppose these figures already familiar to the
audience through Geoffrey of Monmouth's *Historia* and
French romances inspired by it[1].

7. NARRATIVE ELEMENTS RATIONALIZED
AND ELABORATED.

There are several incidents in the *estoire* which
appear to be based on much older tradition, but which
have been subjected to careful revision in those traits
in which the procedure of the hero seemed rash to a
more cautious age. Other modifications betray the
hand of the courtly redactor.

It seems clear that there is some relation between
certain passages of the *estoire* which we shall discuss,
and the lays of *Lanval* and *Chievrefoil*. The *estoire*
presents a more complex treatment of the incidents
found in Marie's lays. This does not imply that it is
necessarily posterior to them in date[2].

---

[1] cf. Golther, *op. cit.* 1907, p. 73.

[2] Marie's lays are dedicated to Henry II, which would afford
a date between 1154 and 1189. Their author has been identified
with Mary, natural daughter of Geoffrey Plantagenet, count of

a) *Chievrefoil* [1].

In the account of the voyage of Tristan and Kaherdin to Cornwall, after the secret of Tristan's marriage is revealed, we find in the *estoire* a combination of two incidents. The one is the story of a tryst which the lover secures with his mistress almost under the eyes of her husband and her train. The other is the justification of Tristan's boast that Isolt shows more affection to his dog than his wife, who is less fair, shows to him himself [2].

The first incident is recounted in Marie de France's lay of *Chievrefoil* [3]:

The exiled Tristan, longing for Isolt, returns secretly to Cornwall. He conceals himself for days in the wood, coming out only at night, in the hope of getting news of the queen. He learns that the king is to hold a feast at Tintagel, and betakes himself to the forest road along which the train must pass. He peels a branch of hazel and cuts it square, writing on it his name and this message: he has been waiting for a long time and planning how he may see her, for he can live no longer without her. With them it is as when the honeysuckle has wound itself around the hazel: both can live as long as they are together, but both must die if they are parted. He places the hazel-branch on the path and retires into the forest.

Anjou, father of Henry II. Geoffrey died in 1151. Mary is mentioned as Abbess of Shaftesbury in 1151 and in 1215 (J. C. Fox, *English Historical Review* XXV, 1910, p. 303—6). Warnke places the date of Marie's lays as 1165. *Die Lais der Marie de France*, *op. cit.*, 1900, XXXV; cf. Warnke, Intr. to *Fables*.

[1] The study on *Chievrefoil* is reprinted with slight changes from *Romania* XXXVIII, 196—218.
[2] cf. Chapter II, R.
[3] Karl Warnke, *Die Lais der Marie de France*, Halle 1900, No. XI, p. 181.

As the queen comes riding by, she perceives and recognizes the message. She commands her train to halt,
and withdraws alone with Brangien into the forest,
to meet her lover.

In the *estoire,* as we have said, this incident is
combined with another[1]:

Tristan has excused himself to Kaherdin for his
neglect of his wife by declaring that she has
shown less love for him than another fairer Isolt
gladly shows, for his sake, to his dog. To test this
assertion the two set out for Cornwall. They are
received secretly by Dynas, whom Tristan sends to
Isolt to inform her of his straits and to ask her to
save him in the following manner: let her arrange
the most magnificent train possible and set out for
Blanche Lande. On the road thither there is a thorn
bush near a hunting booth. In this Tristan will be
hidden, and will shoot a twig into her horse's mane.
She is to stop at this sign, and caress the dog with
so much fervor that Kaherdin will be compelled to acknowledge his boast justified. Dynas goes to Tintagel,
and succeeds in drawing the queen's attention to
Tristan's ring. Isolt recognizes the sign and contrives
a private interview with him. On hearing Tristan's
message the queen immediately arranges a hunting
party in accordance with his directions. When she
sees the twig she commands her train to halt. After
caressing the dog, she approaches the bush, and
pretends to address the birds, bidding them bear her
company that night at Blanche Lande. Galiag
is sent to the king to say that the queen is ill and
can proceed no farther. The lover is received in the
queen's tent.

---

[1] *OX* 6255—6662.

To understand the relation of these two versions to each other it will be useful to examine the other versions of the incident in the twelfth century. From a comparison of them it will be possible to trace the general line of development.

In Heinrich von Freiburg's *Tristan*[1] the episode is the same as in Eilhart, except that here the final touch to Tristan's plan is given by the queen. It is she who sends word to Tristan to throw a twig on her path from his place in the thornbush. She will send Tantrisel to pick it up. It is prearranged for the king to precede Isolt. It is Andret who is sent to notify the king that she must stop where she is for the night. The messenger is to remain with the king if darkness overtakes him on the way. The precautions for Tristan's admission to Isolt's tent are elaborated.

In the English *Sir Tristrem*[2] the episode appears in a very confused form:

Tristan brings Kaherdin to Cornwall in order that he may see Brangien and the Isolt whom Tristan has declared fairer than his wife. He has already shown him their statues in the hall of images. Isolt has received no word of his coming. She has just heard of his marriage, and has angrily saddled her horse and gone for a ride, attended by several of her maids. Tristan and Kaherdin, under a fig-tree along her path, see her and Brangien approaching with their two dogs. Isolt stops. Tristan sends Kaherdin forward to show her the ring. The queen recognizes it, pretends sudden illness, and stays two

---

[1] Edited by Reinhold Bechstein, *Heinrich's von Freiburg Tristan*, Leipzig 1877, p. 170, ch. VIII.

[2] Edited by Kölbing, *Die nordische und die englische Version der Tristansage*, Heilbronn 1878, 1882, II, stanza CCLXXX ff.

nights there. Gorvenal guards the privacy of the
lovers. There is no mention of Mark.

In the *Tristramssaga*[1] the motive of Tristan's
return to Cornwall is the same as in *Sir Tristrem*.
Here also both the twig and the previous message
have disappeared.

Tristan and Kaherdin learn that the queen's train is
to spend the night in a certain place, and conceal themselves, apparently in disguise, along the route. Both step
forward and greet the queen and Brangien. Fearing
recognition by the others, the lovers confine themselves
to a few words. 'Ride off now, stranger knight', says
the queen, 'detain us no longer'. The train proceeds
to the place that has been appointed for the night.
There is no pretense of illness, but the queen passes
the night alone with her maids until her lover appears.

The version of Ulrich von Türheim[2] is similar
to that of Heinrich von Freiberg and Eilhart von
Oberge, except that no provision is made for a signal.

When the party reaches the thornbush, the queen,
after dismounting and caressing the dog, makes a sign
for Tristan to approach. Tristan retires again at a
warning from Brangien, after receiving from the queen
careful directions as to where to find her tent. Andret
appears with a message from the king, saying that he
has taken another route. Isolt complains bitterly, and
declares she is too ill to proceed farther. Andret,
returning to the king, adds the insinuation that her
illness is only an excuse. The king's suspicions are
lulled by Brangien and Paranis, and the lovers pass
the night together undisturbed.

---

[1] Kölbing, *op. cit.*, I, Cap. LXXXVII, p. 100; cf. Kölbing's
translation, *op. cit.*, p. 194, l. 1 ff.

[2] Ulrich von Türheim's continuation, p. 497 ff. of *Tristan
und Isolt von Gottfried von Strassburg*, ed. H. F. Massmann.
Leipzig 1843, l. 1022 ff.

The French Prose Romance[1] preserves only the point of departure for this adventure.

A comparison of the texts in which the episode appears leads us to the following classification:

A. A form in which the request for the meeting is carved on a piece of bark, the bark placed on Isolt's path, and her finding it left to chance: *Chievrefoil.*

B. A form which speaks of a previous communication that puts Isolt in possession of all the facts entrusted in *A* to the bit of bark and to the situation, and notify her that she is to expect a piece of bark (or twig) at a certain place and at a certain time, as a signal that her lover is awaiting her: Eilhart von Oberge; Heinrich von Freiberg.

C. A form in which, in the same situation, the bit of bark (or twig) is lacking or replaced by a conventional signal: *Sir Tristrem*; the *Saga*; Ulrich von Türheim.

It has already been shown[2] that the form *C* is posterior to form *B*. It is improbable that the form *B* is earlier than *A*, because in that case we could not account for the disappearance, in group *A*, of the communication by messenger and ring, on which the whole episode depends in *B*, and which a twelfth century French poet would have no motive in abandoning. But on the supposition that *A* is the original form, it is easy to account for the introduction, in *B*, of the previous communication, as the addition of a twelfth century French writer to whom the device

---

[1] Löseth, *Le roman en prose de Tristan*, Paris 1891, p. 46, p. 60 § 75a; Bédier, *op. cit.* II, 269, 871.

[2] Bédier II, 274—5.

employed in *A* was unfamiliar and seemed precarious. Moreover, a previous communication notifying Isolt to be on the lookout for a piece of bark at a special spot at a specified time makes the piece of bark and its carving entirely superfluous, although the scene and circumstances of the action as well as the prologue and epilogue of *Chievrefoil*, point unmistakably to the fact that it constitutes the main factor of the episode.

Let us therefore consider further the possibility that *A* offers the original form of the episode: The manuscript *S* of *Chievrefoil* gives the following reading at line 61:

'Ceo fu la sume de l'escrit
Qui fu el baston que je (= j'ai) dit
Que lunges ot ilec esté...'

At line 109:

'Pur la joie qu'il ot eüe
De s'amie qu'il ot veüe
Par le bastun qu'il ot escrit
Si cum la reine l'ot dit
Pur les paroles remembrer
Tristram ki bien saveit harper
En aveit fet un nuvel lai.'

The Norse translation [1] is equally uncompromising in defining the role of the 'bastun':

'Nu war ristid a stavenom at Tristram hafde
thar lengi bedir', etc.

---

[1] Edited by Keyser und Unger, *Strengleikar eða Liodabok*, Christiana 1850, p. 66—67.

Manuscript H[1] seems to make a timid attempt
to reduce the role of the writing on the 'bastun'. At
line 61:

> 'Ceo fu la sume de l'escrit
> Qu'il li aveit mandé e dit
> Que lunges ot ilec esté.'

At line 109:

> 'Pur la joie qu'il ot eüe
> De s'amie qu'il ot veüe
> *E pur ceo kil aveit escrit*
> Si cum la reine l'ot dit
> Pur les paroles remembrer
> Tristan ki bien saveit harper
> En aveit fet un nuvel lai.'

The reading of S is preferable, it seems to us, in
both cases, because it is the only reading that brings

---

[1] Warnke edits MS. *H*, but adopts the reading of S in
various cases, in *Chievrefoil*. Among them is line 109. He accounts for his departure from *H* here as 'durch den Sinn er-
fordert'. M. Foulet points out (*Zeitschr. f. rom. Philol.* XXXII, 280):
'Il lui a échappé que le vers 109 est dans un étroit rapport avec
le vers 62 et qu'il faut se tenir, dans l'un comme dans l'autre
cas, à la leçon de *H* ou à la leçon de *S*.' Cohn (*Zeitschr. f. frz.
Spr. u. Lit.*, XXIV², p. 15) objects to S at line 109 on the insufficient ground that 'bastun' appears here as the direct object of
'escrire'. M. Foulet (*op. cit.*, p. 280, n. 1) cites the discussion of
Cohn to support his rejection of S, but rejects Cohn's reading
of *H*, which indeed, with its construction of 'la reine' as dative,
is objectionable syntactically, and gives the very unsatisfactory:
'um das, was er geschrieben hatte, in der Weise, wie er es der
Königin gesagt hatte, d. h. wortgetreu, um die Worte dem
Gedächtnis zu überliefern'. Foulet's interpretation of *H* is
more satisfactory: 'Pour conserver le souvenir de la joie qu'il
avait eue à revoir la reine et des paroles qu'il lui avait envoyées,
Tristan, sur la demande de la reine (si cum la reine l'ot dit), fit
un lai nouvel'. It seems to me that *H* alters at 62 and 109 from
the rationalistic considerations that influence Foulet, *op. cit.* 279 ff.
Syntactically there is not sufficient reason for rejecting either
reading.

the title, prologue, and epilogue [1] into relation with
the episode: I will tell you how, about whom, and of
what, the lay of the honeysuckle was made: Once
Tristan, in order to secure a meeting with Isolt, carved
on a hazel rod a pretty simile about their love and
the hazel and the honeysuckle, and put it on her path.
She found it and recognized its purpose, and they had
a happy meeting. In order to remember the pretty
verse that he had thus carved and that had brought
about their tryst, he made a lay, at her request,
and this is the lay that is called by the French
Chievrefoil [2].

In the voyage of Tristan and Kaherdin to Cornwall in the *estoire*, the *Chievrefoil* incident remains
intact: Tristan, hidden in the forest along the path
which he knows the queen is to traverse, attracts her

---

[1] It appears from the opening of the lay, that Marie is
providing, or pretending to provide, a setting for a lyric lay
called *Chievrefoil*. The same implication is found in other lays,
e. g. *Strandarliod*, ed. Keyser and Unger, *Strengleikar*, Christiana
1850. The contents of this lay are implied by the epilogue (1. 109 ff.)
to be the message which Tristan wrote on the bark: Tristan
made a new lay, called *The Honeysuckle*, for joy of the meeting
secured by the bark, and, as the queen suggested to him, in
order to remember the words he had written on it. Similarly
Foulet, *op. cit.* 284, with the difference that M. Foulet believes
the message to have been sent previously by letter, as is implied
by the reading of MS. *H*. Miss Rickert, *Marie de France, Seven
of her lays*, New York 1901, p. 98, by her translation of the
epilogue, creates the difficulty which she discusses at page 193
and dismisses as insoluble. It is interesting to observe that the
Norse translator (*Strengleikar, op. cit.* 66—67) falls into the same
mistake. *Si cum la reine l'ot dit* is best rendered, with Foulet,
at the queen's request, and *pur les paroles remembrer*, with Foulet
and Cohn, as taking up again the thought of *pur la joie qu'il ot
eüe*, etc. cf. Cohn, *Arch. f. neuere Spr.*, 106, 439 ff. — The extant
lyric lay called *Lai du Chievrefoil* (Bartsch, *Chrestomathie de
l'ancien français*) has no connection with Tristan.

[2] This is also the way Ahlström and Warnke interpret
the lay. Ahlström, *Studier i den Fornfranska Lais-Litteraturen*,
Upsala 1892, p. 147; Warnke, *op. cit.*, p. cxli.

attention by shooting a twig into her horse's mane. She recognizes that her lover is near, contrives to break the journey, and he spends the night with her. But here she has already been notified as to exactly the spot where Tristan is stationed; the twig has become a mere signal; it is no longer *parée* or *quarrée*, to say nothing of bearing a message. But though become superfluous, it still retains, in a situation exactly similar to that of *Chievrefoil*, a ghostlike semblance of its old function. It is completely suppressed in the versions given in Ulrich von Türheim, in the *Saga*, and in *Sir Tristrem*. In the last two, the lover attracts the attention of his lady as she passes by among a troop of enemies, not by a message carved on a branch, nor by a branch without a message, but by sending his friend, or appearing himself, for a moment, on her path.

It is impossible to escape the conviction that the episode in the form in which Marie related it, was not quite in accordance with twelfth century habits. The difficulties, however, allowed themselves to be obviated by a little precaution in the form of a preface. And gradually the ingenious preface became so extensive that it crowded out the original device, or permitted it to remain only as an insignificant superfluity. It is interesting to observe that the whole development is determined by an increasing sensitiveness to considerations of caution. From the first suggestion of a previous message by letter, in manuscript *H* of *Chievrefoil*, to the elaborate precautions of Ulrich, each new touch can be traced to the anxiety of the poet lest the carved bark miscarry or fall into the hands of enemies, lest Tristan mistake the place of the queen's tent, lest Mark appear inopportunely, etc. etc. To guard against these possibilities, precautions are

multiplied, and we have a whole host of go-betweens
— Kaherdin, Brangien, Dynas, Tantrisel, etc. — invented to insure the safety of the lovers' meeting.
But this cautious temper of the redactors is in
direct contradiction to the characteristic feature
of the situation, namely that the lover seeks access
to his lady in the midst of a hostile cavalcade
on the open high-road. The characteristic feature
is therefore scarcely likely to have been their invention [1].

b) *The chips on the stream.*

A similar development is evident in comparing
the texts of another episode in which Tristan uses
the same device to secure a meeting. He carves a bit
of bark and sends it down the stream which flows
through or past Isolt's chamber. In several cases the
passage is brief enough to bear quotation. In *Sir
Tristrem* [2] it runs as follows:

'Tristrem was in toun,
In boure Ysonde was don.
Bi water he sent adoun
Light linden spon:
He wrot hem al with roun;
Ysonde hem knewe wel sone.
Bi that Tristrem was boun,
Ysonde wist his bone,
To abide.
Er a morwe none
Her aither was other biside.'

---

[1] For a discussion of its origin see Ch. VI, infra.
[2] Kölbing II, stanza CLXXXVII.

The passage in the *Saga* [1]:

When Tristan heard of the king's departure, his mind was entirely reassured, and he pretended to be sick, and stayed at home to see if perhaps he might find an opportunity to meet the queen. And then he took a branch and whittled fair shavings so skilfully that no one had ever seen their like: for when they were cast into the stream they were not damaged but floated like foam on the water and no current could destroy them. Whenever Tristan wanted to talk with Isolt, he cast the chips into the stream which ran beside the tower and in front of the sleeping room of the queen, and she knew at once and perceived by these ruses his intention of coming.

In Eilhart [2]:

The king has dismissed Tristan from the court. Separated, the lovers languish. Isolt sends Brangien to tell Tristan he must find means of seeing her. He promises that he will meet her that very night in her orchard. Moreover, whenever, night or day, she finds a branch on the stream that flows through her chamber, she is to wait and see if it is followed by a bit of bark on which is carved a five-pointed cross. Whenever she finds this in the stream, she may know that Tristan is under the linden near its bank. The ruse is repeatedly successful.

In Gottfried [3] also, Brangien is sent to tell Tristan that Isolt desires to see him. Here it is she who invents the device and instructs him in its use:

---

[1] Translated from Kölbing, *op. cit.* I, cap. LIV, p. 68, 1. 25; cf. translation of Kölbing, *op. cit.* p. 167, 1. 18 ff.

[2] Synopsis from Lichtenstein, *op. cit.*, 1. 3278—3355, cf. 3490—3494; cf. ch. II, I supra.

[3] Edited by Karl Marold, *Gottfried von Strassburg Tristan*, *I. Teil*, *Text*, Leipzig 1906, 1. 14427 ff.

'Sô nemet ein oleboumes rîs
Und snîdet spaene in lange wîs
Und zeichent die mit nihte mê,
Wan machet einhalp ein T
Und machet anderhalp ein Î
Daz niwan der êrste buochstap sî
Von iuwer beider namen dar an,
Und leget dâ weder zuo noch van
Und gât zem boumgarten în;
Ir wezzet wol daz bechelîn,
Daz von dem brunnen dâ gât
Hin dâ diu kemenâte stât,
Dar în sô werfet einen spân
Und lât in fliezen unde gân
Hin vür der kemenaten tür;
Dâ gân wir zallen zîten vür
Ich und diu fröudelôse Isôt,
Und weinen unser herzenôt.
Als wir in danne ersehen dâ,
Dâ bî bekennen wir iesâ,
Daz ir dâ bî dem brunnen sît,
Dâ der oleboum schate gît.'

In the French Prose Romance[1] the device by which the corresponding meeting is arranged is not mentioned.

It would seem that Thomas took the precaution to prepare Isolt for the signal on the stream by having Tristan send her a message by Brangien. The trait is found only in Gottfried, but is apparent from other passages that the redactor of the *Saga* has greatly abridged his source, and *Sir Tristrem* in its elliptical style often omits important links in the narrative. For the incident of the chips on the stream then, only

---

[1] Löseth, *op. cit.* p. 186, § 282.

the stages *B*, represented by Eilhart and Thomas, and *C*, represented by the Prose Romance, survive in the extant texts. We are not fortunate enough to possess here, as in the case of the *Chievrefoil* incident, an episodic poem which preserves the incident in a simpler form.

In both cases the *estoire* represents stage B: A conservative but critical redactor introduces a new and more rational trait (the messenger), retaining the traditional feature (the piece of bark) in a subordinate position.

c) *Tristan's boast of his distant mistress.*

1. The story.

It is a curious fact that the *Chievrefoil* tryst is combined in the *estoire* with another theme which also appears in one of Marie's lays: When Kaherdin reproaches Tristan for his indifference to Isolt of Brittany, Tristan justifies himself by declaring that there is a woman who in love for him and in beauty far surpasses the daughter of Howel. Kaherdin requires him to prove his statement. Tristan brings him to Isolt in Cornwall and shows that his boast is justified[1].

This incident involves elements which go back ultimately to popular tradition[2]. The story with which they are usually associated there is as follows:

---

[1] cf. ch. II, Q R.

[2] See bibliography in R. Köhler's notes to Marie's *Lanval* in Warnke's edition of Marie's Lays (Halle 1900, cvi — cxviii). Add J. W. Wolf, *Deutsche Hausmärchen*, Göttingen 1851, p. 198; G. von Gaal, *Märchen der Magyaren*, Wien 1822, *Fischermärchen* 127—75; Dunlop-Wilson, *History of Prose Fiction*, London 1888, II, 402 n. cf. also the Old Irish story *The Debility of the Ultonian Warriors*, ed. Windisch, *Berichte der Kgl. sächs. Gesells. der Wiss., Phil.-hist. Kl.*, 1884, p. 340; English: E. Hull, *The Cuchullin Saga*, p. 97.

The hero, a fisherman's son, is adopted by a water nymph and brought up in her realm. After a number of years, he is seized with a desire to revisit his native land. His mistress gives her permission on condition that he will not speak of her. While he is there a high-born lady offers him her love. He refuses it, declaring that his mistress is far superior to her. When he is required under a heavy penalty to prove his statements, he is in despair, realizing that he has forfeited his lady's favor by violating his promise. She appears at the critical moment, summoned by a magic ring which she has given him. All are forced to acknowledge that the meanest of the handmaids that attend her surpasses the woman he has disdained. But although his mistress has thus saved her hero, she does not pardon him. She disappears, leaving him no token. He must seek her through the world, wearing out iron-shoes before he regains her at last.

Certain elements of this story were current in literary form, in the period when the *estoire* was composed, in Marie de France's lay of *Lanval*[1] and in the anonymous lay of *Graelent*[2]. It is improbable that these lays are adaptations of the Tristan episode, for they contain many more traits characteristic of the traditional versions of the theme — the supernatural qualities of the lady, her forbidding the hero to speak of her, the helplessness of the lover when required to produce her; her displeasure with him for boasting of her;

---

[1] K. Warnke, *Die Lais der Marie de France, Bibliotheca Normannica*, Halle 1900, No. V, p. 86.

[2] Roquefort, *Poésies de Marie de France*, Paris 1820, I, 487 —541; Barbazan et Méon, *Fabliaux et contes*, Paris 1808—23, IV, 57 ff.; G. Gullberg, *Deux Lais du XIIIe Siècle*, Kalmar (Sweden) 1876.

the final reconciliation, etc.[1] The Tristan story, on the contrary, contains nothing that cannot be accounted for from the *Lanval* and *Graelent* lays and the necessity of adapting the incident to the rest of the narrative.

The hero, on his arrival in a new country, is offered the love of a high-born lady and disdains it. He is reproached by her or by her relatives.

In *Lanval*:

> 'Vassal, vus m'avez mult mesfait!
> trop començastes vilein plait
> de mei hunir e avillier
> e la reïne laidengier[2].'

In Eilhart:

> 'wir habin es lastir[3].'

He is required, under a heavy penalty, to produce his mistress and prove his statement.

In *Lanval*[4]:

> 'un sairement l'en guagera,
> e li reis le nus pardurra.
> E s'il puet aveir sun guarant
> e s'amie venist avant

---

[1] In these lays, and in other literary versions of the theme, the hero, instead of sojorning in the realm of the fairy, is able to summon her by means of a talisman, and to enjoy her favor secretly in his own land.

[2] *Lanval, op. cit.,* V, 365—9.

[3] *OX* 6219.

[4] *Lanval* 451—63; cf. *Graelent,* ed. Barbazan, 1. 465 ff.:

> 'C'au chevalier face amener
> Celi qu'il i oï loer,
> E dont i fait si grant vantance:
> Entre nos dex soit la mostrance;
> S'ele est si bele, quite en soit,
> Ou se ce non, faites m'en droit
> Del mesdit e de le blastenge.'

e ceo fust veirs que il en dist,
dunt la reïne se marrist,
de ceo avra il bien merci,
quant pur vilté nel dist de li.
E s'il ne puet guarant aveir,
ceo li devum faire saveir:
tut sun servise pert del rei,
e sil deit cungeer de sei.'

In Eilhart[1]:

.'. . . „ich brenge ûch dar
daz ir wol werdit gewar
daz ich ûch wâr habe gesagit,
und ab ich lîge, daz ir habit
ûwir vorderunge ûf mich."
Kehenis sprach „daz lobe ich".
Dô muste Tristrant vil lîse
geloben [sîne gesellin] Kehenîse
und sîme vater bî trûwin
daz he wedir quême zû der vrawen
vil schiere und sie sêge,
und ob Kehenis jêge
daz he nicht wâr hête
daz er im denne tête
swaz he selbe wolde.'

At the critical moment a number of ladies present
themselves. As each rides up, the judges, marvelling
at her beauty, take her to be the one of whom the
hero has boasted. At last their mistress appears, like
the sun, surpassing all in brilliancy. She descends from
her palfrey. In *Lanval* she addresses the king; in
Tristan she caresses her lover's dog.

---

[1] *OX* 6249—63.

Both contain the detail that she lets fall her
mantle as she descends from her palfrey, in order that
all may judge her beauty.

In *Lanval*[1]:

> 'Devant le rei est descendue,
> Si que de tuz fu bien vëue.
> Sun mantel a laissié chaeir,
> Que mielz la peüssent veeir.'

In Eilhart:

> 'die koningîn dô nedir trat[2]:
>
> . . . .
>
> den mantel lîz sie nedir hangen[3].'

After she has spoken, she again wraps it around her[4]:

> 'Dô dese rede was getân
> dô nam die koninginne sân,
> iren mantel umme sich wedir.'

The beholders declare that the boast is justified.

In *Lanval*[5]:

> 'N'i a un sul ki n'ait jugié
> que Lanval a tut desraisnié.
> Delivrez est par lur esguart.'

In Eilhart[6]:

> '..... Kehenis der snelle
> sprach „lîber mîn geselle,
> du salt dîner trûwe lôs sîn“.

The folk tales and lays then relate how the hero
regains the favor of his mistress, for he has incurred

---

[1] *Lanval* l. 619—623.
[2] *OX* 6575.
[3] *OX* 6606.
[4] *OX* 6631—4.
[5] *Lanval* 645—8.
[6] *OX* 6597 ff.

her displeasure by breaking his promise not to speak of her. The displeasure of Isolt against Tristan for not obeying a request made in her name, and her subsequent relenting, may be a substitute for this.

2. The boast of the lady's beauty.

In Thomas' *Tristan*, as in the lays and the popular versions, the superior beauty of the lady and her maids constitutes the lover's boast. This feature was no doubt also in the *estoire*. There are the following traces of it in the German poem.

Tristan bids Dynas tell Isolt to come in state to Blanche Lande, bringing with her in the procession a train of ladies gorgeously adorned:

> 'Ouch hîz he die koningîn betin
> daz si vil vrauwen brêchte mete,
> gar wol gezîret
> und hêrlîche gebalîret
> als einer koninginne zême
> und hobeschlîchen quême[1].'

With the coming of Camille, Kaherdin confesses that he knows of no one more beautiful:

> 'dô dûchte Kehenis ungefûg
> daz icht schôners mahte gesîn[2].'

At Brangien's approach, he is still more overcome:

> 'he muste ir doch den prîs lân[3].'

The appearance of the queen is represented as

---

[1] *OX* 6347—53.
[2] *OX* 6464—6.
[3] *OX* 6493.

the coming of the sun, compared to which her maids
were as clouds:

'do irsach her ein gelûchte
daz im selbin des gedûchte,
wie der sunnen wêrin zwû[1].'

This simile, a favorite in French courtly romance,
is further developed, and we have at last Kaherdin's
acknowledgment to himself that she far surpasses his
sister[2]:

'„ez enwart nî schôner wîp:
jâ, leidir mîner swestir lîp
enmag ir nicht gelîchen“.'

And his acknowledgment to Tristan[3]:

'ich wêne he zû Tristrande sprach,
he sêge nî sô schône ein wîp.'

The decision of the judges in *Lanval* is similar:

'Ceo qu'il en jugerunt par dreit,
li reis otreie que si seit[4].'

3. The boast of the lady's affection.

The account of Tristan's boast in the *estoire* is
marked by an additional feature. Not only must Kaherdin acknowledge that Queen Isolt is fairer than
his sister, he must also be convinced that she shows

---

[1] *OX* 6513—6.
[2] *OX* 6537—40.
[3] *OX* 6608—10.
[4] *Lanval* 643—5; cf. *Graelent*, ed. Barbazan, 1. 631—5:

N'i ot un seul, petit ne grant,
Ki ne desist bien en oiant,
Qu'ensanble li, a tel mescine,
Qui de biaute vaut la Rôine.

more love, for Tristan's sake, to the dog that he has
given her, than his wife shows to him himself.

The proverb *qui m'aime il aime mon chien*[1] was
probably already current in the twelfth century. We
read in *Dolopathos*[2]:

> 'On sert lo chien por lo signor,
> Et por l'amor au chivalier
> Baise la dame l'escuier'.

We have also the converse form:

> 'Ki volontiers fiert vostre cien,
> Ja mar querés qu'il vus aint bien[3].'

The caresses given by the lady to her dog are
a favorite theme for the envious sighs of the lovers
of the next few centuries. Mellin de St. Gelais, Ronsard,
and Sidney ring the changes on the lines:

> Ha! petit chien, que tu as de bonheur
> Si tu avois le sens pour le comprendre[4]!'

This devotion of Isolt to Tristan's dog is one of
the extravagences of courtly sentiment characteristic
of the *estoire*. The dog again appears in its richly ornamented case in the procession described in the Thomas
version. But its reason for being has disappeared.
Thomas has suppressed the portion of Tristan's boast
that concerns the dog, together with the other passages

---

[1] Le Roux de Lincy, *Le livre des proverbes français*, Paris
1859, I, 170.
[2] *Dolopathos*, ed. Brunet et Montaiglon, Paris 1856,
l. 10, 429 ff.
[3] *Graelent*, ed. Barbazan, l. 547—9.
[4] Mellin de St. Gelais, in *Annales poétiques ou Almanach*,
Paris 1778, III, 91. Cf. Ronsard, *Les amours, premier livre*,
LXXVIII, ed. Blanchemain, Paris 1857, p. 45; Sidney, *Astrophel
and Stella*, LIX.

of his source that illustrate an ideal which displeased him[1]. He confines Tristan's boast to the superior beauty of Isolt of Cornwall[2].

8. THE SECOND ISOLT: THE PSYCHOLOGICAL PROBLEM.

a) The. story in the Tristan texts.

The treatment in Eilhart of Tristan's marriage with the second Isolt is condensed in the extreme[3]. Tristan is received into the besieged castle of Howel and is led into the presence of the ladies. Kaherdin promises him that he will find his sister the fairest woman he has ever seen[4].

'dû mûst des vorwâre jên,
daz nî wart kein schôner wîp.
si mochte wol eines koninges wîp
wesin âne lastir.'

Tristan asks him her name[5].

'„wie heizet dîne swestir?"
„geselle, sie ist Îsalde genant."
dô wênte der hêre Tristrant
daz sie on hête irkorn.
he dâchte „ich habe Îsaldin vlorn:
Îsaldin habe ich wedir vunden."
in den selbin stundin
quam he daz her sie sach.
îdoch zwâre her nî en sprach,
he wuste schôner wîp wen sie.'

---

1 cf. Bédier II, 274—80.
2 cf. Bédier I, 336 ff.
3 cf. supra, ch. II, P Q.
4 OX 5682—6.
5 OX 5686—96.

It seemed to him, says the poet, when he heard
that her name was Isolt, that she had sought him out.
It is Isolt he has lost, it is Isolt now that he finds.
In the same hour he sees her. But of the fairer Isolt
that he knows he says no word.

By Tristan's aid, Howel succeeds in putting down
the rebellion led by Rivalin, the rejected suitor for
his daughter's hand. When peace is established, Kaherdin, fearful to lose so excellent an ally, urges Tristan
to accept his sister in marriage. Tristan manifests no
unwillingness, and the arrangement is made [1].

In the briefest manner and without explanation, we
are told that Tristan did not consummate his marriage [2].

> 'mit dem edelin wîgande
> was sie mêr denne ein jar
> (daz hôrte ich sagin vor wâr)
> daz sie nî wart sîn wîp.
> daz vortrûg die vrauwe âne nît.'

At the end of the year, Isolt is his wife only in
name. The secret is discovered. Tristan justifies himself to her indignant brother, as we have seen, by
taking him to Cornwall and proving to him how far
his wife's devotion to him is inferior to that of Isolt
of Ireland. He parts from Queen Isolt in anger, however, and when he returns to Brittany, he consummates his marriage, and lives happily with his wife
and her kin.

> 'dô vorkôs ouch [her] Tristrant
> ûf sînen gesellin Kehenîsen
> und gewan dar nâch zu wîbe
> sîne swester dorch den zorn.

---

[1] *OX* 5690—6137.
[2] *OX* 6138—43.

> dô wart ouch die vêhede vorkorn
> die ir vatir zû im getrûg.
> dô hâten vroude genûg
> Tristrant und daz wîp sîn [1].'

In MS. 103 of the Prose Romance, Tristan's purpose of withholding himself from his wife seems to have been abandoned for some time before his last visit to Cornwall. It is not clear in this version from what motive or at what time Tristan thus broke his allegiance to Queen Isolt.

We have only the following passage in regard to it [2]:

> Ung jour se jesoit en son lit et estoit presque gari, si lui print volenté de gesir avec sa femme, si just avec elle et en fist sa volenté; et quant il ot fait son desir, si chay emprès elle tout pasmé aussi comme tout mort.

The service to Howel of Brittany whose daughter Tristan received as a reward was probably a traditional exploit; the redactor of the *estoire* was too conservative to reject it. But in order to palliate Tristan's disloyalty to Queen Isolt, he represents him as more or less forced into the marriage. He dwells on his indifference to his wife, emphasizes it by introducing the story of the boast of the fairy mistress, and represents Tristan as consummating the marriage only after he has been driven away from Queen Isolt with blows.

Thomas' revision of the story at this point is just what we should expect. In pious deference to tradition, the redactor of the *estoire* had spared the old even while he introduced the new. He had retained the tradition of the marriage as a real marriage, but he

---

[1] *OX* 7070—8.
[2] Bédier II, 374—5; cf. Löseth, p. 375, n. 4.

had extenuated Tristan's faithlessness by making him
defer consummating it. Thomas was of no such divided
allegiance between the tradition and the new ideal. He
recognized that if Tristan was to be represented as
remaining loyal to Isolt, even when married to another,
it was desirable to represent him as remaining loyal
to the end. He accordingly effaced entirely the trait
of the consummation of the marriage. The passages
in which Thomas defines his attitude toward his sources
make it sufficiently clear that this is the explanation
of the difference between the two versions.

'Thomas iço granter ne volt,
E si volt par raisun mustrer
Que ico ne put pas ester[1].

Il sunt del cunte forsveié
E de la verur esluingné,
E se ço ne volent granter,
Ne voil jo vers eus estriver;
Tengent le lur e jo le men:
La raisun s'i provera ben[2]!

.Pur essemple l'ai issi fait
E pur l'estorie embelir,
Que as amanz deive plaisir[3].'

b) *The lady as a reward in mediaeval romance.*

There is nothing strange in the fact that there
should have existed a tradition of Tristan's accepting
the lady offered him in reward for his service. Most
primitive heroes have a large number of wives, and in

---

[1] Bédier I, 378, l. 2134—37.
[2] Bédier I, 378, l. 2151—7.
[3] Bédier I, 417, l. 3146—9.

the French poems about Gawain, as in the German
romance *Lanzelet*, the hero is *wipselig* to an astonishing degree[1]. Having accomplished an exploit and
won the lady attached to it as a prize, the knight
promptly rides off and leaves her. When he has accomplished the next exploit, and is given the next lady,
both poet and hero have forgotten the first. In those
romances which attained sufficient vogue to invite careful redaction in the twelfth and thirteenth centuries,
this polygamous character of the traditional hero was
felt to be a disturbing factor. The difficulty was sometimes persistently overlooked, as in the case of *Lanzelet*,
or some means was devised to meet it. Sigurd's in-
constancy is explained as due to a drink of forget-
fulness. By this means his adventure with Brynhild
and his marriage with Gudrun are combined in the
Volsungasaga with tragic effectiveness[2]. In cheerful
and edifying romances such as *Horn*[3], *Bevis*[4], and *Guy
of Warwick*[5], the hero is represented as refusing the

---

[1] *Hist. Litt.* XXX, Index; s. v. *Gauvain*, K. A. Hahn, *Lanzelet
von Ulrich von Zatzikhoven*, Frankfurt 1845.

[2] c. 20, 21. Sigurd's betrothal to Sigrdrifa (Brynhild?) is
recounted in the Edda in the *Sigrdrifumǫl*. According to other
accounts, *Fǫfnismǫl*, *Sigurþarikviþa skamma*, and *Helreith*,
Sigurd does not see Brynhild until after his marriage with
Gudrun. For a discussion of the development of the tradition
see R. C. Boer, *Untersuchungen über den Ursprung und die Ent-
wicklung der Nibelungensage*, *Ztschr. f. dtsch. Philol.* XXXVII,
303 ff. esp. 322. For a different interpretation cf. Sijmons, *Sigfrid
und Brunhild*, *Ztschr. f. dtsch. Philol.* XXIV, 1—32. F. Panzer,
Sigfrid, München 1912, p. 240.

[3] *Das anglonormannische Lied vom wackern Ritter Horn*,
ed. Brede and Stengel, Marburg 1883.

[4] *Das anglonormannische Boeve de Haumtone*, ed. A. Stim-
ming, Halle 1899; similarly *Der festländische Bueve de Hantone*,
Fassung I, ed. A. Stimming, Gesellschaft für romanische Literatur,
Band 25, Dresden 1911, CLXXXVI—CXC, CC.

[5] The French text is inedited. The English redactions are
late. For the passage in question cf. *Guy of Warwick*, ed.
J. Zupitza, *Early English Text Society*, London 1875, Version I,
Pt. I, l. 3948 ff.; *Guy of Warwick* (Auchinleck ms.), ed. Zupitza,
E. E. T. S., London 1888, p. 237 ff.

IV. THE DATE OF THE *ESTOIRE*.

reward of his second achievement and returning to his first love. Horn refrains from marrying the proffered Lenburc because he has not forgotten the promised Rigmel. Bevis, who is already married to Josiane, refuses to accept the hand of the princess won by his exploits. Guy of Warwick remembers at the marriage altar that he is betrothed to another, and returns to her.

In these cases the hero's problem is simple enough: he has only to withstand pressure brought upon him from the outside and remain faithful to his first love. In Marie de France's *Eliduc* [1], in *Ille and Galeron* [2], and in *Galerent* [3], the poet is not satisfied with thus recording the conflicts of the hero in battle. He depicts him as torn by an inner struggle. He delights in analyzing his divided mind. His interest in the story is not in the hero's exploits, but in the question of what combination of the conflicting powers, Love, Duty, Pity, etc., will be victorious in the hero's mind.

In order to compare the various treatments of the hero confronted with the necessity of choosing between a first and a second lady, it will be convenient to have before us an outline of the features common to the versions we have studied.

At an early age the hero is driven from home and is received in a foreign court, where he lives until he is knighted. *Bevis, Horn, Ille, Tristan* (partly). Not in *Eliduc* or *Galerent*.

He becomes invaluable to his lord. He wins an important victory and is advanced in favor. The lord has a

---

[1] *Die Lais der Marie de France*, ed. K. Warnke, *Bibliotheca Normannica* III, Halle 1900, no. XII, p. 186.
[2] *Ille und Galeron*, ed. W. Foerster, *Romanische Bibliothek*, VII, Halle 1891.
[3] *Le roman de Galerent Comte de Bretagne par le trouvère Renaut*, ed. Anatole Boucherie, Montpellier 1888.

daughter or sister (in *Tristan* a wife) with whom the hero becomes involved in a love affair. *Guy of Warwick, Horn, Ille, Galerent, Tristan.*

For some reason the hero departs from this court and goes to another, where he is unknown. *Guy of Warwick, Bevis, Horn, Eliduc, Ille, Galerent, Tristan.*

He conceals his identity. The realm is attacked (by a rejected suitor of the lady *Bevis, Eliduc, Galerent, Tristan*), and the lord is unable to defend it. *Guy, Bevis, Horn, Eliduc, Ille, Galerent, Tristan.*

The hero proves a valuable ally, and by his prowess obtains the victory for his lord. *Guy, Bevis, Horn, Eliduc, Ille, Galerent, Tristan.*

The lord decides to give his daughter in marriage to the hero, or she offers herself to him. *Guy, Bevis, Horn, Eliduc, Ille, Galerent, Tristan.*

The secondary elements in the different stories are of course varied. In order to understand the solutions offered by the various poets for the problem that the hero is now facing, it will be necessary to pass their versions in review and to consider the interest shown in the psychological possibilities of the situation, the poet's manner of accounting for the hero's connection with the second lady, and his attitude toward the woman he rejects.

When Horn is offered the emperor's daughter Lenburc, he replies that his rank does not permit him to aspire to her hand, and that he is already betrothed to a maiden of his own station, whom he intends to marry if she has remained true to him[1].

'Reis gentil e vaillant, ne sui pas de teu gent
K'entre moi e Lenburc façuns noceiement;
Mais le rei mun seignur defendrai vassalment,
Tant cum erc ovek li mar avera dutement

---

[1] *Horn et Rimenhild, op. cit.* 3658—72. Similarly 3808—72.

De feluns Sarasins qui li facent torment.
Mès en Bretaine fui vallet en mun jovent,
Od un prodome i fis un poi arestement.
Une fille qu'il ot vers moi fist aliement,
Si k'ele m'avereit e joe li tut ensement;
Fille est d'un vavasur e tel sunt mi parent:
Bien sumes paringals e d'un ordeinement.
Jà ne prendrai muillie[r] od mun dreit escient
Tant ke sache si vers mei s'a tenu leaument
E cum ert de nostre amur, s'ele me tendra covent.'

The poet makes no effort to develop the psychological possibilities which the situation offers.

In *Bevis* the redactor is similarly indifferent. The lady of Civile insists on marrying the hero, although he has repulsed her advances and told her that he is in search of his lost wife Josian. The discussion becomes heated, and the lady threatens to have him beheaded. At this Bevis agrees to go through the ceremony of marriage [1].

'„Bele soure", dist Boves, „ceo estre lessez,
Je ne le forai pur kan ke vus avez."
Key vus dirai plus pur estre losengé?
Mes tant out entre els parlé e tensé,
Ke li un a l'autre i est mult iré,
E la dame li manasse pur le chef coper.
„Dame", dist Boves, „lessez moi parler!
Par ceo covenant te prenderai a mulier
Ke, si Josian ne repeyre, o le vis cler,
En se set ans, ne voile plus aloygner,
Jeo vus prenderai a femme par vostre congé".'

The lady accepts this arrangement. The formal ceremony is performed, but the marriage is not con-

---

[1] *Boeve de Haumtone, op. cit.* 2875—86.

summated. When the seven years are over the maiden-wife demands the fulfilment of the promise [1].

'Set ans ont ensemble conversés,
Que unkes ov lui n'out charnel amistez.
Un jur ad la dame Boun apelez:
„Orefost de vus averai ma voluntez.“
„Bien purra estre“, dist Boves li senez.'

The lost Josian appears just in time. The lady of Civile yields gracefully and receives Tierri as a husband.

We have the same objective handling of the situation here as in Horn. Bevis' resistance is not complicated by any inclination or feeling of obligation toward the second lady.

c) The second lady in the psychological romances.

In another group of romances the poet's interest is in the situation as a psychological problem. Of these we shall first examine Marie de France's lay *Eliduc*. The wife of the hero is dismissed with two lines [2].

'Sa femme en la terre larra;
A ses humes cumandera
Que il la guardent leialment.'

The beauty and charm of the second woman is emphasized, and the interest is concentrated on the conflict in the hero's mind [3].

---

[1] *Boeve de Hauntone, op. cit.* 2954 — 9.
[2] Warnke, *Die Lais der Marie de France*, Halle 1900, p. 188, l. 71—4.
[3] *Eliduc* 314—27.

'Tuz est murnes e trespensez;
pur la bele est en grant esfrei,
la fille sun seignur le rei,
que tant dulcement l'apela
e de ceo qu'ele suspira.
Mult par se tient a entrepris
que tant a esté el païs
que ne l'a veüe sovent.
Quant ceo ot dit, si se repent:
de sa femme li remembra,
e cum il li asseüra
que bóne fei li portereit
e leialment se cuntendreit.'

The poet describes the similar trouble of the young girl, who at last decides to send the hero a ring and girdle. She rejoices to learn that Eliduc has accepted the tokens, and is happy in the prospect of his long sojourn at the court. She knows nothing of the hero's trouble; she does not guess how he is torn between love for her and loyalty to his wife[1]:

'Ne saveit rien de la dolur
u il esteit, puis qu'il la vit.
Unkes n'ot joie ne delit,
fors tant cum il pensa de li.
Mult se teneit a mal bailli,
Kar a sa femme aveit premis,
ainz qu'il turnast de sun païs,
qu'il n'aimereit si li nun.
Ore est sis quers en grant friçun.
Sa leialté voleit guarder;
mes ne s'en puet niënt oster

---

[1] *Eliduc* 458—77.

que il nen eint la dameisele,
Guilliadun, ki tant fu bele,
de li veeir et de parler
e de baisier e d'acoler;
mes ja ne li querra amur,
que ne li turt a deshonur,
tant pur sa femme guarder fei,
tant pur ceo qu'il est od le rei.'

The king encourages the interest of his daughter
and the young knight in each other. News comes
which necessitates the return of Eliduc to his own
country. He regrets that he has ever seen Guilliadun,
for he realizes that separation will perhaps mean death
to both of them [1]:

'„A las," fet il, „mal ai erré!
Trop ai en cest païs esté!
Mar vi unkes ceste cuntree!
Une meschine i ai amee,
Guilliadun, la fille al rei,
mult durement e ele mei.
Quant si de li m'estuet partir.
Un de nus estuvra murir
u ambedous, estre ceo puet.'

Yet he must not fail in his duty to his lord and
to his wife. His love is unlawful [2].

'Jeo ne puis mie remaneir,
Ainz m'en irai par estuveir.
S'a m'amie esteie espusez,
nel suferreit crestïentez.
De tutes parz va malement.'

---

[1] *Eliduc* 585—94.
[2] *Eliduc* 599—604.

He does not tell Guilliadun that he is married.
He tells her only that he must depart. Her distress is
so great that he promises to go or stay as she may
command. She begs him to take her with him[1].

'„Od vus“ fet ele, „m'en menez,
puis que remaneir ne volez!
U si ceo nun, jeo m'ocirai;
ja mes joie ne bien n'avrei “.'

He promises to come back for her. When he
reaches his home, he grieves so bitterly that his wife
realizes that he is devoured by some secret distress.
On the day appointed he returns to Guilliadun, and
secretly sets off with her to his home.

A tempest threatens to destroy the ship, and the
mariners attribute it to Eliduc's sin in bringing her.
The girl thus learns that her lover has a wife in the
country where she is going. She falls into a death-like
swoon. Eliduc conceals her body in a chapel near his
home, and comes thither secretly each day to watch
her. His wife learns the cause of his trouble; she
succeeds in finding the girl and restoring her to life.
She then withdraws to a convent and leaves the lovers
to marry each other. Later Guilliadun withdraws to the
same convent. Eliduc enters an adjoining monastery.

The purpose seems to be to elucidate the problem
which the situation poses: the conflict between the
rights of love, which the poet considers sacred, and the
rights of marriage universally recognized. The attitude toward received standards of morality is respect-
ful. The hero is entirely under their dominion', and
regards the love he feels for Guilliadun as sin. He
yields to it against his own conscience and with no

---

[1] *Eliduc* 679—683.

hope of anything but condemnation for his conduct.
The first wife withdraws to a convent to allow the
lovers to enjoy their love without sin, and they themselves later enter the religious life.

Ille et Galeron presents a similar situation [1] and
deals with the same problem. The forces pitted
against each other are different. Love is here on the
side of Duty, and Pity, although strongly reinforced
by circumstance, makes but a faint resistance. The
conflict is introduced as follows: The hero leaves his
wife because he has lost his eye in a tournament, and he
fears that she will disdain him. He goes to Rome, where
the daughter of the Emperor is seized with love for
him. The Emperor, who has a great admiration for
Ille, offers her to him in marriage, and will accept no
refusal. The hero is forced to confess that he already has a wife. The Pope declares that unless the
wife appears within a given period, Ille must marry
the Emperor's daughter. In the meantime Galeron has
left her home, and Ille's search for her proves fruitless.
The wedding of Ille and Ganor is prepared. But the lost
wife appears at the church door, and the Emperor's
daughter is rejected [2].

> 'Il set bien k'ele l'aime et prise
> Mais Galerons l'ama ançois.'

The fact that the object of the hero's love is
in this case his wife is of secondary importance.
The poet is interested, here as in the preceding case,
in painting the clash of Love with hostile powers.
Although [3]

> 'Prestre, raisons et drois et lois'

---

[1] *Ille et Galeron, op. cit.*
[2] *Ille et Galeron,* 4651—3.
[3] *Ille* 4656.

are here on the side of Love, there is still a strong
force against it. Ganor, whom the hero is on the
point of marrying, is passionately in love with him.
But, whereas the love of the second woman for Eliduc
roused a pity that reinforced his own desire, the pity
roused by Ganor's passion is hostile to Ille's own love.
The conflict between love for Galeron and pity for
Ganor is the centre of the poet's interest[1]:

'De vos ai pitié mervillose,
Si aim de cuer verai [m]espouse.
De l'amor qui est entre nous,
De la pitié que j'ai de vous,
Me destraint si l'angoisse et grieve,
A poi que li cuers ne me crieve.
Amors et pities me justicent
Et mout deversement m'atisent.

. . . .

Dix! que ferai por cou ataindre?
Ou por pitié ichi remaindre
Et envers amors vilener,
U laissier ceste chi[2] pener
Et ferai ce k'a amor taint?'

It is needless to say that after several hundred
lines of struggle, here as in *Eliduc*, *Amors* is the
victor. Pity and Duty, when measured against Love,
are alike powerless.

In *Galerent*, which is a combination of the motifs
of *Ille et Galeron* and Marie de France's *Le Fraisne*,
the hero is similarly a prey to conflicting impulses.
Galerent has accepted the offer of the hand of Florie
on account of her likeness to his lost love *Le Fraisne*.

---

[1] *Ille* 4827—35; 4845.
[2] *ceste chi* is Ganor.

As the day of the marriage approaches, he becomes
more and more disturbed in mind[1].

'Dieux! comment m'en puis je deffendre
A m'onneur de ce mariage?
Elle est a un homme si, sage
Fille, qui [a] tante vertu.
S'or te demande: „Veus la tu?"
Comment te peuz tu assentir
A respondre oil sans mentir?
Mauvaisement je ray en sens
Que mariage fait assens.
. . . .
Si prendray fame pour ses dens,
Et pour ses yeulx, et pour sa bouche,
Quant de si peu m'amie touche
Celle [ne] n'em porte que l'ombre!'

Here the conflict is of Love against Honor, and
here, as in the other cases, it is Love that wins[2].

d) *The psychological problem in the Tristan texts.*

Let us now examine the treatment of the second
Isolt in the *Tristan* story. The poem of Eilhart does
not dwell on the psychological interest of the situation,
but the narrative itself shows clearly the opinions of
the poet on the questions which the situation is introduced to illustrate. The poet subordinates the second
Isolt relentlessly. He reduces her role to that of a
mere foil for his main heroine. As in the other
romances in which the purpose is to tempt the hero,
the proffered maiden has the name of his lost love[3].

---

[1] *Galerent, op. cit.* 6845—65.
[2] v. Appendix III for a discussion of these romances.
[3] *OX* 5686—92.

'„Wie heizet dîne swestir?"
„geselle, sie ist Îsalde genant."
dô wênte der hêre Tristrant
daz sie on hête irkorn.
he dachte „ich habe Îsaldin vlorn:
Îsaldin habe ich wedir vunden".'

Similarly in the English *Horn*, the first maiden
is called Rimenhild, the second Reynild; in *Eliduc* the
women are Guildeluec and Guilliadun; in *Ille* they are
Galeron and Ganor. In *Le Fraisne* and in *Galerant*,
the names Le Fraisne and La Coldre, and Fraisne and
Florie are intended to be suggestive one of another.

At every point in his account of the relation of
Tristan with Isolt of Brittany, the poet makes clear
that the cause of his hero's interest in her is really his
yearning for the other Isolt. The mediaeval hero had
a naïve egoism which is shocking to our modern conscience. Neither the poet nor the hero asks himself
if he is wronging the second Isolt. The saint who
refused a bishopric to go into the wilderness to seek
his own soul's salvation had no regret for the souls that
he might thus be leaving to perish. Tristan on his
marriage night, remembering the distant Isolt, has no
thought for the young bride by his side. It is of the
other Isolt he is thinking, and of the sovereign power
of love. Here Duty and Desire are the opposing forces,
and here, as ever, Love is victorious.

Meager as the account in Eilhart is, nothing is
omitted that would illustrate the soreness of the hero's
trial. The rival is given the name of the woman he
loves. She is of extraordinary beauty. He is destitute
of hope, not only of ever possessing the first Isolt, but
of ever seeing her. If he offends the family of the
second Isolt, his very life is in peril. But he does not

falter. In defiance of duty and despite desire, the second Isolt is his wife merely in name. Love, even in despair, is all exacting; other duties, even the duty of marriage, other desires, even the desire of the flesh, are as naught to it.

In the incident that follows, the supremacy of love is further illustrated. Called to account by the relatives of the second Isolt, and threatened with death for his neglect of his obligations to them, Tristan has only to prove that the love of his mistress for him surpasses that of his wife. When Kaherdin sees Isolt's devotion to Tristan's dog, he freely and completely acquits him. Love alone constitutes obligation. It is to the Isolt who loves him most that Tristan is bound[1].

The psychological conflict is elaborately described in the French Prose Romance[2].

> Tristan regarde Yseult et l'aimme durement, et pense que, s'il la pouoit avoir, il la prendroit volentiers, si en omblieroit l'autre Yseult. Tristan cuide bien qu'il puisse omblier l'autre Yseult pour ceste par moult de raisons, car il voit bien qu'il la tient contre droit et contre raison: et si n'est nul, s'il le savoit, qu'il ne le tensist a mauvais et a traitre. Pour ce s'acorde il qu'il vault mieux qu'il prenge ceste Yseult et leisse l'autre Yseult.

We are told that this Isolt is deeply in love with Tristan. One day when he is riding with her brother, Tristan loses himself in a reverie and becomes so absorbed that he falls from his horse. Kaherdin implores him to confide to him the cause of his abstraction, and Tristan confesses that it is on account of Isolt that he languishes. He declares that he cannot live without her. Kaherdin rejoices to hear this, believing that it is of his sister that Tristan speaks. He re-

---

[1] *OX* 6181 ff.
[2] Bédier II, 365—6.

proaches him for having so long concealed his desire.
Tristan sees that his friend has misunderstood him,
but he does not reveal the truth. Howel is delighted
to give his daughter to so valiant a warrior, and
Tristan cannot refuse to accept her [1]:

> Tristan espousa Yseult. Et furent les neupces et la
> feste grans. La nuyt vint que Tristan deust aler couchier
> avec Yseult; mais l'autre Yseult lui defent qu'il ne gise a
> sa femme charnellement, mais l'acoler ne le baisier ne lui
> deffend elle mie. Tristan se coucha emprès Yseult tout nu
> a nu, et le luminaire luisoit si cler que Tristan pouoit bien
> veïr la beauté d'Yseult. Elle avoit la gorge tendre et
> blanche, les yeulx vers et rians, les sourcilz bruns et bien
> assis, face pure et clere. Et Tristan la baise et acole. Et,
> quant il lui souvient de Yseult de Cornouaille, si a toute
> perdue sa volenté du surplus faire. Ceste Yseult lui est
> devant, et l'autre Yseult est en Cornouaille qui lui deffend,
> si chier com il a son corps, que a ceste ne face chose qui
> a villennie tourne. Ainsi demoure Tristan avec Yseult sa
> femme.

They are almost a year thus [2].

> En ceste partie dit le conte que Tristan et Kehedin
> chevauchoient ung jour ensemble, si souvint a Tristan qu'il
> avoit ung an qu'il avoit perdue Yseult, si commence a
> plourer trop durement. Kehedin, quant il le voit plourer,
> si sceut bien que c'estoit de grant destresse de coeur et lui
> dit: 'Sire, par la foy que vous devés a la riens du monde
> que vous plus amés, dittes moy pour quoy vous ploures'. —
> 'Kehedin', fait Tristan, 'moult m'avés conjuré; mais, se vous
> me convenanciés que a nulli ne le diriés ne mauvais gré
> ne m'en sariés, je le vous diroye'. Et Kehedin lui con-
> venance loyaument. 'Kehedin', fait Tristan, 'j'aimme par
> amours une dame qui me fu emblee huy a ung an'. Et
> lors lui conte la verité de s'amour. 'Et sachiés', fait Tristan,
> 'que je vous puis bien rendre vostre seur toute pucelle; car
> j'ayme tant Yseult que je ne me mefferoye envers elle pour

---

[1] Bédier II, 368—9.
[2] Bédier II, 370—1.

nulle riens'. — 'Sire', dit Kehedin, 'moult me merveille de
ce que me dittes, et non pour tant bien vous en croy. Mais
or me dittes, cette dame que vous amés est elle belle?' —
'De sa beauté', fait Tristan, 'ne fault mie a parler, car en
tout le monde n'a si belle, et si n'aimma oncquez femme
tant homme comment elle m'aime'. — 'Certes', dit Kehedin,
's'elle est si belle et elle vous aimme tant comment vous
dittes, se vous l'amés je ne vous en blasmeray ja'.

The sentiments attributed to Tristan in the Prose
Romance are those indicated in the account of Eilhart:
Tristan is drawn to the second Isolt by her name
and by the yearning for his lost love. He is
pressed into marriage with her by her family, who
are misled by his interest in her name and influenced
by their eagerness to attach him to themselves.
Through no fault against love, he is brought into a
position in which it seems absolutely impossible to
remain loyal to Isolt. The beauty of Isolt of Brittany
is the supreme trial. But the hero does not falter.
Simply: *L'autre Yseult est en Cornouaille qui lui def-
fend.* All other considerations are not only overborne,
but easily overborne by this one. All things done *for
Isolt's sake* are easy.

Thomas, more disposed to paint his lovers in their
human frailty, represents his hero as suffering cruelly
in preserving his loyalty. The struggle is depicted
in a long passage, of which we quote but a few lines[1]:

> 'Il out boen voleir de li faire,
> Mais l'amur le fait molt retraire.
> Gente la sent, bele la set,
> E volt sun buen, sun desir het;

---

[1] Bédier I, 286, l. 659—65; cf. note. *Voleir* is here used to
indicate the craving of the flesh; *desir*, the yearning for the
lost Isolt.

Car s'il n'en oust si grant desir,
A son voleir poust asentir:
Mais a sun grant desir s'asent.'

Thomas' treatment is in the manner of the dia-
lectics of Crestien de Troyes and Andreas Capellanus,
but, in contrast to that of the Prose Romance, it is
an effort to make the lovers more human and less the
exponents of the theory of courtly love.

Of the traits that we have here discussed as associating the *estoire* with the poetry of the latter half of the
twelfth century, none seems to us more striking than
Tristan's failure to consummate his marriage. The
passage is the expression of a romantic idealism to
which no age perhaps has ever been entirely deaf.
But it would be a daring idealist, even today, after
eight centuries of the idealization of romantic love,
who would venture to represent his hero as refraining
from consummating his marriage out of loyalty to a
passion steeped in shame from its beginnings, and to
a woman lost to him now forever. It is a conception
that seems to us historically impossible previous to
the society for which *Cligès* and *La Charrette* were
written. Only in such a society could an idealistic
poet have dared so plainly to assign to marriage a
second place.

9. A *TERMINUS AD QUEM* FOR THE *ESTOIRE*: THE DATES OF THE EXTANT REDACTIONS.

Let us now examine the dates of the *Folie*, Béroul,
the continuation of Béroul, Thomas, and Eilhart, and
see if the date which we are inclined to assign to the
estoire, a date following somewhere during the period

of activity of Marie de France and Crestien de Troyes, is compatible with them.

On the ground of the numerous irregularities in its declensional forms, M. Bédier places the *Folie Tristan* of the Berne manuscript in the first years of the thirteenth century [1].

For the continuation of Béroul a *terminus a quo* is furnished by the line [2]

'les mains gourdes por le mal d'Acre'

which is an allusion to the epidemic among the crusaders during the siege of Acre in 1190 and 1191 [3]).

M. Muret discusses the date for the version of Béroul as follows: The versification is less archaic and the declensions are less well preserved in Béroul than in the *Brut* and the *Roman de Rou* (1155—1175). Moreover the rhymed couplet is used with a freedom hardly conceivable previous to Crestien de Troyes. The poem must therefore have been written at a date posterior to 1165 [4].

Gaston Paris considered it possible to date the version of Thomas by the following method: Both *Cligès* and Thomas contain a play on the words *mer, amer, l'amer*. This word-play is more neatly introduced, and more appropriate in Thomas than in *Cligès*. According to Gaston Paris, Crestien must therefore have been imitating Thomas, and since *Cligès* was written about 1170 [5], Thomas' *Tristan* must have been written before that time [6]. M. Bédier accepts this conclusion [7].

---

[1] *La Folie Tristan,* ed. Bédier, p. 84.
[2] Béroul 3853.
[3] Muret, *Béroul,* Int. p. cxiv.
[4] Muret, *Béroul,* Int. p. cxiv—v.
[5] *Journal des savants,* 1902, p. 303.
[6] *Journal des savants,* 1902, p. 354—5.
[7] II, 55.

Professor Foerster considers that the word-play was original with Crestien and that Thomas imitated it [1].

Since directly opposite conclusions can be sustained with equal plausibility in the interpretation of this evidence, it cannot be considered decisive in fixing the date. The *terminus ad quem* for the version of Thomas is still to be sought. A *terminus a quo* is fixed by the fact that it contains about thirty lines from Wace's *Brut*. Thomas must therefore have composed his poem at a date subsequent to 1155.

10. THE POEM OF EILHART AND THE DAUGHTER OF ELEANOR OF POITOU.

The only redaction for which we have an approximately definite date is that or Eilhart von Oberge, 1185 — 1189 [2]. This redaction was composed for Mathilda [3], daughter of Eleanor of Poitou and Henry II of England, who married the duke of Saxony, Henry the Lion, in 1168. Her husband became involved in a struggle with Frederick Barbarossa. As a result he was exiled for a period of three years. He left for Normandy with his wife and family in the late summer of 1182, and was received by Henry II with great cordiality. Mathilda remained in Normandy until 1184, when she accompanied her father to England. Her husband joined her there

---

[1] Foerster, *Cligès* [3], Introduction, lxvi—viii, and Wilmotte, *L'évolution du roman français aux environs de 1150* (Bull. de l'Acad. roy. de Belg. 1903, n° 7). p, 67.

[2] E. Gierach, *Zur Sprache von Eilharts Tristrant*, Prager Deutsche Studien IV, Prag 1908, 254—5.

[3] Gierach, *op. cit.* p. 243—55, § 106.

shortly afterward. They returned to Germany in 1185 [1].

We have a glimpse of these three years of exile at the Anglo-Norman court in two poems addressed to Mathilda by the troubadour Bertran de Born, in 1182 [2]:

In the first the poet laments the chains in which his lady has cast him, and from which he can never be released. She is so lovely that he must die unless she gives him a kiss. But this wish is too bold, for she surpasses by far the three beautiful sisters of Turenne. Since the superiority of her mind is as great as that of her body, he must realize that his love is hopeless. He knows that she can never be his. She can choose among the noblest barons, for she is the essence of excellence. The beauties he has celebrated up to this time are in comparison to her as sand beside gold. The dulness and pettiness of the court of Argentan would certainly have been his death, had it not been for the sweet form and the gracious pitying face, the fair reception and conversation of the Saxon princess [3].

In the second lyric the poet speaks of his approaching departure for Limousin. In his greeting to the beauties of the south he adds the warning that they must now seek another to celebrate them, for the love that he feels for the loveliest in the world makes him cold to every other. Yes, he sees in advance that when he is at home again he will be unable

---

[1] A. Richard, *Histoire des comtes de Poitou* 778—1204, II, Paris 1903, v. index *Mathilde, fille de Henri II et Aliénor, femme de Henri duc de Saxe.*

[2] A. Stimming, *Bertran de Born, sein Leben und seine Werke*, Halle 1879, 21—5; cf. A. Thomas, *Poésies complètes de Bertran de Born*, Toulouse 1888, XIII ff.; A. Stimming, *Bertran von Born*, Halle 1892, p. 16, 17, 125—9.

[3] Stimming, 1879, p. 141, No. 9; Stimming, 1892, p. 125, No. 34: A. Thomas, *op. cit.* 125—8.

to withstand the longing for her, and will set out once
more for Normandy. The graciousness with which
she has received him has made his heart hers forever.
How could it be otherwise? She is young, noble, sin-
cere, of royal blood, and perfect in all fair attributes.
Indeed she is so far above all others that even the
imperial crown would be honored by her wearing it.
With delight he remembers the hours he has passed
with her; she bade him sit on a gorgeous carpet and
conversed graciously with him. When he heard her
delightful conversation, and enjoyed her kindness,
when he saw her white teeth, her slender, delicate
body, and her rosy fresh color, he lost his heart
forever [1].

The Provençal biographer gives a similar account
of Mathilda, and relates the following incident in connection with the second poem: During the winter,
Richard (Cœur de Lion, brother of Mathilda) and
Bertran had set out on a journey to inspect the
troops. Supplies were extremely scarce in the camp,
and it happened one Sunday that the friends passed
the whole morning without food. Instead of giving
way to vexation, Bertran called to mind the image of
the princess and composed the poem [2].

The lyrics are of course conventional enough.
We do not offer them as a portrait of Mathilda. True
or false as they may be, a princess who had listened
to the praises of Bertran de Born and who had been
one of the central figures in the court of Eleanor,
would be acquainted with the newest poems of courtly

---

[1] Stimming, 1879, p. 160; Stimming, 1892, No. 35. 19;
A. Thomas 122 — 5.
[2] Stimming, 1879, p. 24. 109; Stimming, 1892, p. 127;
A. Thomas, *op. cit.* 122.

love. Such a production, we imagine, was the Tristan romance which, on her return from the Anglo-Norman court in 1185, she confided to Eilhart von Oberge to put into German verse.

C. CONCLUSION.

Thomas', far from being the first to introduce courtly ideas into the tradition of Tristan[1], modified the extravagant lengths to which those ideas were carried in his source. In Kaherdin's adventures with Camille and Gargeolain, the *estoire* seems to show the influence of themes which appear frequently in the courtly lyric of the thirteenth century. In the account of the unconsummated marriage, and of Isolt's anger against Tristan, the *estoire* represents an idealization of unlawful love that can be compared only with that in *Cligès* and *La Charrette*. The redactor is acquainted with the stories of the Arthurian knights, and it appears from his treatment of them that they were already well known to his audience. There seems to be some

---

[1] Gaston Paris contrasted the primitive character of the Tristan romance with the artificiality of the poems of Crestien (*Revue de Paris* 1894, Avril, 138 ff., esp. 163). Novati, although still under the influence of Paris, saw that his statements did not hold good for the version of Thomas (*Studj di filologia romanza*, II, 399—408). This version, it seemed to him, showed the beginnings of the doctrines of courtly love. He contrasted its courtly character with the primitive traits in Béroul. The extant fragment of Béroul breaks off at a point previous to the courtly passages which we have discussed in this chapter. But in Eilhart's poem these courtly passages form the continuation of a narrative which contains all the primitive traits that are in Béroul. There are survivals of this combination in Thomas. There is no doubt that Eilhart and Thomas had these contradictory features from the *estoire*.

relation between the incident of Tristan's first return to Cornwall from Brittany, and the lays of *Lanval* and *Chievrefoil*. None of the extant redactions of the *estoire* antedate the last decades of the twelfth century. It would seem that the *estoire* was written very shortly before them [1].

---

[1] For a discussion of the traces of older tradition in the *estoire* see chapters V and VI. In the introduction to the third edition of *Cligès*, Professor Foerster expresses the opinion that the reconstructions of M. Bédier and Professor Golther represent *bereits eine spätere, stark veränderte und unverhältnismässig vermehrte Umarbeitung eines älteren Urtristan, den wir also als Ur-Urtristan bezeichnen müssen.* lxiv, cf. lxv ff.

V. POPULAR TRADITION
IN THE *ESTOIRE*[1]: ITS NARRATIVE
TECHNIQUE.

A. INTRODUCTION.

So completely are the materials of the story of
Tristan and Isolt transmuted by the tragic fatality
that broods over the whole, that we are likely to forget in how many passages the narrative is a mosaic
of incidents that have been related of hundreds and
hundreds of nameless heroes in every tongue. They
are the same incidents that we hear told around the
peat-fire in remote districts of the Scottish highlands
today, and that we may find tomorrow recorded in a
Hebrew text of the ninth century. We may collect and
compare twenty versions of each story, we may collect
and compare a hundred or a thousand, and while we
are collecting and classifying them, a shepherd on
the Sicilian hills, and a pauper in the almshouse in
Kerry, and a dozen others in a dozen other spots,
will have created a dozen and two versions more.
Each, whether he heard the new version from another
or made it himself from the old, will tell it as nearly

---

[1] We reserve for discussion in Chapter VI the portions
of the Tristan story that may show marks of Celtic influence.

as he can in terms of the life he knows. Some elements of strangeness he will leave, but those only
that are vital to the narrative and that he thinks
his father would have understood even if he does not.
And since all over Europe the conditions of existence
among people whose interest in such stories is alert,
are more or less similar, it is impossible to say, when
we find the tale tricked out in chivalric finery in a
twelfth century French romance, whether the poet
drew it from one source or another.

The imaginative stores of primitive fiction seem at
first glance to be endless. But when we have examined a large body of European popular tales, we are impressed with the fact that they consist of a very
limited number of elements combined in an infinite
number of ways. The materials of popular tradition
are like a child's set of blocks. They may be arranged in a great many different combinations, but
the units are always the same. By the study of a
considerable number of versions of a given story, taken
down from oral tradition, it is possible to gain an
approximate idea of the limits within which the popular account may vary.

Such folk-tales are the fabric of a great part of
mediaeval literature. They form the material of its
fiction and often of its history. Only very slowly does
realism, the interest in things as they are, gain ground.
The naïve indifference to probability and the uniformity
of type of these popular tales, wherever we find them,
betray their origin in oral tradition.

The Tristan romance contains a considerable
number of such stories. In the hands of Thomas,
Gottfried von Strassburg, and the redactor of the
French Prose Romance, their improbabilities are
effaced, their rigid lines softened into greater har-

mony with the narrative of which they are part,
and their details modified to carry out the individual
purpose of the redactor. But in the *estoire* they appear
in their characteristic popular form, with only the
slight modifications necessary to fit them to the narrative and the addition of a few details that reflect
customs familiar to the French redactor. Everything
individual in the particular folk-tale utilized by the
redactor, however, has been suppressed. So far as we
can distinguish, his source may have been one of the
colorless composite versions that we draw up from
the comparison of a hundred narratives. The individual traits that are added are traits drawn from
contemporary twelfth century society; the modifications
that are made are the slightest that may serve to reconcile the tale with the other incidents of the romance.
It is obvious that it is useless to try to trace more
definitely the origin of such parts of the romance. By
observing the manner in which this material is combined in the *estoire*, we may, however, be able to form
some idea of the literary method of the redactor and
his predecessors.

B. THE QUEST OF THE PRINCESS.

1. THE ACCOUNT IN TRISTAN.

The story of the quest of a bride for Mark is told
in the *estoire* somewhat as follows[1]:

> When Tristan returns from Ireland, healed of the wound
> received from the Morholt, Mark resolves to make him his

---

[1] *OX* 1337—2258. There are so many minute points t
bc discussed in connection with this incident that it seems desir
able to give a rather detailed synopsis of it here. Cf. ch. II, E

heir. The envious courtiers insist, however, on the king's taking a wife. He refuses. Learning that the refusal is attributed to his influence, Tristan joins the barons in a second petition. Mark appears to yield, but secretly plans to elude the courtiers' purpose. While seeking a device, he observes two swallows drop a long hair over which they have been quarreling[1]. When the council enters, he declares that he will marry the princess to whom the hair belongs. They wish to know who this is, but Mark is as ignorant as they. To allay the suspicions of the barons, Tristan announces that he himself will seek the lady. The king thanks him and prepares a ship. The poet comments on the folly of this undertaking. After a month of aimless sailing, Tristan commands the boatmen to avoid Ireland and declares that they must make a thorough search through all lands. The boat is, however, driven by a storm to the shore on which Tristan was healed. He knows that, in revenge for the death of the Morholt, every person who approaches this shore is put to death. With evil forebodings he plans a ruse. The Irish king, angered by the nearness of the boat, commands the marshal to go down and kill those on board. Tristan offers the marshal a golden cup, and asks him to tell the king that they are merchants come from England to sell food, that they have met ships on the way, and have thus been warned of their danger, but rather than lose their cargo they have determined to risk the approach and seek permission to trade. While the marshal returns to report to the king, Tristan and his men wait in anxious foreboding.

They learn from a passer-by that a dragon is devastating the country and that the king has promised to give his daughter to anyone who will destroy him.

> 'he dâchte he wolde sînen lîp
> wâgin um daz selbe wîp,
> und ouch durch den willen,
> daz die sîne gesellen
> mochten alsô genesen;

---

[1] I find no mention in the Tristan texts of the color of s hair. Isolt is alluded to in the Béroul version as *Yseut a la ne bloie* 1546, 3699, *la bele franche au chief bloi* 3536.

> und dâchte im sulde libir wesin,
> daz he von dem worme vortorbe,
> den daz he âne wer irstorbe[1].'

Tristan accomplishes the exploit successfully[2]. Burned by the flames of the dragon, he lies down by a spring. Here he is found by Isolt and Brangien. On regaining consciousness he recognizes Isolt's hair as that of the princess he is seeking. He smiles at the thought, and Isolt, not knowing the reason, asks herself if it is because she has left some task undone. She remembers that she has not cleaned his sword, and hastens to do so. She recognizes by the gap in it, and by the piece she has preserved, that it is the weapon that killed the Morholt. At first she is determined on revenge, but she falters when Brangien reminds her that Tristan alone can save her from marriage with the coward who falsely claims to have killed the dragon. The Irish king pardons Tristan for having slain the Morholt, and gives him his daughter to be the bride of Mark.

2. COMPARISON OF THE ACCOUNT IN TRISTAN WITH POPULAR VERSIONS.

Stories of the quest of a bride for a king are universally current in popular fiction. In the popular forms we almost invariably find five narrative steps[3]. The

---

[1] *OX* 1611—19.

[2] For the details of the combat with the dragon, v. C infra.

[3] The following is a list of the stories I have examined. M. Gaster, *Fairy tales from MSS. of the 9th and 12th centuries*, *Folk Lore* VII, 1896, p. 232, discussed in Köhler, *Kleinere Schriften* II, 333, from a later version in Christoph Helwig, *Jüdische Historien* I, ch. 15. — Hahn, *Griechische und albanesische Märchen*, Pt. I *Griechische Märchen*, No. 37, discussed by Köhler, *Kleinere Schriften* II, 339. — G. Maspero, *Les Contes populaires de l'Egypte ancienne*, Paris 1882, p. 5 ff. *Le conte des deux frères*, discussed by Liebrecht, *Germania* XI, 81. — W. Radloff, *Proben der Volksliteratur der türkischen Stämme Südsibiriens*, St. Petersburg 1872, IV, 373, No. 3. — Cosquin, *Contes populaires de Lorraine* II, 290 ff. — Grimm, *Kinder- und Hausmärchen*, No. 6, cited by Köhler, *Aufsätze über Märchen*, ed. J. Bolte und E. Schmidt, Berlin 1894, p. 24 ff. — Basile, *Pentamerone* IV, 9; cf. Liebrecht's translation

story-teller has, it is true, for each step, the choice of a
large number of narrative units, but, like the child's
playing blocks, they are all ready to his hand. 1. *A
king determines to seek a wife.* The narrator may send

of the *Pentamerone* II, 116, no. 39, cited by Köhler, *Aufsätze
über Märchen*, p. 29. — Collections of folk-tales: Köhler, *Kleinere
Schriften* II, 328—346, reprinted from *Germania* XI, 1866, 389
—406; Liebrecht, *Germania* XII, 81 ff.; Cosquin, *Contes populaires
de Lorraine*, I, lxv ff., II, 290 ff.; Köhler, *Aufsätze über Märchen
und Volkslieder* 24 ff. — Scattered folk-tales of this type: E. S. Hartland, *Legend of Perseus;* III, 170; MacInnes and Nutt: *Waifs and
Strays of Celtic Tradition*, II, 2 ff.
    Among others, the following epic treatments: *The Wooing of
Clovis*, Aimoinus I, 13, 14; Greg. Tur. II, 28, translated by the
brothers Grimm *Deutsche Sagen*, Berlin 1865, No. 430, cf. Rajna,
Le Origini dell' epopea francese, ch. III. — *The Wooing of Olaf:*
Snorre Sturlasson *Heimskringla*, ed. C. R. Unger, Christiania
1868, p. 309, Ch. 92. — *Saga Didriks Konungs af Bern*, ed.
C. R. Unger, Christiana 1853: Osantrix ch. 53 ff.; Attila 64 ff.;
others passim. — *Gaungu Hrólfs Saga*, ed. Rafn in *Fornaldar
Sögur Nordrlanda* III, Copenhagen 1830, p. 235—364, resumé in
Golther, *Die Jungfrau mit den goldenen Haaren* in *Studien zur
Literaturgeschichte, M. Bernays gewidmet*, Leipzig 1893, p. 169—72.
Haralds-saga Hringsbana, Ms. A. M. 298 II (collated with 298 I
and Rask 31), Copenhagen. Dr. H. G. Leach has kindly communi-
cated to me a resumé of this saga. Cf. E. Kölbing, *Beiträge zur
vergleichenden Geschichte der romantischen Poesie und Prosa des
Mittelalters*, Breslau 1876, p. 227—229 for rimur version. —
Kudrun[4], ed. E. Martin, *Germanische Handbibliothek*, Halle 1902.
Aventiure V ff. — *Der grosse Wolfdietrich*, ed. Adolf Holtzmann,
Heidelberg 1865, stanza 12—236. — *König Rother*, ed. H. Rückert,
Deutsche Dichtungen des Mittelalters, Leipzig 1892, I ff. — *Sankt
Oswald,* ed. Ettmüller, Zürich 1835, l. 27 ff., resumé in Paul Piper,
Die Spielmannsdichtung, Deutsche National-Literatnr I, 157. —
The Pursuit of Diarmuid and Grainne, ed. O'Grady, *Ossianic
Society Transactions*, 1855, p. 1 ff.
    Some of the stories examined represent the *Quest* in sub-
ordination to or in combination with a story of some other type,
e. g., with the type called by Köhler *Der Bartlose:* Here the
servant, having forced his master to exchange identities with him,
compels him to perform all manner of services for him, among
them the Quest, *Kleinere Schriften* II, 340; or *Der treue Johannes*,
where the characteristic of the story is the faithfulness of the
friend who protects the hero from dangers of which he has been
forewarned, *Aufsätze über Märchen*, p. 24. The stories of the
Quest generally include further complications, and are not logic-
ally complete until the marriage of the hero with the heroine.
Our interest does not extend, however, beyond the five narrative
elements which we have indicated.

the king himself, or he may have the task performed
by a proxy. 2. *There must be a motive for the king's
decision.* The narrator may attribute it to a natural
desire to marry, or he may represent it as due to the
influence of others. 3. *The king must choose a princess.*
The hero may have a clue to her identity or know her
by report. The token and the report are subject to a
considerable number of variations. 4. *The hero must
have definite directions for his journey.* He may either
possess them already or secure them by the conventional
folklore methods, the favorite being that he is guided by
animals bound to him by gratitude or kinship. 5. *The
hero must win the princess.* This he may do by ruse,
or by violence, or by services.

The hero may disguise himself and obtain the
princess by a trick. He may pretend that he is a
merchant and decoy her to his ship. He may accomplish certain tasks and receive her as a reward.
The tasks are conventional in popular tradition: to
procure the water of Paradise and Hell, or the water
of Beauty, or the water of Life and Death; to procure a talisman that has fallen into the sea, or is
in the possession of the youth who drives the sun; to
collect a great number of small scattered objects, such
as pearls, or grains of meal; to select the princess
from her many sisters, being allowed to see only her
feet; to swim in boiling water; or to kill a giant or
other monster [1].

---

[1] For previous discussions of the episode see Golther, *op.
cit.*, 1887, p. 15—16; *op. cit.*, 1907, 19—20; Golther, *Neue Jahr-
bücher für das klassische Altertum, Geschichte und deutsche Literatur*, XVII, 1906, 698—702; Piquet, *L'originalité de Gottfried
de Strasbourg*, Lille 1905, 181—190. — For discussions of the
folk-tale, see Köhler, Cosquin, Liebrecht, *loc. cit.* A above; Cosquin,
Romania V, 106—107. — For discussions of the episode in the
epics, see Golther, *Geschichte der deutschen Literatur (Deutsche
National-Literatur), Die Brautfahrt in der Spielmannsdichtung,*

Only one of the characteristic steps in the
narrative of the folk-tales is lacking in Tristan. In
the former the hero invariably receives information,
as we have seen, as to the identity and whereabouts
of the princess from some kindly disposed person, or
from animals who are attached to him by ties of kinship or gratitude. In Tristan this step is omitted.
Instead of it we have the hero drifting aimlessly
about at sea, and being driven at last by a storm to
the coast of Ireland — exactly what had happened
to him on the voyage for healing. On that occasion:

'dô gîng daz schif aftir wegin
verre ûf den wilden sê.

. . . .

wen daz hers nicht mê gerûchte,
wâ daz schifchin hin gîng.
ein grôz wint in dô gevîng
und treip in kein Îrlant
und warf in ûz ûf daz sant
vor eine borg des koningis.
den tôd den wênte he hân gewis,
dô he sach wâ daz he was[1].'

In the Quest of the Princess of the Swallows'
Hair[2]:

---

p. 97—110; Paul Piper, *Die Spielmannsdichtung (Deutsche
National-Literatur)*; Suchier, *Französische Literaturgeschichte*,
p. 19, 28; Godefroid Kurth, *Histoire poétique des Mérovingiens*,
Paris 1893, p. 237—251; Rajna, *Origini dell' Epopea francese*,
ch. III; Golther, *Studien zur Literaturgeschichte, M. Bernays
gewidmet*, Hamburg 1893, p. 172 ff. — For a discussion of the
incident in Tristan cf. Bédier II, 180—1. M. Bédier is mistaken
in saying that in the folk-tales the king sends the hero on the
quest because he wishes to get rid of him. This is not always
the case.

[1] *OX* 1148—62.
[2] *OX* 1477—80, 1494—1500, 1505—9, 1512—4.

'einen mânen vûrin sie ûf dem sê,
daz sie gesâgin nicht mê,
wen himel unde vlût.

. . . .

dô hûb sich von den winden
ein stormwetir vreissam.
den kîl ez mit gewalt nam
und mit michellîcher macht
und warf in an der selbin nacht
rechte hen kein Îrlant.

. . . .

'alhîr wart ich geheilet:
ich wêne wir sîn vorteilet,
daz uns sô leide geschê hie,
als mir dô lîbe ergie.

. . . .

sulle wir komen hinnen,
daz mûz mit grôzin listen geschîn.'

The poet utilizes the circumstance that Ireland is
hostile to Cornwall in consequence of the death of the
Morholt, to account for a trait which he adopts from
the folk-tale — the hostility of the princess' father,
who allows no suitors to land in the kingdom[1].

A favorite ruse of the wooer in the folk-tales
is to pretend that he and his men are merchants[2].
In Tristan the account of the famine in Ireland in
the Voyage for Healing serves to explain this *motif*.
The hero pretends that he is bringing provisions to

---

[1] cf. Oswald 1. 268 ff.; *Rother*, ed. Rückert I, 1. 80 ff.; cf.
Piper, *Spielmannsdichtung*, I, 89 ff.; *Der grosse Wolfdietrich*, *op.
cit.*, story of Hugdietrich, stanza 16 ff.
[2] e. g., Grimm, *Kinder- und Hausmärchen*, No. 6, discussed
in Köhler, *Aufsätze über Märchen* 24; G. B. Basile, *Il Pentamerone*
IV, 9; cf. Liebrecht's translation II, 116, cited by Köhler, *op.
cit.*, p. 29.

the distressed country. In the folk-tales and popular
epics the maiden is lured on board the ship in order
to examine the merchant's goods[1]. The strangers then
lift anchor and sail away. This plan is followed at
two other points in the Tristan story. In the version
of Thomas, the Norwegian merchants thus kidnap the
youthful hero[2]. In the *estoire* the messenger sent by
the dying Tristan to Cornwall employs the same ruse
with the complicity of Isolt[3]. Only partial use of it
is made in the quest. When the ship is cast on the
Irish shore, Tristan tells the coast-guard that he
is a merchant, and thus procures a respite for his
party[4]. But he has been thrown upon the shore of
Ireland against his will. He has no intention of de-
coying the princess to his ship. Indeed, he does not
know that the princess of whom he is in search
lives in this land. He even undertakes the combat
with the dragon without knowing that he is thus to
win the princess whom he seeks. In the folk-tales,
a combat with a dragon is a familiar means of winning the lady. But in Tristan the hero accomplishes
the exploit with no other thought than to win favor
with the Irish king and thus insure the safety of
himself and his companions[5] in an inhospitable country.
It is only after she has been already won that he
discovers that the princess of this land is the one of

---

[1] cf., e. g., *Kudrun*, ed. E. Martin, *Germanische Handbibliothek*, Halle 1902, Aventiure V—VIII.

[2] Bédier I, ch. IV.

[3] MS. 103, ed. Bédier, Thomas II, 385—8 relates the incident
in detail. Eilhart gives a very condensed account. *OX* 9327—41.

[4] In the *Saga* the poet confides to the reader that Tristan
was uncertain whether he should devise some ruse to lure the
princess on the ship or try to get her by violence or by fair
means. Kölbing XXXIV, p. 43, l. 12 ff. The redactors of the
Tristan story were probably all more or less acquainted with the
different types of the story.

[5] *OX* 1608—19.

whom he is in search. — Not until he is found by
Isolt overcome by the fiery breath of the dragon
does he realize that his quest is accomplished[1].

3. THE ADAPTATION OF THE FOLK-TALE TO THE PRE-CEDING NARRATIVE IN TRISTAN..

a) The heroine of the Voyage for Healing and the heroine of the Quest.

The redactor's unwillingness to furnish the hero
or the reader with a clue to the identity of the
princess, is peculiar to the Tristan story. We have
found nothing similar to it in the popular versions.

As we have shown in Chapter III[2] it is possible to
account for it only on the supposition that two episodes,
originally without connection, the story of a quest for
healing, and the story of the quest for an unknown
princess have been introduced independently, and
that the redactor of the *estoire* has modified them
only as much as is absolutely necessary. By
preventing the appearance of the heroine in person
in the story of healing, he has guarded against the
immediate recognition of the hair as belonging
to her[3]; by not giving the hero the directions
with which the other stories furnished him as to
the identity and the whereabouts of the Princess of
the Swallows' Hair, he further postpones the identification of the two heroines. He represents Tristan
as setting forth on the sea, here as in the *Tantris*

---

[1] *OX* 1863—72.
[2] Chap. III B 1 d, e, f.
[3] It would of course be natural for Pro to have seen Isolt.
cf. Bédier II, 212.

episode, without any effort at direction, or idea of a
goal. Eilhart cannot refrain at this point from a
criticism of the proceding:

> 'Ez was eine grôze kintheit,
> daz he sô michel erbeit
> bestunt umme den wint [1].'

But the redactor has succeeded, without any expense of invention, in enriching the story of Tristan
by two interesting exploits [2].

*b) The hero of the Voyage for Healing and the hero
of the Quest.*

The poet gives the hero the pseudonym Pro in
the first adventure, and makes Isolt heal Tristan by
messenger. In the second he gives him a new pseudonym, Tantris, and in this adventure for the first time
allows him to meet Isolt face to face. The Princess
of the Swallows' Hair is not known by Tristan —
nor by the reader — to be the princess who has
healed the hero, and the wooer is not known by Isolt
nor by the Irish, to be the Pro whom her plaster has
healed. It is a striking fact that in the Eilhart version
there is no reference to the previous visit throughout
the whole account of the quest or the remainder of the
romance. Tristan never reveals himself and is never

---

[1] *OX* 1473—6.
[2] The hypothesis that the episodes were originally independent obviates the difficulties in connection with the Tantris
recognition, which M. Bédier dismisses as insoluble, on his hypothesis of the unity of the narrative *ab incipio.* These are:
1. why Eilhart modified the episode of the healing of Tristan
by Isolt, modifying a 'donnée primitive et essentielle' and sub-
stituting a 'cure bizarre du blessé par messagers'; 2. why Eilhart does not contain the recognition of Tristan as Tantris.
Cf. Bédier II, 212, 221 i, 228.

recognized as the hero of the preceding adventure. Why does this recognition never take place? For the same reason, we believe, that we have postulated in regard to the identification of the heroine — because the episodes were originally separate, and the first redactors who introduced them into the same narrative did not work with a sufficiently free hand to amalgate them completely. The identification of the merchant of the second episode with the Pro of the first, like the identification of Mark's bride with the Isolt who had healed that Pro, was a process that took some time. Provision for such contingencies as the recognition of one personage by another is one of the marks of a regard for probability which is foreign to popular poetry and is still imperfect in the *estoire*.

Thomas, more critical, and bolder in his handling of the tradition, recognized the advantage to the plot to be secured by identifying the heroine of the quest from the outset with the heroine of the preceding adventure[1]. In reading the *estoire* the question could not fail to occur to Thomas, here as in a later incident[2]:

---

[1] Bédier I, Chap. XII. Cf. Gottfried's polemic against the Swallows' Hair 8605—8633, also *Sir Tristrem* 1366. There are numerous examples in popular literature of the development from the quest of an unknown princess to the quest of a known one, e. g., we have folk-tales of a definite princess called the Golden Haired Beauty, which are almost certainly developments of those of a princess sought by the token of her hair. Cf. Cosquin, *op. cit.* II, 302. The contrary process is almost inconceivable. Certainly it does not represent the tendencies of the Eilhart version; cf. Eilhart's criticism of Tristan's voyage to seek the Princess of the Swallows' Hair *OX* 1473—7. The scene of the recognition of Tristan as the slayer of Morholt in the Thomas versions betrays the Eilhart version as its point of departure. Cf. Piquet I, 109.

[2] 2143—2149. At the point in the story at which Tristan sends a messenger to Cornwall to beg her to come and heal his wound, Thomas departs from the version of the episode given in the *estoire* on the ground that in the redaction of it which he knew Tristan is said to have sent Gorvenal as messenger.

'E coment poüst il venir
Sun servise a la curt offrir
Al rei, as baruns, as serjanz,
Cum fust estrange marcheanz,
Si que hum issi coneüz
N'i fust mult tost aparceüz?'

In the later incident he substitutes Kaherdin for Gorvenal as the messenger; in the incident of the quest he provides for the inevitable recognition [1].

c) The merchant ruse.

The redactors leave the merchant ruse standing, although by the introduction of the dragon episode it has lost its value as a means of winning the princess, and is also superfluous as securing a welcome for Tristan. They retained it, no doubt, because it fell in with their tendency to multiply precautionary devices. It probably did not disturb them in the least that here, as in the voyage of Tristan and Kaherdin to Cornwall [2], the enterprise has become overburdened, in the course of transmission, with an accumulation of *motifs*, any one of which alone would insure its success.

d) The slayer of the Morholt and the wooer of Isolt.

α) The enigmatical smile.

The recognition of the wooer of Isolt as the slayer of the Morholt appears already in the Eilhart

---

[1] cf. 2107 ff.
'Seignurs, cest cunte est mult divers,
E pur ço l'uni par mes vers.'
[2] cf. supra, Chapt. IV B 7 a.

version. It is introduced by a method frequent in mediaeval fiction: the enigmatical smile of a person conscious of a secret arouses the curiosity of the person to
whom the poet wishes the secret to be made known,
the observer questions the person who has smiled, and
the latter is forced to explain the cause of his amusement[1]. In the recognition of Tristan as the slayer
of the Morholt the poet is forced to modify the device
slightly, for he has to bring about a double revelation:
Tristan's smile is caused by his recognition of Isolt as
the princess he is seeking for Mark, and her curiosity
about it leads to her recognition of him as the slayer
of the Morholt, by reminding her to clean his sword[2].
In the Thomas version, the first recognition having
become unnecessary, the examination of the sword,
caused in Eilhart by Tristan's smile, loses its motive.
The redactor is therefore reduced to attributing it to
mere curiosity[3]. It is clear that the point of departure
is in the *estoire*. The device is one that would readily
occur to a twelfth century poet.

β) Minor examples in the Tristan story of similar technique.

It may be worth while to cite other examples of
the simplicity of narrative technique which we find
in the *estoire*. We find something equivalent to the
enigmatical smile in a later episode in Tristan: Isolt,

---

[1] Similarly in a story in von der Hagen, *Gesammtabenteuer*
II, no. XXI, *Das Häselein*. Dr. Paton in *Publications of the
Modern Language Association*, XXII, 237; *Folklore* XVI, 1905,
419 ff.; O'Grady, *Silva Gadelica* II, 278—9; Benfey, *Orient und
Occident* 1864, II, 152, Frazer, *Arch. Review* I, 1888, 169—75;
R. Schmidt, *Märchen des Straparola*, p. 324; Larminie, *West Irish
Folk Tales* 17, 18.
[2] *OX* 1863—95.
[3] Bédier I, Ch. XIV, 132, II, 227—8.

Tristan's maiden wife, utters an exclamation when
the water splashes up under her robe. This arouses
Kaherdin's curiosity. He asks her what she has said,
and the poet is thus able to bring about the discovery
of the maiden marriage [1].

We have another example of similar technique
in the *estoire* in the scene on the road to the Blanche
Lande. Isolt is aware that Tristan is concealed in a
thorn-bush beside the road. She wishes to let him
know where he is to seek her that night. To do so
without exciting suspicion she addresses the birds
singing in the thorn-bush, begging them to fly thence
with her to the forest of the Blanche Lande and stay
with her there:

> 'dô sprach die vrauwe âne nît
> zu den vogelin die dâ sungin
>
> . . . .
> . . . . vlîget mit mir hinnen
> (des wil ich an ûch sinnen)
> zu Blankenwalde dâr ich sì
> und sît mir noch hînacht bî[2].'

In the similar incident that follows the poet is
confronted again with the necessity of appointing the
time and place for a meeting between the lovers. Not
wishing to repeat the same device, and yet apparently
unable to find another, he represents Isolt as standing
before the thornbush, and appeals to his audience for
conjectures as to how she conveyed the necessary information to Tristan:

> 'wie sie ez ane vînge
> daz sie sprêche ir lîbez lip?

---

[1] *OX* 6148—81.
[2] *OX* 6610—20.

wuste ich daz sie in icht
nâch ir schîre hîze komen!
sage, hâstû nicht vornomen,
ab sie es icht hîze?
„ich wêne sie des nicht lîze."
„wie wênestû?" „ich getrûwe ez wol."
„und wie dû?" „nein, ich sol
eir gedenken, eir ich trûwe."
„sô wizze daz in die vrauwe
in langer zît nî gesach!"
„ich wêne, ich des wol trûwen mach
daz sie in wêrlîche
bat vlîzlîche
nâch ir schiere komen dar
und wîsete on al rechte war[1].'

In other cases the poet represents his characters
as possessed of necessary information without disturbing himself as to how they obtained it. For example,
he feels it desirable that Tristan should express dis-
approval of Isolt's attempt upon Brangien's life. He
therefore tells us that Tristan learned of the plot
from Gorvenal and was angry[2]. The poet does not
trouble himself with the question of how Gorvenal
could have learned it. At the close of the romance
he puts the lament for the unhappy fate of the
lovers into the mouth of Mark, representing him in
a similar vague way as learning of the potion after
their death

'zewâre man im sagete,
daz hête gemachit ein trang[3].'

---

[1] *OX* 7628—45.
[2] *OX* 3067—76.
[3] *OX* 9470—2.

In the visit to Arthur's court the poet also takes it for granted that Tristan's relations with' Isolt are known to the knights there[1].

It is necessary for Isolt of the White Hands to know that the dying Tristan has sent for the queen. The poet makes no effort to explain how she gained this knowledge. He merely says:

> 'ich enweiz wer ez dô sagete
> Tristrandes wîbe[2].'

Thomas and the Prose Romance, more conscious of literary responsibility, provide independent explanations. The former tells us that Isolt listened at the wall while Tristan gave his directions to the messenger[3]. The Prose Romance (MS. 103) tells us that the messenger's daughter knew the secret and told it to the wife of Tristan[4].

Béroul and Thomas make similar efforts to supplement the account found in Eilhart in the incident of the Flour on the Floor. In Eilhart we are merely told that the wound of Tristan breaks open from the effort of leaping into Isolt's bed[5]. The poet does not inform us how Tristan got the wound. Béroul and Thomas furnish independent explanations. Béroul tells us that Tristan had been wounded in a boar hunt[6]; Thomas explains that Tristan had been bled that day[7].

---

[1] *OX* 5118—21.
[2] *OX* 9346—8.
[3] Bédier I, 396, ll. 2595—2639.
[4] Bédier II, 388.
[5] *OX* 3926—8.
[6] Béroul 716—20.
[7] Bédier I, Ch. XXIV, 203.

4. THE VALUE OF THE INCIDENT OF THE QUEST IN THE TRISTAN NARRATIVE.

The story of the wooing by proxy was valuable in the Tristan romance as preparation for the tragedy to follow. In the folk-tales of the quest by proxy, the lady won almost always remains the acquisition of the wooer [1]. The sympathies of the reader are inevitably with the hero of the quest rather than with a lay figure.

The story has accordingly more than once been used to introduce a tragedy of unlawful love. The Norse rimur of Harald Hringsbane [2] is the story of a fatal passion between the hero and the bride whom he has been sent to bring home to his father. In the *Thidreks saga* [3], Randver, the son of Eormenrich, goes to woo Swanhild for his father. 'It were more fitting that he should woo her for himself', says Bikki. The jealous father has his son hanged. Tennyson saw the value of sending Lancelot to woo Guinevere for Arthur [4]. Boccaccio and other commentators of Dante recount a similar story of Paolo and Francesca [5].

---

[1] E. g., the old king meets his death in an experiment with the water of death brought by the youth. Köhler, *loc. cit.* II, 328 ff.

[2] Kölbing, *Beiträge zur Kenntnis der älteren isländischen rimur*, in *Beiträge zur vergleichenden Geschichte der romantischen Poesie*, Breslau 1876, p. 227.

[3] *Thidreks saga af Bern*, ed. H. Bertel, Copenhagen 1905, 231—9.

[4] Tennyson, *Idylls of the King, Guinevere.*

[5] Boccaccio, Commentary to the Divine Comedy (*Inferno*, Canto V), Florence 1724, vol. 5, fac. 312 ff. Passage reprinted in Baldassarre Lombardi, *La Divina Commedia di Dante Alighieri*, Padova 1822, p. 125 n. b. A similar account by another Florentine commentator is reprinted in Scartazzini, *La Divina Commedia*, Leipzig 1874, I, p. 45, note A.

Everything in the treatment of the Quest in
Tristan betrays a redactor moulding the incident
with the conscious purpose of throwing into greater
relief the lines of a biographical tradition already
formed. The poet seems to have adopted the story
of the swallows' hair because it offered a method by
which Isolt might be made the wife of Mark without
Mark's being disloyal to Tristan. By this means Mark
endeavors to avoid refusing the demands of the
barons, and yet to escape the necessity of marrying.
Tristan's undertaking the quest is, to be sure, as
Eilhart remarks [1], a very midsummer madness. But
it was perhaps hardly less so to the poet who first
introduced it into the Tristan story than it is to us.
The imagination of writers of mediaeval romance
seems to have clung with peculiar fondness to stories
of deliverance from a dragon, and the Tristan poet
succumbs with the rest. Of the other supernatural
paraphernalia of the story of the Quest of the Princess
of the Golden Hair, the helpful animals, the extraordinary tasks demanded of the wooer, there is no trace.

C. THE SLAYING OF THE DRAGON.

The account of the slaying of the dragon belongs
to the group of stories which we shall discuss in the
next chapter in connection with the tribute demanded
by the Morholt. The Morholt episode is rationalized:
the Morholt is made an ordinary knight and the
struggle with him is represented as an ordinary chivalric combat. The incident of Tristan's combat with the

---

[1] *OX* 1473—6.

dragon, on the contrary, preserves almost all the typical features of primitive tradition. We are told that the monster is ravaging the country, destroying human beings and cattle with his fiery breath [1]. Tristan stations himself in a recess and attacks him, when he approaches, with spear and sword. This may be a reminiscence of the numerous stories, among them that of Siegfried, in which the hero digs a pit and attacks the dragon from below [2].

When he has slain the monster, Tristan cuts out its tongue and preserves it as evidence of his exploit. This trait also is typical, occurring almost invariably in popular accounts of the slaying of monsters [3]. It seems to represent a primitive practice. The tongue is of course a convenient trophy to carry.

In almost all the accounts of the slaying of a dragon, the hero is represented as falling into a

---

[1] cf. E. S. Hartland, *The Legend of Perseus*, London 1896, III, chs. XVI—XIX, cf. Hertz [2], *Tristan und Isolde*, 523; Golther, *Die Sage von Tristan und Isolde*, München 1887, p. 16; *Hist. Litt. de la France* XXX, 88 ff.; 116 ff.; 267 ff.; Cox, *Cinderella* 522; *Guy of Warwick*, ed. Zupitza, *EETS* (2nd or 15th century version, couplets) l. 6812 ff.; same from Auchinleck and Caius Manuscripts, p. 374—5 ff.; C. Hippeau, *La chanson du chevalier au cygne et de Godefroid de Bouillon*, Paris 1877, II, 210; cf. L. A. Paton, *The Story of Vortigern's Tower*, in *Radcliffe College Monographs* XV, Boston 1910, 14—15 for further bibliography.

[2] cf. supra Ch. II E; F. Panzer, *Studien zur germanischen Sagengeschichte* I, *Beowulf*, München 1910, p. 297—9, 305. II *Sigfrid*, 1912, p. 26 ff.

[3] cf. Golther, 1887, p. 15; A. Ritterhaus, *Die Neuisländischen Märchen*, Halle 1902, p. 38; E. S. Hartland, *The Legend of Perseus* III, Appendix, Table C; Frazer, *The Golden Bough*, 1900, II, 421 n. 2 (extensive bibliography); *The Sick-bed of Cuchulainn*, Atlantis I, 371; *Mélusine* III, 303; R. Köhler, *Kleinere Schriften*, 1900, III, pp. 303, 399, 430. — Frazer, *loc. cit.*, suggests that this custom is due to the primitive belief that the slain animal remains in relation with his tribe, and that cutting out his tongue prevents him from telling his fate to the live animals and thus frightening them away.

profound sleep, either before or after performing the exploit. In many cases, while waiting for the coming of the monster, he lays his head in the maiden's lap and is awakened only when her tears fall upon his face. In Tristan it is after the accomplishment of the exploit that the hero goes to a brook to refresh himself, and, lying down beside the water, falls asleep [1]. In some stories he awakes after a time and goes to the king to claim the reward. Tristan first regains consciousness when he feels Isolt bending over him. In this trait we see the hand of the conscious artist.

While the hero is sleeping, an impostor almost invariably discovers the dead dragon, and seeing traces of the struggle and no sign of the hero, infers that the victor has been devoured by the monster. He accordingly presents himself before the king as the slayer of the dragon and claims the reward [2]. In many cases he brings the dragon's head to confirm his account. When the real hero appears, he proves the falsity of the impostor's statements by producing the tongue. The use of head and tongue as proof and counterproof appears in Tristan only in the version of Thomas [3]. It is useless to attempt to decide whether this was the version of the *estoire* or whether Thomas is here supplementing the account by a detail which was familiar to him from other versions.

A combat with a dragon was a bit of narrative that could be fitted into almost any romantic biography.

---

[1] Hartland, *Perseus* III, Appendix, Table D.
[2] Hartland, *Perseus* III, 30, 47—8, Table C; cf. *Tyolet, Rom.* VIII, p. 47, 1. 485 ff. — *Robert le Diable*, ed. F. Löseth, *Soc. des anc. textes fr.* 1903, 1. 4006 ff.; Ritterhaus, *Neuisländische Märchen*, p. 42 (extensive bibliography).
[3] Bédier I, 117—41.

It has been interpolated, as Professor Röttiger has shown, into one manuscript of the Prose Romance, by a redactor acquainted with the *estoire*[1].

D. BRANGIEN.

1. THE SUBSTITUTION IN THE MARRIAGE BED ON THE WEDDING NIGHT.

For the maidservant to take the place of the bride on the wedding night is a frequent element in stories from popular tradition[2]. It forms the climax of a group of tales usually known as *The Forgotten Bride*. In this the maidservant is the heroine:

A girl who cherishes the hope of regaining a lover who has forgotten her, seeks service with the woman to whom he is about to be married. The bride, who has lost her virginity, begs the servant to take her place on the marriage night. The youth discovers that his bride has deceived him, and recognizes in the maidservant his lost betrothed[3].

---

[1] *op. cit.* 26. No other manuscript of the Prose Romance contains it. This fact seems to us to bear out the suggestion that the Prose Romance, extensively altered as it obviously is in its present form, is based on a version independent of the *estoire* and, perhaps, anterior to it.

[2] OX 2725—863; cf. supra Ch. II F; cf. P. Arfert, *Das Motiv von der untergeschobenen Braut in der internationalen Erzählungsliteratur*, Rostock dissertation, Schwerin 1897; *Revue des traditions populaires*, 1907, p. 1 ff.; M. Cox, *Cinderella*, Folk Lore Society, London 1892, p. 478 n. 8; 483 n. 14; 481 n. 13; F. J. Child, *English and Scottish Popular Ballads* s. v. *Substitution of maidservant*; *Zeitschr. des Vereins für Volkskunde*, VIII, 1898, p. 87, 90; Hertz, *Tristan und Isolde*[5], 533—5; B. Barth, *Liebe und Ehe im altfrz. Fablel*, *Palaestra* 97, Berlin 1910, p. 127; Golther, 1887, p. 18; Freymond, *Zeitschr. f. frz. Spr. u. Lit.* XVII, 128 n. 1; Köhler, *Kleinere Schriften* II, 399.

[3] Arfert 34.

There are numerous ballads of a bride who fears
discovery on her marriage night because a stranger
knight has robbed her of her virginity. She prevails
on another to take her place, but the deceit is
miraculously revealed. It develops that the bridegroom himself[1] was the stranger knight. In a group
of pious tales which illustrate the power of penitence,
the deceit on the wedding night forms one of a long
series of a woman's crimes[2].

In the type of story of which *Berte aus grans
piés* is the best known example, the maidservant, by
a ruse, usurps the place of the guiltless bride on the
marriage night. She contrives to keep the position
of queen and drives away the rightful bride. After
many years the deceit is discovered and the guilty
woman is punished[3].

In the Norse rimur of *Harald Hringsbane*, to
which we have referred in our discussion of the
quest, the ambassador and the bride whom he is
bringing home are seized during the voyage with a
fatal passion for each other. Harald decides to give
the maidservant to the king, and to keep the princess
for himself. On his arrival he conceals the latter
with a peasant family. Here the incident of the substitution takes on an entirely different significance
owing to its combination with the theme of the wooing
by proxy and its subordination to the love story. In
this case the popular elements are in the hands of an
artist who consciously subordinates events to character.

The substitution on the wedding night is utilized
in the Tristan story because of the poet's conviction

---

[1] Arfert, p. 44.
[2] Arfert, p. 39 ff., *Brangäne Erzählungen.*
[3] Arfert, p. 59 ff.

that the lovers belong first to each other. It has no consequences in the following narrative. Brangien fulfils the promised service and withdraws. She never betrays the secret. The poet seems to feel that this is her penance for her unfaithfulness to her charge.

2. THE MURDERERS.

A similar bit of popular tradition is found in Isolt's bribing the two men to do away with Brangien and to bring back to her a token of their deed[1]. The murderers are moved to pity and spare their victim, deceiving their master by a false token taken from some animal.

The story was current in many versions, and variations of detail must have been familiar to almost any redactor. Sometimes the murderers wait for the victim at the fountain; sometimes they take her to the forest. Sometimes one stays to guard her while the other returns to announce the accomplishment of the deed.

Critics of the Tristan story have endeavored to determine, by a comparison of this incident in Thomas and in Eilhart, which of the two treatments is the more primitive[2]. The task seems to us impossible. M. Bédier rejects the Eilhart version because the murderers are there represented as falling upon Brangien at the fountain in the castle grounds, and one murderer as being left to guard her while the other returns to report to the queen[3]. M. Bédier considers these traits less primitive because they make

---

[1] OX 2863—3081; cf. supra Ch. II G; Bédier I, 158; cf. Golther 1887, op. cit., p. 17; Cox, Cinderella 475; Hertz[5], 533, 536, 567; Scheler, Berte aus grans piés, Bruxelles 1874, p. 11 ff.
[2] Bédier II, 243; Zenker, Rom. Forsch. XXIX, 331—3.
[3] OX 2967—74.

the story less probable. Brangien's screams, he objects,
would have been heard at the castle, and Isolt's suspicions would have been aroused by the failure of the
second murderer to return with his companion. It
seems to us unlikely that these considerations would
have influenced a popular narrator. Probability is
not a primary concern in popular tradition. Variants
in such details, in cases where both variants are
supported elsewhere in popular tradition, are value-
less, it seems to us, in throwing light on the relation
of two literary versions. Variants of this sort are the
only ones that we find in the stories of Brangien.

We should also hesitate to consider the version of
which we have the earliest written record as necessarily the most primitive. Professor Zenker takes this
ground in citing the fact that a version which presents details in closer agreement with Eilhart than
with Thomas is found in the oldest manuscript in
which the story has been noted as occurring in western
Europe — the *Book of Leinster* [1]. A traditional story
may, however, have undergone more modifications at
the hands of one narrator in the ninth century than it
presents in versions taken down from oral tradition
a thousand years afterward [2]. The incidents about
Brangien are merely additional evidence that the
romance has drawn largely from popular tradition,
and that this material appears in the *estoire* with very
slight modifications.

When threatened with death by the two murderers, Brangien recounts her services to the queen, declaring that she has never deserved this fate.
Among the sacrifices that she has made for Isolt

---

[1] *Romanische Forschungen* XXIX, 383.
[2] cf. Herodotus version, of *The Blades at the Bed*, v. infra.

she relates the following: When they departed
from Ireland together, she and her young mistress
received from the queen two white chemises. Isolt's
was soiled during the voyage, and Brangien, yielding
to her pleading, lent her own to the princess for her
wedding night [1].

We find frequently in oral tradition that a shirt
is given by a wife to her husband with the assurance
that as long as it remains white, he may be confident
of her faithfulness. It will become spotted if she is
false to him [2]. There is hardly room to doubt that
in the mind of the popular narrator the appearance
of the shirt actually did indicate the virtue of the
giver. The Tristan redactors are far from this naïve
attitude. If this trait had ever formed part of the
Tristan story in its original context and with its
original literal meaning, it would have been modified
or obliterated in the course of the development of
the tradition, by redactors who disapproved of such
credulity. But here, as in the story of the substitution
on the wedding night, the traditional context is ignored,
and the trait is presented with no effort to rationalize
it. The story appears to be adopted as an allegory,
a convenient manner of treating a delicate subject.

3. ALLUSIONS TO BRANGIEN IN THE FOLLOWING NARRATIVE.

After the incident of the Tryst under the Tree,
Brangien practically disappears from the narrative. She

---

[1] *OX* 2912—59.
[2] Grimm, *Deutsche Sagen*, Berlin 1866, No. 537; Child,
Ballads 1, 268 (extensive bibliography); Hartland, *Perseus* II,
25. 27. The faith token in Eastern tales is usually a flower.
cf. *Tristan*, Prose Romance, Bédier II, 345.

is not present, as we might expect, in the trying scenes of
the condemnation of the lovers, nor to welcome them on
their return from the .forest.   In the episode in which
Tristan justifies his boast to Kaherdin, she is utilized
to form a unit in the series of beautiful women of
which the climax is Isolt, and to protect the lovers
that night from disturbance from the king.   The
central figure of the sub-plot in this episode is, however, Camille, who here appears for the first time[1].
In the following visit, Camille has entirely replaced
Brangien, and we are informed in twenty lines,
without any particulars, that Brangien is dead[2].   We
are tempted to account for this peculiar combination
as follows: The story of Camille and her pillow
belongs with passages of later date and more courtly
character than those in which Brangien figured[3].   The
narrative being modified, at some stage in the development of the tradition, to include the incident of
Camille, the timid redactor retained for its heroine
the name which appeared in the account he appropriated.   In order to explain the absence of
Brangien, who would naturally have had this rôle
in the older tradition, he hit upon the explanation
that she was dead.   It seems hardly possible that a
poet with liberty to create his story, would have
arbitrarily condemned Brangien to a colorless exit
from the romance, merely to invent another person,
of the same attributes, to take her place.   The fact
that Thomas, with his less conservative attitude toward the tradition, and his tendency to unify the
narrative, promptly effaced the upstart Camille and

---

[1] *OX* 6468 ff.
[2] *OX* 7560—82.
[3] cf. Ch. IV.

extended the role of Brangien [1] through the latter portion of the story, is, it seems to us, a point in favor of this view.

E. THE TRYST UNDER THE TREE.

The means by which Tristan makes known to Isolt his presence at the fountain will be discussed among the elements of the Tristan story that seem to be survivals of Celtic tradition. The ruse by which the lovers deceive the king when he overhears their interview there, presents nothing strikingly original. When Tristan has reached the trysting place and sent the signal, he notices the image of the king in the water [2]. In order to warn Isolt he refrains from advancing to meet her according to his custom. She is thus put on her guard, and she too discovers the presence of the king. They accordingly take care that their bearing and conversation shall convince him of their innocence. This account may easily have been put together from such stories as the following:

A prince of Sind feigns madness in order to protect himself from the jealousy of his brother. The latter is suspicious and sets a spy upon him. The spy observes him from a tree, while he is praying. The prince, seeing the shadow of the spy, convinces his brother of his madness by rending his garments and rushing away screaming [3].

---

[1] Bédier I, p. 330 ff, Ch. XXXIV.
[2] The fountain is the ordinary place for lovers' meetings in the courtly as well as the popular lyric. A. Jeanroy, *Les origines de la poésie lyrique au moyen âge*, Paris 1904, p. 161, 199.
[3] Rainaud, *Fragments arabes et persans inédits, relatifs à l'Inde*, Paris 1845, p. 25 ff.

Although the scene is different, the circumstances
and the principle of the ruse are the same as in
Tristan in several stories in the *Pantschatantra*, and
the *Cukasaptati* [1]. For example: A woman who has
invited her lover to meet her, discovers, as she approaches him, that her husband is observing her from a
a place of concealment. She accordingly pretends to be
on terms of innocent friendship with her companion and
relates to him a story that will reassure the listening
husband. She tell him that she has invited him because
she has learned from the goddess that the one means
to insure long life to her spouse is to preserve her
chastity in the arms of another. The husband's
anxiety as to his wife's virtue is entirely set at rest.
He discredits the informers who have aroused his
suspicion and overwhelms with gratitude the pair
that have deceived him.

F. THE BLADES AT THE BED.

1. THE ACCOUNT IN TRISTAN.

On account of its frank barbarity, and because
it required a background more primitive than a
twelfth century feudal castle, M. Bédier included the
incident of the Blades at the Bed among the Celtic
features of the tradition [2]. The knights of Arthur
are all quartered, as the reader will remember, in

---

[1] Benfey, *Pantschatantra*, Leipzig 1859, II, Bk. 3, XI, 258
—61; cf. Richard Schmidt, *Çukasaptati*, Kiel 1894, p. 35 (XIX),
45 (XXIII).
[2] Bédier II, 158—9; cf. G. Huet, *Sur un épisode du Tristan
d'Eilhart d'Oberg*, *Romania* XXXVI, 50 ff.

the same sleeping apartment with the king and queen. Mark places the blades at the bed of Isolt: Tristan is wounded in approaching her. He returns to his bed, bewailing his mischance. With the friendly purpose of diverting suspicion from him, the other knights purposely wound themselves in a similar manner. It is accordingly impossible for Mark to convict Tristan[1].

2. MARKING THE CULPRIT.

A device to mark a criminal in the act of committing a crime is a feature of the folk-tale of the Master Thief. In this story the clever rascal thus marked, finding it impossible to remove the evidence of his guilt, saves himself by branding a number of innocent persons in a similar manner.

The oldest recorded example of this story is in Herodotus[2], but numerous versions from popular tradition present traits of the story lost or consciously modified in the Greek version. The context in which the double ruse usually occurs is the following[3]:

A youth has distinguished himself by a series of clever thefts. All efforts to convict him have been vain. One of the traps set for him is the following:

---

[1] *OX* 5304—462, Ch. II. O.

[2] Herodotus II, 121.

[3] For a discussion of this story and an extensive bibliography, cf. R. Köhler, *Kleinere Schriften*, ed. Bolte, Weimar 1898, I, 200—10; W. A. Clouston, *Popular Tales and Fictions*, London 1887, II, 115 —65, 480; G. Huet, *Romania* XXVI, 50 ff. Add Ed. Huber, *Bull. de l'école franç. d'extreme Orient* IV, 1904, *Etudes de littérature bouddhique*, Le Trésor du roi Rhampsinite, p. 701 ff.; J. Rivière, *Recueil de contes populaires de la Kabylie du Djurdjura*, Paris 1882, p. 13 ff. (*Les deux frères*). Add F. Boas, *Indianische Sagen von der nordpazifischen Küste Amerikas*, Berlin 1895, p. 27, no. 11; p. 37, no. 4; p. 41, no. 5; Jas. Teit, *Traditions of the Thompson River Indians*, Boston 1898, p. 62, no. XVI.

A number of suspected persons are invited to sleep
in the palace. The prince is convinced that the master
thief and he alone will be bold enough to approach
his daughter, and he directs her to mark him by
cutting off his moustache. His expectation is justified.
But the rogue is not convicted. He goes to the
other knights and cuts the moustache of each in
the same way as his own. The prince sets another
trap: the girl is to cut off the rascal's hand. But the
master thief has armed himself with the hand of his
dead brother, and on the following day no one-handed
man is to be found. Having received overwhelming
proof of the youth's superior cunning, the prince ab-
dicates in his favor.

3. SLEEPING ARRANGEMENTS.

This story, with variations of detail, appears
very frequently in mediaeval literature, and has been
collected in widely different districts from popular
tradition. It implies very primitive sleeping arrangements, such as may be found among primitive tribes
today, and as are recorded of the Celts and Teutons
in their earliest records. The right side of the house
is the men's side; the left side is the women's side[1].
The description of the houses in Old Irish literature
is similar. For example the royal house prepared for
King Conchobar is described, in *Fled Bricrend*, as
follows:

The House was made on this wise: on the plan
of Tara's Mead-Hall, having nine compartments from
fire to wall, each fronting of bronze thirty feet

---

[1] E. S. Hartland, *Folk Lore* XVII, 1906, p. 480; Frazer,
Totemism and Exogamy, London 1910, II, 328, 341; O'Curry,
Manners, I, CCCLIII.

high, overlaid with gold. In the forepart of the
palace a royal couch was erected for Conchobar, high
above those of the whole house. It was set with
carbuncles and other precious stones which shone
with a lustre of gold and silver, radiant with every
hue, making night look like unto day. Around it
were placed the twelve couches of the twelve heroes
of Ulster[1] .... The half of the palace was set apart
for Conchobar and his retinue of valiant Ulster heroes;
the other half [was reserved] for the ladies of Ulster
attending on Mugan, daughter of Eochaid Fedlech,
wife of King Conchobar[2].

In the story of the Conception of Cuchulainn it
is said[3]:

> They feared that Conchobar, in a moment of drunkenness,
> had rendered his sister pregnant, for she slept beside him.

Among the Teutons, as among the Celts, both
sexes lived together and slept in the same room. At
evening the floor was strewn with straw or rushes,
and each lay down under or in front of the bench
where he had sat. In order to guard against in-
decencies, lights were kept burning through the night.
The men lay at one side of the room, the women at
the other[4].

In the twelfth century in France, the sleeping
arrangements were more commodious. The master and
mistress slept in one room, the maidservants to-

---

[1] *Fled Bricrend,* ed. E. Windisch, *Irische Texte* I, Leipzig
1880, p. 254 ff. Engl. translation by G. Henderson (*Irish Texts
Society*), § 2.
[2] *op. cit.* § 12.
[3] Windisch, *Irische Texte* I, 139, l. 10—11, 26—27; cf. translation by L. Duvau in d'Arbois de Jubainville, *L'épopée celtique en
Irlande,* Paris 1892, p. 38. § 6, *Rev. Celt.* IX, 12.
[4] K. Weinhold, *Die deutschen Frauen in dem Mittelalter,*
Wien 1882, II, 107.

gether in another, and the men servants together in
a third. But it is certain that the accomodations,
especially during seasons of hospitality, were often
inadequate, and the host had to make what shift he
could to shelter his guests[1].

The story we are discussing is no doubt, in its
origin, the product of a society in which the men
and women slept in the same room. But its popularity persisted after these conditions had changed. In
certain versions of the story the redactor explains
that the quartering of the men in the same room
with the princess was an unusual arrangement[2]. In
other versions the writers find it desirable to suppress
the trait that the princess sleeps in the same room
with the men. They tell us that she slept in a room
apart[3]. The hero is thus forced to make a second
visit to her apartment, in order to get the box
containing the color with which she marked him.
Two of the redactors of the Tristan story, Heinrich
von Freiberg[4] and the redactor of the French Prose
Romance[5], modify the incident in this way.

But most of the redactors appropriate the story
in its original form. In *Il Pecorone* of Ser Giovanni,
the girl lies in the midst of the knights[6].

---

[1] Schultz, *Höfisches Leben*, I, 96 (bibliog.); *Flamenca*, ed.
P. Meyer, l. 200—8; Ulrich von Zatzikhoven, *Lanzelet*, ed. K. Hahn,
l. 831; *La chanson des Saxons par Jean Bodel*, ed. F. Michel,
Paris 1839, II, 169, l. 12 ff.

[2] *Mélanges tirés d'une grande bibliothèque*, Pt. V, *Romans
du seizième siècle*, sect. I, Paris 1780, H, p. 273 ff. (*Histoire du noble
chevalier Berinus*).

[3] *Li romans de Dolopathos*, ed. C. Brunet and A. de
Montaiglon, Bibliothèque Elzeverienne, Paris 1856, l. 6247—9.

[4] Heinrich von Freiberg, *Tristan*, ed. Bechstein, Ch. IV.

[5] Bédier II, 355—6; Löseth § 48.

[6] Ser Giovanni, *Il Pecorone* IX, 1.

il Doge fe fare in una sua sala venticinque letta, dove ciascun di questi giovani dormiva nel suo; e poi fece fare nel mezzo della sala un ricco letto dove dormiva la figliuola.

Similarly, in the version of the *Seven Sages* edited by Rajna,

'nela zanbra con voi lei starase[1].'

In the *Histoire du noble chevalier Berinus*, the knights sleep in beds around the hall with the princess in the midst[2].

Likewise in *De Deif van Brugghe*, a Low German poem of the fourteenth or fifteenth century,

'und jewelyk up synen bedde lycht
und juwe dochter ys darmede[3].'

Eilhart also preserves the story in its original form, remarking that the kings of Tristan's time were not well provided with sleeping rooms[4].

The primitive character of the sleeping arrangements does not furnish, as M. Bédier was inclined to believe, an indication that the incident belonged to the Celtic tradition of Tristan.

4. THE SHARPENED BLADES.

In the stories of the Master Thief, the girl, being the accomplice of the father, can always be depended upon to mark the rascal when he comes to her.

---

[1] *Storia di Stefano, figliuolo d'un imperatore di Roma, versione in ottava rima del libro dei sette savi*, ed. Pio Rajna, Bologna 1880, Canto IX, p. 99.

[2] *Mélanges tirés d'une grande bibliothèque*, H, p. 273 ff.; cf. Clouston, *op. cit.* II, 129.

[3] *ZfdA.* V, 1845, p. 385—404, lines 616—8 cited.

[4] *OX* 5285—300.

Isolt, on the contrary, is in league with Tristan. It
is accordingly necessary for the Tristan redactor to
arrange some other means to mark the person who
approaches her. The device was not far to seek. In
a number of versions of the Master Thief the king
discovers the passage by which the thief enters to
steal the royal treasure and protects himself by placing
a trap around the vessels containing it. This trap
consists of wheels provided with razor blades[1].

In another widely current folk-tale, sharpened
blades are set to wound a lover endeavoring to
approach a lady. The story is best known in Marie
de France's lay of *Yonec* and the Countess of Aulnoy's
Blue Bird. Here the lover visits his mistress in the
form of a bird. The jealous husband, or stepmother,
learning of his visits, has knives, razors, and daggers
fixed outside the window. The bird is wounded on
these instruments.

> 'Des engins faire fu hastis
> a ocire le chevalier.
> Broches de fer fist granz furgier
> e acerer les chiés devant:
> suz ciel n'a rasur plus trenchant[2].
>
> . . . .
>
> devant la dame el lit descent,
> que tuit li drap furent sanglent
> E le veit le sanc e la plaie.
> mult anguissement s'esmaie[3].
>
> . . . .

---

[1] F. M. Luzel, *Contes populaires de basse Bretagne*, III, 356,
368; cf. *Melusine* I, 18, I, 587; J. Rivière, *Recueil de contes populaires de la Kabylie du Djurdjura*, Paris 1882, p. 13 ff.
[2] ed. Warnke, *Lais, op. cit.*, *Yonec* VII, 1. 288—93.
[3] *Yonec* 319—23.

Il n'i puet dunc demurer mes,
kar sa plaie seignot adés.
A grant dolur s'en est partiz
E le siut a mult halz criz.
Par une fenestre s'en ist[1].

The same device appears frequently in folk-tales
and mediaeval romances[2]. In the story of the *Fan
Prince*, the jealous sisters place pieces of broken glass
on the heroine's bridal bed.

In a less fantastic account in the Norse *Cormacsaga*[3] we find the hero hindered by a similar means
from approaching his lady.

> It happened one day that Cormac came to Tongue.
> Stangerd was in the big room sitting on the dais. Thorweg's
> sons were sitting in the big room and were ready to make
> an assault on Cormac as he walked in; and Thorkel had
> set a drawn sword on one side of the door and Narve set
> a scythe on a long handle on the other side. But when
> Cormac came to the hall door *he perceived their trickery, for
> Stangerd beckoned to him; and he held up his shield and
> drove it* against the scythe and bent it, and hit the sword
> *with the iron bound edge of it* and broke a great shard out
> of it, and he turned back forthwith and quoth the verse:

> The scythe struck against Hrungne's footstand [the shield]
> The sword got a shard cut out of it.

---

[1] *Yonec* 337—42.
[2] O. M. Johnston, *Publications of the Modern Language
Association of America*, XX, 1905, p. 330 ff.; *Romania* X, 122—4;
Harvard, *Studies and Notes in Philology and Literature*, VIII
(A. C. L. Brown, *Iwain*), p. 75—82; *Voyage of Bran*, ed. Meyer and
Nutt, I, 78; *Hero Tales of Ireland*, ed. J. Curtin, p. 168—72;
Myths and Folk Lore of Ireland, ed. J. Curtin, p. 94; E. S. Hartland (*Primitive Paternity* II, 65) notes that it is a custom among
the Tiyans for a knife to be placed in the door frame while one
husband is with a woman, in sign to the other husbands that
entrance is forbidden them.
[3] G. Vigfusson and F. York Powell, *Origines Icelandicae*,
Oxford 1905, *Cormacsaga* II, 327, § 5.

5. CONCLUSION.

The treatment of Arthur and his knights in the incident of the Blades at the Bed inclines us to attribute it, in its present form, to a French redactor of the latter half of the twelfth century. As is conventional in early French Arthurian romance, it is Gawain who seeks a means of saving Tristan, and it is Kay who hits upon the scheme of having all the knights mark themselves similarly. It is to the generosity of his friends and not to his own ingenuity, as in the case of the Master Thief, that the hero owes his escape.

G. THE FOOTPRINT ON THE FLOOR.

The spreading of the flour on the floor[1] is another attempt to trap the Master Thief. In the traditional account he outwits his enemies in this case as in the other by a counter-ruse. The Tristan redactor does not adopt the counter-ruse, for he must bring about the condemnation of the lovers and the flight to the forest.

An Italian version of the *Master Thief* gives what we take to be the traditional *denouement*[2]. In this story the branding of the culprit and the spreading of the flour upon the floor are both employed in the hope of convicting the rascal. The girl is directed to mark the youth each time that he comes to

---

[1] *OX* 3821—943.
[2] Rajna, *Storia di Stefano, versione in ottava rima del libro dei sette savi*, p. 100 stanza 34, p. 102 stanza 41.

her. The hero perceives the mark after he has been branded three times. He then goes to the beds of the others and marks each of them three or four times. On returning to rest he notices for the first time the flour on the floor. He accordingly completes his work by tracing and retracing his steps from each bed to the bed of the girl as many times as he has marked each youth.

In the Tristan story the hero perceives the trap and avoids it by leaping to Isolt's bed. The story must proceed, however. Tristan must be convicted. When the dwarf gives the alarm, and Tristan knows himself discovered, he leaps back to his own bed. He is weakened by loss of blood, for his wound has burst open. His foot touches the floor in one spot. Lest this should seem too slight an indication of guilt, the poet adds that Isolt was covered with the blood from Tristan's wound. This last trait may be due to the influence of the story of the Blades at the Bed.

H. INCIDENTS ASSOCIATED WITH ARTHURIAN ROMANCE.

1. INTRODUCTION.

In a considerable number of incidents loosely connected with the main narrative, none of which bear marks of survival from a primitive period of the tradition, Tristan is brought into contact with Arthur and his knights. These incidents are stories universally current in mediaeval fiction. The treatment of Arthurian tradition in them is characteristic of

French romance of the period of the extant redactions.
It would seem, therefore, that we owe them to French
redactors. The purpose of introducing them into the
narrative seems to have been to associate Tristan
with a popular cycle with which his story had a
certain affinity.

2. THE AMBIGUOUS OATH.

The story of the ambiguous oath in the continuation of Béroul is connected with the Arthurian
cycle by the account of Isolt's begging Arthur
to be witness to her justification. The incident is
as follows[1]:

> Although Tristan has gone into exile, the three barons
> still continue to torment the king. One day as he stops
> to watch some peasants burning thorns to fertilize the soil,
> the barons remind him that Isolt has not yet publicly proved
> her innocence. They insist on his requiring her to do
> it. Unreasonable as the demand is, Mark fears to anger
> his barons; they have strong castles and great power
> to injure him. Isolt notices his trouble and prevails upon
> him to tell her the cause. She offers to justify herself
> publicly by an oath, with King Arthur as witness. She
> sends a message to Tristan, who has not really gone into
> exile, but has concealed himself in order to be in readiness
> to serve her. He is to disguise himself as a leper and
> be at the *Mal Pas* on the day appointed. Tristan enters
> into the plan in high spirits. The messenger proceeds
> to Arthur's court, inquiring his way of a shepherd
> whom he meets playing his pipe. Arthur is delighted to
> hear from Queen Isolt, and promises in advance anything
> that she may ask. There is general sympathy for Isolt
> among his knights, and dire threats are made against the
> barons. Arthur's courtiers, magnificently dressed, set out

---

[1] Béroul 3032—4269.

for Mark's court, telling stories as they go. The leper is already at the *Mal Pas*. He recounts unblushingly the cause and course of his disease, begging alms for charity's sake. Arthur takes off his gaiters and gives them to him; Mark gives him his ermine head covering. When the three barons pass, they inquire of the wretch the best way to avoid the mud. Tristan does not miss the opportunity to plunge them into the deepest of it. Isolt prevails upon Dynas, her escort, to allow her to cross last, and alone. From the other side of the pass the court are all watching her. She ties up the trappings of her horse and sends it across unburdened. Then she calls to the leper. He demurs, but she prevails upon him to carry her over on his back. He falls with her. When she leaves him, she refuses to give him alms. 'He is a rascal', she declares, 'and has plenty in the leather sack under his mantle'. The kings are amused. They encamp at the Blanche Lande that night. At daybreak preparations are made for the ceremony. The relics are arranged on a rich cloth. Arthur reproves Mark for suspecting his wife. Isolt takes her place between the two kings, and Gawain stands near the relics. Isolt volunteers the oath. She calls God and the saints to witness that she has had intercourse with none,

> 'Fors le ladre qui fist que some,
> Qui me porta outre les guez,
> Et li rois Marc mes esposez[1].'

The spectators can endure no more. 'It is enough', says Arthur. He declares that from this time those who accuse Isolt will have to reckon with him. The assembly disperses.

In the Thomas version the incident is similar, but there is no association of it with Arthur. It is introduced directly after the attempt to prove the lovers' guilt by the flour on the floor. But the evidence against them is not conclusive: Tristan has succeeded in his leap, and the only indication of the

---

[1] Béroul 4207—10.

lovers' guilt is the blood in the two beds. Mark requires Isolt to justify herself by the ordeal of the red hot iron. Certain details of the incident are also different from the version of Beroul. Tristan is disguised as a pilgrim; he carries the queen from the boat to land. Isolt's appearance and behaviour are calculated to inspire pity for her miserable state, rather than admiration for her beauty and courage[1].

It is possible that the episode was in the *estoire*, and was omitted by Eilhart[2].

The story of the ambiguous oath was one of the most popular tales of feminine ruse in mediaeval fiction. It is found in the *Çukasaptati* and other oriental story books[3]. It appears in the Norse *Grettissaga*[4] and in many other occidental versions[5]. The details vary, but the general circumstances are the same, and the equivocation is always of the same character.

A woman is accused of having had unlawful intercourse with a certain man. She is guilty of the charge. Her lover disguises himself as a repulsive

---

[1] Bédier I, 203, XXIV; cf. II, 259—63, esp. 261, for a discussion of the principle underlying the modifications made by Thomas.

[2] cf. supra Ch. III, p. 105, 106.

[3] *Çukasaptati*, ed. Richard Schmidt, Kiel 1894, p. 30 (15th story); *Pantschatantra,* ed. Benfey, 457—59, § 186; *Mongolische Märchen, Die neun Nachtragserzählungen des Siddhi-Kür,* Innsbruck 1868, ed. B. Jülg, p. 111; *Mélanges de littérature orientale,* ed. Cardonne, la Haye 1788, p. 23. (*La femme justifiée.*)

[4] *Grettissaga,* ed. R. C. Bœr (*Altnordische Sagabibliothek,* 8), Cap. LXXXIX.

[5] H. von Wlislocki, *Die Episode des Gottesgerichtes in Tristan und Isolde unter den transsilvanischen Zeltzigeunern und Rumänen, Zeitschr. f. vergl. Lit.-Gesch.* I, 457; Erwin Rohde, *Der griechische Roman,* Leipzig 1900, p. 515, § 484 n. 1; E. B. Cowell, *The Jataka,* Cambridge 1895, no. 62; Dunlop-Liebrecht, *Geschichte der Prosadichtung,* Berlin 1851, p. 500, no. 4; For further bibliography v. Köhler, *Kleinere Schriften* I, 513.

beggar, or as a fool, and contrives to touch her in the sight of her accusers. When she is called upon to swear to her innocence she declares that no man has ever touched her except her husband and the wretched being who has approached her in their sight. The ordeal proves the truth of her statement, and her accusers must perforce be satisfied.

The story was frequently told in connection with the magician Virgil[1]. Persons accused of crime who protested their innocence, were allowed to take an oath, holding the hand meanwhile in the mouth of a bronze serpent made by Virgil. If the oath was false, the hand was bitten off. A certain woman, accused of adultery, claimed the privilege of attesting her innocence by this means. She had previously arranged with her lover that he should disguise himself as a fool and stand beside her, apparently by chance, in the crowd. She then swears, in the presence of all, that she has had no more to do with the man with whom she is accused of sin than with the fool beside her. She withdraws her hand unhurt, for she has told no lie. Virgil, comprehending the ruse, and piqued that a woman should outwit his art, destroys the oracle.

We shall not attempt to determine the origin of the accounts in the Tristan redactions[2].

---

[1] D. Comparetti, *Virgilio nel medio evo*, Livorno, 1872 II, 280; du Meril, *Mélanges archéologiques et littéraires*, Paris 1850, *Extrait de la Fleur des histoires*, p. 444 ff.

[2] Previous studies on the Ambiguous Oath: J. Grimm, *Deutsche Rechtsaltertümer*, Leipzig 1899, II, 574; Hertz[5], *op. cit.* 544—6; Golther, *op. cit.* 1907, 28—9, 59—63; *op. cit.* 1887, 13—15.

I. TRISTAN'S DISGUISES.

1. GENERAL.

The disguise which the lover assumes in order
to verify the ambiguous oath of his mistress is different in different stories. There are legions of instances in mediaeval fiction in which the hero disguises himself in order to accomplish a purpose. It
seems futile to attempt to classify them. They occur
in ballads, romances, and history with inevitable uniformity. The favorite disguises are of course those
of wandering classes, such as traders, pilgrims, lepers,
minstrels, and fools. All of these occur in the tradition of Tristan. Each poet rings the changes on the
theme, elaborating it in each case with details chosen
to please his particular audience. We have one of
these stories in the Welsh triad [1]:

> Tristan, son of Tallwch, disguised as a swineherd, tended
> the swine of Mark, son of Meirchyon, while the swineherd
> went with a message to Isolt. Arthur, Mark, Kay, and
> Bedivere came all four, but they did not succeed in carrying
> off a single sow, either by ruse, or violence, or theft.

2. TRISTAN THE FOOL.

*a) The account in Tristan compared with the popular
versions.*

The experience of the lover who disguises himself as a fool in order to approach his lady appears
in numerous versions in mediaeval story books. It

---

[1] cf. supra, Ch. I, p. 2 n. 1.

is curious to observe how closely the narrative of Tristan[1], although it suppresses most of the characteristic features, corresponds to the traditional story in the details which it has preserved[2].

In *Die halbe Birn*, as in Tristan, the idea of the disguise has been suggested by another.

In Eilhart:

> 'dir ist daz hâr abe geschorn.
> swer dich eir hête irkant,
> dû wordest denne im genant,
> sô weiz her nicht, wer dû bist.
> nû soldest dû mit diner list
> aleine dar hin gân
> und einen kogilroc nemen an,
> tôrlîche dû gebâre:
> sô wênen die hûtâre
> dû sîst ein rechter affe[3].
>
> . . . .
> he trûg einen kolben grôz[4].'

Similary in *Die halbe Birn*.

> 'Werfent von iu dise wât
> und verandernt iuch, daz ist min rât,
> Und werdent ze eime tôren,
> lânt iu obe den ôren
> Daz hâr [alles] garwe abe nemen;
> diu kleit diu tœrlîche(e) gezemen,
>
> ein[en] kolben swaer' alsam ein blî
> Den nement ze eime leite stabe[5].'

---

[1] cf. Ch. II, W.
[2] F. Liebrecht, *Zur Volkskunde*, Heilbronn 1879, p. 141—54.
[3] *OX* 8700—10.
[4] *OX* 8722.
[5] F. von der Hagen, *Gesammtabenteuer*, Stuttgart 1850, I, x, p. 207—25, l. 141—55. *(Die halbe Birn.)*

The hero gratefully accepts the suggestion, and carries it out. His actions in both stories are similar, and cause similar amusement and consternation.

> 'he was sô affenlîch getân
> und hâte solch gebêre,
> daz sie wânden er wêre
> gewislîche ein tôre.
> sie zogin in bî den ôren
> und begundin mit im spiln:
> des leit he von in harte vil [1].'

But when Andret tries to tease him he is not so patient, and barely lets him go with his life [2].

Similarly amusing to the bystanders is the fool in *Die halbe Birn*

> 'beide, wîp unde man
> Sahen in vür einen gief;
> . . . .
> si machten alle ûz im irn grûs
> Und triben mit ime irn schimpf [3].'

But here too the fool does mischief

> 'vaste sluog er umbe sich,
> Mit sînre herten kiulen
> maht' er starke biulen
> Den knehten die dâ liefen
> Und ime „tore"! riefen;
> Doch muosten si'z ver guot hân
> von dem tôrehten man;
> Wan der mit tôren schimpfen wil,
> der muoz verdulden narren spil [4].'

---

[1] *OX* 8764—70.
[2] *OX* 8771—87.
[3] *Die halbe Birn*, l. 184—94.
[4] *Die halbe Birn*, l. 198—207.

The fool's place is under the steps, the humble
refuge traditional in mediaeval narratives[1], *under die
treppin in irer kemenâtin*, says Eilhart. *Vür der
kemenâten tür*, says *Die halbe Birn*[2]. The lady learns
of the presence of the fool, and invites him to her.
She has a comfortable place given him, usually before
the fire. In Eilhart:

> 'des tôren hîz die vrauwe dô
> gar vlîzlîche plegen
> und hîz im dô zu wege
> stetelîchen betten
> undir die treppin
> in irer kemenâtin
> dâ wart her wol berâtin[3].'

In a similar story, cited by Liebrecht:

> 'Do sprach die fraw bald: „Lat in rein"!
> Wir welln heint frolich mit im sein.
>
> . . . .
>
> Zum ofen furten sie in do
> Dass im die wermd anschin dest bass,
> Wan er gar fast erkaltet was[4].'

In *Die halbe Birn*:

> 'In die kemenâten
> sizzen si in bâten
> Nider zuo dem viure[5].'

In the typical story, as in Tristan,

---

[1] *OX* 8928—30; cf. *Girart de Roussillon*, trad. P. Meyer,
Paris 1884, p. 242, n. 1 (bibliography).
[2] *Die halbe Birn*, l. 227.
[3] *OX* 8924—31.
[4] Liebrecht p. 148, l. 59—61, 72—5.
[5] *Die halbe Birn*, l. 251—4.

'gûte vûge hâte he dar zû
daz ez nîman enwiste [1].'

But in the typical story the lady grants her favor
because she believes the fool really mad, taking
advantage of the immunity from discovery thus
furnished her.

The remainder of the traditional story is not used
in Tristan.

b) *The cheese.*

The Tristan redactor relates that the fool is given
a piece of cheese while he is on the voyage.

'dô wart im kêse gegebin
den he solde ezzin.
do enhâte he nicht vorgezzin
sîner lîben vrauwen:
den kêse stachte he taugen
in sîne kogele în
und brâchte in der koningîn
und az swaz he anders mochte haben [2].'

When he comes before Isolt he declares that he
will prove his devotion to her

'dô greif he in die kogele sîn
und zôch den kêse her vore [3].'

. . . .

---

[1] *OX* 8936—8; cf. Liebrecht p. 148, 1. 62—87; *Die halbe
Birn,* 1. 330—94. Similarly in the others cited by Liebrecht.
[2] *OX* 8750—57. The cheese is also mentioned in the French
Prose Romance, Bédier II, 375—6, in Ulrich von Türheim's continuation of Gottfried von Straßburg, ed. H. F. Massmann, Leipzig
1848, p. 559, and in Heinrich von Freiberg, *op. cit.* ll. 5144, 5191,
5198.
[3] *OX* 8868—70.

„nû nemet, mîn lîbe vrauwe,
ich sage ûch bî mîner trûwe:
wêrit ir mir nicht sô lîp,
ich brêchte ûch daz kleinôt nît" [1].'

He insists on putting into the queen's mouth a
bit of the cheese that he has carried seven days in
his hood.

This emphasis on the cheese in the account of
the disguise of fool was not so meaningless to the
mediaeval French audience as it is to us. Various
proverbs testify to this fact.

'jamais homme sage
ne mangea fromage [2]

a fol fourmage [3].'

Qui mains en mange
est tenu le plus sage [4].

Cheese is physic for gentlemen
and meat for clowns [5].'

The association of cheese with the professional
fool must have been generally understood. Robert II
of Artois (d. 1302) had a court fool, Pierre du Tau,
whose seal bore a cheese as an emblem. He signs a
receipt for his board and lodging as follows:

---

[1] *OX* 8873—7.
[2] Cited by Legrand d'Aussy, *Vie privée des Français*, II, 61.
[3] Le Roux de Lincy, *Le livre des proverbes français*, Paris
1859, I, 238.
[4] *Lean's Collectanea, Proverbs, Folk Lore, and Superstitions*,
collections of V. S. Lean, Bristol 1902, I, p. 501, cited from
G. Meurier, *Colloques*, Anvers 1558.
[5] *Lean's Collectanea, loc. cit.*, cited from Harl. MSS 6395
(*sic*).

'ou quel tesmòignage
je qui ne suis pas sage,
ai scellée cette page
de mon scel a fourmage [1].'

Seals were carried by the middle classes, merchants, artisans, and even by peasants, in the middle ages. They are usually little round seals without counter-seals, with the inscription *sigillum* or *scel* followed by the name. In the field is found either a coat of arms or an emblem suggestive of the profession of the owner [2].

c) Other attributes of the mediaeval fool.

The other attributes of the fool that are mentioned, the shorn head and the club, are also proverbial. We have found the following allusions to the shorn head.

'E pour lui plus encore confondre
Tous les cheveux ly ferent tondre
comme à un fol marquiçon [3].'

'Tête de fou ne blanchit jamais [4].

The club is also mentioned.

'Au plus fol baille on la maçue [5].'

---

[1] Jules Marie Richard: *Une petite-nièce de Saint Louis, Mahaut, Comtesse d'Artois et de Bourgogne* (1302—29), Paris 1887, p. 112.

[2] A. Giry, *Manuel de Diplomatique*, Paris 1894, p. 648; Paul de la Croix, *Mœurs, usages et costumes au moyen âge*, Paris 1878, p. 247 ff.

[3] Du Cange, s. v. *capillorum detonsio*.

[4] Le Roux de Lincy, *op. cit.* I, 244, from *Dictionnaire de l'Académie*, edit. 1835.

[5] Le Roux de Lincy, I, 239.

'Gardez le fol! gardez le fol!
Qui tient la maçue en son col¹.'

'Que Diex me destorne de carete, k'ele ne verse
sor moi; de brait de petit anfant par nuit, de rechane-
ment d'asne, de machue de fol. ...²'

'Ci dit que le villain Dangier
Chaca l'Amant hors du vergier
A une maçue à son col:
Si ressembloit et fel et fol³.'

3. TRISTAN THE MONK.

a) The account in Tristan.

In an episodic German poem found in a manuscript
of Gottfried von Strassburg⁴ we have a story of
Tristan's disguising himself as a monk and in that
character gaining secret access to the queen.

> Tristan receives an invitation to a festival at Arthur's
> court. He is to bring with him his dearest lady. The
> invitation puts him in a grievous dilemma: if he refuses it,
> he will offend his host; if he goes, he must take his wife
> Isolt of Brittany, and will thus offend his lady. He finally
> follows Gorvenal's counsel and accepts. The poem gives a
> long, elaborate description of Tristan's clothing and that of
> his wife, and of the horses of the party. Tristan is received

---

¹ *Tristan*, ed. F. Michel, II, 209, cited from Méon, *Nouveau
Recueil de fabliaux et contes inédits*, II, 183, l. 311.
² Cited by F. Michel, *Tristan*, II, 210, from *La Riote du
Monde*, p. 8.
³ F. Michel, *Roman de la Rose*, I, 96.
⁴ H. Paul, *Tristan als Mönch, Deutsches Gedicht aus dem
13. Jahrhundert, Sitzungsberichte der Münchener Akademie der
Wissenschaften*, 1895, p. 317 ff.; Nachtrag 1896, p. 687, 692.

with great honor and forced to take a place at the Round
Table. Kaherdin is also given a place. But that night he
has a dream in which Queen Isolt appears to him and
reproaches him because she, who has many a time ventured
life and honor for him, is now disdained for another. The next
day, as he is riding in the forest with Gorvenal they come
upon a dead body. A plan occurs to Tristan. He disfigures
the corpse in such a manner as to make it appear to be
himself, puts on the dead man's garments, and, taking the
body to a monastery near by, pretends to have slain Tristan
and to seek forgiveness. He takes on the habit of a monk,
calls himself Brother Wit and vows penitence. The body
is brought to Arthur's court, the monk accompanying it.
One after another, Gorvenal, Arthur, Guinevere, Kaherdin,
and Isolt lament the death of Tristan. Brother Wit,
standing by, is well satisfied with the grief expressed.
The body is sent by sea to Cornwall, where there are further
lamentations. Isolt conceals her grief, and, even when pressed
by Mark, refuses to take part in the general mourning.
She insists, however, on watching alone at the bier that night.
But she abandons the plan when she learns from Gorvenal
that Tristan is really alive. She meets him at the fountain,
and then retires to her room. She begs Mark, eager as
ever for her comfort, to send her Brother Wit, who is a
physician from Salerno. Under his ministrations she slowly
regains her health. Tristan at last reluctantly returns to
Parmenîe.

b) *The feigned death of the lover.*

The poet has here taken a well known popular
theme as the basis of his narrative, the story of
a lover who feigns death in order to get possession
of the woman he loves. This story is universally
current in European tradition. In English its typical
form is the ballad of *Willie's Lyke-wake*[1]. One of
the versions is the following:

---

[1] F. J. Child, *English and Scottish Popular Ballads*, I, 247,
cf. III, 503.

'„O Willie, Willie, what makes thee so sad?“
And the sun shines over the valley
I have loved a lady these seven years and mair
Down amang the blue flowers and the yellow.

„O Willie lie down as thou were dead,
And lay thy winding-sheet down at thy head.

And gie to the bellman a belling-great
To ring the dead-bell at thy love's bower-yette“

He laid him down as he were dead,
And he drew the winding sheet oer his head.

He gied to the bellman a belling-great
To ring the dead-bell at his love's bower-yett

. . . .

When that she came to her true lover's gate
She dealt the red gold and all for his sake.

And when she came to her true lover's bower,
She had not been there for the space of half an hour,

All that she came to her true lover's bed,
And she lifted the winding-sheet to look at the dead.

He took her by the hand so meek and sma,
And he cast her over between him and the wa.

„Tho all your friends were in the bower,
I would not let you go for the space of half an hour.“

„You came to me without either horse or boy,
But I will send you home with a merry convoy“ [1].'

--- -- ---

[1] Motherwell's MS. p. 187, given in Child I, 252.

c) The mutilation of the corpse.

The redactor has here combined the tale with
another, the story of a hero who, wishing to reap
some benefit that will accrue from his own death,
mutilates a dead body until it cannot be identified, and
passes it off as his own. In the ballad of *Robin Hood
and Guy of Gisborne*, Robin Hood has slain Guy of
Gisborne. He nicks the dead knight's face so that it
cannot be recognized, throws his own green gown
over the body, puts on Guy's horse-hide garb, and blows
Guy's horn. The sheriff understands from the sound
that Guy has slain Robin, and thinks it is Guy that
he sees coming in the horse-hide. The supposed Guy
is offered anything that he will ask, but he will take no
reward except the boon of serving the knave as he
has served the master. This having been granted him,
he hastens to Little John, frees him, and gives him
Sir Guy's bow. They both escape[1].

In the *Sqyr of Low Degre*, a similar deceit is
practised by the enemies of the hero. They disfigure
a dead body and make the lady believe that it is the
corpse of the of the hero[2]. In Saxo Grammaticus'
Danish history a certain hero kills his slave and
makes it appear that the body is his own[3].

In stories of Gawain, frequent mention is made
of the death of the hero, various knights pretending
to have executed this deed of prowess[4]. The author

---

[1] Child, *op. cit.*, III, 89.
[2] Ed. Hazlitt, *Early Popular Poetry*, London 1866, II, p. 47,
l. 641 ff.; cf. Hales and Furnivall, *Bishop Percy's Folio Manuscript*,
London 1868, III, 266.
[3] *Saxo Grammaticus*, Bk. VI, 174 ff.
[4] *Hist. Litt. de la France*, XXX, 80, 243.

of *Tristan Mönch* would not have found it difficult to reconcile his story with the biography in the same way as is implied in the stories of Gawain; the hero reappears and vindicates his identity by his prowess; his friends then realize that they have been mistaken in having believed the body to be his.

d) Conclusion.

The account of *Tristan Mönch* shows at every point the influence of late French Arthurian romance. It opens with a festival at Arthur's court. It dwells on the relation between Guinevere and Lancelot. It represents Tristan as given a place at the Round Table. It insists upon the courtly ideal of loyalty to mistress above loyalty to wife. The familiarity of the audience with the Tristan story is clear from the numerous allusions to Tristan's fame as a lover, and from the representation of Mark, who is treated with the open contempt which characterizes the attitude of the later redactors. The fame of physicians from Salerno and the romance of Renard are frequently referred to. The long laments of each of the personages for the death of Tristan show the popularity of the *Totenklagen* [1]. The author does not seem without an inclination to create in this poem a satirical treatment of the *moniage* theme so popular in mediaeval fiction.

---

[1] Otto Zimmermann, *Die Totenklage in den altfranzösischen chansons de geste, Berliner Beiträge zur germ. und rom. Philol.* XIX, Berlin 1889.

4. TRISTAN THE MINSTREL.

a) The incident in Gerbert's continuation and in the 'estoire'.

The account of *Tristan ménestral* in Gerbert's continuation of the *Perceval* of Crestien de Troyes [1] also belongs to a late stage in the development of the story. The ability in wrestling, in playing the harp, and in the tournament, which Tristan displays in this narrative, will be spoken of in the next chapter. The incident is similar to the account in Eilhart [2] of the visit of Tristan to the court of Arthur. The same effort is made to bring Tristan into close relation with the Arthurian heroes, to show him honored by Arthur and equal in prowess to Gawain. In both, the poet represents Gawain as greeting Tristan and making him his particular friend [3]. He and Tristan then compare their strength in a friendly encounter, and Tristan overcomes Gawain as he has overcome Lancelot [4]. Such proofs of Tristan's superiority to the other Arthurian knights are alluded to in general terms in Eilhart, which contains a detailed account of Tristan's vanquishing in a joust the *schevalier Delakors* (apparently a *chevalier de la cour*). In Eilhart Gawain conjures Tristan in Isolt's name to confess to him that it was he who defeated Delakors. Tristan declares that he has never denied a request thus made, and acknowledges the victory. When Gawain learns how much Tristan desires to see his lady, he devises a scheme

---

[1] ed. J. Bédier and J. Weston, *Romania* XXXV, p. 497 ff.
[2] *OX* 5016—304.
[3] *OX* 5026—30; cf. *Tristan Ménestral* l. 446—50.
[4] *OX* 5030—59; cf. *Tristan Ménestral* l. 411—43.

similar to that which we find in Gerbert. In Eilhart night
falls on them when they are far from home at the hunt,
and they seek hospitality at Mark's court. In Gerbert
they present themselves in the guise of minstrels [1]. In
Eilhart the ruse of the Blades at the Bed follows,
and Mark is outwitted and put to shame; in Gerbert
the relations of guests and host are more amiable [2].

It may be, as Professor Golther suggests [3], that
Tristan Ménestral is an expurgated version of the
incident in Eilhart which contains the Blades at the
Bed. In the same way, the second meeting at the
Blanche Lande [4], recounted in Eilhart, may be a
variant of the first [5]. The points of similarity between
them are striking and numerous. The scenario of the
first seems to have been utilized for the second, partly
as a pendant to it, to emphasize to the reader Tristan's
subjection to his lady's will, partly, perhaps, owing to
a real poverty of invention. In both cases we have
Tristan setting out with a companion for Cornwall,
their arrival in Lidan, Tristan's message taken by
Dynas to Isolt, the lover hidden with his companion
in the thornbush, the ruse to inform him of the place
for the meeting, the precautions taken against discovery by Isolt's escort, Andret, and the tryst at the
Blanche Lande [6].

5. CONCLUSION.

The stories of Tristan's returns to Isolt are
drawn to a great extent, as we have seen, from

---

[1] *Tristan Ménestral* 1. 495 ff.
[2] *OX* 5304 ff.; *Tristan Ménestral* 1. 940 ff.
[3] Golther, *op. cit.*, 1907, p. 228 ff.
[4] *OX* 7445—695.
[5] *OX* 6255—7081.
[6] cf. Ch. II, S. T.

stories universally current in popular tradition and
in mediaeval fiction. They are but loosely connected
with the *estoire*. Some of them were perhaps introduced by one redactor, some by another.

J. TRISTAN'S ENEMIES.

1. ANDRET.

We have distinguished among Tristan's enemies
in the court of Mark, three or four barons, Andret,
the nephew of the king, and a dwarf. The name
and character of Andret suggest the Modret who is
familiar from Geoffrey of Monmouth as the false
nephew of Arthur [1]. According to Geoffrey, Arthur
entrusts his nephew with the charge of his kingdom,
when he sets out to do battle with the Romans.
During his absence Modred seizes Arthur's throne and
wife. The poet's sympathy with Tristan would lead
him to give his enemy a name which possessed un-
pleasant associations for his hearers. We shall find
the same tendency in the choice of the names of two
of the barons [2].

2. THE DWARF.

a) The names.

The instrument of Andret in the earlier portion
of the love story is a dwarf. In Eilhart he is called

---

[1] Prof. Golther expresses a similar opinion (*op. cit.*, 1907,
p. 34). Also Muret, *Romania* XVI, 322—3; cf. Ch. VI A, infra.
[2] cf. infra.

Aquitain[1]; in Gottfried *Melôt petit von Aquitân*[2]. In the other texts no name is given him. The diminutive suffix *et* is popular for names of dwarfs in French narratives: Guivret, Picolet, Espiet[3]. Of *ot*, also a French diminutive suffix, we have found only one example, a dwarf called Gralot, in one of the *Miracles de Nostre Dame*[4]. In Béroul the dwarf is called Frocin, perhaps from Freoc, a name found in some eighth century entries in the Cartulary of Redon[5]. *in* is a diminutive suffix in both Celtic and Romance languages. It is the commonest ending for names of dwarfs in French and German. We have found the following examples in French texts: Pippin, Galopin, Basin[6]; and the following in German romances imitated from the French: Albewin, Laurin, Delofin, Lorandin, Merzelin, Malgrim (rhymes *mîn, sîn*)[7].

---

[1] *OX* 3390—8; cf. 3931; for previous discussions of the name of the dwarf, cf. Bédier I, 191; II, 246 note d (M. Bédier seems to have overlooked *OX* 3931); Golther, *Literaturblatt für rom. u. germ. Philol.*, 1904, col. 51; Hertz[2] p. 531, n. 97.

[2] ed. Marold, *Index* s. v.

[3] *Erec* ed. Foerster, *Romanische Bibliothek, Index*, s. v. Guivret; *Bataille de Loquifer, Hist. Litt. de la France* XXII, 533 (Picolet); *Maugis d'Aigremont, Hist. Litt.* XXII, 702 ff. (Espiet); *Bataille de Loquifer, Hist. Litt.* XXII, 537 (Gringalet)

[4] ed. Paris and Robert, *Soc. des anc. textes* II, Miracle XII, rubr., 328. 354, 360.

[5] Béroul 320, 470, 645, 1328; cf. Bédier II, 118 n.

[6] Pippin in *Ogier de Danemarck*, ed. Barrois, *Romans des douze pairs*, 1842, VIII, IX, 1. 9946; Galopin in *Elie de St. Gille*, ed. G. Raynaud, *Soc. des anc. textes*, 1879, 1. 1180 ff.; Basin in *Jehan de Lanson, Hist. Litt.* XXII, 574. For a discussion of these and other dwarfs see F. Wohlgemuth, *Riesen und Zwerge in der altfranz. Erzähl.-Dicht.*, Stuttgart 1906, p. 80 ff.

[7] A. Lütjens, *Der Zwerg in der deutschen Heldendichtung des Mittelalters*, Breslau 1911, *Germ. Abh.* 38; Wohlgemuth, *op. cit.*

b) The account in Tristan.

Andret says that he knows of a dwarf not far away who is able to read the past and future in the stars. It may be possible to learn from him whether the suspicions in regard to Tristan and Isolt are well founded. The barons are pleased with this idea, and Andret goes to seek the dwarf, and secure his services. The dwarf consults the stars and declares that Tristan is indeed guilty. He offers to prove this to the king or lose his head. He stations the king in the tree under which the lovers are to meet. When he sees that Tristan's ruse is successful, the dwarf flees. Some time later Dynas, happening to find the little creature in the wood, and ignorant of the cause of the king's anger against him, brings him back to the court and reinstates him in the king's good graces. When the dwarf is consulted a second time, he maintains his assertion that Tristan is guilty. The barons then prevail upon the king to put his nephew again to the test [1].

The account of Béroul is the same, except that the fact that the dwarf is attached to the court is brought out more clearly. He is alluded to in connection with the king as *son nain* [2]. There are a few more details given as to his appearance. He is the *nain boçu Frocin* [3]; we are told that *li nains fu cort, la teste ot grose* [4]. His ability to read the stars is also emphasized.

---

[1] *OX* 3389—3626, 3772—3862
[2] Béroul 385.
[3] Béroul 320.
[4] Béroul 1329.

Thomas divests the dwarf of his divinatory powers. He declares that this is not according to the true story — Thomas' usual way of rejecting the version of the *estoire* when he wishes to introduce a modification of his own [1].

c) *The dwarf in mediaeval French literature.*

The dwarf is a familiar feature in the French *chansons de geste* and Arthurian romances. Picolet, a dwarf in the *Bataille de Loquifer*, is described as follows:

'Tos est velus et noirs com aversier,
Le poil ot lonc, bien le puet l'en trecier,
Li vens li fet onder et baloier.
Plus tost coroit montaignes et rochier,
Qu'à plaine terre ne brachet ne levrier.
S'il ert levés lo mains à l'esclairier,
Quatrevins liues coroit ains l'anuitier [2].'

The dwarf is usually described as about three and a half feet in height, and sometimes as of extraordinary strength. He carries a whip. Some of the dwarfs named are described as beautiful. Anonymous ones of hideous aspect are also frequent. These are black skinned, with disproportionately large heads. They are sometimes said to be hairy from head to foot, with great beards and long nails. The most important characteristic, however, is that they are hunchbacked [3]. In some romances the dwarf is represented as having divinatory gifts. In some cases

---

[1] Bédier I, 196—8, esp. note.
[2] *Bataille de Loquifer, Hist. Litt.* XXII, 533.
[3] Wohlgemuth, *op. cit.* p. 80—83.

the poet attributes to dwarfs the power of transforming themselves at pleasure [1].

The dwarf in Béroul and Eilhart falls in perfectly with this typical character. There is even a curious indication that there may have been associated with him some story of the ability to transform himself into an animal. It is a popular superstition that persons having some animal feature, such as Mark's horse's ears, owe it to some escapade in which they changed themselves into an animal by means of magic. The return transformation not having been entirely successful, they find themselves burdened with a lasting remnant of their temporary animal form [2]. Mark's observation, when the secret of his deformity is discovered, may point to some such tradition:

> '. . . Ce mal,
> Que j'ai orelles de cheval,
> M'est avenu par cest devin . . .[3]'

Dwarfs appear frequently in the poems of Crestien de Troyes and in other romances. They accompany the hero on his journeys, perform various services for him, and sometimes direct him on his perilous quests. Their directions are often of question-

---

[1] Wohlgemuth, *op. cit.* p. 83, 93.

[2] It may be that the story of the king with horses' ears rests on the belief that by the use of sorcery men could change themselves into beasts, but that animal characteristics, for example the hoof, might remain upon their return to human shape. v. J. von Negelein, *Das Pferd im arischen Altertum,* Königsberg 1903, p. 10 ff. (*Teutonia* II). Cf. also J. Grimm, *Deutsche Mythologie,*[3] p. 621, Göttingen 1854; Apuleius, *Metamorphoses,* Bk. 10, *Zeitschr. d. Ver. f. Volkskunde,* 1902, p. 21.

[3] Béroul 1343—6. On the episode of the horses' ears cf. infra, Ch. VI A.

able value, however, and their intentions do not seem
to have been always disinterested[1].

In *Macaire*, a person of somewhat the same character as Andret makes use of the court dwarf to bring
a false charge against the queen. Here the dwarf himself is found in the bed beside the sleeping woman[2].

We have record of the custom of court dwarfs
accompanying the royal party as early as the eleventh
century. In the two German redactions of Alberic
de Besançon's *Alexander*, made independently of each
other, we find mention, at the same point in the narrative, of five hundred dwarfs, richly clad and *wol
erzogen*, who accompany Queen Candacis:

'uf ir spur funf hundert getwerg giengen[3].'

Similarly, in the Chronicle of Johannes de Oxenedes,
in the year 1249, we find the entry:

'Tempore sub eodem quidam homuncio aetatis
habens annorum XVIII staturae fuit vix tripe-
dalis, nomine Johannis, quem quasi prodigium
regina secum duxit[4].'

The household accounts of Mahaut, countess
of Artois and Bourgogne, mention several dwarfs
maintained at different times at the court, apparently
in the quality of court fools, who seem to have been
great favorites of the countess. Certain items of
costume give reason to believe that the court dwarf
was an important figure in entertainments[5].

---

[1] cf. Wohlgemuth, *op. cit.* 99 and passim.
[2] *Macaire*, ed. F. Guessard, Paris 1866. (*Les anciens poètes
de la France*), l. 113 ff.
[3] Cited by Lütjens, *op. cit.* 19 from *Basler Bearbeitung* 3805,
cf. Strass. *Alex.* V, 6063—9.
[4] Cited by Schultz, *Höfisches Leben* I, 207; cf. 498, 500.
[5] Jules Marie Richard, *Une petite-nièce de Saint Louis,
Mahaut, Comtesse d'Artois et de Bourgogne*, Paris 1887, p. 112.

d) The dwarf in mediaeval Irish literature.

It is interesting to observe that mediaeval Irish literature reflects similar conditions. Here, as in French literature, we have two types, the beautiful clever little creature who is a general favorite, and the deformed malevolent being who inspires dread and loathing. We cite two examples of the first class, the dwarfs of Finn and Cuchulainn. The following is the account of the former:

'A dwarf it was that stalwart Finn obtained: such was the excellence of his memory that he retained by heart all whatsoever in both east and west he chanced to hear. *Cnú deireoil* was the man's name: in Ireland he was not unknown: beloved was the wee urchin that was expert in speech, whose cognomen was *Cnú deireoil*[1].'

Finn found this dwarf one day when he was lying on a green bank and was lulled to sleep by fairy music. The little creature is only four fists in height. Finn succeeds in finding a wife for him, Blathnaid, a woman of the fairy people. She is skilled in embroidery and is able to foretell the future[2].

We have the following verses in their honor:

'Little Cnu, Cnu of my heart,
The small dwarf who belonged to Fionn;
When he chaunted tunes and songs,
He put us into deep slumbers.

---

[1] S. H. O'Grady, *Silva Gadelica* I, 212_{12}, 203_{10}; II, 116, cf. 240, 229.
[2] O'Grady, *Silva Gadelica* II, 117, 230, 242.

Blathnaid, the youthful maid,
Who was never betrothed to man under the sun,
Except to little Cnu alone,
O, Patrick, sweet was her mouth[1].'

We also have an account of how Cuchulainn got his dwarf Senbecc:

When he saw a little man in a purple dress and a small boat of bronze under him .... on the Boyne, without rowing at all. Cuchulainn took him on his hand together with his boat.

The dwarf has a magic cloak and shirt that will fit any man great or small, an invulnerable shield, and a magic spear. He also has a marvellous harp on which he plays a melody that puts Cuchulainn immediately to sleep[2].

The poet Atherne has three malicious dwarfs. He stations them around his house in order that their truculent looks and rude words may drive away anyone who comes to seek hospitality or presents an unwelcome request[3].

The dwarfs were associated by the Irish with the Tuatha De Danaan, a mythical race who were credited with gifts of sorcery. The Irish were acquainted also with a race of pigmies which they called the Lupracan[4]. Of the latter we find Welsh equivalents in the *Book of Taliessin* and the *Black Book of Carmarthen*[5]. It is unnecessary to suppose

---

[1] *Trans. Ossianic Society* IV, Dublin 1859, 4, 10. I am indebted to Professor Bergin for this reference.

[2] *Rev. Celt.* VI, 182—4.

[3] J. Rhys, *Celtic Folk Lore* 681; cf. Meyer, *Contributions to Irish Lexicography*, s. v. *corr.*

[4] cf. O'Grady, *Silva Gadelica* I, 240_{10}; II, 269.

[5] Cited by Rhys, *Celtic Folk Lore* 432; *Book of Taliessin* VII, 135; *Black Book of Carmarthen*, fo. 9 b. ed. G. Evans, *The Black Book of Carmarthen*, Pwlheli 1906.

that the writers we have quoted, Irish, French, or German, had even a very vague idea of the mythological connections of the dwarfs of which they wrote. Their descriptions seem to us to be based wholly on the contemporary custom of maintaining a court dwarf in somewhat the same capacity as a court fool.

e) Bedenis le Nain.

In examining the names Nampêtenis in Eilhart, and Bedalis in the Prose Romance, M. Bédier concludes that this personage must have been called in the original story *le Nain Bedenis*, corrupted in the German to Nampêtenis. He comments on the account as follows: Why a dwarf? Our redactors do not tell us, and we do not know. There is certainly something here that escapes us. There must have existed a form of the adventure where this trait was explained [1].

It does not seem to us necessary to suppose that the name *Bedenis le Nain* implies that the personage in question was really a dwarf. The epithet *dwarf* may have been used ironically.

Thomas describes Tristran le Naim as tall and large and well formed:

---

[1] II, 135—137.

[2] An examination of charters shows that already in the eleventh century sobriquets were tending to petrify. Several brothers or a father and son bear the same appelative. Its original meaning was, to be sure, still so obvious that when several persons of the same name are spoken of, the name is put in the plural, preceded sometimes by the article, Henricus et Radulfus les Fievres, Ricardus et Colinus les potiers, &c. All the sobriquets that one finds in charters of this epoch have not become family names. Those of them which have not are preceded by *dit* or *qu'on dit* or *cognomento*. Giry, *Traité de diplomatique*, 367, 369. For bibliography cf. 352 n.

'Lungs ert e grant e ben pleners,
Armez ert e beas chevalers [1].

. . . .

Il respunt: „ceste novele aim.
Jo ai a nun Tristran le Naim" [2].'

In Eilhart we are told

'[der stolze] Nampêtenis:
der was ein harte kûne degin.
den helt vûrte he aftir wegin,
he twang in umme sicherheit [3].'

In thus introducing him as more than a match
for Kaherdin, and in his entire subsequent treatment
of the character, the poet gives no hint of any
appropriateness to him, other than ironical, of the
appelative *the dwarf.*

3. THE HOSTILE BARONS.

a) *Their number.*

Eilhart is uncertain as to the number of the
hostile faction that plots against Tristan. In one of
the few fragments of his poem that survive in a
twelfth century redaction, we are told that Tristan
was hated at the court

'von einem rîchen *herzogen*
und von vier grâvin [4].'

---

[1] I, 379, ll. 2187—9.
[2] I, 380, ll. 2208—10.
[3] *OX* 5986—5990.
[4] ed. Lichtenstein, p. 16, A. VIII, 63—4.

In accordance with this, the prose redaction of
Eilhart mentions at first only five enemies, Andret
and four barons [1].

Some lines later, when Andret makes his accusation
against Tristan to the king, he appeals to these four
as witnesses, and adds: ·

> 'und ob es zu schulden keme, das unser nit genug
> were an fünffen, so seind noch zwen, die auch
> darumb wissent [2].'

Some mention of seven must have appeared at
this point in the original; for the redactor of the
thirteenth century poetic version (X) apparently also
found it. To patch up the inconsistency he alters the
einem and *vir* of the preceding passage to the following

> 'von *dren* bôsin herzogin
> und von vîr grâbin [3].'

He distinguishes five who are especially hostile
to Tristan, namely, Andret and four others [4]. Neither
of these subdivisions is of any significance for the
narrative. They are shifts made by the two redactors independently to avoid an inconsistency of
the original.

In the Béroul version the allusions to Tristan's
enemies are vague [5]. In the Tryst under the Tree
no number is specified. The incident of the Footprint
on the Floor introduces for the first time a trio of
barons [6]. In the continuation of Béroul the members

---

[1] ed. Pfaff, p. 63, l. 16.
[2] ed. Pfaff, p. 65, l. 9—12.
[3] *OX* 3086—8.
[4] *OX* 3154—8.
[5] Béroul 26, 44 &c.
[6] Béroul 581.

of the trio are named[1]. The redactor is so far, how
ever, from bringing his continuation into harmony
with the main narrative that he overlooks the fact
that one of the barons had been slain by Gorvenal
in the forest, and represents them all as still active
against the hero[2].

It is possible, perhaps, to account for the seven,
five, and three of Eilhart and Béroul, if we suppose
that the *estoire* somewhere mentioned Tristan's enemies
as four, inclusive of Andret. Eilhart took the number
to be exclusive of Andret, and by this misunderstanding, got the number five. Finding some passages mentioning the enemies of Tristan as three,
and others, including Andret, mentioning them as
four, not recognizing that these were the same
group, he gives the number seven. Béroul did not
disturb himself with calculations. He merely introduced the hostile faction active in each episode as it
appeared[3].

It seems to us probable that in the *estoire,* as in
Béroul, different groups figured in different episodes,
and that the poet made no effort to connect them with
each other. Eilhart tried to combine the scattered
notices. We find him doing the same thing in regard
to the first and second visit to the hermit Ogrin[4].
Of these he recounts the first as an introduction to
the second, whereas in Béroul they are mentioned as
they take place, the one at the beginning of the life
in the forest and the other at the end. Similarly
we find Béroul giving the account of the limitation

---

[1] Béroul 3465—7; 78.
[2] cf. Muret, *Béroul,* Int. Xff.
[3] This explanation is based on that given by M. Muret,
Romania XVI, 319 ff.
[4] *OX* 4702—30.

of the potion just at the moment of the abatement
of its influence[1]. It is clear that no mention had been
made of such a limitation in the narrative that preceded the extant fragment.

These different groups of Tristan's opponents:
the three barons, Andret, the dwarf, and others,
perhaps represent personages introduced into the
tradition by different redactors.

b) Their names.

Of the names given to the trio of barons in the
continuation of Béroul, two have been satisfactorily
identified. Guenelon is the classic traitor of the
Carolingian cycle[2]. Godoïne is probably the Saxon
Godwin who was exiled in 1051 at the instigation
of the Normans at the court of Edward the Con-
fessor. He returned the following year, owing to
a reaction against Norman power. At his death
in 1053, his son Harold succeeded to the rule of
England which he had virtually held. Such an adversary as Godwin could not but have been odious
to the Normans, and it is natural that after the
Conquest his name should be a synonym for traitor
among the Anglo Normans[3]. Denoalen seems to be a
Breton name[4].

Since the hostile barons are nameless except in
the continuation of Béroul, it seems unjustifiable to
draw conclusions from these names as to the develop-

---

[1] 2133—41.
[2] Bédier II, 124 n. 1; *Romania* XXXV, p. 100—1.
[3] F. Lot, *Romania* XXXV, 1906, 605—7.
[4] Bédier II, 123.

ment of the tradition previous to that redaction. We should infer from the names merely that the redactor of the continuation of Béroul was familiar with certain well-known French, Breton, and Saxon traditions[1].

K. THE LOVER'S COMPANION REWARDED WITH THE LADY'S MAID: KAHERDIN AND CAMILLE.

It is usual in the romances and the *chansons de geste*, as in later fiction, for the lover who makes a visit to his lady to be accompanied by a friend or attendant. Thus Kaherdin accompanies Tristan when he goes to his tryst with Isolt at the Blanche Lande; Tristan accompanies Kaherdin when he goes to his tryst with Gargeolain[2].

It would be unfair to expect the companion to share the hazards of the enterprise and have no part in the spoils. Such disinterested service was indeed not expected. It appears from numerous narratives[3] that it was considered no more than courtesy for the lady to give one of her maids to her lover's companion to remain with him while be was waiting. The texts permit no doubt as to the significance of this favor.

---

[1] M. Bédier attaches considerable significance to this point, II, 124—9.

[2] *OX* 6655 ff., 9050 ff.

[3] A. Preime, *Die Frau in den altfranzösischen Fabliaux*, Cassel 1901, p. 63 ff.; Krabbes, *Die Frau im altfranzösischen Karlsepos*, Marburg 1884, p. 73; Schultz, *Das höfische Leben zur Zeit der Minnesänger*, I, 597.

In *Fierabras,* Floripas gives her maids directions[1]:

'Chaiens a .v. pucieles de moult grant signourie;
Je ne sai plus que dire: cascuns praigne s'amie,
Tant que nous i serons, menerons boine vie.'

In *Girbert de Metz*[2] Blanchefleur offers her maids
to the knight in no ambiguous terms:

'Pucelles ai en mes chambres gentis
Filles a princes et a contes marchis,
Je vos otroi le baisier à delis
Et l'acolleir et l'autre chouse ausi.'

Similarly Gahariet receives one of the maids of Ydain.

'Ydain l'a par la main baillie
Gahariet, qui la reçut
O lui manga et o lui jut[3].'

The maid assents with more or less unwillingness.
Camille inquires of her mistress:

'„wêre uch lîp, vrauwe hêre,
daz ich vorlore mîne êre?"
„nein mir", sprach die koningin[1].'

Of a lady's maid in one of the *fabliaux* it is said

'Et cele i vait mout à enviz,
Mais escondire ne l'osoit[5].'

In another version

---

[1] *Fierabras,* ed. A. Kroeber et G. Servois, *Les anciens poètes de la France,* p. 118, l. 3916—19.

[2] E. Stengel, *Romanische Studien* I, 521, l. 18 ff.

[3] Cited by Schultz, *Höfisches Leben* I, 597.

[4] *OX* 6743—6.

[5] Montaiglon et Raynaud, *Recueil général des fabliaux,* VI, 81.

'— J'irai donc, puisque le voulez
Et ferai vo commendement[1].'

A humorous treatment of the situation is found
in the romance of Gaydon. Here Gautier, the
companion, desires to remain true to his wife. It
is only under protest that he has accompanied
the lover to his tryst; he knows that they will
attempt to persuade him into an adventure on his own
account, and he refuses to go except on condition
that he shall not be asked to enter a tent. At her
mistress' instigation, the maid seeks the exemplary
Gautier where he is standing under a tree. She ridicules his virtue sharply and decides

'Qu'ainz mais ne vi si vilain chevalier.
Nus gentiz hon qui d'armes weult prisier
Ne déust ja tel home acompaingnier[2].'

In *Flamenca* the lover has obtained one interview
with his lady in the presence of her two maids. When
he comes again he brings with him two of his cousins.
He tells his lady that he wishes they might enjoy
the acquaintance of her maids. She assents gladly,
and, leaving the four together, withdraws with him
alone into an apartment beyond[3].

In the incident of Kaherdin and Camille the companion is too eager. His punishment consists in being
deceived in his expectations at the very moment when
he congratulates himself on his success. He cuts a
ridiculous figure, and the lady is not chary of her
taunts.

---

[1] Montaiglon et Raynaud, *op. cit.* VI, 183.
[2] *Gaydon* ed. F. Guessard, *Les anciens poètes de la France*
p. 248, 265, 269; citation p. 271, l. 8985—8.
[3] ed. P. Meyer, *Bibliothèque francaise du moyen âge*, Paris
1901, 6400 ff.

L. THE MAGIC PILLOW: CAMILLE.

1. SLEEPING CHARMS.

The device by which the poet creates a laugh
at Kaherdin's expense, in the account of his adventure
with Camille, is based on a universal superstition:
the belief in sleeping charms. In all sorts of primitive
records we find charms for inducing sleep [1]. Music is
of course frequently mentioned. One means is to write
certain runes on the cushions. The letter inserted
between the sheets in a story in the *Gesta Romanorum* [2]
is probably a modification of this device. Another
means is the sleep thorn, such as Odin puts into the
garments of Brynhild. A Welsh charm runs:

> 'Take a goat's horn and write the names of the seven
> sleepers thereon, making a knife-haft of it. The writing
> should begin at the blade and these are their names:
> Anaxeimeys, Malchus, Marsianus, Denys, Thon, Serapion,
> Constantynn. When the names are inscribed, lay the knife
> under the sick man's head unknown to him, and he will
> sleep [3].'

2. THE GALLANT OUTWITTED.

These sleeping charms offer dramatic possibilities
that are frequently utilized in traditional narrative.

---

[1] cf. F. J. Child, *English and Scottish Popular Ballads* V,
Index, s. v., *Sleep, induced by charms* (bibliog.); K. Nyrop, *Den
oldfranske heltedigtning*, Copenhagen 1883, p. 77 n.; G. Paris,
Journal des Savants, 1902, p. 442; Cox, *Cinderella* p. 481, nos. 13,
14; Liebrecht, *Zur Volkskunde*, 162 ff., 217; *Clári Saga*, ed. Cederschiöld, *Altnordische Sagabibliothek*, 12, Int. § 1 ff.; Grundtvig,
Danmarks gamle folkeviser II, no. 81, p. 337.
[2] ed. Oesterley p. 603, no. 195.
[3] E. S. Hartland, *Y Cymrodor* IX, 243.

In the story of the forgotten bride, for example, the denouement is thus brought about:

The heroine has lost the hero by enchantment or ill-luck. She follows him, and finds him on the eve of another marriage. By means of a bribe she prevails upon the bride to allow her to sleep with him. The bride consents, because she trusts in a charm to keep her lover unconscious until morning. On the third night, however, he throws away the sleeping draught and recognizes his lost bride [1].

In folk-tales collected in Sweden, Denmark, Greece, and other countries, we find a story similar to the incident of Kaherdin and Camille.

A man undertakes to subdue a maid, and she to outwit him. He comes to the trysting place, but is rendered unconscious by a sleeping charm. When he awakens she ridicules him, and taunts him with his defeat [2].

There is a Scotch Gaelic story to the same effect: a girl preserves herself by magic from suitors who have paid for the privilege of spending the night with her:

'They went to rest, and when she had laid down, she asked the lad for a drink of water from a tumbler that was on the board on the further side of the chamber. He went; but out of that he could not come, as he held the vessel of water the length of the night. „Thou lad", said she, „why wilt thou not lie down?" But out of that he could not drag till the bright morrow's day was ... He went, under shame and disgrace ...'

Two other suitors are similarly served [3].

---

[1] Arfert, *Das Motiv der untergeschobenen Braut. op. cit.* p. 34.
[2] cf. Child, *Ballads* I, 390 ff.
[3] J. F. Campbell, *Popular Tales of the West Highlands*, Edinburgh 1890, I, 86—7.

A form of this story is current as a ballad in Germany under the titles *Der Jäger*, *Des Jägers Verdruss* &c.

A hunter meets a girl on the heath and takes her with him to his hut. There they pass the night. She rouses him in the morning and proclaims herself still a maid. The hunter is so chagrined that he would like to kill her [1].

In the ballad of *Broomfield Hill* the narrative is not entirely clear.

Here a knight and a 'lady bright' make a tryst at Broomfield Hill. The knight is to come in the morning, the lady in the afternoon. A witch tells her that she need have no fear; her love will have fallen asleep when she comes. Let her scatter the blossom of the broom upon his head and feet. He will then sleep on. She will put her rings upon his fingers as a token that she has been so nearly in his possession. When the knight awakens, he finds himself outwitted. He reproaches his hawk and his steed for not having roused him, and sets off in pursuit. But no step is so swift as the maiden's in her flight [2].

In some stories of sleeping charms, collected from oral tradition, the knight, although defeated the first night and the second, discovers the trick on the third, and, preserving himself from the charm, accomplishes his purpose [3].

The story appears in the Middle Ages in various literary forms. In the *Gesta Romanorum* [4] it is included in a form similar to that in the Scandinavian popular versions.

---

[1] cf. Child, *loc. cit.* I, 393.
[2] Child, *op. cit.* I, 394—9.
[3] Passim in bibliography given in note to L1, *supra*.
[4] ed. Oesterley p. 603, no. 195.

Here, however, the knight, having twice paid a thousand marks and been twice befooled, engages for a third night. He consults a philosopher on his situation and learns that his sleep is due to a letter between the sheet and coverlet of his bed. After he has removed this he succeeds in overcoming the lady. The same story, with differences of detail, is found in the French *Dolopathos*, a version of the Seven Wise Masters, in German versions, in the Italian *Il Pecorone*, and in others [1].

The Norse *Clári Saga*, translated from a Latin poem, includes this incident in a story of the taming of a shrew [2].

The hero, seeking vengeance for a slight put upon him by the princess, comes to her in disguise and arouses her covetousness by displaying a coin. He offers it to her on condition that he be allowed to enjoy her favor. Twice she tricks him by a sleeping draught, but the third time her maidservant betrays to him the secret of the drink, and he is enabled to escape its influence.

The sleeping draught is also utilized in the German romance *Wolfdietrich* [3].

The hero sees a number of heads displayed on pikes, and determines to undertake the exploit in which the owners of the heads have failed. Marpali, the daughter of the pagan Belian, is in the habit of receiving Christian knights who come to the fortress. The heads on the pikes are those of knights who have passed the night with her and have failed to subdue

---

[1] cf. Child, *loc. cit.* I, 391—3.
[2] G. Cederschiöld, *Clári Saga*, Halle 1907, *Altnordische Sagabibliothek* 12.
[3] *Der grosse Wolfdietrich*, ed. A. Holtzmann, Heidelberg 1865, § 1060 ff.

her. The maiden is more favorably disposed to Wolfdietrich and keeps him from partaking of the sleeping
draught that caused the failure of his predecessors.

In several twelfth century French romances, the
heroine, for one reason or another, wishes to withhold
herself from the embraces of her husband. In *Orson
de Beauvais*, the *Enfances Guillaume*, and *Raoul
de Cambrai* we find her accomplishing her purpose by
means of a sleeping charm[1]. In some cases the charm
is so wrought that the husband, in his dream, believes
himself to be accomplishing his purpose, and never
knows that he has been deceived.

The nearest approach to a significant literary treatment of the theme is in the *Cligès* of Crestien de Troyes,
in which Fenice preserves herself for her lover by deceiving her husband by means of a sleeping charm[2].

The Tristan poet cleverly utilizes this bit of story
as the ruse by which Camille, in the manner of the
shepherdess in the pastourelle, outwits the too confident lover.

M. THE SUBSTITUTED SWORD.

In Béroul and Eilhart the king takes Tristan's
sword and leaves his own in its place. In Béroul he
likewise exchanges Isolt's ring for his own[3]. These
traits do not appear in Thomas. In Béroul the

---

[1] *Orson de Beauvais*, ed. G. Paris, *Soc. des anc. textes*, Int.
LVIII and note. *Raoul de Cambrai*, *Soc. des anc. textes*,
§ CCLXXXIX ff., § CCCIII ff.; *Les Enfances Guillaume*, *Hist.
Litt.* XXII, 477.

[2] *Cligès*, ed. W. Foerster, l. 3207 ff.

[3] *B* 2027—30, 2043 ff., 2084—8, 2109—11.

king's intention in leaving the tokens is represented
as friendly. He reflects that when the lovers awaken
and find them, they will know that he has discovered them and has had pity on them[1]. But he seems
to forget the incident immediately and completely.
The redactor fails signally to utilize it for the subsequent narrative; it appears in his version in gro-
tesque inconsequence. Eilhart does not explain Mark's
motives, but he later represents him as influenced
by the memory of the incident to receive graciously
the overtures of the lovers when, after the expiration of the potion's influence, they seek a reconciliation. In both Béroul and Eilhart the lovers, far
from interpreting the tokens as Béroul declares they
were intended, are terrified, being convinced that the
king will return with his men and destroy them.
They flee at once from the place, and until the expiration of. the potion's influence, lead a life of perpetual
fear[2]. In the Thomas versions this terror of the
lovers is replaced by satisfaction in the reflection on
the chastity of their attitude[3], and Mark, convinced
of their innocence[4], recalls them at once to the court[5].

The substitution of the king's sword for Tristan's,
and the lovers' terror on finding the token, have close
parallels in mediaeval romance and popular tradition.
The belief that it is unsafe to waken a sleeping man
is universal among primitive peoples[6]. This superstition persists in mediaeval literature as a scruple

---

[1] B 2001—25.
[2] B 2063—133; OX 4647—701.
[3] S LXVI, 81, 14—20; E CCXXXIII, 2559--62; G 17658
—63.
[4] For the sword placed between a sleeping couple, see
B. Heller, Rom. XXXVI, 36—49, and XXXVII, 162—3. cf. also
infra Ch. VI.
[5] S LXVI, 81, 21—9; E CCXXXIII, 2562—4; G 17663—96.
[6] G. L. Gomme, Handbook of Folklore, London 1890, p. 61.

of honor or courtesy[1]. The person who comes upon
the sleeper usually leaves some token of his presence
and goes quietly away[2].

We have found examples where a man comes
upon his wife or daughter sleeping with one of his
vassals, and withdraws without awakening them,
leaving, however, a token of his presence. In these
cases there is no sword between the sleeping couple.
The discovery is a discovery of guilt.

In the Spanish romance *Gerineldo* there is
a liaison between the king's daughter and his
chamberlain. The father, awakening from a terrible
dream, finds Gerineldo absent. He suspects his
whereabouts. He finds the couple sleeping, and,
placing his sword between them, silently withdraws.
His idea is to let them know that he has been there.
After his departure the girl awakens. She rouses
her lover, and he tries to escape. He is met by the
king in the garden. The lovers are saved by a fortunate accident, and flee to another land[3].

---

[1] cf. *OX* 7475—98.
[2] cf. supra, *Ballad of Broomfield Hill.*
[3]   'Tomó la espada en la mano,
            En gran saña va encendido:
            Fuérase para la cama
            Donde á Gerineldo vido.
            El quisiér alo matar;
            Mas crióle de chiquito.
            Sacara luego la espada,
            Entre entrambos la ha metido.
            Porque desque recordase
            Viese cómo era sentido.
            Recordado habia la infanta,
            É la espada ha conocido.
            — Recordados, Gerineldo,
            Que ya érades sentido,
            Que la espada de mi padre
            Yo me la he bien conocido.'

J. Wolf and Hofman, *Primavera y flor de Romances*, Berlin 1886,
II, 166. Cited in Hertz[5], p. 551.

In the Old Irish epic *Táin bó Cúalnge*, the intruder takes the sleeper's sword from its sheath and departs with it.

> 'It is there then that Ailill said to his charioteer Cuillius,
> „Find out for me to-day Medb and Fergus. I know not what
> has brought them to this union. I shall be pleased that a
> token should come to me by you."
>
> Cuillius came when they were in Cluichre. The pair
> remained behind, and the warriors went on. Cuillius came
> to them, and they heard not the spy. Fergus' sword happened
> to be beside him. Cuillius drew it out of its sheath and
> left the sheath empty.'

Fergus is taunted by Ailill and deprived of his sword. Later, when he can do so more conveniently, Ailill avenges himself by killing Fergus[1].

In another redaction of the same story, the spy substitutes a sword of wood[2].

In the Provencal biography of the troubadour Raimbaut de Vaqueiras, a father discovers his favorite asleep with his daughter. He covers the sleepers with his own mantle, and takes away that of the lover. When Raimbaut awakens, he understands what has happened. He takes the cloak and, going straight to his lord, kneels down before him and asks his forgiveness. The marquis, who loves Raimbaut, forgives him, and in order not to betray him to those present, phrases the pardon in such a way that they think it is for the offence of taking the coat[3].

---

[1] W. Faraday, *The Cattle Raid of Cúalnge*, London 1904, p. 44, 51, 134, translation from the *Leabhar na hUidhre version*; cf. d'Arbois de Jubainville's translation, *Rev. Celt.* XXIX, 163, XXX, 162.

[2] *Táin bó Cúalnge*, ed. E. Windisch, Leipzig 1905, p. 414; cf. 858. From the *Book of Leinster*.

[3] Chabaneau, *Les biographies des troubadours*, Toulouse 1885, p. 87.

Since the disposition of the person who leaves the token varies greatly in the versions we have examined, they throw little light on the puzzling passage in Tristan.

N. CONCLUSION.

In our study of the popular tradition contained in the story of Tristan, we have been able sometimes to discern the methods of the redactor who put the narrative into the form in which we find it in the *estoire*. The timidity of his treatment is its most striking characteristic. Incidents which we find in popular literature as independent stories are combined with each other with the slightest possible modification. The most important example of this timidity in combining incidents is the treatment of the Voyage for Healing and the Quest for the Princess of the Swallows' Hair.

The adaptation of older tradition to more modern taste is frequently manifest. Here again the method of the narrator is timid in the extreme. Unwilling to abandon the old, but acutely conscious of how strange the account must appear to his audience, he frequently substitutes for the archaic feature, a trait more in accordance with contemporary customs and ideas, at the same time retaining the traditional trait in an unobtrusive position. We have had numerous examples of this procedure. The hazel on the high-road is retained, and the account of the messenger to the castle is added; the chips on the stream are retained, and the account of the messenger to the town is introduced; Brangien is retained as a lay figure, although Camille has taken her place. We shall find other examples in the next chapter.

Repetitions do not disturb this redactor. In several cases we find in his narrative two variants of the same incident. We have discussed the *Flour on the Floor* and the *Blades at the Bed*, the first and second meetings at the Blanche Lande, and the accounts of Tristan's being driven by the wind to the coast of Ireland.

We have also had occasion to note the simplicity of the narrative technique in cases in which it was necessary to explain how a character obtained information upon which the progress of the narrative required him to act. The enigmatical smile or remark of another personage arouses his curiosity, and he thus discovers the important secret. In this way Isolt's curiosity is aroused by the smile of Tristan, and she is led to examine his sword. She thus learns that it is he who has slain her uncle. Other examples of this device are the exclamation of Isolt of the White Hands to the splashing water, and the words of Queen Isolt to the birds in the thorn-bush.

Similarly characteristic of the simplicity of the narrative technique is the redactor's irresponsibility as to knowledge or conduct which he attributes to his characters. He makes no effort to explain how Tristan got the wound which led to the success of the ruse of the Flour on the Floor. There is no attempt to explain why Tristan placed the sword between himself and Isolt. There is no effort to tell the reader how the second Isolt learned the significance of the color of the sails, or how Gorvenal knew of Isolt's attempt against Brangien's life, or how Mark learned of the potion.

TRISTAN AND ISOLT

A Study of the Sources of the Romance

VOLUME II

VI. AN EXAMINATION OF THE *ESTOIRE* FOR TRACES OF CELTIC TRADITION.

A. THE NAMES IN THE *ESTOIRE*.

From our study of the relation of the extant texts it would seem that we are safe in assuming that the names in the Eilhart version were in the *estoire*. We submit to the reader a brief statement of the conclusions that better qualified investigators have reached in regard to the origin of these names[1].

In some of the incidents the personages bear French names: Blankeflur (Thomas, *Blancheflor*)[2], Ûgrîm (Béroul, *Ogrin*)[3], Aquitain (Gottfried, *Melôt petit von Aquitân*), Thomas, ·*Melot* (?)[4], *Delekors scheualier*[5] (*chevalier de la cour?*), Gymêle von der Schitrîêle[6] (Prose Romance, *Camille*)[7].

---

[1] We confine our examination to the names in Eilhart, although by so doing we may be omitting a few that were found in the French original. M. J. Loth in his *Contributions à l'étude des romans de la Table Ronde*, Paris 1912, seems to us to have fallen frequently into the error of attributing to the *estoire* names that were introduced by later redactors. For examples see *Romanic Review* 1912, III, 431—5.

[2] Bédier II, 124—5, and note 1.

[3] Bédier II, 124, and note 3.

[4] cf. supra, Ch. II J; Ch. V J 2.

[5] Bédier II, 118 n.

[6] Lichtenstein, cxciii—iv; Bédier II, 118 n; cf. J. Kelemina, *Untersuchungen zur Tristansage*, Teutonia 16, Leipzig 1910, 7562.

[7] Bédier II, 377.

The origin of the names *Perenis*[1] and *Andret*[2] is a matter of dispute.

Of the Celtic names, some may be survivals of the Celtic story, others may have been introduced by the redactor of the *estoire*, or a French predecessor. The French redactors, whether they wrote on the continent or in England, would naturally be familiar with the more usual names of their Celtic neighbors. Our knowledge of the phonology of the Celtic dialects previous to the twelfth century is not sufficiently accurate to permit definite conclusions as to exactly which Celtic dialect or dialects the names preserved in the Tristan texts represent.

The name Tristrant (Thomas: *Tristan, Tristran*; Béroul: *Tristran, Tristrant*), probably of Pictish[3] origin, seems to have been transmitted to the French by the Welsh or Cornish. The name Îsalde (Béroul: *Iseut, Yseut*; Thomas: *Isolt, Ysolt, Isol, Ysode, Yselt, Yseut*) has been connected with various Germanic names: Ethylda, Iswalda, and Ishild. Its origin has also been sought in the Welsh Essylt[4]. Opinion is also divided in regard to the name Môrolt (Béroul: *Morho[u]t*; Thomas: *Morholt*)[5].

---

[1] Bédier II, 122, attributes it to the Bretons; Loth 99. 103. 107, is doubtful.

[2] Bédier II, 120, attributes it to the Bretons or Welsh; Loth 93—4, considers it an Anglo-Saxon name.

[3] Zimmer (*Zts. f. frz. Sp. u. Lit.* XIII, p. 73) identifies Tristan with the Drest filius Talorgen who reigned over the Picts from 780 to 785 (*Annals of Tigernach; Annals of Ulster*, Rolls Series). This view has been generally accepted. Cf. Bédier II, 105—8, and bibliography. Also E. Brugger, *Archiv für das Studium der neueren Sprachen und Literaturen*, vol. CXXIX, p. 134 ff. M. J. Loth rejects this identification, *op. cit.* 16 – 23. 95 — 6. He considers the name Tristan to be of Welsh or Cornish origin, transmitted to the French by writing.

[4] For this name, as for Tristan, cf. Bédier II, 112—5, and bibliography, Loth 23—30. 95.

[5] cf. Bédier II, 117. 136; Golther, *op. cit.* 1907, p. 17. 21; J. Loth, *op. cit.* 29, note 1. The question is discussed infra Ch. VI C 1.

The word *mark* is attested from the earliest times equally among the Celts and Teutons as a common noun meaning *horse*[1]. Among the Welsh and Irish we find numerous stories dating from an early period, of a king Mark or Eochaid (Ir. *ech* = *horse*) who had horse's ears, and of an unfortunate servant who possessed the secret. This story, the reader will remember, is told, in the Béroul version, of the uncle of Tristan[2]. The barons one day ask the dwarf what it means that he and the king have so much talk together. The dwarf is drunk, and declares foolishly that he is willing they should know, but does not wish to break his faith to the king. He offers to lead them to the Gué Aventuros, and, arrived there, to put his head into the ditch by the hawthorn-tree and tell the thorn. The plan is carried out. The barons then return to the king and tell him that they know his secret. The king is angry, and, declaring that the misfortune of having horse's ears has come upon him through the dwarf, draws his sword and kills him.

The details of the Celtic versions are the same as those found universally in popular tradition[3]:

A king has some animal member (the ears of a horse, goat, or ass, or the head of an ape). Wishing to guard the secret, he kills one after another the persons who act as barber to him. At length the hero is called upon to perform the office. He escapes, but

---

[1] Old Irish *marc*, Welsh *march*; Old Norse *marha*; O. H. G. *marah*; M. H. G. *marc, march*; O. E. *mear*.

[2] Béroul 1306 — 51.

[3] *Revue Celtique* II, 197 (fifteenth century manuscript); K. Meyer, *Stories and Songs from Irish Manuscripts, Otia Mersiana* III (tenth century); *Cymmrodor* VI, p. 181—3; Cambry, *Voyage dans le Finistère en 1794—5* (Paris, no date) II, 287; *Revue Celtique* XXXII, 413.

must promise never to reveal the secret. He is so much oppressed by it that he seeks relief, usually at the advice of others, by telling it to some inanimate thing, usually a chink or aperture in wood or stone. Some plant grows from the spot, and out of it a musical instrument is made. This instrument, when played, utters the words: 'The king has horse's ears'.

When the secret is made known [1], the king either leaves the country or repents and reveals his deformity [2].

The story appears in a very corrupt form in Tristan. Of the nine [3] steps in the narrative, which most of the popular versions retain, the Tristan poet has dropped all but three, and changed the character of the story by making the possessor of the secret tell it to the aperture with the confessed purpose of being overheard by human beings. It is impossible to decide, without more data than we possess, what was the intention of the poet in introducing the episode into the Tristan narrative. The words of Mark, when he is about to kill the dwarf in punishment for having betrayed his

---

[1] The manner in which the secret is made known varies slightly in the different versions.

[2] *Ovid, Metamorphoses,* Bk. XI, iv; B. Jülg, *Mongolische Märchen,* Innsbruck 1868, p. 46—51; *Archiv für slavische Philologie,* XIV, 1892, p. 148—50; *Archivio per lo studio delle trad. populare* III, 1884, p. 370; Wuk Stephanowitch Karadschitsch, *Volksmärchen der Serben,* Berlin 1854, translation by the author's daughter Wilhelmina, p. 225—8; A. Coelho, *Contos populares portuguezes,* Lisboa 1879, p. 117, no. 50. For further references see Roscher, *Ausführliches Lexikon der griechischen und römischen Mythologie,* under *Midas.*

[3] 1. The king has the ears of an animal. 2. The king has the habit of killing his barber. 3. The hero is called upon to act as barber. 4. The hero escapes death on condition that he will not reveal the secret. 5. The hero is oppressed by the secret. 6. A cure is suggested. 7. He is to tell the secret to an inanimate thing. 8. The inanimate thing betrays the secret. 9. The king's behavior on hearing of the betrayal.

secret[1], suggest that Béroul had in mind some episode, now lost, which accounted for the king's disfigurement. It is also imposible to decide whether the incident is an integral part of the story and belongs to a very old stratum of the narrative[2], or whether it is a mere scrap of Celtic tradition, added by some late *conteur* without any appropriateness except in the name[3].

There is a tradition of a King Mark of Cornwall in the *Vita Sancti Pauli Aureliani*[4], a sixth century saint, composed from Welsh sources by an Armorican monk, Wrmonoc of Landevenec, in 884. We are told that while the saint was living in Britain, rumors of his virtues reached the ears of Mark, King of Cornwall, of whom the hagiographer speaks as of great renown.

---

[1] Béroul 1343—6; cf. supra, Ch. V J 2 c, p. 244 ff.

[2] For previous discussions of this episode v. Muret, Béroul, p. viii; Bédier II, p. 143. 156, n. 3; Golther, *op. cit.* 1907, p. 107—8.

[3] We have noted the name Mark independently of this story in the following Celtic sources: 1. Margg or Morc, steward of the King of the Fomori, *Book of Leinster*, fac-simile 160 a (cited by Rhys, *Hibbert Lectures*, p. 590 n.); 2. Marc, one of the foes killed by Cuchulainn in the *Táin, Leabhar na h-Uidhri*, cited by Rhys, *Hibbert Lectures*, 590 n.; 3. March, *The Book of Llan Dav, Liber Landavensis*, ed. Gwenogwryn Evans, Oxford 1893, p. 225, l. 2—3. 235, 10; 4. March, *Mabinogion*, ed. J. Loth I, 299; in compounds J. Loth, *Crestomathie Bretonne*, Paris 1890, pp. 50, 219.
The use of the word *horse* as a proper name is seen in the Germanic Hengist, Horsa (cf. J. Grimm, *Mythologie*[3], p. 621); in Greek compounds of ἵππος (cf. Fick, *Griechische Personennamen*, p. 393), and in Sanskrit (cf. von Negelein, *Zeitschrift des Vereins für Volkskunde*, 1902, p. 21, n. 2). Cf. Apuleius, *Metamorphoses*, Bk. 10. An animal member (such as horse's ears) might be the characteristic of the offspring of a human being and a beast. For transformations of men into animals cf. Negelein, *loc. cit.*; J. Grimm, *Mythologie*[3], 1047 ff.; Kittredge, [*Harvard*] *Studies and Notes* VIII, p. 149 ff. There is a curious example of the superstition under discussion ·included in the story of Diarmaid and Grainne. See O'Grady's edition, *Ossianic Society Transactions* III, p. 129 ff.

[4] AA. SS. mens. mart., vol. II, p. 114 a. Cf. *Revue Celtique*, vol. V, p. 431.

'Interea cum haec et alia multa bona opera Dei gratia cooperante in illo agebantur, fama ejus regis Marci pervolat ad aures quem alio nomine Quonomorium vocant. Qui eo tempore amplissime producto sub limite regendo moenia sceptri, vir magnus imperiali potentiae atque potentissimus habebatur, ita ut quatuor linguae diversarum gentium uno ejus subjacerent imperio.'

King Mark accordingly sends for the saint, and having convinced himself of his excellent qualities offers him complete ecclesiastical authority in his realm. The saint, however, steals away secretly, being unwilling to accept pontifical authority.

The following names of minor characters are generally held to be Celtic: The name *Brangêne* (Béroul, *Brengain*, &c.; Thomas, *Bringvain* &c.)[1] has been identified with the Welsh Branwen. In Tînas of Lîtan (Béroul, *Dinas of Lidan*, Prose Romance *Dynas*)[2] the French poet is, perhaps, interpreting as the name of a person the Welsh (or possibly the Cornish) words for *great fortress*. *Kehenis* (Thomas, *Kaherdin*)[3], *Pleherin* (Thomas, *Breri?*)[4], Rivalin (Thomas, *Rivalen*)[5], Havelîn (Thomas, *Hoël*)[6], and Kurvenâl (Thomas, *Guvernal*; Béroul, *Governal*)[7] are also Celtic. Utânt (Thomas *Huden*; Béroul *Hu[s]dent*[8]) has been conjectured to have a Celtic origin.

---

[1] Bédier II, 119; Loth 103—4.

[2] F. Lot, *Romania* XXIV, p. 337; similarly Loth, 90—92. 104; M. Muret· identifies Lidan with Lidford, a village in Devonshire, formerly known as Hlydanford, v. glossary in his edition of Béroul.

[3] Bédier II, 119—20, considers the name Kaherdin Breton or Welsh. Loth 104, says it cannot be Breton. He believes it to be Cornish.

[4] Bédier II, 120, Welsh or Breton.

[5] Bédier II, 122. 124—5; Loth 99—100.

[6] Bédier II, 123; F. Lot, *Rom.* XXIX, 380—402; Loth 99.

[7] Bédier II, 119 – 20; Loth 103.

[8] Loth 106.

The following names have not been explained: Rîôle[1] (Prose Romance, *Agrippes*), Galîag[2], Mîlîag[3], Garîôle (Prose Romance, *Gargeolain*)[4], Nampêtenis (Prose Romance, *Bedalis*)[5], Parlasîn[6], Plôt[7], Pîloise[8].

Blankenlant (Blanche Lande)[9], and Blankenwalt[10] might be found in more than one district in Norman England and France. Britanjâ[11], Karahes (Carhaix)[12], and Tintanjôl[13] would probably be known to French poets of the twelfth century. Lîtan (Lidan), as we have seen, has been localized in Wales. For Gânôje[14] various suggestions have been brought forward. Lohenois has been identified with the Pictish territory Lothian south of the Firth-of-Forth[15].

There is one passage that seems to show a rather intimate acquaintance with the geography of Brittany and Cornwall. The poet knows that there is a St. Michael's Mount in each.

> 'zu Kurnevâles dâr ouch hîz
> eine stat rechte alsô die:
> vor wâr mag ich daz sagen hie,

---

[1] Rîôle (von Nantis) *OX* 5542. 5709. 5732. 5774. 5787. 5799. 5811. 6033. 8581. 8595.
[2] *OX* 6471. 6546. 6568; cf. Bédier II, 118 n.
[3] *OX* 6472; cf. Bédier II, 118 n.
[4] Bédier II, 118 n.
[5] Bédier II, 118 n.; 135. M. Bédier proposes *le Nain Bedenis*.
[6] *OX* 8268; Lichtenstein cxlv.
[7] *OX* 8374. 8400; cf. Golther 1907, p. 79.
[8] *OX* 7131 ff.
[9] *OX* 6284. 6396. 7521. 7541. 7606; Loth 78—9. 80—2. 125—6.
[10] *OX* 6619.
[11] *OX* 3878. 5020. 5021.
[12] *OX* 5557 and *passim* ff.
[13] *OX* 74 and *passim* ff.
[14] *OX* 4997; F. Lot, *Romania* XXV, 16—8.
[15] F. Lot, *Romania* XXV, 16. XXVII, 608; Loth, *Revue Celtique* XVI, p. 86; Bédier II, 108; Loth, *Contributions* 88.

daz sie hîzen beide
zû sant Michelssteine
und wâren vil nâch ebin rîche
und jârmarket was dâ gelîche:
zu sente Michahêlis misse
enwart dô nicht vorgezzen
grôz jârmarket alle jâr[1].'

The names in the *estoire* point to the same conclusion as that which we have arrived at from a study
of its narrative elements. The poem is based on a
Celtic romance. Many of the incidents in it are drawn
from the common fund of European folk-lore. Others
show the influence of French courtly literature of the
latter half of the twelfth century, including the popular
matière de Bretagne.

B. THE BIRTH AND ACCOMPLISHMENTS OF TRISTAN AND MINOR TRAITS OF HIS STORY.

1. THE CONCEPTION AND BIRTH OF TRISTAN.

We have studied the elements of the *estoire* which
seem to betray the influence of a courtly redactor of
the latter half of the twelfth century, and have thus

---

[1] *OX* 7384—94. This passage is corrupt in MS. D and in
the prose redaction. In Béroul Ogrin goes to the *Mont* to pur-
chase garments for Isolt when Tristan brings her back from the
forest.

'Li hermites en vet au Mont,
Por les richeces qui la sont.
. . . .
Ogrins l'ermite tant achate
Et tant acroit et tant barate
Pailes, vairs et gris et hermine,
Que richement vest la roïne.'   2735 ff.

Cf. Loth, *op. cit.* 86—7.

arrived at an approximate date for the composition
of the poem. We have studied the narrative technique
in the passages whose elements, current everywhere
in popular tradition, it was impossible to trace to one
origin rather than another. We shall now examine
the portions of the *estoire* which did not fall under
either of these categories. We shall study them with
especial reference to the question so frequently posed
and so variously answered, of the possible Celtic origin
of the tradition. For completeness we shall include in
the discussion the fragments of tradition outside the
estoire to which a Celtic origin has been assigned.

Before asking ourselves whether the account of the
birth of Tristan in the *estoire* goes back to an older
tradition, it is desirable to examine birth-stories
which are actually preserved to us dating from more
primitive times. The following account shows the
curious belief that conception is caused by a worm
swallowed in a drink of water[1].

> Findchoém, Cathbad's daughter, Amargein's wife,
> suffered from 'hesitation of offspring', so that she bore no
> children. But a certain druid met her and said: 'If my
> fee were good', quoth he, 'you would bear a noble son to
> Amargein.' — 'That will be true', quoth she, 'good shall
> be thy fee from me.' So the druid said: 'Come to the well
> tomorrow, and I will go with thee'. So on the morrow the
> twain fare forth to the well, and the druid sang spells and
> prophecies over the spring. And the druid said: 'Wash
> thyself therewith, and thou wilt bring forth a son, and no
> child will be less pious than he to his mother's kin, to wit,
> to the Connaughtmen.'
>
> Then the damsel drank a draught out of the well, and
> with the draught she swallowed a worm, and the worm was
> in the hand of the boy (as he lay) in his mother's womb,
> and it pierced the hand and consumed it.

---

[1] Windisch, *Irische Texte* III, p. 392—3, ed. W. Stokes,
Cóir Anmann (Fitness of Names) § 251.

In another case conception is caused by eating a mess of pottage[1]:

> After the end of a time Cormac, king of Ulster, 'the man of the three gifts', forsook Echaid's daughter, because she was barren save for one daughter that she had borne to Cormac after the making of the pottage which her mother — the woman from the elf-mounds — gave her. Then she said to her mother: 'Bad is what thou hast given me: it will be a daughter that I shall bear.'

In the Life of Saint Molasius of Devenish[2] we are told that the holy man's mother dreamed 'that she got seven fragrant apples and the last apple of them that she took into her hand, her grasp could not contain it for its size; gold (as it seemed to her) was not lovelier than the apple'. Her husband interprets the dream as promising 'an offspring excellent and famous, with which the mouths of all Ireland shall be filled', an interpretation justified, of course, by the saint's birth. The dream prophetic of the birth and future greatness of the hero is an element that appears in many stories. It may be that, as this story was originally told, Molasius was the direct result of his mother's eating the apple. The same manuscript indeed contains an account of the saint's blessing a cup of water and giving it to a childless woman to drink with the intention that she should thereby become pregnant. We are told that the very noble bishop Finnacha was the result[3].

As the significance of conception became more clearly understood[4], distinguished heroes were credited

---

[1] *Revue Celtique* XXII, 18.

[2] S. H. O'Grady, *Silva Gadelica* I, 18 II, 19. The *Life* dates from the sixteenth century.

[3] *loc. cit.* I, 23. II, 23.

[4] E. S. Hartland, *Primitive Paternity*, London 1910 II, 249 ff. The author speaks of the Irish stories I, 9.

with extraordinary fathers, and marvellous stories associated with their conception. The heroes of primitive Aryan tradition are almost all born out of wedlock [1]. The father is a god or hero from afar [2].

In the following version of the *Conception of Cuchulainn*, there is a combination of various primitive ideas:

Dechtire . . . asked for a drink in a copper vessel. They brought her a drink. As she lifted the vessel to her lips, she felt a little animal in the liquid. And when the creature had been removed from her lips, no one saw anything more. The creature gave a sudden leap, carried by the breath of Dechtire.

She went to sleep then, and during the night she saw something: a man came to her and spoke to her. He told her that she was pregnant by him. It was he who had brought her into the country with her companions; it was by him that they had been guided under the form of birds. The child she had brought up was he; and now it was he who had entered her womb and who would take the name Setanta. He was Lugh, son of Ethniu.

---

[1] In primitive societies the question of légitimacy is of small importance. Bastards are at no disadvantage in primitive law. In societies in which the mother-right prevails, the mother alone counts as the source of kinship; the identity of the father is a matter of no consequence. The male relative most directly responsible for the child is the maternal uncle. Even in the communities where father-right exists, the illegitimate children are usually accepted into the family. If the father of a bastard does not take it, it enters into the mother's family and inherits in due course from the father. Hartland, *Primitive Paternity* II, 178; cf. *Ancient Laws of Ireland, Book of Aicill* cxlvii.

[2] J. G. von Hahn, *Sagwissenschaftliche Studien*, Jena 1876, *Arische Aussetzungs- und -Rückkehr-Formel*, p. 341 ff. A. Nutt: *The Aryan Expulsion- and -Return Formula in the Folk and Hero Tales of the Celts, Folk Lore Record* IV, London 1881, p. 1—44.

The young girl became pregnant then. There was great dispute about it among the Ulstermen, for she was known to have no husband. They feared that Conchobar, in a moment of drunkenness, had rendered his sister pregnant, for she slept beside him. Conchobar then betrothed his sister to Sualdam, son of Rôg. Sore was her shame, to go to her husband pregnant. She went to the tree of ..., vomited, and lost the germ that she bore in her womb, and became virgin again. She gave birth to a son, and the son was the child of the three years. And he bore the name of Setanta until he killed the dog of Culann the smith: it was only then that he was called 'the hound of Culann', Cuchulainn [1].

Here a conservative redactor seems to be trying to combine two accounts, one in which Cuchulainn is represented as conceived by the god Lugh (entering into the mother's womb in the form of a little animal?), and a second in which he is represented as of legitimate birth.

There is something similar in the account of the birth of Conchobar:

Ness goes to the river Conchobar to seek a drink for Cathbad her husband. She strains the water in the cup through her veil, and brings it to him.

'Let a light be kindled', said Cathbad, 'that we may see the water.' There were two worms in the water. Cathbad bared his sword over the woman with intent to kill her. 'Drink thyself, then,' said Cathbad, 'what thou wouldst have me drink, or thou wilt be killed, if thou drink not the water.' Then the woman drinks of the water twice, and she drinks a worm at either draught. Thereupon the woman grew pregnant for as long a time as every woman is pregnant, and some say that it was by the worms that she was pregnant, But Fachtna Fathach was the leman of the maiden, and he caused this pregnancy instead of Cathbad, the noble druid [2].

---

[1] *Compert Conchulaind* MS. *LU*, ed. *Irische Texte* I, p. 138—9. We have followed the French translation of L. Duvau, *Légende de la Conception de Cúchulainn, Revue Celtique* IX, p. 12.

[2] *Compert Concobuir, Revue Celtique* VI, 179—80.

Mongán, like Cuchulainn, is represented as the son of a god:

> Fiachna Lurga, the father of Mongán, was sole king of the province . . . A message went from Aedán to him that he would come to his aid. . . . Then Fiachna went across. He left his queen at home. While the hosts were fighting in Scotland, a noble-looking man went to his wife in his stronghold in Rathmore of Moylinny. At the time he went there were not many in the stronghold. He asked the woman to arrange a place of meeting. . . . 'If we, I and thou, make love, then wilt bear a son thereof. That son will be famous: he will be Mongán . . .'
>
> And Fiachna returned to his country. And the woman was pregnant and bore a son, even Mongán son of Fiachna . . . So that this Mongán is a son of Manannán mac Lir, though he is called Mongán son of Fiachna[1].

In the society which the redactor of the *estoire* addressed somewhat more modern ideas prevailed. It was desirable[2] that the hero should be of legitimate birth. In the Norse redaction of the version of Thomas Tristan resents the slight upon his birth made by the usurper Morgan.

> 'You have lied, Duke, for I was begotten in honest wedlock, and that I will prove to you if you dare to press the matter further[3].'

In this statement the poet sets to rest whatever uncertainties may have been lingering in his readers' minds from acquaintance with older versions of the story. In all the extant versions Tristan is born, although perhaps not conceived, in lawful wedlock[4].

---

[1] Meyer and Nutt, *The Voyage of Bran* I, 44—5.

[2] cf. Huet, *La légende de Charlemagne bâtard, Le Moyen-âge* XV, 161—73.

[3] ed. Kölbing, *op. cit.* XXIV [30], p. 28, l. 22.

[4] In Eilhart the account of the union of Blanchefleur and Rivalin is hurried over. Rivalin is represented as serving Mark as a vassal for the purpose of gaining Mark's sister. Dr. Kele-

In all of them the circumstances of his birth are tragic. In Eilhart, the child is cut from the dead mother's womb[1], a trait familiar in popular tradition[2]. In the redaction of Thomas, Blanchefleur gives birth to Tristan in the throes of her grief for her dead husband[3]. In the Prose Romance, Helyabel, deserted by the faithless Meliadus, brings forth her child in the forest[4].

It is usual in primitive stories for the hero to be brought up in obscurity, to display extraordinary powers in his youth, and then, coming to a brilliant assembly, to surpass the greatest in the land[5]. Some of these characteristics we find in the *estoire*, all of them in the redaction of Thomas. The latter seems to have supplemented his source by a considerable number of elements drawn from the familiar story known as the Exile and Return[6].

---

mina, *Studien zur Tristansage* (*Teutonia* 16), p. 83—91 et passim, has objected that the terms in which Rivalin's hope is expressed

> 'daz wart umme daz getân,
> daz her gerne wolde hân
> sîn swestir ze einem wîbe (*OX* 83—6)

do not necessarily imply marriage. Dr. Kelemina accordingly infers that Tristan is represented in Eilhart as an illegitimate child. This inference seems to us unwarranted. If Rivalin hopes to receive Blanchefleur from Mark, it can hardly be on other terms than those of lawful marriage. Mark's graciousness to Tristan when he learns that he is his sister's son is also proof that the poet intended to represent Rivalin's union with Blanchefleur as conforming to his hearers' ideas of honor. For the expression *ze wîbe hân* as implying marriage cf. Gierach, *Deutsche Literaturzeitung*, February 11, 1912.

[1] *OX* 99—101.
[2] cf. references in Bédier II, 197; also *Waifs and Strays of Celtic Tradition, Argyllshire Series* IV (*The Fians*, London 1891), p. 285. The hero of Persian legend, Rustem, had to be cut from his mother's womb. Similarly, in Germanic tradition, Volsung, cf. Grimm, *Deutsche Mythologie*, Göttingen 1854, I, p. 361.
[3] Bédier I, Ch. II.
[4] Löseth, § 16 from MS. 334 fo. 28; similarly Bédier II, 322.
[5] cf. J. G. Hahn, *Sagwissenschaftliche Studien, loc. cit.*
[6] Bédier I, Ch. II—X; cf. II, 197.

The story of the conception and birth of Tristan
in the extant texts contains no traits that cannot
be accounted for as the invention of a French poet
of the twelfth century. The names of the hero's father
and mother support this view[1]. Whether these accounts
are modifications of a Celtic tradition or the invention
of the French redactors, it is impossible definitely to
decide[2].

If there was a Celtic story of Tristan's birth, it
was of the character of the Old Irish accounts that
we have cited. It would be manifestly impossible to
present such a story to a twelfth century French
audience. The story of Rivalin in the *estoire*, and of
Meliadus in the French Prose Romance may be the
survival of a Celtic tradition of a god or hero coming
from afar and, after the conception of the child, disappearing, like Lugh and Manannán, into the unknown.
Tristan's close association with Mark, his maternal
uncle, would be natural in such a tradition. The
figure of Rivalin is drawn with considerable uncertainty[3] in the extant texts. No two accounts of his
history agree, and Tristan's interest in his paternal
inheritance[4] is extremely slight.

---

[1] cf. Bédier II, 125.

[2] For previous dicussions of the tradition of the birth and
childhood of Tristan cf. Golther (1907) 142—7; Deutschbein,
Studien zur Sagengeschichte Englands, Cöthen 1906 I, 121 ff.

[3] cf. Bédier II, 194—5 and notes. Also *OX* 8135—205,
8553—75. In Eilhart the death of Rivalin occurs some years
after Tristan has married and is established in Brittany. When
he hears the news he decides to pay a visit to Queen Isolt before
setting out for his own land. He and Gorvenal go to Cornwall,
disguised as minstrels. They return to Brittany, muster several
hundred men, and set out for Lohnois, where Tristan remains two
years. He then leaves the realm in charge of Gorvenal, and returns to Brittany. We have a similar treatment of the hero's
regaining his inheritance in the romance of *Lanzelet*, ed. K. A.
Hahn, Frankfurt a. M. 1845, 8041 ff.; and in Crestien's *Erec* 6510.

[4] For the location of Lohnois cf. F. Lot, *Romania* XXV,
16—18.

2. THE ACCOMPLISHMENTS OF TRISTAN.

a) *Feats of strength and skill.*

1. Jousting, wrestling, &c.

Like the other heroes of popular romances of the
twelfth century[1], Tristan excelled in the accomplishments
cultivated by the knights of the time. Gorvenal's
teaching is thus described:

> 'her lîz ez spelin unde tobin
> mit andern kindern genûch
> und lêrte in grôzin gevûch
> mit hendin und mit beinen
> werfen mit den steinen,
> loufin unde springen,
> listlîchin ringen,
> die schaft schîzen
> nâch manlîchen genîzen.
> her hîz in wesin milde
> und lêrte in mit dem schilde
> ritterlîchen rîten,
> und wie he in strîte
> slûge mit dem swerte[2].'

Wace mentions similar exercises in which a knight
is expected to be proficient.

> 'Si ont les chevaliers josté
> E li baceler escrémi
> Pière jeté, lancié, sali[3].'

---

[1] For wrestling cf. *e. g.*, *Lanzelet* 282; *Trojanerkrieg* 6172 ff.;
Gr. Wolfdietrich 264; *Walberan* 1038; *Parzival* 538$_{19}$; *Doon de
Mayence*, p. 280—2; Crestien de Troyes, *Erec* 5994 ff.; Hartmann
von Aue, *Erec* 9280—5. For the others, cf. A. Schultz, *Höfisches
Leben, op. cit.* Index s. v. *Tjost, Steinwerfen, Lanze, Springen.*

[2] *OX* 138—52.

[3] Wace, *Roman de Brut*, ed. Le Roux de Lincy, Rouen 1836,
4443—6.

Jousting, fencing, putting the stone, hurling the lance[1], wrestling[2], and leaping, are accomplishments in which Tristan's surpassing skill is emphasized in various texts.

Wrestling is one of the chief exercises of the Old Irish heroes. We are told, for example, of Cuchulainn:

> When they were wrestling he threw the same three times fifty of them under him on the ground and all of them together were not sufficient to throw him[3].

2. Leaping.

Tristan's ability in leaping is emphasized at several points in the narrative. When the flour has been strewn on the floor, and a footprint would incriminate him, he reaches Isolt's bed by a leap[4]. When he is being led to death, he begs to be allowed to stop in the chapel to pray, and saves himself by leaping from its window into the sea[5]. When he is asked in Isolt's name to take part, in his pilgrim disguise, in the sports of Mark's courtiers, he distinguishes himself above all the rest by an extraordinary leap[6]. We may regard these feats as exaggerations of such agility as that with which the French poets were familiar, or we may consider them to be paler descriptions of such feats as we find recounted of Celtic heroes.

The most striking of Tristan's leaps is that from the chapel window. It will be remembered that he is convicted by the footprint on the floor, and condemned,

---

[1] cf. *OX* 7794—7822; cf. infra.
[2] cf. Gerbert's continuation of *Perceval, Tristan Ménestral, Romania* XXXV, p. 507, l. 411 ff.
[3] Windisch, *Táin bó Cúalnge, op. cit.,* p. 120.
[4] *OX* 3926—8.
[5] *OX* 4098—142.
[6] *OX* 7794—822.

according to Béroul[1], to be burned, according to
Eilhart[2], to be broken on the wheel. On his way to
be punished he obtains leave from his guards to stop
in the chapel to pray. He forces his way through
the little window, and leaps down from the cliff into
the sea.

The accounts vary in detail[3]. In none of them is
there expressed, but in all of them there is more or less
implied, the idea that M. Bédier has emphasized as underlying the series of incidents from the footprint on the floor
to the return from the forest: God delivers the lovers
by two miracles; he saves Tristan by the leap from
the chapel; he saves Isolt by delivering her from the
lepers. For this poet it is not the fact that proves
the crime, but the judgment which God sends upon it[4].

Tristan's escape by leaping from the chapel on
the cliff becomes more significant when we consider
that to be hurled over a precipice is one of the
punishments for capital crimes in primitive law. The
penalty of unchastity among the Britons was to be
hurled over a cliff. In Gildas' *Breviarium* a miracle
is feigned to save a mother from this doom[5]. Dion
Cassius, speaking of the mildness of the Roman penalties,
says that many means of deliverance are left to the
condemned. For example, if a prisoner is hurled from the
Capitol as a punishment, and escapes, no further penalty
is exacted. One of the questions argued in the schools
was the case of the vestal precipitated from the Tarpeian
rock and saved by the grace of Vesta. Opinion was
divided as to whether she should be given over a second

---

[1] Béroul 882—4.
[2] *OX* 4016.
[3] Cf. also the French *Prose Romance*, Bédier II, 358.
[4] Bédier II, 183—6.
[5] Cited by Nutt, *Folk Lore* IV, p. 34.

time to punishment. The rigorists held that judgment should be carried out, declaring that an accident should not interfere with the law. The partisans of mercy considered that heaven had intervened in favor of the vestal, and that its decree should be respected. At every period of Greek history we read of religious ceremonies for occasions when human beings, criminals or priests, were hurled from a rock as a punishment, with the idea that God might nevertheless spare them from death [1].

It may be that to the readers of Tristan who were interested in the moral aspect of the situation, there was some association between the fact of Tristan's leap from the chapel and the question of his innocence in the eyes of heaven. The incident may have meant to the contemporaries of Béroul and Eilhart, and to previous redactors, not only the escape which it means to us, but a miraculous intervention in sign of the hero's innocence. That Tristan had indeed committed the crime was not significant. What was significant was that his will was innocent. It was the potion that was responsible for the deed.

The leap of Tristan is prodigious when compared with the accounts of leaping in French romances. It is not extraordinary compared with those in Irish ones. One of the traditional feats of the Irish hero was the salmon leap. It is frequently referred to in the Irish romances. For example, in *Bricriu's Feast* [2]:

> Fighting from ears of horses and over the breaths of men-folk, springing in air like a salmon when he springeth the spring of the heroes.

---

[1] For the examples from Greece and Rome, see Gustave Glotz, *L'ordalie dans la Grèce primitive*, Paris 1904, p. 92 ff.

[2] *The Feast of Bricriu*, ed. G. Henderson, *Irish Texts Society*, London 1899, § 25.

Rarest of feats he performeth, the leap that is birdlike he leapeth. Bounding o'er pools of water, he performeth the feat *cless nonbair.*

Again, in the same romance[1]:

He then mused within himself as to the leap his fellows leapt over the fort, for their leap was big and broad and high[2]. Moreover, it seemed to him it was by leaping it that the valiant heroes had gone over it. He essayed it twice and failed. 'Alas!' Cuchulainn quoth, 'my exertions hitherto about the Champion's Portion have exhausted me, and now I lose it through being unable to take the leap the others took.' As he thus mused, he essayed the following feats: He would keep springing backwards in mid-air a shot's distance from the fort, and then he would rebound from there until his forehead would strike the fort. Anon he would spring on high till all that was within the fort was visible to him, while again he would sink up to his knees in the earth owing to the pressure of his vehemence and violence. At another time he would not take the dew from off the tip of the grass by reason of his buoyancy of mood, vehemence of nature, and heroic valor. What with the fit and fury that raged upon him he stepped over the fort outside and alighted in the middle at the door of the palace. His two footprints are in the flag on the floor of the hold at the spot where was the royal entrance. He thereafter entered the house, and heaved a sigh.

Extraordinary leaps are frequently mentioned of Diarmaid, an Irish hero, who, as we shall see later, is strikingly similar to Tristan in many ways[3].

---

[1] *op. cit.* § 88.
[2] These comrades had in reality been thrown over the fort by the giant, but Cuchulainn does not know this. Cf. Henderson, *op. cit.,* § 82.
[3] cf. *The Pursuit of Diarmaid and Grainne,* ed. S. H. O'Grady, *Transactions of the Ossianic Society,* Dublin 1855; re-edited for the Society for the Preservation of the Irish Language, Dublin 1895, passim; cf. infra.

3. Harping.

Tristan's ability to play the harp and to make lays is mentioned in almost all the extant texts. It is referred to in *Chievrefoil*[1]:

'Tristram, ki bien saveit harper,
en aveit fet un nuvel lai.'

In Eilhart he takes only his harp and sword with him when he sets out in his rudderless boat[2]. In Thomas and in the Prose Romance, and probably in the *estoire*, the king hears or hears of his harp playing, and his attention is thus attracted to the little boat[3]. In Thomas Tristan teaches Isolt to play the harp[4]. The incident of the Harp and the Rote will be discussed later. In Gerbert's continuation of *Perceval*, when Tristan, disguised as a minstrel, visits Mark's court, he plays the lay of *Chievrefoil* before the king. Isolt knows that it is Tristan; he would never, she is sure, have taught that lay to another[5].

The references in Old Irish literature to skill in the playing of the harp are too numerous to cite. We shall give one characteristic example[6]:

> Now Lugh and the Dagdae and Ogma pursued the Fomorians, for they had carried off the Dagdae's harper, whose name was Uaitne. Then they reached the banqueting-house in which were Bres son of Elatha and Elathan son of Delbaeth. There hung the harp on the wall. That is the harp in which the Dagdae had bound the melodies so that they sounded not until by his call he summoned

---

[1] *Chievrefoil* ed. Warnke, *Lais* (1900), p. 185, l. 112—4.
[2] *OX* 1134—8.
[3] Bédier II, p. 209 h., and note; cf. Bédier I, p. 94; II, 330; Löseth § 29.
[4] Bédier I, Ch. XI, p. 97.
[5] *Tristan Ménestral*, *Romania* XXXV, p. 512, ll. 758—88.
[6] *Revue Celtique* XII, 109.

them forth. .... Then the harp went forth from the wall,
and killed nine men, and came to the Dagdae. And he
played for them the three things whereby harpers are
distinguished, to wit, sleep-strain and smile-strain and
wail-strain. He played wail-strain to them, so that their
tearful women wept. He played smile-strain to them, so their
women and children laughed. He played sleep-strain to
them, and the hosts fell asleep. Through that (sleep) the
three of them escaped unhurt from the Fomorians though
these desired to slay them.

4. Imitating the songs of birds.

Such accomplishments as we have mentioned up
to this point are not inappropriate to French heroes.
Tristan's feats of agility, on the other hand, and his
ability to imitate the songs of the birds are comparable
in French tradition only to the accomplishments of
minstrels and jongleurs, whereas in Irish they are still
appropriate to heroes.

The latter gift is mentioned in an account of one
of those secret visits of Tristan to Isolt which form
the favored theme of episodic poems[1]: Isolt is lying
in Mark's arms when she hears at the fountain in the
garden below the voice of Tristan:

> 'humain language deguisa,
> cum cil qui l'aprist de pec[e]a:
> Il cuntrefit le russinol
> la papingai [e] l'oriol,
> E les oiseals de la gaudine[2].'

From his earliest years Tristan has had this gift:

---

[1] The incident is narrated, as an example, in the *Donnei
des amants*, a thirteenth century French poem on the art of love.
Romania XXV, p. 508 ff.

[2] *loc. cit.* ll. 463—8.

'De grant engin esteit Tristrans:
Apris l'aveit en tendres anz;
Chascun oisel sout contrefere
Ki en forest vent ou repeire.
Tristrans feseit te[l] melodie
Od grant dousur ben loinz oïe
N'est quer enteins de murdrisur.
Ke dę cel chant n'eüst tendrur[1].'

She braves the dangers that surround her, the king in whose arms she lies, the ten knights that guard, and the dwarf that follows her, and joins her lover in the garden.

To imitate birds seems to have been an accomplishment not uncommon among French minstrels of the twelfth and thirteenth century. Giraut de Calanson and others mention this among other tricks of the minstrel trade[2].

'Sapchas trobar
E ben tombar
E ben parlar e jocs partir;
Taborejar
E taulejar
E far sinphonia brogir,
E paucs pomels
Ab dos coltels
Sapchas girar e retenir
E chanz d'auzels
E bavastels
E fay los castels assalhir,
E citolar

---

[1] *loc. cit.* ll. 475—83.
[2] K. Bartsch, *Denkmäler der provenz. Lit.*, Stuttgart 1856, p. 94; cf. Bartsch, *Grundriss der provenz. Lit.*, p. 25, § 21.

E mandurar
E per catre sercles salhir.'

In *Karlmeinet* this accomplishment is possessed by certain minstrels [1]:

Ouch quam da sulch reis, De kunde harde waele Schallen as de nachtegale. Ind ouch sunderlingen Nach anderen vogelen singen. Sulche pyffen, als de re, Sulch as der pawe schre.

In the Old Irish story *The Tragical Death of Aife's Only Son* we find a hero possessed of this accomplishment [2].

> They saw the boy coming towards them across the sea, a skiff of bronze under him, and gilt oars in his hand. In the skiff he had a heap of stones. He would put a stone in his staff-sling, and launch a stunning shot at the birds, so that he brought down . . . and they alive. Then would he let them up into the air again. He would perform his palate feat, between both hands, so that the eye would not reach it (?). He would tune his voice for them, and bring them down for the second time. Then he revived them once more.

5. Juggling.

Tristan is adept in another art which the lower classes of French minstrels share with the Old Irish heroes. He is able to balance planed sticks. According to the *Folie* [3]

'Je ai sailli et lanciez jons
Et sostenu dolez bastuns'

---

[1] *Karlmeinet* ed. A. von Keller, Stuttgart 1858, p. 440, 1. 54 ff. Cf. for other examples Schultz, *Höfisches Leben* I, 570.
[2] ed. Kuno Meyer, *Eriu, Journal of the School of Irish Learning*, Dublin I, 114—5.
[3] *La Folie Tristan* 184—5; cf. *Rom.* XL, 86—8.

The second line seems to be in allusion to the juggling
frequently mentioned among the tricks of the lower
classes of minstrels. We are told in *Des deux Bordeors
Ribauz* [1]:

> 'Ge sai joer des baasteax
> et si sai joer des costeax.'

We have seen the same boast in the passage quoted
from Giraut de Calanson, and may find, on turning
the pages of almost any mediaeval romance, similar
descriptions of popular entertainment.

In Ireland the education of the hero included more
varied and infinitely more difficult feats of this character.
In a primitive society agility and dexterity of movement
must constitute a hero's claim to distinction. Each of
the Old Irish heroes had certain feats peculiar to himself, besides those which were more or less generally
practised.

The following list from the *Táin bó Cúalnge*
allows us to form, from its very unintelligibility,
some idea of the elaborate character of the Irish
hero's feats [2]. Many of the words are doubtful.

> The feat with the apples, the feat with the blades, the
> feat with the shield held horizontally, the feat with the
> dart, the feat on the rope, the feat with the body, the cat
> feat, the hero's salmon leap, the cast with the staff-
> sling, the leap over an abyss (?), the whirl (?) of a valiant
> champion, the feat of the *gae-bolg*, the ... of swiftness,
> the feat with the wheel, ... the over-breath feat ... the
> hero's cry, the blow with adjustment, the side stroke,
> the mounting on the lance and straightening his body on
> its point.

---

[1] ed. Montaiglon and Raynaud, *Recueil des Fabliaux* I, p. 11.
[2] cf. Windisch, *Táin bó Cúalnge, Irische Texte*, Extraband,
278—83 and notes.

The following are the conditions of entrance into the band of Irish heroes known as the Fiana[1].

> Of all these again not a man was taken until he were a prime poet versed in the twelve books of poesy. No man was taken till in the ground a large hole had been made (such as to reach the fold of his belt) and he put into it with his shield and a fore-arm's length of a hazel-stick. Then must nine warriors, having nine spears, with a ten furrows' width betwixt them and him, assail him, and in concert let fly at him. If past that guard of his he were hurt then, he was not received into Fianship.
>
> Not a man of them was taken till his hair had been interwoven into braids on him, and he started at a run through Ireland's woods; while they, seeking to wound him, followed in his wake, there having been between him and them but one forest bough by way of interval at first. Should he be overtaken, he was wounded and not received into the Fianna after. If his weapons had quivered in his hand, he was not taken. Should a branch in the wood have disturbed anything of his hair out of its braiding, neither was he taken. If he had cracked a dry stick under his foot [as he ran] he was not accepted. Unless that [at his full speed] he had both jumped a stick level with his brow, and stooped to pass under one even with his knee, he was not taken. Also, unless without slackening his pace he could with his nail extract a thorn from his foot, he was not taken into Fianship; but if he performed all this he was of Finn's people.

6. The twigs in the wall.

a) The trick.

There is a striking instance of the dexterity of Tristan in a curious passage in the latter part of the

---

[1] *The Enumeration of Finn's People*, ed. S. H. O'Grady, *Silva Gadelica* I, 92—3. II, 99—100. Professor K. Meyer places this text in the twelfth century. *Fianaigecht*, R. I. A. *Todd Lecture Series*, XVI, xxx.

romance. Tristan has accompanied Kaherdin to his
tryst with Gargeolain[1].

> 'nu geschôz er mit dem rîse baz
> denne îman anders dô tête.
> dô saz der helt stête
> und schôz ein rîs in die want.
> dar nâch schôz er zu hant
> abir einez in daz,
> dar nâch baz und î baz
> einez in daz ander.
> daz nam die vrauwen wunder,
> daz er sô wol dâ mete schôz.
> des spils vil lutzel in vordrôz:
> der wand beschôz er sô vil
> und tet den frawen daz zu spil
> daz er sich nicht verdâchte.
> daz schîzen in dô brâchte
> in ein tôtlich arebeit
> do er wedir kein Karahes reit.'

When the husband returns[2]

> 'dô gîng he unde nam ware,
> waz die vrauwin tâtin.
> boben in der kemenâtin,
> dâ sach he daz rîs steckin
> daz Tristrant der kûne recke
> hâte geschozzin in die want.
> do gedâchte der wîgant
> „diz schîzen nîman kan
> wen Tristrant der eine man:
> her hât ez sicherlîche getan“

> und dâchte an sînem mûte sân,
> Kehenis wêre mit im dâr.'

Similary in the French Prose Romance [1].

Puis passent oultre et defferment la porte et tous les
autres huys et s'en viennent en la chambre ou Gargeolain
estoit, et estoit toute la chambre jonchie de joncs vers et
nouveaulx, et encourtinee d'une courtine la plus belle et la
plus riche qui oncques fust ... et Tristan s'en va d'autre
part et les leisse ensemble, et print une poingnee de joncs
et se couche sus l'erbe tout envers, et commence les joncs
a lancher et atacher en la courtine l'un dedens l'autre.
Helas! oncques si mal jeu(s) ne fist! Mais il ne se donnoit
garde, car il le faisoit pour soy esbanoyer.

The husband returns and hastens to his wife's room,

[Il] se leisse cheïr eu lit tout envers et voit les joncs
fichiés en la courtine, si commence tout a fremir, car bien
sceut que c'estoient des gieux Tristan.

Tristan seems to be able to cast the rushes into
the curtain one into the other, in such a way that
the first remains there and each following one lodges
in the one before it, and remains attached to it. Both
redactors mention that no one else is able to perform
this feat.

The treatment of the passage by Ulrich von
Türheim and Heinrich von Freiberg show that these
later redactors did not understand it, or did not consider it suitable to present to their audience. The
passage in Heinrich von Freiberg [2] is as follows:

> 'nu vuorte sie den ritter wert
> in eine kemenâten sân,
> und sîn geselle Tristan

---

[1] Bédier II, 380.

[2] Heinrichs von Freiberg *Tristan*, ed. R. Bechstein, Leipzig
1877, ll. 6072—9. 6103 ff. Cf. Ulrich von Türheim, ed. Massmann, p. 575, l. 35 ff. 577, l. 6 ff.

hie ûze bî den vrouwen bleip;
die zît kurzt er in und vortreip
mit hübschen dingen sunder zil,
der er konde mêr dan vil.'

Both Heinrich and Ulrich attribute the discovery of
the two gallants by the husband to the garland that
falls from Kaherdin's head into the moat. This trait,
the dropping of the garland, is found also in Eilhart
and the French Prose Romance. In their source, in
this case as in the incident of the sign on the highroad
and the whittlings on the stream, the more primitive
trait and the more modern one doubtless stood side by
side. The more primitive trait was preserved and the
new one was added [1]. The subsequent redactors, however, recognizing the tautology, suppressed definitively
the older trait, and emphasized the more modern one.

Tricks with osier rods are probably more or
less universal in primitive communities. Games with
rushes, twigs, grasses &c. are popular among French
peasants [2]. Irish stories frequently mention jugglers'
tricks with rushes [3].

We find an account of a feat resembling that in
Tristan in the Old Irish epic, *The Feast of Bricriu* [4]:

---

[1] For the examples of garlands worn by the knights in the
summer time cf. Schultz, *Höfisches Leben* I, 312; also Müller,
Mittelhochdeutsches Wörterbuch, s. v. schapel. Cf. Heinrich von
Freiberg, 6103 ff.

[2] Sébillot, *Folk Lore de France* III, 520—7.

[3] E. g. S. H. O'Grady, *Silva Gadelica* II, 200: to take nine
straight osier-rods, and (the while they stood on one leg, and
had but one arm free) to dart them upward to rafter and to
roof-tree of the building, he that did this catching them again
in the same form. Another trick p. 320.

[4] Ed. Henderson, *Fled Bricrend*, § 65. Professor Kuno
Meyer has suggested the modifications introduced into the translation. Henderson has *anon* for *then*; *tossed up* for *threw*; *joined
together* for *in a row*.

Cuchulainn then sought out the women-folk and took
thrice fifty needles from them. These he threw one after
the other. Each needle went into the eye of the other till
in that wise they were in a row. He returned to the
women and gave each her own needle into her hand. The
young braves praised Cuchulainn.

It is frequent in American Indian stories for a
chain of arrows to be made from the sky to the
earth.· The following is a characteristic account:

Snail cried out: 'I see it (the arrow) sticking in the
sky.' . . . So the next time Snail aimed the arrow while
Wren pulled it. And it flew and stuck there. Then they
shot arrow after arrow, and each stuck in the notch of the
one preceding, and made a chain reaching down to the
earth [1].

There is a curious echo of the situation in Tristan
in one of Straparola's *novelle* [2].

A lover visits his lady in secret. He has taken himself
off before her husband returns. But one day, some time
afterward, as the latter glances up from his bed, he notices
on the wall very far from him and very high, certain marks
which he recognizes as the traces of spittle. Seized with
jealousy, he tries to spit the same distance, but fails. He
knows then that his wife is unfaithful, and exacts of her
an ordeal. She escapes by means of an ambiguous oath of
innocence similar to that taken by Isolt.

β) The intrigue.

It is possible that the poet of the *estoire* (or one
of his predecessors) has remodelled, in the story
of Kaherdin and Gargeolain, an adventure originally belonging to Tristan. It is very probable that
Tristan, like other traditional heroes, had other

---

[1] L. Farrand, *Traditions of the Quinault Indians*, Jesup
North Pacific Expedition, New York 1902, vol. 2, p. 108.

[2] Straparola, *Piacevoli Notte* IV, Favola II.

adventures in love besides those with Isolt. Many
other love stories besides his tragic relation with
Grainne are told of the hero of the Old Irish tale
The Elopement of Diarmaid and Grainne. So numerous were these stories that he was known as *Diarmaid na mban,* Diarmaid of the women[1].

We have a story of Tristan in this character in
his tryst with the wife of Segurades, related in the
French Prose Romance[2]. A peculiar trait in this incident is given in the *Tavola Ritonda,* and is found also
in the story of Gargeolain and Kaherdin in Eilhart.

Tristan is summoned by the lady to enjoy her
favor. The Italian redactor says[3]:

> Vero è che la donzella avea preso marito di sedici
> giorni dinanzi, non che ancora si fossono congiunti in-
> sieme: imperò ch' egli era usanza a quel tempo, che quando
> gli cavalieri prendeano dama, egli stavano trenta giorni,
> ch' eglino si congiugnessono insieme; e ciascuno giorno
> insieme udivano messa, acciò che Iddio perdonasse loro
> l' offense, e anche perchè perdeano loro virginitade e veni-
> vano al conoscimento carnale; e pregavano Iddio che di lor
> uscisse frutto che fosse pro al mondo e grazioso alla gente
> e degno a Dio, e che portassono loro matrimonio con leanza.

It will be remembered that Gargeolain is represented as having promised her lover that before
she would receive her husband, she would grant him
a tryst and her love. At a later point in the narrative
Kaherdin reminds Gargeolain of what she had promised
him to do before she would take her husband. The
passages read as follows[4]

---

[1] Cf. e. g. O'Grady, *Silva Gadelica* II, Index, *ua Duibhne*;
Revue Celtique XXXIII, p. 175, § 49. p. 178, § 80. p. 168, § 25. For
a comparison of the story of Diarmaid with that of Tristan cf. infra.

[2] Löseth § 34.

[3] Ed. Polidori, *Collezione di opere inedite o rare* VIII, i, 93.

[4] *OX* 7945—50.

'Nû hâte die vrawe lîse
gelabit Kehenîse
eir sie einen[1] man nême,
ab he zû ir quême,
sie wolde in ummevân.

. . . .

Kehenis sie dô manete
swes sie im gelabit habete
eir sie iren man nême[2].'

This is a less explicit statement of the situation described in the *Tavola Ritonda*[3].

It is a general practice among primitive peoples to defer the consummation of a marriage for a fixed period. The idea seems to be that a temporary renunciation of a dangerous satisfaction will obviate the risks it ordinarily involves. The fear of sexual intercourse is possibly due to the belief that weakness and effeminacy may be produced by contagion from the woman and loss of strength of body and soul. Sometimes a child or an old woman is placed between the newly married pair to keep them apart[4]. The period of abstinence varies from one week to two months.

Such customs were encouraged by the mediaeval church, which was disposed to regard marriage as a necessary evil, and to foster any tendency to mitigate its sensual character. From the fifth century the

---

[1] iren, MS. H.

[2] *OX* 7989—92.

[3] The passage in the *Tavola Ritonda* is drawn perhaps from a manuscript of the French Prose Romance which was less abridged at this point than those represented in our modern editions.

[4] E. Crawley, *The Mystic Rose*, London 1902, 343—7. For the child placed between the couple of the Old Irish story cf. *Liadain and Curithir*, Appendix V.

church had recommended, if not actually commanded, that marriage should be left unconsummated for three nights after the wedding. Intercourse was also forbidden during Lent, for the week after Easter, the week after Pentecost, and three days before partaking of the communion. It was also prohibited on the eve of Sundays, feast days, Wednesdays, Fridays, and fast days [1].

This custom would seem to be reflected in the passages in Eilhart and the *Tavola Ritonda*. In the latter, and in the similar incident in the French Prose Romance, the gallant who is favored by the lady in preference to her husband is Tristan. It may be that the poet of the *estoire* has here transferred to Kaherdin the favor which the Prose Romance represents as granted to Tristan.

Such a change would be easily accounted for; the poet wished to clear the tradition of an adventure which detracted from its romantic idealism. In his version the incident is subordinated, and treated, as we have shown in a preceding chapter, in the manner of the fashionable court lyric of the time [2]. The name of the heroine, Gargeolain [3], and the record of Tristan's extraordinary dexterity may be fossils of an earlier period of the tradition.

Thomas rejects the entire episode, with the following comment [4]:

'Plusurs de noz granter ne volent
Ço que del naim dire ci solent,

---

[1] F. Roeder, *Die Familie bei den Angelsachsen, Studien zur Englischen Philologie* IV, p. 130—3.

[2] Cf. supra Ch. IV.

[3] Professor Kuno Meyer remarks, in answer to a personal inquiry, that the first syllable looks like the Celtic *garg*.

[4] Bédier I, p. 377. 2125—8. 2134—7.

Cui Kaherdin dut femme amer.

. . . .
Thomas ico granter ne volt,
E si volt par raisun mustrer
Que iço ne put pas ester.'

His proof that there is no truth in the incident
is based on the observation that if things had really
happened as they were represented in this other
version, if Kaherdin had had his tryst with Gargeolain and if Tristan had accompanied him, and if
the husband had discovered their visit, and if Kaherdin
had been killed, and Tristan wounded, and if the
wounded Tristan had sent Gorvenal across the sea to
bring Isolt, — then Gorvenal would certainly have been
recognized and Isolt could not have escaped with him
to come to Tristan. In other words, since one of the
sequence of events in the *estoire* is impossible, the
whole is to be discredited.

The real reason for Thomas' rejection of the
passage is that the traditional incident, even when
transferred to Kaherdin, offends his taste. He does
not wish to represent Tristan even as assisting in
such an escapade. He therefore substitutes a final
adventure more worthy of his hero. Having treated
unlawful love as a tragedy in the main plot, he cannot
look upon it lightly here. He does not approve of
the moral *insouciance* in questions of conjugal infidelity
which is reflected, if our interpretation be correct,
in the latter part of the *estoire* from the *chansons
de mal mariée*. Thomas was an idealist who held
himself aloof from the vagaries of sentiment of his
time.

Our interpretation of this incident may be fanciful.
It is offered only as a suggestion in line with the

processes which we see at work in the evolution of
the story as a whole.

7. The hazel on the highroad; the chips on the stream.

We have shown in the preceding chapter our
reasons for believing that the version of Marie de
France represents the simplest extant form of the incident of the hazel on the highroad. In the incident
of the chips on the stream we have suggested that,
in earlier versions, the workmanship of the whittlings
was a sufficient sign to Isolt that her lover was on
the bank of the stream. No one else could have
fashioned the chips in just that deft way. We have
seen also that accomplishments such as these were
so unfamiliar to the French poets who transmitted the
accounts that they were modified, and their function
in the narrative served by more familiar devices. It is
probable therefore that we should seek elsewhere for
their origin.

We find some interesting parallels in Irish romance. With the episode of the chips sent down the
stream the following Irish instance has already been
compared[1]:

> ... Slechtaire discovered an underground cave, wherein
> they (he and the other kinsmen and allies of Sengarmain,
> with whom Finn is at feud) dwelt for a long time. Every
> night they used to go forth from it a-raiding, and one day
> they found, on Luachair Aine, Find's son Ossian alone. They
> make a prize (?) of him and carry him off to their dwelling.
> There Ossian cut a chip from a spearshaft (which Crim-

---

[1] Ed. and transl. by Stokes, *Revue Celtique* XV, p. 446 ff.
Cited by Kuno Meyer, *Ztschr. f. rom. Phil.* XXVIII, p. 353, in
connection with Tristan. The *Rennes Dindsenchas*, in which the
passage is found, is a collection of stories that belongs in part
to the ninth century.

thann had given him to trim), and cast it into the stream
from the well [1], so that it got to Áth na Féile, 'the Ford of
the Feale', where Find was dwelling. Then Find took the
chip in his hand and said: 'Ossian made this'. And Find's
men ascended the stream to its source and saw the earth-
cave in which were Criblach and the rest, and dug into it.
Then Criblach fled, but Find overtook her in Airer Criblaige
(and there he killed her) [2].

---

[1] Houses built over a stream are referred to elsewhere in
Celtic and in Scandinavian literature. In the *Destruction of Da
Derga's Hostel,* ed. Stokes, *Revue Celtique* XXII, p. 316, § 146, we
read: 'The cupbearers found no drink for him in the Dodder (a
river) and the Dodder had flowed through the house.' O'Curry,
Manners and Customs of the Ancient Irish, London 1873,
I, cccxviii, cites passages from the ancient laws of Ireland by
which physicians and other persons were obliged or permitted to
build their houses over a spring. He adds: This custom of having a spring of water in the living room, or in the dairy of a
farm-house, covered over with a movable flag, has come down
to the present time in some remote districts of the country. Cf.
also Kuno Meyer, *Ztschr. f. rom. Phil.* XXVI, 716. XXVIII, 353.
In Scandinavian literature, the *Christne Saga, Biskopa Sögor,*
i, p. 33 ff., contains a tale of Thorwald the Far-Farer in which is
described a gathering of Christian and heathen Norsemen: 'There
was a great hall, as was then much the custom, and there ran
a little brook across the hall, well-cared for. But neither side,
Christian or heathen, would eat with the other, and therefore
the counsel was taken, to hang a curtain across the hall in the
midst where the brook ran.' *Origines Icelandicae,* ed. Vigfússon
and Powell, Oxford 1905, I, 410. In the *Grettir saga* Thorsteinn
meets Spes in a chamber under which the sea flows. Being discovered, Thorsteinn escapes through a trap-door in the floor, and
swims to safety. Reaching land, he takes a burning log, and
holds it up, as a signal to Spes that he is safe, *Grettir Saga
Asmundarson,* ed. R. C. Boer, Halle 1900, p. 303—5. M. Bédier,
op. cit. II, 157, has called attention to the fact that *Robert le
Diable* contains a description of a stream conducted by a canal
through the chamber of the heroine from a spring in the garden.
The circumstance is, however, not utilized in the narrative;
cf. *Robert le Diable,* ed. E. Löseth, Paris 1903, X, n. 2, and
ll. 1231 ff. 3500 ff. The present town of Chaudesaigues in France
has a system of canals by which the warm streams characteristic
of the place are conducted along the ground floors of the houses,
cf. Joanne, *Dictionnaire géographique et administratif de la
France,* Paris 1892.

[2] F. Lot, *Romania* XXIV, 322, and George Henderson,
Bricriu's Feast, London 1899, p. 143, have called attention to
the utilizing of the stream as a signal bearer in the story of

In the versified form of the story contained in the *Book of Leinster*[1], a manuscript written before 1150, it is said that what Ossian cast into the stream was a ball that he had made of the chips from the spearshaft.

A similar incident, in which the characteristic chips floating down the stream serve to betray the hero to his enemy, is found in the story of *Diarmaid and Grainne*[2].

Diarmaid was making dishes, and the shavings which he was making were going down with the burn to the

---

Blathnat and Cúroi. Here Blathnat pours milk into the water to notify her lover, who is farther down the stream, that the moment has arrived for carrying out their plan; cf. *The Tragic Death of Cúrói mac Dári*, ed. and transl. by R. I. Best, *Ériu, Journal of the School of Irish Learning* (Dublin) II, Pt. I, p. 20 ff.; Kuno Meyer, *Revue Celtique* VI, 187 — 8 for another version; also *Dindsenchas of Findglais*, ed. and transl. by S. H. O'Grady in *Silva Gadelica*, II, 482. 530 ff.; *Rennes Dindsenchas*, ed. and transl. by Stokes, *Revue Celtique*, XV, 448 ff.; the poem of *Brinna Ferchertne*, ed. and transl. by Kuno Meyer, *Zts. f. celt. Philol.*, III, 40 ff. The date of the first and last is the tenth century. The reader will note, however, that the parallel it not close, the milk being only a preconcerted signal, as in groups B and C of the Tristan texts, and the stream not passing through the house. For the reference to Henderson's note I am indebted to Mr. F. N Robinson, of Harvard University. Hertz, *Tristan und Isolde von Gottfried von Strassburg*[2], p. 532, cites an incident from a ninth century Chinese story where a man and woman correspond by means of a floating red leaf.

[1] Cf. Stokes, *Revue Celtique*, XV, 448.
[2] J. F. Campbell, *Popular Tales of the West Highlands*, Edinburgh 1862, III, 43. The *Elopement of Diarmaid and Grainne* is mentioned in the list of tales in the *Book of Leinster*, facsimile, p. 190, col. 1, l. 9, and is alluded to in a gloss in an eleventh century manuscript; cf. *Revue Celtique*, XI, 126. Several incidents of the story are contained in tenth century texts (edited by Kuno Meyer, *Revue Celtique*, XI, p. 125, and *Zts. f. celt. Philol.*, I, 458). Two poems from the *Book of the Dean of Lismore*, probably dating from the fifteenth century, have been published by O. J. Bergin, J. H. Lloyd, and G. Schœpperle in the *Revue Celtique* (XXXIII, 41—57, 158—80). A discussion of the development of the tradition is given in the introduction to these articles. The complete story is extant only in late manuscripts, and in folk-tales collected within the last two centuries.

strand. The Fiantan were hunting along the foot of the strand ... Finn took notice of the shavings at the foot of the burn. 'These', said he, 'are the shavings of Diarmaid.' — 'They are not; he is not alive', said they. — 'Indeed', said Finn, 'they are'.

In another version[1] we read:

Fingal saw a speal that Diarmaid cut off a stick in the water, and immediately knew that Diarmaid was in the woods thereabout, for the speal curled round nine times, and it was s ... quarters long; there was none in Ireland that could do the like.

In another version[2]:

One day my generous king,   And his Fenians who were not
                                          [timorous,
Were hunting along dark glens.   We went down to the strand.
Then my king saw   In front of the true man of strength
                                          [of Ireland,
A shaving in form of a pure white roll,   Folded nine times,
                                          [coming to the sea.
He caught it in his white hand,   And he gazed sharply
                                          [and keenly,
He me assured it with his comely foot,   And its length was
                                          [five feet and a span.
Then he spoke fiercely,   'It is Diarmaid who. made this in
                                          [all truth,
And none of the men of Cormac,   Or the swordsmen of
                                          [the Fianna.'

A similar story is told of Finn and Ferchess, son of Comman. Since this particular version is alluded

---

[1] *Leabhar na Feinne*, vol. I, Gaelic Texts, Heroic Gaelic Ballads collected in Scotland, chiefly from 1512—1871, arranged by J. F. Campbell, London 1872, p. 128, H. 26. We have discussed this incident in connection with the *Death of Diarmaid* in the *Revue Celtique*, XXXIII, p. 158—60.

[2] *Rev. Celt.* XXXIII, 171. I have adopted the translation of W. J. Watson, *Celtic Review* VIII, 266, for *sliseag na cuartaig fhinn* 'a shaving in a form of a pure white roll' instead of the rendering which I gave in the *Revue Celtique*.

to in *Cormac's glossary* (s. v. ringcne)[1], it is clear that it was current in the ninth century[2].

> Finn ua Báiscne went on the track of Ferchess (son of Commán) to avenge Mac Con (for 'tis Finn that was leader of his Fian), until he slew him at the end of seven years at the Pool of Ferchess on the Bann, when he found the chips carried down by the river which Ferchess had set free.

The points of similarity between the Irish and the Tristan episodes are:

1. The hero fashions chips in a manner so individual that they are sure to be recognized by those who know him (ODTF)[3].

2. He sends some of them down a stream (ODTF).

3. This stream flows through a house (OT).

The hero sends the chips from this house (O).

The hero sends the chips to a person dwelling in this house (T).

4. They are found and recognized (D) by the person for whom they are intended (OT), and notify him (her) of the hero's presence along the stream (ODTC).

> The device is of the same sort as that used in *Chievrefoil*: the hero fashions his bit of bark and confides it to the path of the person to be notified.

> But there are more striking parallels to the *Chievrefoil* episode.

---

[1] ed. W. Stokes, Calcutta 1868, p. 142.

[2] ed. Kuno Meyer, *Fianaigecht, R. I. A. Todd Lecture Series* XVI, xxi, p. 38—9; cf. Zimmer *ZfdA.* XXXV, p. 115.

[3] O refers to the episode about Ossian; D to the episode about Diarmaid; F to the episode about Ferchess; T to the *Tristan* episode.

1. An episode in the Old Irish saga *Táin bó Cúalnge*[1] (the *Leabhar na h-Uidhri* version)[2]:

'I am forced to go to a tryst with Fedelm Noichride[3], from my own pledge that went out to her' [said Cuchulainn].

He made a spancel-withe[4] then before he went, and wrote an ogam[5] on its peg[6], and threw it on the top of the pillar . . .

---

[1] It is generally agreed that the *Táin* was compiled and written down in the seventh century; see Ernest Windisch, *Die altirische Heldensage Táin bó Cúalnge*, Leipzig 1905, lxviii, lxxxv. The oldest version is contained in the *Leabhar na h-Uidhri* (*Book of the Dun Cow*), written before 1106, which has been published in fac-simile by the Royal Irish Academy, Dublin 1870. It has been translated by Winifred Faraday, *The Cattle Raid of Cúalnge*, London 1904. Another version is contained in the *Book of Leinster*, a manuscript of the middle of the twelfth century, which has been published in fac-simile by the Royal Irish Academy, Dublin 1880. This version has been edited and translated into German by Windisch, *op. cit.* A French translation containing passages from both manuscripts was made by M. d'Arbois de Jubainville *L'enlèvement du Taureau divin et des vaches de Cooley*, 3 parts, Paris 1907 ff., Pt. I. An edition by J. Strachan and J. G. O'Keeffe, based on the *Yellow Book* of *Lecan*, a fourteenth century manuscript, with variants from the *Leabhar na h-Uidhri* version, with which it is substantially identical, appeared in *Ériu*, vol. I, Part. II ff. (Supplement).

[2] I have quoted from the *Leabhar na h-Uidhri* version because it is less diffuse than that of the *Book of Leinster*. The translation is Miss Faraday's, *op. cit.*, p. 10—13; cf. Windisch, *op. cit.*, p. 66—74; d'Arbois de Jubainville, *op. cit.*, 51—4.

[3] 'Gloss incorporated in the text: that is with her servant.' Miss Faraday's note.

[4] 'This was a twig twisted in the form of two rings; joined by a straight piece, as used for hobbling horses and cattle.' Miss Faraday's note. *The Book of Leinster* version adds: 'und that den Reifen um den dünnen Teil des Pfeilersteins bei Ard Cuillenn. Er rückte den Reifen, bis er auf das Dicke des Pfeilersteins kam.' Windisch, *op. cit.*, p. 68.

[5] For studies on ogam writing see R. A. Stewart Macalister, *Studies in Irish Epigraphy*, London 1897, 1902, 1907; d'Arbois de Jubainville, *Académie des Inscriptions et Belles-lettres, comptes rendus des séances de l'année 1881*, pp. 20—7. For references to ogam writing in the romances, see O'Curry, *op. cit.*, I, cccxli—iv, also Index, vol. III, 689; Douglas Hyde, *A Literary History of Ireland*, London 1899, p. 105—22. Ogam inscriptions, like runes, were carved on wood or stone. In the passages here cited it appears that Cuehulainn's writing was in one of the ordinary

They [the four who went ahead of Medb's army] found the withe that Cuchulainn threw, and perceived thè grazing that the horses had grazed. For Sualtaim's two horses had eaten the grass with its roots from the earth; Cuchulainn's two horses had licked the earth as far as the stones beneath the grass. They sit down then, until the host came, and the musicians play to them. They give the withe into the hands of Fergus Mac Roich; he read the ogam that was on it.

When Medb came, she asked: 'Why are you waiting here?'

'We wait', said Fergus, 'because of the withe yonder. There is an ogam on its peg, and this is what is in it: „Let no one go past till a man is found to throw a like withe with his one hand, and let it be one twig of which it is made; and I except my friend Fergus.[1] — Truly', said

more or less complicated ogam alphabets; that it was not in cipher, intelligible only to Fergus, as O'Curry and Hyde seem to suppose, is shown by the fact that in the second passage it is 'one of them' and not Fergus, who reads it.

[6] I. e. the piece of wood that holds the withe together. I am indebted to Professor Kuno Meyer for this translation. Miss Faraday leaves a blank.

[1] Cuchulainn puts the army under a *geis* not to proceed until one of them complies with his demand of a *fír-fer*, i. e. that the withe shall be removed under the same disadvantages under which it was placed on the pillar stone. The *fír-fer*, literally *the truth of men*, is the demand that the person challenged shall submit to the same conditions as the person challenging; cf. *Cuchulainn's Death.*, ed. Stokes, *Revue Celtique*, III, 184: 'I wish,' says Lugaid, 'to have the truth of men from thee.' — 'What is that?' says Conall the Victorious. — 'That thou should use only one hand against me, for one hand only have I.' — 'Thou shalt have it', says Conall the Victorious. So then Conall's hand was bound to his side with ropes, cf. Windisch, *Táin*, p. 72, n. 6; *Irische Texte*, I, *Wörterbuch*, under *fír*, p. 550. This prohibition of Cuchulainn's constitutes what is known in Irish literature as a *geis*; cf. Windisch, *Irische Texte mit Wörterbuch*, Leipzig 1880, p. 590. Such taboos are a feature of the Irish saga. Each hero has his particular *geasa*. For instance, Cuchulainn was under a *geis* not to go to a cooking hearth and consume the food; he was not to eat his namesake's (hound's) flesh; cf. *Cuchulainn's Death*, ed. Stokes, *Revue Celtique*, III, 176. Fergus must not leave a feast before it ended, cf. Windisch and Stokes, *Irische Texte*, II, 159. The violation of a *geis* was practically never ventured by an Irish hero, no matter by whom imposed,

Fergus, 'Cuchulainn has thrown it, and they are his horses that grazed the plain.'

And he put it in the hands of the druids; and Fergus sang this song:

'Here is a withe, what does the withe declare to us?
What is its mystery?
What number threw it?
Few or many?

Will it cause injury to the host,
If they go a journey from it?
Find out, ye druids, something therefore
For what the withe has been left.

— of heroes the hero who has thrown it,
Full misfortune on warriors;
A delay of princes, wrathful is the matter,
One man has thrown it with one hand.

Is not the king's host at the will of him,
Unless it breaks fair play?
Until one man only of you
Throw it, as one man has thrown it.
I do not know anything save that
For which the withe should have been put.
Here is a withe.'

Then Fergus said to them: 'If you outrage this withe', said he, 'or if you go past it, though he be in the custody of a man, or in a house under a lock, the — of the man who wrote the ogam on it will reach him, and will slay a goodly slaughter of you before morning, unless one of you throw a like withe.' — 'It does not please us, indeed, that one of us should be slain at once', said Ailill. 'We will go

---

or how unreasonably. Thus Deirdre succeeds in prevailing upon Nóisi to take her from Conchobar: 'A ces deux oreilles', s'écrie-t-elle, 's'attacheront la honte et le ridicule, si tu ne m'emmènes avec toi'. Ed. Windisch, *Irische Texte*, I, p. 72, § 9, transl. by d'Arbois de Jubainville, *L'Epopée celtique en Irlande*, Paris 1892, p. 226. The piety with which the Old Irish hero observed the *geis* is similar to that with which the French knight observed requests made in his lady's name. Cf. supra, pp. 132—6; and Eilhart, 6840 ff., where the hero must risk his life sooner than disregard an unreasonable request made 'dorch sîner vrauwin willen'.

by the neck of the great wood yonder, south of us, and we will not go over it at àll.'

In the *Book of Leinster* version Ailill's decision is slightly different[1]:

We will betake ourselves to the protection of this great forest until morning. There we will pitch our tents, and take up our quarters.

2. Another episode in the Old Irish saga *Táin bó Cúalnge* (the *Leabhar na h-Uidhri* version)[2]:

Then Cuchulainn went round the host till he was at Ath Gabla. He cuts a fork there with one blow of his sword, and put it on the middle of the stream, so that a chariot could not pass it on this side or that. Eirr and Indell, Foich and Fochlam (their two charioteers) came upon him thereat. He strikes their four heads off, and throws them on the four points of the fork . . .

Then the horses of the four went to meet the host, and their cushions very red on them. They supposed it was a battalion that was before them at the ford. A troop went from them to look at the ford; they saw nothing there but the track of one chariot and the fork with the four heads, and a name in ogam written on the side. All the host came then.

'Are the heads yonder from our people?' said Medb.

'They are from our people and from our choice warriors', said Ailill.

One of them read the ogam that was on the side of the fork; that is: 'A man has thrown the fork with his one hand; and you shall not go past it till one of you, except Fergus, has thrown it with one hand.' . . .

'Avert this strait from us, O Fergus', said Medb.

---

[1] Windisch, *op. cit.*, p. 74—5; d'Arbois de Jubainville, *op. cit.*, p. 54.

[2] Faraday, *op. cit.*, 14 ff.; cf. the *Book of Leinster* version, Windisch, *op. cit.*, 82—99; d'Arbois de Jubainville, *op. cit.*. 56—60.

'Bring me a chariot then', said Fergus, 'that I may take it out, that you may see whether its end was hewn with one blow.' Fergus broke then fourteen chariots of his chariots, so that it was from his own chariot that he took it out of the ground, and he saw that the end was hewn with one blow.

In the *Book of Leinster*[1], Fergus, having broken seventeen chariots, is commanded by Medb to desist:

'Stop, O Fergus', she says, 'if you were not with the army we should already have reached Ulster. We know why you do this, to delay and hinder the army until the Ulstermen recover from their weakness.'

The army encamp on the spot for the night.

3. Another episode in the Old Irish saga *Táin bó Cúalnge* (the *Leabhar-na h-Uidhri* version)[2]:

Then they reached Mag Mucceda. Cuchulainn cut an oak before them there, and wrote an ogam in its side. It is this that was therein: that no one should go past it till a warrior should leap it with one chariot. They pitch their tents there, and come to leap over it in their chariots. There fall thereat thirty horses, and thirty chariots are broken. Belach n-Ane, that is the name of that place for ever.

They are there till next morning; then Fraech is summoned to them: 'Help us, O Fraech', said Medb. 'Remove from us the strait that is on us. Go before Cuchulainn for us, if perchance you shall fight with him.'

Fraech is killed in a struggle with Cuchulainn. Fergus springs over the oak in his chariot. They then proceed until they reach Ath Taiten.

---

[1] Windisch, *op. cit.*, 92 – 3; d'Arbois de Jubainville, *op. cit.*, 59.

[2] Faraday, *op. cit.*, 35; cf. O'Curry, *op. cit.*, I, cccxliii, n. 595. This episode does not occur in the *Book of Leinster* version, cf. Windisch, *op. cit.*, p. 172, note; d'Arbois de Jubainville translates the text of the *Leabhar na hUidhri* to supplement the *Book of Leinster* version at this point, *op. cit.* p. 85.

4. A less striking parallel in a story of Finn[1]:

> Finn once came into Tethba with his Fiann, and went on a hunting excursion. Lomna staid at home, and as he was walking without, he saw Coirpre, a champion of the Luigne, lying secretly with Finn's woman. Then the woman besought Lomna to conceal it. It was grievous to him to be concerned in betraying Finn. Then Finn came (back), and Lomna cut an ogam in a four square rod, and this was on it: 'An alder stake in a pale of silver. Deadly night shade... A husband of a lewd woman (is) a fool among the well-taught Fiann. There is a heath on bare Ualann of Luigne.' Finn then understood the story, and he became disgusted with the woman.

The points of similarity to *Chievrefoil* in the Irish episodes from the *Táin* are:

1. A person knows that a troop is to pass along a certain path.

2. He has reason for wishing to delay their march.

In Tristan, to allow him a meeting with Isolt.

In the first Irish episode cited, to allow him a meeting with Fedelm Noichride [or her maid].

In the second Irish episode cited, to gain time.

In the third Irish episode cited, to gain time.

3. He carves a message[2] on a piece of bark and places it on their path[3].

---

[1] Ed. Stokes, *Three Irish Glossaries*, London 1862. Under the words *orc tréith*, p. 34. Translated in *Cormac's Glossary*, ed. O'Donovan and Stokes, Calcutta 1868, p. 129. This passage belongs to the oldest codex, and was written, says Stokes (*Three Irish Glossaries*, XVIII), 'if not in the time of Cormac (831—903), at least within a century after his death'. Similarly Zimmer, *ZfdA.*, XXXV, 38.

[2] Teutonic as well as Celtic messages would naturally be carved on wood. Runes carved on wood are mentioned as messages by Venantius Fortunatus, Bishop of Poitiers, in the sixth century. See Oscar Montelius, *Kulturgeschichte Schwedens*, Leipzig 1906, p. 210. For Celtic messages carved on wood see references above.

[3] A stanza of an Anglo-Norman political song directed against one of the ordinances of Edward I. is interesting in this connection:

4. The troop pass; the message is found and read.

5. The halt is secured.

6. The purpose of the ruse is achieved.

Owing to the great dissimilarity in the underlying forces in the two situations and the complete difference of *milieu* which they represent, it would be absurd to hope to establish anything approaching a connection between the Tristan episode and the particular Irish fragments that have come down to us. But the device to bring about the halt and delay of a hostile troop is strikingly similar in both. The procedure of the hero, in the specifically Irish form in which it appears in the *Táin* episodes, was practically sure to be effective; in the simpler form in which it appears in Tristan, on the contrary, it presents all manner of difficulties. These difficulties were realized keenly, as we have seen, by the French redactors of the Tristan narrative, and have been emphasized again and again by the modern critics[1] who have discussed

---

'Cest rym fust fet al bois desouz un lorer,
La chaunte merle, russinole, et cyre l'esperver;
Escrit estoit en parchemyn pur mout remenbrer,
E gittè en haut chemyn, qe um le dust trover.'

Thomas Wright, *Political Songs of England*, London 1839, p. 236. The purpose of the writer here, however, goes no further than to attract the attention of anyone who chances to pass. I am indebted to Professor Schofield for calling my attention to this passage.

[1] M. Sudre (*Rom.*, XV, 551) does not attempt to interpret Ms. *S*. but, following the reading of *H*, supposes that Tristan 'l'avait avertie de ce signal qu'il lui dоnnerait, en lui écrivant...' Miss Rickert (*op. cit.*, 193) remarks: 'We cannot suppose that Tristram wrote out in full the message of which the „import" fills seventeen lines. Even if it had been possible, Yseult could not have read it as she rode along, nor was there any need for her to do so, as the branch served merely to indicate Tristram's whereabouts'. M. Foulet (*loc. cit.*, 279) calls attention to 'combien il est invraisemblable que Tristan ait pu faire tenir tant de choses sur une baguette de coudrier, ou que Marie ait voulu nous le laisser entendre!' And (p. 280): 'Si attentive que fut Iseult, pouvait-elle se douter que son ami était soudainement revenu d'exil

the episode. We are strongly tempted to explain them as due to the loss of the specifically Irish superstitions[1] of which we have examples in the episodes from the *Táin.* We have the process of the disintegration of the episode from manuscript *S* of *Chievrefoil* to Ulrich von Türheim before our eyes[2]. It seems probable that the same tendencies of compromise had been at work before Marie de France as after her.

If we admit that our twelfth century French Tristan was originally a Celtic Drostan[3], it is difficult to resist reconstructing, in our imagination, the episode we have just been studying as this Drostan might have figured in it. Shorn of his twelfth century French trappings and restored to his Celtic *milieu*, we can

---

après une longue année d'attente? Ne risquait-elle pas de passer à côté de la branche sans la voir?' He therefore takes advantage of the ambiguities introduced by Ms. *H* to form the following hypothesis: 'Il y a parfaitement eu un message, où était exprimée tout au long la comparaison de leur amour à la coudre et au chèvrefeuille et où se trouvaient les deux beaux vers que nous venons de citer, mais c'était une lettre que Tristan avait expédiée quelques jours avant.' M. Bédier (I, 194 n.), influenced by the same considerations of caution, in reconstructing the Thomas *Tristan*, rejects *Sir Tristrem* and *the Saga*, in which Tristan throws the message into the stream on the bare possibility of Isolt's finding it. 'Pour que la ruse ait chance de réussir, il faut qu'elle ait été concertée entre les deux amants; sans quoi le ruisseau pourrait charrier des branchages pendant des jours et des jours sans qu'Isolt, non avertie, les remarquât.' He accordingly accepts the testimony of Gottfried, which represents Isolt as sending Brangien to Tristan, telling him exactly where and when to meet her and instructing him to send the chip down the stream as a signal.

[1] The *geis* and the *fír-fer,* cf. note above.
[2] cf. supra, Ch. IV, pp. 138—50.
[3] As do Zimmer, *Zts. f. f. Sp. u. Lit.,* XIII, 73; d'Arbois de Jubainville, *Revue Celtique,* XV, 405—8; F. Lot, *Rom.,* XXV, 22; Bédier, II, 106; Golther, *Tristan und Isolde in den Dichtungen des Mittelalters und der neuen Zeit,* Leipzig 1907, p. 15; E. Brugger, *Archiv für das Studium der neueren Sprachen und Literaturen,* CXXIX, 134.

imagine this Drostan as taking some such means as did Cuchulainn to bring about the delay of the troop and to secure opportunity for his tryst. A challenge carved on a spancel-withe would run little risk of being overlooked on a high road. It might safely fall into the hands of the first person who passed that way and be read to the whole army. The hero could depend upon a people to whom the *geis* was sacred and the *fír fer* not to be denied. The march of the troop once arrested, he could rely on his own cunning to effect a meeting with a person already informed of his presence by some characteristic of his message.

The prologue — the hero deftly peeling and shaping the piece of bark, carving his message, and then withdrawing into the forest — is preserved in Tristan. But it would be impossible for a twelfth century French poet to adopt completely the procedure of Cuchulainn. The impressiveness of ogam writing, the binding character of the *geis,* and the demand of a *fír fer* were ideas specifically Irish. Even at the expense of leaving a slight gap in the narrative, in the shifting of the scene from Ireland to courtly France such ideas would have to be sacrificed. As far as bringing about the halt of the army was concerned, it was sufficient for the hero to indicate to his beloved his desire for a meeting. In a society dominated by chivalric ideals, the lover could trust her to her being able to arrange a meeting with him. The poet was therefore free to fill out the content of the carving with any assurance of love he chose.

But, having thus simplified the character of the message, the French poet is forced to take it for granted that it will fall into the hands of the very person for whom it is intended. To a naïve listener the question would perhaps not occur as to how the bark could be counted upon to reach the one person for whom it was designed, and be read by her in the midst of a hostile troop without incurring suspicion. But that the question *did* occur to twelfth century redactors, and with disastrous consequences to the original form of the episode, the preceding investigation of the texts that followed Marie's lay has shown[1].

The considerations which incline us to the belief that the Tristan episodes in question are based on Celtic traditions are: first, there are other traces in the story of Tristan, of its Celtic origin; second, the episode in question has been shown to be a relic of a pre-French stage of the tradition; third, the Irish parallels to the incident include not only both the carved bit of wood and the device of leaving it upon the path, but the employment of it, through the appeal to peculiarly Irish superstitions, to bring about the halt of a hostile army. Our suggestion of a Celtic origin for this incident accords with the facts of the development as we have been able to trace it in the extant texts, with the evidence of the Irish parallels, and with general probability. Our study proves no more, however, than that the *Chievrefoil* episode *may* be a survival of some such specifically Irish practice as we have seen in the *Táin* episodes.

b) *Tristan master of primitive arts:* arc-qui-ne-faut.

Tristan is regarded as having introduced various arts. In Eilhart he is said to have been the first to fish with a bent hook[2]. Béroul tells us that Tristan

---

[1] Ch. IV, p. 146—7.
[2] *OX* 4539—41.

invented the *arc qui ne faut*. While the lovers are living in the forest, Tristan's dog Husdent finds them, and lest his barking should betray them, Tristan teaches him to bring down the game without making a sound[1].

The *arc qui ne faut*[2], regarded by Gaston Paris and M. Bédier as a Celtic trait, in reality presents no characteristics that associate it especially with the Celts. It is represented as a trap consisting of a bow and arrow. When it is placed in position the arrow flies against any object that touches its cord. This trap is also mentioned in Geoffrey Gaimar's *De Gestis Regum Anglorum* (1147—51)[3]. The death of King Eadmond (1016) is described as due to an *arc qui ne faut*, set by the traitor Eadric.

> 'Edriz out fait un engin feire
> *l'arc ki.r e faut* eissi set treire,
> si rien atuehe sa cordele
> tost pot oïr male novele.'

The king is invited to seat himself, and the bow is so arranged that the arrow strikes him from below[4].

> 'Treskil sasist sur la sette,
> El fundement li fiert la saiette.
> Amunt li vint treskal pomun,
> [Unc ne parurent li penun]
> De la saiette kot[5] el cors,
> Ne neient del sanc nen issi fors.'

---

[1] *OX* 4541—6; cf. Béroul 1437—637.
[2] Béroul 1752—74.
[3] Geffrei Gaimar, *Lectorie des Engles*, ed. Hardy and Martin (*Rolls Series* 1888), ll. 4409 ff., cited by Muret, Béroul, ix.
[4] Gaimar, *op. cit.*, ed. Hardy and Martin, 4421 ff.
[5] I have not attempted to emend this passage.

Henry of Huntingdon (d. circa 1155)[1] and William of Malmesbury (d. circa 1142)[2] give an account of Eadmund's death similar to that in Gaimar, but no details are mentioned. According to them it was the son or the accomplices of Eadric who, concealed in the pit above which the king was seated, plunged the steel into his body[3].

The account of the introduction of arts and the invention of weapons is a characteristic feature of traditions of primitive heroes[4]. In Irish tradition, for example, the *gœ-bolga* of Cuchulainn, a peculiar weapon which he alone possesses, has an Eastern origin assigned to it[5]. A certain Briun is represented in an Irish poem as having invented the *tathlum* or slingstone of artificial composition[6]. Labraidh Loingsech is said to have been the first to invent the green broad spears[7]. Similarly, in Greek tradition, Peleus is credited with the invention of the hunting knife[8].

---

[1] *Historia Anglorum*, ed. T. Arnold (*Rolls Series*), p. 185 ff.

[2] *De gestis regum anglorum*, ed. W. Stubbs (*Rolls Series*) p. 217.

[3] Automatic arrangements are not infrequently mentioned in the Arthurian romances. In *La Vengeance Raguidel* (*Hist. Litt. de la France*, XXX, p. 57) the lady plans to invite her unfaithful lover to look through the window at her treasures. The panel which closes the window is fitted with a razor. This she will drop to cut off his head. There is a portcullis fitted with a razor-blade mentioned in Crestien's *Yvain*, l. 907 ff.

[4] These traditions seem to bear out the epithet *gallofydd* or *galltofydd*, given to Tristan in the Welsh triad 43. M. J. Loth translates it *maître ès machines*. Rhys and Evans, *Y Mabinogion*, Oxford 1887, p. 304; J. Loth, *Les Mabinogion*, Paris 1889, II, p. 238, cf. I, p. 337—8 note on *ovydd*.

[5] O'Curry, *Manners and Customs of the Ancient Irish* II, 311—2.

[6] O'Curry *Manners* II, 252.

[7] *op. cit.* II, 257.

[8] Serv. Vergil. Aen. 9, 505. For the development of the tradition see Roscher, *Ausführliches Lexicon der griechischen und römischen Mythologie*, s. v. Peleus (u. Akastos).

c) *Minor traits in Tristan story.*

1. Heads as trophies.

A bit of savagery which is mentioned frequently in Old Irish romances is practised, according to Béroul, by Tristan and Gorvenal [1].

One day Gorvenal comes upon one of the barons hunting in the forest. He stations himself behind a tree, and, when the baron is sufficiently near, falls upon him from his ambush and cuts off his head. He carries it in his hand to the cabin where Tristan is sleeping, and suspends it by the hair from a forked branch, to greet his master when he awakens. The huntsmen find the dead body of the baron, and think it is Tristan's work. They shun that part of the forest thereafter.

In the *Táin bó Cúalnge*, Cuchulainn, meeting four enemies, cuts off their heads, and attaches each to one of the four prongs of a fork he has cut from a tree in the wood. One of the Old Irish warriors boasts that, since the first day he held a javelin in his hand, he has not often slept without the head of a Connaught man as a pillow. Examples of Old Irish heroes who, having slain their enemies, carry the heads with them as trophies, are too numerous to quote [2].

In the continuation of Béroul [3] there is an incident very similar to the one we have just discussed. The similarity is especially striking from the fact that the continuator is apparently oblivious of the fact that

---

[1] Béroul 1656—750.
[2] ed. Windisch, *Táin*, p. 82—3; cf. 420. For similar examples, cf. d'Arbois de Jubainville, *Táin Bó Cúalnge*, Int. p. 29, *L'Épopée Celtique en Irlande*, Paris 1892, p. 97. 113. 116. 138. 139. 141. 347. 352. 353; cf. A. H. Leahy, *Heroic Romances of Ireland*, London 1905, I, p. 10.
[3] cf. Muret, *Béroul* xvi—ii.

the personage whose death he is relating has already been beheaded in the earlier portion of the romance. The details in the two accounts are slightly different[1].

In the second, Tristan, making his way through the forest to meet Isolt, sees Godoïne approaching. He conceals himself behind a tree with the intention of killing him from this ambush. But Godoïne escapes him. Denoalent, however, approaching with his hunting dogs, falls into his hands. Tristan kills him. He cuts off the braids of his hair, and carries them to Isolt as proof of his achievement.

The long hair mentioned in both incidents gives no clue to the origin of the stories, for, curiously enough, the fashion of wearing the hair long, characteristic equally of primitive Celts and primitive Teutons, was revived in the twelfth century in France, and the church declaimed against it in vain[2].

---

[1] Béroul 4354—95; 4435—40.

[2] For allusions to the long hair worn by primitive Irish heroes, and the ignominy attaching to the loss of it, cf. Windisch, *Táin*, *op. cit.*, p. 246; d'Arbois, *Epopée*, p. 369—70; Windisch, *Irische Texte* III, 465 (*Tochmarc Ferb*); K. Meyer, *Stories and Songs*, *Otia Merseiana* II, p. 90; O'Mahony's Keating, p. 283; Windisch, *Táin*, p. 246.

For references to the long hair worn by primitive Teutons see Grimm, *Deutsche Rechtsaltertümer* I, 395. 469. II, 287; *Kudrun*, ed. Ernst Martin, *Germanische Handbibliothek*², II, Halle 1902, p. 78, n. 341. p. 81, n. 355.

For a history of the fashions in wearing hair in France see Jules Quicherat, *Histoire du costume en France*, Paris 1875, Primitive Celts p. 2. 4. 10; French, from 290—490 A. D., p. 70; from 490—752, p. 82 ff. 95; from 752—888, p. 109; from 888—1090, p. 142; from 1090—1190, p. 158; from 1340—1380, p. 228.

For the accounts of Saxo Grammaticus and Giraldus Cambrensis about the way the Irish wore their hair, see Saxo, Bk. V, § 169; Giraldi Cambrensis, *Opera* (ed. J. F. Dimock, *Rolls Series*) VI, p. 185.

For previous discussions of the relation of the two episodes in Béroul, see Muret, Béroul, x—xiii, xvi—xviii; Bédier, *op. cit.* II, 151. Cf. Muret, *op. cit.* glossary *s. v.* treces.

2. Petit Crû and the bells.

α) The incident.

Other traits in connection with Tristan, unusual in French romance, appear frequently in Celtic stories. There is the charming incident of Petit Crû, preserved only in the version of Thomas [1]:

> While Tristan is in exile, he enters the service of a certain duke, by whom he is honored and cherished for his prowess. When the duke sees that he is always heavy-hearted, he seeks to divert him, and sends for his chief treasure, a marvellous little dog which he has from Avalon, the country of the fairies. This dog is of extraordinary beauty; from whatever side one looks at it, it shines with innumerable colors. If one looks at it from the front it appears white, black, and green. If one looks at it obliquely it looks red as blood; sometimes one would think it dark brown, and again light red. From the side, one cannot tell what color it is, for it seems to have none. It was a fairy that gave it to the duke. Never was there a dog so beautiful, so delicate, so agile, so gentle, and so obedient. The servants bring it in by a golden chain. When it is freed, it shakes its body, and the little bell that it wears on its neck sounds with so sweet a tinkling that Tristan forgets all his sorrow. His heart and senses are so strangely moved that he forgets even his love. No one living, when he heard that sound, could fail to be altogether consoled and filled with joy and to forget every other desire.

> Tristan determines to obtain the dog for Isolt, to free her from her grief for him. But he is too wise to make known his wish at once. One day the duke declares that there is nothing he would not give to be delivered from a giant that is coming to carry off the tribute of cattle which he levies yearly upon the people. Tristan succeeds in destroying the giant. When the delighted duke tells him to name his reward, he asks for Petit Crû.

---

[1] Bédier I, Ch. XXV.

He sends it to Isolt by a messenger. She has built
for it a beautiful golden niche, and has it carried with her
wherever she goes. But when she perceives that the
tinkling of the bell makes her forget her grief, and that
with her grief she forgets Tristan, she reproaches herself
bitterly that she should be gay while her lover is sad.
She tears the little bell from the dog's neck, and from
that moment it loses its magic power.

The tale of the giant and his tribute belongs to
the type of popular stories which we shall discuss
in connection with the Morholt. Even the trait that
the hero's attention is attracted by the sound of
cattle led across the bridge, and that he then makes
inquiries and learns of the tribute, we have found in
an account in the life of St. Judicael, and might find
perhaps in many others [1].

Lap-dogs were popular among German and French [2]
as well as Celtic [3] ladies in the Middle Ages. They
seem to have been held in both countries as a great
luxury. We read in the Welsh laws [4]:

> The pet animal of a king's wife or his daughter is a
> pound in value. The pet animal of a [breyr's] wife or his
> daughter is half a pound in value. The pet animal of
> a taeog's wife or his daughter is a curt penny in value
> because they ought not to keep pet animals.

---

[1] For giants in Tristan v. Hertz [5]; 547, Hertz [2] 538; Bédier I,
289, n. l. 715; Golther (1887), p. 19. For the trait in the life of
St. Judicael cf. A. de la Borderie, *Histoire de Bretagne*, Rennes
1905, I, p. 481.

[2] Weinhold, *Deutsche Frauen im Mittelalter* I, 109; Grimm,
Deutsche Rechtsaltertümer I, 487; Schultz, *Höfisches Leben* I, 450;
Herrig's *Archiv* XLVI (1870), 425 — 64, (*Der Hund in den
romanischen Sprachen*); Veldeke, *Eneide,* ed. O. Behaghel, Heilbronn 1882, 1766.

[3] Cormac's *Glossary,* ed. W. Stokes, p. 111, *s. v.* Mug-Éime;
Revue Celtique XV, p. 293. 310; *Voyage of Bran,* ed Meyer and
Nutt I, 81, § 23; *Ancient Laws of Ireland* I, 145. IV, 120.

[4] A. W. Wade-Evans: *Welsh Mediaeval Law*, Oxford 1909,
p. 254 — 5.

The lady treated her lap-dog with great consideration, and usually carried it in front of her on her horse when she rode. A lap-dog was a favorite gift from a lover.

β) The colors of the dog.

We find many accounts, both French and Irish, of dogs and horses of strange and varied coloring[1].

It may be that the horses and dogs were artificially colored in order to obtain this effect. We find the following passage in *Renaut de Montauban* in regard to the coloring of a horse:

> 'Maugis ot pris une herbe qui mult ot grant bonté;
> Au pont del branc d'acier a l'erbe pestelé;
> D'ew froide et de vin l'a molt bien destempré,
> Puis en a Baiart ters, le pis et le costé,
> Dont fu Baiars plus blans que n'est flors en esté.
> Puis en a oint Renaut; es le vos tot mué;
> En l'aé de .xv. ans ainsi l'a figuré[2].'

The practice of coloring domestic animals is believed by Jähns to have been introduced from the East, and to have established itself in Europe through the influence of the Crusades. As late as the sixteenth

---

[1] L. A. Paton, *Studies in the Fairy Mythology of Arthurian Romance, Radcliffe Monographs*, no. 13, Boston 1903, p. 230; D. Hyde, *Beside the Fire*, p. 15; *Silva Gadelica*, ed. S. H. O'Grady II, 333; *Wooing of Fraech*, in R. Thurneysen, *Sagen aus dem alten Irland*, Berlin 1901, p. 116. *Le roman d'Aubery le Bourgoing*, ed. P. Tarbé, Reims 1849, p. 62₂₆. *Fierabras*, ed. Kroeber and Servois, Paris 1860, 4109. *La chevalerie Ogier de Danemarche*, ed. Barrois, Paris 1842; Foerster, Crestien de Troyes, *Erec*, 5319 ff. Hartmann, *Erec*, 7307 ff.; Veldeke's *Eneide*, ed. Ettmüller, Leipzig 1852, 148₁₅ ff.; *Wigalois*, ed. F. Pfeiffer, Leipzig 1847, 68₁ ff.; *Carmina Burana*, ed. J. A. Schmeller, Stuttgart 1847, p. 161.
[2] *Renaus de Montauban*, ed. H. Michelant, Stuttgart 1862, p. 127, l. 4 ff.

century, he says, it was a favorite custom to dye the tail and mane and even the leg, red. Many of the old equestrian treatises contain directions how to obtain the 'turkish red' color for this purpose[1].

There is an elaborate description of a horse of many colors given to Tristan by Morgan le Fee in *Tristan Mönch*, an episodic poem of late origin found in one of the manuscripts of Gottfried von Strassburg[2].

We cite a few of the numerous Celtic passages in regard to colored dogs and horses.

> Then looked he at the color of the dogs, staying not to look at the stag, and of all the hounds that he had seen in the world, he had never seen any that were like unto those. For their hair was of a brilliant shining white, and their ears were red; and as the whiteness of their bodies shone, so did the redness of their ears glisten[3].

> 'O Ciaran', says his mother, 'do not now spoil the dyestuff for me; but let it be blessed by thee'. So when Ciaran blessed it there never was made, before or after, dyestuff as good as it, for though all the cloth of the Cenél Fiachrach were put into its *iarcáin*, it would make it blue, and finally it made blue the dogs, and the cats, and the trees against which it came[4].

---

[1] M. Jähns, *Ross und Reiter*, Leipzig 1872, II, 133; cf. O'Curry, *Manners and Customs* I, cccciv—v; F. Bangert, *Die Tiere im altfranzösischen Epos*, Marburg 1885, § 50. 62. 68—71 is not inclined to believe that the remarkable colors mentioned in the French romances are due to dyeing; A. Kitze, *Das Ross in den altfranzösischen Artus- und Abenteuerromanen*, Marburg 1888, p. 19—22, n. 120, offers no comment.

[2] Ed. H. Paul, *Tristan als Mönch, Sitzungsberichte der Münchener Akademie der Wissenschaften* 1895, p. 317 ff., l. 353—442; cf. supra, Ch. V, I, 3, p. 234 ff..

[3] *Pwyll, Prince of Dyved, The Mabinogion*, ed. Lady Guest, London 1849, III, 38.

[4] *Lives of the Saints from the Book of Lismore*, ed. W. Stokes, *Anecdota Oxeniensia*, p. 267, § 4076.

It is interesting to observe that Tristan's dogs, Husdent and Petit Crû, are the only ones in French romance which are given names. In Irish romance, on the contrary, in which, as in Tristan, hunting plays so important a part, the names of dogs are frequently mentioned.

> 'Goll', asked Cormac, 'what hounds were those?' — 'Bran and Sceolang held by Finn', replied Goll: 'Adhnuaill and Féruaine by Ossian; Iarratach and Fostadh by Oscar; Baeth and Buidhe by Dermot; Breac and Luath and Láinbhinn by Caeilte; Conuall and Comrith by mac Lughach'[1].

β) The bells.

In the story of Petit Crû, there is one trait that seems to us peculiarly Celtic — the description of the little bell that soothed the griefs of those who heard it. Cormac's branch, one of the familiar talismans of Irish romance, has a similar property[2].

> One day, at dawn in Maytime, Cormac, grandson of Conn, was alone on Múr Tea in Tara. He saw coming towards him a warrior, sedate (?), grayhaired. A purple, fringed mantle around him. A shirt, ribbed, gold threaded next (?) his skin. Two blunt shoes of white bronze between his feet and the earth. A branch of silver with three golden apples on his shoulder. Delight and amusement enough it was to listen to the music made by the branch, for men sore-wounded, or women in child-bed, or folk in sickness would fall asleep at the melody which was made when that branch was shaken . . . .
>
> . . . .
>
> At the end of a year the warrior comes into his meeting and asked of Cormac the consideration for his branch. 'It shall be given', says Cormac.
> 'I will take (thy daughter) Ailbe today', says the warrior.

---

[1] Cf. O'Grady, Silva Gadelica, In Agallamh I, 204. II, 231.
[2] Cormac's Adventure in the Land of Promise, Irische Texte III, 211—3; cf. Silva Gadelica II, 308; Voyage of Bran I, p. 2, n. 3. For passages in Irish romance descriptive of the power of music, cf. supra, Ch. VI, B. 2 and 3.

So he took the girl with him. The women of Tara utter three loud cries after the daughter of the king of Eriu. But Cormac shook the branch at them so that he banished grief from them all and cast them into sleep.

That day month comes the warrior and takes with him Cairpre Lifechair (the son of Cormac). Weeping and sorrow ceased not in Tara after the boy, and on that night no one therein ate or slept, and they were in grief and exceeding gloom. But Cormac shook the branch at them, and they parted from (their) sorrow.

Another account of Cormac's branch corresponds still more closely with the account in Tristan[1].

And this was the manner of that branch, that when anyone shook it, wounded men and women with child would be lulled to sleep by the sound of the very sweet fairy music which those apples uttered, and another property that branch had, that is to say that no one upon earth would bear in mind any want, woe, or weariness of soul when the branch was shaken for him, and whatever evil might have befallen anyone, he would not remember it at the shaking of the branch[2].

---

[1] *Trans. Ossianic Society* 1855, p. 213—4.

[2] Two other traits to which a Celtic origin has been ascribed we include here for want of a more appropriate place. Attention has been called to the description of the castle of Tintagel, in the *Folie Tristan* of the Douce manuscript

'Li lius ert beus e delitables,
Li païs bons e profitables,
E si fu jadis apelez
Tintagel li chastel faez.

Chastel faé fu dit a dreit,
Kar dous faiz l'an tuz se perdeit
Li païsant dient pur veir
Ke dous faiz l'an nel pot l'en veir,

Ne hom del païs ne nul hom,
Ja si grante guarde en prenge l'on,
Une en ivern, autre en esté;
So dient la gent del vingné.'
                (*La Folie Tristan*, ed. Bédier, p. 20, l. 129 ff.).

Such, says M. d'Arbois de Jubainville, is the castle of the Irish magician Cúroi, which could be rendered inaccessible

C. THE VOYAGE FOR HEALING AND THE OLD IRISH IMRAMA.

1. THE TRIBUTE TO THE MORHOLT.

In the opening of the Tristan story we are told that Mark is at war with the king[1]

'gewaldig zû Îberne'

on the nights when the master was absent. In the *Feast of Bricriu* it is said: 'In what airt soever of the globe Cúroi should happen to be, every night o'er the fort he chaunted a spell, till the fort revolved as swiftly as a mill-stone. The entrance was never to be found after sunset' (*Fled Bricrend* § 80; Windisch, *Irische Texte* I, 295; ed. G. Henderson, *Irish Texts Society*, p. 102—3).

Another passage from the *Folie Tristan* of the Douce manuscript has been compared to a description in the *Wooing of Etain*. The passage in *Tristan* is the following:

'Reis', fet li fol, 'la sus en l'air
Ai une sale u je repair.
De veire est faite, bele e grant;
Li solail vait par mi raiant;
En l'air est e par nues pent,
Ne berce e ne crolle pur vent.
Delez la sale ad une chambre
Faite de cristal e de lambre.
Li solail, quant main leverat,
Leenz mult grant clarté rendrat.'

(ed. Bédier, *La Folie Tristan*, p. 27, l. 301).

The passage in the *Wooing of Etain*: 'And he made a bower for Etain with clear windows for it through which she might pass, and a veil of purple was laid upon her; and that bower was carried about by Mac Oc wherever he went. And there each night she slept beside him by means that he devised, so that she became well-nourished and fair of form; for that bower was filled with marvellously sweet-scented shrubs, and it was upon these that she thrived, upon the odour and blossom of the best of precious herbs.' (ed. Windisch, *Irische Texte* I, p. 130; trans. A. H. Leahy, *Heroic Romances of Ireland* I, 7; cf. Zimmer, *ZfdA.* XXVIII, p. 587).

We see no connection between these passages. Cf., however, d'Arbois de Jubainville, *Revue Celtique* XXII, 133; Bédier II, 157.

[1] *OX* 59.

or, in another manuscript[1],

'ze Schotten und Yberne'.

We are not told how the struggle ended; we learn only that one of the princes who has come to Mark's aid wins the king's sister as his reward, and takes her back with him to his own land. Of their union is born the child Tristan. About fifteen years later a champion of the king of Ireland, who has reduced to subjection all the surrounding realms, turns his attention to Cornwall, and demands that Mark send him the tribute which he has withheld for more than fifteen years[2]. *Vreislich*[3] and *grûwelich*[4] is the Morholt, and Cornwall trembles before him. He is sister's husband to the king of Ireland, and he has the strength of four men. He requires as tribute every third child born in the Cornish land during the last fifteen years. If Mark will not give them willingly, he will take them himself, youths and maidens. The boys shall be his own, and the girls he will put in a brothel to earn him silver pennies late and early.

Traditions of human tribute are universal in primitive societies. Many localities preserve the memory of monsters, half man, half beast, who formerly inhabited the country and, issuing forth from their lairs, carried off the passers-by from time to time[5].

The following are a few examples of this belief which survive in France. In Gascony we hear of horned beings who dwell underground among the rocks.

---

[1] MS. *H.* v. Lichtenstein, p. 29, note to l. 59.
[2] *OX* 351 ff.
[3] *OX* 355.
[4] *OX* 798.
[5] E. S. Hartland, *Legend of Perseus* III, 1—95; Sébillot, *Folk Lore de France* I, 463 ff.; *Trans. Oss. Soc.* II, 62—71; cf. supra Ch. V C, The slaying of the dragon, p. 203 ff.

They have the bodies of men, but tails and hairy legs like goats. It is believed that these creatures will live till the end of the world, but that they cannot rise for the judgment day. When they used to live in Gascony they carried off the fairest maidens of the country. They have no horned women like themselves[1].

The caves of Bugey are believed to be the haunt of a mysterious being to whom men used to bring large bowls of milk to the entrance of the caverns that sheltered him by turn. He is a creature sad as death; he walks with bent head and draws back into his cave rather than talk with his benefactors[2].

A grotto of Périgord used to be frequented by a monster who fed upon the flesh of passers-by. A cavern in a mountain called Rez de Sol, in Auvergne, used to be inhabited by a ferocious being, half man, half beast, who devoured the inhabitants of the surrounding country[3].

Among the many stories of dragons current in popular tradition in France, there is one from Villedieu-lès-Bailleul in Normandy of a monstrous serpent that used to be the terror of the neighboring districts. To calm his rage the inhabitants presented him the first fruits of harvest and the purest milk of the herds. At times he required a young girl, whom he dragged to his cave and devoured[4].

Beowulf and the *Grettir Saga* are literary expressions of similar traditions. Professor Panzer, in his study of the former, gives a number of examples of folk-tales which relate how the inhabitants of the devastated country secure peace from a dragon by

---

[1] Sébillot, *op. cit.*, I, 463.
[2] Sébillot I, 464.
[3] Sébillot I, 464.
[4] Sébillot I, 469.

offering to him at regular intervals a sheep, a calf, or a young girl. The victims are usually chosen by lot[1]. It is unnecessary to multiply instances of this practise. Welsh and Irish popular tales are rich in them.

These monsters are frequently represented as dwelling in or near the water. It is possible that the name Morholt, of which the first syllable signifies in the Celtic languages *sea,* and in the Germanic *marsh,* may be connected with this belief[2]. M. Joseph Loth suggests the etymology **mori-solto-* < an old Celtic **mori-spolto-,* he who cleaves the seas. **spolto-,* remarks M. Loth, has given the Welsh *hollt,* Cornish and Breton *folt* — (Cornish *felja,* to cleave, Breton *faota* for *falta*)[3].

There naturally associates itself with the superstition of the monster, an account of the delivery of the country from him. Such narratives are frequent in saints' lives, epics, and pseudo-historical accounts, as well as in folk-tales. The two French folk-tales last cited are concluded satisfactorily in this way.

---

[1] F. Panzer, *Studien zur germanischen Sagengeschichte* I, *Beowulf,* p. 276 ff.

[2] *Morhold* is a Germanic name, cited by Foerstemann, *Altdeutsches Namenbuch*[2], 1118, from Frankish documents of the eighth century. Cf. Hertz[5], 517; Hertz[2], 511 ff.; Golther (1907), p. 17. Dr. H. G. Leach and Professor Axel Olrik, who have aided me in searching for it in Scandinavian documents, have found no trace of it. Cf. O. Rygh, *Gamle Personnami Norske Stedsname,* Kristiana 1901.

It is improbable that the name Morholt has been substituted, as Golther suggests (1907, p. 17), for a lost Celtic name connected with *mor.* It is difficult to believe that French poets would have substituted for an unknown Celtic name an unknown Germanic one. The name Morholt is unknown in France. E. Langlois, *Table des noms propres de toute nature compris dans les chansons de geste imprimées,* Paris 1904; Longnon, *Polyptique de l'Abbaye de St. Germain des Prés,* Paris 1895. The substitution of the well-known Morant (cf. Langlois, 470) would not have been astonishing, but this form first occurs in the English *Sir Tristrem.*

[3] *Contributions, op. cit.,* 29 n.

The *Legenda Aurea* of Jacobus de Voragine represents the citizens of Silena in Libya as suffering from the visits of a dragon who had his lair in a swamp near the town. In order to appease him, the citizens determined to offer two sheep daily. When their flock failed, they substituted one sheep and one human being. The victim was chosen by lot from the sons and daughters of the citizens. The lot at last falls upon the king's daughter, who is delivered by St. George[1].

We have another example of the use of this folk-tale with emphasis on the demand of tribute in the story of the Minotaur. This was a monster, half man, half bull, which Minos kept captive in the Cnossan labyrinth and fed with the bodies which the Athenians were obliged at fixed times to send as tribute. This tribute was the result of a war waged by Minos in revenge for the death of his son Androgeos, who had been slain on Attic soil. The vanquished Athenians had been compelled to promise to send to Minos annually for nine years seven youths and seven maidens, according to most accounts chosen by lot. They were finally delivered by Theseus[2]. Delivery from a similar tribute is recounted in Pausanias[3] as an exploit of Kleostratos.

The biblical Moloch and the Carthaginian Saturn, to whom human sacrifice is offered, belong to the same class of monsters.

---

[1] E. S. Hartland, *The Legend of Perseus,* in his chapter on the *Rescue of Andromeda, op. cit.* III, pp. 1—95, has brought together a great number of variants of this story.

[2] Daremberg, *Dictionnaire des antiquités grecques et romaines, Minotaurus;* Roscher, *Ausführliches Lexikon der griechischen und römischen Mythologie, s. v.*

[3] IX, 26, 5.

Among the Irish, stories of human tribute paid to monsters are almost invariably associated with the Fomorians[1]. The accounts of the Fomorians show a gradual process of rationalization which is, perhaps, suggestive, of the development which the story of the Morholt underwent previous to the redaction of our extant Tristan texts.

The modern Irish word *fomhair, famhair, foghmair* (pronounced *foar*) is ordinarily used for giant. It seems to have had this meaning as early as 1100, for it is so used in the *History of Monsters*[2], *that is the Fomori and the Dwarfs* in the *Book of the Dun*

---

[1] The reader must be on his guard against attaching too much importance to the similarity between the names *Morholt* and *Fomori* 'As to Morholt and Fomori', says Prof. Kuno Meyer, in answer to a personal inquiry, 'I do not see how any connection is possible. Do not forget that Fomori was accented on the first syllable; the *m* is *mh* (pronounced *w*)'. The effort to connect the two was first made by Muret, *Romania* XVII, 606; XXVII, 112. Deutschbein, *Beiblatt zur Anglia* XV, 20, and Golther (1907) 17, repeat the suggestion. It is possible that the *mor* in the two words is identical in origin.

Deutschbein, *Beiblatt zur Anglia* XV, 16 ff., compares the story of the Morholt in Tristan with an Irish story of a princess offered as tribute to the Fomorians, and delivered by Cuchulainn (*Revue Celtique* XXIX, 141). This Irish episode is in place in a discussion of the Morholt only as representing one of the innumerable folk-tales originating in local traditions similar to those which gave rise to the pseudo-historical accounts of the Fomorian tribute. The mere fact that it exists in a very old manuscript gives no significance to the analogue. In discussing this incident, Rhys (*Hibbert Lectures*, p. 595) justly remarks that the Fomori here assume the place occupied by the dragon in the legends of other lands and that the episode is the familiar folk-tale of the winning of a princess, with the usual heightening of interest by the concealment of the identity of the hero. Nutt pronounces it 'a folk-tale arbitrarily altered', and Hartland, who cites his opinion (*Perseus* III, 50), agrees with it.

The episode has moreover been proved beyond a doubt by Irish scholars (Zimmer, *ZfdA.* XXXII, 240; Meyer, *Revue Celtique* XI, 435 ff.) to be an interpolation that has no connection, either with the story in which it stands, or with the adventures of Cuchulainn, or with the Fomorians.

[2] d'Arbois, *Cours de la littérature celtique* II, 92—3.

Cow, and by Giraldus Cambrensis[1]. All the extant accounts reflect the impression made upon the Celts by the Scandinavian pirates, whose ravages in the western isles date from 795. To this Keating's etymology is traceable: 'It is wherefore they used to be called Fomorians, namely from their being committing robbery on sea. *Fomhóraigh*, i. e., along the seas[2].' The Fomorians had originally no connection with the Scandinavians. There are indications that they were a race of monsters. The name of one of their leaders, Cichol Gri cen Chos (Cricenchos?), means the Footless. In a poem quoted by Keating, he is referred to as Cíocal the stunted, of withered feet[3]. A pseudo-historical account of the invasions of Ireland in a twelfth century manuscript describes the Fomorians as having only one eye and one hand. Some of them appear to have had only one hand and one foot, others to have been horned[4]. The names of one of their tax collectors, Morc (Horse), and one of their kings, Echaid Echchenn (Horsehead) lead Rhys to class them with the Luchorpáin and Goborchinn, monsters with their upper parts animal and lower parts human. Rhys explains the word Fomorian as meaning *under the seas*, and considers the race as imaginary creatures who originally had their abodes in or beneath the lakes and the sea, whence they paid unwelcome visits to the land[5].

---

[1] *Topographia Hibernica* III, § 2, ed. Dimock (*Rolls Series*), p. 141, l. 27. 142, l. 7.

[2] Keating, *History of Ireland*, ed. Comyn I, p. 183.

[3] ed. Comyn I, 163. The editor adds the note or *hairy-legged?*

[4] d'Arbois, *Cours* II, 92—6. 99. 103, following a passage in the *Leabhar na h-Uidhri* (before 1100), analogous to one which in the Book of Leinster serves as an introduction to the *Lebar Gabála* (*Book of Invasions*).

[5] J. Rhys, *Hibbert Lectures*, p. 592 ff.

We are told that after the death of Nemed, the Fomorians settled in Tory Island and levied upon Ireland an annual tribute of two thirds of the sons and daughters of the inhabitants, and two thirds of the grain and milk. This tribute was brought to the island by the subject people every year on the night before the first of November[1]. The extortions of the Fomorians are mentioned again and again in the succeeding periods of Irish history[2]. The most famous account of delivery from the tribute paid to them is in the story of the *Second Battle of Moytura*. This tradition, which dates as far back as the tenth century is extant only in a manuscript of the fifteenth. The language presents some eleventh century forms[3].

---

[1] cf. *Catha Neimid re Fomorchaib*, d'Arbois, *Catalogue de la Littérature épique d'Irlande*, Paris 1883, 56. Zimmer, *ZfdA*. XXXII, 196 ff., following the *Book of Leinster*.

[2] For discussions of the character of the Fomorians in Irish literature, v. O'Curry, *Lectures on the Mss. Materials*, Index; O'Curry, *Manners*, Index; O'Curry, *Atlantis* IV, 234, 164, n. 148, p. 159; vol. III, 390; J. Rhys, *Hibbert Lectures*, Lecture VI, p. 593; d'Arbois, *Le Cycle Mythologique*, *Cours* II, Index; *Epopée* 393—448; *Catalogue* 56; Zimmer, *Berl. Akad. der Wiss.* 1891, p. 312; Zimmer, *ZfdA.*, XXXII, 196 ff.; Stokes, *Revue Celtique* XII, p. 52—130; Meyer and Nutt, *Voyage of Bran* II index, *s. v. Fomorians*.
Allusions to the Fomorians are found in poems of Cinaed hua Artacain, and Eochaid hua Flainn, and in Cormac's *Glossary*, texts previous to the tenth century. Cf. infra.

[3] Stokes, *Revue Celtique* XII, p. 63 § 25 ff. This tale exists only in a fifteenth century manuscript, Harl. 5280. Stokes points out that it contains several loan-words from Old Norse 'which can hardly have been naturalized in Ireland before the tenth or eleventh century, and one which points to the fourteenth. Of the grammatical forms, many are, doubtless, Old Irish . . . On the whole the language is of considerable antiquity'. *Revue Celtique*, XII, p. 53.
D'Arbois de Jubainville, *Epopée*, p. 394 ff., attempts to distinguish the interpolations (none of which have been included in our résumé) and dates the 'rédaction primitive' as far back as 900. He bases this conclusion chiefly on the fact that quotations from our text are found in the *Leabhar na h-Uidhri* and in Cormac's *Glossary*. He cites allusions to the second battle of Moytura in poems of Cinaed hua Artacain who died in 975, and of Fland Manistrech, who died in 1056.

The story of the *Second Battle of Moytura,* which
relates Lugh's abolishing the Fomorian tribute, bears
a general similarity to the story of Tristan's delivery
of Cornwall from tribute to the Morholt. We offer
a synopsis of it as suggestive of how the account of
the Morholt, if indeed it is a traditional element,
may have appeared in earlier versions of the Tristan
story.

Now when Bres had assumed the kingship, the Fomorians bound their tribute upon Ireland, so that there
was not smoke from a roof in Ireland that was not under
tribute to them. But when the Tuatha de Danann deposed
Bres they ceased to pay the tribute, and now the Fomorians
had come with a terrible host to impose their tribute and
their rule perforce. Never came to Ireland a host more
horrible or fearful than that host of the Fomorians. The
men from Scythia of Lochlann and the men out of the
Western Isles were rivals in that expedition.

A young warrior, fair and shapely, with a king's
trappings, was coming with his band to Tara where the
Tuatha de Danann were feasting. The doorkeeper asks
his lineage, and he replies that he is Lugh, son of Cian,
son of Dian-cecht (of the Tuatha de Danann) and of Ethne,
daughter of Balor (of the Fomorians). The Fomorians and
the Tuatha de Danann had made a truce fifteen years
before, of which this marriage was the confirmation. The
door-keeper further asks the youth 'What art dost thou
practise; for no one without an art enters Tara'. The youth
offers himself as a wright, but is refused, since they have
a wright already; then as a smith, a champion, a harper,
a hero, a poet, a sorcerer, a leech, a cup-bearer, a brazier.
But all these they have already. Lugh says again: 'Ask
the king whether he has a single man who possesses all
these arts, and if he has, I will not enter Tara'. The king
then commands that the chessboards be brought, and the
stranger youth wins all the stakes. Then the king says:
'Let him into the garth, for never before has man like
him entered this fortress'. He entered the fortress then
and sat down in the sage's seat, for he was a sage in
every art.

Then the great flagstone, (to move) which required the
effort of four score yoke (of oxen), Ogma hurled through
the house so that it lay on the outside of Tara. This was
a challenge to Lugh. But Lugh cast it back, so that it
lay in the centre of the palace; and he put the piece
which it had carried away into the side of the palace and
made it whole.

'Let a harp be played for us', say the hosts. So the
warrior played a sleep-strain for the hosts and for the king
the first night. He cast them into a sleep from that hour
to the same time on the following day. He played a wail-
strain so that they were crying and lamenting. He played
a smile-strain, so that they were in merriment and
joyance.

Now Nuada (the king), when he beheld the warrior's
many powers, considered whether he (Lugh) could put
away from them the bondage which they suffered from the
Fomorians. So they held a council concerning the warrior.
This is the decision to which Nuada came, to change seats
with the warrior. So Lugh went to the king's seat, and
the king rose up before him till thirteen days had ended.

. . . .

Now when provision (?) of the battle had then been
settled, Lugh and Dagdae and Ogma went to the three
gods of Danu, and these gave Lugh the . . . of the battle;
and for seven years they were preparing for it and making
their weapons.

Then the Fomorians march till their . . . were in Scetne.
'The men of Ireland venture to offer battle to us', says
Bres to Indech. 'I give this anon', says Indech, 'so that
their bones will be small unless they pay their tributes'.

Because of Lugh's knowledge, the men of Ireland had
made a resolution not to let him go into the battle. So
his nine fosterers are left to protect him. They feared an
early death for the hero, owing to the multitude of his
arts. Therefore they did not let him go forth to the fight.

But Lugh had speech as to their arts with every one
of the leaders in turn, and he strengthened and addressed
his army so that each man of them had the spirit of a
king or a mighty lord.

Then when the battle followed, Lugh escaped in disguise
from the keeping in which he was so that it was he who

was in front of the battalion of the Tuath Dea. So then
a keen and cruel battle was fought between the tribe of
the Fomorians and the men of Ireland. Lugh was hearten-
ing the men of Ireland that they should fight the battle
fervently so that they should not be any longer in
bondage. For it was better for them to find death in protecting their fatherland than to bide under bondage and
tribute as they had been. Wherefore then Lugh sang this
chant below, as he went round the men of Eriu.

. . . .

Lugh and Balor of the Piercing Eye met in the battle.
An evil eye had Balor. That eye was never opened save
only on a battlefield. Then he and Lugh met.

'Lift up mine eyelid, my lad', says Balor, 'that it
may see the babbler who is conversing with me'. The
lid is raised from Balor's eye. Then Lugh cast a sling-stone
at him which carried the eye through his head.

Then the battle became a rout, and the Fomorians were
beaten to the sea.

Both the story of Tristan and the Morholt, and
of Lugh and the Fomorians are accounts of a people
suffering under a tribute imposed by a foreign power[1].
This tribute includes a certain proportion of the
children of the country. The tax collectors come with
an army by sea to take the tribute by force if necessary. Fifteen years previous to the opening of
the story, the kingdom had had a struggle with the
enemy, and it had resulted in a truce. At this time
a child had been born, one of whose parents was of
high birth among the subject people and the other
was from another land. The boy has been brought
up among the stranger people and, now become a
youth, sets out to the realm of his other parent and

---

[1] J. Rhys (*Hibbert Lectures*, 607 ff.) calls attention to the
similarity between the tradition of the Fomorians among the Irish,
and that described in the *Mabinogion* and called in the Welsh
triads the scourge of March Malaen.

offers his services to the king. He is graciously received on account of his surprising ingenuity and strength. After a council, the charge of delivering the country from the tribute is put into his hands. He exhorts the subject people to defy the oppressors. The king is unwilling to let him engage in combat on account of his youth, but he nevertheless attacks the champion of the tyrants and kills him. He is thenceforth associated with the people whom he has delivered.

We do not cite these traits with the idea of establishing by means of them a relation between the story of Tristan and that of Lugh, but as an example of a characteristically Celtic story similar to that of the Morholt. In the extant texts there is nothing in the account of the tribute to the Morholt nor of Tristan's encounter with him that could not have been appropriated from twelfth century French tradition and literature.

We find mention of tribute similar to that demanded by the Morholt in numerous French romances, among them the *Roman d'Aquin*, where *trente pucelles* are among the exactions of the Norse from the Bretons[1]. Crestien reckons among the exploits of Yvain the destruction of two monsters to whom the king of the Ile des Pucelles promises an annual tribute of thirty maidens[2]. The account of the hero's birth and accomplishments and of his coming to offer his services to the distressed people, is such as might be found in the story of any primitive hero. The account of the actual encounter with the Morholt, as we shall see in the following pages, is entirely in accordance

---

[1] Ed. Sonon des Longrais *Soc. des bibliophiles Bretons,* Nantes 1880, CXIV.

[2] Ed. Foerster, l. 5279—84.

with twelfth century customs in France and England,
and has many analogues in twelfth century French
romance.

There are indications, however, in the account of
the voyage for healing made by Tristan after he has
been wounded by the Morholt, that the person from
whom Tristan received the poisoned wound was
originally a supernatural being, very recently rationalized by the redactors into an Irish champion, the
uncle of Isolt. We are therefore inclined to recognize
in the Morholt tribute, in spite of the conventional
chivalric features which it presents in the extant texts,
the survival of a tradition of considerable antiquity.

2. THE ISLAND COMBAT.

The Morholt comes with his army in the direction
of Cornwall. He sends messengers to Mark offering
to defend his right to the tribute in a judicial duel.
Tristan accepts the challenge, and arrangements are
made for the combat. It is to take place on an island.

a) The place of combat in the conventional chivalric duel [1].

The advantages of an island or a boat in the
middle of a stream as a meeting place for rival powers
seem to have been appreciated throughout the Middle

---

[1] The following study on the island combat appeared in
Radcliffe College Monographs, no. 15, Boston and London 1910,
p. 27—50. I am deeply indebted to Miss Hope Allen and Professor
Schofield, who had the labor of putting the article through the
press during my absence from America. The references to the
island combats in the *Eneas* and *Sone de Nausay* appear here
for the first time.

Ages. An early instance of this recognition of the
stream as a sort of neutral territory is the treaty
signed by Athanaric the Visigoth and the Emperor
Valens, where the contracting parties met on a boat
in the Danube[1]. Another, much later (1215), is Magna
Carta, signed on an island at Runnymede. Similarly,
the tradition of the tribute levied by the Fomorians
on Ireland represents it as being brought yearly to
the plain of Magh Céidne, which lies between the
rivers Drowse and Erne[2].

For the judicial combat the island position would
be especially favorable. Disturbances from the crowd
or interference from friends of one or the other of
the combatants would be effectually prevented. On
the other hand, the spectators would be afforded a
favorable position to watch the combat from the
opposite shores or from boats along the stream. Fair
play on the part of the champions would be further
assured by the fact that the island offered a natural
boundary beyond which neither could withdraw.

An examination of mediaeval accounts of judicial
duels[3] shows that these considerations were universally appreciated. The single combats in the Old Irish
epic take place at the ford of a river, a position offering similar advantages[4]. The Norse term *holmgang*
(going to the island) and numerous accounts in the

---

[1] Ammian. Marc. xxvii, 5. 9, cited by Keary, *The Vikings
in Western Christendom*, London 1891, p. 35.

[2] Keating, *History of Ireland*, ed. Comyn, *Irish Texts Soc.*
I, 180—1.

[3] It is unnecessary, of course, to state that the judicial
combat is a prehistoric Aryan custom. Readers will recall the
description of the duel between Menelaus and Paris in the *Iliad*.
For the history of the judicial combat, see Lea, *Superstition and
Force*, Philadelphia 1892.

[4] Cf. *Die altirische Heldensage Táin bó Cúalnge*, ed.
Windisch, Leipzig 1908, passim.

sagas[1] show that the Scandinavians usually selected an island as the place for a judicial duel.

It is our purpose here to show that the island combat was familiar in twelfth century France, and that the Tristan-Morholt duel offers no peculiarity which is not richly paralleled in accounts of the conventional chivalric duels there. A study of the descriptions of the judicial duel in mediaeval romances and chronicles shows that the details in connection with the island are as stereotyped as those of the other formalities.

The preliminaries of the Tristan combat fall in exactly with the type established by Pfeffer and Schultz as the conventional description of the judicial duel in mediaeval literature[2]. They comprise the following:

a) The Indictment (Pfeffer a)[3].

The Morholt claims the tribute which he declares is justly due him.

O. He accompanies the message with an offer to prove his right to it by single combat or general battle. P 7, 6—13; X 404—442; Č 12, 17—14, 3.

---

[1] See Vigfússon, *Icelandic Dictionary*, p. 280, under *holmganga*; Paul Du Chaillu, *The Viking Age*, London 1889, I, 563 —577.

[2] M. Pfeffer, *Die Formalitäten des gottesgerichtlichen Zweikampfes, Zts. f. rom. Philol.* IX (1885), 1—75; A. Schultz, *Höfisches Leben zur Zeit der Minnesinger*, Leipzig 1889, II, 165; O. Leibecke, *Der verabredete Zweikampf in der altfranzösischen Literatur*, Göttingen 1905. For the reference to Dr. Leibecke's dissertation I am indebted to my friend Miss Hibbard of Mount Holyoke College.

[3] The references to the versions of *Tristan* are as follows:
O — Eilhart von Oberg.
T — Thomas:
    S — *Saga*.
    E — *Sir Trestem*.
    G — Gottfried von Strassburg, *Tristan*, ed. Marold.
R — *Le Roman en Prose de Tristan*, ed. Löseth.

> T. The Morholt comes in person: single
> combat or general battle are the
> implied alternatives. S 30, 21—25;
> ch. xxvi (32); E lxxxvi—xci; G 5954
> —5973.

b) The Challenge (Pfeffer *b*; Schultz, p. 159).
His claim is denied and a judicial combat is
agreed upon.

> O. Mark sends word to Morholt, ap-
> pointing the time and place for the
> combat (no mention of gage). P 13,
> 10—15; X 709—723; Č 24, 3—13.

> T. Tristan personally denies before
> the assembly and before Morholt
> that the tribute is justly due.
> Morholt challenges him to single
> combat and Tristan accepts. S 32,
> 19—34, ch. xxvii (34) — xxviii (36)
> (glove); E xcii (ring); G 6264—6496
> (glove).

c) The Vigil (Pfeffer *d*; Schultz, p. 164).

> R. Tristan passes the night in prayer
> in the church (Bédier II, 326 n. 1;
> Löseth, § 28).

d) The Mass (Pfeffer *e*; Schultz, pp. 164, 167).

> R. Tristan hears mass on the morning
> of the combat (Bédier II, 326 n. 1;
> Löseth, § 28).

e) The Prohibition against Interference from the
Spectators (Pfeffer *b*; Schultz, p. 167).
G 6731—6736.

f) The Combat (Pfeffer *i*).

   I. The time of the combat (Pfeffer *i*, *I*).

      1. Appointment of the day (Pfeffer *i*, *I*, *1*).

         O. Mark appoints the third day for the combat. Morholt receives the message on the second day, and sets out preparing to meet his opponent on the next, i. e. on the third day. P 13, 11, 21; X 715. 742; Č 24, 6.

         T. (?) S 34, 1—2; ch. xxvii (35). The combat follows the challenge immediately.

         E. The time is not specified.

         G. The combat is deferred till the third day after the challenge.

      2. Appointment of the hour (Pfeffer *i*, *I*, *2*; Schultz, p. 169).

         O. The combat is to begin in the morning. P 13, *zu rechter streytzeyt*; X 733. 743; Č (24)6. (25)2.

         T. (?) S, E, G, not specified.

Schultz has overlooked the fact that the place of combat is frequently an island, and Pfeffer passes it over in a note[1]. It seems desirable, therefore, to analyze here at length, in connection with *Tristan*, the twenty-two versions — Old French, Latin, and Middle English — of the fifteen instances of island

---

[1] Schultz, *op. cit.* II, 165—6; Pfeffer, *op. cit.*, p. 62, § 4. Correct Godefr. 1870 to 4974. Leibecke, whose work was unknown to me when I prepared this chapter, mentions that an island is frequently the place of combat. He cites (p. 61) some of the passages I have given, and one that I had not seen: *Sone von Nausay*, ed. M. Goldschmidt, Tübingen 1899, 5073.

combats (thirteen of them from French romances, one
from Geoffrey of Monmouth, and one from the annals of
Jocelin of Brakelond) that have come to our notice [1].
They all appear in a conventional setting, and the
treatment of them is lacking in any indication that they
were considered extraordinary. The examples cited
seem sufficient, therefore, to establish the fact that the
practice, so well suited to the requirements for a
judicial duel, was widespread and frequent.

The following is a list of the island combats that
we have examined. The abbreviations indicated will
be employed in the analysis:

1. The duel between Henry of Essex and Robert of
   Mountford.
   > Jocelin — *Chronica Jocelini de Brakelonda*
   > (Annals of the Monastery of St. Edmund),
   > Camden Society [2].

2. The duel between Arthur and Flollo.
   a) Geoffrey — *Gottfried's von Monmouth Histo-
      ria Regum Britanniae*, ed. San Marte, Halle
      1854.
   b) Wace — *Le Roman de Brut*, ed. Le Roux
      de Lincy, Rouen 1836.
   c) Layamon — *Layamon's Brut*, ed. F. Madden,
      London 1847.

3. The duel between Roland and Olivier.
   > Girard — *Le Roman de Girard de Viane*,
   > ed. Tarbé, Rheims 1850.

---

[1] Several of these have been already cited; cf. Bédier I, 84
n. 2; Kölbing, *Germania* XXXIV, 190—5; Pfeffer, *op. cit.*, p. 162;
Golther, *Tristan* (1907), p. 17; Kölbing, *Sir Bevis of Hamtoun*,
E. E. T. S., 1894, pt. III, p. 350, note to l. 4141.
[2] I am indebted to Dr. K. G. T. Webster for this reference.

4. The duel between Ogier and Charlot and between Sadoines and Karahues.

Ogier (Chevalerie) — *La Chevalerie Ogier
de Danemarche*, ed. J. Barrois, Paris 1842.

5. The duel between Ogier and Brunamon.

Ogier (Enfances) — *Les Enfances Ogier,·*
ed. A. Scheler, Brussels 1874.

6. The duel between Helyas and Macaire.

Chev. Cygne — *Monuments pour servir à
l'histoire des provinces de Namur, de Hainaut
et de Luxembourg, Le chevalier au cygne et
Godefroid de Bouillon*, ed. Baron von Reiffenberg, Brussels 1846, Vol. IV.

7. The duel between Cornumaran and Aupatris.

Godefroi — *La Chanson du Chevalier au
Cygne et de Godefroid de Bouillon*, Paris
1874—1876, Vol. II.

8. The duel between Sir Torrent and the giant
Cate.

Sir Torrent — *Torrent of Portyngale*, ed.
E. Adam, E. E. T. S., London 1887.

9. The duel between Guy and Amorant.

a) *Guy of Warwick* (couplets), *G. & A.* — *The
Romance of Guy of Warwick*, the second or
fifteenth century version, ed. Zupitza (from
the paper MS. Ff. 2, 38 in the University
Library, Cambridge), E. E. T. S., London
1875. 1876.

b) *Guy of Warwick* (Auchinleck MS.), *G. & A.
The Romance of Guy of Warwick*, ed. Zupitza
(from the Auchinleck MS. and from MS. 107
in Caius College), E. E. T. S., London 1883.
1887. 1891.

10. The duel between Guy and Colebrande.

    a) *Guy of Warwick* (couplets), *G. & C.* — See above.

    b) *Guy and Colebrande* — *Bishop Percy's Folio MS.*, ed. Hales and Furnivall, London 1868, Vol. II.

11. The duel between Bevis and Yvor.

    a) *Boeve* — *Der Anglonormannische Boeve de Haumtone*, ed. A. Stimming (*Bibliotheca Normannica* VII), Halle 1899.

    b) *Bevis* — *Sir Bevis of Hamtoun*, ed. Kölbing, E. E. T. S., London 1885. 1886. 1894.

12. The duel between Otuel and Roland.

    a) *Otinel* — *Gui de Bourgogne, Otinel, Floovant*, ed. Guessard, *Les Anciens Poètes de la France*, Paris 1858.

    b) *Otuel* — *The Taill of Rauf Coilyear*, with the fragments of *Roland and Vernagu* and *Otuel*, ed. S. J. Herrtage, E. E. T. S., London 1882.

    c) *Duke Rowland and Sir Otuell* — *The Sege off Melayne* and the *Romance of Duke R. and Sir O. of Spayne*, ed. Herrtage, E. E. T. S., London 1880.

13. The duel between Aeneas and Turnus.
Eneas, ed. Salverda de Grave, *Bibliotheca Normannica* IV, Halle 1891.

14. The duel between Sone and Aligos. *Sone* — *Sone von Nausay*, ed. M. Goldschmidt, Tübingen 1899.

15. The duel between Tristan and Morholt.

We can now make an analysis of the features connected with the place of combat, including here the parallels from the above works.

I. The place of combat
(Pfeffer. *i*, ii; Schultz, pp. 165—7).

A. *Tristan.* An island in the sea.

O. P 13, 4. Auff den word.

X 711. Bî den sê ûf ein wert.

Č (island characteristics effaced)[1].

T. S (island characteristics effaced).

E xciv. þe yland was ful brade,.
þat þai gun in fiȝt.

G 6727.

Ein kleiniu insel in dem mer,
dem stade sô.nâhe unde dem her,
daz man dâ wol bereite sach,
swaz in der insele geschach.
und was ouch daz beredet dar an.
daz âne dise zwêne man
nieman dar în kaeme,
biz der kampf ende naeme.
daz wart ouch wol behalten.

La Folie Tristan (MS. Berne ed. Bédier, 100)..
En l'ile ou fui menez a nage.

R. (Löseth, § 28; Bédier II, 326 n. 1). Island of Saint Samson.

Cf. *Erec* 1247—1251.

Onques, ce cuit, tel joie n'ot
La ou Tristanz le fier Morhot
An l'isle saint Sanson vainqui,
Con l'an feisoit d'Erec iqui.

---

[1] For the absence of the island characteristics in the Czech redaction of Eilhart and in the Saga, see Appendix I.

B. Parallels in mediaeval literature.

    1. The island is in the sea.

        Sir Torrent 1248.

> Then take counsell kyng and knyght,
> On lond that he shold not ffyght,
> But ffar oute in the see,
> In an yle long and brad.

        Guy of Warwick (couplets), *G. & A.* 7965.

> To an yle besyde the see,
> There the batayle schulde bee.

        Guy of Warwick (couplets), *G. & C.* 101. 31.

> In a place, where they schulde bee,
> Yn an yle wythynne the see.

    Guy and Colebrande 202.

> Then the Gyant loud did crye:
> to the King of Denmarke these words says
>   [hee,
> "behold & take good heede!
> yonder is an Iland in the sea;
> ffrom me he can-not scape away,
> nor passe my hands indeed;
> but I shall either slay him with my brand,
> or drowne him in yonder salt strand;
> ffro me he shall not scape away."

    Sone 5073.

> En une ille qu'en mer estoit.

    2. The island is in a river.

        Ogier (Enfances).

> Fu Karahues en l'isle voirement,
> Il et Sadoines, armés moult gentement.
>   2618.

Seur les estriers chascuns d'aus .ii. s'estent,
Droit vers le gué s'en vont mult fierement.
2642.

Entre Charlot et le Danois Ogier
Orent le gué passé par le gravier. 2658.

En l'isle furent tout .iiii. li baron. 2711.

Chevalier au Cygne 1631.

Derière le palais au fort roy Oriant
Avoit une rivière moult bielle et bien
[courant,
Qui une ille entre deulx aloit avironnant,
L'ille fu longe et lée demy-lieue durant;
Là fù li camps frumés et derière et devant.

Godefroi 4947.

Chil sont remés en l'isle, où l'erbe est
[verdoians.

Otinel 324.

Entre .ii. eves en ont mené Rollant;
Ce est le pré où furent combatant
Li dui baron, quiconqu'en soit dolant.

Otuel 418.

þere þe bataille sscholde be.
Al a-boute þe water ran.

Duke Rowland and Sir Otuell 379.

þay broghte þam by-twene two watirs
[brighte —
Sayne, and Meryn le graunte, þay highte,
Als þe bukes gan vs saye —
In to a Medowe Semely to sighte,
There als these doghety men solde fighte
With-owiten more delaye.

Ogier (Chevalerie) 2959.
> Li baron furent en l'ille enmi 'l'erbage.

Guy of Warwick (Auchinleck), *G. & A.* 96. 4.
> Þan speken þai alle of þe batayle:
> Where it schuld be, wiþ-outen fayle,
> þai token hem to rede.
> þan loked þai it schuld be
> in a launde vnder the cite:
> þider þai gun hem lede.
> Wiþ a riuer it ern al about:
> þer-in schuld fiȝt þo kniȝtes stout.
> þai miȝt fle for no nede.

Geoffrey, p. 130. 53.
> Conveniunt uterque in insulam quae erat
> extra civitatem.

Sir Bevis 4141.
> In an yle vnder þat cité,
> þar þat scholde þe bataile be.

Jocelin, p. 52.
> Convenerunt autem apud Radingas pu-
> gnaturi in insula quadam satis Abbatie
> vicina.

Layamon 23, 873.
> He wende to þan yllond: mid gode his wepne.
> he stop vppe þat yllod: and nam his stede
> [on his hond.
> þe men þat hine þar brohte: ase þe king
> [þam hehte.
> lette þane bot wende: forþ mid þan watere.

Wace 10, 278.
> Es vous les deux vassax armés
> Et dedens l'ille el pré entrés.

Eneas 7838.

> et manda li qu'a l'uime jor,
> en une isle desoz la tor,
> fust la bataille par els deus [1].

II. The champions arm
(Pfeffer i, III).

A. *Tristan.*

O. Mark arms Tristan with his own hands. P 13, 21—25; X 750—775; Č ——.

T. Both Tristan's and Morholt's equipment are described. S 34, 7—24, ch. xxviii [36]; E ——; G 6505—6525, 6538—6725.

The hero parts from his friends at the shore (not mentioned by Pfeffer, but frequent).

O. Tristan embraces Mark and sets off for the place of combat, commended to heaven by the weeping spectators. P 13, 25—14, 4; X 775—788; Č 25, 5—16.

T. Same with different details. S 34, 19—23, ch. xxviii [36]; E ——; G 6791—6795, additional exhortation of Tristan to Mark, 6758—6791.

B. For parallels, see Pfeffer, p. 43; Schultz, p. 164.

---

[1] This island is not mentioned in Virgil's *Aeneid*. 'Ce qui est assez curieux', says the editor, 'dans *Eneas* le combat se fait pourtant sur la terre ferme, comme la suite le montre'. Cf. Salverda de Grave, *Eneas* LXVII. The lack of further mention of the island does not seem to us to mean that the combat did not take place there, v. infra. Cf. *Eneas* 9290.

III. The champions cross over to the island.

A. *Tristan.* In separate boats.

O. X 787.

Zu dem schiffe dô der helt gîng.
mit dem zôme he sîn ros bivîng;
he nam sînen schilt und sîn swert
aleine vûr he ûf den wert.

P. 14. 5.

Hiemit gieng herr Tristrant ʒů schiff, nam
mit im sein pfärdt, schilt und schwerdt,
und fůr allein in den wörd . . . Morholt
kam im entgegen gefaren.

Č (island characteristics effaced;
see Appendix I).

T. S (island characteristics effaced;
see Appendix I).

E xciiii.

Þai seylden into þe wide
wiþ her schippes tvo.

G 6736.

Sus wurden dar geschalten
den kemphen zwein zwei schiffelîn,
der ietwederz mohte sîn,
daz ez ein ors und einen man
gewâfent wol trüege dan.
nu disiu schif diu stuonden dâ.
Môrolt zôch in ir einez sâ;
daz ruoder nam er an die hant,
er schiffete anderhalp an lant.

. . . .

Nu Tristan ouch ze schiffe kam,
sîn dinc dar în zuo sich genam,

beidiu sîn ors und ouch sîn sper;
vorn in dem schiffe dâ stuont er.

. . . .

sîn schiffelîn daz stiez er an
und fuor in gotes namen dan.

B. Parallels in mediaeval literature.

1. In separate boats.

Sir Torrent.

The Gyaunt shipped in a while
And sett him oute in an yle,
That was grow both grene and gay. 1260.
To the shipp sir Torent went,
With the grace, god had hym sent,
That was never ffayland. 1278.
Whan sir Torrent in to the Ile was brought,
The shipmen lenger wold tary nought,
But hied hem sone ageyn. 1284.

Sone 5095.

Appareillie fu la nes
Et Sones est dedens entrés
Et si doi varlet awec lui
E maronnier, n'i ot autrui.

2. Both champions in the same boat.

Godefroi 4944.

Sor l'iaue de Quinqualle, qui est rade et
[corans,
Estoit apareilliés .i. moult riches chalans.
Li Aupatris i entre et avoc lui Balcans;
Outre l'en ont nagié à .xiiii. estrumans.
Puis revinrent ariere, nus n'i est demorans.

Guy of Warwick (Auchinleck MS.), *G. & A.*, 97. 1.

Ouer þe water þai went in a bot.

3. When it is only necessary to cross a ford in order to get to the island, they ride or swim.

Ogier (Chevalerie) 2774.

> A ces paroles, rois Brunamons s'entorne,
> Dessi au Toivre ne s'aresta-il unques.
> Poinst le ceval, si se féri en l'onde,
> Et li cevalx l'enporta tot droit outre;
> Unques la sele n'en moilla ne la crupe,
> Et li Danois le bon destrier golose:
> 'Dex! dist-il, pères qui formas tot le monde,
> Se toi plaist, Sire, cel bon ceval me done!'

Boeve 3583.

> Le gué passent, oltre se sont mis.

Beves 4143.

> Ouer þat water þai gonne ride.

Otuel 417—443.

> Al a-boute þe water ran,
> þer was noþer man ne wimman,
> þat miȝte in riden no gon,
> At no stede bote at on;
> & þere otuwel in rood,
>
> .   .   .   .
>
> Ouer þe water þe stede swam,
> & to londe saf he cam.

IV. The spectators are gathered on the opposite shore.

A. *Tristan.*

O.   P. 14. 2—4.

> Er küsst in, trückt in an sein brust,
> unnd rûfft umb hilff in die hôhe der hym-
> mel, er und als sein volck.

X 746.

An dem stade bî dem mere
vîlen sie nedir an daz velt;
ûf sô slûgen sie ir gezelt.
dô sie wârin ûf geslagin,
dô hîz der koning her vore tragin
sîn stêlîne harnas.

Č (island peculiarities effaced).

T.　　　　S (island peculiarities effaced).

E xcviii.

Mark the batayl biheld
And wonderd of þat fiȝt.

G 6501.

Dô kam al diu lantschaft
und volkes ein sô michel kraft,
daz daz stat bî dem mer
allez bevangen was mit her.

B. Parallels in mediaeval literature.

1. The spectators are gathered on the opposite
shore and seek to secure elevated places.

Geoffrey, p. 130. 54.

Populo expectante . . . Britones ut pro-
stratum regem viderunt, timentes eum pe-
remptum esse, vix potuerunt retineri, quin
rupto foedere in Gallos unanimiter irruerunt.

Wace 10, 278.

Dont véissiés pule fremir,
Homes et femes fors issir,
Saillir sor mur et sor maisons,
Et réclamer Deu et ses nons.

Layamon 23, 883.

> þa me mihte bihalden:
> þe þer bihalues weoren.
> folc a þan uolde:
> feondliche adredde.
> heo clumben uppen hallen:
> heo clumben uppen wallen.
> heo clūben uppen bures:
> heo clumben uppe tures.
> þat comp to bihalden:
> Of þan tweom kingen.

Jocelin, p. 52.

> Convenit et gentium multitudo, visura
> quem finem res sortiretur.

Godefroi 4956.

> Tex .c. mil les esgardent, qui en sont esfrois
> Car c'erent lor ami, si dotent, ce est drois.
> Li borjois et les dames sont monté
> [as defois,
> Es tors et es bretesches et es murs de liois,
> Por véir la bataille des .ii. vassax adrois.

Boeve 3607.

> Kant ceo veient paien, al gué sont feru ...

Bevis 4169.

> Alle, þat siȝen hem wiþ siȝt,
> Seide, neuer in none fiȝt
> So stronge bataile siȝe er þan
> Of Sarasin ne of cristene man.

Otinel 575.

> A ces paroles vint .i. colon [volant];
> Karles le vit et tote l'autre gent.
> Saint Espirit sus Otinel descent.

Otuel.

King Charles wiþ hise kniȝtes bolde,
Was come þe bataille to bi-holde. 503.
A whit coluere þer cam fle,
þat al þe peple miȝten se. 577.

Duke Rowland & Sir Otuel 487.

Charlles herde those wordes wele.
(Of the Saracen during the fight.)

Ogier (Chevalerie) 2943.

Francois le voient, mult en sont esmari,
E l'empereres qui France a à tenir
Andeus ses mains vers le ciel estendi.

Guy of Warwick (couplets), *G. & C.*, 10, 305.

Now the Danes prowde bene
And seyde þemselfe þem betwene,
That Gye was þen ouercomen.

Guy & Colebrande 387.

& then the Danish men gan say
to our Englishmen, 'well-away
that euer wee came in your griste!'

Sir Torrent 1281.

All the lordys of that contre,
Frome Rome unto the Grekys se,
Stode and be-held on lond.

Sone 5241.

Chil de saint Joseph l'ont vëu.

2. The people watch the combat from boats on the river.

Chevalier au Cygne 1638.

Ly gent de la chité, li bourgois, li siergant
Aloient entre l'ille à batiaus batellant.

3. In one case a number of the most distinguished spectators are allowed on the island.

Chevalier au Cygne 1711.

> Et! Dieus! qu'il y avoit de grant
> [peuple assamblé!
> Le camp y véist-on autour avironné
> Tellement qu'il estoient si drut et sy sierré
> Que jusqu'en la rivière estoient avalé.
> Et ly roys Orians et son riche barné
> Estoit droit as feniestres de son palais listé;
> Et la royne estoit amenée ens le prés,
> Pour la justiche faire d'icelle cruauté.

V. A further touch characteristic of the island scene is introduced.

A. *Tristan.*

1. The hero, upon reaching the island, pushes off his boat, declaring that one will be sufficient for the return.

O.   X 794.

> Der kûne degin Tristrant
> sîn schef gar harte hafte
> und stîz dô mit dem schafte
> Môroldes schef an den sint.

P 14. 8.

Morolt kam im entgegen gefaren; der hefft sin schif und stiess her Tristrant seins[1] verr hindan.

Č (island peculiarities effaced).

T.   S (island characteristics effaced).

---

[1] Reading of MS. W.

E xciii.

Moraunt bond his biside
And Tristrem lete his go;
Moraunt seyd þat tide:
'Tristrem! Whi dos tow so?'
'Our on schal here abide,
No be þou never so þro,
Ywis!
Whether our to liue go,
He haþ anouʒ of þis!'

G 6796.

Sîn schiffelîn er fliezen liez
und saʒ ûf sîn ors iesâ.
nu was ouch Môrolt iesâ dâ:
'sage an', sprach er, 'was tiutet daz
durch welhen list und umbe waz
hâstû daz schif lâzen gân?'
'daz hân ich umbe daz getân:
hie ist ein schif und zwêne man,
und ist ouch dâ kein zwîvel an,
belîbent die niht beide hię,
daz aber binamen ir einer ie
ûf disem werde tôt beliget,
sô hât ouch jener, der dâ gesiget,
an disem einen genuoc,
daz dich dâ her zem werde truoc'.

B. Parallels in mediaeval literature.

1. A similar incident.

Guy and Colebrande 218.

& as soone as hee to the Iland come was,
his barge there he thrust him ffrom;
with his ffoote & with his hand
he thrust his barge ffrom the Land,

with the watter he lett itt goe,
he let itt passe ffrom him downe
     [the streame,
then att him the Gyant wold ffreane
why he wold doe soe.
then bespake the Palmer anon-right,
'hither wee be come ffor to ffight
til the tone of vs be slaine;
2 botes brought vs hither.
& therfore came not both together,
but one will bring vs home.
ffor thy Bote thou hast yonder tyde,
ouer in thy bote I trust to ryde;
& therfore Gyant, beware!'

2. The hero breaks his sword, and, calling to the
boatman, sends him to bring another, and with
it wine.

Girard 142, 31.

'Sire Rollant, je vos en sai bon gré,
Puisque m'avez ainsi asseuré.
Sé il vos plaist por la vostre bonté,
Reposés vos .i. petit en cel pré,
Tant que je aie au maronier parlé,
Qui m'a issi en ceste ile amené'.
Et dist Rollant: — 'A vostre volanté'.
Et Olivier au corage aduré
Vint à la rive. N'i a plus demoré; ...
Le maronier appelle isnelemant.
Et dist li Quens: 'Amis, à moi entant!
Va à Viane tost et isnelemant,
Et di Girars mon oncle le vaillant
M'espée est fraite joste le heuz devant.
Envoit m'en une tost et isnelemant; ...

Si m'envoit plain bocel de vin ou
　　　　　[de pimant;
Car grant soif a le niez Karl, Rollant'.
'Sire', fait il, 'tot á vostre commant'.
En sa nef entre si s'en tornat atant.
D'autre par l'ague en est venus najant.

3. In several of the accounts of single combats
related of Guy of Warwick, the giant, becoming
thirsty, begs to be allowed time to go down
to the shore and drink; Guy gives him permission, but when he himself, shortly after,
becomes thirsty, the giant refuses him the same
privilege. Guy leaps into the water, however,
defending himself at the same time. *Guy of
Warwick* (Auchinleck), *G. & A.* 1144; *ib.*, Caius
MS. 8325; *ib.*, couplets 8105; *Guy and Colebrande* 271.

4. The giant attempts to escape by wading, but
the hero stones him to death in the water.

Sir Torrent 1295.

The theff couth no better wonne,
In to the see rennyth he sone,
As faste as he myght ffare.

5. The king is prevailed upon to interfere, and,
going down to the shore, calls across the water
to the combatants.

Godefroi 5134.

Venus est al rivage, si lor crie à haut ton,
'Seignor, estés tot coi, par mon
　　　　　　[Deu Baratron!
Se mais i ferés colp, j'en prendrai
　　　　　　[venjoison'.

VI. His opponent attempts to bribe the hero.

(cf. Pfeffer, *f*). An offer more closely corresponding to that in *Tristan* is found very frequently in Old French poems; cf. *Girart* 133, 23. 135, 12; *Ogier* (*Chevalerie*) 2788—2803; *Guy, G. & A.*, Auchinleck 1230—1240, Caius 8442—8454; *ib., G. & C.* 2650—2660, 10, 700—10, 710; *Guy* (couplets), *G. & A.* 8206—8215; *G. & C.* 10, 312—10, 332; *Guy & Colebrande* 348—363; *Otinel* 511—530; *Duke Rowland & Sir Otuell* 517—540, *Sone*, 5129—5163, 5203—5208.

A. *Tristan.*

O. Morholt, impressed by Tristan's courage as manifested by his abandoning his boat, offers to share his lands with him and to make him his heir if he will give up the fight. Tristan refuses. P 14, 12—15. 17; X 807—852; Č 25, 15—27. 8.

T. Morholt, having succeeded in wounding Tristan, offers to take him to his sister for healing and to share his goods with him, if he will abandon the fight. Tristan refuses. S 35, 20—36, ch. xxviii [37]; E___; G 6935—6980. G also contains a previous offer, on the part of Morholt, corresponding to O, above, 6799—6837.

VII. The champions return from the island.

1. Mention is made of a boat.

A. *Tristan.*

T.   S (island characteristics effaced).

E 1096.

Wiþ sorwe thai drouȝ þat tide
Moraunt to þe se

And care.
With ioie Tristrem, þe fre,
To Mark, his em, gan fare

G. 7090.

Sus kêrte er wïder zuo der habe,
dâ er Môroldes schif dâ vant;
dâ saz er în und fuor zehant
gein dem stade und gein dem her.

B. Parallels in mediaeval literature.

Godefroi 5147.

Li Sodans a tost fait une nef aprester,
S'i a envoié outre por ax .ii. amener.
Quant orent fait la barge d'autre
          [part ariver,
L'Aupatris i entra, n'ot cure d'arester;
Et cil les aconduirent, n'i volrent demorer.

Guy of Warwick (couplets), *G. & A.* 8313.

Wyth the boot he came passynge
And caste hyt to Tryamowre þe kynge.

Guy of Warwick (Auchinleck), *G. & A.* 134, 1.

Ouer þe water he went in a bot,
& present þer-wiþ fot hot
þe king, sir Triamour.

Sir Torrent 1310.

He said: 'Lordys, for charite,
A bote that ye send to me,
It is nere hand nyght!'
They Reysed a gale with a sayll,
The Geaunt to lond for to trayll,
All men wonderid on that wight.

Whan that they had so done,
They went to sir Torent ful sone
And shipped that comly knyght.

Sone 5254.

Au port vient, une nef trouva
Et les notonniers aprestés.
Sones est en la nef entrés.
Dont l'ont le maronnier passé
Et en l'ost des Escos mené.

2. No mention is made of a boat.

A. *Tristan.*

O.   P 16, 5.

Also ward der streit gescheiden, dem
eiŋen zů freüd, dem andern zů klag. Künig
Marchs holt sein ôhem mit freüden und
gesang; ...... und fůren mit freüden heim.
... Aber die traurig schar von Irland holten
iren kempffer auch.

X 932—6.

Dô wart geholt Tristrant
mit vroudin und mit gesange.
ouch beiten nicht lange
die Môrolden man.

Č (island characteristics effaced).

B. Parallels in mediaeval literature.

Layamon 23, 992.

Ardur þe riche:
wende to londe.

Girard 156, 33.

Le Dus Rollant est fors de l'ile issus.

Girard 157, 31.

Dedans Viane est Oliviers venus;
Le grant bernaige est encontre venus.

3. The narrator takes the return for granted and
proceeds with the story without alluding to it.
Geoffrey 130. 53; Wace 10, 353; *Chev. au Cygne*
2043; *Guy of Warwick* (couplets), *G. & C.* 10, 369;
Guy & Colebrande 393.

All the details of the engagement itself in *Tristan*
are recognized commonplaces.

It is clear from the preceding analysis that in
the description of Tristan's combat with Morholt we
have a stereotyped incident of mediaeval French
literature, offering no peculiarities for which we should
be justified in seeking parallels farther afield.

b) *The Norse* Holmganga.

Twenty-five years ago, however, Sarrazin, in an
article on *Germanische Sagenmotive in Tristan und
Isolde*[1], suggested that the island combat in Tristan
was a peculiarity that pointed to Scandinavian influence. Since then the incident has been repeatedly
cited by *Tristan* critics as an instance of a Norse
holmganga, although no characteristics of the *holmganga*
have been given to support the assertion[2].

---

[1] *Zts. f. vgl. Lit.* I (1887), 262—72.
[2] cf. W. Hertz, *Tristan von Gottfried*[5], p. 519, n. 52; Golther,
Tristan, Munich 1887, p. 24; Golther, *Tristan und Isolde in den
Dichtungen des Mittelalters und der neuen Zeit*, Leipzig 1907,
p. 16—7; F. Piquet, *L'Originalité de Gottfried de Strasbourg*,
Lille 1905, p. 154, n. 5; Löseth, *Le Roman en prose de Tristan*,
Paris 1891, p. 20, n. 1; Muret, *Romania*, XVI, 304; Kölbing,
Sir Bevis of Hamtoun, E. E. T. S., III, 350, note to l. 4141.

Let us look a little more closely at the Norse
holmganga to see what similarities it may offer to the
Morholt combat. Although the *holmganga* is frequently
mentioned in the sagas, our information regarding it
is almost entirely drawn from the *Kormaks-saga*[1]. The
significant passage is the following[2]:

After that Cormac went to meet his men. Berse
and his men were come thither þy this time and many
other men to see their meeting. Berse spake: 'Thou,
Cormac, hast challenged me to a *holmganga*, but I
offer thee an *einvigi* instead. Thou art a young man,
and little tried, and there are points to be known in
the *holmganga*, but none at all in the *einvigi*'. Cormac
spake: 'I would just as soon fight a *holmganga* as an
einvigi. I will risk this and in everything match
myself with thee.' 'Have thy way,' says Berse.

It was the law of *holmganga* that there should be a
cloak of five ells in the skirt and loops at the corners.

They must put down pegs with heads on one end that
were called *tiosnos*.

He that was performing must go to the *tiosnos* so that
the sky could be seen between his legs, holding the lobes
of his ears, and with this form of words [form lost]; and
afterwards was performed the sacrifice that is called *tiosno-sacrifice*.

There must be three lines round about the cloak of a
foot breadth; outside the lines there must be four posts,
and they are called *hazels*, and the field is *hazelled* when
this is done.

---

[1] cf. Vigfússon, *Icelandic Dictionary*, p. 280, under *holm-ganga*.

[2] Ch. x; ed. Möbius, Halle 1886; ed. Valdimar Asmundarson,
Reykjavik 1893; *Islendingasögur* 6, translated in Vigfússon,
Origines Icelandicae, Oxford 1905, II, 322; and I, 320—1; cf.
diagram of holmgang ground in Du Chaillu, *The Viking Age*,
London 1889, I, 565; also Collingwood, trans. of *Kormakssaga*,
Ulverston 1902.

A man shall have three shields, and when they are gone then he shall step upon the skin though he have left it before, and then he must defend himself with weapon henceforth.

He shall strike first that is challenged.

If one of them be wounded so that blood come on the cloak, they shall not fight any longer.

If a man steps with one foot outside the hazels, he is said to flinch [lit. goes on his heel]; but if he step outside with both feet, he is said to run.

His own man shall hold the shield for each of them that fight.

He shall pay holm-ransom that is the more wounded, three marks of silver as holm- ransom.

It is thus clear that the Norse used the term *holmganga* with a very particular application, and that the extension of it by *Tristan* scholars to the Morholt combat is entirely without justification. The Scandinavian duel, in so far as we know it to have been different from the French chivalric duel, is paralleled at no point by *Tristan*. On the contrary, our examination of the latter in connection with similar combats in contemporary narratives brings out most clearly the fact that the *Tristan* story is at this point entirely under the influence of French chivalric conventions.

c) The Island of Saint Samson.

The Prose Romance[1] names the island of Saint Samson as the place where the combat was fought. Crestien's *Erec* contains an allusion to the same effect:

---

[1] ed. Löseth § 28; cf. also Index *s. v.* Saint Sanson; Bédier II, 326.

'Onques, ce cuit, tel joie n'ot
La ou Tristanz le fier Morhot
An l'isle saint Sanson vainqui,
Con l'an feisoit d' Erec iqui'[1].

It is possible that the Eilhart version, with its habitual avoidance of names, has here omitted the name Saint Samson. The indications which it gives would correspond to this localization[2].

Thomas, who has suppressed the messengers, and brought the Morholt in person to the court of Mark, has effaced this localization, and makes the combat take place just off the coast of Tintagel.

There is nothing in the account of the combat with Morholt to differentiate it from what appears to have been the universal practise at the time of the redaction of the extant texts. It may or may not represent an older tradition remodelled according to contemporary taste. The indications that the Morholt adventure is a survival of a more primitive tradition receive neither confirmation nor denial from the account of the combat.

3. SECLUSION OF THE INVALID.

The wound received by Tristan at the hands of the Morholt becomes so offensive that he begs Mark to have built for him a little house by the sea, far from everyone. Those who accompany him when he is borne thither mourn him as one dead[3]:

---

[1] ed. Foerster 1247—51.
[2] cf. supra, p. 102—4.
[3] *OX* 1071—83.

'dâ wart der siche în getragin
mit unmêzigen clagin
obir lût und tougen.
dô worden lûter ougen
trûbe von weinen,
dô man den helt reinen
ûz der stad in daz hûs trûg.
lûte volgeten im genûg
die alle sêre clageten,
daz sie vorlorn habeten
alsô den wigant.
sîne wunde im sô sêre stang
daz se in medin gemeine'.

The Prose Romance retains a shadow of this
description in the sentence [1].

> Tristan se fait apporter a une fenestre sur la mer, et
> commença la mer a regarder et pensa une grant piece.

This account reflects a custom frequent in primitive
communities. A person dangerously ill is removed
from his house. A hut is built for him at a distance
from the other dwellings, and he is transported thither
and avoided. Mourners, homicides, warriors at certain
periods, women in childbirth, girls at their first cata-
menia, and all those who have come in contact with
the dead, are similarly isolated for definite periods.
Contact with ordinary society is forbidden the person
under taboo, and when the period is over, everything
that has been touched by him is burned.

The king is permanently isolated. His divinity
is considered as a fire which, under proper restraint,
confers endless blessings, but if allowed to break

---

[1] Bédier II, 328.

bounds, burns and destroys all it touches. He is therefore shut up in his palace, and only certain persons
are allowed to look at him. It is considered dangerous
to partake of food that has been touched by him or
to wear clothes that have belonged to him[1].

We find traces of these customs in Greek literature.
The story of Philoctetes is a survival very similar
to that which we have in Tristan. While the Greeks
are at Tenedos after the sacrifice of Iphigenia,
Philoctetes is bitten by a serpent. The wound refuses
to heal, and the stench becomes so great that the
Greeks, unable to endure his presence, expose him on
the island of Lemnos. There the sick man lives alone,
his only nourishment being the birds he can shoot
with the bow left him by Hercules. Fragments of
this story occur in numerous Greek writings. Certain
of the classic writers explain that Philoctetes is thus
abandoned by the Greeks on account of the evil smell
of his wound. Sophocles adds that his cries disturbed
the sacrifice. The latter considers, however, that the
treatment of the wounded man was inhuman, and he lays
the blame on Odysseus. Ovid excuses the Greek leader
on the ground that the decision was approved by all.
According to him, Odysseus believed that Philoctetes'
wound might heal sooner if he were left alone on
the quiet island. Later writers also represent the
isolation at Lemnos as an opportunity for healing[2].
This humane interpretation is hardly true to the
original story.

Tristan's little hut on the shore seems to us to
be a survival of the same primitive custom that we

---

[1] Frazer, in *Ency. Brit. s. v. taboo; Folk-Lore* XI (1900),
p. 346; G. L. Gomme, *Handbook of Folk-Lore*, London 1890, p. 49;
cf. Piper, *Höfische Epik, Deutsche National-Literatur* III, 264.
[2] Roscher, *Ausführliches Lexikon der gr. u. röm. Myth.* 2319.

find in the story of Philoctetes. In both cases the
redactors whose accounts have come down to us belonged to a society that had abandoned the practise.
The ideas out of which it grew had long been unfamiliar.

4. THE RUDDERLESS BOAT.

Tristan has been living in his hut for some time
when he decides to commit himself in a little boat
to the waves. Eilhart accounts for his resolution as
follows [1]:

'he gerûchte, ab he nimmir mê
alsô siech zu lande qûeme.
he bat daz man in nême
und trûge in in ein schiffelîn:
dâ wolde he eine inne sîn
und ûf dem irsterbin.
do wolde he eir vorderbin
ûf dem wazzer eine,
den he die lûte gemeine
vorterbete mit gestanke:
des wârin sîne gedanke.'

He bids farewell to Gorvenal, telling him to wait
for him one year, and if he does not return, to go
to his father and tell him to take him as a son, in
Tristan's place. He bids his sword and harp be placed
with him in a little boat without oars or rudder. There
is general lamentation as he is borne down to the
sea, and the winds and waves carry him where they

---

[1] *OX* 1094—1104.

will. He would rather die alone on the water than destroy the people with the smell of his wound.

The voyage in a rudderless boat is a' favorite story in Old Irish literature[1]. In the extant examples of it the hero who thus sets out is usually impelled by religious motives. The enterprise is a penance appointed by a spiritual director or undertaken voluntarily. The extant accounts are almost all influenced by Christian ideas.

The voyage of Mael-duin[2]:

A mysterious person, appearing to a voyager, reproaches him for his covetousness, and obtains from him a promise of obedience. The stranger then directs him to throw all his riches into the sea. He continues: 'Go now, and in the stead in which thy boat shall pause, stay therein'. He is given as provision a cup of whey water and seven cakes. Putting forth alone, without oars or rudder, he is borne to an unknown goal by the wind and waves.

The voyage of the Húi Corra[3]:

A party of jesters see a boat departing on which are embarked the three sons of Conall the Red, 'robbers and brigands going on their pilgrimage', by the command of St. Columba, 'to seek the Lord on the sea and on the mighty main'. The leader of the jesters, stricken with contrition, joins them of his own accord. Then he went on board their boat and they were thinking whither they should go. 'Whithersoever the wind shall take us', says the bishop. Thereafter they shipped their oars and offered themselves to God. They visit marvellous islands, the description of which constitutes the interest of the story.

---

[1] In the tenth century list of tales in the *Book of Leinster* (cf. d'Arbois, *Catalogue de la littérature épique de l'Irlande*, Paris 1883, p. 151 ff.), one of the most important categories is that of the *Imrama* (Voyages).

[2] *Revue Celtique* X, 85—7. For date and composition see Zimmer, *ZfdA.* XXXIII, 147—82.

[3] *Revue Celtique* XIV, 39; cf. Zimmer, *ZfdA.*, XXXIII, 182—211.

The voyage of Snedgus and Mac Riagla[1]:

Snedgus and Mac Riagla had been directed by Columba to watch the departure of sixty couples of the men of Ross who had been condemned to put to sea in open boats 'that God would pass his judgment upon them'. When the two had assured themselves that the condemned were not trying to evade their fate, 'they bethought them of wending with their own consent into the outer ocean on a pilgrimage, as the sixty couples had gone, though these went not with their own consent'. They abandon their oars, and leave their voyage to God. The story relates the wonders which they see.

The tidings of the three young clerics[2]:

Three young clerics set out in a boat with three loaves and a cat. When they have reached the open sea, they throw away their oars and rudder, and commend themselves to God. They reach an island, and spend the rest of their lives as hermits.

Voyage of Maelduin (second example)[3]:

Mael-duin, having set out with his companions to avenge his father, is driven from his course by the wind. And even after morning they saw nor earth nor land, and they knew not whither they were going. Then said Mael-duin: 'Leave the boat still, without rowing, and let it be brought whithersoever it shall please God to bring it'. They come to marvellous islands, the description of which constitutes the interest of the story.

We find in a Saxon chronicle[4]:

891 þrie Scottas comon to Aelfrede cyninge on anum bate butan aelcum gereþrum of Hibernia, þonon hi hi be-

---

[1] Revue Celtique IX, 18; cf. Zimmer, ZfdA. XXXIII, 211—9. The Adventure of St. Columba's Clerics, Revue Celtique XXVI, 133 is another account of the same adventure.

[2] Zimmer, ZfdA. XXXIII, 132; Gaidoz, Mélusine IV, 6—11; Stokes, Lives of the Saints from the Book of Lismore (Anecdota Oxoniensia 1890) VII—X.

[3] Revue Celtique IX, 462 ff.; cf. ZfdA. XXXIII, 147—82.

[4] John Earle and Charles Plummer, Two of the Saxon Chronicles, Oxford 1892, I, 82.

staelon forþon the hi woldon for Godes lufan on elþiodignesse
beon, hi ne rohton hwaer.

Se bat waes geworht of þriddan haelfre hyde þe hi on
foron, 7 hi namon mid him þaet hi haefdun to seofon nihtum
mete; 7 þa comon hie ymb .vii. ni' t to londe on Cornwalum
7 foron þa sona to Aelfrede cynir ͜e; þus hie waeron genem-
nde, Dubslane 7 Macc bethu 7 Maelinmun.

Life of St. Tathan [1]:

In order to avoid being made king, St. Tathan, following
the command of an angel, goes to the sea-coast, and, finding
a little ship, unsupplied with rudder or rowing gear, is
carried by the wind to Britain.

Life of St. Brynach [2]:

The saint, troubled by his increasing fame, goes alone
to the sea and, not finding a ship, places a piece of rock
on the water. Committing himself altogether to God, he is
carried the length of the British sea and brought to the
port of Milford.

In the *Voyage of St. Brendan* [3]:

The idea of abandoning the oars comes to the
men when they have already lost control of the boat
on account of the wind.

Post XV vero dies cessavit ventus et ceperunt navigare
usque dum vires eorum defecerunt. Confestim sanctus Bran-
danus cepit illos confortare atque monere dicens: 'Fratres,
nolite formidare: Deus enim noster adjutor et nauta et guber-
nator est. Mittite intus omnes remiges et gubernacula,
tantum dimittite vela extensa et faciat Deus sicut vult de
servis suis et de sua navi'. They come to marvellous

---

[1] *Cambro British Saints*, ed. W. J. Rees, Llandovery 1853,
p. 256. 581. On his Irish origin see p. 591, n. 1.

[2] *Cambro British Saints*, ed. W. J. Rees, Llandovery 1853,
p. 6, 291. On his Irish origin see p. 289, n. 1.

[3] *Sanct Brandan*, ed. Carl Schroeder, Erlangen 1871, p. 7.

islands, the description of which constitutes the interest of the story [1].

A similar incident occurs in the story of *Liadain and Curithir* which we have cited at length in Appendix V. We have no reason to believe that the idea of such a voyage of adventure was confined to the Irish. We have found an Annamite story of a husband who, taking the body of his dead wife, commits himself on a raft to the winds and the waves. The raft is borne to the Eastern Paradise, and the wife is restored to life [2]. In the romance of King Horn and in certain versions of the widely diffused Constance story [3], a person commits himself of his own accord to the chance of the waves [4].

---

[1] Most of the above instances have already been mentioned by Deutschbein, *Sagengeschichte Englands*, Cöthen 1906, p. 69 ff.

[2] E. S. Hartland, *Perseus* II, 340, cited from A. Landes, *Contes et Légendes Annamites*, Saigon 1887, 207 (no. 84).

[3] cf. Piper, *Höfische Epik* II, 372; Kittredge, (*Harvard*) *Studies and Notes in Philology and Literature* VIII, 241.

[4] The exposure of a child in an open boat is an incident to be met almost everywhere, from the story of the infant Moses and the legend of Sceaf to the modern newspaper. There are wide-spread instances of this as a means of punishment. We see examples of this in the Irish Imrama (*The Sons of Hui Corra* and the men of Ross in *Snedgus and Mac Riagla*). The mother of St. Kentigern, being discovered pregnant, was thus punished (*Lives of St. Ninian and St. Kentigern, ed. Forbes* 1874, p. 167. 249—50). Similarly Ovid, in a mediaeval German rhymed chronicle (Grimm, *Deutsche Rechtsaltertümer* II, 285), and a girl in the legendary *Vita Offae secundi* (quoted by Grimm, *ibid.* 285). In *Kinder- und Hausmärchen* no. 16 the false wife is put into a leaky ship and set adrift. Grimm speaks of finding instances in legal records (*Rechtsaltertümer* II, 286 citing *Monumenta boica* II, 507) and quotes from the story of King Karl and Radbod (Old Frisian), a passage which gives the criminal the choice between this and other punishments. Exposure in an open boat is a frequent method of getting rid of an enemy without bloodshed. In the *Life of Findchua of Bri Gobann,* a lad, Ciar Cuirchech, is put to sleep with intoxicating liquor and then put into a coracle with one oar on the sea (Stokes, *Lismore Lives,* p. 95. 242. 3157 ff.). Instances of persons voluntarily submitting themselves to the chance of the winds and waves are rare.

5. HEALING AT THE HANDS OF THE ENEMY.

In Eilhart the poet confides to the reader that no one but Isolt, the niece of the Morholt, can heal Tristan's wound. Tristan himself is given no inkling of this[1]. The prose redaction of Eilhart contains an additional passage which leads us to believe that in the *estoire* Tristan was represented as conscious of this possibility: the redactor takes the trouble to deny, quite gratuitously, that Tristan knew anything of the sort[2].

> auch weste er solicher kunst nit bey ir, er het es sunst mit seiner listigkeit wol dartzu gebracht das ym hilff durch sy wer geschehen.

In the *Saga* and in Gottfried, hence probably in Thomas, Morholt declares to Tristan that he can be healed only by his sister Isolt[3]. In Malory we have the following rendering of the same idea[4]:

> Thenne the king lete sende after alle manere of leches and surgens bothe unto men and wymmen and there was none that wolde behote hym the lyf. Thenne came there a lady that was a ryght wyse lady and she said playnly unto King Mark and to Sir Tristram and to alle his barons that he shold never be hole but yf Sir Tristram wente in the same countrey that the venym came fro and in that countrey shold he be holpen or els neuer.

There are traces of this feature in the French Prose Romance[5]. From these indications we are in-

---

[1] *OX* 1015—25.

[2] ed. Pfaff 17, 12—5.

[3] Bédier I, Ch. X, p. 87—8.

[4] Malory, *Morte d'Arthur*, ed. O. Sommer, Bk 8, Ch. 8 Malory's version is based on a lost manuscript of the French Prose Romance. Cf. Sommer, III, 279—90.

[5] Löseth § 29; Bédier II, 328. In these versions the idea of seeking healing in *the same country that the venym came fro* is lost.

clined to believe that the *estoire* contained some survival of this trait.

There is still another sign that in the source of the extant versions Tristan was directed to seek healing at the hands of the Morholt's kinsmen. M. Bédiér has ingeniously suggested that the name Pro of Iemsetir, which Tristan gives on being questioned by the Irish king, is an anagram for *Isot pro mire*[1]. If Tristan gave this name he would seem to have undertaken his voyage with the conscious purpose of seeking Isolt of Ireland.

Gottfried traces with charming delicacy the direction of Tristan's thought. As his wound becomes more and more ill-smelling and he realizes how obnoxious his presence is to his friends, he remembers what the Morholt has told him of Isolt of Ireland.

> 'ouch was sîn meistez ungemach,
> daz er daz alle zît wol sach,
> daz er den begunde swaeren,
> die sîne friunde ê waeren,
> und erkande ie baz unde baz
> Môroldes rede; ouch hete er daz
> ê males dicke wol vernomen,
> wie schoene und wie vollekomen
> Îsôt sîn swester waere;
> wan von ir floug ein maere
> in allen den bîlanden,
> diu ir namen erkanden:
> diu wîse Îsôt, diu schoene Îsôt,
> diu liuhtet alse der morgenrôt.

---

[1] Bédier II, 211—2. The poet may, however, have used the anagram without intending to imply such an intention on the part of Tristan.

Tristan der sorchafte man
hie gedâhte er zallen zîten an
und wiste wol, sollte er genesen,
daz enkunde niemer gewesen
wan eine von ir liste,
diu disen list dâ wiste
diu sinnerîche künigîn[1].'

Tristan's little boat is driven to the shores of Ireland. The music of his harp draws the attention of the Irish king to the wretched man thus cast upon the island. Tristan gives his name as Pro of Iemsetir, and explains that he is a merchant minstrel who has been attacked and left in this plight by pirates. The king sends to his daughter for a plaster, and after several failures she at last prepares one that heals him[2].

Tristan is thus saved by the kinswoman of the enemy who wounded him, the person who, as the German prose redaction says,

'was ym günstiger zesterben, dann zu leben'[3],

Striking as this seems to us, it is a theme popular in primitive fiction.

Stories of healing received at the hands of the person who inflicted the wound or of his kinsmen, are widely diffused. Greek literature offers an interesting example in the story of Telephus wounded by the lance of Achilles[4].

---

[1] ed. Marold, 7283—304.
[2] *OX* 1150—1220.
[3] ed. Pfaff, p. 17, l. 11.
[4] Welcker, *Griechische Tragödie* II, 477 ff. (*Rheinisches Museum*, Sup. II, Pt. 2); L. Preller, *Griechische Mythologie*, Berlin 1875, II, 417—419; C. Pilling, *Quomodo Telephi fabulam et scriptores et artifices veteres tractaverint* (dissertation Halle 1886); E. Gerhard, *Die Heilung des Telephos, Drittes Programm zum Berliner Winckelmannsfest*, Berlin 1843, p. 5—6.

On their expedition to Troy, the Greeks first land
at Mysia. In the mistaken idea that it is Trojan
territory they plunder the country. Telephus withstands
them stoutly, but is at last wounded in the leg by
Achilles. The Greeks are repulsed and return home.
The wounded Telephus seeks the counsel of the oracle
at Delphi, and receives the answer that the author
of the wound must heal it. Knowing the danger he
incurs by entering the land of the Greeks, he disguises
himself as a lame beggar, wearing a Mysian cap and
bearing a bag for crusts and a cruse for water. He
waits before the house of Agamemnon. Clytemnestra
appears, and he prevails upon her to help him. At
her suggestion he seizes the little Orestes, and seeks
sanctuary with the child before the altar. He pretends
to be a merchant who has fallen upon evil fortunes
and been wounded by the Mysians. The suspicion
of Ulysses is aroused, and the stranger's identity is
discovered. In the meantime it has been revealed to
the Greeks that Troy cannot be taken by them unless
they are led by Telephus. They then join in begging
Achilles to cure him. Achilles replies that he knows
nothing of medicine. Ulysses, however, interprets the
oracle: 'Apollo does not mean thee; it is the lance
that he calls the author of the wound'. Telephus is
accordingly healed by Achilles with the rust of the
spear that had wounded him.

There is a similar incident in the Norse saga of
Harald Hringsbane [1]:

---

[1] The resumé is from an abstract of *Haralds-rímur Hringsbana* which Kölbing considers must represent a lost saga; see
E. Kölbing, *Beiträge zur Kenntnis und kritischen Verwertung
der älteren isländischen Rímurpoesie* in his *Beiträge zur vergleichenden Geschichte der romantischen Poesie und Prosa des
Mittelalters*, Breslau 1876, p. 227. In a saga representing the
same story, examined in manuscript by Dr. H. G. Leach, to whom

Hermod, fatally wounded by Harald, declares with his last breath that his sister will avenge him. She only, he says, is able to heal the wounds he has given his slayer; but she will not do it, for she loves her brother supremely. Harald leaves his companions, and sets out to seek healing. For a twelvemonth he remains in the desert, his wound growing daily worse. At last he meets Hertrygg, Hermod's sister's son, who is seeking the murderer of his uncle. Disguised as an old man, Harald presents himself to him, and they swear blood-brotherhood. Harald then reveals himself, and Hertrygg is forced by his oath to spare him. He must also assist him to obtain healing from his sister.

The Norse *Aliflekkrsaga* recounts a similar incident [1]:

The troll woman Nótt comes one night in a dream to Aliflekkr and strikes him with a whip, saying that she is avenging her brother Gloðaugi. The wounds she has given him, she declares, cannot be healed except

---

I am indebted for my acquaintance with it, this incident appears in different form. Harald, wounded, as in the *rímur*, by a man who would avenge Hring, is healed by a dwarf who chances to find him (Ch. XV — VII, MS. A. M. II, 298, Copenhagen). This saga, apparently unknown to Kölbing, represents, in Dr. Leach's opinion, a later development than the *rímur*.

[1] F. Jónsson, *Den Oldnorske og Oldislandske Litteraturs Historie*, København 1898, III, 115 conjectures that the story was written down about 1400. The earliest *rímur* belong to the seventeenth century. The resumé was made by Dr. Leach from two vellum manuscripts, one of the fifteenth century, the other of the sixteenth century, in the Arna Magnean collection. Chapters I—VII have been edited by O. Jiriczeks in *Zts. f. deutsche Philol.* XXVI, 17—22. The portion concerned with the voyage for healing is not included. Cf. Finnur Jonsson *op. cit.* III, 114. Ward, *Cat. of Rom.* I, 846. This incident of striking in a dream by a supernatural woman, who inflicts wounds which can be healed only by herself or her kin, is remarkably similar to the incident in the *Sickbed of Cuchulainn;* cf. below.

by one of her brothers. If they are not healed in ten years, the victim will die. Thorbiarg, Aliflekkr's wife, prepares ships, and takes her husband in search of cure. In all the quarters of the earth the best leeches fail. In India they learn that Nótt has three brothers; two of them, Seggur and Liðr, have an ointment that will heal anyone not destined to die, but they dare not use it without the consent of Jotunoxi, the third brother. Jotunoxi lives in a land at the confines of the earth, peopled by giants and giantesses. Aliflekkr and his wife set out under assumed names as brother and sister. Jotunoxi consents to allow Aliflekkr to be cured if Thorbiarg will be his wife. She agrees on the condition that he kill Nótt. Jotunoxi then sends them to his brothers with the coveted permission, and Aliflekkr is healed. Jotunoxi kills Nótt, according to his promise, but is slain on his wedding night. Aliflekkr and Thorbiarg sail home to England.

There is an example of healing at the hands of the enemy in an incident in the *Leabhar na h-Uidhri* version of the *Táin bó Cúalnge*[1].

> When Cuchulainn was in this great weariness, the Morrigan [whom he has previously wounded in the head, the eye, and the leg] met him in the form of an old hag, and she blind and lame, milking a cow with three teats, and he asked her for a drink. She gave him milk from a teat.
>
> 'He will be whole who has brought it (?)', said Cuchulainn; 'the blessings of gods and non-gods on you', said he. (Gods with them were the mighty folk that is the dwellers in the sid; non-gods the people of husbandry).
>
> Then her head was healed so that it was whole.
>
> She gave the milk of the second teat, and her eye was whole; and gave the milk of the third teat, and her leg

---

[1] Cited from Faraday, *The Cattle Raid of Cúalnge*, London 1904, p. 81—2.

was whole. So that this was what he said about each thing of them, 'A doom of blessing on you', said he.

'You told me', said the Morrigan, 'I should not have healing from you forever.'

'If I had known it was you', said Cuchulainn, I would not have healed you ever'.

In versions of this incident in the *Book of Leinster*[1] and in the *Cóir Anmann*[2] it is stated that none but Cuchulainn could heal the wounds that he inflicted.

A story of this sort, in which the wound is love, is the *Sickbed of Cuchulainn*[3]:

Cuchulainn wounds one of two mysterious birds, and is immediately stricken with mysterious languor. The same night two women come to him while he sleeps, and strike him, one after the other, until he is almost dead. He falls into a wasting illness. At the end of a year a stranger appears, promising him health and strength if he will come to the country of Fand, who desires his love. One of the mysterious women appears to him again on the spot where he had the vision that caused his illness. She repeats that he can be healed only by Fand. Cuchulainn cautiously sends ahead his charioteer Loeg to learn the nature of the country to which he is invited. Loeg returns with news and with full directions of the battle that Cuchulainn must fight in order to win Fand. Having now an invitation from Labraid, Cuchulainn sets out. He has scorned the summons of Fand because they are from a woman. He wins the victory, possesses Fand for a month, and returns healed.

---

[1] Windisch, *Táin bó Cúalnge*, 330—4; cf. *Rev. Celt.* I, 49; d'Arbois de Jubainville, *Rev. Celt.* XXIX, p. 201.

[2] Windisch, *Irische Texte* III, 354—5.

[3] Windisch, *Irische Texte* I, p. 197—227, edited from the *Leabhar na h-Uidhre*. Cf. d'Arbois de Jubainville, *L'Épopée celtique*, p. 170—208.

In the lay of *Guigemar*[1] the woman who heals is
not identified with the woman who wounds. It seems
justifiable, however, in the light of similar Celtic stories
and the probably Celtic origin of this part of the lay[2],
to supply the trait. We may give the adventure in
the words of the hero as he relates it to the lady
whom he meets at the end of his voyage[3]:

'En bois alai chacier jehui.
Une blanche bisse feri,
e la saiete resortie;
en la quisse m'a si nafré,
ja mes ne quid aveir santé.
La bisse se pleinst e parla,
mult me maldist e si ura,

que ja n'eüsse guarisun
si par une meschine nun.
Ne sai u ele seit trovee!
Quant jeo oï la destinee,
hastivement del bois eissi.
En un hafne ceste nef vi;
dedenz entrai, si fis folie;
od mei s'en est la nes ravie.
Ne sai u jeo sui arivez,
Coment a nun ceste citez.
Bele dame, pur deu vus pri,
cunseilliez mei, vostre merci!'

The lady heals him of the wound, and after many
difficulties the two are united.

In the *Feast of Bricriu or the Exile of the Sons
of Doel Dermait:* we have the following account of

---

[1] Warnke, *Lais* (1900), no. I.
[2] Warnke, *op. cit.* lxxviii—xxx.
[3] Warnke, *op. cit.,* ll. 316—35.

how the wounded man learns the means by which to obtain relief[1].

In punishment for the indignities which have been put upon him, Eoeho Rond pronounces a curse upon Cuchulainn: He shall not rest sitting or lying until he knows what caused the exile of the sons of Doel Dermait. Cuchulainn immediately feels the garment that he wears, the house which he is in, and the ground that is under him, burning and tormenting him. 'Methinks I feel the effect of the curse that Eocho Rond put upon me. I shall die if I do not leave this place'. He takes his arms and goes down to the shore. He puts his question as to the sons of Doel Dermait to the prince of Scotland whom he finds in a boat in the port. 'I do not know', says the young warrior, 'but I have a sea-charm, and it shall be set for you, and you shall have the boat and shall not remain in ignorance'. Cuchulainn seats himself in the boat and is carried to an unknown land. There he receives directions by which he succeeds in finding the kinsmen of Doel Dermait and removing the curse.

The manner in which the hero learns the desperate conditions under which alone he can obtain healing is different in the various narratives we have examined.

In the *Exile of the Sons of Doel Dermait* the enemy who causes the distress of Cuchulainn declares to him at the same time the conditions for obtaining

---

[1] *Fled Bricrend and the Exile of the Sons of Duil Dermait*, ed. with trans. by Windisch, *Irische Texte* II, p. 164 ff. French transl. by d'Arbois de Jubainville, *L'Epopée Celtique*, p. 149 ff. Windisch does not date the story, but calls attention to the fact that 'die Übereinstimmung zwischen den alten Berichten (Diodor und Athenaeus) und den Sagen lässt uns hier echtestes Keltentum erkennen'. He considers that the voyage of Cuchulainn 'hat wieder ganz den alten volkstümlichen Charakter'. p. 171.

relief. These conditions Cuchulainn has no idea how to fulfil. It appears that his task involves the finding of the kinsmen of Doel Dermait, persons who dwell in undiscoverable regions.

In the lay of *Guigemar* also it is the injured enemy who reveals to her victim the means of recovery[1]:

> 'Oï, lasse! jo sui ocise!
> E tu, vassal, ki m'as nafree,
> tels seit la tue destinee:
> ja mais n'aies tu medecine!
> Ne par herbe ne par racine,
> ne par mire ne par poisun
> n'avras tu ja mes guarisun
> de la plaie qu'as en la quisse,
> des i que cele te guarisse,
> ki suffera pur tue amur
> si grant peine e si grant dolur,
> qu'unkes femme tant ne suffri;
> e tu referas tant pur li,
> dunt tuit cil s'esmerveillerunt,
> ki aiment e amé avrunt
> u ki puis amerunt aprés.

In the *Sickbed of Cuchulainn* it is from the messenger of the fairy lady who has wounded him that the hero learns how he is to be healed. In the *Aliflekkrssaga*, the troll woman declares that the wound she has inflicted can be healed only by one of her brothers. Similarly, in *Haralds-saga Hringsbana*, the dying enemy declares that the hero can be cured only by his sister. In the story of Telephus it is not from his enemy, but from the oracle that the hero learns the means of recovery.

---

[1] Warnke, *op. cit.* (1900), *Guigemar*, no. I, 106—22.

The points of similarity in the incidents discussed
are briefly as follows: The hero has been wounded. It
has been declared to him that he shall not have relief
except under certain conditions. He may be healed
at the hands of the person who inflicted the wound or
of his kinsman. He sets out, in some cases placing
himself in a boat without oars or rudder, and confiding
himself to chance or supernatural direction. He comes
to the country of the person who has wounded him,
and succeeds in obtaining relief by ruse at the hands
of his enemy or one of his kinsmen.

In each case the victim, knowing that he can be
cured only by the person or the kinsman of the person
who inflicted the wound, sets out with more or less
certainty of finding him. Since the person of whom
he is in search is of course bitterly hostile to him, he
disguises himself and obtains healing by a ruse. Telephus presents himself as a beggar and, by threatening
Agamemnon through his child, attempts to prevail
upon the Greeks to command Achilles to heal him.
Aliflekkr promises his pretended sister to Jotunoxi on
condition that he heal him. Harald Hringsbane takes
advantage of the oath of blood-brotherhood given him
by his enemy, to wring from him the promise of healing[1]. In Tristan likewise the hero succeeds by ruse
in obtaining healing at the hands of the kinswoman of
his foe.

In the *Sickbed of Cuchulainn* the situation is
different in that the fair enemy from whom the hero
receives the wound inflicts it with no other purpose
than to force him to seek her in her land. The
messengers that direct and the boat that bears him
thither are sent by her. She is a goddess: to her

---

[1] In the *rimur* version he is in the disguise of an old beggar.

the end and the beginning, the desire and the event
are one. *Guigemar* seems to present a similar situation,
but the connection of events is less clear, owing, we
believe, to modifications made by the French redactor.
It appears to be by mere chance that the hero enters
the ship that bears him to the land of healing. We
are not told of any connection between the enchanted
hind, the person who sent the magic boat, and the
lady who receives and heals the hero.

All of these stories are founded on a primitive
belief that a wound establishes some relation between
the victim and the person or weapon inflicting it[1].
We find accounts of this superstition widely diffused.
In Melanesia the friends of the injured man seek the
weapon by which he has been wounded, and place it
in a cool damp place. They believe that they thus
soothe the inflammation of the wound[2]. Pliny directs
a man to spit on his own hand if he wishes that the
wound he has inadvertently caused should heal[3].
Francis Bacon records cures by salving, without the
knowledge of the victim, the weapon that caused the
wound[4]. The Norse *Havamal* recommends 'a hair of
the dog that bit you' among other precepts of leech-
craft[5]. Hrolf Kraki's sword Sköfnung had the property
of being able to heal, by a stone belonging to it, the
wounds which it inflicted[6]. Iphyklus is cured of

[1] Liebrecht, *Zur Volkskunde*, 253. E. S. Hartland, *Perseus* II,
Ch. IX, Ch. X, 133 — 74. Cf. J. G. Frazer, *The Golden Bough*, London
1890, I, 9 — 12; London 1900, I, Ch I. esp. 56 — 61. G. L. Gomme,
Handbook of Folk-Lore, p. 47.

[2] Hartland, *Perseus* II, 171.

[3] Pliny, *Nat. Hist.* XXVIII 36, cited by Frazer, *Golden
Bough*[2] (1900) I, p. 56.

[4] F. Bacon, *Natural History*, cent. X § 998, cited by Frazer,
Golden Bough[2] (1900) I, p. 57; cf. Hartland, *Perseus* II, 169.

[5] *Hávamál*, stanza 138, *Edda, Saemundar hins fróaða*.

[6] *Hrolf Kraka saga*, Cap. 50, *Fornalddars.* I, 93 — 102.

impotence, according to Apollodorus, by the rust of
the instrument that has castrated a ram[1]. In the
Tuti-Nameh we are told that the bites of a certain
ape could be cured only by a plaster made from
its blood[2].

Such beliefs, of which the literary records might
easily be multiplied, survive among the peasants of
parts of England and Germany to this day. If a man
cuts himself with a hoe or a scythe, he cleans the
implement with oil. An object that has caused a
wound, whether it be a thorn, a rusty nail, a pair
of scissors, a flat iron, or what not, is carefully greased
or bound, and put away in a cool place. In some
cases it is put away dry; in other cases damp, in
order to accumulate rust. These measures are taken
in the belief that the inflammation and poisoning of
the wound it has dealt are thus avoided. In Central-
Australia relatives grease themselves and submit to
a diet in order to hasten the recovery of their
kindred[3].

This superstition appears to have been familiar
to the writers of French romance. In some of the
versions of the Grail story it is said that the lance
which had wounded the Fisher King could alone heal
him[4]. In the *Tale of Balin* in the *Huth Merlin*[5]
we hear of a slain knight who could be avenged
only by the *tronchon meismes* by which he had been
killed. In the same story it appears that the youth

---

[1] *Apollodorus* I, Chapter 9, § 12.
[2] *Tuti-Nameh*, ed. von Rosen, Leipzig 1858, I, 132.
[3] Frazer[2], *op. cit.* (1900) I, 58—9; cf. 30—4.
[4] *Queste del Saint Graal*, ed. Furnivall, 51—2, summary of
A. Nutt in *Studies on the Legend of the Holy Grail*, London 1888,
p. 51.
[5] *Merlin*, ed. Paris and Ulrich. *Soc. des. anc. textes fr.*
(1886) II, 6.

who has been wounded by Garlan, can be healed
only by his enemy's blood[1]. In *Meriaduc* a knight
is wounded by a certain sword, and can be healed
only by a second blow from the same weapon[2].
The Dutch romance *Torec*, a late compilation from
various French sources, tells of a poisoned wound
that can be healed only by the sister of the
enemy's wife[3]. The spear of Achilles is frequently
alluded to by writers of amatory verse in the twelfth
and thirteenth century as having the property of
healing the wounds it made[4]. Dante refers to it as
follows:

'Od' io che soleva la lancia
D'Achille e del suo padre esser cagione
Prima di trista e poi di buona mancia[5].'

The person who has caused the wound seeks in
the same range of ideas a means to aggravate it.
He and his friends drink burning liquids in the belief
that inflammation is thus brought about. They keep
the bow-string of the arrow stiff, and stretch it from
time to time for the purpose of causing a similar
strain in the nerves of the wounded man. The savage

---

[1] *Merlin* II, 22.

[2] *Hist. Litt. de la France* XXX, 240.

[3] Cited by Hertz[5] 565; cf. Paul, *Grundriss* II, 1. Abt. p. 465.

[4] By a misunderstading it is frequently alluded to as the
lance of Peleus. Cf. the study of Paget Toynbee, *Dante Studies
and Researches*, London 1902, p. 137—41. Passages alluding to
the healing lance are cited from Bernart de Ventadour and other
poets, among them Shakespeare (*Henry VI.*, Part. II, Act V, Sc. I,
ll. 100—1):

'Whose smile and frown like to Achilles' spear
Is able with the change to kill and cure.'

[5] *Inferno* XXI, 4--6.

who has bitten the arm of one of his enemies, drinks.
hot water for a similar purpose[1].

Tremendous narrative possibilities are inherent
in this primitive idea. It is a homeopathy not easy
to put in practice. To seek the enemy, defeated or
victorious, on his own ground, involves difficulties
enough, but to prevail upon him to heal the wound
he has himself inflicted calls into requisition all the
hero's capacity for strategem. Toward the man who
could achieve such an undertaking successfully in a
primitive society, the attitude of the barons toward
Tristan as described by Gottfried might well be
justified.

> 'merket wunder, hoerèt her:
> der parâtiere, wie kan er
> gesehendiu ougen blenden
> und allez daz verenden,
> daz er ze endenne hât[2]!'

6. CONCLUSION.

How are we to reconcile the hero's conscious
purpose of seeking healing at the hands of his enemy
with the story of his setting out without oars or
rudder and confiding himself to the mercy of the
winds and the waves? Why, instead of sailing to
Ireland, where he knew the kinsfolk of Morholt were
to be found, did Tristan set out in a rudderless boat
as if he had no hope or goal?

The impulse to throw oneself upon the unknown,
which appears in the Irish *Imrama* and in Tristan

---

[1] Frazer, *Golden Bough*[2] (1900) I, p. 56.
[2] ed. Marold, 8349—54.

is not entirely blind. It is based on the belief in marvellous countries to be found by such an abandonment, countries not to be reached by chart or compass. In such lands the Old Irish pilgrims always arrive. To such a land Cuchulainn is borne for healing at the hands of Fand. Such seems to be that of which the more cautious Aliflekkr learns, after his search through the known quarters of the globe, — a land inhabited by monsters at the confines of the earth. To such a land the Annamite husband is borne, committing himself on a raft to the winds and waves. The juxtaposition, in Tristan, of the rudderless voyage and the cure at the hands of the enemy's kinsman, lead us to believe that such also was the land of the Morholt, — a land of monsters beyond the confines of the earth, a land that cannot be reached by means of chart or compass.

The story of the Morholt, as we have seen, contains striking primitive traits: the hut built for the wounded Tristan, his embarking in a rudderless boat, his securing healing under the name of Pro of Iemsetir from the kinswoman of the Morholt himself. It has seemed possible to discern beneath these fragments of tradition the outlines of a type of story which we have not found elsewhere in French romance, but of which we have examples in Greek, Irish, and Norse literature. The Norse stories in question are late compilations of foreign, perhaps of Celtic, origin. They lack one of the most characteristic features of the Tristan story, the voyage in the rudderless boat. The Greek story is also without this feature. It seems possible, in view of the other Celtic connections of Tristan, that the Morholt story is traceable to Celtic tradition.

D. THE FLIGHT TO THE FOREST AND THE OLD IRISH *AITHEDA*.

1. INTRODUCTION.

We have discussed in Chapter V the portion of the story that follows the voyage for healing — the quest of Isolt, the marriage with Mark, the deceits by which the lovers at first elude suspicion, the desperate shifts by which, suspected, they contrive for a time to maintain their relation unmolested. These incidents the story has drawn to itself from the rich funds of popular tradition in which, everywhere in western Europe, the mediaeval story-teller was at home. With the exception of the incident of the harp and the rote, the portion of the Tristan story which lies between the voyage for healing and the life in the forest consists of incidents that may be found in almost any literature. They may equally well have been introduced into the story of Tristan by one people as by another. Our own opinion is that they were introduced by the French. It was not the habit of the Celts to leave in their typical form the stories which they appropriated. In these passages of Tristan, stories widely current in the Orient and Occident in popular tradition are reproduced with almost no modification.

But with the life in the forest we come to a passage of more distinctive character. Other lovers, to be sure, have fled from their persecutors, and some, in seeking a more hospitable society, have passed through forests and lonely places. Such are Aucassin and Nicolette[1]. Such are Guillaume de Palerne and

---

[1] *Aucassin et Nicolette.* ed. Suchier, Paderborn 1903, § 18—27.

the fair Melior[1]. But Tristan and Isolt, alone of the lovers that we know, have made the wilderness their home, have had no thought of seeking beyond it a more friendly society. These alone establish themselves in the desert, wrenching their scanty sustenance and shelter from reluctant nature. These alone are cut off for years from the world, living without intercourse with any, deprived of every activity and every responsibility. In the closely woven fabric of feudal society, they alone have no relation, no place. In the account of their life in the forest, Tristan and Isolt are unique in French romance. In other passages of their story we have found glimpses of a spirit and of customs that are not French. But in the life in the forest we find Tristan and Isolt associating themselves definitively with the company of the star-crossed lovers of Old Irish romance.

Nous avons perdu le monde et le monde nous[2], says Isolt to Tristan. The solitude of their forest life is peopled for the French poets by no tales of other lovers who have felt and lived as they. But the Celtic Grainne sings her lover to sleep in the forest with stories of many another that has shared their fate[3]:

---

[1] *Guillaume de Palerne.* ed. H. Michelant, *Soc. des anc. textes. fr.* Paris 1876, 1. 3023 ff. Similarly in *William of Palerne,* ed. W. W. Skeat, London 1867, 1. 1764 ff. In *Islenzkar Pjodsögur og Afíntýri,* Leipzig 1864, *Saga af Geirlangu og Groðara,* p. 379—80, and *Saga af Jónides Kóngssyni og Hildi Kongsdottur,* p. 418, two lovers flee to the forest and, pursued, change themselves into birds. The step-mother discovers and kills them. In one of the lays included in the Norse *Strengleikar,* two lovers flee to the forest and shelter themselves in a cave. A shepherd brings them provisions. In a terrible snow-storm they perish of cold and hunger. I am indebted to Mr. Sigurdur Nordal for the first two Norse references.

[2] Löseth, § 51.

[3] *Duanaire Finn,* ed. Mac Neill, *Irish Texts Society* V, Gaelic p. 84, Eng. p. 197. *The Sleep Song of Grainne.*

Sleep a little, a blessing on thee! above the water of the spring of Trénghart; little lamb of the land above the lake, from the womb of the country of strong torrents.

Be it even as the sleep in the south of Dedidach of the high poets, when he took the daughter of ancient Morann in spite of Conall from the Red Branch.

Be it even as the sleep in the north of fair comely Finnchadh of Assaroe, when he took stately Sláine in spite of Failbhe Hard head.

Be it even as the sleep in the west of Aine daughter of Gailian, what time she fared by torch light with Dubhthach from Doirinis.

Be it even as the sleep in the east of Degha, gallant and proud, when he took Coinchenn daughter of Binn in spite of fierce Dechell of Duibhreann.

Stories like that of Tristan and Isolt in the forest were numerous among the Celts. They constitute one of the important categories in the list, made in the tenth century, of the tales that every poet is bound to know[1]. Under the rubric: *Aitheda (Elopements)* we find the following[2]:

The Elopement of Mugain with Fiamain.

The Elopement of Deirdre with the sons of Uisnech.

The Elopement of Aife, daughter of Eoghan, with Mesdead.

The Elopement of Naise, the daughter of Fergus, with Nertach, son of Ua Leith.

The Elopement of the wife of Gaiar, son of Derg, with Glas, son of Cimbaeth.

---

[1] The *Imrama*, mentioned above, constitute another group of such tales.

[2] *The Book of Leinster*, Facsimile published by the Royal Irish Academy, Dublin 1880, pp. 189—90; printed in E. O'Curry, *Lectures on the manuscript materials of Ancient Irish history*, Dublin 1873, p. 590. Cf. d'Arbois de Jubainville, *Catalogue*, 34—8, 259 ff.

The Elopement of Blathnait, the daughter of Pall, son of Fidhach, with Cuchulainn.

The Elopement of Grainne with Diarmait.

The Elopement of Muirn with Dubhruis.

The Elopement of Ruithchearn with Cuana, the son of Cailcin.

The Elopement of Erc, daughter of Loarn, with Mureadhach, the son of Eoghan.

The Elopement of Dighe with Laidcnen.

The Elopement of the wife of Ailill, the son of Eoghan, with Fothudh Canann.

To these may be added

The Elopement of Emer with Tuir Glesta, son of the king of Norway[1].

Such a category is unknown in Old French literature. There the lover carries on his intercourse with his lady under the convenient shelter of the husband's roof, and does not find salt the taste of the husband's bread. In the more highly developed society which we find on the continent, the social order is too strong for such open revolt as we find in the Irish stories. The individual has not the courage to live in open defiance of the society to which he belongs. He cannot trust entirely to his own ingenuity and endurance, his own resourcefulness and self-sufficiency. He dares not struggle for existence, as these Irish fugitives have dared, his hand against every man's and every man's hand against his. Tristan alone of French heroes, by virtue of accomplishments which distinguish him strikingly from his fellows, is capable of it.

---

[1] ed. K. Meyer, *Rev. Celt.* VI, 184—5.

2. TRISTAN AND ISOLT AND THE OLD IRISH STORY OF DIARMAID AND GRAINNE.

a) Introduction.

Only a few scanty fragments of the Irish *Aitheda* have come down to us[1]. It has seemed worth while to try to piece one of them together, and to compare it with the romance of Tristan.

The tradition of Diarmaid and Grainne descends in an unbroken line from the ninth century to the present day. Its hero, Diarmaid, is one of the Fianna, bands of roving warriors of which we have traces in Ireland as early as the sixth century[2]. We have already discussed the accomplishments of Tristan, and pointed out analogues to them among the feats of the Old Irish heroes. The Fianna were especially remarkable for strength and agility[3]. The exploits and adventures of their various chiefs were the subject of numberless stories. In the course of development of Irish literary tradition most of these adventures came to center in Finn ua Baiscne or Finn mac Umall, represented in the extant texts as the supreme leader of the Fianna, and his companions, Caoilte, Ossian, Diarmaid and others. These adventures are accounts of extraordinary feats, of incredible enchantments, of earthly and unearthly loves, of impossible quests, of far-fetched scruples of

---

[1] *The Elopement of Deirdre with the Sons of Usnech* is discussed below. *The Elopement of Blathnait with Cuchulainn* was probably the same story that is preserved in *The Tragic Death of Curoi mac Dari*, discussed below in connection with *The Harp and the Rote.*

[2] K. Meyer, *Fianaigecht, R. I. A. Todd Lecture Series* XVI, Int. viii ff.

[3] cf. supra Ch. VI B.

honor. They are intensely individualistic in spirit; they are but slightly influenced by feudal ideas; their interest centers not at all in a cause or in battles for a cause; their paganism is intact.

With these heroes Tristan is allied in his adventures as in his accomplishments. It is not in fight shoulder to shoulder that we find Tristan at his best, although the French redactors have not allowed him to remain devoid of distinction in the abilities in which their own heroes excelled. What is most characteristic of Tristan is his nimbleness of hand and foot, his extraordinary possession of his five senses, and his fertility in ruses. Tristan can tune his voice to the birds, Tristan can take prodigious leaps, Tristan can snare the fish and trap the game. He can break the deer as none other can do it. He can teach his dog to bring down the prey without a sound. The mark of his hand is distinguishable by its superior cunning from that of any other, the whittlings which he makes will float on any current, and the sign that he leaves on the highroad is recognized at once as his. By him alone can the twigs be shot into the wall so that they will enter, the one into the other, and remain fixed in a line. With such accomplishments as these Tristan might well meet the requirements for entrance into the band of the Fianna. Among the heroes of French romance they isolate him.

French redactors, in adopting a Celtic elopement story, would very naturally modify it to some degree of conformity with the stories of unlawful love which were popular in France. It may well be due to them that the story of the flight to the forest is reduced to a subordinate element, whereas the situation of Isolt at the court, and Tristan eluding the vigilance of Mark to secure meetings with her, is elaborated in numerous episodes. Some incidents, moreover, which in Celtic stories would have belonged to the period of the life in the forest, seem to have been shifted by the French redactor, for one reason or another, to other positions· in the narrative[1]. We shall not attempt to trace any but general similarities between the Tristan story and the particular Irish romance which we have examined. Our purpose is merely to show that the former, in so far as it is not explicable by French literature contemporary with the extant redactions, seems to be a survival, in an alien atmosphere, of an Old Irish elopement story.

b) Fragments of the story of Diarmaid and Grainne in texts anterior to the tenth century.

The full title of the story of *Diarmaid and Grainne*, which is the *Aithed* that we shall take to compare with the story of Tristan and Isolt, is *Aithed Grainne ingine Corbmaic la Diarmaid ua n-Duibni*, (*The Elopement of Grainne, daughter of Cormac, with Diarmaid, grandson of Duibne*)[2]. The *Aithed* itself is unfortunately lost. Certain fragments of the story are extant, however, in tenth century texts, and from these we can discern the general outlines of the original romance.

Diarmaid, the nephew of Finn mac Umaill, is one of his chief's closest friends and most trusted warriors. Grainne, the daughter of Cormac the high king of Ireland, is Finn's wife.

---

[1] cf. e. g. infra, *The Harp and the Rote, The Splashing Water*.

[2] d'Arbois, *Catalogue*, p. 35, cf. clv and p. 176. 7. 32 and 3.

One of the few fragments of tradition regarding them that dates from the tenth century is the account of Finn's wooing of Grainne[1]. This relates Grainne's unwillingness to become Finn's wife. She requires, as the condition of her marriage with him, a couple of every wild animal in Ireland. This attempt to evade Finn's suit is, however, unsuccessful. With the help of Caoilte, Finn brings the bridal gift demanded.

> Then in an unlucky hour Grainne was given to Finn, for they never lived in peace until they separated. Finn was hateful to˙ the maiden and such was her hatred that she sickened of it.

She confesses to her father her feeling toward her husband. Finn, overhearing her words, declares that it is time for them to separate.

There is an allusion in a gloss in the *Amra Coluimb Chille* of the ninth century[2] to Grainne's love for another.

> And Grainne sang: There is one for a long look from whom I should be thankful: for whom I would give the whole world, O Son of Mary, though it be a privation.

According to the *Tochmarc Ailbe, ingine Cormaic hui Chuind la Find húa mBáiscne (The Wooing of Ailbe, daughter of Cormac grandson of Conn, by Finn grandson of Baiscne)*, an unpublished tale of the tenth century[3], there was strife between Cormac and

---

[1] ed. K. Meyer, *Zts. f. Celt. Philol.* I. 458. Prof. Meyer dates this in the ninth or tenth century. *Fianaigecht, R. I. A. Todd Series* XVI, p. xxiii.

[2] Ed. Stokes *Rev. Celt.* XX, p. 156 — 7; Meyer, *Rev. Celt.* XI, 126, prints: *Ut dixit Gráinne ingen Cormaic fri Find*, citing *Rawl. B* 502, fo 56 a 2.

[3] MS. H. 3. 17, p. 827 — 31. Meyer, *Fianaigecht* xxiv, places this in the tenth century.

Finn, the cause being that Grainne had come to hate Finn, and had set her love on Diarmaid, son of O'Duibhne.

An allusion in the *Book of Aicill*, a law tract of the ninth century[1], shows that already at that time the story of the elopement of Diarmaid and Grainne was traditional. It appears further that Lughaid was present when the elopement took place[2]. The line[3]

'Grainne eloped with thee, O Lughaidh'

is cited to illustrate the legal responsibility of witnesses.

The *Uáth Beinne Étair* (*The Hiding in the Hill of Howth*)[4] of the tenth century[5], gives a dramatic

---

[1] *Ancient Laws of Ireland*, ed. R. Atkinson, *op. cit.* III, clxii, n.

[2] *Op. cit.*, III, 533. The scene of the elopement in the *Tóruigheacht Dhiarmada agus Grainne* (*The Pursuit of Diarmaid and Grainne*) is a feast at the house of Cormac in Tara, v. ed. S. H. O'Grady, *Transactions of the Ossianic Society*, Dublin 1855; re-edited for the *Society for the Preservation of the Irish Language*, Dublin 1895, in two parts. The oldest manuscript noted by d'Arbois de Jubainville, *Catalogue*, p. 249, is R. I. A. 23 L 27, 1736—8. Mr. J. H. Lloyd informs me that one of the manuscripts in the Royal Irish Academy belongs to the middle of the seventeenth century. We have cited the *Oss. Soc.* edition by pages, the other by paragraphs. In oral tradition it is frequently during a feast that Grainne is overcome with love for Diarmaid (cf. stanzas 16—8, p. 56, *Rev. Celt.* XXXIII) and begs him to elope with her. It is not until some time later, however, that she succeeds in prevailing upon him to go; cf. J. F. Campbell, *Popular Tales of the West Highlands* (cited *W. H. T.*), Edinburgh 1862, III, p. 39. 54. 56; J. G. Campbell, *The Fians* (cited *F*), *Waifs and Strays of Celtic Tradition* V, London 1891, p. 53, p. 55; J. F. Campbell, *Leabhar na Feinne*, London 1872, (cited *L. F.*), p. 153. 154. In O'Grady, p. 55 (I, § 7) there is no mention of the love spot.

[3] This Lughaidh, son of Daire Derg, is mentioned in the genealogical lists of the *Book of Leinster*, p. 311 ff., and in Rawlinson B. 502. 128 a. He is frequently mentioned among the Fenian heroes. In the *Pursuit of Diarmaid and Grainne* he is represented as one of those present when Grainne eloped with Diarmaid. ed. O'Grady, p. 50 (I, § 5).

[4] Ed. Meyer, *Rev. Celt.* XI, p. 125 ff.

[5] Meyer, *Fianaigecht*, p. xxiv.

moment in the life of the fugitives. They have taken
refuge in a cave, and the old woman who is serving
them is about to betray them. They are saved by
the foster-father of Diarmaid, Aonghus of the Brugh,
one of the Tuatha de Danann[1].

c) The transmission of the other portions of Diarmaid and Grainne.

The comparison of the Tristan story with that
of Diarmaid and Grainne involves difficulties on both
sides. The Celtic tradition of Tristan was modified
by the French poets almost beyond recognition, and
brought into conformity with French customs and
French habits of thought. The tenth century story
of *Diarmaid and Grainne* has survived in Ireland and
Scotland only in fragments, and these often in late
redactions, at the hands of men to whom the life it
reflected was almost as strange as it was to the French
poets. In consequence we find the story of Tristan distorted in the direction of French chivalry, and the story
of Diarmaid, even in those fragments of it which are
preserved to us in sixteenth century manuscripts, sadly
corrupted by oral transmission. Fortunately there is
a third set of documents that aids us in determining
the original tradition — ninth and tenth century Irish
texts recounting similar adventures of other heroes,
and preserving, in a more primitive form, the incidents
which appear in *Tristan and Isolt* and in *Diarmaid
and Grainne*.

---

[1] Aonghus has a similar role in the *Pursuit*. Cf. O'Grady,
p. 71. 148. 150. 168 (I § 21. 23. 26. 34).

d) General similarities between Tristan and Isolt and Diarmaid and Grainne.

Like the story of *Tristan and Isolt*, the story of *Diarmaid and Grainne* is the tale of a trusted warrior who is driven by a strange fatality to take away the wife of his friend and king. By this he cuts himself off from all human ties. The fugitives are tracked like wild beasts. They sustain themselves in the wilderness, unconscious, in their love for each other, of hardships and privations.

e) The love-potion.

The fatality that draws the two lovers together is expressed in *Diarmaid and Grainne*, as in *Tristan*, in terms of popular superstition. In oral tradition everywhere in Scotland and Ireland, Diarmaid is represented as possessed of a mark called a *love-spot* which makes him irresistible to any woman who sees it[1]. For this trait no manuscript evidence of early date happens to survive, but Diarmaid's charm for women is always alluded to in Old Irish romance. The fifteenth century lay of the *Death of Diarmaid* in the *Book oʒ the Dean of Lismore*, for example, is prefaced by the line

'This is the tale that makes women sorrowful[2]'

and closes with the lament[3]:

---

[1] Cf. versions collected from oral tradition cited.
[2] *Rev. Celt.* XXXIII, p. 163. 166, Stanza 6, line 3.
[3] *Rev. Celt.* XXXIII, p. 165. 168. Stanza 25.

'Master (?) and charmer of women,
Son of O Duibhne of swift victories,
Wooing has not lifted her eyes
Since the clay was placed on his cheek'.

According to tradition, Grainne catches a glimpse of this love-spot and is at once consumed with passion for Diarmaid. She tries to persuade him to take her away from her husband. He attempts in a manner characteristic of popular tradition to evade her[1].

> 'I will not go with thee; I will not take thee in softness, and I will not take thee in hardness; I will not take thee without, and I will not take thee within; I will not take thee on horseback, and I will not take thee on foot.'
>
> She, however, went to a fairy woman and got garments made from mountain down. She came with this garment on, riding on a he-goat in the dusk of the evening, when it was neither light nor dark; and thus it could not be said that she was clothed or unclothed, on foot or on horseback, in company or without company, and consequently was deemed free from the spell laid upon her.

Grainne might have had recourse to a love-potion, but she takes the method of putting a *geis* upon Diarmaid to go with her. The *geis* is a peculiarly Irish taboo which any individual seems to have been at liberty to impose upon any other, and which, if disregarded, entailed moral degradation and swift retribution[2].

---

[1] *W. H. T.* (*West Highland Tales*) p. 40, F. (*The Fians*), p. 52—3. Similarly *L. F.* (*Leabhar na Feinne*) 153. 154. This ingenuity in accomplishing an apparent impossibility is discussed by Köhler, *Kleinere Schriften* III, p. 514; cf. Grimm, *Kinder- und Hausmärchen*, no. 94.

[2] cf. Windisch, *Irische Texte mit Wörterbuch* I, Leipzig 1880, p. 590, s. v. *Geis*. Such prohibitions or interdicts are a characteristic feature of Irish romances. v. supra.

Diarmaid and Grainne are thus marked by fate for the tragic issue. She is under the spell of the *love-spot*, and he under the *geis*. They cannot escape — they must go with each other. They cannot defy their fate, and, subject to it, they must defy every human tie.

Similarly, in the story of the *Exile of the Sons of Usnech*, preserved in the *Book of Leinster*, a manuscript written before 1150, Naisi resists the advances of Deirdre, wife of King Conchobar, and refuses to take her from her lord. When she puts a *geis* upon him he is forced to yield[1].

In Tristan it is a love-potion that introduces the tragic necessity. The belief in love-charms is universal among primitive peoples. There is no literature that does not contain traces of it. We cite several examples from classic literature.

Lucian describes a witch preparing a love charm. She takes some portion of the man's clothing, or a few hairs, and hanging them on a nail, fumigates them with incense. Then, sprinkling salt on the fire, she pronounces the name of the woman, coupling with it the name of the man. Further spells are muttered to the twirling of a spindle, and the charm is complete[2]. Ovid describes a charm for a similar purpose, but expresses his scepticism as to the efficacy of such measures. He declares that potions are injurious to the brain, and concludes:

---

[1] 'Two ears of shame and mockery shalt thou have', she cried, 'if thou take me not with thee'. Ed. Windisch, *Irische Texte* I, p. 73. d'Arbois, *Epopée*, p. 226; A. H. Leahy, *Heroic Romances of Ireland*, London 1905, I, p. 95. Cf. infra.

[2] Lucian, *Hetaerae*, Dial. IV.

'Sit procul omne nefas! ut ameris, amabilis esto,
Quod tibi non facies solave forma dabit[1].'

Horace describes the kidnapping of a boy for the
purpose of obtaining his marrow and liver to make
a love charm[2]. Juvenal attacks potions among the
magical arts used by women against their husbands[3].
Pliny describes various ingredients, such as the hair
of a wolf's tail, a morsel of the forehead of a horse,
or of a certain fish, as excellent, according to superstition, for love potions[4]. Suetonius ascribes Caligula's
crimes to a love-potion administered by his wife[5].
Plautus also refers to the havoc played by a love-
potion[6]. According to popular belief, love-potions sometimes caused madness.

These allusions of the Latin poets illustrate
characteristics of the superstition which appear universally. We find similar practises among peasant
communities today.

A love-potion plays a part in a story in the Old
Norse *Heimskringla*[7].

> There rose to meet him Snowfair, daughter of Swasi,
> fairest of women, and gave to the king a cup full of honey
> mead. Then took he together the cup and the hand of her,
> and straightway it was as if hot fire came into his skin and
> therewith would he be by her that very night. But Swasi
> says it may not be, but if need sway him, but if the king
> betroth him to her and take her lawfully. So King Harald

---

[1] Ovid, *Ars Amatoria* II, 106—8.
[2] Horace, *Epodes* V, 37—8.
[3] Juvenal, *Satires* VI, 609—13.
[4] Pliny VIII c. 22. 42. IX, 25.
[5] Suetonius, *Lives of the Caesars, Caligula*, ch. 67.
[6] Plautus, *Truculentus*, Act I, Sc. I, ll. 22—4.
[7] Snorri Sturluson, *Heimskringla*, trans. W. Morris and
Eiríkr Magnússon, London 1893, I, 119.

betrothed him to Snowfair and wedded her; and with such longing he loved her that he forgat his kingdom, and all that belonged to his kingly honor.

He will not leave her even when she is dead. Not until years afterward, when the worms crawl out of her body, is he freed from the spell and able to leave her side.

Love charms are frequently mentioned in Old Irish literature. In the *Conception of Mongán and Dubh Lacha's Love for Mongán*[1]:

> And Mongan put a love-charm into the cheeks of the hag, and from the look which the king of Leinster cast on her he was filled with her love, so that there was not a bone of his of the size of an inch, but was filled with love of the girl.

He is so eager for her that he offers his own wife to Mongan in exchange for her.

In the *Rennes Dindshenchas*[2]:

> Maer, wife of Bersa of Beramain, fell in love with Find son of Cumall, and she formed nine nuts of Segais with love-charms, and commanded Ibuirne son of Dedos to deliver them to Find, and told Find to cut and eat them. 'Nay', says Find, 'for they are not nuts of knowledge but nuts of ignorance, and it is not known for what they are, unless an enchantment for drinking love". So Find buried them a foot deep in the earth.

In the Irish saints' lives we find the theme under ecclesiastical treatment. In the *Life of St. Brynach*[3]:

> She endeavored by every means to enthral the servant of God with her snares of alluring pleasure; and from the performance of better things she endeavored to allure him

---

[1] Meyer and Nutt, *Voyage of Bran,* London 1897, I, 69. 82.
[2] *Rev. Celt.* XV, p. 334.
[3] *Cambro-British Saints*, ed. W. G. Rees, Landovery 1853, p. 291.

to luxurious habits; she mixed wolfsbane with lustful ingredients formally prepared, she ceased not to get it for him
to drink; but she prepared the mixture. in vain; the holy
servant of God did not thirst for such a cup; but refused it and
as the apostle advised, he avoided the assaults of fornication.

In the *Life of St. Brigit*[1]:

There was a certain man biding in Lassair's church,
and his wife was leaving him and would not take bit nor
sleep along with him; so he came to Brigit for a spell to
make his wife love him. Brigit blessed water for him and
said: 'Put that water over the house, and over the food,
and over the drink of yourselves, and over the bed in the
wife's absence'. When he had done this, the wife gave exceeding great love to him, so that she could not keep apart
from him, even on one side of the house; but she was always at one of his hands.

The Old Irish law and medical tracts also contain provisions in regard to love charms[2].

The following passage from the *Heptads*, an Old
Irish law tract, makes provision in the case of the
administration of a potion for the separation of the
parties when its influence abates[3].

There are with the Feinne seven women who though
bound by son and security are competent to separate from
cohabitation whatever day they like; and whatever has been
given them as their dowry is theirs by right: ... a woman
to whom her mate has administered a philtre when entreat-
ing her so that he brings her to fornication ....

It was before entering into the law of marriage the
philtres were given to her and it is when in the law of
marriage *the effect* became *apparent* upon her (*sic*); and he
pays the 'smacht' fine of cohabitation for it; and there are due

[1] *Lives of the Saints from the Book of Lismore,* ed. Whitley
Stokes, *Anecdota Oxoniensia,* 1890, I, § 1478.
[2] *Ancient Laws of Ireland, op. cit. Senchus Mor* I, 176₅, 181.
[3] *Ancient Laws of Ireland* V, p. 293. 297. The *Heptads*
are referred to in the *Senchus Mor* I, 252—3. For the age of
the *Senchus Mor* cf. I .ix. Cf. O'Curry's trans., *Manners and
Customs* I, clxxvff.

dowry and honour-price and body-fine to her, and *liberty* to
separate from him; or 'eric' according to the nature of the
philtres, and she has her choice either to separate or to
remain in the law of marriage. And this is the second place
in the Brehon law in which there is a 'smacht' fine of cohabitation paid by a person for the damage he did before
coming into the law of marriage.

In some of these accounts the kindling of love is
regarded as brought about by a simple aphrodisiac,
in others by supernatural agency. In every case one
person is desirous of influencing the will of another.
In *Tristan and Isolt*, on the other hand, the two
persons are equally victims in their passion for each
other. The account of the drinking of the potion
is intended to emphasize the irresponsibility of the
lovers for their passion. The drink was brewed by
the mother of Isolt to seal more firmly the bond of
her marriage with Mark. By a fatality for which
they are in no wise responsible, it seals upon Tristan
and Isolt the fetters that should have bound her to
her lord[1]. In the story of *Diarmaid and Grainne* also,

---

[1] It is clear that the poet who invented this passage desired
to emphasize the fact that the lover's error was due to no weakness or evil intention, and that they were the innocent victims of
an unkindly fate.

In France as in other European countries in the twelfth
century it was part of the wedding ceremony to offer a drink to
the couple after the consummation of the marriage. They are
brought to the bridal bed by their friends and, after they have
been left to themselves for a while, the nearest relatives, sometimes the whole company, enter the room and bring them a
strengthening drink.

Isolt requests the custom of her country to be followed, and
no lights to be in the room on her wedding night. It is frequently
mentioned in the romances that a light was kept burning in the
bed-chamber. In many cases, persons of different sexes slept in
the same room. There are several allusions in Middle High
German poems to the bridegroom's putting out the lights. For
example, in the *Nibelungen Lied*, *diu lieht begunde bergen diu
Gunthers hant* (l. 961), *diu lieht verbarg er schiere under die
bettewat* (l. 1005).

both hero and heroine are victims of a supernatural influence.

We have found no other account in which, as in *Tristan*, the influence of a love-charm is described as lasting always, but as suffering a diminution in strength at the end of a certain number of years. This feature of the *estoire* seems to us to be a modification of the romance as first conceived. We should ascribe it to a redactor who wished to continue the story beyond the period where it originally ended — the return from the forest. In the *Elopement of Grainne with Diarmaid*, and in the *Elopement of Deirdre with Naisi*, as we shall see, the lovers are lured back from their exile by promises. On their return, Naisi is treacherously slain by King Conchobar, and Deirdre taken into his power. By similar trickery, Finn succeeds sooner or later in bringing Diarmaid from his hiding place and getting possession of Grainne. The continuator of the Tristan story brought the lovers back from the forest, but postponed the tragic ending. The *Pursuit of Diarmaid and Grainne* is in a similar stage of development. Here also the lovers return from the forest under the king's pardon, and the tragedy is deferred.

Our own inclination is to attribute the origin of the idea of the love-charm in *Tristan and Isolt* to the people who sealed their tragic lovers with a similar mark. We should place Tristan and Isolt, not with Cligès and Soredamors, not with Parides and his empress in *Eracles*, but with Deirdre and Naisi, with Diarmaid and Grainne, and the company of those whose stories have been cherished for generations among the Celts.

The potion may have been introduced by a French redactor to replace a Celtic *motif*, such as the *geis* or the *love-spot,* which would have been less suggestive to a French audience.

Old French literature is not without examples of magic drinks. Medea, in the *Roman de Troie,* and Thessala in *Cligès* are versed in sorcery. In Béroul and the first part of Eilhart the naïve popular conception of the potion is preserved. In the latter part of the *estoire* there are clear indications of an effort to bring the relation of the lovers into accord with a more courtly ideal. The poet is far from regarding love, as the Tristan narrative postulates it, as a baleful influence which may paralyze a man's powers and cripple his activity. In Thomas, in Gottfried, and in the French Prose Romance, the potion has become almost entirely symbolical of the idea of courtly love. The story of Lancelot and Guinevere, which draws its material to so large an extent from the Tristan tradition[1], probably owed its popularity, if not its origin, to the demand for an amorous hero better representative of this ideal than Tristan. It is no doubt due to the fact that Lancelot did not blindly drink the poison of love, but sought the cup of his own will, that he superseded Tristan in the favor of many twelfth century readers. The conception of love of the twelfth century French poets had no affinity with tragedy. Love was an activity for

'fins cuers et bone volontez[2]'

---

[1] cf. e. g. *Mort Artu,* An Old French Prose Romance of the thirteenth century, being the last division of 'Lancelot du Lac', ed J. D. Bruce, Halle 1910.

[2] J. Brakelmann, *Les plus anciens chansonniers français,* Paris 1870—1871, p. 47, *Crestien de Troies* II, 24—34; cf. infra chapt. VI, E 2 b.

increasing a man's effectiveness, and quickening in him the desire to do noble deeds.

f) The life in the forest.

There are numerous passages in Béroul and Eilhart describing the life of Tristan and Isolt in the forest:

'Aspre vie meinent et dure:
Tant s'entraiment de bone amor
L'un por l'autre ne sent dolor.

. . . .

„Sire j'an Yseut a mervelle,
Si que ne dor ne ne somelle.
De tot est ja li consel pris:
Mex ain o li estre mendis
Et vivre d'erbes et de glan
Qu'avoir le reigne au roi Otran."

. . . .

Au bois se tient, let les plains chans.
Li pain lor faut, ce est grant deus;
De cers, de biches, de chevreus
Ocist asez par le boscage.
La ou prenent lor herbergage
Font lor cuisine e lor beau feu;
Sol une nuit sont en un leu'[1].

As a gloss in the *Amra Coluimb Chille*, which dates from the ninth century, we have a quatrain about Diarmaid and Grainne which might almost be put in the mouth of Tristan[2].

---

[1] Béroul 1364 ff. 1401 ff. 1424 ff.; cf. also 1279 ff. 1636 ff.; Eilhart 4515 ff. 4566 ff. 4692 ff. 5647 ff.
[2] ed. Stokes, *Rev. Celt.* XX, 264—5.

As Diarmaid said: Good is thy share, o Gráinne, better
for thee than a kingdom, the dainty flesh (*sercoll*) of the
woodcocks, with a drop of smooth mead.

There is another description of the life of two
lovers in the forest in the *Elopement of Deirdre with
Naisi*[1].

And for a long time they wandered about Ireland, in
homage to this man or that; and often Conor sought to slay
them, either by ambuscade or by treachery; from round
about Assaroe, near to Ballyshannon in the west, they
journeyed, and they turned them back to Benn Etar, in the
north-east, which men today call the Mountain of Howth.
Nevertheless the men of Ulster drove them from the land,
and they came to the land of Alba, and in its wildernesses
they dwelled.

Deirdre afterward alludes to their forest life as
follows:

'Naisi, with mead of delicious hazel-nuts
(came), to be bathed by me at the fire,
Ardan, with an ox or boar of excellence,
Aindle, a faggot on his stately back.

Though sweet be the excellent mead to you
which is drunk by the son of Ness, the rich in strife,
there has been known to me, ere now, leaping over
                                            [a bank,
frequent sustenance which was sweeter.

---

[1] *The Elopement of Deirdre with Naisi* is extant in the
story of the *Exile of the sons of Usnach*, contained in the *Book
of Leinster*, a manuscript written before 1150. Ed. Windisch,
Irische Texte I, 67—82, trans. d'Arbois de Jubainville, *L'Epopée
Celtique en Irlande*, Paris 1892, p. 217 ff.; another version in
Windisch, *Irische Texte* II, Heft 2, 109—84 with translation and
bibliography by Stokes. The passage cited is from the translation
of A. H. Leahy, *Heroic Romances of Ireland*, London 1905, p. 95,
based on the text of Windisch I.

When the noble Naisi spread out
a cooking hearth on hero-board of tree,
sweeter than any food dressed under honey
was what was captured by the son of Usnach.

Though melodious to you each month
(are the) pipers and horn-blowers,
it is my open statement to you today
I have heard melody sweeter far than these.

For Conor, the king, is melody
pipers and blowers of horns,
more melodious to me, renowned, enchanting
the voice given out by the sons of Usnach.

Like the sound of the wave the voice of Naisi,
it was a melodious sound, one to hearken to for ever,
Ardan was a good barytone,
the tenor of Aindle rang through the dwelling place' [1].

The remainder of the song is a lament for her
lover Naisi.

In the *Sleep Song for Diarmaid,* a poem dating
somewhere between the twelfth and sixteenth century,
Grainne sings of the life with her lover in the
forest [2].

O fold of valour of the world west from Greece,
over whom I stay (?) watching, My heart will well-
nigh burst if I see thee not at any time.

The parting of us twain is the parting of children
of one home, is the parting of body with soul, hero
of bright Loch Carmain.

Caoinche will be loosed on thy track: Caoilte's
running will not be amiss: never may death or

---

[1] Leahy, *op. cit.* I, 187.
[2] *Duanaire Finn,* ed. Mac Neill, *Irish Texts Society, op. cit.*
Text, p. 84, trans. p. 198.

dishonour (?) reach thee, never leave thee in lasting sleep.

This stag eastward sleepeth not, ceaseth not from bellowing: though he be in the groves of the black-birds, it is not in his mind to sleep.

The hornless doe sleepeth not in the tops of the fair-curved trees: it is a noisy time there, even the thrush does not sleep.

The duck of numerous brood sleepeth not, she is well prepared for good swimming; she maketh neither rest nor slumber there, in her lair she does not sleep.

Tonight the grouse (?) sleepeth not up in the stormy heaths of the height: sweet is the sound of her clear cry: between the streamlets she does not sleep.

g) The splashing water.

It is unwillingly that Diarmaid leaves his uncle's court to follow his uncle's bride. He takes her away not because he desires to do so, but because he must choose between this and the loss of his honor. He takes his resolution: He will go with Grainne, but he will do Finn no wrong. When they are overtaken therefore, as overtaken they must be, she shall be returned to her husband unharmed. Grainne is, however, not content with this. She gives Diarmaid no peace, tempting him continually. The *Reproach of Diarmaid*, a poem in the *Book of the Dean of Lismore*, implies this [1]

'Thou hast ruined me, O Grainne.
thou hast brought shame on the son of Cumhall;
to be as I am in distress
is a load I cannot endure.

---

[1] *Rev. Celt.* XXXIII, 52—4. Italics indicate doubtful words

I left play and uproar
for a companion, which is more shameful;
I left women without an attendant,
and thou hast ruined me, O Grainne.

I left merriment and delight,
banquet and festive group and laughter;
I left the play of poets;
And thou hast ruined me, O Grainne.

Caoilte the *Swift* and Mac Lughach,
a pair never put to shame —
their anger was not very good toward us[1]
thou hast ruined me, O Grainne.

The unloverlike attitude of Diarmaid in this lay
is not accounted for in what survives of tenth century
tradition, unless by the mention, in the *Tochmarc Ailbe*[2]
and in the *Amra Coluimb Chille*[3], that it was Grainne
who set her love on Diarmaid. We may perhaps infer
that Diarmaid was less eager than she for the elopement. A more complete explanation of Diarmaid's attitude is found in an incident which unfortunately has
come down to us only in documents of a later date.

On their flight Diarmaid makes his bed at some
distance from Grainne's, or puts a stone between
them[4]. He leaves uncooked meat behind him at every
resting place as a sign to Finn that his wife is un-

---

[1] Dr. W. J. Watson, *Celtic Review* VIII, 265, suggests *am
faithche 'nuair ruaidheadh roinne*, on fields when points would
be reddened.

[2] MS. H. 3. 17, p. 827—31. I am indebted to Mr. R. I. Best
for the following lines from the beginning of the story: There
was strife between Cormac and Finn, the cause being that Gráinne
had come to hate Finn, and had set her love on Diarmaid son of
O'Duibhne.

[3] cf. supra, VI D 3 c.

[4] cf. the incident of the separating sword in Tristan, infra,
p. 430.

touched. Grainne taunts him with cowardice, and uses
every means to tempt him. The following is a part
of the account that appears in all the versions[1]:

> She took heart and began to walk by Diarmaid's side
> boldly. A light jet of water splashed up through the toes
> of her foot till it struck up to her thigh, and she said to
> herself softly and guardedly
>
> > 'A plague on thee streaky splash,
> > Thou art bolder than Diarmaid.'
>
> 'What is that you said, O Grainne?' asked Diarmaid.
> 'It is of no importance,' said Grainne.
> 'Not so', said Diarmaid, 'I shall not rest until I know
> it, for I think I heard part of it.'
> Then Grainne said timidly, shyly, and modestly: 'O
> Diarmaid, great as is thy valor and bravery in battles and
> encounters, methinks this light splash of water is bolder
> than thou.'
> 'That is true, O Grainne', said Diarmaid, 'and although
> I have been keeping myself from thee for a long time for
> fear of Finn, I will no longer endure thy reproaches. Truly
> it is hard to trust women.'
> It was then that Diarmaid first made a wife of Grainne,
> and took her into the thicket. He killed a wild deer that night,
> and they ate their meal then, their fill of flesh and pure water.

---

[1] *Rev. Celt.* XXXIII, p. 47—8, from *R. I. A.* MS. 3 B. 8, f. 312
of the *Pursuit of Diarmaid and Grainne.* The *Ossianic Society*
edition of O'Grady's manuscript gives a less detailed account,
p. 108. The passage is not translated, p. 109. In the edition of
the *Society for the Preservation of the Irish Language* the passage
is entirely suppressed. I am indebted to Professor Kuno Meyer
for calling my attention especially to this passage. R. Köhler
has already noted the similarity between it and the Tristan incident, *Kleinere Schriften, op. cit.* II, 346—7. The incident
appears invariably in the stories collected from oral tradition, cf.
West Highland Tales p. 56: They went away, and they travelled
together three days and three nights. They were crossing a
river, and a little trout rose and struck her, and she said 'Thou
art bolder than Diarmaid. If thou couldst go on shore!' . . .
cf. *The Fians* 55: Grainne put her feet in a pool of water and
some of it splashed on her. She said: 'I am so long a time
going with the third best hero of the Fians, and he never approached so near'. Then Diarmaid left broken bread behind him.

This is from the *Pursuit of Diarmaid and Grainne.*
The popular accounts are similar.

Singularly enough, as the reader will remember,
the very same incident appears in Tristan[1]. But in
Tristan it is told of Isolt of Brittany. There is no
reproach upon the Isolt of the forest life, as upon
Grainne, for having led the hero to his ruin. It is
another Isolt ·whom Tristan resists, and who thus
resents his indifference.

'eines tagis dô geschach
daz der koning und die koningîn
und Tristrant und daz wîp sîn
unde Kehenis dâ mete
ûf eime tîfen wege retin
zu Karahes nâ bî der stad.

Îsaldin pfert dô trat
in einen gereinetin pfûl
daz ir daz wazzir ûf vûr
bî dem knî undirz hemede.
sie sprach, „wazzir, dû bist vromede,
daz dir mûzze misselingen.
wie getorstestû î gespringen
sô verre undir mîn gewant
dar noch nî ritters hant
getorste komen, noch en quam?"

ir brûder Kehenis daz vornam
und sprach, des en wêre nît.
dô was der vrauwen leit geschît
daz her daz hâte gehôrt,
îdôch sô sprach sie die wort:
„daz ich sage, daz ist wâr"[2].'

---

[1] *OX* 6134   80.
[2] *OX* 6144—65.

The incident is slightly modified. The significant remark to the water is not made in the presence of the hero, nor intended for him. It is made by Isolt of the White Hands as she rides along with her brother. Only indirectly, if at all, does she hope to bring about a change in the attitude toward her of the man she loves. The cause for that attitude in *Tristan* is, moreover, entirely different from that in *Diarmaid and Grainne*. In the French romance it is due, as we have shown, to an idealization of unlawful love characteristic of the latter half of the twelfth century. In *Diarmaid and Grainne* it is due to the hero's loyalty to his friend and lord. In *Tristan* the incident is a mere bit of narrative technique to bring about the revelation of a secret[1]. In the Irish romance it is organic. It is an important link in the heavy chain of circumstance that binds the hero to his tragic fate. The frank expression of the woman sounds strange in the courtly French romance, following, as it does, the refinements of sentiment which explain the sham marriage, and preceding Isolt's homage to Tristan's dog. It belongs naturally to the more primitive attitude of mind reflected in *Diarmaid and Grainne*.

h) The harp and the rote.

There is another incident which illustrates Diarmaid's unwillingness to betray Finn. Although it is recounted at length only in late versions, it may have become attached to the story at an early date[2].

A stranger, who seems to be a supernatural being, enters the cave in which the lovers have taken refuge,

---

[1] cf. supra. Ch. V B d.
[2] *WHT* 41. 55. 61; *F* 53. 55. 56; *LF* 153. 154.

and he and Diarmaid engage in a game of dice.
Diarmaid loses, and the stranger demands Grainne as
the stake. Diarmaid is compelled in honor to re-
linquish her and departs. Later he comes to the
cave in the disguise of a beggar. Grainne recognizes him when he offers her the first piece of
salmon he has roasted, for she knows that he is
under a *geis* [1] never to eat or drink in the
presence of a woman without offering her the first
morsel. He engages in a struggle with the stranger,
kills him, and leaves the cave. Grainne follows
him, overtakes him at dawn on the mountain
Sliabh Gaoil, and attempts to effect a reconciliation
with him.

The *Reproach of Diarmaid*, a fifteenth century
poem in the *Book of the Dean of Lismore*, of which we
have already quoted several stanzas, seems to belong in
this setting, and seems to refer to it in the following
stanza [2]:

> . . . . . cave . . .
> *it is no cause* of laughter *to me;*
> keeping a little cave;
> thou hast ruined me, O Gráinne.

---

[1] According to oral tradition, supported by the *Pursuit of
Diarmaid and Grainne*, Diarmaid's *geasa* were the following:
not to eat or drink in any place where there was a woman without giving her the first morsel, not to hear the cry of the hounds
without following the hunt, not to watch a game without helping
the losing player, not to refuse his comrades anything they should
ask of him. *LF*. 153. 156; O'Grady, p. 78. 174—6. 144 (I § 23,
II § 37, II § 22). Cf. *The Death of Diarmaid, Rev. Celt.* XXXIII,
162 ff. Here Finn asks Diarmaid to measure the venomous boar
against the bristle, and he does not refuse. Cf. *Rev. Celt. loc. cit.*
175 n. 5 and references: Diarmaid helps the losing chess player.
Cf. *loc. cit.*, p. 172: Diarmaid insists on following the hounds.
Cf. also *WHT* 57.

[2] *Rev. Celt.* XXXIII, p. 52. 54, stanza 7; cf. the suggestions
of Dr. W. J. Watson, *Celtic Review* VIII, 265—6.

An elaborated version of this lay has the following[1]:

Diarmaid: Why should I take thee as a wife, O woman, although thy voice is soft, — the woman who forsook the king of the Fiann, And forsook me afterward as surely.

Grainne: Even though I did leave Finn ... And although I forsook thee afterward, when I was altogether despondent,

I will never forsake thee now, But true love to thee forever growing,` [shall be] like fresh branches on the bough. With gentle warmth throughout my life.

Diarmaid: Fulfil thy promise, O woman, [and] although thou hast tormented me with sorrow, I will accept thee as my wife, although thou didst choose the great giant.

The episode is found in numerous versions of the story of Diarmaid and Grainne. In some, it exercises an important influence on the story. In certain versions, the stranger, entering, attempts to embrace Grainne, and Diarmaid slays him. In these versions it is at this point that Diarmaid yields to Grainne, for she taunts him by comparing his boldness with that of the stranger[2].

In another version it is not through his own fault that Diarmaid, after the coming of the cave man, is unable longer to leave the uncooked meat as a sign to Finn. Grainne has given herself to the stranger. Diarmaid kills him when he discovers her dishonor, and remains to the end faithful to his lord. Finn, knowing nothing of this, and finding the sign no longer, believes that it is Diarmaid who has betrayed him. Accordingly, when he overtakes him, he brings about

---

[1] *Rev. Celt.* XXXIII, p. 56, stanzas 19—22; Text *LF*, p. 153.

[2] *F* 54. 55. This is a variant of the taunt about the splashing water discussed above.

his death: Diarmaid's innocence is afterward discovered, and Grainne is buried alive[1].

The reader of Tristan will at once recognize the similarity of the story to the incident of the harp and the rote, lost in the version of Eilhart, but preserved in the *Folie Tristan* of the Berne manuscript, in the Prose Romance, and in Thomas. The account in the *Saga* is as follows[2]:

A stately ship arrives from Ireland, and the master of it, magnificently apparelled, enters the presence of the king and queen. The latter recognizes him at once, for he has long loved her, and has come hither for her sake. She tells the king his race and lineage, and bids him do him honor. The king invites him to eat from his own plate. The stranger says that he is a minstrel, and will on no condition part for a moment from the ornamented golden harp which he carries under his cloak. After the meal, the king asks him to play. The stranger refuses except for a reward. The king promises he shall have what he wills. He plays twice, and then demands Isolt. The king refuses; the stranger declares that a liar is unworthy to be king. He appeals to Mark's council, declaring that he is ready to maintain his right in

---

[1] *F* 57. Grainne is buried alive according to the following versions also: *LF* 162a, stanza 82. 164a, stanza 30, 164b, stanza 13; *F* 60. 2.

The *Pursuit* preserves in other contexts a few details which are found, in the oral versions, in connection with the episode of the stranger: the mention of Diarmaid's characteristic manner of dividing the fish, p. 80—1 (1 § 23); cf. *LF* 153b; the dwelling in the cave; Grainne asks Diarmaid for his knife, p. 96—7 (1 § 39); cf. *WHT* 42: 'Wouldst thou eat bread and flesh, Diarmaid?' [says Grainne]. 'Needful were I of it if I had it'. 'Here I will give it to thee. Where is a knife will cut it?' 'Search the sheath in which thou didst put it last', said Diarmaid. Grainne, ashamed, takes the knife out of the side of Diarmaid. She had aided the stranger against him. Similarly *LF* 153b.

[2] Kölbing I, 60, Cap. II.

single combat. All advise Mark to keep his word; no one dares undertake the combat. The stranger carries the weeping queen to his ship, but the departure is delayed by the tide.

In the meantime Tristan returns from the hunt and, learning the news, disguises himself as a minstrel and hastens to the shore. He finds the stranger trying to divert the distressed queen. Tristan is promised a mantle and a good robe if he can dry her tears by his playing.

While Tristan plays, the stranger forgets that the tide is rising, and that it is time to set out. When the water has risen above the gang-board, Tristan offers to carry the queen to the ship on his horse. As soon as he has her safely up, he is off, flinging a taunt to the helpless stranger[1] for his folly.

The details in *Sir Tristrem*[2] and Gottfried[3] vary, but not in any way that we can perceive to be significant. The *Folie Tristan* of the Berne manuscript contains the following passage[4]:

'Po vos manbre de Gamarien,
Qui ne demandoit autre rien
Fors vostre cors qu'il en mena
Qui fu ce qui vos delivra?

. . . .

Resanble je point a celui
Qui sol, sanz aïe d'autrui,
Vos secorut a cel besoin
A Guimarant copa lo poin?'

---

[1] It is apparently by inadvertence that the *Saga* has represented the stranger as riding into Mark's court.

[2] Kölbing II, p. 50, CLXV ff.; cf. Bédier I, Ch. XXIX.

[3] l. 13 110 ff.; cf. *Folie Tristan*, Douce MS. ed. Bédier p. 45, l. 765 ff.

[4] ed. Bédier, p. 99, l. 380 ff.; cf. n. *Il n'y a qu'une ressemblance vague et probablement accidentelle entre son aventure et celle du harpeur d'Irlande.*

The incident appears in the Prose Romance in a greatly modified form[1].

In Old Irish romance we find analogues to the incident of the harp and the rote in which the details that are puzzling in the Tristan story[2] and in *Diarmaid and Grainne*, are perfectly appropriate.

We shall turn now to the analogues in Old Irish literature. One of them is the story of the *Wooing of Etain*[3]:

a) Etain the wife of Midir, king of the fairy folk of Bri-Leith, after being beaten about by the winds for a thousand years through the magic arts of the jealous Fuamnach, is reborn as the child of an

---

[1] ed. Löseth, p. 36 § 43; Bédier II, 346.

[2] We have examined versions of the story in connection with Guinevere and other mediaeval heroines in Appendix IV.

[3] Section *a* exists only in the *Leabhar na h-Uidri (LU)*, a manuscript written before 1106; section *b* is found in *LU* and in *Egerton* 1782, a fifteenth century manuscript; section *c* exists in *LU* and, in a modified form, in *Eg.* and in the *Rennes Dindsenchas*; section *d* is found in *Egerton*, the *Rennes Dindsenchas* and other fragmentary accounts. Cf. Nettlau, *Rev. Celt.* XII, p. 232—9. The texts of *Eg.* and *LU* have been edited by Windisch, *Irische Texte* I, 113 ff.; *LU* 130 b 19—132 a have been edited with interlinear translation by A. Leahy, *Heroic Romances of Ireland*, London 1906, vol. II, p. 145 ff. A translation of the complete story, from *LU* and *Eg.*, is given by Leahy, *op. cit.* I, 3—33. We have printed in Appendix V a portion of Leahy's translation, p. 23—7. Ed. Müller, *Rev. Celt.* III, 350 ff. has edited the portion of *Eg.* corresponding to Windisch, *op. cit.* § 1—15 with an English translation. Stokes has edited, with an English translation, the *Rennes Dindsenchas* (prose), *Rev. Celt.* XV, p. 290—1 § 3, *Raith Esa*. Ed. Gwynn has edited, with an English translation, the *Metrical Dindsenchas*, *Royal Irish Academy*, *Todd Lecture Series* IX, p. 3 ff. *Rath Esa*. The *Togail Bruidne Da Derga*, *Rev. Celt.* XXII, 13—8, ed. Stokes, with an English translation, contains the courtship of Etain by Eochaid. L. C. Stern, *Zts. für celt. Philol.* V, 522 ff., edits fragments from a sixteenth century manuscript. Cf. A. Nutt, *Rev. Celt.* XXVII, 325. Nettlau, *Rev. Celt.* XII, 229 ff., gives an account of the manuscript authority for the various portions of the story, and a highly condensed summary. Zimmer, *Zts. f. ver. Sprforsch.* XXVIII, 587 ff. gives a more detailed summary, based on a collation of the manuscripts.

Ulster warrior, and becomes the wife of Eochaid, king of Ireland. In her childhood, a mysterious and magnificent personage once appears to her, accosts her as the wife of Midir, and sings a prophetic song.

b) Again, shortly after her marriage, Midir appears to her three times mysteriously, and reminds her of their former relation and its tragic ending. She refuses to return with him unless he obtains her husband's consent.

c) Early one summer morning Midir approaches and greets Eochaid as he sits in his tower overlooking the country. He proposes a game of chess, and insists on playing for a stake of fifty horses. He loses the first game. For the second he suggests that the winner shall appoint the wager. He loses this time also, and is required by Eochaid to perform a number of difficult tasks. They play a third game on the same terms. Midir wins. He demands a kiss and his two hands about Etain. Eochaid asks a month's delay. On the day appointed the king sets guards within and without the house. At nightfall the stranger appears in the midst of the armed forces surrounding the queen, and demands her. He reminds the king of his promise, and her, in a touching song, of her pledged word, and the delights of his land. Eochaid concedes only the permission to embrace her in the presence of all. Midir takes his weapons in his left arm, and the woman under his right, on the floor before them. The heroes rise in indignation, but see only two swans, disappearing in the direction of the Fairy Hill. For a year the king seeks his wife in vain.

d) At last a druid finds out, by some tricks with ogam, that she is in the Fairy Hill. After a nine year's siege Midir is forced to surrender Etain.

In this story the stranger is a supernatural personage. The period of his possession of Etain in
Fairyland is an important part of the story. The
poet describes effectively the mysterious appearance
of Midir to his lost wife. He dwells on his haughty
dictation of terms to Eochaid. Representing the stranger
as having paid two heavy losses without remonstrance,
he leaves the king no pretext to refuse to pay his
pledge. The poet dwells on his mysterious appearance,
through locked doors, the ineffectual precautions of
Eochaid, the song in which he reminds Etain of her
life with him and the loveliness of his land, the transformation of both into swans. The mysterious character of his realm, which Eochaid seeks a year in vain,
and finds, at last, only with the aid of magic, is another
point by which his supernatural character is emphasized.

We include also the resumé of a similar story,
told of Dubh Lacha, wife of Mongan[1]:

Mongan, king of Ulster, covets the kine of the
king of Leinster. The latter refuses to give them to
him except on condition of 'friendship without refusal'.
Mongan agrees, and takes the kine home with him.
Shortly after his arrival home, the king of Leinster
appears and demands Dubh Lacha, Mongan's wife.

---

[1] Edited and translated by Kuno Meyer, *Voyage of Bran*,
London 1895, I, p. 58 ff., from the *Book of Fermoy*, a fifteenth
century manuscript. The list of historic tales in the *Book
of Leinster* (written before 1150) mentions *The Love of Dubh
Lacha for Mongan* among the tales that every poet is obliged
to know. See E. O'Curry, *Lectures on the MSS. Materials*,
p. 592. 243; cf. d'Arbois, *Catalogue*, 206. Mongan appears in
the eighth century verse portion of Bran's voyage, and various
fragments relating to him are found in the *Leabhar na h-Uidhri*
(written before 1106) and other manuscripts. *The Book of
Leinster*, p. 41 c, mentions him in a list of the kings of Ulster.
The texts in which he appears are edited and translated by
Meyer in *Bran* I, 42 ff. For a discussion of the Mongan cycle see
Nutt, *Bran* I, 136 ff.

Silence fell upon Mongan. And he said: 'I have never heard of anyone's giving away his wife.' — 'Though thou hast not heard of it,' said Dubh Lacha, 'give her, for honor is more lasting than life.' Anger seized Mongan, and he allowed the king of Leinster to take her with him [1].'

She obtains from the latter, however, the promise that he will not claim her body for a year. At the end of that time Mongan shifts his shape, and sets out for the wedding feast as the son of the king of Connaught. He brings with him a hideous hag whom he has transformed for the occasion into the shape of Ibhell of the Shining Cheek. By the power of a love-charm the king of Leinster falls in love with her and offers Dubh Lacha in exchange for her. Mongan craftily accepts, and departs with his wife on the swiftest steeds in the king of Leinster's stables.

A similar story is told of Mongan's mother [2]:

Fiachna Finn is losing great numbers of his army by a flock of venomous sheep let loose upon them by his enemy, the king of Lochlann. One day he saw a single tall warlike man coming toward him, wearing a green cloak of one color, and a brooch of white silver in the cloak over his breast, and a satin shirt next his white skin. A circlet of gold was around his hair, and two sandals of gold under his feet. And the warrior said: 'What reward wouldst thou give to him who would keep the sheep from thee?' — 'By my word', said Fiachna, 'whatsoever thou ask, provided I have it, I should give it.' — 'Thou shalt have it to give', said the warrior, 'and I will tell thee the reward'. — 'Say the sentence', said Fiachna. The stranger then demanded Fiachna's wife for the night, and revealed his identity. He was Manannan, son of the god Lir.

---

[1] *Voyage of Bran, op. cit.* I, 75.
[2] *Voyage of Bran, op. cit.* I, p. 72.

Here we have only the first portion of the incident. The supernatural being appears to the king, and induces him, in reward for a service, to promise an indefinite boon. But the demand is not based on any previous claim to the woman, and involves only the possession of her for a night.

A similar story is told in Welsh of Rhiannon, the bride of Pwyll, Prince of Dyved[1].

A stranger arrives at the wedding feast of Pwyll, salutes the company, and declares that he has come to make a request. Pwyll promises that it shall be granted, whatever it be. Having reminded him of the dishonor attaching to the breaking of one's pledged word, the stranger demands Rhiannon, the bride. He is Gwawl, son of Clut, a magnificent and powerful personage, to whom she has previously been promised to wife. Rhiannon reproaches Pwyll for his rashness, but declares that he must not break his word. She teaches him a ruse by which he may avoid losing her. She will obtain a year's respite. On the day set for her marrige with Gwawl, Pwyll is to enter the hall in the disguise of a beggar, and ask, as a gift, sufficient food to fill a little sack which she gives him. It is a magic sack and will remain empty, however much is put into it. Gwawl will remark that it is slow in filling. The beggar is then to advise him to press down the contents of the bag with his foot, and to declare that by this means alone it can be filled. Pwyll will then tie Gwawl

---

[1] *Pwyll, Prince of Dyvet*, one of the *Mabinogion*, ed. Rhŷs and Evans, Oxford 1887; trans. J. Loth, *Les Mabinogion*, Paris 1889; Lady Charlotte Guest: *The Mabinogion*, numerous editions. For date v. J. Loth, *op. cit.* I, 9: *Ces quatre récits appartiennent au cycle gallois le plus ancien et sont sans doute un reste du patrimoine commun aux Gaëls et aux Bretons.*

in the bag, and signal to his men to enter from the wood.

All turns out as she has planned. Gwawl makes the rash promise and puts his foot in the sack. He is compelled to pledge himself to give up his claim to the bride and to pay a heavy ransom for his own release.

A similar story is told of Blathnad[1].

Cúroi engages with Cuchulainn and the heroes in an expedition to seize the treasures and the daughter of Mend, king of Falga. He promises to obtain entrance into the fortress on condition that his companions allow him his choice of the booty. 'Thou wilt get it', said Cuchulainn. — 'Then', replied he, 'Blathnad is my choice of the treasury'. Cuchulainn now attempts to modify the bargain, but Cúroi carries away the princess. Cuchulainn pursues and overtakes them. In the struggle that ensues, Cúroi is victorious. He succeeds in maintaining possession of Blathnad, and leaves Cuchulainn with shorn head, outraged, and bound head and heels. For a year Cuchulainn searches for Blathnad. He at last learns where Cúroi is concealing her. He attacks the fortress, and wins her back.

---

[1] *The Tragic Death of Cúroi Mac Dári* has been edited from the *Yellow Book of Lecan*, col. 776 (fac-simile ed. *R. I. A.*, p. 123) by R. I. Best, in *Ériu* II, 18. A shorter version, from MS. *Laud* (Oxford) 610 fol. 117 a, has been edited by Kuno Meyer, *Rev. Celt.* VI, 187—8. *The Vision of Ferchertne*, relating the same story, has been edited (in part) from *Laud* 610, fol. 117 b, by Kuno Meyer in *ZCP*. III, 40 ff. *Egerton* 88, fol. 10 a ff. contains another, version printed by Best, *loc. cit.* The date of these versions is placed by Meyer, *ZCP*. III, 41, and Best, *Ériu* II, 18, as the tenth century. The various *Dindsenchas* of Findglais also record the recovery of Blathnad by Cuchulainn. Cf. *Silva Gadelica* II, 482. 530; *Rev. Celt.* XV, 448 ff. There are other inedited accounts. The account of the abduction of Blathnad by Cúroi, forming as it does only a prologue, is merely sketched in the above narratives. Further details are given in Keating. v. O'Mahony's ed. p. 282. Cúroi is frequently mentioned in Old Irish literature.

Such stories of a woman won and lost by ruse between mortals and immortals seem to have been a favorite type among the Celts. The tale might go on indefinitely in a circle of loss and recovery, the distinction between loss and rescue depending on the point where the reader takes up the story, or on the sympathy of the story-teller with the mortal or the immortal lover. The ruse of Mongan to recover his wife from the king of Leinster is equivalent to Midir's ruse to reclaim his from King Eochaid. The first part of the Etain story has as much right to be termed a recovery as the last; it depends entirely upon whether we take Midir's or Eochaid's point of view.

The Celtic type, as represented by the Old Irish versions[1] and by Tristan, is as follows:

A magnificent and mysterious stranger appears to the king[2]. His race and lineage are known only to the queen, to whom he has a claim owing to some previous attachment[3]. He gives a display of skill, in recognition of which[4] the king promises him any boon he shall name[5]. He demands the queen[6]. The king hesitates, but, taunted with having compromised his honor, unwillingly accedes[7]. The stranger departs with the queen, no one daring to lift a hand to prevent him[8]. The husband later pursues and recovers the lady by ruse or magic[9].

---

[1] The stories studied are referred to as follows: *T:* Tristan; *E:* Etain; *M:* Mongan; *P:* Pwyll; *C:* Curoi; *F:* Fiachna Finn.
[2] *TEF.*
[3] *TEP.*
[4] *TEMCF.*
[5] *TEMPCF.*
[6] *TEMPCF.*
[7] *TEMCF.*
[8] *TEMC.*
[9] *TEMPC.*

In Tristan and in some versions of the Guinevere story[1] it is the husband who rashly gives away his wife to the stranger, and her lover who afterward regains her.

The substitution of the lover for the husband as rescuer, and the consequent division of the interest between the stranger, the husband who loses, and the lover who rescues the lady, is foreign to the Irish stories. The development of it can be clearly traced on French soil in connection with Guinevere[2]. In the episode in *Diarmaid and Grainne* the loser and the rescuer are still the same person, but popular narrators have corrupted the details of a tradition which they did not understand. Owing to the variations in its interpretation in the corrupt versions that are alone extant, it is impossible to determine what was the bearing of the incident on the tenth century romance. It may have been, as we find it in Tristan, purely episodic.

To explain the Tristan version various hypotheses suggest themselves. Perhaps the most plausible is that the original context of the episode, in *Tristan* as in *Diarmaid and Grainne*, was the life in the forest.

Some French redactor, anxious to remove from Tristan the shade of odium that attaches to the loss of the lady, and with less concern for the character of Mark, would seem to have transferred the episode from its original context to the period of the king's possession of Isolt. The emphasis on the power of music in the incident of

---

[1] v. Appendix.
[2] In Appendix IV we have given a detailed discussion of the incident of the *Harp and the Rote.*

the *Harp and the Rote* recalls the smile-strain
the sleep-strain, and the wail-strain of Old Irish
romance[1].

i) The separating sword.

There is another trait in Diarmaid and Grainne
which may throw light on a puzzling passage which
occurs in all the Tristan texts. While he is with
Grainne in the forest, Diarmaid always makes his bed
at a distance from Grainne's[2]. When they are in a
cave, he takes his place always at the farthest end.
It is thus that the stranger is able to reach Grainne
before him. In one version we are told that every
night Diarmaid put a cold stone between himself and
Grainne[3].

When Mark comes upon Tristan and Isolt sleeping
in the forest, he finds a sword between them. Béroul
does not account for Tristan's placing it there[4]. Eilhart
declares that it was a habit of the lovers to sleep thus,
and expresses his personal opinion that it was a strange
one[5]. Gottfried explains that Tristan, having guessed,
from the barking of the hounds on the preceding day,
that Mark and his party are in the forest, places the
sword in this position as a ruse to deceive anyone who
may chance to discover them[6]. M. Bédier has shown
that the version of Gottfried is posterior at this
point[7].

---

[1] cf. supra VI B 2 a 3.
[2] *W H T* p. 41. 43. 55; *F* 53. 56; O'Grady, 28.
[3] *The Fians*, *op. cit.* 56. In another Old Irish romance,
The Meeting of Liadain and Curithir, a little boy sleeps between
the lovers. Cf. App. V B.
[4] *B* 1805—6.
[5] *OX* 4581—93.
[6] ed. Marold 17 398—421.
[7] Bédier I, 244—5 n.

The incident is characteristic of the peculiar relation of Diarmaid and Grainne in their flight to the forest. In the Tristan story, on the other hand, it is incomprehensible. Every redactor from Eilhart to Swinburne has been embarassed by it. Why did Tristan place the sword between himself and Isolt? Eilhart's words are:

> 'Dô hâte Tristrant einen sete,
> des volgete im die vrauwe mete:
> swen sie sich gelegetin
> und mit ein andir redeten
> daz ez in dûchte genûch,
> sîn swert er ûz der scheide zôch
> und legete ez zwischin sich und sie;
> daz en wolde der helt nie
> dorch kein ding gelâzen.
> wan sie en soldin slâfen,
> daz swert en lêge zwischin in.
> daz was ein vromder mannes sin
> und quam im doch zu heile sît[1].'

The fact remains, however, that a poet who really meant us to believe that his hero had such a habit would have made for us another story, — the story of Diarmaid and Grainne perhaps — not the story of Tristan and Isolt. And perhaps it was a story like that of Diarmaid and Grainne that he really made; it may be the French redactors who have changed it[2]. The separating sword is perhaps a fossil of Celtic tradition[3].

---

[1] *loc. cit.*

[2] It is they who have brought it so well into accordance, in spirit and in matter, with French customs and feeling, that M. Bédier found in it but a few passages to which a French origin might not be assigned.

[3] v. supra Ch. V M, *The Substituted Sword.*

j) The dog in the forest.

There are several incidents of the life in the
forest in the Tristan story, which appear there without any vital connection with the narrative. In the
story of Diarmaid and Grainne similar incidents lead
to the tragic conclusion.

After Tristan's departure, his dog grieves violently
for him. He is let loose and follows the track of his
master through the forest. The fugitives are terrified
when they hear him approaching. Gorvenal insists on
placing himself in the way to meet and kill the dog.
Tristan and Isolt unwillingly withdraw. They all believe that the dog is followed by Mark and his men.
When Gorvenal sees that the dog is alone, he takes
him up on his horse, and sets out to join the lovers.
Losing the way, he puts the dog down on the ground,
and is guided by him to Tristan[1].

According to numerous versions of *Diarmaid and
Grainne*, it is one of Diarmaid's *geasa*[2] never to hear
the barking of the hunting dogs without following the
sound. Finn knows this, and, coming to a district where
he believes Diarmaid to be, lets loose the hounds on
he track of a wild cat there. Diarmaid hears the
sound, and in spite of the pleadings of Grainne, goes
out and joins the hunt. By the treachery of Finn he
meets his death[3].

---

[1] Béroul 1437—1637; *OX* 4368—511; cf. the interesting
suggestion of Röttiger, *op. cit.* p. 23, that this passage in Eilhart
(ll. 4457—63) is connected with the passage in Béroul (1678—9.
1693—6) where Gorvenal, from the ambuscade of the tree, kills
one of the three hostile barons. Cf. Muret, *Int.* Béroul, x—xii.

[2] cf. supra VI B.

[3] *LF* 158. 161; cf. *Zts. f. Celt. Philol.* V, 564—5; *F* p. 56 ff.;
WHT 43.

In the *Pursuit of Diarmaid and Grainne*, when Finn and his men are on the track of the fugitives, we read[1]:

> And Oisin (who is friendly toward Diarmaid), spoke: 'We are in danger lest Diarmaid and Grainne be yonder, and we must needs send him some warning; and look where Bran is, that is the hound of Finn Mac Cumhaill, that we may send him to him, for Finn himself is not dearer to him than Diarmaid ... And Oscar told that to Bran. Bran understood that with knowledge and wisdom, and went back to the hinder part of the host where Fiann might not see him, and followed Diarmaid and Grainne by their track until he reached Doire dha Bhoth, and thrust his head into Diarmaid's bosom, and he asleep.
>
> Then Diarmaid sprang out of his sleep, and awoke Grainne also, and said to her: 'There is Bran, that is the hound of Finn Mac Cumhall, coming with a warning to us before Finn himself.' — 'Take that warning', said Grainne, 'and fly'. — 'I will not take it', said Diarmaid, 'for I would not that Finn caught me at any [other] time, rather than now, since I may not escape from him'.

These passages are not sufficiently similar, and the texts of the Diarmaid and Grainne versions are too corrupt, to justify any conclusions as to the relation of the one to the other. They are interesting, however, as showing the general likeness of the elements that went to make up the two romances[2].

---

[1] ed. O'Grady, p. 65; cf. *The Fians*, p. 55: 'Bran was sent after him, and he was caught. It was then he was sent to kill the boar and Finn made him measure it against the bristles.'

[2] There is another glimpse of the lovers in *Tristan and Isolt* which resembles a scene in the story of *Diarmaid and Grainne*.

One hot morning Tristan, returning weary from the hunt, lies down to sleep in the hut beside the sleeping Isolt. He lays his sword between them, but their lips touch, and his arm is around her neck. A forester, chancing to pass, catches sight of them, and hastens away to tell Mark what he has seen. (*B* 1774—1850; *OX* 4594—616).

In *The Pursuit of Diarmaid and Grainne*:

As for Finn I will tell you [his] tidings clearly. He departed not from the tracking until he reached Doire dha bhoth, and he

k) The whittlings on the stream.

We have already discussed, in connection with
his accomplishments, the incident of the chips which
Tristan˘ whittled so deftly and sent down the stream
to Isolt[1]. In Tristan the incident has no important
bearing on the narrative. In several versions of the
Diarmaid and Grainne story, a similar incident is
fraught with tragic consequences. One of the whittlings
made by Diarmaid flows down the stream. Finn, who
is hunting in the woods near, knows that it is Diarmaid
who has made it; *for the speal curled round nine times,
and it was ... quarters long; there was none in Ireland
that could do the like.* It is then, according to several
of the versions, that Finn lets loose his dogs[2].

l) The continuation: stolen visits of Tristan to Isolt.

In the hunt introduced by the two incidents just
discussed, Finn treacherously brings about Diarmaid's
death.

---

sent the tribe of Eamhuin in to search out the wood, and they
saw Diarmaid and a woman by him. They returned back again
where were Finn and the Fianna of Erin, and Finn asked of them
whether Diarmaid and Grainne were in the wood. 'Diarmaid is
there', they said, 'and there is some woman by him [who she is
we know not]', for we know Diarmaid's track and we know not
the track of Grainne' (ed. O'Grady, p. 289, Pt I § 18).

There is a similar scene in the story of Deirdre and Naisi:
Now one day the high-steward of the king went out in the
early morning, and he made a cast about Naisi's house, and saw
those two sleeping therein, and he hurried back to the king,
and awaked him. (Leahy, *op. cit.* I, 96.)

The incident is, however, not of sufficient importance to
be insisted upon. It might be found in romances entirely un-
related.

[1] Supra. Ch. VI B 2 a 7.
[2] *I.F* 158 b. The reader will recall the versions of the
complete incident cited above VI B 2 a 7.

We have said above that in the *Pursuit of Diarmaid and Grainne,* a version made by a redactor desirous of softening the old story in accordance with modern taste, Diarmaid is represented as making terms with Finn, returning from the forest, and living for some years in peace[1]. In the voluntary return of Tristan and Isolt from the forest and the following incidents of the Tristan story, it may be that we have an analogous literary phenomenon. The calamity was averted, the tragic ending of the story was post-poned, in each case, by a redactor willing to meet the desire of his audience for a continuation. As an example of how easily the material which constituted these stories lent itself to continuations, one of the tenth century fragments of the *Diarmaid and Grainne* tradition referred to above might be cited. Here the hero's foster-father, Aonghus of the Brugh, appears at a crucial moment, and miraculously carries Grainne to a place of safety. The hero is able to save himself, and the lovers are thus preserved for further adventures. By such methods, a good story might be indefinitely prolonged in mediaeval romance as in popular tradition.

The incidents which form a considerable part of the continuation of the Tristan story, the stolen visits of Tristan to Isolt, are of a character to which we may find analogues anywhere in mediaeval fiction. The Celtic stories of this type are not more or less similar to Tristan, so far as we have been able to determine, than are those of any other literature.

---

[1] cf. supra VI D 2b; ed. Meyer, *Rev. Celt.* XI, p. 125 ff.: *Uath Beinne Etair (The Hiding in the Hill of Howth).* The *Uatha, Tales of Hiding,* constitute a class of stories mentioned in the list in the *Book of Leinster*; cf. the *Aitheda, Tales of Elopement;* the *Imrama, Tales of Voyages,* discussed above.

We cite as a Celtic analogue to *Tristan Mönch* the following story from *The Conception of Mongan and Dubh Lacha's Love for Mongan* [1].

Mongan has lost his wife Dubh Lacha in consequence of a rash promise similar to that which we have discussed in connection with the harp and the rote. She is now queen of Leinster.

> 'And for that while Mongan was in a wasting sickness continually. . . . .
>
> . . . .
>
> Mongan took on himself the shape of Tibraide (the priest), and gave Mac an Daimh the shape of the cleric, with a large tonsure on his head, and the . . . on his back. And they go onward before the king of Leinster, who welcomed Tibraide and gave him a kiss, and 'Tis long that I have not seen thee, O Tibraide' he said, 'and read the gospel to us and proceed before us to the fortress. And let Ceibhin Cochlach, the attendant of my chariot, go with thee. And the queen, the wife of the king of Ulster, is there and would like to confess to thee'. . . . And Mongan went onward to the front of the fortress in which Dubh Lacha was. And she recognized him. And Mac an Daimh said: 'Leave the house all of ye, so that the queen may make her confession'. . . . And he closed the bower after them and put the glazen door to it, and opened the window of glass. . . . And Mongan sat down by her shoulder and gave her three kisses and carried her into bed with him and had his will and pleasure of her. . . .'
>
> Mongan outwits his enemies and escapes safely. He makes repeated visits to Dubh Lacha, and succeeds repeatedly, by dint of the fertility of his wits, in gaining access to her in one disguise or another.

The similarity is not close. The lover who puts on a disguise in order to gain access to his mistress

---

[1] Meyer and Nutt, *Voyage of Bran* I, 58 ff. 70 ff. Translation p. 76 § 11. p. 77 § 15. § 16.

is familiar in many lands.[1] The incident lends itself
easily to variations in detail. It is probable that
similarities would be found in versions entirely independent of each other.

m) The conclusion in the poems[2].

The closing incident in the poetic versions is
similar, as has been pointed out[3], to the ending of
the story of Œnone, whom Paris loved before he knew
Helen. When he is wounded by the poisoned arrows
of Hercules, he sends for her to come and heal him.
He dies on hearing that she has refused to come.
When she hastens after the messenger with her herbs
and simples, she arrives too late. She kills herself,
and is buried with Paris in the same grave.

Into a story of this type the Tristan poet has
introduced the theme of the signal of the sail and the
fatal error, a theme which is familiar from the story of
Theseus[4]. Theseus departs to carry tribute for the second
time to Crete. Aegeus tells the pilot to take white
sails with him and to hoist them on the return in case
his son succeeds in killing the Minotaur. The expedition is successful, but Ariadne is stolen from Theseus
by Bacchus. In his grief at her loss Theseus forgets
the instructions of his father, and does not put up

---

[1] We have spoken in our discussion of the *Harp and the Rote*
(cf. *h* supra) of Diarmaid's coming to the cave in the disguise of a
beggar. Cf. examples cited by Golther, *Die Sage von Tristan und
Isolde*, München 1887, p. 18: Jänicke, *Deutsches Heldenbuch* IV,
XL—XLII; Grundtvig, *Danmarks gamle folkeviser* I, 271; III, 796;
Landstad, *Norske folkeviser*, no. 59.

[2] E. Brugger, *Herrigs Archiv* CXXIX, 134, announces a
forthcoming article, entitled *Zu Tristans Tod.*

[3] Golther (1907) 20—3.

[4] Bédier (II, 137—41; cf. Bédier, *Romania* XX, 485) believes the Tristan poet read the story in Servius, note to Bk. III,
l. 74 of Virgils *Aeneid.*

the white sail. Aegeus, thinking his son dead, throws himself from the citadel.

Stories of the signal of a sail would naturally be found in all countries bordering on the sea. The device is simple enough, and the idea of making one color denote good news and the other bad, is not far to seek. It constitutes an essential element in an Irish folk-tale of which we have collected several examples[1]. In these stories the wrong sail is purposely hoisted in order to mislead the person on shore.

> Finn succeeds in engaging the services of a personage called the Lad of the Skins. The Lad's wife will not allow her husband to depart with Finn except on condition that the latter will bring him home alive or dead. The exploit on which the Lad sets out is successfully accomplished, but in returning home he is killed by an old sorcerer. Finn has promised the wife that he will indicate by the sails whether her husband is alive or dead. If her husband is dead, the intention of the woman is to sink the vessel by means of her magic arts before it touches the shore. But her husband is sincerely devoted to Finn. He therefore tells Finn that even in case of his death, he must hoist the sail that indicates his safe return. Thanks to this ruse Finn disembarks in safety[2].

---

[1] *Rev. Celt.* XXXII, 185—6 and notes 3 and 4.

[2] The following Irish folk-tale offers more striking similarities to the Tristan story, but since it is the only example we have, and since we have not been able to trace it to older Irish literature, we offer it with reservations. A maiden is called from the side of her lover, whose wounds she is tending, to visit her dying father. The wounded man sends a messenger day after day to the top of the highest hills to look for the ship which is to bear her back. His enemy, who has introduced himself into the household in disguise, offers to go out to meet the ship which is to bring her, and to raise a signal, red, if all is well, and black, if the princess is dead. When he reaches the boat he persuades the princess to raise the death signal, saying that her lover will have the greater joy to see her living. On seeing the signal, the prince kills himself in despair. The enemy, rejoicing, kills the princess also. *Waifs and Strays of Celtic Tradition* V, *Argyllshire series,* ed. A. Campbell, London 1895, p. 76.

n) The conclusion of the French Prose Romance and of the Old Irish stories. The eye at the window.

The French Prose Romance of Tristan preserves an ending different from that which we find in the poems.

> Or dit li contes que un jour estoit Tristans entrés es chambres la royne et harpoit un lay qu'il avoit fait. Audret l'entendi et le vint conter au roy, Marc; Tristans estoit désarmés, si que le roy le ferist mortelment parmi l'eschine d'un glaive envenimé que Morgain li ot baillié ... Tristans congnut bien que il estoit féru à mort; il ne pot le roy ateindre et, pour ce, s'en vint d'autre part en la court à val et monta le premier cheval qu'il trouva; si s'en fuit de Tintaguel et s'en vint au chastel de Dinas[1]. . . . . .
>
> . . . .
>
> Quant Tristans vit apertement qu'il estoit à la mort venus, il regarde entour soi et dist: Seigneur, je muire, je ne puis plus vivre; à Dieu soyés tout commandé. Quant il ot dite ceste parole, il dist à la royne Iseult: Amie or m'accolés, si que je fine entre vos bras. Si finerai adonc à aise, ce m'est avis. Iseult s'incline sur Tristan, quant ele entent ceste parole; ele s'abaisse seur son pis. Tristans la prent entre ses bras, et quand il la tint seur son pis, il dist si haut que tuit cil de léans l'entendirent: Des ore ne me chaut quant je muire, puis que je ai ma dame avoec moy. Lors estraint la royne de tant de force que il li fist le cuer partir, et il méesmes morut en tel point. Si que bras à bras et bouche à bouche moururent li dui amant, et demourèrent en tele manière embraciés. Mort sont amdui et par amour, sans autre comfort[2].

The Prose Romance, for all its modifications and interpolations, seems to us to preserve in this ending a tradition, if not older than that of the poems, at least independent of them[3]. It is difficult to believe

---

[1] P. Paris, *Les manuscrits français de la bibliothèque du roi*, Paris 1836, I, 200 ff.

[2] *op. cit.* 208 ff.; cf. Löseth § 546 ff.

[3] cf. *supra* Ch. I, pp. 9—10.

that it was written by a poet who was acquainted with the version of the poems. It represents a much simpler stage of the story, involving only the three main characters — the husband, the wife, and the lover. The vengeance comes, as in the Celtic stories, from the injured husband. In this account there is no trace of the second Isolt. It is striking also that this redactor does not attribute to Isolt the extraordinary powers of healing credited her by the poems. It has been seen in our examination of the fusing of the episodes of the voyage for healing and the quest of Isolt, that these were originally distinct. It is impossible to tell in what order the parts which now constitute the narrative were assimilated. It may be that the ending of the Prose Romance goes back to a period of the tradition before the second Isolt, or perhaps even the story of the voyage for healing, had been introduced into it. It is hardly conceivable that this ending should have taken the place of the one we have in the poems after the tradition of Isolt's healing powers had become established by the incident of the rudderless voyage, and after the second Isolt had come to constitute an element in the story.

There are some curious additional traits in the version of this incident in the *Tavola Ritonda*. Here it is Andret who first finds the lovers together. Mark, peering into the window, sees Tristan and Isolt bent over the chess board [1].

Trapassata che fu la notte e venuto il giorno, e Tristano e Isotta stando in tanta allegrezza, e giucando a scacchi e cantando sotto boce uno sonetto, lo quale sonetto Isotta fatto

---

[1] *La Tavola Ritonda (Collezione di opere inedite o rare,* vol. 8), ed. F. L. Polidori, Bologna 1864, I, 495 ff.

avea in quel punto per Tristano; e lo sonetto dicea cosi: . . .
E cantando e giucando gli due leali amanti, e stando in
tanto diletto, sì come volle la disavventuranzia, Adriett,
nipote dello re Marco, passa quindi e, udendo il canto,
conobbe la boce di Tristano, e allora, correndo, se ne va
allo re Marco e si gli conta la novella. E lo re Marco, si
come uomo irato, sanza niuno provvedimento, si tolse i'mano
lo lanciotto che la fata mandato gli avea, e vassene alla
camera: e mirando per una finestra ferrata, e vedendo
Tristano ch' era i' giubba di seta, ed era inchinato al giuoco
ch' egli facea con Isotta, lo quale molto gli dilettava; allora
lo re, per mal talento, si gli lanciò la lancia e ferillo nel
fianco dal lato manco.

The continuation of Béroul breaks off with a
similar scene [1].

Gondoïne, one of the hostile barons, peers into
the window of the chamber where Tristan and Isolt
are together. Isolt perceives the head at the window.
She pretends to be curious to know how to manipulate
Tristan's bow and arrow. When her lover has drawn
the bow and put the arrow in place, she directs her
eyes to the window. Tristan follows her with his gaze,
and sees the head of Godoïne. The bow is ready, and
the arrow flies. It enters the head of the spy.

In some earlier version of Tristan, this incident
in the continuation of Béroul may have been a prelude
to the tragic ending preserved, with characteristic
modifications, in the late and courtly version of the
Prose Romance. There is a striking similarity between
it and the incident which introduces the catastrophe
in a version of *The Elopement of Deirdre with Naisi* [2]:

---

[1] Béroul 4413—87.

[2] ed. Windisch, *Irische Texte* II, 138, l. 403—20, trans.
p. 167, l. 405 ff. Cf. d'Arbois, *Epopée*, p. 272. This incident does
not occur in the *Book of Leinster*, cf. supra VI D 3 f n. 2. The
manuscript in which it is contained, the *Glenn Masáin*, Advocates
Library, Edinburgh, was probably written in the fifteenth century.

And Trén-dorn moved forward, and came to the hostel, und found the doors and the windows shut; and dread and great fear seized him, and this he said 'There is no proper way to approach the sons of Usnech, for wrath is on them.' And after that he found a window unclosed, in the hostel, and he began to look at Naisi and Deirdre through the window. Deirdre looked at him, for she was the most quick-witted there, and she nudged (?) Naisi, and Naisi looked after her look and beheld the eye of that man.

And thus was he himself, having a dead man of the men of the draught-board, and thereof made he a fearful successful cast, so that it came to the young man's eye . . . . interchange was made between them, and his eye came on the young man's cheek, and he went to Conchobar having only one eye, and told tidings to him from beginning to end.

o) Conclusion.

The conclusion of the Prose Romance is closely allied with the conclusion of the Old Irish stories which we have examined. The Celtic elopement tale out of which the French redactor made the story of Tristan and Isolt may have represented the lovers as lured back from the forest under promises from Mark, and Tristan as treacherously slain by the jealous king on their arrival. Let us compare the scene of the return from the forest in Béroul, with that in the story of Naisi and Deirdre.

In Béroul, Tristan receives the promise of Mark that he may bring back Isolt, and that they will be received on friendly terms[1]:

'D'ui en tierz jor, sanz nul deçoivre,
Est li rois prest de lié reçoivre.

---

[1] Béroul 2767—82.

> Devant le Gué Aventuros
> Est li plez mis d'eus et de vos:
> La li rendroiz, iluec ert prise.'

The description of the scene of the return in Béroul is as follows[1]:

> 'Seignors, au jor du parlement
> Fu li rois Marc a mout grant gent.
> La out tendu maint pavellon
> Et mainte tente de baron:
> Loin ont porpris la praerie.
> Tristran chevauche o s'amie;
> Tristran chevauche et voit le merc.
> Souz son bliaut ot son hauberc;
> Quar grant poor avoit de soi,
> Por ce qu'il out mesfait au roi.'

The · description of the return in the story of Deirdre and Naisi:

The men of Ulster urge King Conor to recall the sons of Usnach from their exile[2].

'Let them come to us then', said Conor. . . . The news was brought to them.

'This is welcome news for us', they said; 'we will indeed come' . . . And the sons of Usnach went on, accompanied by Fiacha, Fergus' son; until they came to the meadows around Emain. . . . .

The sons of Usnach stood upon the level part of the meadows, and the women sat upon the ramparts of Emain. And Eogan came with his warriors across the meadow, and the son of Fergus took his place by Naisi's side.

---

[1] Béroul 2767—77.
[2] A. H. Leahy, *Heroic Romances of Ireland*, London 1905, I, 97. Leahy writes *Conor*. Other translators retain the Irish orthography *Conchobar*.

In the Old Irish romance the tragic conclusion immediately follows. What Tristan merely feared that day when he put on his hauberk to meet Mark at the Gué Aventuros, here comes to pass.

> And Eogan greeted them with a mighty thrust of his spear, and the spear brake Naisi's back in sunder, and passed through it. The son of Fergus made a spring, and he threw both arms around Naisi, and he brought him beneath himself to shelter him, while he threw himself down above him; and it was thus that Naisi was slain, through the body of the son of Fergus. Then there began a murder throughout the meadow, so that none escaped who did not fall by the points of the spears, or the edge of the sword, and Deirdre was brought to Conor to be in his power, and her arms were bound behind her back[1]. . .
>
> Deirdre lived on for a year in the household of Conor; and during all that time she smiled no smile of laughter; she satisfied not herself with food or with sleep, and she raised not her head from her knee[2]. . . .
>
> Now upon the morrow they went away over the festal plain of Macha, and Deirdre sat behind Eogan in the chariot; and the two who were with her were the two men whom she would never willingly have seen together upon the earth, and as she looked upon them, 'Ha, Deirdre', said Conor, 'it is the same glance that a ewe gives when between two rams that thou sharest now between me and Eogan!' Now there was a great rock of stone in front of them, and Deirdre struck her head upon that stone, and she shattered her head, and so she died[3].

In *Diarmaid and Grainne* also, as we have seen, the lover is treacherously killed in a similar way by the jealous king. In some versions Finn takes back Grainne.

---

[1] *op. cit.* 97.
[2] *op. cit.* 98.
[3] *op. cit.* 102.

In *Liadain and Curithir*, another Old Irish story of tragic love, the woman survives her lover, and at last dies of grief[1].

It seems to us probable that the popularity of the Tristan story led some redactor to defer the tragic conclusion by bringing the lovers back safely from the forest to the court of Mark. Further adventures were added, most of them dictated by ideals of courtly love. The scant account which the Celtic elopement story gave of Tristan's birth and childhood was supplemented from various sources. The tragedy was complicated by the introduction of the second Isolt, and a new tragic ending was substituted for the old.

This new ending is probably the work of a French poet. As we have indicated in Chapter IV, there seems to have been a tradition that Tristan delivered the land of Howel and received his daughter as a reward[2]. It must have been a French poet, and it seems to have been a poet of genius, who, for an audience deeply imbued with the theories of courtly love, rendered this incident significant by representing Tristan as remaining true to Isolt in spite of his marriage. It was perhaps the same poet who gave us the catastrophe which we find in the poems, with its echoes of the voyage for healing and of the unconsummated marriage.

The most important stages of the tradition of Tristan previous to the extant versions seem to us to be roughly as follows:

A. A Celtic *Aithed* similar to the story of *Diarmaid and Grainne*. Its ending, similar to that of the French

---

[1] cf. infra, Appendix V.
[2] cf. supra p. 160 ff. and infra Appendix III.

Prose Romance, was on the return of the lovers from the forest.

B. The first French romance, modifying *A* for a French audience and incorporating new material, some of it, perhaps, from Celtic sources.

C. The *estoire*, a redaction of this version, reproducing *B* and incorporating more new material. To this belong, perhaps, (1) a fuller account of the birth and childhood of Tristan; (2) a number of episodes from the general fund of mediaeval fiction; (3) a continuation containing incidents that illustrate the doctrines of courtly love; and (4) a new ending, the messenger sent to the healing Isolt, and the story of the sails.

E. THE TRAGIC CONFLICT IN *TRISTAN AND ISOLT* AND IN OLD IRISH ROMANCE

1. UNLAWFUL LOVE IN OLD FRENCH LITERATURE.

Accusations, true and false, of unlawful love, serve to fill out many a mediaeval romance, besides the considerable number to which they furnish a central theme. The punishment threatened, and in some cases inflicted, is burning at the stake[1]. The woman

---

[1] cf. Pio Rajna, *Le fonti dell' Orlando Furioso*[2], Florence, 1900, pp. 154 ff.; F. J. Child, *English and Scottish Popular Ballads*, II, 113; J. D. Bruce, *Mort Artu*, Halle a. S. 1910, p. 283 note to p. 108 ll. 27 ff.

is given an opportunity to justify herself, either by a champion, in judicial combat, or by an ordeal.

Adultery occurs frequently in episodes in the *chansons de geste*, it is frequently mentioned in the *fabliaux*, and it forms one of the favorite themes of courtly romance. In all of these we find the admirable husband who is indulgent toward his unfaithful wife just as often as the old and jealous husband, ridiculous in his misfortune. The version of Eilhart presents Mark in the one character, and the French Prose Romance in the other.

The love of a gifted vassal for the lady of his lord is the frequent theme of the lyrics of the troubadours. The story of Tristan is the oft-repeated tale which we read in the biography of Bernard de Ventadour, fabulous if you will, but no less important for literary history[1].

> E Bernart venc bels hom et adreitz, e saup ben trobar e cantar et era cortes et enseignatz. E'l vescoms de Ventedorn, lo sieus seigner, s'abellic mout de lui e de son trobar e de son chantar, e fetz li grand' honor. E'l vescoms de Ventedorn si avia moiller bella e gaia e ioven e gentil; et abellic se d'en Bernart e de las soas chanssos, et enamoret se de lui et el de lieis, si q'el fetz sos vers e sas chanssos d'ella, de l'amor q'el avia ad ella, e de la valor de la dompna. Mout duret lonc temps lors amors anz qe'l vescoms, maritz de la dompna, ni las autras gens s'en aperceubessen. E qan lo vescoms s'en fo aperceubutz, en estraigniet en Bernart de si, e pois fetz la moiller serrar e gardar. Adoncs fetz la dompna dar comiat a'n Bernat, e fetz li dir qe 'is partis e is loignes d'aquella encontrada.

---

[1] Appel, *Provenzalische Chrestomathie*, Leipzig 1907, 189—90.

2. THE ATTITUDE TOWARD UNLAWFUL LOVE IN *TRISTAN AND ISOLT.*

a) In the part of the estoire *previous to the return from the forest.*

On close examination it appears that the various extant redactions reflect important variations of moral sentiment. Even in the same redaction it is often clear that different series of events were conceived under widely different moral premises. There are three sharply defined conceptions of the potion to be distinguished in the earliest Tristan texts. The first is that of the portion of the Béroul-Eilhart version previous to the return of Isolt to Mark and the exile of Tristan. The second is that of the Eilhart version from the return from the forest to the end of the romance. The third is that of Thomas [1].

In Béroul and Eilhart the passion of the lovers is the direct effect of a potion. It dominates their entire being, making them indifferent to their infidelity to Mark, indifferent to the sinfulness of their love, indifferent to their social ruin, indifferent to danger, indifferent to every consideration except the means of maintaining their relation. With all the orthodox

---

[1] We have already discussed the diminution in the influence of the potion at the expiration of a certain period, a trait which appears in Béroul, Eilhart, and the *Folie Tristan* of the Berne manuscript, but which is lacking in the version of Thomas and the Prose Romance. In Béroul, as the reader will remember, the abatement of the potion's influence is related in two long monologues and a dialogue. Their change of sentiment, although developed at less length, is apparent in Eilhart and in the *Folie* also. It has already been shown that these versions are here faithfully following their source, whereas Thomas, who avoids this lessening of the power of the potion, is revising it. Cf. supra Ch. III, p. 72—84; cf. *Rom.* XL, 277—97.

Christian horror of their sin, they feel themselves, as a result of the potion, under a diabolical compulsion.

The more closely we examine the attitude of Béroul and Eilhart, the more forcibly we are struck with their anxiety to emphasize the fact that the lovers are not responsible for their conduct. We are told that Tristan's deception of Mark in lying with Isolt on her wedding night while the unsuspecting king was with the servant Brangien was *nichein untrûwe*[1] but, like his *grôzen unmâze*[2] in leaping across the flour on the floor, was *âne sînen dang*[3] and all due to *der vil unsêlige trang*[4]. Mark himself acknowledges this when he learns of the potion, after the lovers' death[5].

This idea is most strongly emphasized toward the close of the life in the forest[6], in the passage in which the overwhelming influence of the potion is represented as expiring. Completely dominated by the fatal drink, the lovers had been unconscious of their suffering and privations. When the good hermit had urged them to repentance, Tristan had replied[7]

'Sire, par foi,
Se ele m'aime (en bone foi,
Vos n'entendez pas la raison),
S'el m'aime, c'est par la poison.'

---

[1] *OX* 2838—48.

[2] *OX* 3918.

[3] *OX* 2843. 9490. Also 2367 cf. *OP* 57,10: 'Doch mag es rechtlich nit betrieglikeit sein, weil er solichs nit aus eignem mutwillen und frefel geton hat, sunder aus schickung und würkunge materlicher kunst, vor offt genent.'

[4] *OX* 2844. 3915. Also 2368; cf. *OP* 82,16: 'nit aus schickung und ordnung der natur, sunder aus krafft und würckung des getrancks, das sy getruncken hetten.'

[5] *OX* 9490.

[6] cf. supra Ch. III, p. 72—5.

[7] Béroul 1381—4.

Isolt had likewise declared[1]:

> 'Sire, por Deu omnipotent,
> Il ne m'aime pas, ne je lui,
> Fors par .i. herbé dont je bui,
> Et il en but: ce fu pechiez'.

As Tristan expresses it in the Czech translation of Eilhart[2]: 'It is laid on us by God; we are powerless to resist it.' They had departed from the hermit without absolution. But now that the term appointed is complete, the compulsion is lifted. The other values of life — the emoluments of knight-hood, their relations with the world, their duty to Mark, and their affection for him — take on again their normal significance. The lovers proceed in the orthodox manner to seek from the pious hermit remission of their sins, absolution, and counsel for amendment[3].

> 'Por qoi la joie pardurable
> Porron ancore bien merir'[4].

b) In the part of the estoire *subsequent to the return from the forest.*

The attitude toward the relation of the lovers which we find in the continuation of the romance which appears in the *estoire* is entirely different. The account of Tristan's refraining from consummating his marriage, and of the displeasure of Queen Isolt against him on account of his supposed

---

[1] Béroul 1413—7.
[2] *OČ* 224,6 (*ZfdA.* XXVIII, p. 321). Similarly *OX* 4720—9; *OP* 101,25—102,4.
[3] Béroul 2265—89.
[4] Béroul 2276—8.

failure to respond to a request made in her name[1]
illustrates a conception of love of an entirely different
order from that which we have found in the first part
of the romance. The author of the *estoire* tried to
veneer the first part to make it correspond with the
second. But the poet who conceived the second
part, if he had been free to deal with the story as a
whole, would have suppressed the love-potion and
effaced the lovers' repentance and voluntary return
from the forest.

The treatment of the potion and of the expiration
of its influence in the *estoire* is the work of a poet to
whom the love of Tristan and Isolt was an unlawful
and unholy thing, a passion explicable and capable of
commanding sympathy only from the fact that it was
due to a malign influence for which the lovers were
not responsible. This attitude is still apparent in some
passages of Béroul and Eilhart. It even survives in
the poem of Gottfried. When Brangien discovers that
the lovers have drunk the potion, and realizes the
cause of their illness, she says to Tristan[2]

'lât diz laster under uns drîn
verswigen unde beliben sîn'.

The feeling that the love of Tristan and Isolt is
laster, is *pechié*[3], *puterie*[4], is never quite effaced from
the story. It is most strongly emphasized, as we have
said, in the account of the return from the forest
in Béroul and Eilhart. What follows in the Eilhart
version is the expression of an entirely different
attitude. Here Isolt is represented as exacting from

---

[1] cf. supra Ch. IV.
[2] Gottfried, ed. Marold 12147—9.
[3] Béroul 700.
[4] Béroul 407.

Tristan an obedience so exaggerated that she treats
him with the greatest severity because he appears
to have refused a request made in her name. Here
Tristan is represented as refraining from accomplishing his marriage on account of a scruple for which
we may search in vain outside the peculiar idealization of illegitimate love which we find in the circle
of *Cligès* and *La Charrette*. Here, finally, Tristan
is represented as losing his life in furthering Kaherdin's *amour* with Gargeolain the wife of Bedenis, an
enterprise for which neither hero nor poet feels any
moral compunction. This portion of the *estoire* is
dominated by a conception of love — whether legitimate or illegitimate — as invading the hero through
his eyes, arousing in his heart a noble aspiration to be
worthy of the beauty which he beholds, and awakening
in him valor and courtesy. The service of love is a
voluntary service, which the lover joyfully accepts
with his whole mind. As Gottfried expresses it[1]:

'Liebe ist ein alsô saelic dinc,
ein alsô sæleclîch gerinc,
daz nieman âne ir lêre
noch tugende hât noch êre.
sô manecwert leben, sô liebe frumet,
sô vil sô tugende von ir kumet,
owê daz allez, daz der lebet,
nâch herzeliebe niht enstrebet'.

To poets with this ideal of love, the treatment of
the potion in Béroul and Eilhart is not only unsym-
pathetic, it is actually repugnant. It degrades a deity.
The following lyric expresses Crestien's attitude[2].

---

[1] ed. Marold 187—94.
[2] J. Brakelmann, *Les plus anciens chansonniers français,*
Paris 1870—1, p. 47.

'Onques del bevrage ne bui
Dont Tristans fuz enpoisonez,
Mais plus me fait amer que lui
Fins cuers et bone volentez.
Si ne m'en doit savoir mal gré
Quant de rien efforciez n'en fui
Fors de tant, que mes eus en crui,
Par qui sui en la voie entrez,
Dont ja n'istrai, n'ains n'i recrui.'

Heinrich von Veldeke also feels that the potion
detracts from the merit of love, which should be a
voluntary service[1].

'Tristrant môste sonder danc
stâte sîn der koninginne,
want hem poisûn dartoe dwanc
mêre, dan die kracht der minne.
des sal mir die gôde danc
weten, dat ich nien gedranc
alsolhen wîn, end ich si minne
bat dan he, end mach dat sîn.
wale gedâne,
valskes âne,
lâ mich wesen dîn,
ende wis du mîn.'

The second part of the *estoire*, together with
Crestien's *Cligès* and *La Charrette*, form the three
most curious expressions of the courtly ideal of love.
Each is the treatment of a problem in the new system
of ethics which the new ideal involved. In *La Charrette* unlawful love is put before chivalric honor:
Lancelot courts ignominy in the tournament at his

---

[1] Piper, *Höfische Epik, Deutsche National-Literatur* I, 69.

lady's command. In *Cligès* unlawful love is put before
the duty of wife to husband: Fenice, married to Alix,
preserves her virginity for her lover. In *Tristan* it
is put before the duty of husband to wife: Tristan
refrains from consummating his marriage with Isolt
of the White Hands for the sake of a hopeless and
forbidden love.

η) In Thomas.

Thomas modified to some extent this exaggerated
expression of the courtly ideal. He suppressed Isolt's
anger against Tristan for not submitting to unreasonable demands made in her name, although it was
necessary for him to change the narrative considerably
in order to do so [1]. His attitude toward love is still,
however, in marked contrast to that which we find in
the treatment of the return from the forest in Eilhart
and Béroul. To him the potion is not the instrument
of destiny to which the lovers submit against their
will; it is the symbol of Amors, a divinity worshipped
and blessed. Thomas' lovers, if we are to believe
Gottfried, accept and rejoice in their fate. In the
first part of the *estoire*, on the other hand, their
passion is not only forbidden by society; it is felt by
the lovers themselves to involve the infringement of a
moral law. This moral law the poet accepts without
question. In Thomas and Gottfried, on the contrary,
there is no law but love. There is a social order, to
be sure — there is honor in the eyes of the world (*êre*),

---

[1] cf. supra Ch. IV, p. 128—32; cf. Bédier II, 270—6. Thomas
does not allow Isolt to believe the accusation against Tristan. He
shifts the quarrel to the subordinate characters, Brangien and
Kaherdin.

and there is Tristan's faith to Mark (*triuwe*).   Love,
however, is a more powerful deity [1]:

> 'in muoten harte sêre
> sîn triuwe und sîn êre
> sô muote in aber diu Minne mê,
> diu tete im wirs danne wê:
> si tete im mê ze leide
> dan Triuwe und Êre beide'.

Even Mark bows to the lovers' passion and gives
them his permission to go together to the forest [2]:

> 'sît ich nu an iu beiden sihe,
> daz ir ein ander alle zît
> wider allem mînem willen sît
> lieber dan ich iu beiden sî,
> sô weset ouch beide ein ander bî,
> als iu ze muote gestê:
> durch mîne vorhte lât nimê'.

Here Thomas departs widely from the tradition
in which the lovers escaped to the forest from worse
than death, and Mark could find no punishment cruel
enough for their crime.

3. TRISTAN'S DISLOYALTY TO MARK.

With the first coming of Tristan to Mark's court
the poet of the *estoire* begins to prepare for the tragic
struggle which is to form the theme of his narrative.
Mark receives the stranger youth graciously and treats

---

[1]   ed. Marold 11 771—6.
[2]   ed. Marold 16 596—63.

him with generous kindness. He grants his request
for arms, although it is premature; he is so fond
of him that he is unwilling to allow him to undertake the combat with the Morholt; his distress is
increased when he learns that the young knight is
his sister's son. When the others desert Tristan on
account of his wound, Mark remains with him. He
is grief-stricken when his nephew insists on setting
out alone on the sea; he is overjoyed when he returns
in safety. He makes every effort to withstand the
barons' demand that he shall marry, and when he
can refuse them no longer, he submits on condition
that they bring him a princess impossible to obtain.
His purpose of resistance is unexpectedly thwarted by
Tristan himself, who insists on undertaking the quest.
He makes every effort to dissuade his nephew from
the enterprise which is to bring such direful consequences upon them both. At every point the poet
dwells upon the tenderness of Mark toward Tristan,
and on the relation of confidence and affection that
exists between them.

The tragedy of Tristan and Isolt in the *estoire*
is thus not merely a conflict of human passion with
the laws of an organized society. It is not only in-
quietude as long as the lovers successfully keep their
relation secret. It is not only danger when they maintain it in defiance of society and of its most powerful
member. The situation has a tragic quality deeper
than that of a war with society, more poignant than
that of the transgression of moral law. It is the
tragedy of outraged friendship. It is man's love for
woman at war with man's loyalty to man.

It has already been pointed out that in many
cases the effort of Thomas to rationalize the story is
successful at the expense of the character of Mark.

In order to suppress the incredible account of the
swallows' hair in the story of the *Quest*,. Thomas
effaces the point which had been made with so much
care in his source, namely that Mark had recourse to
this resolve as a strategem to evade the demands of
the barons [1]. While appearing to be willing to accept a
bride, he demands one impossible to obtain, the Princess
of the Swallows' Hair. The reply which Mark gives
the barons in Thomas is that he will marry if they
find him a fitting wife. To be sure the king none
the less arouses their antagonism by his preference
for Tristan and his evident unwillingness to marry. In
the account of the footprint on the floor, the ambiguous oath, the banishment of the lovers, and the discovery in the garden, the character of Mark suffers
constantly from Thomas' modification of his source.
The king appears vacillating and inconsistent, now
suspicious and now foolishly trustful, as the narrative
demands. The character clearly defined in Eilhart
and blurred in Thomas is entirely distorted in the
French Prose Romance. In this version Mark is the
personification of cowardice and perfidy. In the episodes which constitute the continuation of Béroul and
in the other fragments of Tristan tradition, the character of Mark is determined, as we might expect, by
the narrative which the poet is exploiting.

In Eilhart alone we have a clearly marked development in Mark's feeling for Tristan. His tenderness and loyalty struggle against the increasing weight
of evidence until his nephew's guilt is proved beyond
possibility of doubt. From that moment he is
unrelenting. The Mark of Eilhart is long in being
convinced. At first he is passionately loyal, and

---

[1] Bédier II, 215—8; supra Ch. III, 84—8.

unwilling to listen to the voice of suspicion. When
he surprises his nephew and the queen in each other's
embrace, he is quick to anger, but when he hears their
conversation under the pine-tree he is no less quick to
acknowledge that he has misinterpreted an innocent
affection. The footprint on the floor is at last absolute
proof. From that instant Mark is implacable. No
punishment seems to him severe enough[1]:

> 'he sprach, daz he ir minne
> gerne sô gar zubrêche
> daz man dar von sprêche
> die wîle die welt wêre'.

He cannot wait until the dawn to punish. He is
deaf to entreaties[2].

> 'der koning von zorne nedir saz
> und begunde burnen als ein kole'.

When Tristan escapes him, by the leap from the chapel[3],

> 'dô wolde der koning sînen mût
> irkûlen an der vrauwin'.

When the leper suggests that life with his band
would be more horrible for Isolt than burning at the
stake, he does not hesitate to give her the worse fate[4].
He even takes revenge upon Tristan's dog, commanding
the wretched animal to be hanged[5].

Eilhart tells us that Mark's punishment of Isolt
was looked upon with disfavor in the land[6], but he

---

[1] *OX* 3962—6.
[2] *OX* 4036—8.
[3] *OX* 4246—8.
[4] 4256—92.
[5] 4368—85.
[6] 4296—302.

does not indicate that the king ever regretted it. To
be sure Mark stays his hand when he finds the lovers
sleeping in the forest. The poet gives us no clue to
Mark's feelings, and the scene is a puzzle[1]. So much,
however, is clear: the sword between the pair does
not convince him of their innocence, and Tristan makes
no attempt, even in the letter written by Ogrin, so
full of protestations of innocence in Béroul, to persuade
the king that he is not guilty[2]. Before his counsellors
Mark defends the innocence of his wife, and he is willing
to take her back. But he will not permit Tristan to
remain in the land[3]. Tristan pleads[4]:

> 'nû vorgebit mir die missetât
> daz ûch got von himele lône!'
> 'so muste mich got hônen,
> ab ich ez tête umme daz.
> ja ist ûch mîn herze sô gehaz,
> daz ich ûch nî mê mag werdin holt'.

Tristan continues his pleading, but Mark is in-
exorable[5].

> 'ûwers dînstes begere ich nît.'
> 'war umme, hêre?' 'daz wil ich sagin:
> dâ habe ich lastir unde schadin
> vil von ûch gewonnen.'

Tristan insists[6]

> 'wolt ir mir nicht gonnen
> daz ich in ûwerm lande sî?'

---

[1] cf. supra Ch. V, 261—5.
[2] 4844—61.
[3] 4863—90; cf. 4915—30.
[4] 4930—6.
[5] 4940—4.
[6] 4944—6.

Mark's reply is[1]

> 'nein, ir wêret mir zu nâhe bî.
> ir mûzet ûch enweg haben:
> ich wil ûch wol vorclagen.'

In Eilhart's poem these are Mark's last words to Tristan. His character is rigorously consistent — tender, generous, loyal, quick to anger, and quick to forgive anger suddenly roused. But he is terrible when once convinced that he has been betrayed, and unrelenting. The love of the betrayed husband for the betrayer forms as important an element in this tragic treatment as the passion of the lovers for each other.

The treatment of this passion as in itself tragic is unique in Tristan among twelfth century French romances. To understand its appearance there, let us study the development of the moral and social ideal of which the love of Tristan and Isolt is a violation.

4. THE ATTITUDE TOWARD UNLAWFUL LOVE IN PRIMITIVE SOCIETY.

Promiscuous as may seem to us the practices of primitive tribes in sexual relations, one principle is clearly distinguishable: the wife is the property of the husband. He who has bought her has the right to use her or to dispose of her as he wills. Wives are lent or rented in the same manner as horses and fields. A man who owns a field may make a contract with his neighbor by which he gives him the privilege of cultivating it and enjoying the produce. But if the neighbor undertakes to cultivate

---

[1] 4946—9.

the field without the owner's consent, the action is considered theft, and the owner demands an indemnity. A man demands a fine for the infringement of his right to the exclusive use and disposal of his wife in the same way that he demands a fine for the unauthorized use of his fields for cultivation or of his cattle for breeding purposes [1].

Primitive law-books offer suggestions of what might be an equitable settlement of differences [2] arising from the violation of these rights. It appears that there was no machinery to enforce such a settlement. If the injured person was not satisfied with the fine designated, or if the offender was unwilling to pay it, the former might satisfy himself by what means he could. He must expect, however, that the latter, in his turn, might employ a similar procedure. In the case of adultery on the part of a wife, it seems to have been generally recognized that it was just for the husband to kill the thief. If he desired to sacrifice his property to his passion, he was of course at liberty to kill his wife also.

5. THE ATTITUDE TOWARD UNLAWFUL LOVE IN OLD IRISH LITERATURE.

The earliest extant Irish literature reflects in most instances the customs of a society in this stage of development. The accounts of the conceptions and

---

[1] cf. O. Schrader; *Reallexicon der indogermanischen Altertumskunde*, s. v. Ehebruch; E. Westermarck, *The Origin and Development of the Moral Ideas*, London 1906—8, I, Ch. XXVI. II, p. 446—51.

[2] cf. d'Arbois de Jubainville, *Etudes sur le droit celtique*, Paris 1895, I, Ch. I.

births of the Old Irish heroes, and the *Aitheda* [1], the
elopement stories of which we have spoken, are for
the most part uninfluenced by Christian standards
of sexual morals. The Old Irish saints' lives frequently betray a similar pagan attitude. All manner of
relations which Christian morality stamps as unlawful and unnatural, are recounted of the saints and of
their parents with apparent unconsciousness of their
inappropriateness [2]. In the Old Irish epic, as in the
primitive societies we have just discussed, adultery is
considered by the husband as an infringement of his
property rights, which he tolerates or punishes according to his convenience. The husband may find it preferable, if his wife's lover is useful to him, to spare him.
For example, Ailill, although he knows that there is a
liaison between his wife Medb and the Ulster outlaw
Fergus makes no effort to punish the offender. On one
occasion he satisfies himself that his suspicions are
correct by sending a spy to bring him a token of
the fact. The spy finds the couple sleeping. He takes
the lover's sword from his side, and, stealing away
silently, brings it to the king [3]. Ailill then taunts
Fergus, and refuses for a time to return him the
sword. It is not until he can do so conveniently that
he avenges himself [4].

> Now on a certain day the whole host went into the
> lake to bathe. 'Go down, O Fergus', said Ailill, 'and drown
> the men'. — 'They are not good in water', said Fergus,

---

[1] cf. supra Ch. VI D.
[2] cf. Zimmer, *ZfdA.* XXXIII, p. 283—5 n.
[3] W. Faraday, *The Cattle Raid of Cualnge*, London 1904,
p. 44. 51. 134, translation from the *Leabhar na h-Uidhri version;*
cf. d'Arbois de Jubainville's translation, *Rev. Celt.* XXIX, p. 163.
XXX, 162; cf. ed. Windisch, Leipzig 1905, p. 414, cf. p. 858, from
the *Book of Leinster* version; cf. supra.
[4] Kuno Meyer, *The Death Tales of the Ulster Heroes,*
R. I. A., Todd Series XIV, 32—5.

Nevertheless he went down. Medb's heart could not bear
that, so that she went into the lake. As Fergus entered
the lake, all there was of gravel and of stones at the bottom
of the lake came to the surface. Then Medb went till she
was on the breast of Fergus, with her legs entwined around
him, and then he swam around the lake. And jealousy
seized Ailill. Then Medb went up.

'It is delightful what the hart and the doe are doing
in the lake, O.Lugaid', said Ailill. — 'Why not kill them',
said Lugaid who never missed his aim. — 'Do thou have a
cast at them'! said Ailill. — 'Turn my face towards them',
said Lugaid, 'and bring a lance to me!' Fergus was wash-
ing himself in the lake, and his breast was towards them.
And his chariot is brought to Ailill, so that it was near
him; and Lugaid threw the lance, so that it passed out
through his back behind. 'The cast has gone home'! said
Lugaid.

It is related that when the son of the high king
made a royal progress through Ireland, the wife of a
different chieftain was offered him each night [1].

The elements of the tragedy of Tristan and Isolt
are present, however, among the Irish as among the
most primitive societies, in the fear of vengeance
from the husband, and in the sense of dishonor,
developing from this fear, attaching to the prohibited
relation.

6. THE ATTITUDE TOWARD UNLAWFUL LOVE IN OLD IRISH LITERATURE UNDER CHRISTIAN INFLUENCE.

In sharp contrast to this pagan attitude, we find
in Old Irish narratives dating from a very early
period, side by side with such accounts as we have

---

[1] Cited by Zimmer, *ZfdA*. XXXIII, 284 n, from *LL* 299 a, 35 ff.
The *Bóroma*. Ed. Stokes, *Rev. Celt.* XIII. 54.

mentioned, an attitude of mediaeval Christian asceticism toward questions of sexual intercourse. We shall consider only the question of adultery. The punishment of the woman is usually burning. We cite a few examples[1]:

Cormac's *Glossary*, a document of the eighth or ninth century, gives the following etymology of the word *druth*: 'harlot', *dír-aedh* is she, *i. e.* to burn her were right, because *aedh* is 'fire'.

In the *Book of Leinster*, written before 1150, we read that it was customary to burn any woman who violated her betrothal[2]. Various other documents show the prevalence of this punishment. In a passage of the Old Irish laws, the judge says to the woman accused of adultery: 'Your crime is proved and you are found guilty. I will not put you to death, but I adjudge you a dishonored grave with the three shovelfuls of disgrace upon your body'[3].

There is the following account in the *Adventures of Art, son of Conn, and the Courtship of Delbchaem*[1].

It was on that very day the Tuatha de Danann happened to be gathered in council in the Land of Promise, because of a woman who had committed transgression, and whose name was Bécuma Cneisgel, daughter of Eogan Inbir, that is, the wife of Labraid Luathlam-ar-Claideb. And Gaidiar, Manannan's son, it was that had committed the transgression. And this was the sentence passed on her as regards herself: to be driven forth from the Land of Promise, or to be burned according to the counsel of Manannan, and Fergus Findliath, and Eogan Inbir, and Lodan son of Lir, and Gaidiar, and

---

[1] *Cormac's Glossary*, ed. Stokes, Calcutta 1868, p. 59.
[2] *LL* 287 b 7. Cf. Meyer, *Contributions to Irish Lexicography*, Halle 1906, s. v. *Airnaidm*. I am indebted to Professor Bergin for this reference.
[3] O'Curry, *Manners and Customs* I, p. cccxxiii, n. 561.
[4] *Eriu* III, p. 150—3.

Gaci Gormsuilech, and Ilbrec son of Manannan. And their counsel was to banish her from the Land of Promise. And Manannan said not to burn her lest her guilt should cleave to the land or to themselves.

7. UNLAWFUL LOVE AS A TRAGIC *MOTIF* IN OLD IRISH LITERATURE.

Old Irish romance is rich in stories of tragic love. Only through an intimate acquaintance with the great body of imaginative literature that has been edited in the past thirty years is it possible to form an idea of the persistence with which this theme recurs. No more than a small fraction of the wealth of romance that existed in Ireland previous to the tenth century has survived, but in what we have, the note of tragic passion is sounded with a hundred variations. Students of mediaeval romance are disposed to look upon French literature, from its superiority to that of the neighboring peoples, as highly developed. They are disposed to consider that, whatever tradition of Tristan the Celts may have had, it must have been of a rudeness of sentiment corresponding to the primitive character of their material civilization. There could be no greater error. Ireland possessed in the tenth century a literature of romantic love of a depth and refinement of senti-ment of which France had not dreamed.

In Appendix V we have printed passages from several Old Irish stories of tragic love. The narrative rests in many cases on beliefs and customs that are strange and frequently unintelligible to us. But even with this immense disadvantage, the reader cannot fail to be impressed by the depth and purity of their tragic quality. Only the chief points of the stories seem to have been written down, apparently merely to aid the memory in oral narration. But even these synopses are in the grand style.

In the story of Deirdre and Naisi, *The Exile of the Sons of Usnech*[1], the elements of the tragic conflict are on the one hand the passion of the lovers, and on the other the social order. Naisi takes Deirdre from Conchobar in defiance of the laws of feudal society, and brings upon himself the enmity of its most powerful member.

In *Liadain and Curithir*[2] the struggle is not with outward circumstances. It is a struggle of love and conscience. Liadain has already taken the vows when her lover comes to her. Saint Cummine, to whom they turn for direction, endeavors to resolve the conflict by uniting them in one of those spiritual marriages dear to the church. His effort fails. Curithir must therefore depart. Liadain follows him, full of remorse now for having denied him. When he hears that she is coming, he sets out in a rudderless boat on a pilgrimage upon the sea. She returns and ends her life in grief and prayer for him.

In the *Sickbed of Ailill*[3] we have again a story of unlawful love in which the tragedy is in the transgression of a moral law. This story involves in a curious way the theme which we have discussed in connection with the incident of the harp and the rote. Ailill is stricken with love for the wife of his brother Eochaid, the high king of Ireland, and falls into a wasting sickness. When Eochaid goes on his royal progress through Ireland, he leaves his wife behind to take care of his brother, who is near death. When she at last discovers the cause of his illness,

---

[1] Appendix V A, infra.
[2] Appendix V B, infra.
[3] Appendix V C, infra.

she resolves to heal him [1]. Here, as in Tristan, the
lover struggles between his passion for the woman
and his loyalty to her husband. By the intervention
of Midir, who corresponds to the stranger in the story
of the harp and the rote, Ailill is cured of his
sickness without the loss of her honor.

In the story of *Diarmaid and Grainne*, there is
an added element of tragedy: Diarmaid, like Tristan,
is deeply attached to the husband whom he betrays.
The lovers suffer, not only from the hostility of the
social order which their passion sets at defiance, not
only from the vengeance of the most powerful of its
members, but from the consciousness of having violated
an inner law, of having broken their faith to one whom
they love. Even in the mutilated fragments of *Diarmaid
and Grainne* which have come down to us, and even
in the corrupt versions drawn from oral tradition, this
element still survives. In the lay in the *Dean's Book*
from which we have already quoted, Diarmaid laments [2]:

'Thou hast ruined me, O Gráinne.
thou hast brought shame on the son of Cumhall;
to be as I am in distress,
is a load I cannot endure.

. . . .

From Finn himself of joyous heart —
from him *we used to get* welcome;
I *left* the delight of his house,
and thou hast ruined me, O Gráinne'.

---

[1] At this point the narrative has been interpolated by a
later redactor whose attitude toward adultery is similar to that
which we find in Béroul and Eilhart. When Etain appoints the
tryst she says: "'Tis tomorrow it shall be', and he adds 'but it
shall not be in the abode of the lawful monarch of the land that
this felony shall be done'.

[2] *Rev. Celt.* XXXIII, 52—4. The son of Cumhall is of course
Finn. The words in italics are uncertain.

In a later version of the same lay[1]:

> I am like a deer or a stag, Passing my days along remote glens. None desires to see me, Of all who were kin to me in the house of hosts.
>
> I have forsaken all my people, Those who were brighter in nature than snow on the hillside. Their hearts were loving and generous to me, Like the sun high in the sky.
>
> But now they have become full of hatred toward me, Like an ocean that does not ebb, Since thou didst beguile me, O Grainne. O, thy love hath been of ill omen to me!
>
> . . . .
>
> I can never again return To the Fianna of Erin *whose companies were great;* My character is more hateful to Finn Than the terror of a monster of sharpest *bristles.*

It is related in some of the oral versions that Grainne tried for a long time without success to prevail upon Diarmaid to elope with her. She taunted him so far that Diarmaid went to Finn himself, and put to him the question: 'Is it best to bear reproach, or decay'? Finn's answer was: 'Do not decay while you live, my sister's son.' It was some time after this, says the narrator, that Diarmaid went off with Grainne[2], 'but where he passed the night he left unbroken bread to show that he was still blameless'.

The services of Diarmaid to Finn, the many exploits which they undertook together, and the many times that Diarmaid saved Finn from a situation of great peril form an important body of the stories of the Fianna[3]. The theme is a favorite one in oral tradition to this day.

---

[1] *Rev. Celt.* XXXIII, 55; cf. text, J. F. Campbell, *Leabhar na Feinne*, London 1872, p. 153; cf. suggestions of W. J. Watson, *Celtic Review* VIII, 265.

[2] J. G. Campbell, *The Fians, op. cit.,* p. 53. 55—6.

[3] cf. e. g. *Silva Gadelica* I, 265 ff.; II, 300 ff.; *Rev. Celt.* XXXII, 188 ff. 191 ff.

In the lay of the *Death of Diarmaid*, extant in
numerous versions, Diarmaid, as he lies dying, reminds
Finn of some of these services[1].

'One drink from thy cup, O Finn, O man of sweet and
pleasant words, Since I have shed much of my blood, Bring
me a drink from the well.' . . . .

'I have never injured thee, Yonder or here, from east
or from west, But (it was) Grainne who carried me off
captive, when she caused me to break my word.' . . . .

'If thou didst remember the day of Suibhne. There is
no need to be recalling it; I killed eight hundred and three
men for thee', ...

'In Bruidhen Caorthainn thou wast prisoner, O Finn,
I was good to thee, When the White-toothed one was wounding thee, And thou wast in distress and in *combat*. . . .

'Another day I was of service to thee, In Tara when
thou wast in distress, I was victor in the house, Protecting
thee from every combat. . . .

'Three king's sons of Inis Tire-fo-thuinn, I killed them
all in spite of their resistance; and I washed thee in their
blood, Though thou hast overcome me with cruelty'. . . .

'If thou didst but remember the day of Conall . . . [When]
Cairbre and his people were before thee, Thyself and thy
Fenians in thy train, O sad is my face toward Ben Gulbain!'

8. CONCLUSION.

Our study of the traces of Celtic elements in the
earliest extant versions of the Tristan story leads us to a
conclusion that reconciles the opposing views of Gaston
Paris and M. Bédier. The story of Tristan as it was
first conceived, and conceived in no less of tragic
beauty than in the forms in which we now have it,
was Celtic. Gaston Paris, in the glowing pages in
which he discusses it, speaks to us of the story as it

---

[1] *Rev. Celt.* XXXIII, p. 173—5; text, *Leabhar na Feinne*,
p. 158b.

was[1]. The story of Tristan as we have it, in Eilhart, in Béroul, and in Thomas, *is* French, and M. Bédier, in his discussion of it, speaks to us of the story as it *is*[2].

In the present study we have tried to show, by examining in detail Celtic romances of a character similar to Tristan, that the stories current among the Celts in the twelfth century not only reflect a *milieu* entirely different from that with which the twelfth century French poets were familiar, but that they imply sentiments, emotions, conceptions of honor, moral ideas — an entire psychology, different from that of the French. A Celtic story would have to be altered, in fact almost transformed, before it could be presented to a French audience. The poet must infuse into the Celtic lovers the spirit of French chivalry. He must supply them with a French background. He must adapt them to French life. He must complete their story according to French ideas. He must connect them with the literary figures familiar to a French audience. He must modify, efface, transform, supplement, create.

Such seems to have been the work of the poet who first conceived the idea of presenting the story of Tristan to a French audience. Such seems to have been the work of the poet of the *estoire*. Such was the work of the poets whom we find telling the story in the latter part of the twelfth century. Such has been the work of every poet that has told it to this day[3].

---

[1] *Revue de Paris*, April 1894, p. 152 ff.

[2] II, 186—8.

[3] Macpherson and the modern Anglo-Irish poets have attempted to do something similar for other Celtic heroes. They have made them interesting to their contemporaries by infusing into them the spirit of their own time. A translation of the stories as the Old Irish poets told them would have been incomprehensible to the eighteenth century. The naïve objectivity of the original narratives would fail to charm the readers of today who are ravished by the poems of William Butler Yeats and Fiona Macleod.

VII. CONCLUSION.

The romance of Tristan, as far back as we can trace it in France, had already enjoyed a considerable period of popularity. Its nucleus is a Celtic elopement story. In the earliest extant texts this story has been almost transformed in accordance with French taste. The few biographical details it may have contained have been supplemented from sources generally accessible to French *conteurs*, and numerous incidents have been added. Fragments of the Celtic elopement story have been taken out of their original setting and introduced in contexts where they illustrate more effectively the conception of a French poet of the latter half of the twelfth century. Among these are the splashing water, the chips on the stream, the harp and the rote, the hazel on the highroad, and the twigs in the wall.

In appropriating the Celtic romance, the French poets had re-created it in terms of their own imagination and feeling, giving it as a background the social conditions with which they were familiar, and introducing details from the life around them. Each successive redactor had brought it more perfectly into accordance with French ideas. In the incident of the anger of Isolt against Tristan and her penance of the hair shirt, and in the account of the unconsummated marriage with Isolt of the White Hands,

we can see how conceptions of love peculiar to
the French poetry of the latter half of the twelfth
century had become an integral part of the once
Celtic story.

Since we have no information as to his source,
it is hazardous to attempt to define too accurately
what was the contribution of the poet who composed
the *estoire*. The parts are still discernible — the
Celtic elopement story, which had already been adapted
for French hearers, some supplementary French and
Celtic material in regard to Tristan's birth and youthful exploits, some episodes, among them those about
Brangien, and the incidents from the return from the
forest to the end of the romance. This last portion is the
work of a very recent court poet. In the *estoire* these
materials are still very imperfectly assimilated. The
story of the potion and of the return from the forest
is rebel to the courtly poet's purpose of representing
Tristan and Isolt as perfect servants of love. The
bridge between it and the courtly continuation is very
imperfectly built. The incidents from popular tradition,
which constitute a considerable part of the romance,
have been very slightly modified; the redactor has
introduced them into the biography almost exactly
as he found them, merely suppressing, in each, the
one or two traits of the independent folk-tale which
were in contradiction with other passages of the
narrative.

The reader will recall a characteristic example
of the use of this method. Where we find in popular
tradition the story of the healing of the hero at the hands
of his enemy, the cure is performed in person. In Tristan,
however, where this story and the story of the quest
of an unknown princess are placed in juxtaposition
and credited to the same hero, this trait must be

suppressed; it would completely alter the character of the second tale if the Princess of the Swallows' Hair were at once known to be the princess of hostile Ireland. In the popular versions of the story of the quest for the princess, the wooer ascertains her identity before setting out. The poet of the *estoire* suppresses this trait; for, in a combination of the quest story with the story of the voyage for healing, he could have preserved it only at the expense of more important traits in the traditional form of the story. Thomas, on the other hand, does not hesitate to sacrifice the more important elements. To avoid the awkward device of having Isolt heal Tristan by a messenger, he abandons the story of the Swallows' hair. He allows Tristan to see Isolt on the first visit, and to set out to obtain her rather than In quest of an unknown princess. Throughout the romance we have seen similar instances of the conservatism of the *estoire* and of the bolder treatment of Thomas.

That the author of the *estoire* was not Crestien de Troyes seems sufficiently clear from a comparison of the literary technique of the former with that of the poet of Champagne[1]. It is possible that Crestien had some hand in the composition of the latter part of the romance. The unconsummated marriage, the story of Tristan's boast, the dog which Isolt carries in state, her anger against a lover who fails to turn his horse when the request is made in her name, the penance of the hair-shirt, are such as may indeed be the work of Crestien. It may be that his patron ordered a continuation of the romance, and that

---

[1] cf. supra. Ch. V.

'Cil qui fist d'Erec et d'Enide

. . . .

et del roi Marc et d'Iseut la blonde[1]'

is responsible for some of the incidents preserved in the *estoire*.

Such theories are interesting, but have no objective value. We know nothing of the character of Crestien's

'del roi Marc et d'Iseut la blonde.'

His *Cligès* seems to be an effort to remodel the Tristan story according to a different moral ideal. The particular version on which it is based is a matter of dispute[2]. It seems to us impossible to affirm more than that Crestien was acquainted with a version of the Tristan romance that presented the same general outlines as the portion of the *estoire* previous to the return from the forest. No distinct resemblances to the portions we have discussed in Chapter IV are noticeable in it.

We have endeavored to show that the *estoire* and *La Charrette* belong together as being the most striking expressions of the twelfth century idealization of unlawful love. In *La Charrette*, Lancelot holds so highly his love for the wife of Arthur that he kneels at her bed before he enters it, and sacrifices his chivalric reputation for her whim. In the *estoire*, Tristan holds so highly the unlawful love of a woman whom he can never see again nor ever hope to possess, that he regards his wife as a temptation, and refrains from consummating his marriage.

---

[1] *Cligès*, ed. W. Foerster, *Romanische Bibliothek*, Halle 1910, l. 1—6.

[2] *Cligès*, *op. cit.* Int. (ed. 1901); cf. G. Paris, *Journal des savants* Feb., June, August, November 1902; A. G. van Hamel, *Cligès et Tristan*, *Romania* XXXIII (1904), 465—89; cf. Foerster *Cligès*[3], Halle 1910, Int.

The question of the relation of Marie de France to the Tristan tradition is another problem which it seems impossible to solve on the evidence available. As we have shown in our study of *Chievrefoil*, that lay presents, in a simpler form, an incident which appears in the *estoire* combined with another of Marie's lays. It has been suggested that Marie was acquainted with the *estoire*, and that she purposely simplified the incident[1]. This explanation is of course possible, but we are inclined to reject it; the opposite tendency is constantly to be observed in the development of the tradition.

Another mooted question is the interpretation of the passage in Thomas in regard to Breri[2]. We agree with M. Bédier in seeing in this a mere device on the part of Thomas to cover his modifications of the tradition by citing as his source a name which, it appears, enjoyed no slight reputation among his hearers as an authority on Arthurian romance[3].

On the question of the channel of transmission of the tradition from the Celts to the French, it seems to us premature, in our present knowledge of the history and literature of the Celtic countries in the Middle Ages, to pronounce[4].

---

[1] Foulet, *Zts. für rom. Philol.* XXXII (1908) 278—89. Cf. *Rom.* XXXVIII (1909), 196—207.

[2] Bédier I, p. 377, l. 2107—24.

[3] Bédier II, 95—9; cf. Weston, *Legend of Sir Perceval* I, 288—93; Edw. Owen, *Rev. Celt.* XXXII, p. 5 ff.; W. J. Gruffidd, *Rev. Celt.* XXXIII, 180—3.

[4] It is because Ireland is the only Celtic country of which we have any considerable literary remains that we have drawn so largely from mediaeval Irish romance in our search for analogues to the Tristan story. This literature seems to have been considered by the Scotch Gaels, whose language was practically identical with that of the Irish, as their own. The few fragments of Welsh romantic literature that are preserved are similar in character. Of the other Celtic peoples there is no romantic literature extant.

APPENDIX I.

THE VALUE OF THE EXTANT REDACTIONS OF EILHART VON OBERGE'S *TRISTRANT* AS REPRESENTING THE *ESTOIRE*.

A. INTRODUCTION.

The original text of Eilhart's poem is not extant. We have fragments of two twelfth century manuscripts (R and M), comprising 611 lines [1]. Of the complete poem we have three redactions. One (X) in German verse, made in the .thirteenth century, is represented by two fifteenth century manuscripts (D and H). It comprises about 9500 lines and, compared with the fragments, shows the effort to improve the imperfect rhymes of the original. The close of the poem of Eilhart is also found in a more diffuse redaction (B) as a ·continuation to Gottfried in one manuscript [2]. A second complete redaction (P) is the prose version, of which the oldest text is the print of 1484 [3]. Finally

---

[1] ed. F. Lichtenstein, *Quellen und Forschungen* XIX, p. 1—25.

[2] ed. F. Lichtenstein, *op. cit.*; cf Int. See also E. Gierach, *Zur Sprache von Eilharts Tristrant, Prager Deutsche Studien* IV, Prag 1908.

[3] ed. F. Pfaff, *Tristrant und Isalde, Bibliothek des literarischen Vereins in Stuttgart* CLII, Tübingen 1881. On the prose texts see *Schlusswort des Herausgebers*, p. 203 ff. Also Gierach, *op. cit.* p. 3 n. 1.

we have a Czech poem (*Č*), which translates the version of Eilhart as far as the wedding night of Mark and Isolt [1].

In a study in the *Sitzungsberichte der philosophisch-historischen Klasse der kaiserlichen Akademie der Wissenschaften* of Vienna (1882, vol. 101, p. 319—438) [2] Knieschek endeavored to show that the Czech redactor worked on a model superior to *D* and *H*. He even considered the model of *Č* superior in certain cases to that of the twelfth century fragments *R* and *M*. Dr. Gierach has pointed out that Knieschek was mistaken in preferring *Č* at any point to the twelfth century fragments [3].

B. A COMPARISON OF *Č* AND *X* WITH THE TWELFTH CENTURY FRAGMENTS.

That our readers may form an opinion of the characteristics of *Č* and *X*, we print in parallel columns the passages of those versions corresponding to the extant twelfth century fragments [4].

---

[1] Translated into German by Knieschek, *ZfdA.* XXVIII, 261—358.

[2] Cited *WSB.*

[3] *op. cit.* IV (1908) p. 5—9.

[4] Italics emphasize modifications introduced by the redactor. Space in brackets calls attention to omissions on the part of the redactor. Words enclosed in brackets are supplied by Lichtenstein in his edition.

TWELFTH CENTURY FRAGMENTS.	THIRTEENTH CENTURY GERMAN REDACTION.	CZECH TRANSLATION.
I (R 1a).	X (= D + H) 1608 — 1622.	$Č\ 57_{21} - 58_{20}.$
1 dâ wart abir wol schîn	da wart abir wol schîn	da wart *wider* offenbar,
2 daz der hêrre Tristrant	daz *die unvorvērte* Tristrant	*dass dem Tristram das gar nicht*
		[*furchtbar war*
		und dass der weise mann
4 was ein chuone wîgant.	was ein kûner wîgant.	war aller tapferkeit voll.
5 er gedâhte, er wolde sînen lif	he dâchte he wolde sînen lîp	er gedachte bei sich *und sagte:*
6 wâgen umb daz magedîn	wâgin um daz *selbe wîp*,	*'ich will wagen mein* leben [ ]
7		*und will mich deshalb der not*
		[*unterziehen,*
8 und joh durh den willen	und ouch durch den willen,	*ob ich könnte meine* genossen
		[*befreien*
9 daz die sîne gesellen	daz die sîne gesellen	*vom tode und von dieser grossen*
		[*not*
10		*und von mancherlei arbeit.*
11 des baz gedingen muosen:	mochten alsô *genesen*;	*das will ich gutwillig lieber tun*;
12 und sold er den lip verliesen,	und *dâchte im sulde* libir *wesin*,	denn es wird mir auch zu.
		[*sterben lieber sein*

TWELFTH CENTURY FRAGMENTS. I (R 1a).		THIRTEENTH CENTURY GERMAN REDACTION. X (= D + H) 1608—1622.	CZECH TRANSLATION. Č 57$_{21}$ — 58$_{20}$.
13	daz taete er vil gerner von [dem wurme¹	daz he von dem worme vor- [torbe,	im kampfe mit diesem schlim- [men wurme,
14	den er âne wer sturbe.	den daz he âne wer irstorbe.	als dass ich hier ohne kampf [würde *schmählich getötet.*'
15	Zehant des morgenes vruo	Zu hant des morgenes vrû	gleich morgens sehr früh
16			*seine rüstung ward zugerichtet;*
17	dô wâfenôt er sih dar zuo	wâpente he sich dar zû	mit dieser rüstete er sich tüch- [tig zu
18	*Tristrant der helt guot*		
19	vil harte vlízichlíche.	gar vlizicliche	
20	und reit vil manlíche:	und reit *vormezzenlíche*	und ritt dorthin sehr tapfer.
21		*dâ he grôzen prís gewan.*	
22	wan er was ein chuone [degen.	[ ]	*und wie* er war ein tapferer [mann:

¹ Knieschek (p. 336) considers that lines 13 and 14 are best preserved in Č and H (1617 *daz he von dem wurm sturb | wann ön wer so verdurb*). Gierach (p. 5) shows that Lichtenstein was right in preferring D to H as representing X, and that R is néarer the original than Č. Both X and Č derive from a model in which the imperfect rhyme of R *wurme : sturbe,* had been suppressed.

TWELFTH CENTURY FRAGMENTS.	THIRTEENTH CENTURY GERMAN REDACTION.	CZECH TRANSLATION.
I (R 1a).	$X (= D + H)$ 1608—1622.	$\check{C}$ 57$_{21}$—58$_{20}$.
23 al eine reit er after [wegen]	[ ]	dorthin ritt er auf diesen weg [allein,
24 Fragment breaks off	. . . .	*keine hilfe er mit sich nahm.*
		.
II (R 1b).	X 1655—1677.	$\check{C}$ 60$_{11}$—61$_{12}$.
1 . . . . . . swert in der hant;	dô hâte he sîn swert in der hant.	[ ]
2 joh brante der serpant	[joch] brante im der serpant	so verbrannte ihm *Sarpand* der [drache
3 das ros undir im ze tôt.	sîn ros undir im tôd.	*sein gutes* pferd, *dass er allein* [stand,
4		*dass er da unter ihm auf der* [stelle starb,
5		*weshalb er vil übles litt.*
6 an lief in der helt gôt,	an lif in der helt gût,	*zu fuss lief auf den drachen der* [held wacker

TWELFTH CENTURY FRAGMENTS.	THIRTEENTH CENTURY GERMAN REDACTION.	CZECH TRANSLATION.
II (R 1 b).	*X 1655 — 1677.*	*Č* 60$_{11}$ — 61$_{12}$.
7	*wen he sînes lîbes gerte.*	*und verwundete ihn mit dem* [schwerte sehr,
8 er hiu in vil vaste	her heu in [ ] *mit dem swerte*	*dem allerbesten allerschärf-* [sten —
9 mit dem besten sahse		*man hätte es ihm nicht mit rotem* [golde bezahlt
10		*wie kein mann ein so gutes* [hatte,
11 daz inchein sîn genôz [truoch.	*daz he an sîner hant trûg:*	*mit dem man so hauen konnte.*
12 swâ man iz mit zorne [sluoch,	swâ *he ez mit zorne slûg,*	*denn rasch vertilgte er den* [drachen
13		*und verwundete ihn mit dem* [schwerte an der seite.
14		*es konnte vor ihm nichts be-* [stehen.
15 dar ne mohte niuht vor be- [stân.	dar en mochte nicht vor be- [stân.	

TWELFTH CENTURY FRAGMENTS. II (R 1 b).	THIRTEENTH CENTURY GERMAN REDACTION. X 1655—1677.	CZECH TRANSLATION. Č 60_{11} — 61_{12}.
16		es musste alles auseinander [gehen.
17 der helt dô den sich genam:	[der helt dô den sige genam]	da nahm der herr Tristram den [sieg,
18	an dem trachin, der was grôz.	
19	swie vele her des sint genôz,	
20 den chouft er vil tiure,	her kouftez doch vil tûre	doch es kam ihm dies [ ] teuer;
21 wan er was von dem fiure	wan he was von dem vûre	denn von dem feuer dieses [drachens
22 nâh ze tôde verbrunnen.	nâ zu tode vorbrunnen.	war er beinahe zu tode ge-[brannt.
23	den sege hâte he gevunnen	
24	mit menlichir deginheit.	
25 er sneit im ûz die zungen	die zungin her im ûz sneit.	dann schnitt er ihm aus dem [rachen die zunge
26 und stah si in sîn hosin.	her stackte sie an sîne hâte;	und steckte sie in die tasche in [den beutel.

TWELFTH CENTURY FRAGMENTS. II (R 1 b).	THIRTEENTH CENTURY GERMAN REDACTION. X 1655—1677.	CZECH TRANSLATION. Č 60_{11}—61_{12}.
27 .	*und ist ûch wol zu mûte,*	
28 .	*sô mogit ir daz gerne losen:*	
29 dô chêrt er gegen einem [mose,	*dô kârte he zu einem mose,*	und es wandte sich *der held* [zum wasser,
30 dâ wold er sih chôlen:	*dâ wolde he kûlen sich.*	*damit er von diesem brande nicht* [*käme zu schaden.*
31 dô wart der schône	*dô was der degin herlich*	da ward der held *so verbrannt.*
32 von dem fiure	.	.
.		

III (R 2 a).	X 1725—1843.	Č 63_4—68_{15}.
1 im gaebe sîne tohter.	*he solde sîne tochtir hân.*	dass er ihm seine tochter wolle [geben.
2	*dô sprach der koning rîche*	
3 der ch[un]ich erne mohte	'*ich welde denne tûn bôslîchen,*	*er gab ihm darauf die antwort,*

TWELFTH CENTURY FRAGMENTS. III (R̆ 2 a).	THIRTEENTH CENTURY GERMAN REDACTION. X 1725—1843.	CZECH TRANSLATION. Č 63_4—68_{15}.
4 des niht wol wider chomen,	sô *magich* des nicht wedir komen;	*dass er ihm das alles erfülle,*
5 joh hêt er gerne baz ver-[nomen,	doch hête *ich* gerne baz vor-[nomen,	aber der könig *wollte* gerne [*sicherheit gewinnen,*
6 wer den trachen slûge.	wer den trachen slûge.'	wer den drachen mochte er-[schlagen.
7 'daz waere vil ungevuge'	'daz wêre [ ] ungefûge'	da sagte der *treulose* schaffner:
8 sprah der truhsêze	sprach der truhsêze	'das wären wunderbare nach-[richten,
9 'daz ih mih des vermêze,	'daz ich mich des vormêze	dass ich dürfte je sagen
10 ob iz waere gelogen'.	daz doch wêre gelogen.'	eine lüge *und dies als wahrheit* [*erzählen.*'
11 den hêrren hêt er nâh be-[trogen:	den koning hête he nâ be-[trogin;	und *damit* teuschte er *den könig* [*so,*
12 er wan[*de daz ez*] wâr waere.	he wânde daz ez wâr wêre.	dass er glaubte es wäre wahr-[heit.
13 der chunich dô daz maere	der koning dô daz mêre	da begann der könig diese [märe

TWELFTH CENTURY FRAGMENTS.	THIRTEENTH CENTURY GERMAN REDACTION.	CZECH TRANSLATION.
III (R 2 a).	X 1725 — 1843.	Č 63$_1$ — 68$_{15}$.
14 sîner tohter selbe sagete,	sîner tochter selbe sagete,	selbst seiner tochter sagen,
15 daz der truhsatze habete	*wie* der trogsêze habete	dass der schaffner *sein dienst-*[mann
16 si gewunnen ze wîbe	sie gewunnen ze eime wîbe	sie *von ihm* erworben habe als [frau.
17 mit sîn selbes libe	mit sîn selbis libe	[ ]
18 vil harte mänliche,	gar harte menlîche,	[ ]
19 und sprah offenlîche,	und sprach offenlîche,	und er begann offen zu sprechen [zu ihr,
20 er solde si im ze wîbe geben.	[he solde sie im] zu wîbe gebin:	dass er sie solle haben zur frau
21 ouch mohte sí in gerne [nemen,	daz mochte sie vil gerne *lebîn*	und sie ihn könnte gerne [nehmen;
22 wan er hêt erslagen den [serpant.	dorch daz he irslûg den serpant.	denn er habe *sich nicht ge-*[fürchtet,
23		diesen drachen *zu töten.*
24 dô sprah diu vrowe al zehant	dô sprach die vrauwe al zuhant	es zögerte darauf die jungfrau [nicht, zu antworten:

	TWELFTH CENTURY FRAGMENTS. III (R 2 a).	THIRTEENTH CENTURY GERMAN REDACTION. X 1725—1843.	CZECH TRANSLATION. Č 63_4 — 68_{15}.
25	'vater, daz geloube mir,	'vatir, daz geloube mir,	'könig, vater! du kannst das [wol glauben,
26	er ne hât niht rehte gesaget [dir.	he hât nicht rechte gesaget dir.	dass er *ihm selbst nicht getötet;*
27	jo begieng er nie dehein vru-[micheit:	her begîng doch nî vromigheit.	*denn* er begieng nie eine tüch-[tigkeit.
28	wâ nam er nû die manheit	wâ nam he nû die manheit,	*wie durfte er nun diese mannes-[tat verrichten*
29	daz er in torste bestân?	daz her in torste bestân?	*und den wilden drachen be-*[stehen?
30	nû lâ dînen muot zigân	lâz dînen mût zugân	lass jetzt deinen gedanken [fahren
31	und vernim die wârheit [rehte:	und vornim die wârheit rechte:	und vernimm die wahrheit [recht
32	sage dem guoten chnehte	sage dem gûten knechte	und sage dem guten knechte,
33	daz er bîte biz morgen vrô.'	daz he beite biz morgen vrû.'	dass er bis morgen lasse seine [frist.'

	TWELFTH CENTURY FRAGMENTS. III (R.2 a).	THIRTEENTH CENTURY GERMAN REDACTION. X 1725—1843.	CZECH TRANSLATION. Č 63_4 — 68_{15}.
34	dô tet der chunich alsô.	der koning sprach, 'ich wil [daz tû.'	so tat der könig ihm das
35			und keine antwort gab er [darauf.
36		Dô diz was irgangen,	
37		do begunde harte irlangin	
38		deme trogsêzen, sundir wân.	
39	Der truchsatze manete	den koning manete he sân,	dann begann der schaffner den [könig zu mahnen,
40	den chunich des er habite	sînen hêren, daz he tête	was er ihm versprochen,
41	gelobet mit sîner wârheit:	als he gelobit hête bî sîner rechtin wârheit.	dass er ihm wolle erfüllen.
42	im was inneclîche leit	[ ]	das war ihm zu hören leid;
43	daz er iz sô lange vriste.	[ ]	denn er sollte ihm so lange [trügen[1].

---

[1] The translation given in *ZfdA* 64₁₆ is: *denn er sollte sie nicht so lange betriegen.* In his study in *WSB,* *loc. cit.,* Knieschek gives the line as we have printed it, corresponding to *R.*

488   TRISTAN AND ISOLT,

TWELFTH CENTURY FRAGMENTS.	THIRTEENTH CENTURY GERMAN REDACTION.	CZECH TRANSLATION.
III (R 2 a).	X 1725 — 1843.	Č 63_4 — 68_{15}.
45 nû vernemet, mit welhen [listen	[ ] vornemet, mit welchir [*wisheit*	nun vernehmet das alle,
46		wie mit *sehr grosser* list
47 vrowe Ŷsalde dô ervûre,	[frauwe Îsolde dô ervûre]	die jungfrau *Izalda* das erfuhr,
48 ob er den trachen slûge	*wer* den trachin irslûge!	ob er den drachen erschlug. sie [sagte
49 si sprach zuo Peronîse	sie sprach zu Perenîse	zu *Permenys, ihrem kämmerer,*
50 daz er braehte lîse	daz he brêchte lîse	dass ihr *die* pferde *wären bereit,*
51		*wenn es sein wird morgen sehr* [*früh,*
52 driu phärith als iz tagete.	*die* pfert, swenne ez tagete.	wenn es schon tag würde.
53 Brangênen sî dô sagete,	Brangênen sie sagete,	Zu Brangenena,
54 einer ir junchvrouwen,	[ ] irer juncfrauwin,	[ ] ihrer kammerfrau, sie [sagte:
55		ʻob der schaffner den drachen [erschlug, *das weiss* [*ich nicht,*

TWELFTH CENTURY FRAGMENTS.	THIRTEENTH CENTURY GERMAN REDACTION.	CZECH TRANSLATION.
III (R 2 a).	X 1725—1843.	Č 63_4—68_{15}.
56 si wolde selbe schouwen,	sie wolde *balde* schauwin,	doch will *ich* das selbst *morgen* [sehen,
57 wie der wurm gewunt [waere.	wie der worm gewunt wêre.	wie dieser drache *erschlagen* [wäre.
58 Peronîs der chameraere	Perenîs der kemmerêre	Permenis [ ]
59 der brâhte diu pharit frô.	brâchte ir die pferd vrô.	brachte der frau die pferde früh,
60 ûf sâzen sî dô	ûf sâzin sie dô	auf die *er mit Brangenena* sich [setzte.
61 und rîten gelîche.	und retin *ilentlîchin.*	und sie ritten hin *ganz heimlich,* [*wo dieser drache lag.*
62 diu schône vrouwe rîche	*zu hant* die vrauwe rîche	die jungfrau, *des königs reiche* [*tochter,*
63 Tristrandis slâwe dô gesach;	Tristrandes slâwe dô gesach.	verfolgte Tristrams spur;
64		*und als sie dieselbe ganz er-* [*blickte,*
65 ze Peronîse sî dô sprah	*Brangênen* sie dô zû sprach	sagte sie zu *Brangenena* unver- [züglich:

TWELFTH CENTURY FRAGMENTS. III (R 2 a).	THIRTEENTH CENTURY GERMAN REDACTION. X 1725—1843.	CZECH TRANSLATION. Č 63$_4$—68$_{15}$.
66 'sî wâ diz ros was beslagin	'sich, wie daz ros was beslagin.	'sieh, wie war dies pferd be-[schlagen,
67 daz den helt hâ[t her] ge-[tragen	daz hât den helt her getragin,	auf dem hieher *gekommen* war [der heldenhafte mann,
68 der den trachin bestunt!	der den trachin *irslûg*.	der den drachen bestand.
69		*und ihn des lebens beraubte.*
70 daz ist uns allen wol [chunt:	*merke ebin den gevûg*	doch uns ist das wol bekannt:
71 man besleht niht diu ros hî.	die ros man hîr nicht besleit	*so* beschlägt man bei uns die [pferde nicht.
72	*als an desir slâwen geit.*	
73 swanne sô er chomen sî,	[ ]	woher er immer gekommen ist
74 dirre der hie geriten is,	desir die hîr geretin is,	der, der hier geritten ist,
75 des sît ze wâre gewis,	des wes sichir und gewis,	[ ]
76 der h[â]t geslagen den ser-[pant.'	der hât irslagin den serpant'.	der hat diesen drachen er-[schlagen
77		*und ihm seines lebens beraubt.'*

	TWELFTH CENTURY FRAGMENTS. III (R.2 a).	THIRTEENTH CENTURY GERMAN REDACTION. X 1725—1843.	CZECH TRANSLATION. $\check{C}$ 63_4—68_{15}.
78	dô quâmen die vrouwen al [ze[h]ant	dô quâmen die vrauwin al zu [hant	und es ritten gleich die jung- [frauen dorthin,
79	dâ der trache lach tôt.	dâ der trache lag tôt.	wo des drachen *toter leib* lag.
80	dô vunden sî den schilt [gôt	dô vundin sie einen schilt *rôt*	da fanden sie einen schild [gut,
81	v[e]rbrunnen alsô garwe,	besengit alsô garwe	*vom feuer* sehr verbrannt,
82	daz si in bî der varwe	daz sie ihn bî der varwe	und sie konnten nach seiner [farbe
83	nemohten niht erchennen.	nicht mochtin irkennen;	nicht haben eine unter- [scheidung,
84		*die was doch eteswenne*	*wessen schild das mochte sein*
85		*gewesen licht und tûre.*	*oder woher er mochte dorthin* [kommen.
86	ouch lach daz ros besenget,	*ouch vunden sie von dem vûre*	und auch *erblickten sie dort*
87		*ein ros vorbrant vil gare,*	sein verbranntes *ross,*
88		*des nâmen sie ernstlîchen ware.*	
89	daz si chûme ercnanden	*idoch sie wol erkandin*	dass sie es kaum unterscheiden,

TWELFTH CENTURY FRAGMENTS.	THIRTEENTH CENTURY GERMAN REDACTION.	CZECH TRANSLATION.
III (R.2a).	X 1725—1843.	Č 63_4 — 68_{15}.
90 daz iz in dem lande	daz es in den landin	dass in diesem lande das pferd [nicht war
91 niht was *gezogen.	nicht gezogen noch gevallen [was,	aufgezogen, noch wussten wo- [her es gekommen wäre.
92	als ich in dem bûche las;	
93	ouch habe ich die rede ver- [nomen:	
94 'owî, war ist der helt [chomen	'owê, wâ ist der helt hen komen	und sie sagten: 'o weh! wohin [ist der held gekommen,
95 der ditze ros her reit?'	der diz ros her reit?'	der dieses pferd hatte?
96 sprah diu frowe gemeit	sprach die vrauwe gemeit	[ ]
97 'wie gern ih daz wiste!'	'wie gerne ich daz erfunde,	weh mir! wie gerne wüsste [ich das[1]
98 sie sprah aber enrihte	ab ich in vinden kunde.	wenn ich ihn wo lebend träfe!

---

1 We substitute here the reading given by Knieschek WSB 326, cf. n. 2. The reading given in ZfdA is wie gerne würde ich ihn sehen.

TWELFTH CENTURY FRAGMENTS. III (R.2a).	THIRTEENTH CENTURY GERMAN REDACTION. X 1725—1843.	CZECH TRANSLATION. $Č\ 63_4—68_{15}.$
99 'in habent die mordaere [erslagen,	die mordêre habin in irslagin.	vielleicht haben ihn diese treu-[losen getötet
100 er liget hie etteswâ bi-[graben.'	he lît hîr eteswâ begrabin.'	und irgendwo heimlich be-[graben.'
101 Zuo Peronîse sî dô sprah,	Di vrauwe Perenîsin bat,	zu Permenis sie begann zu [reden,
102 daz er sûhte daz grab,	daz he sûchte daz grab.	dass er wollte das grab suchen,
103 ob er iz vinden mohte.	[ ]	ob er es wo möchte finden[1].
104 sie˙ sprah, swer sô sôhte	[ ]	[ ]
105 daz er funde den degen,	ab he vunde den degin,	und wenn er ihn irgend fände,
106 sie wold ihn hundirt mark [geben.	sie welde im hundirt mark [gebin.	dass er dafür ein grosses ge-[schenk erhalte,
107		sie wollte ihn reich machen,
108		dass er ihr müsse dafür [danken.

[1] WSB 327. The translation given in ZfdA is ob er ihn möchte wo finden.

32*

TWELFTH CENTURY FRAGMENTS. III (R 2 a).	THIRTEENTH CENTURY GERMAN REDACTION. X 1725—1843.	CZECH TRANSLATION. Č 63$_4$—68$_{15}$.
109 dô ne sôhten sî niht lange,	dô sûchtin sie nicht lange.	da suchten sie ihn [ ] sehr [lange,
110		bis sie suchend zur seite aus- [einanderliefen.
111 ê Brangêne cham gegangen	[ ] Brangêne quam gegangin	dann lief Brangenena dorthin
112 zuo dem mose dô er lach.	zû dem mose dâ he lag.	zum sumpfe, da wo Tristram lag.
113 diu junchvrowe in gesah,	dô die juncvrauwe ersach	da erblickte ihn die jungfrau [bald
114 den helm glizen	den helm glizen sô ein glas,	und sah den helm leuchtend [wie gold.
115 sam ein carbuncel wîze.	schôre sie dar komen was.	bald kam sie dorthin zu ihm
116	ir dûchte daz her sich regete,	und fand ihm noch lebend.
117		zu ihrer frau sie eilte,
118		keine verzögerung sie tat
119	zu der vrauwin sie dô redete	und sagte zu ihr: ich habe
120 'ih hân den helt funden	'ich habe den helt vundin	diesen helden gefunden
121 vil harte ungesunden.	vil harte ungesundin.	und gar sehr ungesund:

TWELFTH CENTURY FRAGMENTS.	THIRTEENTH CENTURY GERMAN REDACTION.	CZECH TRANSLATION.
III (R.2 a).	X 1725—1843.	$Č\ 63_4—68_{15}.$
122 nû chomit îlande here,	nû komet bald îlende here,	darum eile bald zu ihm,
123 ob ir in mohtet ernern',	ab ir in mochtet irneren'	wenn du ihm gesundheit [gönnen willst,
124 sprah diu guote Brangêne.	sprach Brangêne die gûte.	[ ]
125		ob wir ihm irgendwie heilen [können
126		und damit seine gesundheit [verlängern.'
127 der vrowen wart vil lêve:	der vrauwen wart wol zu [mûte:	der jungfrau war dies sehr [lieb
128		und auf alle weise war ihr das [angenehm.
129 dô sî des siechen wart [gewar,	dô sie des hêren wart geware,	und als ihn die jungfrau er-[blickte,
130 vil schiere cham si dar,	sie quam vil schîre dare.	sprang sie zu ihm sehr bald,
131 den helm sî im abe bant.	den helm sie im abe bant.	seinen helm band sie ihm vom [kopfe los

TWELFTH CENTURY FRAGMENTS. III (R 2 a).	THIRTEENTH CENTURY GERMAN REDACTION. X 1725—1843.	CZECH TRANSLATION. $Č\ 63_1—68_{15}.$
132		*und mit weisser hand verband* [*sie seine wunden.*
133 do gehôrte wol Tristrant	do irhôrte wol her Tristrant	das hörte herr Tristram wol,
134 daz dâ wâren vrôwen:	daz dâ wârin vrauwin:	dass dies *jungfrauen* wären
135 ûf warf er die ôgen	he begunde *sie schauwin*	[ ] und fragte sie, *weshalb*
136 und vrâgete wer dâ waere	und vrâgete wer dâ quême	*sie zu ihm gekommen wären*
137		[*aufblickend*
138		*und warum sie zu ihm ge-* [*kommen wären*
139 der im den helm naeme.	der im den helm abe nême.	*und* den helm ihm vom kopfe [*genommen.*
140 Diu vrowe antwurt im dô	Di vrauwe im dô antworte	die jungfrau ihm da ant- [*wortete:*
141 ne habe neheime vorhten nû.	'nu en habe, helt, keine vorte,	'hab keine furcht, *das wisse,*
142 er wirt	he wirt dir vil wol wedir.'	dass dein helm dir wird gegeben
Fragment breaks off	·	·

	TWELFTH CENTURY FRAGMENTS. IV (M 1 a).	THIRTEENTH CENTURY GERMAN REDACTION. X 2811—2853.	CZECH TRANSLATION. Č 104_{20}—106_3.
1	[des] ûch diu frowe heizit [biten,	des ûch mîn vrawe lêst betin,	'du kannst das tun wol,
2			was sie dich bitten wird,
3			das kann dir nicht schaden,
4			dass du ihr das zu liebe tust
5	daz ir irn [lantsite]	das ir iren lantsetin	und ihres landes sitten nicht [veränderst.'
6	[mit] ir wellent begân.'	mit ir wollit begân.'	[ ]
7	dô vrâgite der cuon[ing [sân,]	dô vrâgete der koning sân,	da fragte ihn der könig,
8			dass er ihm das zeige,
9	[waz sitis] ir lant habite?	waz setis ir land hête?	welche gewohnheit das sein [sollte
10			der er sich sollte unterziehen.
11	Tristrant ime sagete,	dô sprach der held stête,	da sagte ihm Tristram:
12	da [ensolde niht] lihtis sîn,	bî dem bette solde nicht lichtes [sîn,	'es soll da kein licht sein, das [weiss ich,

	TWELFTH CENTURY FRAGMENTS. IV (M 1 a).	THIRTEENTH CENTURY GERMAN REDACTION. X 2811—2853.	CZECH TRANSLATION. Č 104_{20}—106_3.
13	suwenne sô diu cuonigîn	swenne sô die koningîn	wo meine jungfrau mit dem [manne liegen soll
14	[zu dem êrsten bî im lêge],	zu dem êrsten bî im lêge,	und das erste nachtlager mit [ihm soll haben,
15	durh daz si nieman ne [sêge	daz sie nîman gesêge	damit sie niemand sehe,
16	bis [siu morgens ûf ge]-[stunde.	bis des morgens daz sie ûf [stunde.	dass sie sich davon nicht schäme [ ].
17	wie wol er ir des gunde!	wie wol he ir des gunde,	[ ]
18	spra[ch der cunig ze] sîneme neben:	sprach der koning zu sînem [nebin	es sprach der könig zu seinem [neffen,
19			indem er ihm darauf seine [hand gab:
20			diese gewohnheit will ich nicht [ändern
21	er wolt im den gew[alt [geben]	[ ]	[ ]

TWELFTH CENTURY FRAGMENTS.	THIRTEENTH CENTURY GERMAN REDACTION.	CZECH TRANSLATION.
IV (M 1 a).	X 2811—2853.	Č 104_{20}—106_3.
22 [daz er] selbe wêre	[ ]	[ ]
23 des nahtis kamerêre,	und hîz in kemmerêre wesin,	und *du sei* ihr kämmerer
24 daz [er die lîht leschte,]	daz er die licht leschte,	und lösche das *brennende* licht.
25 wande er wol weste	wen her wol weste	[ ] Tristram wuste wol von [dieser sache:
26 wie iz gescien solt[e]	wie ez [gescîn] solde,	[ ] das muste alles sein,
27 [und suwaz] diu ᵛrowe [wolte,	und swaz die frauwe wolde	[ ] was der frau gefallen [mochte.
28 daz er daz alliz tête,	daz her daz alles tête,	[ ] das *tat* er alles
29 [mit vlîze er in des bête]	mit vlîze er in des bête.	[ ]
30		*uf keine weise er daz änderte.*
31 Der kamerêre Tristant	Der kemmerêre Tristant	Der kämmerer Tristram da
32 sich der kameren under-want,	der kemenâtin sich undirwant,	der kammer selbst sich unter-[wand.
33 dô der cuo[ning slâfin solde.]	dô der koning slâfin solde;	als der könig sollte schlafen [gehen
		Č breaks off.

As a result of his comparison of these versions Knieschek believes that we are justified in relying on the Czech version throughout[1]. In the portions of the poem not covered by the fragments[2], he accordingly attributes to an interpolator all traits in X and P that are not corroborated by $\check{C}$. His conclusions have been generally accepted[3].

In the portions of the poem for which twelfth century fragments are available for comparison, $\check{C}$ and X present no variants on which our study would throw light. It may, however, be of assistance to the critic who next takes up the problem of the relation of the extant texts to express here the doubts that have occurred to us in the course of our work on the *estoire*, as to the correctness of Knieschek's conclusion for the following portions of the poem.

C. A COMPARISON OF $\check{C}$ AND X IN PORTIONS OF THE STORY FOR WHICH NO TWELFTH CENTURY TEXT IS EXTANT.

1. The harp on the rudderless voyage.

We shall first discuss the cases in which Knieschek rejects traits given in X and P, and lacking in $\check{C}$.

---

[1] Knieschek concluded that $\check{C}$ used an original text of Eilhart, not a redaction. *WSB* 340—1. Gierach (*op. cit.* 5) pointed out that the model of $\check{C}$ was not an original text, but considered it a redaction distinctly superior to that used by X.

[2] We are discussing only the portion of the poem translated by the first Czech redactor, not the continuation.

[3] Schroeder, *Deutsche Literaturzeitung*, 1883, col. 154; Pfaff, *Literaturblatt für rom. u. germ. Philol.* 1884, col. 3; Lambel,

Knieschek rejects the trait, given in X and P, that Tristan took his harp with him in the rudderless boat[1]. The passage in X is as follows:

'do bat der hêre nicht mê
mit im an daz schif tragin,
wen sîne harfin, hôrte ich sagin,
und sîn swert des he begerte[2].'

The passage in P is:

Hiemit ward er getragen in das schiflin mit grosser klage, mitt im sein schwert uund ein härpffen[3].

When questioned by the king of Ireland, Tristan says:

'ich was ouch ein speleman[4]'

and in the prose redaction:

'unnd bin ein spilman[5].'

In $\check{C}$ we have only:

'er hiess sich auf das schiff bringen schwert
und rüstung[6].'

Knieschek believes that the mention of the harp is the work of an interpolator under the influence of Gottfried von Strassburg. Gottfried says

---

Mitteilungen des Vereins für die Geschichte der Deutschen in Böhmen, XXII, 226; E. Muret, *Romania*, XVI, 293; E. Gierach, *Zur Sprache von Eilharts Tristrant*, op. cit. 9.

[1] *WSB* 407.
[2] *OX* 1134—8.
[3] *OP* 18$_{27}$.
[4] *OX* 1186.
[5] *OP* 19$_{19}$.
[6] *OČ* 37$_{15}$.

'sîne harpfen er besande,
die fuorte er ouch von lande
und sînes dinges nie niht mê[1]'

and Tristan, in accounting for himself to the king of
Ireland

'ich was ein höfscher spilman[2].'

Let us examine the other redactions of the *estoire*
to see if they contain this trait. In the French Prose
Romance Tristan plays the harp when he finds himself cast upon the Irish coast. The king hears the
melody, thinks it *faerie*, and goes down to the shore
to investigate[3]. The German redactions *X* and *P* have
the same situation, except that we are not told how
the king's attention was attracted to the little boat[4].
In the *Folie Tristan* of the Oxford manuscript, and
in the version of Thomas, Tristan attracts attention
in the harbor by playing on the harp, and the report
of his skill reaches the ears of the queen.

In the former text Tristan recalls his landing in
Ireland as follows:

'Mais jo fu naufrez e chitifs.
Od ma harpe me delitoie,
Je n'oi confort, ke tant amoie.
Ben tost en oïstes parler
Ke mult savoie ben harper;
Je fu sempres a curt mandez
Tut issi cum ere navrez[5].'

---

[1] ed. Marold 7363—5.
[2] ed. Marold 7564.
[3] ed. Löseth § 29.
[4] The redactor also neglects specifically to mention the fact
that Tristan produced the tongue to disprove the seneschal's boast.
OX 2165 ff. He also fails to specify that Tristan returned by
boat from the island after the combat with the Morholt. Cf. infra.
[5] Bédier, *La Folie Tristan*, p. 29, l. 352 ff.

All the redactions of Thomas contain the trait.
According to the *Saga* [1]:

> Now Tristan began to play the harp and to
> display the other courtly arts in which he was
> master, and rumors of his beauty ' and accom-
> plishments soon spread abroad.'

According to *Sir Tristrem* [2]

> 'In his schip was that day
> Al maner of gle
> And al maner of lay,
> In lond that might be.
> To the quen tho seyd thay,
> Morauntes soster, the fre,
> Ywounded swiche a man lay,
> that sorwe it was to se
> And care.'

According to Gottfried [3]

> 'wan daz diu jugent Tristanden
> mit munde und ouch mit handen
> ir zeiner kurzewîle twanc,
> daz er ir harphete unde sanc.'

Since the trait is preserved in all the redactions
except the Czech translation of Eilhart, it would seem
probable that in the *estoire* Tristan was represented
as taking the harp with him on his rudderless voyage.
The poem of Eilhart, like the other versions of the
estoire, probably contained the trait, X and P preserved
it, and $\check{C}$, or its model, suppressed it.

---

[1] ed. Kölbing, *op. cit.* 1, p. 38$_{6-8}$.
[2] ed. Kölbing II, 1189 ff.
[3] ed. Marold 7541 — 5.

2. The combat on the island.

Knieschek includes the description of the island combat of Tristan with the Morholt among the interpolations made by a redactor whose version was the source of X and P [1].

The reasoning by which Knieschek arrives at the conclusion that the description of the island combat is an interpolation is the following: $\check{C}$ three times asserts that the combat took place upon a mountain; there is no allusion whatever to a ship. In other cases in which $\check{C}$ misunderstands the original, he involves himself in a net of inconsistencies. Since he does not do so in this case, it must be that he preserves the original reading. The presence of the boat in PX must accordingly be due to the influence of G. The incident of Tristan's pushing off the boat into the sea when he disembarks on the island, is consistently carried out in G by Tristan's return in the Morholt's bark. It is left incomplete in OX 932, OP 16₆. The lines in X 'do watt geholt Tristrant mit vrouden und mit gesange, ouch beiten nicht lange die Morolden man' represent an original account in which there had been no question of an island. There is the following verbal similarity between G and XP. In Gottfried: 'sin schiffelin er iesa nam zuo dem stade hafte er daz'. G 6746. In the prose redaction of Eilhart: 'Morholt kam im entgegengefahren. der hefft sin schif.' 14₇. In OX, this is corrupted to 'sin schif gar harte hefte,' 795. This similarity of X and P to G cannot be due to chance. $\check{C}$ does not abridge. Hence we must suppose X and P dependent upon a redaction made posterior to G, hence in the thirteenth century.

These arguments seem to us to be open to the following objections: We have no proof that $\check{C}$ is incapable of abridging. It is hardly to be doubted that Gottfried knew and utilized Eilhart (cf. Piquet, *op. cit.*). The fact that $\check{C}$ mentions a mountain not once but several times is no proof that he is correctly translating his original. Lichtenstein's suggestion (*ZfdA.*, *Anzeiger* 10, p. 11) that $\check{C}$ read *berc* for *wert* is entirely plausible. If he misunderstand (or changed) the

---

[1] *WSB* p. 408—10.

word *wert* once, he would misunderstand (or change) it again. Knieschek rejects the possibility that $\check{C}$ has modified his source on the ground that he was incapable of carrying out such a change without involving himself in inconsistencies. But, as we shall see, his account is full of inconsistencies.

The significant points in which P differs from $\check{C}$ in this passage are in the mention of *island* in three places where $\check{C}$ has *mountain*[1], and in the additional words

 'der hefft sein schif, und stiess her Tristrant seins ferr hindan[2]'

The first point is explained by Lichtenstein's suggestion that $\check{C}$ read the *wert* of his Bavarian or Austrian original as *berc*[3]. The other differences are the inevitable results of this misunderstanding.

In every case in which it differs from PX the reading $\check{C}$ is unsatisfactory: $\check{C}$ has the reading

 'dann ging der held zu seinem speere[4]'

where P has

 'Hiemit ging herr Tristrant zu schiff[5].'

In X and P the Morholt inquires in surprise why Tristan has pushed off the boat. Tristan replies

 'wir sîn beide here komen
 durch schaden und durch vromen
 die wir hie mogen gewinnen.
 ir komet wol hinnen
 in einem schiffe der helt
 dem der sege hie wirt gezelt[6].'

---

[1] *OP* 24₈, ₂₅; 25₁₄.
[2] *OP* 14₇₋₉. MS. *A*.
[3] *ZfdA.*, *Anzeiger* X, p. 11.
[4] *OČ* 25₁₂.
[5] *OP* 14₄, similarly *OX* 787.
[6] *OX* 801—7.

P is less clear. The phrase *in einem schiffe* is implied:

> 'Wir seyen beyd herkommen, das wir schaden
> oder frummen hie holen wollen. Ey, sprach
> Tristrant, er kommet wol von hinnen, wer den
> syg behelt, ich weys fürwar [1].'

In $\check{C}$ the Morholt asks Tristan why he has come alone [2].

> 'sprach er: „sage mir, lieber jüngling,
> warum bist du so heldenhaft allein gekommen?“
> der held Tristram gab ihm die antwort:
> „wegen nichts anderem, als weil wir zusammen
> [geladen sind,
> damit irgend einer vorteil oder schaden nehme,
> wem gott zu siegen gönnen wollte“.'

In X and P the Morholt is surprised to see Tristan pushing off the boat, and asks him why he has done it. Tristan replies that each has come to vanquish or be vanquished, and that one boat will suffice the victor. The passage in P seems to us to be a less clear expression of the idea we find in X. $\check{C}$, who, whether intentionally or not, has suppressed the traits in regard to the island, does not even preserve the implication which we have in P.

There is a further indication that in Eilhart the combat was localized on an island: Gottfried has borrowed from Eilhart the offer of friendship which the Morholt makes to Tristan immediately upon perceiving this act of reckless courage [3], before recounting the similar offer which, in his model Thomas, the Morholt

---

[1] OP 14_{9-12}.
[2] $O\check{C}$ $25_{16}-26_1$.
[3] $6799-837$.

makes after wounding Tristan [1]. The fact that the first
offer is not found in Thomas, that Gottfried's description
of the combat betrays the influence of Eilhart at other
points[2], and that all the extant redactions of Eilhart
contain it, would indicate that it was in the original
German poem. It is difficult to believe that $\check{C}$, in which
alone the speech is inexplicable, being unmotivated by the
pushing off of ·the boat, should represent the original
setting for it. In the other four texts, in which it is
clearly motivated, it is inextricably bound up with
the island combat. It would seem therefore that the
island combat was found in the original text.

Knieschek considers the fact that the boat is not
alluded to in XP in connection with the return, to mean
that the previous mention of it in these texts is due
to an interpolation. It really means that in a description
familiar to the readers, the details were not insisted
upon. This is shown by a comparison of the description
of the return in Tristan with that in other island combats in contemporary romance in France and England.

In a few of them, as in *Sir Tristrem* [3] and *Gottfried* [4], mention is made of a boat.

*La chanson du chevalier au cygne et de Godefroid
de Bouillon* [5].

'Li sodans a tost fait une nef aprester,
S'i a envoié outre por ax .ii. amener.
Quant orent fait la barge d'autre part ariver,
L'Aupatris i entra, n'ot cure d'arester;
Et cil les aconduirent, n'i volrent demorer.'

---

[1] 6935 — 80.
[2] cf. Piquet, *op. cit.* ch. X *et passim.*; Bédier II, 81 — 6;
Lichtenstein cxcv — cxcviii.
[3] ed. Kölbing II, 1. 1096 ff.
[4] ed. Marold, 1. 7090 ff.
[5] ed. Hippeau, *op. cit.*, Paris 1874 — 6, II, 5147.

Guy of Warwick (couplets) [1],

'Wyth the boot he came passynge
And caste hyt to Tryamowre the kynge.'

Guy of Warwick (Auchinleck) [2],

'Ouer the water he went in a bot,
& present ther-with fot hot
the king, sir Triamour.

Torrent of Portyngale [3],

'He said: „Lordys, for charite,
A bote that ye send to me,
It is nere hand nyght!"
They Reysed a gale with a sayll,
The Geaunt to lond for to trayll,
All men wonderid on that wight.
Whan that they had so done,
They went to sir Torent ful sone,
And shipped that comly knyght'.

In some of them, as in P [4] and X [5] of Eilhart, the return is alluded to, but the means of transportation is not mentioned:

Le roman de Girard de Viane [6],

'Le Dus Rollant est fors de l'ile issus

. . . .

Dedans Viane est Oliviers venus;
Ce grant bernaige est encontre venus.'

---

[1] ed. Zupitza, *op. cit. EETS*, London 1875—6, 8313.
[2] ed. Zupitza, *op. cit. EETS*, London 1883. 1887. 1891, 134, 1.
[3] ed. E. Adam, *EETS*, London 1887, 1310 ff. Similarly in *Sone von Nausay*, ed. M. Goldschmidt, *op. cit.* 5254 ff.
[4] *OP* 16 5.
[5] *OX* 932—6.
[6] ed. Tarbé, Rheims 1850, 156, l. 33; 157, l. 31.

Layamon's *Brut*[1],

> 'Ardur the riche
> wende to londe.'

In other versions the narrator does not even stop to mention the return. He trusts the audience to take it for granted[2].

Let us review the treatment of the place of combat in the Tristan texts: The French Prose Romance and the *Folie Tristan* of the Berne manuscript both relate that the combat took place on an island. Two redactions of Thomas (Gottfried and *Sir Tristrem*), localize the combat on an island[3]. The *Saga*, which is a more condensed version, gives no details further than that the combat took place on a shore[4]. In two redactions of Eilhart (*P* and *X*) the combat takes place on an island; the localization on the island is lacking in the third, *Č*. That the omission of the details about the place of combat would suggest itself to a redactor as a means of abridging the narrative is seen by a comparison of the Caius MS. of *Guy of Warwick* with the Auchinleck MS.[5]

---

[1] ed. Madden, London 1847, 23. 992.

[2] Geoffrey of Monmouth, *Historia Regum Britanniae*, ed San Marte, Halle 1854, 130$_{53}$; *Le Roman de Brut*, ed. Le Roux de Lincy, Rouen 1836, 10. 353; von Reiffenberg, *Monuments pour servir à l'histoire des provinces de Namur* etc., *Chevalier au Cygne* op. cit. 2043, *Guy* of Warwick (couplets) 10. 369; *Bishop Percy's Folio MS.* ed. Hales und Furnivall, London 1868, II, *Guy and Colebrande* 393.

[3] cf. supra.

[4] ed. Kölbing I, ch. XXVII [36], p. 34, l. 4.

[5] Both edited by Zupitza, London 1883. 1887. 1891. Auchinleck MS. 96, 7 ff.; Caius MS. 8157 ff.

Auchinleck	Caius MS.
Þan loked þai it schuld be	Caius MS.
In a launde under þe cite:	
Þider þai gun hem lede.	
Wiþ a riuer it ern al about:	
þerin schuld fiȝt þo kniȝtes [stout.	
þai miȝt fle for no nede.	
Ouer þe water þai went [in a bot,	Forth they wente to that [bateyle
On hors þai lopen fot hot,	Hastily, with-oute fayle,.
þo kniȝtes egre of mode.	In a feld with-owte the [Cyte:
	Þer was hyt ordeyned [to be
	. . . .
	When they com there they [schuld fyght.

The desire for abridgment probably explains the version of the *Saga*. To explain that of *Č* we would suggest the misunderstanding of *wert* as *berc* and the unfamiliarity of the Czech redactor with island combats. There is hardly room for doubt that the trait was contained in the *estoire*. It seems probable also that it was preserved in Eilhart.

3. *The love-monologue.*

There is a third important point in which Knieschek considers that the versions X and P show the work of an interpolator[1]. They develop at greater length than does *Č*, the monologue in which Isolt, on

---

[1] *WSB* 410 ff.

feeling the effects of the love-potion, reasons with herself as to the cause of her sudden passion. Of this monologue as given in *XP*, lines 2436 — 551 are lacking in *Č*.

Lichtenstein had called attention to certain striking verbal similarities between these lines and the love monologue in Veldeke's *Eneide* [1]. He had seen in them a proof that Veldeke was acquainted with Eilhart's poem; for it appeared to him impossible that a poet acquainted with Veldeke should have ventured to use the imperfect rhym which we find in *X*. Behaghel, editing Veldeke's poem some years later, argued from what he considered the more perfect adaptation of the passages in question to the context of Veldeke, that in the *Eneide* they were in their original context [2]. Knieschek takes the absence of the passage in *Č* to be proof that it was not in the original version of Eilhart, but is borrowed, by the redactor of *XP*, from Veldeke's *Eneide* [3].

Let us compare the portions of the monologue preserved in *Č* with the corresponding passages in *X* and *P*.

With the beginning of Isolt's reflections, *Č*'s inability to follow the delicate thread of the thought becomes manifest [4]. Their trend in *X* is as follows [5]: She declares that her heart is disturbed on account of the loved foe Tristan. Having spoken the word *foe* she regrets it, reminding herself that it is this foe's love alone that would make her happy. She reflects on her desire for him, then on her need of him. This leads her to

---

[1] *op. cit.* clxxxviii.
[2] Behaghel, *Eneide*, Heilbronn, 1882, Int. clxxxviii—cxcvii.
[3] *WSB* 412.
[4] In two places *Č* has grossly misunderstood the original. *OX* 2374—7; cf. *OČ* 90_{3-6}; *OX* 2380—3; cf. *OČ* 90_{7-11}.
[5] *OX* 2400—20.

the thought that he may disdain her. If he disdains
her, can she be well-disposed toward him? Yet how
could she be *ill*-disposed to one of such valor?

The connection between these ideas is just such
as we find habitually in similar monologues in French
courtly romance. In each new sentence a word of
the preceding one is taken up, questioned, and refined
upon. $\check{C}$ has lost the delicate filaments of transition.
It is only upon supplying them from X, as indicated
by the italics of the following reconstruction, that $\check{C}^1$
becomes coherent. It is also necessary to suppress
the portions of $\check{C}$ which we have enclosed in brackets[2].

> O weh! weh mir armen, welches leid habe ich in meinem
> herzen um diesen *lieben leiden* mann Tristan, [dass mir
> nicht geziemt zu sagen diesen Not, doch]. *Ach, wie torste
> ich sprechen so, ja* ich wäre dessen froh, wenn ich wüsste
> ob ich ihm bin lieb. Ohne ihn ist mein tod. Er benimmt
> mir essen und trinken. *Wie mag ich ihm denne holt sin?*
> *Holt, warumme spreche ich daz? Wie mochte ich im sin*
> *gehass?* Was kann zwischen himmel und erde besseres sein
> und in aller schöpfung, als der mann überaus stark.'

Isolt asks herself how it has befallen her to love
one who has refused to take her from her father
except for another. According to *PX*, she asks herself
what means she shall take to turn her thoughts from
him[3]. According to $\check{C}$ she considers what *person* she
can find to deliver her[4]. It appears from what follows
in both that the version of X is the correct one.

Isolt tells herself that, since Tristan does not love
her, she must overcome her love for him. But to over-

---

[1] $\check{C}$ 91_9 $_{22}$'; cf. OX 2400—20.
[2] The passage is from Knieschek's translation. Brackets indicate passages where $\check{C}$ seems to us to bungle his original. Italics
represent passages which we have supplied from $O\check{X}$.
[3] OX 2439—52; OP 48_{20} $_{23}$.
[4] $O\check{C}$ 92_{21}—93_2.

come it means death to her. Rather than die she will tell him. But if she tells him he will think ill of her, and if he thinks ill of her she will lose life and honor too. Since she must lose life in either case, she will die silent. No, life is too precious; she will tell him. He is not hard hearted; he will pity her. In this passage also $\check{C}$ gives a garbled version which becomes intelligible with the aid of X[1].

[Mein liebes] herz, gedenke nicht mehr an diesen held; denn ich will meinen [leidvollen] sinn abwenden von ihm [mit Schande] *wie mochte ich daz vulenden daz ich mich von im zoge'? ich vorchte daz es mir nicht entoge, ab ich des wolde beginnen;* [doch] mir scheint es besser dass ich ihn liebe, als dass ich darum mein leben gebe *wen worde ich nicht sîn wîp, so bin ich sichirlîchin tôd. eia, wiste he nû mine nôd die ich nâch sime libe hân! wie sal ich ane vân daz he vorneme mine clage?'* [und] so wähne ich dass ich es [selbst] sagen muss.' Und sie sagte zu sich: '*Owê* wie soll ich es tun? [Er kann übel denken von dieser meiner rede. Es kann ohne zweifel, mich dunket es gut, wenn es mir auch schädlich ist]. *waz ab he obele dar zû gedenke, sô her wol mag, sô vorwinne ich den tag wedir in nû noch nimmer mêre. ich wêne daz ich mîn êre wage',* sprach daz *schône wîp.* Ich will [selbst] meine ehre bewahren, wenn ich auch sollte mein leben geben, ehe ich es ihm sage. [doch sicherlich, davon nähme ich schaden; mein leben ist mir lieb. fürwahr, vielleicht ist er geneigt zu verstehen mein minnen, [Er ist kein heide] ich will es lassen an das glück und sage ihm, wie es mag um mich sein. Wer weiss, wie es sich wendet.'

At the two points of the monologue at which $\check{C}$ does not present passages which appear in X, we have the following hints that the Czech redactor is omitting something from his original. $\check{C}$ remarks

---

[1] $O\check{C}$ 93_3—94_6; cf. OX 2564—97.

'wozu der rede mehr
lassen wir davon und schweigen[1]'

where *X* has 2422—35. *Č* remarks

'dann ein wenig zögernd[2]'.

where *X* has 2439—551.

Whether or not we consider the passages interpolated which we find in *XP* and which are lacking
in *Č*, it is difficult to suppose that the garbled form
of the portion given by *Č* represents the original.
A poet sufficiently interested in the psychological
aspect of the occasion to make an analysis of it at
all, would hardly have introduced it in the form in
which we find it there. The Countess Mathilda must
have been easily satisfied if she allowed the German
poet to treat it as the Bohemian has done.

4. *Minor differences.*

Knieschek considers that *X* has suffered other
interpolations besides those in which it is supported by
P. As interpolations peculiar to *X*, Knieschek cites
Tristan's departure for Loonois (lines 244—64), the
arming of Tristan for the combat with the Morholt
(737—78), and the adorning of Tristan's companions to
honor the proxy wooer at the Irish court (2064—87).
He bases his conclusion that these passages were interpolated by *X* on the fact that they appear in a shorter
form in both *P* and *Č*[3].

Let us take up in detail the passages in question.
If we examine *P* closely we find that the absence

---

[1] $92_7 - _9$.
[2] 92_{11}.
[3] *WSB* 417 ff.

of the mention of putting the horses into the ship
(X 259—64) is a mere momentary oversight; a few
lines below ($P\,5_{18}$) the prose redactor tells us that on
disembarking in Cornwall, Tristan and his followers
mount their horses and ride to the court of Mark.

The description of hoisting the sails, which
Knieschek considers an interpolation made by X under
the influence of Veldeke, is an almost inevitable detail
in French romances of the character of Eilhart's source.
We find in the *Roman de Troie*[1]

> 'Les nes furent apareilliees
> E de la terre en mer veiliees.
> Vint e dous furent e non plus:
> Mout lor venta dreit Eürus.'

Likewise in the *Tristan* of Thomas[2]

> 'Le batel i esteit tut prest,
> E la reïne entree i est.
> Nagent, siglent od le retrait;
> Ysnelement al vent s'en vait.
> Mult s'esforcent de l'espleiter:
> Ne finent unques de nager,
> De si la qu'a la grant nef sunt;
> Levent le tref e puis s'en vunt.
> Tant cum li venz les puet porter
> Curent la lungur de la mer,
> La terre estrange en costeiant
> Par devant le port de Witsant,
> E par Buluingne e par Treisporz.
> Li vent lur est portanz e forz
> E la nef legere kis guie.
> Passent par devant Normendie,

---

[1] ed. L. Constans, Paris 1904, l. 4169—73.
[2] Bédier I, 2795—813.

> Siglent joius e leement,
> Kar oré unt a lur talent.'

Eneas[1]:

> 'Troïen tornent de Cartage,
> a lor nes vienent al rivage,
> lor chose aveient apresté
> et molt aveient buen oré;
> traient lor ancres, flotent nes,
> li alquant traient sus lor tres.'

Cligès[2]:

> 'Au port truevent lez la faloise
> Les mariniers dedanz les nes.
> La mer fu peisible et soés,
> Li vanz douz et li ers serains.'

Even those who consider that $\check{C}$ correctly represents the German poet in omitting this detail, would hesitate to assert that it was lacking in the *estoire*, a product of the same school as *Eneas*, *Troie*, and *Cligès*.

K. considers that the description of the preparations for the Morholt combat (X 737—78) are interpolated under the influence of Gottfried. The fact of their absence in $\check{C}$ leads him to this conclusion. Since $\check{C}$ omits all indications that the combat took place on an island, the omission of lines 737—749 is not remarkable. The description of the arming of the hero (X 749—78) as well as of the spectators gathered along the shore (737—749) is one of the stereotyped features of the accounts of island combats in French

---

[1] ed. J. Salverda de Grave, *Bibliotheca Normannica* IV, 1869.
[2] ed. W Foerster, l. 242—6.

romance. It is almost inevitable that both should
be given in the *estoire*, as we find them in X. That
they were indeed given there is shown by the fact
that they appear in the account of the incident given
by the French Prose Romance and in Thomas.

It is not surprising that Eilhart and Gottfried
should be similar; both versions are derived from the
same source, Eilhart directly, and Gottfried through
the intermediary of Thomas. Besides, it appears
frequently that Gottfried, although he followed in
general the poem of Thomas, introduced additional
details from Eilhart[1].

D. CONCLUSION.

Our own inclination is to interpret the evidence
in the cases we have discussed as indicating that X
preserves traits of Eilhart's version that Č has lost.
There may be others who would interpret the
facts as follows: XP has restored, from acquaintance
with other derivatives of the *estoire*, traits which
Eilhart had suppressed. For the purposes of the
present study it is immaterial which of the two
hypotheses is correct[2]. Even those scholars who, like
Knieschek, consider that the text of Eilhart which
the Czech redactor had before him was superior to
that followed by the German redactors, will agree

---

[1] cf. Piquet, *L'originalité de Gottfried von Strassburg*
Lille 1905, passim.

[2] In speaking of the methods of the Czech redactor of certain
mediaeval saints' lives, Jan Jakubec (*Geschichte der čechischen
Literatur*, Leipzig 1907, p. 12) says: 'Der cechische Dichter weicht
in der Bearbeitung von seinen Vorlagen namentlich darin ab, wo
er die fremden Verhältnisse dem čechischen Leser zu entfernt
findet.' — The Čech redactor of the *Alexander* seems to have
treated his source in a similar manner.

that in the traits we have mentioned, as indeed throughout, the redaction in German verse represents better the French original. They will therefore understand our reasons for placing at the opening of our study of the *estoire* an outline of the redaction edited by Lichtenstein.

APPENDIX II.

POINTS IN WHICH M. BÉDIER'S RECONSTRUCTION DIFFERS FROM THE VERSION OF EILHART.

For the convenience of the reader we append a list of the traits given by M. Bédier in his reconstruction of the common source on the authority of other versions than that of Eilhart. We have indicated by italics the passages that we have discussed.

A. Points in M. Bédier's reconstruction which do not seem to us to represent the *estoire*.

    1. p. 258. On awakening and finding the substituted sword the lovers are terrified at first, fearing that the king has gone to bring help. *However, they soon understand his clemency and realize that it will be possible to arrange a reconciliation with him (OBT). Negotiations (OBT)* .... Mark takes back Isolt, and Tristan remains exiled from the court *(OBR)*, by the terms of an

agreement with the king (*OB*). Cf. supra, p. 72—84. We have shown that the return from the forest in the *estoire* is due to the abatement of the influence of the potion.

2. p. 207. *Tantris.* M. Bédier has adopted the heading for this chapter from Thomas. Cf. supra Ch. III, p. 84—9.

3. p. 209. Tristan pretends that his name is *Tantris RTF.* Cf. supra Ch. III, p. 88—9.

4. p. 210. The daughter of the king, Isolt, *undertakes to heal him.* She finally discovers the poison, combats it by herbs, and cures the stranger (*OTRF*). Cf. supra, Ch. III, p. 84—8. We have shown that Isolt heals Tristan by messenger.

5. p. 221. Restored to consciousness, *he confesses that he is Tantris (TR).* Cf. supra Ch. III p. 84—8.

B. Points in which M. Bédier's citation of his sources is incomplete. He might have added Eilhart to the versions he mentions as supporting the following traits in his reconstruction.

1. p. 196. *Loved by all the court,* the young Tristan is now almost of age to be dubbed knight (*TR*). Cf. supra, Ch. III, p. 90.

2. p. 209. Driven toward the coast of Ireland *Tristan played his harp as he neared the shore* (*R* and in part *T*). Cf. supra, Ch. III, p. 90 —1.

3. p. 218. The Irish king offers *half of his lands*, in addition to his daughter, to

anyone who will deliver the country from the dragon *(TR)*, cf. supra, Ch. III, p. 91.

4. p. 233. Such was the virtue of the potion that those who drank it together must love each other *always*, cf. *OX* 2285—8. Cf. supra, Ch. III, p. 91.

5. p. 234. *Or sont entrez en la rote qui jamais ne leur fauldra jour de leurs_vies, car ils ont beu leur destruction et leur mort,* cited by M. Bédier from the Prose Romance, of the fatal effects of the potion. Cf. supra, Ch. III, p. 90.

6. p. 249. The dwarf spreads the flour on the floor and *steals away (TB)*, cf. Ch. III, p. 92.

7. p. 249. *Unperceived by him, Tristan's blood stains the clothes as he lies in Isolt's bed, and when by a new leap he regains his own, the sheets of his bed are stained in turn (TB)*, cf. Ch. III, p. 91.

8. p. 250. *The dwarf sees the two beds stained with blood (BT)* cf. Ch. III, p. 91.

9. p. 258. *At the moment of parting, Isolt gives Tristan a ring to keep in memory of her; whenever he wishes to send her a message, let him send her this ring, and she will fulfil his wishes (BTF)*, cf. Ch. III, p. 92.

10. p. 267. *His attention is drawn by chance to the ring which Isolt gave him at parting (T.* Heinrich von Freiberg). There is insufficient justification for the acceptance of this trait. There is no evidence that Heinrich von Freiberg had access to

the common source. Cf. Bédier II, 268;
Golther, *op. cit.* 1907, 89—90 and bibliog.
Thomas may here represent the common
source, but we have no evidence to prove it.

11. p. 268. *The news of the marriage of Tristan
reaches Cornwall. Grief of Queen Isolt*
(*TR*), cf. Ch. III, p. 93.

12. p. 298. He is admitted to the presence
of Queen Isolt, in order to show her his
merchandise (*RT*), cf. *OX* 9330 *und fûr
mit dem koufman.*

13. p. 300. *Tortured by jealousy,* Isolt of
Brittany tells the dying Tristan that the
sail is black (*RT*), cf. Ch. III, p. 93—8.

C. Points in which there is little data available for
determining the version of the *estoire*. M. Bédier
has followed other versions than Eilhart.
It seems to us that, if there is any choice, the
version of Eilhart is preferable, cf. Ch. III,
p. 98—100.

1. p. 234. *Brangien makes a mistake* (*F.* Escoufle,
and in part *R*), cf. Ch. III, p. 98—9.

2. p. 299. *He charges the daughter of his
messenger from now on to watch for the
approach of the boat; he confides his secret
to her: 'if your father brings my lady Isolt,
the sail of his boat will be all white; if he
does not bring her, it will be all black'. Isolt
of the White Hands wonders to see the frequent
conversations between the young girl and
Tristan, and this constant watch at the shore.*
(*R* only), cf. Ch. III, p. 99.

D. Points in which *T* and *R* agree in giving details not in Eilhart. These points may represent omissions on the part of the German redactor. Cf. Ch. III, p. 100—2.

1. p. 195. The child was given the name Tristan *in memory of the circumstances of his birth* (*TR*).

2. p. 199. The Morholt bases his demand of the tribute on the ground of *ancient custom (TR)*.

3. p. 204. *The queen of Ireland, sister of the Morholt,* and Isolt his niece, take the piece of steel from the Morholt's skull (*TR*).

4. p. 219. Tristan kills the dragon *by one blow which penetrates the jaw to the heart* (*TR*).

5. p. 220. She takes *her mother with her,* and the two go out secretly from the castle *(TR)*.

6. p. 223. Isolt's *mother,* when informed of the discovery that they owe the delivery of Ireland to the slayer of the Morholt, also makes peace with Tristan on condition that he will deliver them from the seneschal (*TR*).

7. p. 240. Isolt prevails upon *two serfs* to lead Brangien into the forest. In Eilhart it is two poor knights.

8. p. 241. Isolt feigns illness, and sends Brangien to seek healing *herbs* in the *forest.* The two serfs will accompany her (*TR*). In Eilhart Brangien is to draw water at the fountain.

9. p. 241. They tie her to a tree and leave her there (*TR*). In Eilhart one of them remains to guard her.

10. p. 244. M. Bédier thinks it impossible to decide whether or not the common source contained the episode of the *Harp and the Rote (TR)*.

11. p. 299. While Isolt is on her way to Brittany to bring healing to the dying Tristan, *he has himself carried each day to the sea shore* and looks out upon the horizon (*TR*).

E. Points in which Béroul and the Prose Romance agree in giving details not in Eilhart. These points may represent omissions on the part of the German redactor. Cf. Ch. III, p. 102.

1. p. 247. Returning to the castle after the tryst under the tree, *the queen tells Brangien what has occurred, and congratulates herself on having escaped the danger and reassured the king* (*BR*).

2. p. 253. *Lamentations of the people when Tristan is condemned to death, his guilt having been proved by the flour on the floor. They recall the anguish that Tristan suffered to free Cornwall when the Morholt came, and they deplore the ingratitude of Mark* (*BR*).

3. p. 253. Tristan leaps from the chapel window and falls on the rock which since that time is *called Tristan's Leap* (*BR*).

4. p. 254. The lovers take refuge in the forest of *Morois* (*BR*).

F. Points in which two other versions agree in giving a detail not in Eilhart. These details may possibly represent omissions on the part of the German redactor. Cf. Ch. III, p. 102—5.

1. p. 201. The island on which the combat between Tristan and the Morholt is fought is called *St. Samson* (*RF* Erec).

2. p. 222. *At last he appeases her with the account of the Swallows' Hair. He tells her that king Mark of Cornwall has fallen in love with her and wishes to marry her* (*F* in part, and *T* in part).

3. p. 265. M. Bédier considers it impossible to determine whether the episode of the *Ambiguous Oath* was contained in the common source or is a parasitic growth. It is contained in *T* and in the continuation of *B*. The source of the latter is unknown.

APPENDIX III.

THE PROBLEM OF THE SECOND ISOLT.

The idea of rejecting, on account of moral scruples, a woman offered him in reward for an exploit, would not occur to a hero of primitive tradition[1]. Genuine popular tradition implies a society in which a multiplication of such rewards causes no difficulty. The

---

[1] cf. *Gold Tree and Silver Tree*, a folk-tale to which Alfred Nutt called attention in connection with *Eliduc (Folk-Lore* III 1892), p. 32. The hero keeps both women assigned him by the story, and they live happily together.

prejudice against accepting more than one is a late social and literary development.

The offer of a second lady in *Horn, Bevis,* and *Guy* is perhaps due to the accretion of two independent traditions. The twelfth century poet accepts both, and combines them as best he can. Marie de France and Gautier d'Arras appropriate the situation for the very sake of the dilemma which it presents. We should classify the stories mentioned in the text (Ch. IV, p. 158—77) as follows:

1. Romances in which the situation of the hero who is offered a second lady is the result of an accretion of traditional incidents.

The hero refuses her. Loyalty is stronger than ambition or fear:

> *Horn,*
> *Bevis of Hampton,*
> *Guy of Warwick.*

2. Romances in which the situation is appropriated by a poet interested in the conflict for which it offers an opportunity.

In spite of Ambition, Fear, Duty, Pity, and the resemblance of the other woman to the one he loves, the hero does not falter. *Amor vincit omnia.*

Love is stronger than Duty: *Eliduc.*
  „   „   „   „ Ambition, Fear, and Pity:
                      Ille et Galeron.
  „   „   „   „ Love's very counterpart:
                      Galerant.
                      Freisne.
  „   „   „   „ all these as well as phy-
                      sical desire: *Tristan.*

34*

Previous investigators have dwelt upon the question of marital fidelity and the question of providing for the rejected lady as the chief points of interest in these stories[1].

These do not seem to us vital. Whether the lover is or is not married, and whether the woman loved is the first or second that has come into his life, is of secondary interest to the poet. The important point is that she is the one chosen by *Amors*. It is a mere chance that it is only in *Eliduc* that *Amors* is on the side of the second woman. Constancy and Marriage, like Pity, Ambition, Fear, and Duty, are looked upon by the poet as distinctly secondary considerations. Violation of any of them may be difficult, may be regrettable, but deference to any of them in opposition to Love would be unpardonable.

The provision for the rejected lady in the *dénouement* of the stories in groups 1 and 2 is interesting only as it illustrates the poet's loss of interest in his secondary characters when they cease to serve

---

[1] *Comptes rendus des séances de l'Académie aes inscriptions et belles-lettres* XV (1887) 571—86; A Nutt, *Folk-Lore* III, 26—48; J. E. Matzke, *Modern Philology* IV, 471—9, V, 211—39.

Matzke (*op. cit.* V, 226—7) groups the texts, with reference to the attitude of the hero and the *dénouement*, as follows:

1. 'The knight is not married to the first maiden but succumbs to the resemblance to her which the appearance of the second maiden suggests. *Lai du Fraisne, Galerant,* and *Tristan.* It will be noted that the exile formula as such is absent here and that the stories are based solely on the resemblance theme.

2. The knight is not married to the first maiden and remains true to her, illustrated by the song of *Horn*.

3. The knight is married to the first maiden and succumbs to the charms of the second, illustrated by *Eliduc.*

4. The knight is married to the first maiden and remains true to his vows. Here belong *Ille et Galeron*, the lost lay from which it derives, and the episodes from *Bueve de Haumtone*.'

his hero. We find several methods of getting rid
of the superfluous lady. The redactors whose
audience insisted on monogamy had two alternatives. In *Bevis* and *Le Fraisne* the rejected lady
is given another husband. In *Eliduc* she goes into
a nunnery. The disappointed women in *Horn* and
Galerant also enter convents. Galeron, after being
reunited with Ille for some years, decides to take
the veil. The hero is thus free to console Ganor by
making her his wife. This compromise is in deference
to the readers whose sympathy has been on the side
of Ganor. Out of regard for the moral sensibilities
of those who have been shocked by Fortune's — or the
poet's — kindness to Eliduc and Guilliadun, we are
told that after a time the lovers decide to enter a
convent. The *dénouement* is merely a means of putting
an end to the story. Its interest concluded for the
poet with the solution of the psychological conflict.

A few centuries later we have examples of the
story in which the interest is concentrated on the
dénouement. This constitutes a third group.

3. Stories in which the situation is appropriated
from an interest in the question of bigamy.

During his stay in the East, the Count of Gleichen
has been saved from death on the condition of accepting
the hand of a Saracen lady. The fact that he has a
wife already has not been considered a valid excuse.
On his return, a dispensation from the pope relieves the
hero's embarassment. He brings the second lady to
his home, and the two wives live happily together.
The story was perhaps suggested by a tombstone
representing a knight reclining between two ladies.
It has been supposed that this sixteenth century
revival of interest in the *Eliduc* theme was due to

Philip of Hesse, who was encouraged by Luther and Melanchthon in his effort to obtain a dispensation in favor of bigamy. Henry VIII had desired this privilege as a solution for his marital difficulties. A similar story was told in France in the fifteenth century of Gilles de Trasignies[1].

The popularity, in the twelfth century, of the story commonly referred to as that of *The husband with two wives*, and the occurrence, in several contemporary romances, of similar psychological treatments of it, sufficiently account for the second Isolt of the Tristan romance[2].

APPENDIX IV.

THE HARP AND THE ROTE: THE STORY TOLD OF GUINEVERE AND OTHER TWELFTH CENTURY HEROINES[3].

A. GUINEVERE.

The same story which we find in Tristan in the incident of the Harp and the Rote is fre-

---

[1] cf. G. Paris, *op. cit.*, 575—8.

[2] Cf. supra. Ch. IV, 158—77. It is unnecessary to seek for a more recondite explanation, as do M. Deutschbein, *Studien zur Sagengeschichte Englands*, *Cöthen* 1906, p. 174 n.; E. Muret, *Zts. f. franz. Sp. u. Lit.* XXXVII, *Referate und Rezensionen*, 173. Similarly J. Loth, *Contributions à l'étude des Romans de la Table Ronde*, Paris 1912, p. 110: *C'est, à mon avis, de la juxtaposition en Cornwall des deux légendes, cornique et armoricaine, et d'un compromis entre les deux, que vient la création des deux Iseuts.*

[3] Gaston Paris has made an exhaustive study of the abduction of Guinevere in *Rom.* XII, 459 ff. He establishes the fact that 'Le conte breton que Crétien a connu sous une forme très altérée avait un fond mythologique: il racontait à l'origine l'enlève-

quently related in connection with Guinevere. The

ment d'une reine par le dieu des morts et sa délivrance par son époux. Par la suite des temps, on avait identifié l'époux avec Arthur, et la reine enlevée avec Guanhumar sa femme. Plus tard encore, le dieu des morts reçut le nom de Melwas, et, confondu sans doute avec un personnage historique, perdit en grande partie son caractère surnaturel; mais la trace de l'ancienne conception persista dans le nom d'„ile de verre“ et de „pays dont nul ne retourne“ donné à son royaume, et dans la description du „pont de l'épée“ qu'il faut franchir pour y pénétrer' (*op. cit.* p. 533). For a discussion of the 'pont de l'épée', see an article by Miss Laura Hibbard in the *Romanic Review*, 1913 (in press).

John Rhys (*The Arthurian Legend*, Oxford 1891, p. 64), mentions the *Wooing of Etain* in connection with a Welsh dialogue which he believes to refer to the abduction of Guinevere by Melwas, suggesting that Crestien had two distinct versions of 'the same mythic incident' to work upon.

G. L. Kittredge (*Harvard Studies and Notes* VIII, 190 n. 2) makes the suggestion that the episode of the abduction of Guinevere is a rationalized version of a story of the same general character as the *Wooing of Etain*.

K. G. T. Webster (*Englische Studien* XXXVI [1906], p. 340) gives a resumé of an unpublished study in which he has developed Professor Kittredge's suggestion. He also points out that in the Middle English *Ballad of King Arthur and King Cornwall*, a relation similar to that between Etain and Midir seems to exist between Guinevere and Cornwall.

W. H. Schofield, in an article on the *Franklyn's Tale*, (*Modern Language Publications* XVI, 405 ff.) cites as parallels in faithfulness to a rash promise, the *Mabinogi of Pwyll*, the *Wooing of Etain*, the story of *Mongan*, *Sir Orfeo*, Gottfried's *Tristan*, *Sir Tristrem*, the episode of Isolt's rash promise to Palamedes in Malory, Hartmann's *Iwein*, and other versions of the abduction of Guinevere. He considers the theme of the *Franklyn's Tale* to be of the same character.

G. L. Kittredge, in an article on *Sir Orfeo* (*American Journal of Philology* VII, 176 ff.), suggests that the non-classical elements of this poem may conceivably be derived from the *Wooing of Etain*. He also calls attention to the marked similarity between the second part of *Orfeo* and the first part of the *Harp and the Rote* episode in *Tristan*.

J. L. Weston *The Legend of Sir Gawain*, London 1897, p. 67 ff., and *The Legend of Sir Lancelot du Lac*, London 1901, p. 40 ff., has chapters on *Le Chevalier de la Charrette*.

We have already devoted a brief discussion to the incident of the *Harp and the Rote* in connection with the tradition of Diarmaid and Grainne in the *Revue Celtique* XXXIII, 48. 51.

The present study offers some new material and seeks to bring the results of previous investigations of the *Guinevere, Orfeo*, and *Franklyn's Tale* episodes into relation with the episode in

oldest version is in a Latin saint's life,. the *Vita Gildae*[1].

Gildas ... entered Glastonbury. Melwas was the reigning king at that time in Somerset, that is the City of Glass; for it took its name from glass, and the

---

Tristan. The Cúroi, Manannan, Garel, Cormac, and Diarmaid texts have not, so far as we know, been previously mentioned in this connection.

    E. Brugger, *Zur Harfnerepisode, Herrigs Archiv* CXXIX, 375—87 appeared while the present study was in the press.

    For discussions of the various Tristan texts see Bédier I, 168—75; II 244; Piquet, *op. cit.* 243—45.

    The theme under discussion is essentially identical with one that has already been discussed in connection with Celtic and chivalric romance — the mortal loved by a fee and lured by her to the Other World. Here, however, the sexes being reversed, the mortal is not lured, but carried off, and masculine initiative gives the tale a more virile character throughout. See Nutt and Meyer, *Voyage of Bran;* A. C. L. Brown, *Iwain,* [Harvard] *Studies and Notes in Philology and Literature* VIII; cf. Windisch, *Táin bó Cúalnge, Irische Texte* V, p. xxxiii, l. 12 and note, p. xc.

    [1] *Vita Gildae,* ed. *Mon. Ger.* XIII, p. 109 (Chronica minora saec. IV, V, VI, VII). For the date see G. Paris, *Rom.* X, 490; Sir T: D. Hardy, *Descriptive Catalogue of materials relating to the history of Great Britain and Ireland,* London 1862, I, p. 151 ff.; Stevenson's Gildas, Int.; E. A. Freeman in *Macmillan's Magazine* XLII, p. 463; Rhys, *Arthurian Legend,* p. 52; T. Wright. *Biog. Brit. Lit.* I, p. 119. 120, II, 166; F. Lot, *Rom.* XXVII, 566; Zimmer, *Zts. f. f. Sp. u. Lit.* XII, p. 248; de la Borderie, *Etudes historiques bretonnes* I, 356. Wright and Lot consider the document as the work of Caradoc of Llancarfan (Lancarvan), and date it between 1145 and 1660. Stevenson and de la Borderie consider it a forgery. The Celtic connections of the document are obvious.

    Gildas ... ingressus est Glastoniam ... Melvas rege regnante in aestiva regione ... Glastonia, id est Urbs Vitrea, quae nomen sumsit a vitro, est urbs nomine primitus in Britannico sermone. obsessa est itaque ab Arturo tyranno cum innumerabili multitudine propter Guennuvar uxorem suam violatam et raptam a praedicto iniquo rege et ibi ductam propter refugium inviolati loci propter munitiones arundineti et fluminis ac paludis causa tutelae. Quaesiverat rex rebellis reginam per unius anni circulum, audivit tandem illam remanentem. illico commovit exercitus totius Cornubiae et Dibneniae; paratum est bellum inter inimicos. Hoc viso abbas Glastoniae comitante clero et Gilda Sapiente intravit medias acies, consuluit Melvas regi suo pacifice, ut redderet raptam. reddita ergo fuit, quae reddenda fuerat, per pacem. et benivolentiam. his peractis duo reges largiti sunt abbati multa territoria.

city was called in early times by that name in the British tongue. Now this city was besieged by King. Arthur with a great host, because of his wife Guennuvar, outraged and stolen by the aforesaid wicked king, and brought hither for the refuge of an impregnable fortress; impregnable because of the fortification of the marshes und river and swamp which were to it a cause of safety. The king had been seeking to get the queen from the rebels for about a year. He heard finally that she was there. Thither moved the whole army of the men of Cornwall and of Devon. Battle between the foes was imminent. Seeing this, the abbot of Glastonbury, accompanied by a clerk and Gildas the Wise, went into the midst of the line of battle, and with peaceful intent advised Melwas to return the stolen queen; thus peacefully and amicably she was restored who should have been restored. After this the two kings presented the abbot with broad lands.

Here the episode is presented in bare outlines very closely corresponding to those of the *Wooing of Etain*, although the assistance in the rescue is given by a pious abbot instead of a magician. It should be noted that here, as in the Irish versions, it is the husband who is the rescuer.

Ulrich von Zatzikhoven's *Lanzelet*[1] relates the incident of the abduction of Guinevere as follows:

---

[1] Ulrich von Zatzikhoven, *Lanzelet*, ed. K. A. Hahn, Frankfurt a. M. 1845, l. 4972—5360, 6710—7423. 'The German poem, which may be dated about 1194, is a translation of a French biographical romance of Lancelot, which must have been written before Crestien's *Charrette*, that is before 1170.' Webster, *Eng. Stud.* XXXVI, 348. Paris, *La Littérature française au Moyen-âge²*, p. 247, dates it 1160. For contrary view see W. Foerster, *Der Karrenritter*, Halle 1899, Int. XLVI, LXXIX. On the Celtic character of the poem, cf. Paris, *Rom.* X, 476—8; Paris, *art. cit.*, p. 471 ff. and Weston, *Sir Lancelot du Lac*, 8 ff. give synopses of the entire romance.

King Valerin, the owner of a marvellous shining castle, made impregnable by a hedge of *grozem ungezibele* guarded by dragons, appears at the court of Arthur, and declares *er solde Ginoveren billichher hân danne Artûs ane wân, wan siu im gemèhelet waere, ê siu wurde hîbaere.* Arthur declares he knows nothing of a previous betrothal of Guinevere, but the stranger says he will establish his claim by. a single combat, giving Arthur a week's time to appoint a champion. He is, however, defeated by Lancelot in the ensuing duel.

A year afterward he attacks and overcomes Arthur and his men while hunting, and takes the queen. The king pursues him to his castle, but the united efforts of all his knights and men cannot prevail against it. At last, by the advice of Tristan, Arthur seeks the magician Malduck. With great difficulty they succeed in penetrating the mysterious country that surrounds Malduck's castle. cross the dangerous bridge which leads to it, and prevail upon him to help them. By his magic he sinks into a heavy sleep the inhabitants of Valerin's fortress and the dragons which guard it. Arthur and his army are thus enabled to enter the castle, to kill all within, and rescue the queen.

The reader may wish to compare the incident as it occurs in Crestien's *La Charrette*[1].

---

[1] Christian von Troyes, *Der Karrenritter (La Charrette) und das Wilhelmsleben (Guillaume d'Angleterre)*, ed. W. Foerster, Halle 1899. For the date see Foerster, *op. cit.* xix, who places it about 1170; cf. G. Paris, *Rom.* XII, 463, who places it between 1164 and 1172; cf. Paris, *Journal des Savants*, Nov. 1901, p. 702, where he dates it 1172. On the Celtic elements see Paris, *Rom.* XII, 498 ff. Paris suggests Welsh connections. Foerster combats the views of Paris in this regard in *Karrenritter* xxxiii ff. Our study leads us to believe that Lancelot, the abduction of Guinevere, and the *Ehebruchsmotiv* were first combined by Crestien.

A stranger, Meleagant, appears at Arthur's
Pentecost feast and declares that he holds many
ladies and knights of Arthur's realm captive in
his kingdom. He declares that if one of Arthur's
knights can overcome him in single combat in the
neighboring wood, he will give up all the prisoners.
If he wins, however, Guinevere must be added to his
spoils. At this point Kay demands a boon of the
king, threatening to quit his service if he is refused.
At the queen's intercession Arthur promises to grant
the request. What Kay asks is permission to
accept the stranger's challenge. Arthur hesitatingly
complies, and Kay departs, accompanied by the queen,
for the place of combat. Gawain reproaches Arthur,
and proceeds to follow them. On the way he meets
Lancelot, whom he does not recognize, and lends him
one of his horses. Shortly afterward he reaches the
wood, and finds bloody traces of the combat. He meets
Lancelot, unhorsed, following a cart driven by a dwarf.
The latter promises Lancelot to bring him to the queen
the next morning on condition that he will mount the
cart. After a moment's hesitation he complies. Gawain
follows on foot. The two knights overcome various
difficulties in the approach to the land of Meleagant,
Lancelot reaching it by crossing a bridge made of a
sword blade, and vanquishing lions by gazing on his
magic ring. He sustains a combat with Meleagant,
and delivers the queen. He had been separated from
Gawain when they decided to approach the castle by
different bridges, and he now sets out in search of
him. He is lured off, however, by a false message,
and treacherously taken captive by Meleagant. It is
Kay and the others who rescue Gawain from drowning,
and set off with Guinevere to Arthur's court. They
have been led by Meleagant to believe that Lancelot

has already arrived. Lancelot succeeds in freeing himself and killing his enemy [1].

The outlines of the Celtic type, preserved in the

---

[1] We have examined a number of other versions of the abduction of Guinevere. In order not to make our exposition too long we shall confine our references to them to the notes.

Hartmann von Aue, *Iwein der Ritter mit dem Löwen*, ed. E. Henrici, Halle 1891, ll. 4530—725. The work of Hartmann, written before 1204 (Henrici, p. vi) is a translation of Crestien's *Chevalier au Lion*, and, though rather more diffuse, follows its source closely. Cf. Piquet, *Etude sur Hartmann d'Aue*, Paris 1898, 99—144.

The Pleier, *Garel von dem blühenden Tal*, ed. M. Walz, Freiburg 1892. As this edition has not been accessible to us we have followed the resume in P. Piper, *Höfische Epik* II, 306. 317. The date of the work is c. 1260—1290. It seems to be a redaction of the Stricker's *Daniel vom blühenden Tal*. The portion referring to the abduction of Guinevere is not found in the Stricker.

Li Romans de Durmart le Galois, ed. E. Stengel, *Bibliothek des lit. Ver. in Stuttgart*, cxvi, Tübingen 1873, l. 4185—340. A late romance.

Sir Thomas Malory, *Le Morte Darthure*, ed. H. O. Sommer, London 1889, Bk. XIX, ch. 1—6, p. 772.

Diu Crône, ed. G. H. F. Scholl, *Bibliothek des lit. Vereins in Stuttgart*, XXVII, Tübingen 1852, ll. 3356—5370, 10113—12588. The assumption of a French source for most of *Diu Crône* is general. See Scholl's introduction, p. xi; cf. O. Warnatsch, *Der Mantel*, p. 120; cf. Webster, *Eng. Stud.* XXXVI, 346, n. 3. Scholl (p. xi) gives the date of the German poem as c. 1220. Its version of the abduction of Guinevere is more archaic than that of Crestien, according to Paris, *Rom.* XII, p. 506.

King Arthur and King Cornwall in F. J. Child, *English and Scottish Popular Ballads* I, p. 279. For a discussion of the similarity of the relation between Guinevere and King Cornwall, and that between Etain and Midir, see Webster, *Eng. Stud.* XXXVI, p. 337 ff.; esp. pp. 347—51.

Livre d'Artus, see Freymond, *Beiträge zur Kenntnis der altfranzösischen Artusromane in Prosa*, *Zts. f. fr. Sp.* XVII, p. 1 ff. — P. 21 ff. gives the contents of version P. from a thirteenth century manuscript. The passage relating to the abductions of Guinevere are 1. p. 34, § 37; 2. p. 35, § 40; 3. p. 45 § 67 and note.

Prose Romance. Cf. Foerster, *Karrenritter*, xxiii, for bibliography; for a discussion of the portion dealing with the abduction and for the date (probably after 1170) see also Paris, *Rom.* XII, p. 485 ff. 497. 534. The source is Crestien's *Charrette*.

Guinevere stories which we have examined[1] and paralleled by Tristan, are as follows:

1. A magnificent and haughty stranger appears to the king[2].

2. He has previously known the queen, and has a claim to her[3]. He has long loved her[4].

3. He demands her, and secures her through the response, on the part of his hearers, to a conception of honor universally recognized by his hearers, (1) Fidelity to an indefinite promise, however rashly given and, however, unreasonably interpreted[5]; (2) the right of anyone to demand that his claim be submitted to the issue of wager of battle[6].

4. An ineffectual attempt is made to check the stranger's purpose[7].

5. The stranger is with difficulty pursued to his realm[8].

---

[1] The texts considered in relation to Guinevere are referred to as follows: $V = Vita\ Gildae$; $Z =$ Ulrich von Zatzikhoven's *Lanzelet*; $HI =$ Hartmann's von Aue *Iwein*; $CC =$ Crestien de Troyes *La Charrette*, the Prose *Lancelot*, Crestien's *Iwain*, *Livre d'Artus*; $GP = The\ Pleier's\ Garel$; $D = Durmart\ le\ Galois$; $HC =$ Heinrich von Türlin's *Diu Crône*; $MM =$ Malory's *Morte Darthur*; $AC = The\ Ballad\ of\ King\ Arthur\ and\ King\ Cornwall$; $A_{1,\ 2,\ 3}$ *Livre D'Artus*; $L_{1,\ 2,\ 3}$, episodes in the Prose *Lancelot*. Cf. the abbreviations used to refer to the Old Irish stories, Ch. VI D 2*h*; T refers to Tristan.

[2] $E, M, F, P, - V, Z, HC, HI, GP, CC, - T.$

[3] $E, P - Z, HC, AC.$

[4] $D, M - T.$

[5] $E, M, F, P, C - GP, HI, CC, - T.$

[6] $Z, CC, HI, HC.$

[7] $E, C, - CC, HI, HC.$ In Z Lanzelet is allowed to win the combat. $- T.$

[8] $E, C, - V, CC, Z, D, M.$

6. The queen is won back: (1) with the help of an army and a magician[1]; (2) by single combat[2]; (3) by a ruse[3].

7. The rescuer is: (1) the king[4]; (2) his devoted vassal[5]; (3) the queen's lover[6].

The typical traits preserved in the Guinevere versions and lost in Tristan are the following. The stranger is the possessor of a mysterious realm. He has been the husband or the betrothed husband of the queen. He is pursued to his domain. It is the husband who achieves the rescue.

One trait which occurs frequently in the Celtic versions appears in Tristan but not in Guinevere: The stranger gives a display of skill, in recognition of which the king promises to grant him any boon he may name.

It is impossible to classify the versions of Guinevere's abduction. Some have undergone greater modifications in some parts, others in others. We might arrange them roughly in some such groups as the following, to show the gradual disintegration of a primitive trait:

(1) Versions in which the taking away of the queen is made dependent upon an indefinite boon: Hartmann's *Iwein, Garel*. (2) Versions in which the taking away of the queen is made dependent upon a wager of battle: *Lanzelet*, Crestien, *Diu Crône*. (3) Versions in which the queen is simply abducted: *Lanzelet*, Malory, *Durmart*.

---

[1] *E, C* (army only), — *V* (an abbot) *Z.*
[2] *CC, HC, D, MM*
[3] *M, P,* — *T.*
[4] *E, M, P, C* — *V.*
[5] *HC, D, HI.*
[6] *CC, GP. T.*

But if we arrange them according to some other apparently primitive trait, the earlier and later stages of development are represented by an entirely different grouping of the versions. If we classify them according to Guinevere's previous relation to the stranger, we get the following grouping. (1) Versions in which Guinevere was the stranger's wife: *Diu Crône*. (2) Versions in which Guinevere was the stranger's betrothed: *Lanzelet*. (3) Versions in which Guinevere was the stranger's paramour: *King Arthur and King Cornwall*. (4) Versions in which Guinevere has been loved by the stranger: Malory, *Durmart*, Crestien (?). (5) Versions in which no relation is mentioned: Crestien (?), Prose *Lanzelot*, *Garel*, Hartmann's *Iwein*.

Again, if we arrange the versions according to the character of the rescuer, we get the following classification: (1) The rescuer is the king: *Vita Gildae*, *Lanzelet*. (2) A knight performs the feat in the service of the king: *Diu Crône*, Hartmann's *Iwein*, *Durmart*. (3) The queen's lover is the rescuer: Crestien, *Garel*, Malory.

Next to the *Vita Gildae*, Ulrich von Zatzikhoven's *Lanzelet* corresponds most closely to the Etain story. In his version, however, the relation of the stranger to the queen is weakened to betrothal, and the test of his claim by wager of battle is substituted for the rash boon. It is interesting to notice that Ulrich cannot bring himself to allow the combat to result to the disadvantage of Arthur's knights. Lanzelet is made to win it. As a result of this modification the stranger goes away empty handed.

Instead of the test of skill, followed by the unexpected demand of the queen as the promised reward, the stories of Guinevere usually substitute a wager of battle, sometimes retaining the rash promise in a subordinate position. The latter is the case in Hartmann's *Iwein* and the *Pleier's Garel.* In these two versions as well as in Crestien, where it is transferred to Kay, the *motif* of the rash boon is feebly handled. The single combat is of course more intelligible to a chivalric audience. The inability of Arthur's knights to compel the stranger to withdraw his claim puts them in a bad light, but it is unavoidable unless the whole first part of the story is to be abandoned. Ulrich retains it, as we have seen, at considerable expense. He makes Arthur's knight win in the single combat, and represents the stranger as appearing afterward and abducting the queen. Most of the chivalric poets prefer to abandon the rash boon entirely, and represent the stranger as abducting the queen at a moment when she is insufficently guarded. The interest of the story is thus entirely concentrated on the rescue of the queen.

The treatment of this rescue in the different versions reflects perhaps as clearly as any other element of the story the development of custom in romance in the twelfth and thirteenth centuries. A single combat between the stranger and the rescuer[1] replaces the siege by the combined forces of the king[2]. The shifting of the role of rescuer from Arthur to Lancelot can be traced by gradual stages. As long as the stranger was a mysterious personage whose previous relations to the queen constituted an important trait of the story, as in *Etain*, it is impossible to conceive of its containing any further complication than that of the struggle between him and the husband. In *Diu Crône, Iwein,*

---

[1] *HC, HI, CC, GP, D, MM, A* 1, 2, 3, *L,* 1, 2, 3, 4.
[2] *V, Z.*

Durmart, and Ulrich von Zatzikhoven's *Lanzelet* the situation remains the same as in the *Vita Gildae,* although the tendency to relegate Arthur to the background forbids the king to achieve the rescue in person. In these versions the hero is Gawain or Durmart, and his motive is disinterested knightly honor. Lanzelet undertakes the duel with Valerin from the same motive. This group offers an easy transition to Crestien and his followers, who make the rescuer the queen's lover. By this time the supernatural character of the stranger and his previous relations with the queen[1] are almost forgotten.

Variations of style in romance are likewise reflected in the difficulties which constitute the interest of the rescue. In *Etain, Lanzelet,* and the *Vita Gildae* they consist chiefly in storming the abductor's castle; in Crestien the reader's concern is centered in the dangerous approach to the stranger's territories, although the single combat, here as in *Diu Crône,* comes in for a share of his interest. The difficult passage of the water surrounding the stranger's realm[2] seems to present a Celtic detail.

---

[1] We may interpret as an allusion to them, the passage in MS. *C,* l. 210—13 of *La Charrette,* where the queen, when she is being led off by the stranger, says,

'an bas por ce qu'an ne l'öist.
„Ha, rois! se vos le sëussiez
Ja, ce croi, ne me leississiez
Sanz chalonge mener un pas"!

and Malory's mention of the fact that the stranger has loved her long.

[2] For a discussion of the realm of Melwas in romance literature, see Paris, *Rom.* X, 490 ff.; XII, 508 ff.; F. Lot, *Rom.* XXIV, 327 ff.

The entrance to the other world in Etain, as in *Sir Orfeo,* is by a hill or rock. There seems to have existed in the earliest Irish literature, in addition to the conception of the other-world

The story of the Harp and the Rote, and the
stories of the abduction of Guinevere seem to be independent developments of a Celtic type. Each presents
primitive characteristics of that type which are lacking
in the other. The *Guinevere* stories are interesting in
connection with the *Tristan* accounts as showing the
gradual effacement of the relation between the
stranger and the queen, the gradual displacement of
the rash boon, and the gradual shifting of the role of
rescuer from husband to lover. The two last processes,
as we have seen, have already taken place in *Tristan*.
On the other hand the *Tristan* version represents from
the point of view of the rash boon, a more perfect form
of the inception of the incident, than any of the *Guinevere*
versions. In the Guinevere versions the rash boon is
modified little by little until it completely disappears.
Minor points, such as the mysterious character of the
stranger and the journey to his marvellous realm,
appear in a more primitive form in certain versions
of the Guinevere story than in Tristan[1].

---

lying within the *sid* or fairy hills, another conception in which
it is a mysterious island beyond the sea.

The adoption of this latter idea is familiar to readers of
Arthurian romance in Crestien's *Erec*, 1. 1946 ff. as the Isle de
Voirre; in the description in the *Vita Merlini* of Glastonbury as
the Insula pomorum, 908—17.

For the same idea of the land of 'âventiure' as shut off by
mountains and water, and inaccessible except by a single entrance,
the passage of which is very difficult, see the Strickers *Daniel
von dem blühenden Tal*, ed. G. Rosenhagen, Breslau 1894, Weinhold
und Vogt, *Germanistische Abhandlungen* No. 9 1. 508 ff. and note.

For discussions of the character of the Celtic other world
see Meyer and Nutt, *Voyage of Bran* I; cf. O'Curry, *MS. Materials*,
504—5; d'Arbois, *Le Cycle Mythologique*, 140 ff.; *Folk Lore* XVIII,
339—40; E. Hull, *Folk Lore* XVIII, 121—66; A. Nutt, *Folk Lore*
XVIII, 445—8; H. Zimmer, *ZfdA.* XXXIII, 257 ff.; Kuno Meyer,
Cath Finntraga, Oxford 1885, *Int.* p. xiii, xi; Kittredge, *Amer.
Journal Philol.* VII, 195.

[1] It is our intention to investigate in a later study the
development of the entire tradition of Lancelot.

B. HEURYDYS.

An analogue to the incident of the Harp and the Rote is also found in a Middle English poem, *Sir Orfeo*[1].

The wife of Sir Orfeo falls asleep in her orchard under an 'ympe tree', and dreams that she is approached by two knights who summon her to the presence of their king. When she refuses, the king appears, followed by a noble train of knights and ladies robed in white and riding snow-white horses. He bids her be in the same place the following day, and declares that he will take her to his beautiful realm, of which he shows her the fair castles and forests and fields. He threatens her with torments if she fails to comply willingly.

The next day Sir Orfeo surrounds the place with guards, but in spite of all his efforts, his wife is borne away mysteriously, and no one knows whither.

The despairing Orfeo abandons his kingdom and, taking his harp, wanders disconsolate in the forests, charming the wild things with his melodies. Sometimes, in the hot summer days, he sees the king of the fairies, hunting or hawking with his rout. At last he approaches them, and recognizes among them his lost wife Heurydys. But she is hurried away

---

[1] *Sir Orfeo,* ed. O. Zielke, Breslau 1880. I have had access only to the edition of Ritson, *Ancient English Metrical Romances,* London 1802, II. The English poem dates from the end of the thirteenth century. It is probably a translation from a French version of a Breton lay. See Kittredge, *Amer. Journal of Philol.* VII, 177. Cf. the *Ballad of King Orfeo,* Child, *English and Scottish Popular Ballads,* Boston 1882. I, 215.

The position of Orfeo, with its fusion of Celtic and classic elements, has been carefully worked out by Professor Kittredge, *loc. cit.*

35*

from him by the others. He follows, and enters after them into the rock leading to their marvellous realm. He knocks at the gate of the castle and receives admittance. The king, having listened to his harping, declares that he will reward him with anything he may demand. Orfeo asks, for his wife. The king refuses at first, but he assents when Orfeo reminds him of the dishonor attached to breaking his word. Orfeo leads his wife to his own country, and takes his place again as king.

The outlines of the Celtic type preserved in *Sir Orfeo* are as follows:

A magnificent and haughty stranger appears to the queen, declaring that he has a claim to her[1]. He comes later to take her away, and does so in spite of the armed band set by the king to guard her[2]. The stranger is with difficulty pursued to his realm[3]. The husband, whose identity is unknown to the stranger, gives a display of skill, in recognition of which the king promises to grant him any boon he shall name[4]. He demands the queen[5].

The traits preserved in *Sir Orfeo*, and not found in *Tristan* or in the *Guinevere* episodes, are:

The stranger appears to the queen, represents to her the beauty of his land and demands that she come thither. The stranger appears mysteriously at a time appointed, and carries off the queen from the midst of the king's guards.

The traits preserved in *Tristan* and not found in *Sir Orfeo* are:

---

[1] *E, O.*
[2] *E, O.*
[3] *E, O.*
[4] *E* (in connection with the inception of the incident) *O, T.*
[5] *E* (in connection with the inception of the incident) *O, T.*

The stranger has previously known and loved the queen. He gives a display of skill in recognition of which the king promises to grant him any boon he may name. He demands the queen. The king hesitates, but taunted with having compromised his honor, unwillingly accedes.

The traits preserved in the *Guinevere* episodes and not found in *Sir Orfeo* are:

There has been a previous relation between the stranger and the queen. The stranger demands and secures her through the response, on the part of his hearers, to a current conception of honor.

It appears from the preceding analysis that *Sir Orfeo* is another example of the Celtic type we have discussed. It is strikingly similar to Etain in the scene where the stranger reappears at the appointed time, suddenly and mysteriously, in the midst of the guards with which the king has surrounded the queen. Unable, if indeed they see the fairy prince, to resist his occult influence, they allow him to carry her off, nobody knows whither. The previous scene, where Midir appears to Etain in a vision, and, reminding her of her former relations with him, exacts from her a conditional promise to follow him to his land, corresponds to the scene in *Orfeo* where the fairy king appears to Heurydys and tells her that she must come with him on the morrow. But the important section lying between them first finds its parallel in the second part of *Orfeo*, where the king of Fairyland loses his prize in a way very similar to that by which, in Etain, he wins her — namely by entering the court of his rival, inducing him to promise an indefinite boon in reward for a display of his skill (in chess in *Etain*, in playing the harp in *Orfeo*), and then demanding his wife. The rash

king hesitates, but, reminded of his honor, reluctantly accedes.

It is interesting to note that in *Sir Orfeo* the
scene of the rescue is exactly the same as the scene
of the abduction in the *Tristan* story[1].

C. STEINGERD.

One might be tempted to see another analogue
in the following incident in the *Cormacssaga*[2], an Old
Norse story of tragic love which presents numerous
points of resemblance to the Tristan story.

Thorvaldr Tinteinn's ship is attacked, and Steingerd (his wife) is stolen. Cormac, the lover of
Steingerd, overtakes the ship of Thorvaldr, and learning the news, pushes on to rescue her. He reaches
the Viking ship, which is moored for the night,
and overcomes the robber. He leaps into the water
with Steingerd and swims to land. When he brings
her back to her husband the latter orders her to
follow Cormac, since he has rescued her so valiantly.
Cormac says that he wishes it. But Steingerd refuses.
Cormac then angrily gives her up to her husband.

The episode offers the following points in common
with the Celtic type: A stranger departs with the

---

[1] cf. *Sir Tristrem* 1827—44; cf. *Sir Orfeo* 410—35.
[2] *Kormaks saga* ed. T. Möbius, Halle 1886, § 26; cf. Vigfússon, *Origines Icelandicae, op. cit.* II, 315 ff.; *Corpus Poeticum
Boreale* II, p. 32 ff. 66 ff. The story of Cormac and Steingerd, one
of the oldest of the Norse sagas, is another tradition of a pair
of star-crossed lovers. Cormac is a passionate and ill-fated bard.
He and Steingerd love each other, but hostile persons are at work
against them, and he loses her. She becomes the wife of Bersi,
and afterward of Tinteinn. Cormac returns again and again to
see her. He dies at last in a strange land with her name on his
lips. The story is handled with the characteristic realism and
restraint of the sagas. It is characteristic of the Norse treatment
that the elements of the tragedy lie in the hero's own nature.

lady, and no one attempts to prevent him. He is pursued, and the lady is recovered. Even taking into consideration the fact that the *saga* presents characteristics that point to Irish influence, the family of the hero, for example, and Cormac's fight with the eels in bringing Steingerd to shore, the similarity in this episode does not seem close enough for us to associate it with the Irish type under consideration. Its similarities to the Tristan episode are more striking. The stranger comes by ship; the scene of the rescue is a ship at anchor. The lover, absent at the time of the abduction, learns the news, and sets out in pursuit. He rescues the lady and turns her over to her husband.

APPENDIX V.

TRAGIC LOVE STORIES IN OLD IRISH LITERATURE.

A. EXTRACTS FROM THE STORY OF THE *ELOPEMENT OF DEIRDRE WITH NAISI* [1].

There was a prophecy before her birth that Deirdre would bring woe to the warriors of Ulster. The warriors would have had her slain, but Conor, the king, declares that she shall be set apart to be his wife [2].

---

[1] cf. bibliography in note supra VI D 2 f. The story is mentioned in the tenth century list of tales in the *Book of Leinster*.

[2] By the translator's kind permission, the following is from A. H. Leahy, *Heroic Romances of Ireland*, London 1905, I, 94 ff.

'The maiden was reared in a house that belonged
to Conor, and she grew up to be the fairest maid in
all Ireland. She was brought up at a distance from
the king's court; so that none of the men of Ulster
might see her till the time came when she was to share
the royal couch: none of mankind was permitted to
enter the house where she was reared, save only her
foster-father, and her foster-mother; and in addition
to these Levorcham, to whom naught could any refuse,
for she was a witch.

Now once it chanced upon a certain day in the
time of winter that the foster-father of Deirdre had
employed himself in skinning a calf upon the snow,
in order to prepare a roast for her, and the blood
of the calf lay upon the snow, and she saw a black
raven who came down to drink it. And 'Levorcham',
said Deirdre, 'that man only will I love, who hath
the three colors that I see here, his hair as black as
the raven, his cheeks red like the blood, and his body
as white as the snow.' 'Dignity and good fortune to
thee!' said Levorcham; 'that man is not far away.
Yonder he is in the burg which is nigh; and the
name of him is Naisi, the son of Usnach.' 'I shall
never be in good health again', said Deidre, 'until
the time come when I may see him.'

It befell that Naisi was upon a certain day alone
upon the rampart of the burg of Emain, and he sent
his warrior-cry with music abroad: well did the musical
cry ring out that was raised by the sons of Usnach.
Each cow and every beast that heard them, gave of
milk two thirds more than its wont; and each man
by whom that cry was heard deemed it to be fully
joyous, and a dear pleasure to him. Goodly moreover
was the play that these men made with their weapons;
if the whole province of Ulster had been assembled

against them in one place, and they three only had
been able to set their backs against one another, the
men of Ulster would not have borne away victory
from those three: so well were they skilled in parry
and defence. And they were swift of foot when they
hunted the game, and with them it was the custom
to chase the quarry to its death.

Now when this Naisi found himself alone on the
plain, Deirdre also soon escaped outside her house
to him, and she ran past him, and at first he knew
not who she might be.

'Fair is the young heifer that springs past me!'
he cried.

'Well may the young heifers be great,' she said
in a place where none may find a bull.'

'Thou hast, as thy bull,' said he, 'the bull of the
whole province of Ulster, even Conor the king of
Ulster.'

'I would choose between you two,' she said, 'and
I would take for myself a younger bull, even such as
thou art.'

'Not so, indeed,' said Naisi, 'for I fear the prophecy
of Cathbad.'

'Sayest thou this, as meaning to refuse me?' said she.

'Yea indeed', he said; and she sprang upon him,
and she seized him by his two ears. 'Two ears of
shame and of mockery shalt thou have', she cried,
'if thou take me not with thee.'

'Release me, O my wife!' said he.

'That will I.'

Then Naisi raised his musical warrior-cry, and
the men of Ulster heard it, and each of them one
after another sprang up: and the sons of Usnach
hurried out in order to hold back their brother.

'What is it,' they said, 'that thou dost', let it not
be by any fault of thine that war is stirred up between
us and the men of Ulster.'

Then he told them all that had been done; and
'There shall evil come on thee from this', said they;
'moreover thou shalt lie under the reproach of shame
so long as thou dost live; and we will go with her
into another land, for there is no king in all Ireland
who will refuse us welcome if we come to him.'

Then they took counsel together, and that same
night they departed, three times fifty warriors, and
the same number of women, and dogs, and servants,
and Deirdre went with them. And for a long time
they wandered about Ireland, in homage to this man
or that; and often Conor sought to slay them either
by ambuscade or by treachery; from round about
Assaroe, near to Ballyshannon in the west, they
journeyed, and they turned them back to Benn Etar,
in the north-east, which men today call the Mountain
of Howth. Nevertheless the men of Ulster drave them
from the land, and they came to the land of Alba,
and in its wildernesses they dwelled. And when the
chase of the wild beasts of the mountains failed them,
they made foray upon the cattle of the men of Alba,
and took them for themselves; and the men of Alba
gathered themselves together with intent to destroy
them. Then they took shelter with the king of Alba,
and the king took them into his following, and they
served him in war. And they made for themselves
houses of their own in the. meadows by the king's
burg: it was on account of Deirdre that these houses
were made, for they feared that men might see her,
and that on her account they might be slain.

Now one day the high-steward of the king went
out in the early morning, and he made a cast about

Naisi's house, and saw those two sleeping therein, and he hurried back to the king, and awaked him: 'We have', said he, 'up to this day found no wife for thee of like dignity to thyself. Naisi the son of Usnach hath a wife of worth sufficient for the emperor of the western world! Let Naisi be slain, and let his wife share thy couch.'

'Not so!' said the king, 'but do thou prepare thyself to go each day to her house, and woo her for me secretly.'

Thus was it done; but Deirdre, whatsoever the steward told her, was accustomed straightway to recount it each even to her spouse; and since nothing was obtained from her, the sons of Usnach were sent into dangers, and into wars, and into strifes that thereby they might be overcome. Nevertheless they showed themselves to be stout in every strife, so that no advantage did the king gain from them by such attempts as these.

The men of Alba were gathered together to destroy the sons of Usnach, and this also was told to Deirdre. And she told the news to Naisi: 'Depart hence'! said she, 'for if ye depart not this night, upon the morrow ye shall be slain!' And they marched away that night, and they betook themselves to an island of the sea.

Now the news of what had passed was brought to the men of Ulster. 'T is pity, O Conor!' said they, 'that the sons of Usnach should die in the land of foes, for the sake of an evil woman. It is better that they should come under thy protection, and that the (fated) slaying should be done here, and that they should come into their own land, rather than that they should fall at the hands of foes.' 'Let them come to us then', said Conor, 'and let men go as securities to them'. The news was brought to them.

'This is welcome news for us', they said; 'we will indeed come, and let Fergus come as our surety, and Dubhtach, and Cormac the son of Conor'. These then went to them, and they moved them to pass over the sea.

But at the contrivance of Conor, Fergus was pressed to join in an ale-feast, while the sons of Usnach were pledged to eat no food in Erin, until they had eaten the food of Conor. So Fergus tarried behind with Dubhtach and Cormac; and the sons of Usnach went on, accompanied by Fiacha, Fergus' son; until they came to the meadows around Emain.

Now at that time Eogan the son of Durthacht had come to Emain to make his peace with Conor, for they had for a long time been at enmity; and to him, and to the warmen of Conor, the charge was given that they should slay the sons of Usnach, in order that they should not come before the king. The sons of Usnach stood upon the level part of the meadows, and the women sat upon the ramparts of Emain. And Eogan came with his warriors across the meadow, and the son of Fergus took his place by Naisi's side. And Eogan greeted them with a mighty thrust of his spear, and the spear brake Naisi's back in sunder, and passed through it. The son of Fergus made a spring, and he threw both arms around Naisi, and he brought him beneath himself to shelter him, while he threw himself down above him; and it was thus that Naisi was slain, through the body of the son of Fergus. Then there began a murder throughout the meadow, so that none escaped who did not fall by the points of the spears, or the edge of the sword, and Deirdre was brought to Conor to be in his power, and her arms were bound behind her back.

Now the sureties who had remained behind, heard what had been done, even Fergus and Dubhtach, and

Cormac. And thereon they hastened forward, and they forthwith performed great deeds. Dubhtach slew, with one thrust of his spear, Mane a son of Conor, and Fiachna the son of Feidelm, Conor's daughter; and Fergus struck down Traigthren, the son of Traig-lethan, and his brother. And Conor was wroth at this, and he came to the fight with them; so that upon that day three hundred of the men of Ulster fell. And Dubhtach slew the women of Ulster; and ere the day dawned, Fergus set Emain on fire. Then they went away into exile, and betook them to the land of Connaught to find shelter with Ailill and Maev, for they knew that that royal pair would give them good enter-tainment. To the men of Ulster the exiles showed no love: three thousand stout men went with them; and for sixteen years never did they allow cries of lamentation and of fear among the Ulstermen to cease: each night their vengeful forays caused men to quake, and to wail.

Deirdre lived on for a year in the household of Conor; and during all that time she smiled no smile of laughter; she satisfied not herself with food or with sleep, and she raised not her head from her knee. And if anyone brought before her people of mirth, she used to speak thus[1]:

'Though fair to you seems the keen band of heroes
who march into Emain that they lately left
more stately was the return to their home
of the three heroic sons of Usnach.

Naisi, with mead of delicious hazel-nuts
(came), to be bathed by me at the fire,
Ardan, with an ox or boar of excellence,
Aindle, a faggot on his stately back.

---

[1] We give the literal rendering of the verses, Leahy, *op. cit.* 187.

Though sweet be the excellent mead to you
which is drunk by the son of Ness, the rich in
[strife,
there has been known to me, ere now, leaping over
[a bank,
frequent sustenance which was sweeter.

When the noble Naisi spread out
a cooking-hearth on hero-board of tree,
sweeter than any food dressed under honey
was what was captured by the son of Usnach'.

. . . .
. . . . .¹

'Whom dost thou hate most', said Conor, 'of those
whom thou now seest?'

'Thee thyself', she answered, 'and with thee
Eogan the son of Durthacht.'

'Then', said Conor, 'thou shalt dwell with Eogan
for a year'; and he gave Deirdre over into Eogan's
hand.

Now upon the morrow they went away over the
festal plain of Macha, and Deirdre sat behind Eogan
in the chariot; and the two who were with her were
the two men whom she would never willingly have
seen together· upon the earth, and as she looked upon
them, 'Ha, Deirdre', said Conor, 'it is the same glance
that a ewe gives when between two rams that thou
sharest now between me and Eogan!' Now there was
a great rock of stone in front of them, and Deirdre
struck her head upon that stone, and she shattered
her head, and so she died.

---

¹ The prose is resumed *op. cit.* 101—2.

B. THE MEETING OF LIADAIN AND CURITHIR[1].

Liadain of the Corco Dubne[2], a poetess, went visiting into the country of Connaught. There Curithir Otter's son[3], of Connaught, himself a poet, made an ale-feast for her.

'Why should not we two unite, Liadain?' saith Curithir. 'A son of us two would be famous'.

'Do not let us do so', saith she, 'lest my round of visiting be ruined for me. If you will come for me again at my home, I shall go with you'.

That fell so. Southward he went, and a single gillie behind him with his poet's cloak in a bag upon his back, while Curithir himself was in a poor cloak. And there were spear heads in the bag also. He went till he was at the well beside Liadain's court. There he took his crimson cloak about him, and the heads were put upon their shafts, and he stood brandishing them.

---

[1] 'The story has reached us in two late MS. copies only (Harl. 5280, p. 26a — 26b [Ha] and H. 3. 18, p. 759). But that it nevertheless enjoyed some popularity in earlier times I conclude from the fact that in the introduction to the song of the Old Woman of Beare, Liadain is mentioned as one of the celebrated women of Corkaguiney (see *Otia Merseiana* I, p. 121) and that one of the quatrains contained in our story is quoted as an example of its metre (treochair) in a metrical treatise of the tenth century (v. *Irische Texte* III, p. 16 § 39 and p. 45. § 63.' K. Meyer: *Liadain and Curithir, An Irish Love-story of the ninth century*, London 1902, p. 8—9. I am deeply indebted to Professor Meyer for permission to reprint the story as a whole. The few slight changes from the published translation are made by him. The reader is referred to the preface of his edition for the linguistic reasons for dating the poem in the ninth century. The notes, except those in brackets, are Professor Kuno Meyer's.

[2] A barony in county Kerry, now Corkaguiney.

[3] The name of the father of Curithir, Doborchu, means 'Otter' (Welsh Dyfrge).

Then he saw Mac Da Cherda[1] coming towards him, a fool, the son of Maelochtraig, son of Dinertach, of the Dessi of Munster. He would go dryshod across sea and land alike. Chief poet he was and the fool of all Ireland.

He went up ,to Curithir.

'Well met!' said Mac Da Cherda.

'So be it!' said Curithir.

'Are you the owner of the court?·

'Not I', said Curithir; 'whence are you yourself?'

'I am the poor fool of the Dessi, Mac Da Cherda is my name.'

'We have heard of you', said Curithir. 'Will you go into the court?'

'I will', said he.

'Do me a favour', said Curither. 'The tall woman who is there, tell her, using your own wits, to come to this well.'

'What is her name?'

'Liadain.'

'What is yours?'

'Curithir, Otter's son.'

'Right!' quoth he.

He goes into the house. She was there in her bedroom with four other women. Down he sat, but no notice was taken of him.

'T was then he said:

'The mansion
Which the pillars support —
If any there be who have made a tryst,
The behest for them is till sunset.

---

[1] As to this character, see the *Vision of Mac Conglinne*, ed..K. Meyer, London 1892, p. 131, and Todd, *Book of Hymns* I, p. 88. He was called 'Boy of Two Arts', 'quia nempe nunc extreme fatuus, mox summe prudens' (Colgan).

O well which art before the house,
It were time some one should visit thee,
Around it larks
Fair, hesitating (?), take flight.

Darkness is on my eyes,
I make nothing of indications,
So that I call Liadain (the Grey Lady)
Every woman whom I do not know.

O woman with the firm foot,
Thy like for great fame I have not found:
Under nun's veil will not be known
A woman with more sense.

The son of the beast [1]
That stays at night under pools,
As he waits for you,
Pale-grey feet with points support him.'

It is after this she went with Curithir, and they put themselves [2] under the spiritual direction [3] of Cummine the Tall, the son of Fiachna.

'Good', said Cummine. 'It is many of my morsels that are offered up. The power of soul-friendship be upon you! Whether for you shall it be seeing, or talking together?'

'Talking for us!' said Curithir. 'What will come of it will be better. We have ever been looking at each other.'

So whenever he went around the grave-stones of the saints, her cell was closed upon her. In the

---

[1] A play on Curithir's patronymic Mac Doborchon, i. e. Otter's son.
[2] She put herself, *Ha.*
[3] Literally, 'soul-friendship.'

same way his would be closed upon him whenever she went.

　　'Tis then she said:

> 'Curithir, once the poet,
> I loved; the profit has not reached me:
> Dear lord of two grey feet,
> It will be alas to be without their company [1]
> 　　　　　　　　　　　　　　[for ever!
>
> The flagstone to the south of the oratory
> Upon which is he who was poet once,
> It is there I often go each day,
> At eve after the triumph of prayer.
>
> He shall have neither cow
> Nor yearlings nor heifers [2],
> Never a mate shall be [3]
> At the right hand of him who once was
> 　　　　　　　　　　　　　　[a poet.'

Curithir says:

> 'Beloved is the dear voice that I hear,
> I dare not welcome it!
> But this only do I say:
> Beloved is this dear voice!'

Says the woman:

> 'The voice which comes to me through the
> 　　　　　　　　　　　　　　[wattled wall,
> It is right for it to blame me:
> What the voice does to me, is
> It will not let me sleep.'

---

[1] Without his company, *H.*
[2] i.e. he shall have neither wife nor children, male or female.
[3] Literally, 'there shall be no thigh bone'.

[She expostulates with Cummine and exculpates herself.]

'Thou man, ill it is what thou dost,
To name me with Curithir:
He from the brink of Lough Seng [1],
I from Kil-Conchinn [2].'

'Sleep by each other to-night!' said Cummine. 'And let a little scholar [3] go between you lest you do any folly'.

It was then Curithir said:

'If it is one night you say
I am to sleep with Liadain, —
A layman who would sleep the night
Would deem it a great thing: the night
[would not be lost.'

It was then Liadain said:

'If it is one night you say
I am to sleep with Curithir, —
Though we gave a year to it,
There would (still) be something about
[which we might talk.'

They sleep by each other that night. On the morrow the little boy is brought to Cummine to be examined on soul and conscience.

'You must not conceal anything', said Cummine; 'I shall kill you if you do.'

---

[1] A lake in Connaught.

[2] The Ui Maic Iar-Conchinn are mentioned as a tribe in Corkaguiney. v. *Otia Merseiana* I, p. 121.

[3] Literally 'a little reader' or 'student' [cf. supra, VI D 2 i].

It is indifferent to him how he dies: — 'I shall flog him if he confess.'

After that Curithir was taken to another church. It was then he said:

> 'Of late
> Since I parted from Liadain,
> Long as a month every day,
> Long as a year every month.'

Liadain says:

> 'If Curithir to-day
> Is gone to the scholars,
> Alas for the sense he will make
> To any who do not know him.'

Cummine says:

> 'What you say is not well,
> Liadain, wife of Curithir.
> Curithir was here, he was not mad,
> Any more than before he came.'

[Liadain repudiates the term 'wife'.]

> 'That Friday[1]
> It was no camping on pastures of honey[2],
> Upon the fleeces of my white couch[3]
> Between the arms of Curithir.'

He however went on a pilgrimage until he came to Kil-Letrech in the land of the Dessi. She went seeking him and said:

---

[1] This stanza seems to refer to the night she was allowed to spend with Curithir.

[2] Literally, 'out-spanning on a honey-field'.

[3] Literally 'little skin, rug'.

'Joyless
The bargain I have made!
The heart of him I loved I wrung.

'Twas madness
Not to do his pleasure
Were there not the fear of the king of
[Heaven.

To him the way he has wished
Was great gain,
To go past the pains of Hell into Paradise.

'Twas a trifle
That wrung Curithir's heart against me.
To him great was my gentleness.

I am Liadain
Who loved Curithir:
It is true as they say.

A short while I was
In the company of Curithir:
Sweet was my intimacy with him.

The music of the forest
Would sing to me when with Curithir,
Together with the voice of the purple sea.

Would that
Nothing whatever of all I might do
Should wring the heart of Curithir
[against me!

Conceal it not!
He was the love of my heart,
If I loved every other.

A roaring flame
Dissolved this heart of mine, —
Without him surely I shall not live'.

But how she had wrung his heart was the haste
with which she had taken the veil.

When he heard that she was coming from the
west, he went in a coracle upon the sea, and took to
strange lands and pilgrimage, so that she never saw
him more. 'Now he is gone!' she said.

The flagstone upon which he was wont to pray,
she was upon it till she died. Her soul went to
Heaven. And that was the flagstone that was put
over her face.

Thus far the meeting of Liadain and Curithir.

C. THE STORY OF AILILL AND ETAIN [1].

Now a year after Eochaid (Airemon) had obtained
the sovereignty, he sent out his commands to the men
of Ireland that they should come to Tara to hold
festival therein, in order that there should be adjusted
the taxes and the imposts that should be set upon
them, so that these might be settled for a period of
five years. And the one answer that the men of Ireland made to Eochaid was that they would not make
for the king that assembly which is the Festival of
of Tara until he found for himself a queen, for there

---

[1] Ed. Windisch, *Irische Texte* I, 113—33. The story is
mentioned in the tenth century list of tales in the *Book of Leinster*.
It is contained in the *Leabhar na hUidhri*, a manuscript written
about 1100. By the kind permission of the translator the following extracts are from A. H. Leahy, *Heroic Romances of Ireland*,
op. cit. I, 23—32.

was no queen to stand by the king's side when Eochaid first assumed the kingdom.

Then Eochaid sent out the messengers of each of the five provinces to go through the land of Ireland to seek for that woman or girl who was the fairest to be found in Erin; and he bade them to note that no woman should be to him as a wife, unless she had never before been as a wife to any one of the men of the land. And at the Bay of Cichmany a wife was found for him, and her name was Etain the daughter of Etar; and Eochaid brought her thereafter to his palace, for she was a wife meet for him, by reason of her form, and her beauty, and her descent, and her brilliancy, and her youth, and her renown.

Now Finn the son of Findloga had three sons, all sons of a queen, even Eochaid Fedlech, and Eochaid Airemm, and Ailill Anguba. And Ailill Anguba was seized with love for Etain at the Festival of Tara, after she had been wedded to Eochaid; since he for a long time gazed upon her. And, since such gazing is a token of love, Ailill gave much blame to himself for the deed he was doing, yet it helped him not. For his longing was too strong for his endurance, and for this cause he fell into a sickness; and, that there might be no stain upon his honor, his sickness was concealed by him from all, neither did he speak of it to the lady herself. Then Fachtna, the chief physician of Eochaid, was brought to look upon Ailill, when it was understood that his death might be near, and thus the physician spoke to him: 'One of the two pangs that slay a man, and for which there is no healing by leechcraft, is upon thee; either the pangs of envy or the pangs of love.' And Ailill refused to confess the cause of his illness to the physician, for he was withheld by shame; and he was

left behind in Frémain of Tethba to die; and Eochaid
went upon his royal progress throughout all Erin, and
he left Etain behind him to be near Ailill, in order
that the last rites of Ailill might be done by her;
that she might cause his grave to be dug, and that
the keen might be raised for him, and that his cattle
should be slain for him as victims. And to the house
where Ailill lay in his sickness went Etain each day
to converse with him, and his sickness was eased by
her presence; and, so long as Etain was in that place
where he was, so long was he accustomed to gaze
at her.

Now Etain observed all this, and she bent her
mind to discover the cause, and one day when they
were in the house together, Etain asked of Ailill
what was the cause of his sickness. 'My sickness',
said Ailill, 'comes from my love for thee'. — 'T is
pity', said she, 'that thou hast so long kept silence,
for thou couldst have been healed long since, had we
but known of its cause.' — 'And even now could I be
healed', said Ailill, 'did I but find favor in thy sight.'
— 'Thou shalt find favor', she said. Each day after
they had spoken thus with each other, she came to
him for the fomenting of his head, and for the giving
of the portion of food that was required by him, and
for the pouring of water over his hands; and three
weeks after that, Ailill was whole. Then he said to
Etain: 'Yet is the completion of my cure at your
hands lacking to me; when may it be that I shall
have it?' — 'T is tomorrow it shall be', she answered
him, ('but it shall not be in the abode of the lawful
monarch of the land that this felony shall be done)[1].
Thou shalt come', she said, 'on the morrow to yonder

---

[1]) Interpolation.

hill that riseth beyond the fort: there shall be the tryst that thou desirest.'

Now Ailill lay awake all that night, and he fell into a sleep in the hour when he should have kept his tryst, and he woke not from his sleep until the third hour of the day. And Etain went to her tryst, and she saw a man before her; like was his form to the form of Ailill, he lamented the weakness that his sickness had caused him, and he gave her such answers as it was fitting that Ailill should give. But at the third hour of the day, Ailill himself awoke: and he had for a long time remained in sorrow when Etain came into the house where he was; and as she approached him: 'What maketh thee so sorrowful?' said Etain. — 'T is because thou wert sent to tryst with me', said Ailill, 'and I came not to thy presence, and sleep fell upon me, so that I have but now awakened from it; and surely my chance of being healed hath now gone from me.' — 'Not so, indeed', answered Etain, 'for there is a morrow to follow to-day.' And upon that night he took his watch with a great fire before him, and with water beside him to put upon his eyes.

At the hour that was appointed for the tryst, Etain came for her meeting with Ailill, and she saw the same man, like unto Ailill, whom she had seen before; and Etain went to the house, and saw Ailill still lamenting. And Etain came three times, and yet Ailill kept not his tryst, and she found the same man there every time. 'T is not for thee', she said, 'that I came to this tryst: why comest thou to meet me? And as for him whom I would have met, it was for no sin or evil desire that I came to meet him; but it was fitting for the wife of the king of Ireland to rescue the man from the sickness under which he

hath so long been oppressed . . . . Why', said she,
'what is thy name?' — 'T is easy to say', he answered, 'Midir of Bri Leith is my name. . . . It was indeed myself', said Midir, 'who long ago put beneath
the mind of Ailill the love that he hath felt for thee,
so that his blood ceased to run, and his flesh fell
away from him: it was I also who have taken away
his desire, so that there might be no hurt to thine
honor . . .'

After all this Etain departed to the house. 'It
hath indeed been good, this our tryst', said Ailill,
'for I have been cured of my sickness; moreover, in
no way has thine honor been stained.' — 'T is glorious
that it hath fallen out so', answered Etain.

And afterwards Eochaid came back from his royal
progress, and he was grateful that his brother's life
had been preserved, and he gave all thanks to Etain
for the great deed she had done while he was away
from his palace.

END.

A SURVEY OF TRISTAN SCHOLARSHIP
AFTER 1911

By Roger Sherman Loomis

Reviews

The reviews of Miss Schoepperle's *Tristan and Isolt* were, broadly speaking, highly favorable. Her critique of Bédier's reconstruction of the *poème primitif* in his edition of Thomas's *Tristan* on the basis of its assumed logical structure and consistency was generally accepted. So, too, was her rejection of his thesis that Béroul, Thomas, Eilhart, the *Folie*, and the Prose Romance were all derived from a French poem of the early twelfth century, created at one stroke by a single author of genius. Her array of parallels between the surviving Tristan texts, on the one hand, and motifs, situations, and stories in circulation at the time, on the other, was taken as evidence that there was a far more important body of tradition in the romance than Bédier had recognized, even though Kelemina and others questioned the validity of particular examples which she adduced.

Most of the reviewers were impressed by the array of analogues culled from Irish literature, and especially by the similarity to the Tristan romance presented by the Irish saga of Diarmaid and Grainne, which, though most of the texts are late, could be traced back to the tenth century, and which told a tragic tale of the compulsive love of a hero for his royal uncle's wife, and of their flight to the forest. Miss Schoepperle's contention that this formed the nucleus from which developed the great medieval romance was received favorably by most critics, not only because of the basic resemblance in plot but also because it afforded an explanation of the curious episodes of the sword separating the two lovers in their forest retreat and of the splashing water. Joseph Loth was almost, if not quite, alone in asserting that adultery and elopement were too commonplace in life and fiction to prove dependence of the romance on the saga.

Not all reviewers were ready to accept Miss Schoepperle's contention that Eilhart's French source, the *estoire*, could be taken as the source of Thomas's poem, Kelemina and Nitze being among the sceptics. Huet and Ferdinand Lot questioned the dating of the *estoire* in the last quarter of the twelfth century, both arguing that the courtly elements were not necessarily attributable to so late a date, and Lot pointing out that it was inconsistent with the dating of Thomas's *Tristan* before Chrétien's *Cligès*. Miss Schoepperle's belief that it was Mathilda, daughter of Henry II and Eleanor of Poitou, who confided a manuscript of the *estoire* to Eilhart von Oberge on her return from England to Saxony in 1185, and that this furnishes a *terminus a quo* for the composition of his translation was challenged and is now pretty generally rejected.

On the whole, the response of scholars to Miss Schoepperle's *Tristan* may be summed up in the concluding words of Joseph Loth:

> L'étude des sagas irlandaises se recommandait d'elle-même; elle pouvait assurer la celticité de traits de moeurs, d'épisodes même qui prêtaient à la discussion.

A ce point de vue, les recherches de Miss Schoepperle sont des plus méritoires. . . . Les analyses des diverses versions du roman sont également faites avec la plus grande conscience, et ajoutent notablement à l'oeuvre de M. Bédier. Les remarques ingénieuses abondent. En somme, le travail de Miss Schoepperle est un véritable miné de renseignements, un répertoire indispensable non seulement à tous ceux qui s'intéressent aux romans arthuriens, mais encore à ceux qui s'occupent du moyen âge et des questions de Folklore.

The Dating and Authorship of Texts

The theory of Bédier that the reference of Bernard de Ventadour to Tristan as the suffering lover of Yzeut could be dated approximately 1154, though unacceptable to Miss Schoepperle, was upheld by Deister as a probability, but has again been vigorously challenged by Delbouille.

The dating and the provenance of Eilhart von Oberge's *Tristrant* are still the subject of debate. The editor of the surviving fragments, Wagner, argued that the dialect was that of the Middle Rhine, not of Lower Saxony, and that the poem must have been written about 1170, and in these views he was supported by Van Dam and Ranke. But Wesle in W. Stammler's *Deutsche Literatur des Mittelalters, Verfasserlexikon,* I (1933), cols. 520-4, was not convinced. In any case the poet must have lived earlier than the official of the court of Brunswick with the same name, of whom records survive.

Similar uncertainty exists as to whether the Béroul fragment was composed by one or two poets. Muret in his edition for the Société des Anciens Textes Français maintained that the first part, which corresponded in substance to Eilhart and which extended to vs. 2754, was the work of a jongleur named Béroul, who twice

referred to himself, and that the rest of the poem was
added by an anonymous author, who not only contra-
dicted his predecessor violently but also used another
source and exhibited certain differences of spirit. Later
Muret conceded the possibility of a single author, and
has had many followers in this opinion. But Miss Schoepperle, though she did not commit herself, distinguished
between the two parts, and recently Raynaud de Lage
has adduced strong arguments from the versification, the
introduction of new characters, and the absence of the
mannerisms of oral recitation in the second part, to
render nearly certain the division of the poem between
two authors. Only the latter part, then, can be assigned,
on the basis of the reference in line 3849 to the epidemic
which the Crusaders suffered at Acre in 1191, to a period
after that date, and the first section may well be twenty
or thirty years older.

Though the *terminus a quo* of Thomas's poem still
remains fixed at 1155, owing to the certainty of his borrowing from Wace's *Brut*, the *terminus ad quem* is still
an open question. A large number of scholars have accepted the arguments of Gaston Paris and Bédier that
Chrétien wrote his *Cligès* as a sort of counterblast to
Thomas's *Tristan* and that he imitated a word-play, preserved in Gottfried's adaptation of Thomas, on *l'amer*
(love), *l'amer* (bitterness), and *la mer* (sea). But not only
did Miss Schoepperle reject the dependence of *Cligès*
on Thomas as unproved, but Hoepffner also pointed out
that certain of the more specific of Chrétien's allusions
to, or imitations of, the Tristan material (such as the
golden hair) were inspired by another version than that
of Thomas. Jirmounsky, in addition to this argument,
showed that the verbal conceit was a commonplace with
Latin authors. R. S. Loomis was unable to find before
1195 examples in art of the repetition of the heraldic

device on shield, lance, pennon, and *conisance,* which Thomas assigned to Tristan le Nain, and hence concluded that the poem could not be much more than ten years earlier. The latest editor of Thomas, Professor Wind, though leaning toward a date after *Cligès,* does not pronounce a final decision. She agrees with Bédier that the poet's professed ignorance of affairs of love does not mean that he was in holy orders, and accepts the general view that he addressed himself to a courtly circle, perhaps to a royal patron. Jonin, however, believes Thomas was a cleric.

The Names in the Early Tristan Romance

Miss Schoepperle adopted a noncommittal attitude to the evidence offered by the names as to the history of the Tristan legend. Bédier, however, even though he minimized the Celtic elements in that legend and believed that all our early texts were derived from a single French poem which owed little to an earlier tradition, somewhat inconsistently defined several stages in the transmission of the story from Pictland to Anglo-Norman Britain by way of Wales, Cornwall, and Brittany, on the basis of the names. Later scholars have added considerably to our information on the nomenclature. The following is offered as an amplification and rectification of Bédier's scheme.

Pictish: Drustan>Tristan.

Welsh: Esyllt>Iselt, Iseut; March>Mark; Branwen> Brenguen; Kae Hir>Kaherdin (assimilated to Turkish Kahedin); Bleddri>Bleheri>Pleherin; Caradoc>Cariado.

Breton: Rivelen>Rivalen; Rivelen + (French) *reis*> Rouland riis, Kanelengres; Rodald>Roald; Morgan>

Morgan; Morald>Morholt, Morhaut; Perinis>Perinis; Donuallen>Donoalent, Denoalan; Godoine>Godoine; Houel>Hoel.

French: Blanchefleur; Guenelon; Orri; Ogrin; Estult le Orgillius.

Of the place-names, some can be identified with certainty. Loenois, Tristan's native land according to Béroul and Eilhart, is Lothian, which then extended from the Firth of Forth to the Tweed; in the Prose *Tristan* it was confused with Leonois, a Breton province. Béroul's Gavoie or Ganoie, whose king was at war with the Scottish king, is Galloway. Carloon or Cuerlion is, of course, Caerleon on Usk. Isneldone, where Perinis found King Arthur, is the Roman fort near Carnarvon, called by the Anglo-Normans "la cité de Snaudone". Tintaguel, needless to say, is the romantic castle of Tintagel. Le Mont in Béroul is St. Michael's Mount, and Loth identified Lancien with the modern parish of Lantyan in Cornwall. Ermonie, mentioned by the English redactor of Thomas as the land of Tristan's father, represents a not uncommon corruption of Armorique, that is, Brittany.

Some identifications are plausible, others mere guesses. The forest of Morrois, to which the lovers retired, may possibly be the wild region of Moray in northern Scotland. The isle of Saint Sanson, where, according to the Prose *Tristan* and Chrétien's *Erec*, the combat with Morholt took place, is probably one of the Scilly Isles of that name, even though this identification puts it far from Tintagel. Béroul surely knew Cornish geography well, but Loth's attempt to place the Blanche Lande, Costentin, the Mal Pas, and Morrois in that county has been met by the reviewers with scepticism. The notion that Leonois, Malory's Lyonesse, was a country lying west of Land's End, which had sunk beneath the Atlantic waves, goes back no farther than the Cornish antiquary Carew in the seventeenth century (*Modern Philology*, L, 162-70).

The Origin and Development of the Legend

Since Bédier and Miss Schoepperle wrote, much has been added to our knowledge of the origin, development, and transmission of the Tristan legend. Even as early as 1891 Zimmer had discovered in the *Chronicles of the Picts and Scots* (977-995) a certain Drest or Drust, son of Talorcan, who reigned about 780, and he had pointed out the equivalence of this name with the Drystan son of Tallwch, who in Welsh texts was the lover of Esyllt, wife of March. This identification was not only accepted by Bédier and many others, but it was confirmed by Deutschbein's proof that a tale about Drust had been interpolated in the ancient Irish saga, the *Wooing of Emer*. In this interpolation alone the Ulster hero Cuchulainn is accompanied by a certain Drust. The setting is the Hebrides, not far from Pictish territory at the mouth of the Clyde. When Cuchulainn arives at the king's court, he hears wailing and learns that a human tribute is to be given over to warriors from Ireland. He kills them, but is himself wounded. Though others claim credit for the victory, the king's daughter does not believe them, and is able to recognize Cuchulainn as he takes a bath. The king offers her to him as a bride, but he refuses. Once granted that Drust was the original hero of this episode, is it not obvious that here is reflected the Pictish source of the Morholt episode and of the discomfiture of the false claimant? By great good fortune, then, we have preserved to us the outline of the original saga which was attached to Drustan, the Pictish king, the nucleus of the famous romance.

If Sidney Hartland's great study of the legend of

Perseus may be relied on, it is probable that the Pictish saga is a descendant of the classical story of Perseus and Andromeda which had drifted far to the northwest. Its localization in this region may possibly have left traces in the geography of the French romances, where Tristan's homeland is Loenois and the forest to which he and Isolt fled was Morrois. Loenois is certainly Lothian, and Morrois is most plausibly identified as the wild region of Moray, the former adjacent to the southern border of Pictland and the latter lying deep within it. Conceivably, therefore, these lands of Tristan's birth and exile may owe their mention in French romance to Drust's original connection with what is now Scotland.

The Pictish saga, besides passing over to Ulster to be incorporated in the Cuchulainn cycle, must have passed southward by way of the Britons of Strathclyde and Cumberland into Wales, and here an extraordinary process of accretion began. The literary remains concerned with Drystan son of Tallwch (except for a very doubtful fragment from the Black Book of Carmarthen which contains the name Diristan) are unfortunately late. Though two Esyllts are listed among the goldentorqued ladies of Arthur's court in *Kulhwch and Olwen* (ca. 1100), Drystan and March son of Meirchiawn are first mentioned in *Rhonabwy's Dream* of the early or middle thirteenth century—strangely enough, among Arthur's counsellors! But there is no proof that the Welsh Drystan material at this stage had been influenced by the French romances, and it is safe to assume that the tradition was considerably older than the texts. Noteworthy is the fact that Drystan, March, and Esyllt are persistently associated with Arthur. In a thirteenth-century ms., Peniarth 16, we read:

> Drystan son of Tallwch, who guarded the swine of March son of Meirchyawn, while the swineherd went

to ask Esyllt to come to a meeting with him. Arthur
was trying to get one pig from among them, either by
deceit or by force, but he did not get it.

A later version magnifies Drystan's cleverness and
prowess by adding March, Kei, and Bedwyr to Arthur
as unsuccessful pig-snatchers. Such evidence as we have,
then, indicates that already in the Welsh stage Drystan
had been attracted into the Arthurian orbit, that he was
noted for exceptional cunning and strength, and that he
was involved in an affair with Esyllt, the wife of March.

This love-affair was evidently the most important
accretion to the Pictish tale of Drust. As already noted
above, it was Miss Schoepperle's great contribution to
show that, as developed in the *estoire*, the tragic story of
Tristan and Isolt showed a marked affinity to the famous
Irish saga of Diarmaid and Grainne and must, in fact,
have been derived, even though indirectly, from some
version of it. For there was a correspondence in the relationship of the three principal characters, Diarmaid
being, like Tristan, the lover of his uncle's wife; there
was a similar compulsive force which brought the lovers
together; in both stories the lovers dwelt for a long time
in the forests, subsisting on game and moving from place
to place. Miss Schoepperle clinched the matter by pointing to parallel incidents, the woman's reaction to the
water which splashed against her leg, and the placing
of a barrier (stone or sword) between the lovers as they
slept. Even though the full form of the *Pursuit of Diarmaid and Grainne* has come down to us in no manuscript
earlier than the seventeenth century, the saga is mentioned in a tenth-century list, and may be centuries
older. Thus the heart of Tristan's love-story is Irish.

If further proof be needed that this saga exerted a
powerful influence on the Tristan romance in the Welsh
stage, it is provided by the short Welsh tale entitled

Ystoria Trystan. This evidence was disregarded by Miss
Schoepperle, Loth, and Kelemina, apparently because
we have no copy earlier than 1550, but Sir Ifor Williams
in his *Lectures on Early Welsh Poetry* declared that the
verse elements were much older than the linking prose
passages, and that the narrative closely resembled the
Diarmaid and Grainne tale in Irish. In fact, there are
nine points of likeness, some of them very specific details.
Significant is the fact that Kae Hir, the Sir Kay of
Arthurian romance, appears as the friend of Trystan and
asks Esyllt to bestow her handmaid on him, just as
Kaherdin appears in Thomas's poem as Tristan's friend
and with Isolt's consent wins her handmaid as his mistress. Of course, the equation of Kaherdin with the
brother of Isolt of the White Hands must have been
made much later in the development of the romance,
since, as Miss Schoepperle argued and as we shall see
in due course, the second Isolt belongs to the last stages.

Two other Irish love-stories may have had some
influence. One is the tragic tale of Deirdre, which has
so strongly appealed to modern Irish poets and play-
wrights. Like the *Elopement of Diarmaid and Grainne,*
it tells of the passion of a young hero, Naisi, for the
destined bride of an old king, their elopement and
wanderings, and the attempts of the king to catch them.
At last, they were persuaded to return with an assurance
of safety, but Naisi was treacherously killed, Deirdre
never smiled again or raised her head from her knee,
and a year later crushed her head against a rock. Miss
Schoepperle proposed, with good reason, that at a
stage before the addition of Tristan's exile and marriage,
the romance had a similar ending with the return of
the lovers from the forest with an assurance of forgiveness from Mark—an assurance broken when he found
the two together. Much less plausible is Thurneysen's

attempt to connect the saga of Cano mac Gartnain with the romance of Tristan. To be sure, this too is a tragic tale of a man's love for another's wife, but except for the fact that the husband's name is Marcan, there is little resemblance. The only certain major Irish influence on Tristan is that of Diarmaid and Grainne.

There are, however, quite a few elements which show enough similarity to motifs or situations in Irish literature to be judged of Celtic origin, but whether derived ultimately from Ireland or derived from similar materials current in Wales or Cornwall or even in Brittany, it is often difficult to determine. According to Cormac's *Glossary* (ca. 900) King Finn had a fool who spied on Finn's wife and revealed her infidelity to his master. Béroul and Eilhart give a roughly similar account of King Mark's dwarf who spied on Tristan and Isolt. Miss Schoepperle cited several instances from Irish literature of chips of wood cast into a stream to convey a message, but none of them corresponds closely enough in the attendant circumstances to be accepted definitely as the source. The same may be said of the analogues she cited for Tristan's carving a message on a hazel rod and laying it on the road where Isolt was to pass, as described in Marie de France's *Chèvrefeuille*. So, too, the voyage of Tristan in a rudderless boat in the hope of healing may well be a Celtic feature, but there is no precise parallel in Irish.

Two episodes, treated by Miss Schoepperle, though they have analogues in Irish, are more closely paralleled in Welsh. Mark, according to Béroul, had the ears of a horse and managed to keep the secret until his confidant, the dwarf, told it to a bush in the hearing of the barons. Essentially the same story was related of March in a Welsh manuscript of the sixteenth century and in the folklore of the Lleyn peninsula as late as 1882. The so-called incident of "the harp and the rote", which involves the abduction of Isolt by a stranger as a result of Mark's rash promise and her rescue by Tristan, is unquestionably Celtic, with analogues in Irish and Arthurian romance, but it comes close enough to the episode of the rash boon in *Pwyll* to render it fairly certain that it was absorbed directly from a variant version of the *mabinogi*. Indeed, as an illustration of Tristan's resourcefulness and skill in music, "the harp and the rote" belongs with the other evidence for Tristan's reputation among the Welsh for cunning—a reputation which in all likelihood was responsible for his later fame as a master of venery.

If one may hazard a reconstruction of the Welsh saga of Drystan, it had little to say of his parentage and boyhood, for it is significant that in the French romances his father's name is Breton and his mother's name French, and his birthplace and early home is Brittany. Probably the story began with his arrival at a royal court and followed the outline of the Pictish tale of Drustan. It continued on the pattern of the Irish saga of Diarmaid and Grainne, the princess of the Pictish tale being carried over and taking the role of Grainne. Drystan, Esyllt, and March were substituted for Diarmaid, Grainne, and Finn. There was no potion exercising its compulsive force on the lovers simultaneously, and though Esyllt may have put a spell on Drystan so that he eloped with her to the forest, he rejected her embraces and placed a stone between them each night. Only after the incident of the splashing water did he yield. After successfully eluding the efforts of March to catch them, the lovers were finally persuaded by the intervention of Arthur to return to the court, but they continued to meet surreptitiously, and, though often suspected, managed to deceive or outwit March. Finally, March discovered them together and murdered Drystan. Esyllt died in her lover's arms or committed suicide. Into some such composite framework minor incidents were fitted —the betrayal of March's secret deformity, "the harp and the rote", Kae Hir's intrigue with Esyllt's maid, and perhaps others from the fund of current non-Celtic fiction. Needless to say, in this oral stage every *cyvarwydd* told the saga with individual and sometimes wide variations from the outline sketched above; some, probably, emphasized the romantic aspect and the lovers' fidelity; others what one might call the *fabliau* elements of bedroom comedy and successful dupery.

Mrs. Bromwich has suggested that in Welsh tradition March's court was in Glamorgan; in any case when the legend traveled south, the centre of the action was moved to Tintagel on the coast of Cornwall, where the ruins ever since have sheltered memories of the famous lovers. This new localization and the choice of the isle of St. Sanson as the site of the combat with Morholt are the only novelties which we can attribute with considerable plausibility to the passage of the legend through Cornwall at this early stage. The alternative situation of Mark's court at Lancien, modern Lantyan, which we find in the first part of Béroul, may well represent a genuine local tradition picked up by the poet, who was certainly acquainted with the country, but since it has left no traces in any other version, it could hardly have enjoyed much currency, and Loth's other geographical speculations, based on Béroul, have been properly received with scepticism.

This elaborate legend of Tristan passed on to Brittany to undergo further change and expansion. Between 1035 and 1045 a lord of Vitré named Triscan or Tristan attained a certain celebrity because of his quarrels with the Duke of Brittany, and his father was named Rivalon or Rivelon. It can hardly be a coincidence that Thomas transferred Tristan's homeland from Loonois to Brittany, assigned him a seneschal with the Breton name of Roald, described his war with the Duke of that land, and, in agreement with Eilhart, called his father Rivalon. Whether this Triscan or Tristan of Vitré and other Triscans of the same period were named after the Welsh Trystan or not, it is hard to say, but it seems fairly clear that the names were confused and that the hero of the French romances derived his father's name and inherited his war with the Duke of Brittany from the historic baron of Vitré. The Breton influence on the early part of the romance and the lack of specifically Celtic ingredients render it most likely that the affair of Rivalon and Blanchefleur, their deaths, and the upbringing of their orphan son by the faithful Roald were innovations, lacking a traditional basis. Probably some ingenious Breton, struck by the similarity of the name Tristan to the French adjective *triste*, invented a new etymology for the name and gave the birth-story a sombre cast.

Three elements in the Tristan romances have counterparts in modern Breton folklore. The story of King Mark's equine ears, current in Finistère in 1794 and for a century afterwards, was presumably imported as a component part of the legend from Wales. On the other hand, the death of the hero on hearing the lie about the sail, which forms the conclusion of the romance in Thomas and Eilhart, bears a close resemblance to a folktale collected on the islands of Ouessant and Molène some fifty years ago and was probably a native contribution. So, too, was Tristan's combat with the dragon which, Van Hamel has shown, is paralleled in modern Breton folklore. This folktale, an offshoot of the Perseus and Andromeda legend, was apparently combined in Brittany with the other version of which Drust was the hero, thus giving us two combats in which Tristan, though victorious, was left severely poisoned, and employing both the discomfiture of the false seneschal by means of the dragon's tongue from the Breton version and the recognition in the bath from the Pictish version.

Tristan's boast of his mistress and its justification by her beauty and even that of her handmaids, as they ride by, form an episode which was classified by Miss Schoepperle as a wide-spread folktale and such it is in modern times; but it may be claimed as a Breton addition, perhaps a Breton invention, since the earliest forms are found in the Breton *lais* of *Lanval* and *Graelent*. Moreover, the corresponding Italian folktales, as Levi has shown, derive from Breton originals through the fourteenth-century *cantare* of *Liombruno* and its many printed editions.

The curious episode of the *Salle aux Images*, the subterranean hall which Tristan had built and where he resorted secretly to caress the statue of Isolt, bears so marked a resemblance to Geoffrey of Monmouth's tale of the subterranean chamber which King Locrine had made and where he was wont to visit secretly his mistress Estrildis that we may feel sure of some relationship between the two narratives. Though the name Estrildis might suggest that Geoffrey had borrowed the story from a Welsh tale of Esyllt, Drystan's mistress, it is hard to see how the episode would have fitted into the saga when, as yet, Drystan had no jealous wife. One may be rightly cautious in accepting Geoffrey's statement that his source was a book brought from Brittany, yet considerable material did come to him from across the Channel, and the odds favor a common Breton source, more or less remote, for both versions of the clandestine visits to a mistress in a subterranean chamber.

Miss Schoepperle was able to cite Oriental parallels for such *fabliau* themes as the Tryst under the Tree and

the Ambiguous Oath, but she did not assert Oriental
derivation. Though these themes were coupled with
Celtic motifs, such as the chips on the stream, the pre-
sumption is that they were not absorbed into the legend
till a late stage, perhaps when Breton story-tellers wandered abroad and added to their repertoire fresh stories
of jealous husbands, wayward wives, and tricky lovers.

The most important discovery concerning the latter
part of the Tristan romance was made by Samuel Singer,
who proved that the idea of a second Isolt, the unconsummated marriage, and the offended brother of the
bride were taken over from the famous Arabic love-story
of Kais and Lobna. Through what channels it had passed
before it came to Brittany, no one can say, but that this
pathetic plot was incorporated at the Breton stage can
hardly be doubted when one considers the geography
and the personages. The Arab romance afforded, moreover, examples of a rarefied passion which, when ascribed to Tristan, raised him high above more earthy
lovers. Like Kais, Tristan, when separated from his lady,
marries another woman for the ultra-romantic reason
that she bears the same name. Like Kais, he is encouraged to do so by her brother. Like Kais, he cannot bring
himself to consummate the marriage and thus gives
offense to her relatives. Like Kais, Tristan, in Eilhart, is
buried with his first love in one grave.

Thus the Celtic and Arabic tales had come from
the West and the East to unite and form a harmonious
whole which was singularly adapted to the expression
in narrative form of the new cult of idealized extra-
marital passion of which the troubadours of Provence
were the lyrical mouthpiece. For Isolt, as for Grainne,
the claims of her husband were as naught beside the
claims of love. For Tristan, as for Kais, the claims of
his wife were as naught beside the claims of love. It

seems probable that at this stage, if not earlier, Tristan as an ideal lover could no longer be depicted as hanging back, like Diarmaid, before the advances of an infatuated woman, and the potion was introduced to bring about a mutual and overpowering attraction. The episode of the separating sword, however, survived as a relic of the older story and as a testimony to Tristan's original resistance to Esyllt's overtures.

It was in Brittany, then, that the legend of Tristan and Isolt was expanded into a tragic love-story on a scale comparable to that of Paris and Helen. Though it included much that was episodic and unessential and much that was hardly above the level of farce, the main structure was grandiose and certain situations afforded opportunities for lofty treatment, of which Thomas and Gottfried von Strassburg took full advantage.

Bleheris

Before the romance came into the hands of the poets, it was an oral tradition. To this fact there is ample testimony. Béroul himself refers scornfully (vs. 1265) to the *conteor;* Peter of Blois testifies that the *histriones* moved their audiences to tears by their fables of Arthur, Gawain, and Tristan. Bédier quoted the significant passage in which Renart, the fox, disguised as a "jongleur breton", asserts his knowledge of lais concerning Tristan and "Dame Iset". Marie de France asserts that she has heard the lai of the Honeysuckle as well as finding it in writing. Thomas is explicit: "Entre ceus qui solent cunter Et del cunte Tristran parler, Il en cuntent diversement: Oï en ai de plusur gent." Indeed, the poets themselves expected to have their stories recited, as is proved by the addresses of Béroul and Thomas to a listening audience. Thomas goes on to invoke, in favor of his statement that Kaherdin accompanied Tristan to Britain, the authority of one Breri, who knew the deeds of all the kings and counts who have been in Britain. Bédier and Miss Schoepperle held that this reference was merely a device to cover the poet's departure from a common tradition, and they may well be right; but even so, the existence of Breri is not disproved. Others have accepted Breri's existence, but have sought to identify him either with a historical bishop named Bleddri (983-1022), or with a landowner of South Wales of the same name, who may have acted as an interpreter between the Welsh and the Normans in the first third of the twelfth century. Both identifications are pure guesses, and are refuted by the fact that Giraldus Cambrensis, about 1194, referred to that famous *fabulator*, Bled-hericus, who came a little before his time. A *fabulator* or *fableor* was a professional story-teller, not an official interpreter or a wealthy landowner, and 1022 is over a century before Giraldus' birth about 1147. Further testimony comes from the Second Continuation of Chrétien's *Perceval* (formerly ascribed to Wauchier), where we read that Bleheris, who was born and brought up in Wales, told a tale of Gawain and a dwarf knight to the Count of Poitiers, who loved it more than any other. Chrétien de Troyes and Eilhart unconsciously reveal an association in their minds between this Bleheris and Tristan, for the first lists Bliobleheris and Tristan together in *Erec*, and the second introduces a minor character under the name of Pleherin. Finally, the author of the so-called *Elucidation*, prefixed to Chrétien's Perceval, mentions a knight of Arthur's Blihos Bleheris, who knew such good tales that no one tired of listening to him. All this testimony, conscious and unconscious, converges to prove that there was a renowned Welsh *conteur* named Bleddri and that he included in his repertoire tales of Tristan.

His visit to Poitiers seems to be confirmed by the fact that two troubadours connected with that household, Bernard de Ventadour and Cercamon, refer familiarly to Tristan as a lover. Kellermann's attempt to dispose of this singularly concordant evidence because the manuscripts vary as to the forms of the name Bleheris and because it was mistakenly attached to a knight of Arthur's court should not be taken too seriously.

If we do recognize the validity of the evidence, we must come to some further conclusions. Bleheris must have been fluent in French in order to be understood at the court of Poitou and to win a reputation on the Continent. His stories must have been derived mainly from the Breton rather than from his native tradition. There is no need to suppose with Brugger that he ever composed in verse; the common medium of the *conteurs* was prose. He must have possessed rare histrionic gifts, for he alone of all the reciters of Arthurian tales has left us his name. Whether we should also ascribe to him a share, small or large, in co-ordinating the mass of materials which made up the Breton heritage and in producing the romance of Tristan substantially as we know it from Eilhart, is a question imposible to answer.

The Early Poets and Their Patrons

According to a hypothesis developed by R. S. Loomis, the influence of Bleheris on the court of Poitou may be detected not only in the alluions of the troubadours to Tristan but also in the fact that scions of that house in the latter half of the century seem to have favored poets who dealt with the theme, briefly or at length. The daughter of Eleanor of Poitou by Louis VII of France, Marie de Champagne, was, for a time at least, the patroness of Chrétien de Troyes, who tells us that he had written a poem on King Mark and Iseut la Blonde. Eleanor's second husband, Henry II of England, is usually identified with the noble king to whom Marie de France dedicated her lais, including *Le Chèvrefeuille*. The Anglo-Norman Thomas, surely a court poet, may have written for Eleanor's circle, since he described the caparison of Tristan's steed as red embroidered with golden lions and this device was probably that of the royal house. Whether this interest on the part of the descendants of the Counts of Poitou was primarily due to the posthumous influence of Bleheris, may be questioned, for, as we have seen, the romance of Tristan must have largely taken shape before his time and there were other *fabulatores* who could make their audiences weep over Tristan's sufferings. In any case, the interest of this same royal house continued into the thirteenth century. King John's regalia included in 1207 a *soi-distant* "sword of Tristram", and there is a fair probability that the Chertsey Tiles which illustrate Thomas's poem were commissioned by Henry III a few years before his death. Edward I before his accession owned a version of the Prose *Tristan*, which came into the hands of Rusticien de Pise. It should be added, of course, that Eleanor of Poitou and her descendants were not the only regal enthusiasts for the Tristan story, but, strange to say, I can find no others recorded before 1339, when Pedro IV of Aragon bought a manuscript of *Meliadus*, a history of Tristan's father.

The Episodic Poems

Levi argued cogently against the thesis that the Breton lais formed a new type which was created solely by Marie de France, and that all examples of later date were mere imitations of her work. He proved the popularity of Marie's *Chèvrefeuille* by citing many allusions. There has been a spirited debate as to the interpretation of this poem. Mrs. Frank, though she overlooks Miss Schoepperle's treatment of the subject, nevertheless agrees that Tristan carved on the hazel rod not only his name but also a message summarized in vss. 63-78, and she cited examples of inscriptions on wooden tablets and wands. She is supported by the Norse translation and by the statement in the poem itself that the Queen "knew all the letters" on the rod,—a strange remark if there were only the letters of Tristan's name. Spitzer, however, regards this as too prosaic an interpretation of the text and argues that the symbolism of the hazel and the honeysuckle was readily divined by the Queen and that there was no need for Tristan to spell it out. Le Gentil very rightly contends that this theory, though attractive, imputes more subtlety to Marie than the poem itself justifies.

Hoepffner, in his edition of the Berne *Folie Tristan*, abandoned his earlier view that this poem and the Oxford *Folie* were derived from a common source, and maintained with solid reasons that the latter was an adaptation of the former in order to harmonize it with Thomas's poem and to arrange in chronological sequence the allusions of Tristan to the past history of his amour.

Various Episodes

Vinaver in his article on the love potion supports Miss Schoepperle's theory that Eilhart and Béroul represent the original tradition which limited the efficacy of the philtre to three or four years, but he suggests that the abatement of its power was merely an illusion in the minds of the lovers. Vinaver also points out, as does M. Marx in his more recent article on the wakening of passion in the lovers, that in Thomas's account they were already enamored of each other before they drank the potion. To Vinaver this seems a deliberate alteration by Thomas of an earlier tradition represented by Eilhart, whereas Marx finds here a vestige of the original version, taken over from a lai.

In another article Marx treats the discovery of the lovers in the forest and notes that according to Béroul King Mark, when convinced by the separating sword of their innocence, leaves his own in its place, substitutes a ring for that which Iseut wears, and places his glove so that it will shield her face from the rays of the sun. Though maintaining that there are analogues for such actions in Irish sagas, Marx believes that they represent a triple claim—investiture by sword, ring, and glove— and that the king thereby asserts symbolically his right to the loyalty of his nephew and his wife.

Ranke in the Schoepperle memorial studies called attention to the fact that the two scenes connected with the ambiguous oath carved on the French ivory casket at Leningrad were immediately preceded by another depicting Tristan and Isolt lying naked in bed together. Eilhart sheds no light on this concatenation since he has nothing to say of the equivocal oath, and neither Béroul II nor Thomas describes an assignation at which the lovers were observed while in bed, and which caused Isolt to resort to the compurgation by oath. Ranke argued from the casket that there must have been such an assignation in the text followed by the carver since otherwise this bedroom scene would have no specific literary basis. Ranke's case would be stronger if there were in the carving any indication of the presence of an observer.

Miss Newstead, taking full account of Miss Schoepperle's findings regarding the chips in the stream and of Krappe's study of the dwarf, has given an excellent analysis of the whole complex of material which went into the Tryst beneath the Tree.

Conclusion

In the last ten years various ambitious attempts have been made to account for the rise and development of the tragic romance of Tristan, among them Mergell's *Tristan und Isolde* (Mainz, 1949) and James Carney's *Studies in Irish Literature and History* (Dublin, 1955), pp. 189-242, but their results are highly speculative. Miss Schoepperle's work remains, after more than forty years, the most solid foundation for research in this vast and fascinating field.

A BIBLIOGRAPHY OF TRISTAN SCHOLARSHIP
AFTER 1911

Bibliographical Guides

J. J. Parry, *A Bibliography of Critical Arthurian Literature for the Years 1922-1929* (New York, 1931). See Index under Tristan Story.

J. J. Parry and Margaret Schlauch, *A Bibliography of Arthurian Critical Literature for the Years 1930-1935* (New York, 1936). See Index under Tristan, *Tristan, Tristan de Leonois* and *Trystan ac Esyllt.*

J. J. Parry, "A Bibliography of Critical Arthurian Literature," in the June number of the *Modern Language Quarterly,* beginning with the year 1940; continued after 1954 by Paul A. Brown.

H. Küpper, *Bibliographie zur Tristansage, Deutsche Arbeiten der Universität Köln,* XVII (Jena, 1941). Reviewed by J. Horrent, *Revue belge de philologie et d'histoire,* XXIII (1944), 357-63.

R. Bossuat, *Manuel bibliographique de la littérature française du moyen âge* (Melun, 1951), nos. 1554-1690. Supplement (1955), nos. 6293-6313.

Bulletin bibliographique de la Société Internationale Arthurienne, No. 1 (1949) to date. See "Index des matières et des oeuvres."

Principal Reviews of Gertrude Schoepperle's *Tristan and Isolt*

J. D. Bruce, *Modern Language Notes,* XXIV (1914), 213-8.

W. Golther, *Englische Studien,* XLVIII (1914-15), 299-306.

G. Huet, *Moyen âge,* XXVII (1914), 380-3.

J. Kelemina, *Anzeiger, Zeitschrift für deutsches Altertum,* XXXVIII (1917), 55-66.

F. Lot, *Romania,* XLIII (1914), 126-35.

J. Loth, *Revue celtique,* XXXV (1914), 379-83.

W. A. Nitze, *Journal of English and Germanic Philology,* XIII (1914), 444-9.

F. Ranke, *Göttingische gelehrte Anzeigen,* 1920, 240-52.

New Editions of Texts

Eilhart von Oberge, *Tristrant,* ed. K. Wagner, *Rheinische Beiträge,* V (Bonn, 1924).

Romance of Tristran by Béroul, ed. A. Ewert, I (Oxford, 1939).

Béroul, *Tristan*, ed. E. Muret, revised by L. M. Defourques, *Classiques français du moyen âge* (Paris, 1947).

Les fragments du Tristan de Thomas, ed. B. H. Wind (Leiden, 1950).

La Folie de Tristan de Berne, ed. E. Hoepffner (Paris, 1934).

La Folie Tristan d'Oxford, ed. E. Hoepffner, 2nd ed. (Paris, 1943).

Chèvrefeuil in *Die Lais der Marie de France*, ed. K. Warnke, 3rd ed. (Halle, 1925), pp. 181-5; in Marie de France, *Lais*, ed. A. Ewert (Oxford, 1944), pp. 123-6; in Marie de France, *Lais*, ed. Hoepffner (Strasbourg, 1921).

Ystoria Trystan, ed. by J. Loth in *Revue celtique*, XXXIV (1913), 366-96; by T. P. Cross in *Studies in Philology*, XVII (1920), 93-110; by I. Williams in *Bulletin of the Board of Celtic Studies*, V, (1930), 115-29. Trans. by R. S. Loomis in Thomas of Britain, *Romance of Tristram and Ysolt* (New York, 1951), pp. xxi-xxvi.

Dating and Authorship of Texts

J. L. Deister, "Bernart de Ventadour's Reference to the Tristan Story," *Modern Philology*, XIX (1922), 287-96.

M. Delbouille, "Les 'senhals' littéraires désignant Raimbaut d'Orange et la chronologie de ces témoignages (Tristan)," *Cultura neolatina*, XVII (1957), 64-72.

J. van Dam, *Zur Vorgeschichte des höfischen Epos* (Bonn, Leipzig, 1923), pp. 13 ff.

L. E. Winfrey, "Kaherdin and Camille; the Sources of Eilhart's *Tristrant*," *Modern Philology*, XXV (1928), 257-67.

G. Raynaud de Lage, "Faut-il attribuer à Béroul tout le *Tristan?*", *Moyen âge*, LXIV (1958), 249-70.

M. M. Jirmounsky, "Quelques remarques sur la datation du 'Tristan' de Thomas," *Archivum romanicum*, XI (1927), 210-22.

E. Hoepffner, "Chrétien de Troyes et Thomas d'Angleterre," *Romania*, LV (1929), 1-16.

M. D. Legge, "Encore la date du *Tristan* de Thomas," *Bulletin bibliographique de la Société Internationale Arthurienne*, No. 6 (1954), 95 f.

F. Whitehead, in *Arthurian Literature in the Middle Ages*, ed. R. S. Loomis (Oxford, 1959), pp. 134-6.

General Studies of the Origin and Development of the Legend

J. D. Bruce, *Evolution of Arthurian Romance from the Beginnings down to the Year 1300, Hesperia*, Ergänzungsreihe 8, 9 (Göttingen, Baltimore, 1923, 1928), I, 153-91.

J. Kelemina, *Geschichte der Tristansage nach den Dichtungen des Mittelalters* (Wien, 1923). Reviewed by Ranke, *Göttingische gelehrte Anzeigen*, 1925, pp. 277-86.

F. Ranke, *Tristan und Isold* (München, 1925).

J. van Dam, "Tristanprobleme," *Neophilologus*, XV (1929-30), 18-34, 88-103, 183-201.

H. Küpper, "Les Etudes françaises sur la légende de Tristan et Iseut," *Revue germanique*, XXVI (1936), 322-35; XXVII (1937), 23-36.

A. Pauphilet, *Le Legs du moyen âge* (Melun, 1950), pp. 107-41.

B. Panvini, *La Leggenda di Tristano e Isotta, studio critico, Biblioteca dell' Archivum romanicum*, XXXII (Firenze, 1951).

H. Newstead, in *Arthurian Literature in the Middle Ages*, ed. R. S. Loomis (Oxford, 1959), pp. 122-33.

P. Jonin, *Les Personnages féminins dans les romans français de Tristan au XIIe siècle, Etude des influences contemporaines* (Aix-en-Provence, 1958).

Celtic Origin and Influences
(See previous section)

R. Bromwich, "Some Remarks on the Celtic Sources of 'Tristan,'" *Transactions of the Hon. Soc. of Cymmrodorion*, 1953, pp. 32-60.

E. Brugger, "Leonois as Tristan's Home," *Modern Philology*, XXII (1924-5), 159-91.

R. S. Loomis, "Problems of the Tristan Legend: Bleheris; the Diarmaid Parallel; Thomas's Date," *Romania*, LIII (1927), 82-102.

E. Brugger, "Zur Harfner Episode," *Archiv für das Studium der neueren Sprachen*, CXXIX (1912), 375-87; "Zu Tristans Tod," *ibid.*, CXXX (1913), 124-36.

J. Loth, *Contributions à l'étude des romans de la Table Ronde* (Paris, 1912). Reviewed by A. Smirnov, *Romania*, XLIII (1914), 119-26; by G. Schoepperle, *Romanic Review*, III (1912), 431-5; by

E. Brugger, *Zeitschrift für französische Sprache und Literatur,* XLVII² (1925), 218-39.

H. Newstead, "King Mark of Cornwall," *Romance Philology,* XI (1958), 240-53.

A. H. Krappe, "Der Zwerg im *Tristan,*" *Romanische Forschungen,* XLV (1931), 95-99.

V. J. Harward, *The Dwarfs of Arthurian Romance and Celtic Tradition* (Leiden, 1958), pp. 198 f.

A. H. Krappe, "Petitcrû," in *Balor with the Evil Eye* (New York, 1927), pp. 157-62.

H. Newstead, "Kaherdin and the Enchanted Pillow," *PMLA,* LXV (1950), 290-312.

H. Newstead, "The Tryst beneath the Tree," *Romance Philology,* IX (1956), 269-84.

A. G. Van Hamel, "Tristan's Combat with the Dragon," *Revue celtique,* XLI (1924), 331-49.

R. S. Loomis, "Le Folklore breton et les romans arthuriens, *Annales de Bretagne,* LVI (1949), 203-10; trans. into English, *Comparative Literature,* II (1950), 289-94.

Oriental Influences

S. Singer, "Arabische und europäische Poesie im Mittelalter," *Abhandlungen der preussischen Akademie der Wissenschaften,* phil.-hist. Kl., No. 13 (1918).

See above, Newstead, "The Tryst beneath the Tree."

Breri or Bleheris

R. S. Loomis, "Bleheris and the Tristram Story," *Modern Language Notes,* XXXIX (1924), 319-29.

E. Brugger, "Der Dichter Bledri-Bleheri-Breri," *Zeitschrift für französische Sprache und Literatur,* XLVII (1924), 162-85.

R. S. Loomis, *Wales and the Arthurian Legend* (Cardiff, 1956), pp. 193-5.

W. Kellermann, "Le Problème de Breri," *Les Romans du Graal aux XIIe et XIIIe siècles, Colloques internationaux du Centre Nationale de la Recherche Scientifique* (Paris, 1956), pp. 137-48.

Various Episodes

E. Vinaver, "The Love Potion in the Primitive Tristan Romance," in *Medieval Studies in Memory of Gertrude Schoepperle Loomis* (Paris, New York, 1927), pp. 75-86.

F. Ranke, "Isoldes Gottesurteil," *ibid.*, pp. 87-94.

J. Marx, "La Naissance de l'amour de Tristan et Iseut dans les formes les plus anciennes de la légende," *Romance Philology*, IX (1955), 167-73.

J. Marx, "Observations sur un épisode de la légende de Tristan" (discovery of lovers separated by sword), in *Recueil de travaux offert à M. Clovis Brunel* (Paris, 1955), pp. 265-73.

Le Chèvrefeuille

E. Levi, "I Lais e la leggenda di Tristano," *Studj romanzi*, XIV (1917), 137-48.

L. Spitzer, "La 'Lettre sur la baguette de coudrier' dans *Le Lai du Chievrefueil*," *Romania*, LXIX (1946), 80-90.

G. Frank, "Marie de France and the Tristram Legend," *PMLA*, LXIII (1948), 405-11.

P. Le Gentil, "A propos du *Lai du Chèvrefeuille* et de l'interprétation des textes médiévaux," *Mélanges d'histoire littéraire de la Renaissance offerts à Henri Chamard* (Paris, 1951), pp. 17-27.

The Prose *Tristan*

E. Vinaver, *Etudes sur le Tristan en prose, les sources, les manuscrits, bibliographie critique* (Paris, 1925).

E. Vinaver in *Arthurian Literature in the Middle Ages*, ed. R. S. Loomis, pp. 339-47.

INDEX NOMINUM.

N.B. Material in Professor Loomis' essay not indexed.

INDEX RERUM.

N.B. Material in Professor Loomis' essay not indexed.

birth of hero, 12, 110, 274—282,
446, 472, 522
— on sea, 12, 110
— stories, 275—282, 462
blades, at bed, 3, 37, 112, 213
—221, 240
on portcullis, 317
blonde Isolt, 187, 474
blood-brotherhood, 379, 385
-drops on snow, 546
-stains, 30, 37, 91, 222, 225, 520
blossom of the broom, 259
Blue Bird, 219
boast of lady, 42, 44, 45, 133,
138, 150—158, 160, 176, 473
boon, rash, 31, 223, 420—430,
436, 528—541
braids as trophies, 319
branch on stream, *v.* whittlings
on stream
branding, *v.* marking
bread, broken, as token, 415, 468
breaking on wheel, 30, 284,
bribery attempted in judicial
duel, 14, 361, 506—507
burial alive, 420
burning at the stake, 30, 446,
458, 464, 465

C

Caesarian operation, 12, 110, 280
caps, red, 56, 57
cave, lovers' refuge, 392, 400,
417—420, 430, 437
chansons à personnages, 124,
128—132
— *de geste,* 79, 117, 121, 254, 474
— *de mal mariée,* 120, 124—128,
452
— *dramatiques, v. chansons à
personnages*

chaplet, 61, 295
character of duped husband,
455—460
charm to preserve virginity, 123
chastel faé, 325 – 326
chastity token, *v.* token
cheese, food for fools, 58—60,
231—233
chemise, 24, 210
chess-man, missile, 440—442
childhood of hero, 12, 282—288,
446, 472, 519
chips on stream, *v.* whittlings
clothing, 234
club, jester's, 58, 60, 228, 233
– 234
common source, 4, 5, 7, 8; *v.*
also *estoire*
companion of lover, 46, 60, 121,
254—256
conception, by eating apple, 276;
by eating pottage, 276;
by drinking water, 276;
by swallowing worm, 275, 277,
278
caused by a god or hero from
afar, 277—281
of Tristan, *v.* birth of hero
conditions, apparently impossible:
to be neither within nor without &c., 402
to obtain pair of every wild
animal, 398;
consummation of marriage, *v.*
marriage
courtesy, 33, 36, 37, 39, 48, 52,
263—265, 418, *et passim, v.*
also *name, in* Isolt's
courtly love, *v. amour courtois*
cue given by Isolt, 45, 52
culture hero, 315—318

V

vassals, rebellious, 55, 58

vine, 65

virginity preserved by magic, 46, 257—261

visits in disguise, 78, 80, 197, 211, 227—241, 434—437; *v.* disguises

voyage for healing, Pro of Iemsetir, 15—17, 445;

 seclusion of the invalid, 367—370;

 rudderless boat, *s. v.*

 harp on rudderless boat, 90—91, 500—504, 519;

 healing from enemy, 375—391; by messenger, 16, 84—88, 194—197, 472—473;

 similarities to quest of princess, 187, 191—192;

 connection with quest of princess, 194—197, 440, 472—473

voyage to Cornwall, 42, *v.* boast, tryst at Blanche-Lande, thornbush, dog

W

wager of battle, *v.* judicial duel

water, of Life and Death, 190, 202;

 of Paradise and Hell, 190

weapon treated instead of wound, 386—387

wert, 505, 510

whip, carried by dwarf, 244

whittlings on stream, 26, 27, 147—150, 265, 301—315, 396, 434, 471

wibe hân, ze, 280

wife locked, 54, 124—128, 447

wirt, 62, 107

wisps in wall, *v.* twigs, rushes

woman, position of, 460—463;

 reward for exploit, 18, 160, 161—163, 187, 193, 203, 445, 524—528

word-play, 178, 376

wounds, of Tristan, 15—16, 30, 37, 58, 63, 93, 201, 367—370, 437—438

wrestling, 12, 239, 282—283

ERRATA.

Page 20, line 23: part read past.

 „ 38, „ 29: hermit „ priest.

 „ 40, „ 30: delete King.

 „ 43, „ 34: „ of Montrelles.

 „ 194, last line: *Tantris* read Pro.

 „ 206, note 1, and page 258, note 1: *untergeschobenen* read *unterschobenen*.

 „ 261, line 22: delete and Eilhart.